Labour Law: Council of Europe

Labour Law: Council of Europe

Fifth Edition

Andrzej Marian Świątkowski

This book was originally published as a monograph in the International Encyclopaedia of Laws/Labour Law and Industrial Relations.

Founding Editor: Roger Blanpain
General Editor: Frank Hendrickx
Volume Editor: Roger Blanpain

Wolters Kluwer

Published by:
Kluwer Law International B.V.
PO Box 316
2400 AH Alphen aan den Rijn
The Netherlands
E-mail: lrs-sales@wolterskluwer.com
Website: www.wolterskluwer.com/en/solutions/kluwerlawinternational

Sold and distributed by:
Wolters Kluwer Legal & Regulatory U.S.
920 Links Avenue
Landisville, PA 17538
United States of America
E-mail: customer.service@wolterskluwer.com

ISBN 978-94-035-4807-4

e-Book: ISBN 978-94-035-4817-3
web-PDF: ISBN 978-94-035-4827-2

This title is available on www.kluwerlawonline.com

The Author

Andrzej Marian Świątkowski (born 17 January 1944 in Warsaw) studied Law and Sociology at the Jagiellonian University in Cracow (1961–1969). He gained a Master of Law (1966) and an Master's in Sociology (1969). After working as a clerk for two years at the district court in Cracow, he received a doctorate in Labour Law from the Institute of Legal Sciences of the Polish Academy of Science in Warsaw (1972).

Dr Świątkowski studied at the Columbia Law School in New York. He gained an LLM in Labour Law from the University of Pennsylvania's Carey Law School (1977) in Philadelphia – an Ivy League school. In Poland, he received a habilitation degree from the Jagiellonian University in Cracow in the field of Labour Law and Social Policy (1976).

Dr Świątkowski spent a year as a distinguished research fellow at the National Institute of Public Management in Washington, DC (1977–1978). After returning to his post at the Jagiellonian University, he was appointed to the positions of extraordinary professor of law (1984) and ordinary professor of law (1991).

Professor Świątkowski spent one semester as a visiting scholar at the New York University School of Law and another semester as a visiting professor at Indiana University. He lectured at various universities in Europe, the United States, Argentina, and Australia. He delivered papers at International Industrial Relations Association congresses in Dublin, Helsinki, Oslo, Sydney, Tokyo and Santiago de Chile.

Professor Świątkowski acted as editor-in-chief of two legal journals, *The Jagiellonian University Yearbook of Labour Law and Social Policy,* published in 1989–1999 in English, and *Studies in Labour Law and Social Policy,* published in 1994 in Polish. He was also a co-editor of the *East–West Review of Social Policy* published by the Catholic University of Brabant in Tilburg. He also served as a member of the editorial board of *Tilburg Foreign Law Review.*

Since 1989, Professor Świątkowski has acted as the coordinator of the Tempus programme on European social law. Under his academic supervision, more than 500 students received Master of Law degrees at the Faculty of Law and Administration of Jagiellonian University. Twenty-one of the post-graduate students went on to earn doctorates in labour law. He reviewed over thirty doctoral and habilitation monographs in Poland. Four of his former doctoral students employed currently at the Jagiellonian University received a habilitation, and three of them were appointed to the positions of Professors of Labour Law at the Jagiellonian University, Faculty of Law and Administration. He also served as an external reviewer of three doctoral theses at the Andhra University in India and one in Vilnius (Lithuania). He was asked to submit a professional opinion to support a candidate applying for an honorary doctorate at Harvard University and a professorship at Vilnius University in Lithuania. Professor Świątkowski has published more than 800 studies, articles, and reviews and more than fifty books in the field of Polish, international, comparative, and foreign labour law, social security law, and social policy.

In 2002, Professor Świątkowski was elected by the Committee of Ministers of the Council of Europe to serve as an international expert on the European Committee of Social Rights (former Committee of Independent Experts) in Strasbourg. In 2005, he was elected Vice-President of that Committee. He served at the European Committee of Social Rights until 31 December 2012. Since 1 October 2014, Professor Świątkowski has been Professor Emeritus at Jagiellonian University. Currently, he is employed at the Jesuit University Ignatianum in Cracow.

Professor Świątkowski is a member of the International Employment and Labour Association (former International Industrial Relations Association) and the Society for Labour Law and Social Security. He was awarded by the European Union the title 'Jean Monnet' professor of European labour law and social security law and, in the United States, an honorary citizenship for the State of Kentucky – 'Kentucky Colonel'.

Table of Contents

The Author 3

List of Abbreviations 13

Part I. The Council of Europe 15

Chapter 1. General Background Information 15

§1. Definition 15

§2. History and Membership 15

§3. Observers, Partners and International Cooperation 16

§4. Structure 16

§5. Aims and Functions 17

§6. Headquarters and Offices 18

§7. Symbols 19

Chapter 2. International Treaties Protecting Labour Rights 20

§1. Introduction 20

§2. The European Social Charter of 1961 21

§3. Additional Protocols 28
I. The Additional Protocol of 1988 28
II. Amending Protocol of 1991 28
III. Additional Protocol of 1995: Establishing a Collective Complaints System 30

§4. The Revised European Social Charter of 1996 31

§5. Reform of the European Social Charter System 44

Part II. Labour Human Rights 49

Introduction: Categories of Labour Human Rights Connected with Work and Methods of Their Protection 49

Chapter 1. Regulation of Individual Labour Human Rights 51

§1. THE RIGHT TO WORK 51
I. Full Employment 51
II. Freedom of Work 58
A. Prohibition of Forced Labour 58
B. Eliminating Forms of Discrimination in Employment 63
III. To Establish and Maintain the Function of General Access to Free Employment Services 71
IV. Vocational Guidance, Training and Rehabilitation 75

§2. THE RIGHT OF NATIONALS TO ENGAGE IN GAINFUL OCCUPATION IN THE TERRITORIES OF OTHER COUNTRIES 78
I. Introduction 78
II. An Obligation to Apply the Existing Regulations in a Spirit of Liberty 81
III. Simplifying Existing Formalities and Reducing or Abolishing Administrative Fees 83
IV. Liberalisation of Regulations 85

§3. THE RIGHT TO JUST CONDITIONS OF WORK 86
I. The Definition of Reasonable Daily and Weekly Working Hours 87
II. Public Holidays with Pay (Article 2 §2) 94
III. Two Weeks' Annual Holiday with Pay 98
IV. The Duty to Eliminate Risks for Workers in Dangerous or Unhealthy Occupations and Provide Them with Additional Paid Holidays or Reduced Working Hours when Possible 103
V. To Ensure a Weekly Rest Period 109
VI. To Ensure Workers Are Informed in Writing of the Aspects of the Work Agreement 113
VII. Protection of Workers Employed in Night Work 114

§4. THE RIGHT TO SAFE AND HEALTHY WORKING CONDITIONS 116
I. According to the European Social Charter 118
A. The Responsibility to Issue Regulations Dealing with Health and Safety at Work 118
B. Obligation to Provide for the Enforcement of Such Regulations by Measures of Supervision 123
C. To Ensure Consultation with Stakeholders in Matters of Industrial Health and Safety 126

II. According to the Revised European Social Charter 127
A. Policies of Occupational Safety and Health 130
B. Occupational Health Services 130

§5. The Right to Fair Remuneration 132
I. Decent Remuneration 133
II. Additional Remuneration for Overtime Work 139
III. The Right of Men and Women to Equal Remuneration for Work of Equal Value 145
IV. The Right of All Workers to a Reasonable Period of Notice for Termination of Employment 152
V. Deductions from Wages 161

§6. The Right of Children and Young Persons to Protection 165
I. Introduction 165
II. A Ban on Employing Children under the Age of 15 Years 165
III. A Prohibition of Employing Persons under the Age of 18 Years in Employment Dangerous or Harmful to Health 169
IV. The Banning of Employment of Children of School Age in Work Affecting Their Education 170
V. Time of Work for Young Workers 174
VI. Remuneration for Young Workers 175
VII. Time of Vocational Training 179
VIII. Annual Holiday for Young Persons 180
IX. Banning the Employment of Young Persons in Night Employment 181
X. Regular Medical Supervision of Young Persons 183
XI. Special Protection of Children and Young Persons against Physical and Moral Dangers 186

§7. The Right of Employed Women to Protection 187
I. Maternity Leave 188
II. Prohibiting the Termination of a Work Agreement with a Pregnant Woman 195
III. Time Off Work for Mothers Nursing their Infants 200
IV. Obligation to Regulate Rules of Employment Concerning Women Workers Employed at Nighttime in Industrial Occupations 202
V. Duty to Regulate the Rules of Employment at Nighttime Concerning Pregnant Women, Women Who Have Recently Given Birth or Women Nursing Their Infants 204
VI. Prohibiting the Employment of Women 204
VII. Prohibiting the Employment of Pregnant Women, Women Who have Recently Given Birth, or Who Are Nursing Their Infants, in Underground Mining and All Other Work of Dangerous, Unhealthy or Arduous Nature 206

§8. The Right to Vocational Guidance 207

§9. The Right to Vocational Training 210
I. The Obligation to Provide or Promote Technical and Vocational Training and Granting Facilities for Access to Higher Technical and University Education 211
II. The Duty of Providing or Promoting a System of Apprenticeship for Young Persons 215
III. Vocational Training for Adult Workers 217
IV. Special Measures for the Retraining and Reintegration of the Long-Term Unemployed 221
V. The Duty of Encouraging Actions Facilitating Vocational Training 222

§10. The Right to Equal Opportunities and Equal Treatment in Matters of Employment Without Discrimination on the Grounds of Sex 226

§11. The Right to Protection in Cases of Termination of Employment 235

§12. The Right of Workers to the Protection of Their Claims in the Event of the Insolvency of Their Employer 243

§13. The Right to Dignity at Work 249

§14. The Right of Workers with Family Responsibilities to Equal Opportunities and Equal Treatment 261

Chapter 2. The Regulation of Collective Labour Rights 266

§1. The Right to Organise 266
I. Forming Trade Unions 269
II. The Freedom of Trade Unions to Regulate Their Internal Organisational Affairs 273
III. The Right of Workers to Join a Trade Union or Elect Not To 276
A. The Right to Join a Trade Union 276
B. The Right Not to Join a Trade Union 277
IV. The Freedom to Carry Out Trade Union Activities 281
A. Negotiating Collective Labour Agreements 281
B. Carrying Out Trade Union Activities in the Territory of the Workplace 284
V. Legal Guarantees Allowing Workers to Freely Associate in Trade Unions 286
A. Prohibiting Discrimination of Workers Based on Their Trade Union Membership and Participation in Trade Union Activities 286

B. Prohibition of Allocating Workers Duties, Which Are Not Being Fulfilled by Workers Participating in a Legal Strike Action 289

VI. Union Freedom and the Right to Associate in Trade Unions for Certain Categories of Worker 290

A. Trade Union Freedom for Civil Servants 290

B. The Right of Police Officers to Organise 291

C. Union Freedom for Professional Militia 293

D. The Right of Migrant Workers, Citizens of a Member State, to Organise 294

E. Aftermath – A prelude to what is happening today 295

§2. THE RIGHT TO BARGAIN COLLECTIVELY 296

I. Introduction 296

II. Joint Consultations Between Workers and Employers 297

III. Collective Labour Agreements 302

IV. Mediation and Arbitration 311

V. Right of Workers and Employers to Collective Action 317

A. Collective Action 317

B. A Legal Strike 320

C. Illegal Strikes 325

D. Restricting the Right to Strike 326

1. Restricting the Right to Strike in Collective Labour Agreements 326

2. Restricting the Right to Strike, as Introduced by the Domestic Legislation of Member States 327

E. Restricting the Number of Entities Entitled to Organise Strikes 328

F. Procedural Requirements Needed Prior to the Commencement of a Legal Strike 329

G. Compulsory Referral of Collective Disputes to an Arbitration Tribunal 332

H. The Obligation to Ensure Continuous Operation of Certain Workplaces 333

I. The Legal Consequences of Collective Action with Regard to Individual Work Agreements 336

1. Strike and the Termination of a Work Agreement 336

2. Strike Action and the Right to Fair Remuneration 338

3. Strikes: Civil Liability and Criminal Responsibility 338

4. Restrictions on the Right to Strike as Imposed by the Courts 340

5. Lockouts 342

§3. THE RIGHT TO INFORMATION AND CONSULTATION 343

§4. THE RIGHT TO TAKE PART IN THE DETERMINATION AND IMPROVEMENT OF WORKING CONDITIONS AND WORKING

ENVIRONMENT 352

§5. THE RIGHT OF WORKERS TO INFORMATION AND CONSULTATION IN COLLECTIVE REDUNDANCY PROCEDURES 356

§6. THE RIGHT OF WORKERS' REPRESENTATIVES TO PROTECTION 362
I. An Obligation to Ensure Workers' Representatives the Protection of Endurance in the Undertaking 367
II. The Obligation to Afford Workers' Representatives Facilities to Carry Out Their Statutory Functions 369

Chapter 3. Necessary Derogations 372

§1. TEMPORARY DEROGATIONS OF THE CHARTER IN CASE OF WAR OR NATIONAL SECURITY THREATS 372

§2. DEROGATIONS NECESSARY FOR THE PROTECTION OF THE RIGHTS AND FREEDOMS OF OTHERS OR FOR THE PROTECTION OF PUBLIC INTEREST, NATIONAL SECURITY, PUBLIC HEALTH, OR MORALS 373

§3. DEROGATIONS OF THE PROVISIONS SPECIFIED BY THE CHARTER TO THE SIGNIFICANT MAJORITY OF WORKERS 374

§4. TERRITORIAL APPLICATION OF THE CHARTER 375

Part III. The Supervision of Complying with the Laws of the European Social Charter 377

Chapter 1. Supervisory Bodies 377

§1. THE COMMITTEE 377
I. Reports Concerning the Ratified Provisions of the Charter 379
II. Reports Concerning Provisions of the Charter That Have Not Been Ratified 385

§2. THE GOVERNMENTAL COMMITTEE 386

§3. THE COMMITTEE OF MINISTERS 391

Chapter 2. Adjudicating Collective Complaints 393

§1. INTRODUCTION 393

§2. ENTITIES ENTITLED TO INITIATE COLLECTIVE COMPLAINT PROCEEDINGS 394

§3. Examining the Admissibility of the Collective Complaint 396

§4. Grounds for Collective Complaint 405

§5. Formal Requirements for Collective Complaint Proceedings 428

§6. Collective Complaint Proceedings 429

§7. Conclusion 430

Selected Bibliography 433

Index 435

List of Abbreviations

AFM	Advance Training and Artistic and Musicals Specialisation Institutions
APeS	Associazione Profesionale e Sindicale
CDS	Confederazione Generale Sindicale
CESP	European Council of Police Trade Unions
CFDT	*Confédération Française Démocratique du Travail*
CFE-CGC	*Confédération Française de l'Encadrement*
CGIL	*Confederatione Generale Italiana del Lavoro*
CGSLB	*Générale des Syndicats Libéraux de Belgique*
CGT	*Confédération Général du Travail*
CGT-FO	*Confédération Génerale du Travail Force Ouvrière*
CM	The Committee of Ministers
CoE	Council of Europe
CPT	European Committee for the Prevention of Torture and Inhuman Degrading Treatment or Punishment
CSC	*Confédération des Syndicats Chrétiens de Belgique*
ECHR	European Convention on Human Rights
ECRI	European Commission Against Racism and Intolerance
ECSR	European Committee of Social Rights
EEA	European Economic Area
EOMA and TU	The European Organisation of Military Associations and Trade Unions
ESC	European Social Charter
ETUC	European Trade Union Confederation
EU	European Union
EUROCOP	European Confederation of Police
EUROFEDOP	European Federation of Employees in Public Services
EYF	European Youth Forum
FFFS	*Fellesforbundet for Sjøfolk*
FGTB	*Fédération Générale du Travail de Belgique*

List of Abbreviations

FIDH	International Federation of Human Rights Leagues
FLP	Federazione dei Lavorati Pubblici e Funzioni Pubbliche
GC	Governmental Committee
GCHQ	British Government Communications Headquarters
GRETA	Group of Experts on Action Against Trafficking in Human Beings
ICTU	Irish Congress of Trade Unions
IFAE	International Federation of Associates of the Elderly
ILO-CEACR	ILO Committee on the Application of Conventions and Recommendations
INGOs	International Non-governmental Organisations
IOE	International Organisation of Employers
LO	Swedish Trade Union Confederation
MFHR	Marangopoulos Foundation for Human Rights
MMW	Monthly Minimum Wage
NCHR	National Centre for Human Rights
Nursing Up	Associazione nazionale sindacato professionisti sanitari della funzione infermieristica
PACE	Parliamentary Assembly of the Council of Europe
QCEA	Quaker Council of European Affairs
RESC	Revised European Social Charter
SAGES	*Syndicat des Agréés de l'Enseignement Supérieur*
TCO	Swedish Confederation of Professional Employees
TSPC	Tripartite Social Partnership Commission
UGL-CFS and SAPAF	Unione Generale Lavoratori – Federazioni Corpo forestale dello Stato and Sindacato autonomo polizia ambientale
UN	United Nations
UNDIS	Unione Nazionale Dirigenti dello Stato
UNICE	Union of the Confederation of Industry and Employers of Europe
USB	Unione Sindacale di Base
UWE	University Women of Europe

Part I. The Council of Europe

Chapter 1. General Background Information

§1. Definition

1. The Council of Europe is the oldest regional organisation established after the Second World War and promotes cooperation between European Member States in the following areas: human rights, democratic development, the rule of law, legal standards and cultural common efforts.[1] It includes the following Member States: Albania, Andorra, Armenia, Austria, Azerbaijan, Belgium, Bosnia and Herzegovina, Bulgaria, Croatia, Cyprus, Czech Republic, Denmark, Estonia, Finland, France, Georgia, Germany, Greece, Hungary, Iceland, Ireland, Italy, Latvia, Lichtenstein, Lithuania, Luxembourg, Malta, Moldova, Monaco, Montenegro, the Netherlands, North Macedonia, Norway, Poland, Portugal, Romania, San Marino, Serbia, Slovakia, Slovenia, Spain, Sweden, Switzerland, Turkey, Ukraine, the United Kingdom.

2. Its population encompasses over 820 million citizens from Reykjavik to Vladivostok. The Council of Europe is an entirely separate international organisation from the European Union (EU), which brings together twenty-eight European Member States. The two separate regional (European) organisations share the same symbols: the flag and the anthem.

§2. History and Membership

3. On 19 September 1946, Sir Winston Churchill mentioned the idea of the 'United States of Europe' at Zurich University. The future structure and aims of such an organisation were discussed by politicians, government representatives and civil society at The Hague in 1948. At that congress, two schools of thought were presented. The first favoured a classical international organisation with the representation of governments. The second preferred a political forum with parliamentarians. Both approaches towards the organisational structure of the present Council of Europe were combined via the creation of the Committee of Ministers and the Parliamentary Assembly.

1. The Council of Europe: An Overview; The Council of Europe in Brief; Council of Europe, 47 states – 820 million citizens; Wikipedia, the free encyclopaedia.

4. The Council of Europe was founded on 5 May 1949 by the Treaty of London. That treaty was signed by ten states: Belgium, Denmark, France, Ireland, Italy, Luxembourg, the Netherlands, Norway, Sweden and the United Kingdom.

Article 4 of the Council of Europe Statute declares that membership is open to any 'European' state. That declaration was interpreted liberally in order to include any Eurasian state with a 'toe-hold' in Europe. The other states below listed joined the Council of Europe as full members: Greece (1949), Turkey (1949), Iceland (1950), Germany (1950), Austria (1956), Cyprus (1971), Switzerland (1963), Malta (1965), Portugal (1976), Spain (1977), Liechtenstein (1978), San Marino (1988), Finland (1989), Hungary (1990), Poland (1991), Bulgaria (1992), Estonia (1993), Lithuania (1993), Slovenia (1993), Czech Republic (1993), Slovakia (1993), Romania (1993), Andorra (1994), Latvia (1995), Albania (1995), Moldova (1995), the Former Yugoslav Republic of Macedonia, now – North Macedonia (1995), Ukraine (1995), Russia (1996), Croatia (1996), Georgia (1999), Armenia (2001), Azerbaijan (2001), Bosnia and Herzegovina (2002), Serbia (2003), Monaco (2004), Montenegro (2007).

Almost all European Member States have acceded to the Council of Europe, with the exceptions of Belarus (human rights concerns), Kazakhstan (human rights concerns) and the Vatican City (a theocracy).

§3. Observers, Partners and International Cooperation

5. The Council of Europe has established the following instruments for cooperation with non-Member States: observer, applicant, special guest and partner for democracy. The Holy See, Canada, Japan, the United States of America and Mexico enjoy observer status within the Council of Europe. Non-Member States may be invited to sign and ratify certain conventions or international treaties set up for the Council of Europe Member States.

6. Cooperation between the Council of Europe and the EU was signed in matters concerning the international enforcement of human rights. Protocol No. 14 of the European Convention on Human Rights (ECHR) allows the EU to accede to the ECHR and to the EU Treaty of Lisbon in order to prevent legal conflicts between judgments of the EU Court of Justice in Luxembourg and those of the European Court of Human Rights in Strasbourg.

7. The Council of Europe holds observer status in the United Nations and is represented in the UN General Assembly. It cooperates with the UN in the areas of human rights, minorities, migration and others.

§4. Structure

8. The statutory institutions of the Council of Europe responsible for the functioning of the organisation include the following:

- the Committee of Ministers is the Council of Europe's decision-making body in matters of policies, activities and budget and comprises the foreign ministers of all Member States or their permanent representatives in Strasbourg;
- the Parliamentary Assembly (PACE) is the political driving force which consists of parliamentarians from the forty-seven Member States;
- the Congress of Local and Regional Authorities is a political forum of representatives of regions and municipalities. It enables the strengthening of democracy and improving of services at local and regional levels;
- the European Court of Human Rights is the permanent judicial institution which guarantees for all Europeans the rights safeguarded by the ECHR adopted in 1950, which entered into force in 1953. The ECHR protects, among other things, the right to: life, freedom and security, freedom of expression, freedom of assembly and association. It prohibits, among other things, forced labour and discrimination in the enjoyment of the rights and freedoms secured by the Convention;
- the Commissioner for Human Rights is an independent institution within the Council of Europe, mandated to promote the awareness of and respect for human rights in the forty-seven Council of Europe Member States;
- the conference of International Non-Governmental Organisations (INGOs) provides a vital link between politicians and citizens and ensures that the voice of civil society is presented on the international forum;
- the Secretary General is the head of the Secretariat of the Council of Europe elected by the Parliamentary Assembly for a term of five years;
- the Secretariat is an administrative body of the Council of Europe employing over 2,300 employees. It ensures that the organisation's offices function properly and fulfils their mandates, as well as implementing the internal policy of the international institution.

§5. Aims and Functions

9. Article 1(a) of the Statute states that 'The aim of the Council of Europe is to achieve a greater unity between its members for the purpose of safeguarding and realising the ideals and principles which are their common heritage and facilitating their economic and social progress.' The Council of Europe Member States commit themselves through conventions, treaties, agreements[2] and cooperate on the basis of common values and common political decisions. Being part of international public law, Council of Europe conventions are open for signature to non-Member States.

10. The Council of Europe's major conventions include:

- the ECHR, which protects civil and political rights and liberties and propagates civilised values and democratic growth of European societies;

2. The key partial agreements include: the Council of Europe Development Bank, the European Directorate for the Quality of Medicines and Health Care (European Pharmacopoeia), the Pompidou Group, the Venice Commission – the European Commission for Democracy through Law.

- the European Social Charter, which protects the economic and social rights of European citizens. It safeguards rights regarding employment, social and legal protection, health, housing, education, free movement and non-discrimination;
- the European Convention for the Prevention of Torture and Inhuman or Degrading Treatment or Punishment, which prevents torture and inhuman treatment in places of detention. It sets and enforces standards with regard to safeguarding the rights of those imprisoned or otherwise deprived of their liberty in the Council of Europe's Member States;
- the Framework Convention for the Protection of National Minorities is concerned with protection of national minorities within the Council of Europe's Member States. It sets out guidelines relating to a wide range of fundamental freedoms, including peaceful assembly, expression, conscience and religion, access to media, language and education;
- the European Cultural Convention promotes and protects cultural diversity throughout Europe, encourages appreciation of national identities which comprise Europe's common cultural heritage, with a focus on languages, history and society;
- the ECHR and Biomedicine safeguards ethical practice in biomedicine;
- the European Convention on Action against Trafficking in Human Beings prevents and combats trafficking in human beings;
- the Convention on Preventing and Combating Violence against Women and Domestic Violence sets out guidelines which target the protection of women and the elimination and prosecution of such acts and monitors implementation and compliance;
- the Convention on the Protection of Children against Sexual Exploitation and Sexual Abuse prevents sexual offences against children, prosecutes the perpetrators of such acts and protects the victims.

11. Monitoring the compliance of Member States with the Council of Europe's conventions and treaties is provided by the following, most important, permanent committees:

- the European Committee of Social Rights (ECSR);
- the European Committee for the Prevention of Torture and Inhuman Degrading Treatment or Punishment (CPT);
- the European Commission Against Racism and Intolerance (ECRI);
- the Group of Experts on Action Against Trafficking in Human Beings (GRETA).

§6. Headquarters and Offices

12. The headquarters of the Council of Europe is in Strasbourg, France. The official languages of the Council of Europe are English and French. The Committee of Ministers, the Parliamentary Assembly and the Congress of Local and Regional Authorities also use German, Italian and Russian for their work.

The Council of Europe's information and project offices are present in a majority of Member States.

§7. SYMBOLS

13. The European flag and the European anthem were chosen and adopted by the Council of Europe before also becoming symbols of the EU. On 25 October 1955, the Parliamentary Assembly unanimously approved the emblem of gold stars on a blue background. 'Against the background of blue sky, the stars form a circle, symbolising union. The number of stars is fixed, 12 being the symbol of perfection and completeness and bringing to mind the apostles, the sons of Jacob, the labours of Hercules, the months of the year.'

On 9 December 1955, the Committee of Ministers adopted the star-studded flag, which was launched officially on 13 December 1955 in Paris.

14. The European Anthem, based on the prelude to the Ode to Joy from Ludwig van Beethoven's Ninth Symphony, has been used by the Council of Europe since 1972. On 5 May 1964, the 15th anniversary of its founding, the Council of Europe proclaimed 5 May as Europe Day. On the occasion of its 50th anniversary in May 1999, the Council of Europe adopted its logo. To avoid confusion with the EU, which subsequently adopted the same symbols in the 1980s, the Council of Europe often uses a modified version with a lowercase 'e' in the centre of the stars, which is referred to as the 'Council of Europe Logo'.

Chapter 2. International Treaties Protecting Labour Rights

§1. Introduction

15. The European Social Charter of the Council of Europe is a term acknowledged by lawyers specialising in international and comparative labour law and social security, as well as by specialists in international social policies, to define the following treaties and international agreements entered into between 1961 and 1996:[3]

- the European Social Charter from 18 October 1961;
- the Additional Protocol to the European Social Charter from 5 May 1988;
- the Amending Protocol to the European Social Charter from 21 October 1991;
- the Additional Protocol to the European Social Charter providing for a system of collective complaints, from 9 November 1995;
- the Revised European Social Charter from 3 May 1996.

The European Social Charter of the European Council is a fundamental international treaty in which labour rights are regulated by labour and social security laws. These rights are regarded as human rights,[4] guaranteeing protection on the European continent.

16. The European Social Charter of 1961, along with the three already mentioned Protocols and the Revised European Social Charter of 1996, are treaties guaranteeing the following labour rights:

(a) regulation of rights through individual labour laws: the right to work (Article 1), the right to just conditions of work (Article 2), the right to safe and healthy working conditions (Article 3), the right to fair remuneration (Article 4), the right of children and young persons to protection (Article 7), the right of employed women on maternity to protection (Article 8), the right to vocational guidance (Article 9), the right to vocational training (Article 10), the right to equal opportunities and equal treatment in matters of employment and occupation without discrimination on the grounds of sex (Article 20), the right to protection in cases of termination of employment (Article 24), the right of workers to protection of their claims in the event of insolvency of their employer (Article 25), the right to dignity at work (Article 26), the right of workers with family responsibilities to equal treatment and equal opportunity (Article 27);
(b) regulation of rights through collective labour laws: the right of workers and employers to organise (Article 5), the right to bargain collectively (Article 6), the right of workers to information and consultation (Article 21), the right of workers to take part in the determination and improvement of the working conditions and working environment (Article 22), the right of workers to be

3. Published in: *European Social Charter: Collected Texts* (Council of Europe Publishing 4th ed. 2005).
4. M. Mikkola, *Social Human Rights of Europe* (Bookwell Ltd 2010).

informed and consulted in collective redundancy procedures (Article 29), the right of workers' representatives to protection and the availability of appropriate facilities (Article 28).

§2. The European Social Charter of 1961

17. The European Social Charter was ratified by eighteen Member States of the Council of Europe. It was presented for ratification on 18 October 1961 in Turin during the Centenary of Italy's unification. On that day, thirteen countries signed the Charter.[5] Appropriately, under Article 35, section 2, the Charter comes into being thirty days after its ratification by competent authorities of five Member States. The European Social Charter came into being on 26 February 1965.[6]

18. The European Social Charter is comprised of two parts. In the first part, Member States (Parties to the Charter) define the standards of social policy as a priority and list them in nineteen points of rights and regulations as follows: the right to work (point 1), the right to just conditions of work (point 2), the right to safe and healthy working conditions (point 3), the right to fair remuneration (point 4), the right to freedom of association in national or international organisations for the protection of their economic and social interests (point 5), the right to bargain collectively (point 6), the right of children and young persons to special protection against physical and moral dangers (point 7), the right of employed women to protection in cases of maternity and other appropriate cases (point 8), the right to appropriate facilities for vocational guidance with a view to helping choose occupations to personal capabilities and interests (point 9), the right to vocational training (point 10). In Part II of the draft of the European Social Charter, nineteen labour rights were codified to which all Member States of the Council of Europe should adhere. The European Social Charter, Article 20(1) encourages Member States to achieve (with the help of particular resources) the goals declared within Part I(a) as well as to ratify at least five out of the ten following regulations of Part II of the Charter: Articles 1, 5, 6, 12, 13, 16, 19(b). Fulfilling at least five out of the seven regulations mentioned under Article 20 §2(b) of the Charter, Member States are obliged to accept at least as many other regulations listed in Part II of the Charter as to make a total number of ten out of nineteen ratified articles or forty-five out of seventy-two paragraphs respectively, in accordance with Article 20 §1(c). The established standards of protecting labour rights by the European Social Charter were constructed in such a way as to allow the ratification of some numbered paragraphs within the nineteen stated articles.

19. The procedure for ratifying the Charter demands that Member States inform the Secretary General of the Council of Europe about the regulation of the Charter

5. Belgium, Denmark, Greece, the Netherlands, Ireland, Luxembourg, Germany, Norway, Sweden, Turkey, the United Kingdom, Italy.
6. After ratification by: Ireland (7 Oct. 1964); Germany (27 Jan. 1965); Norway (26 Oct. 1962); Sweden (17 Dec. 1962); the United Kingdom (11 Jul. 1962).

they have chosen to follow (Article 20 §2). If Member States choose to abide by all regulations of the European Social Charter, there are no legal obstacles standing in their way when handing in their ratifying documents. Belgium and Spain did just this. Filing a declaration to abide by the minimum number of regulations, ten articles or forty-five paragraphs, including five paragraphs listed under Article 20(1)(a) of the Charter, does not stand in the way of increasing the scope of responsibility. All Member State authorities that are party to the agreed international treaty have the right to inform the Secretary General of the Council of Europe at any given time that they will abide by other regulations of the Charter. Additional obligations are regarded as an integral part of the original ratification (Article 20 §3).

Ratifying the European Social Charter in 1961 was not an obstacle to signing and ratifying the Revised European Social Charter. Other Member States, influenced by the case of France, bound themselves by the regulations of the European Social Charter and signed and ratified the Revised European Social Charter. These are mentioned alphabetically. Bracketed is the signing date of the European Social Charter, Revised European Social Charter and protocols; following is the date of ratification if applicable.

Signatures and Ratifications of the 1961 Charter, Its Protocols and the European Social Charter (Revised) as of 1 January 2017 Member States[7]	*European Social Charter 1961 STE 035 Signature Ratification*	*Additional Protocol 1988 STE 128 Signature Ratification*	*Amending Protocol 1991 STE 142 Signature Ratification*	*Collective complaints Protocol 1995 STE 158 Signature Ratification*	*Revised European Social Charter 1996 STE 163 Signature Ratification*
Albania	(2) (2)	(3) (3)	(2) (2)	(2) –	21/9/98 14/11/02
Andorra	(2) (2)	(3) (3)	(2) (2)	(2) –	4/11/00 12/11/04
Armenia	(2) (2)	(3) (3)	(2) (2)	(2) –	18/10/01 21/1/04
Austria	22/7/63 29/10/69	4/12/90 –	7/5/92 13/7/95	(2) –	7/5/99 20/5/11

7. Activity report 2019, European Committee of Social Right, European Social Charter, Council of Europe, pp. 71–73.

Signatures and Ratifications of the 1961 Charter, Its Protocols and the European Social Charter (Revised) as of 1 January 2017 Member States[7]	*European Social Charter 1961 STE 035 Signature Ratification*	*Additional Protocol 1988 STE 128 Signature Ratification*	*Amending Protocol 1991 STE 142 Signature Ratification*	*Collective complaints Protocol 1995 STE 158 Signature Ratification*	*Revised European Social Charter 1996 STE 163 Signature Ratification*
Azerbaijan	(2) (2)	(3) (3)	(2) (2)	(2) –	18/10/01 2/9/04
Belgium	18/10/61 16/10/90	20/5/92 23/6/03	22/10/91 21/9/00	14/5/96 23/6/03	3/5/96 2/3/04
Bosnia and Herzegovina	(2) (2)	(3) (3)	(2) (2)	(2) –	11/5/04 7/10/08
Bulgaria	(2) (2)	(3) (3)	(2) (2)	(4) (4)	21/9/98 7/6/00
Croatia	8/3/99 26/2/03	8/3/99 26/2/03	8/3/99 26/2/03	8/3/99 26/2/03	6/11/09 –
Cyprus	22/5/67 7/3/68	5/5/88 (3)	21/10/91 1/6/93	9/11/95 6/8/96	3/5/96 27/9/00
Czech Republic	27/5/92* 3/11/99	27/5/92* 17/11/99	27/5/92* 17/11/99	26/2/02 4/4/12	4/11/00 –
Denmark	18/10/61 3/3/65	27/8/96 27/8/96	– ***	9/11/95 –	3/5/96 –
Estonia	(2) (2)	(3) (3)	(2) (2)	(2) –	4/5/98 11/9/00
Finland	9/2/90 29/4/91	9/2/90 29/4/91	16/3/92 18/8/94	9/11/95 17/7/98	3/5/96 21/6/02
France	18/10/61 9/3/73	22/6/89 (3)	21/10/91 24/5/95	9/11/95 7/5/99	3/5/96 7/5/99
Georgia	(2) (2)	(3) (3)	(2) (2)	(2) –	30/6/00 22/8/05
Germany	18/10/61 27/1/65	5/5/88 –	– ***	(1) –	29/6/07 –

Signatures and Ratifications of the 1961 Charter, Its Protocols and the European Social Charter (Revised) as of 1 January 2017 Member States[7]	*European Social Charter 1961 STE 035 Signature Ratification*	*Additional Protocol 1988 STE 128 Signature Ratification*	*Amending Protocol 1991 STE 142 Signature Ratification*	*Collective complaints Protocol 1995 STE 158 Signature Ratification*	*Revised European Social Charter 1996 STE 163 Signature Ratification*
Greece	18/10/61 6/6/84	5/5/88 18/6/98	29/11/91 12/9/96	18/6/98 18/6/98	3/5/96 18/03/16
Hungry	13/12/91 8/7/99	7/10/04 1/6/05	13/12/91 4/2/04	7/10/04 –	7/10/04 20/4/09
Island	15/1/76 15/1/76	5/5/88 –	12/12/01 21/2/02	(1) –	4/11/98 –
Ireland	18/10/61 7/10/64	(3) (3)	14/5/97 14/5/97	4/11/00 4/11/00	4/11/00 4/11/00
Italy	18/10/61 22/10/65	5/5/88 26/5/94	21/10/91 27/1/95	9/11/95 3/11/97	3/5/96 5/7/99
Latvia	29/5/97 31/1/02	29/5/97 –	29/5/97 9/12/03	(1) –	29/5/07 26/03/13
Liechtenstein	9/10/91 –	– –	– –	– –	– –
Lithuania	(2) (2)	(3) (3)	(2) (2)	(2) –	8/9/97 29/6/01
Luxembourg	18/10/61 10/10/91	5/5/88 –	21/10/91 ***	(1) –	11/2/98 –
Malta	26/5/88 4/10/88	(3) (3)	21/10/91 16/2/94	(2) –	27/7/05 27/7/05
Republic of Moldova	(2) (2)	(3) (3)	(2) (2)	(2) –	3/11/98 8/11/01
Monaco	(1)	(1)	(1)	(1)	5/10/04 –
Montenegro	(2) (2)	(3) (3)	(2) (2)	(2) –	22/3/05** 3/3/10
Netherlands	18/10/61 22/4/80	14/6/90 5/8/92	21/10/91 1/6/93	23/1/04 3/5/06	23/1/04 3/5/06

Signatures and Ratifications of the 1961 Charter, Its Protocols and the European Social Charter (Revised) as of 1 January 2017 Member States[7]	*European Social Charter 1961 STE 035 Signature Ratification*	*Additional Protocol 1988 STE 128 Signature Ratification*	*Amending Protocol 1991 STE 142 Signature Ratification*	*Collective complaints Protocol 1995 STE 158 Signature Ratification*	*Revised European Social Charter 1996 STE 163 Signature Ratification*
North Macedonia	5/5/98 31/3/05	5/5/98 –	5/5/98 31/3/05	(2) –	27/5/09 6/1/12
Norway	18/10/61 26/10/62	10/12/93 10/12/93	21/10/91 21/10/91	20/3/97 20/3/97	7/5/01 7/5/01
Poland	26/11/91 25/6/97	(1) –	18/4/97 25/6/97	(1) –	25/10/05 –
Portugal	1/6/82 30/9/91	(3) (3)	24/2/92 8/3/93	9/11/95 20/3/98	3/5/96 30/5/02
Romania	4/10/94 (2)	(3) (3)	(2) (2)	(2) –	14/5/97 7/5/99
Russian Federation	(2) (2)	(3) (3)	(2) (2)	(2) –	14/9/00 16/10/09
Saint-Marin	(1) –	(1) –	(1) –	(1) –	18/10/01 –
Serbia	(2) (2)	(3) (3)	(2) (2)	(2) –	22/3/05* 14/9/09
Slovak Republic	27/5/92* 22/6/98	27/5/92* 22/6/98	27/5/92* 22/6/98	18/11/99 –	18/11/99 23/4/09
Slovenia	11/10/97 (2)	11/10/97 (3)	11/10/97 (2)	11/10/97 (4)	11/10/97 7/5/99
Spain	27/4/78 6/5/80	5/5/88 24/1/00	21/10/91 24/1/00	(1) –	23/10/00 –
Sweden	18/10/61 17/12/62	5/5/88 5/5/89	21/10/91 18/3/92	9/11/95 29/5/98	3/5/96 29/5/98
Suisse	6/5/76 –	– –	– –	– –	– –
Turkey	18/10/61 24/11/89	5/5/98 (3)	6/10/04 10/6/09	(2) –	6/10/04 27/6/07

Signatures and Ratifications of the 1961 Charter, Its Protocols and the European Social Charter (Revised) as of 1 January 2017 Member States[7]	*European Social Charter 1961 STE 035 Signature Ratification*	*Additional Protocol 1988 STE 128 Signature Ratification*	*Amending Protocol 1991 STE 142 Signature Ratification*	*Collective complaints Protocol 1995 STE 158 Signature Ratification*	*Revised European Social Charter 1996 STE 163 Signature Ratification*
Ukraine	2/5/96 (2)	(3) (3)	(2) (2)	(2) –	7/5/99 21/12/06

* Date of signature by the Czech and Slovak Federal Republic.
** Date of signature by the State Union of Serbia and Montenegro.
*** State whose ratification is necessary for the entry into force of the protocol.

The last group of countries consists of those which have ratified or signed the RESC without ratifying the earlier international treaty, that is, the European Social Charter.

20. Legal practitioners dealing with the protection of national labour and social security laws treat the European Social Charter with great reserve. Its scope guarantees the protection of chosen legal categories. The Charter protects the following categories of rights: the right to work (Article 1), the right to just conditions of work (Article 2), the right to safe and healthy working conditions (Article 3), the right to freedom of association (Article 5), the right to bargain collectively (Article 6), the right to vocational guidance (Article 9), the right to vocational training (Article 10), the right to health protection (Article 11).

The division of guaranteed rights by the European Social Charter in 1961 was upheld by the following documents: the Additional Protocol to the European Social Charter in 1988, which broadened the scope of protection rights by four further regulations (the right to equal opportunity and equal treatment in matters of employment and occupation without discrimination on the grounds of sex (Article 1)); the right to information and consultation (Article 2); the right to take part in the determination and improvement of working conditions and working environment (Article 3); by the Revised European Social Charter broadening the following eight protection rights: the right to protection in cases of employment termination (Article 24); the workers' right to protection of their claims in the event of insolvency of their employer (Article 25); the right to dignity at work (Article 26); the right of workers with family responsibilities to equal opportunity and equal treatment

(Article 27); the right of workers' representatives to protection and appropriate facilities (Article 28); the right of workers to be informed and consulted in collective redundancy procedures (Article 29).

Apart from the introduction of the first two parts of the European Social Charter, the treaty comprises Parts III and IV as well as the appendix.

Part IV (Articles 21–23) binds Member States to provide reports regarding their fulfilments of duties specified by the Charter as well as binding them to provide copies of reports to social stakeholders. Identical obligations encompass appropriate employer and employee organisations to provide the Secretary General to the Council of Europe with reports. The Charter obliges Member States to file two types of reports: to provide documents specified by the rules ratified by a given country (Article 21) as well as reports dealing with national labour laws that were not ratified by a Member State (Article 22). Copies of such reports should be given by Member States to national employee and employer organisations associated with their international counterparts invited to partake in the Subcommittee of the Governmental Social Committee sittings.

Part V of the Charter was regulated by a mechanism supervising obligations of the Charter regulations undertaken by Member States. The essential supervising element over Member States, seeing whether the standards of the Charter are followed, is the Committee of Experts (Article 24).[8] The reports of Member States and the conclusions of the Committee of Experts shall be submitted for examination to a Subcommittee of the Governmental Social Committee of the Council of Europe (Article 27). The Subcommittee of the Governmental Social Committee, whose role has been taken over by the Governmental Committee, is a political organ. From such a perspective, the content-related reports and conclusions presented by the Committee of Independent Experts and the Governmental Committee analysed the execution of responsibilities ratified by Member States of Part II of the Charter. The results were passed on to the Secretary General by the Committee of Experts, who, in turn, presented the finding to the Advisory Assembly. The Advisory Assembly passed on any remarks made regarding the results to the Committee of Ministers (Article 28). Based on the report of the Subcommittee of the Governmental Social Committee, and after listening to the advice of the Advisory Assembly, the Committee of Ministers, by a majority of two-thirds Member State votes, made the decision to address its essential recommendations to Member States that are Parties to the Charter (Article 29).

21. The responsibility of adjusting national practices and regulations to the standards set in the Charter lies with Member States. The European Social Charter is in force on the national territory of every party. Each Member State defines the territorial scope of the application of the Charter. This is done by a statement addressed to the Secretary General by the Council of Europe. Each Member State has the right to propose amendments to the Charter. This is done by way of an address to the Secretary General of the Council of Europe. Amendments are also passed on to other

8. Originally, this Committee was called the Committee of Independent Experts. This name emphasised the lack dependency between members of the Committee and the authorities of Member States. From 1988, the Committee adopted the name of the Committee.

Member States. The acceptance or rejection of such amendments is decided by the Committee of Ministers. The amendments analysed by the Committee are then passed to the Consultative Assembly for an opinion. Amendments accepted by the Committee of Ministers come into being on the 30th day from the date of informing the Secretary General of their acceptance. The Secretary General officially informs all Member States, as well as the Director of the International Labour Office, of the amendment coming into effect.

22. The whole Charter can be denounced by each Member State after the passing of five years from the date of its coming into effect of the above-mentioned international treaty, with respect to each country or with each following two-year passing period. The denunciation of the Charter is not influential in terms of the obligations of the Charter for the remaining signatories if their number is no fewer than five.

23. An integral part of the Charter is its appendix. In it are defined certain legal terms and regulations which are used within the Charter, such as: 'foreigner', 'work freely entered upon' (Article 1 §2); 'period of notice for termination' (Article 4 §4); 'deductions from wages' (Article 4 §5); 'right to strike' (Article 6 §4), 'young persons shall not be employed in night work' (Article 7 §8).

§3. Additional Protocols

I. The Additional Protocol of 1988

24. The following three protocols complete the Charter: the Additional Protocol of 1988, the Amending Protocol of 1991, and the Additional Protocol of 1995.

The above-mentioned protocol was prepared for Member States to sign on 5 May 1988. It came into force on 4 September 1992, the 30th day from the day the third ratifying document was tendered.

The Additional Protocol of 1988 supplements the catalogue of labour rights protected by the European Social Charter by three extra regulations: the right to equal opportunities and equal treatment in matters of employment and occupation without discrimination on the grounds of sex (Article 1), the right to information and consultation (Article 2), the right to take part in the determination and improvement of working conditions and the working environment (Article 3).

II. Amending Protocol of 1991

25. The Amending Protocol of 1991 is an international document aimed at strengthening the significance of the European Social Charter and the Additional Protocol to the level of the ECHR.

The number of members of the Committee was increased to nine, and their tenures were limited to a maximum of two six-year terms. The grounds for supervision were determined, and the Committee was obliged to check the conformity of domestic legislation, executive regulations and practices with the provisions of the Charter. The Committee was authorised to directly contact the authorities of Member States to obtain additional information or explanations. Members of the Committee were given the right to arrange meetings with representatives of Member States, initiated either by them or by representatives of Member States. Motions and rulings were to be published and passed by the Secretary General to the Governmental Committee, the Parliamentary Assembly and stakeholders entitled to obtain copies of national reports under Article 32 §1 of the Charter. The parliamentary Assembly no longer took part in supervisory procedures of abiding by Charter regulations by Member States. It was decided that the Governmental Committee would prepare decisions for the Committee of Ministers on the basis of rulings of the Committee. In particular, on the basis of rulings of the Committee and reports sent by authorities of Member States, the Governmental Committee chooses, taking into consideration social and economic policy, what recommendations should be addressed to a given Member State. The Government Committee reports, prepared for the Committee of Ministers, are known to the public. The Committee of Ministers analysing reports produced by the Committee and the Governmental Committee adopts, by a two-thirds majority of votes, resolutions concerning the whole supervisory cycle of Member State reports as well as individual recommendations addressed to a given Member State. Reports of the Committee and the Governmental Committee involve a plenary discussion.

The European Social Charter, together with the Protocols, inspired European Communities to pass the Charter of Fundamental Labour Rights for Workers.

26. The Amending Protocol of 1991 has brought important alterations to the administrative structure of the Council of Europe. Until 1989, an organisational body concentrating on obeying the European Social Charter was a part of the Department of Social Affairs. In the period preceding the passing of the Amending Protocol of 1991, all issues connected with the substantial supervision of abiding by the European Social Charter were passed on to the Department of Human Rights, a body responsible for dealing with human rights protection. Until 1989, the Department of Human Rights of the Council of Europe dealt solely with matters of political and civil rights protection: organisational changes, works on increasing the efficiency of supervisory procedures of abiding social rights coincided with extensive political changes in Europe, and introducing free-market economies in former communist countries. The authorities of these countries started showing an increasing interest in matters of the protection of social and economic rights, as they were experiencing serious difficulties with aggressively controlling growing capitalism on their own. They needed patterns to follow. Even though neither the European Social Charter nor the Committee of Social Rights defined patterns of conduct in cases concerning the protection of social rights, the standards determined under the Charter as well as rulings of the Committee of Social Rights, roughly informed the authorities whether domestic labour law and social protection regulations were in conformity with the standards accepted by the Council of Europe, that should be observed by current European countries.

III. Additional Protocol of 1995: Establishing a Collective Complaints System

27. Signatories of the Additional Protocol of 1995 are the following states: Belgium, Bulgaria, Croatia, Cyprus, Czech Republic, Denmark, Finland, France, Greece, Holland, Ireland, Italy, Norway, Portugal, Slovakia, Slovenia, and Sweden.

The Protocol consists of the preamble and sixteen provisions. The Protocol determines subjects entitled to register collective complaints against Member States. It defines a body of the Council of Europe authorised to recognise these complaints. It describes fundamental rules of conduct in cases of collective complaints. The right to register such complaints was granted to some international employee and employer organisations, to other non-governmental organisations of advisable character to the Council of Europe as well as to representative national organisations of stakeholders appointed by Member States.[9] Each collective complaint is analysed by the Committee, which, at the initial stage, debates on the legitimacy of the complaint and then, after hearing the interested sides, makes a ruling stating either a violation of Charter regulations by the charged state or the conformity between Charter provisions and state conduct, in which case the complaint is dismissed. A ruling of the Committee gives the basis for the Committee of Ministers to pass an adequate resolution. Member State authorities against which a collective complaint was registered are obligated to deliver a report to the Secretary General on means undertaken in order to bring the resolution passed by the Committee of Ministers into life. The Additional Protocol took effect on 1 July 1998, on the first day of the month after a month since the day when five Member States[10] filed ratification documents. All countries wanting to join the Protocol in the future will be bound by its regulations from the first day of the month after a monthly period of the ratification date when appropriate documents are filed or the Protocol is adopted or ratified. All Parties to the Protocol can denounce by giving a twelve-month notice period starting on the day when the Secretary General is given a denouncement notification. The Secretary General is obliged to inform all Member States about the following: signing of the Protocol, filing ratification documents, adopting or approving the Protocol, the date when the Protocol takes effect or is denounced, as well as about any other action connected with the Additional Protocol.

28. The Additional Protocol of 1995 created a legal mechanism which has enabled the Committee to supervise Member States effectively following the standards set up by the European Social Charter in 1961 and the Revised European Social Charter in 1996. One of the Council of Europe's bodies recognising collective disputes, an institution independent of Member States, is formed with the highest class of professionals. The Governmental Committee, a political body consisting of the authorities of Member States, does not evaluate rulings made by the Committee. The Council of Europe was allowed to take part in collective complaints procedures if the Committee made a decision differing from the interpretation of

9. Currently, it is only Finland which has agreed that national employee and employer organisations may register collective complaints with the Committee.
10. Cyprus, Italy, Norway, Portugal, Sweden.

Charter regulations, which formed a legal basis for the complaint. A necessary condition for the Governmental Committee to take part in collective complaints procedures in the preceding stage, adopting a resolution by the Committee of Ministers on the basis of a report prepared by the Committee, is to lodge a proposal by the charged Member State and for the Committee of Ministers to pass the bill by a two-thirds majority, allowing the report made by the Committee to be deduced by the Governmental Committee (Article 9 §2 of the Additional Protocol).

§4. The Revised European Social Charter of 1996

29. The Revised Social Charter is an international treaty which modified and took over the former legal regulations of the European Social Charter and the earlier three Protocols protecting labour rights. The original nineteen regulations of Part II of the European Social Charter, utilised in the amended demands for labour rights protection, supplemented by four supplementary regulations by the Additional Protocol of 1988, were enriched by further eight regulations.

The Revised European Social Charter does not replace the European Social Charter. Those Member States, which initially ratified the European Social Charter either with or without the Additional Protocols, and further ratified the Revised European Social Charter automatically cease producing reports which address the obeying of European Social Charter regulations. Member States are no longer bound by the earlier European Social Charter, albeit considering the vast differences in the standards of labour rights protection between the 'old' and 'new' Charter, the discontinuation of abiding by the 'old'. Charter regulations are not influential at the level of such labour rights. Member States, which ratified the European Social Charter, signing the Revised European Social Charter but not ratifying it,[11] are bound by the 'old' Charter. Article B in Part III of the Revised European Social Charter of 1996 regulates the relationship between itself and the European Social Charter of 1961 and the Additional Protocols of 1988.

30. The changes introduced to the first twenty-three provisions of Part II of the Revised European Social Charter dealing with the labour regulation accepted by the European Social Charter are as follows:[12]

- an increase of the right to annual holiday pay from two to four weeks (Article 2 §3);
- first-row Member States were obliged to eliminate risk in dangerous or unhealthy occupations, and when such risk is not able to be eliminated or reduced, Member States became obliged to reduce the working hours or provide additional paid leave for workers engaged in such occupations (Article 2 §4);

11. Austria, Belgium, the Czech Republic, Denmark, the United Kingdom. Ireland, Luxembourg, Slovakia and Spain.
12. Explanatory note to the Revised European Social Charter, European Social Charter, *Collected Texts, supra*, pp. 163 et seq.

- employers should ensure workers are informed by writing, as soon as it is possible, and not later than two months from commencing their employment, of the essential aspects of the contract or employment relationship (Article 2 §6);
- a new obligation was introduced that workers performing night work should benefit from measures which take into account the special nature of their work (Article 2 §7);
- Member States were obliged to formulate, implement and periodically review policy on matters of occupational safety and work hygiene, occupational health and working environment (Article 3 §1);
- a new obligation was introduced to promote a progressive development of occupational health services, with preventative and advisory functions, with a right to access such facilities for all workers (Article 3 §4);
- the scope of competency of stakeholders was broadened, who under the European Social Charter take advantage of engaging in positions dealing with the improvement of safety and hygiene at work (Article 3 §3), to all categories regulated by Article 3 of the Revised European Social Charter;
- a minimum age of 18 was provided for the admission of employment into occupations regarded as dangerous or unhealthy (Article 7 §2);
- the age level of young persons was raised from 16 to 18 years of age, limiting their working hours in accordance with their needs of development and their need for vocational training (Article 7 §4);
- employees under the age of 18 have had their annual paid leave increased from 3 to 4 weeks (Article 7 §7);
- an increase in maternity leave from 12 to 14 weeks (Article 8 §1);
- a broadening of the scope of protecting pregnant workers, including making it unlawful to give a woman notice of dismissal during the period of time she notifies her employer that she is pregnant (Article 8 §2);
- regulated employment for pregnant women, women who have recently given birth, or who are nursing their infants during night hours (Article 8 §4);
- a prohibition on employing pregnant women, women who have recently given birth, on who are nursing their infants in underground mining and all other work considered to be dangerous or unhealthy or arduous in nature and to take appropriate measures to protect the employment rights of these women (Article 8 §5).

31. The new provisions introduced to the Revised European Social Charter (Articles 24–31) guarantee the protection of the following labour rights:

- the right of workers to protection of their employment durability (Article 24), in which the provision forbids employers to terminate employment without valid reasons as well as giving the right to those workers who have had their employment terminated without a valid reason to adequate compensation;
- the right of workers to protect their pecuniary claims in cases of insolvency of their employer (Article 25). Satisfying such claims, or employees' contracts or employment relationships should be done by guaranteeing institutions or a mechanism, which for example, can give precedence to workers in such implementation proceedings;

- the right of workers to dignity at work (Article 26), protecting them from harassment, sexual harassment and mobbing;
- the right of workers with family responsibilities to equal opportunities and equal treatment (Article 27). The above provision has obliged Member States to undertake the appropriate measures to enable such workers to enter and remain in employment and to re-enter employment after the absence due to family responsibilities. Member States are also to take into account workers' needs in terms of conditions of employment and social security, to develop and promote child care services, to allow for the availability of parental leave and to ensure that family responsibilities shall not constitute a valid reason for termination of employment;
- the right of workers' representatives to protection in the undertaking and facilities to be accorded to them (Article 28);
- the right of workers and/or their representatives to information and consultation in collective redundancy procedures (Article 29).

32. The Revised European Social Charter is made up of six parts and an appendix. The first three parts of the Revised European Social Charter were structured according to the standards implemented in the construction of the European Social Charter.

In Parts III, IV, V and VI of the Revised European Social Charter, constructed with provisions which are structured according to the capitals of the alphabet from A to O, the following problems were resolved: supervision of the implementation of the undertakings contained in the Charter (Article C); collective complaints (Article D); non-discrimination for reasons specified within the Charter (Article E); exceptions for a Member State not to abide by the provisions of the Charter (Article F); the introduction of restrictions in the realisation of rules and provisions specified in Part I as well as their effective implementation as specified by Part II of the Charter (Article G); relations between the Charter and domestic law or international arrangements (Article H); means by which a Member State can fulfil its obligations specified in the Charter (Article J); signature, ratification and entry into force of the Charter (Article K); territorial application of the Charter (Article L); principles involved in denouncing the provisions regulated by the Charter (Article M); the legal status of the appendix to the Charter (Article N); notification procedure (Article O).

Until the day of universal ratification of the Revised European Social Charter in Europe, two Charters are current. The fulfilment of the legal obligations outlined by the provisions of both Charters is identically supervised.

Within the Revised European Social Charter, the provision for collective complaints, Article D, has been established. It addresses those Member States which have ratified the Additional Protocol of 1995 and have adhered to the provisions set by the Revised European Social Charter. Such power of Article D of the Revised European Social Charter obligates Member States to be subject to the supervisory standards established by the Revised European Social Charter according to the procedure outlined in the Additional Protocol. Article D(1) of the Revised European Social Charter does not allow the above Member States to withdraw from the obligations set by the Additional Protocol of 1995 dealing with procedures of collective complaints simply because they have ratified the Revised European Social Charter.

Those Member States which have ratified the Revised European Social Charter but are not bound by the provisions of the Additional Protocol of 1995 to the European Social Charter can, during the filing of ratification documents or at any time thereafter, declare by notification addressed to the Secretary General of the Council of Europe that it considers itself bound to the Additional Protocol of 1995 (Article D §2) This provision intends to simplify the procedure for Member States that are connected to the European Social Charter and have ratified the Revised European Social Charter and find reconnaissance in the provisions of the Additional Protocol of 1995. Accepting the obligations of the Additional Protocol is not done so by separate mechanisms; further ratification is usually dealt with by a legislative body or president but rather through notification by authorised government.

Article E of the Revised European Social Charter disallows discrimination based on grounds such as race, colour, sex, language, religion, political or other opinions, national extraction or social origin, health, or association with a national minority. It has in its parameters the protection of all labour rights guaranteed by the Charter. It is modelled on Article 14 of the ECHR. The rulings of the Committee, presented in Part II of this monograph, illustrate the scope of labour rights protection from discrimination.

Temporary exemption from obligations of the Revised European Social Charter and abiding by its standards is allowed only in circumstances of war and other public emergencies threatening the life of the nation. In such circumstances, a nation has the right to take measures derogating from its obligations under the Charter. The scope of being exempt from obligations of the Charter should be in strict proportion to the circumstances occurring in order for derogation to be called for. An essential requirement for allowing such exemption is a Member State's compliance with other obligations set up by international law. Any Member State, which would seek the right of derogation from the Charter, should, within a reasonable timeframe, inform the Secretary General of the Council of Europe of its reasons. The Secretary General should also be informed about the planned period of derogation and the date from which the provisions of the Charter, which it has accepted, will again be fully executed.

Article G §1 of the Revised European Social Charter stipulates that no Member State has the right to restrict the effective realisation of principles and laws outlined within the Charter. This article, however, does introduce an exception to the rule. It states that laws that are accepted and abided by in a democratic society can introduce restrictions in utilising labour rights guaranteed by the Charter when such laws are essential for the protection of rights and freedoms of others or essential for the protection of public order, national security, public health or good customs. Part II of this monograph looks at the decree of the Committee and how the above provision is interpreted. Article G §2 of the Charter determines boundaries by which Member States can utilise the above exception in the provision. The permitted restrictions to the rights and obligations set forth for the entitled by this Charter shall not be applied for any purpose other than for which they have been prescribed (Article G §2).

The Revised European Social Charter set minimum standards for labour rights protection. The provisions of this Charter do not prejudice the provisions of domestic law or bilateral and multilateral international treaties, conventions or agreements, which guarantee an effective right protection (Article H).

33. Introducing the provisions of the Charter and its coming into force in Member States may be done in a manner chosen by the authorities of a given Member State. Following in the footsteps of the undertakings in Article 7 of the Additional Protocol of 1988, Article I of the Revised European Social Charter states that the implementation of the Charter may take place through domestic laws (laws or regulations) or by normative agreements (agreements with workers' organisations) with stakeholders. Implementation may also take place by combining the already mentioned alternative methods regulating such provisions as work rights and social security. Article I of the Revised European Social Charter allows Member States the freedom to choose methods other than the above-mentioned implementation stated by the Charter. It is important that the chosen methods for implementing the Charter be effective.[13]

In the case of some of the provisions of the Charter (Article 2 §1–5 and 7, Article 7 §4, 6, and 7, Article 10 §1–3 and 5, as well as Articles 21 and 22 of the Charter), compliance with the undertakings from these provisions by Member States shall be regarded as effective if the provisions of this Charter are applied to the great majority (80%) of the workers concerned (Article I §2).

Amendments to all six Parts of the Revised European Social Charter are shaped according to the procedure stipulated by Article 36 of the Charter. Despite the fact that this last provision was never implemented due to its restrictive character, Article J of the Revised European Social Charter repeats the latter mechanism so as not to inhibit either Member States or Council of Europe bodies, the legal ability to amend the Charter. Even though the procedure for amending both the Charters is the same, Article J of the Revised European Social Charter stipulates that amendments made to Parts I and II of this Charter can be introduced solely for the broadening of rights guaranteed by the Charter. The concept of 'amendments' does not only hide the possibility of changing the obligating provisions of Parts I and II of the Charter, but it also suggests new protections of labour rights.[14] There are, however, no such restrictions in introducing amendments to the remaining parts of the Charter. Member States that are Parties to the Charter and the Governmental Committee are able to propose amendments to the Revised European Social Charter. All proposals should be addressed to the Secretary General of the Council of Europe. The Secretary General passes on each proposal to each Member State, that is, to all signatories of the Charter. Each proposal for an amendment is considered by the Governmental Committee, and when it is accepted, it is then passed on to the Committee of Ministers. This procedure is not appropriate when proposals are made by the Governmental Committee. All amending proposals considered by the Committee of Ministers to the Revised European Social Charter have the right to be made by all authorities of

13. Explanatory note to the Revised European Social Charter, European Social Charter, *Collected Texts, supra*, p. 159.
14. *Ibid.*, pp. 179–180.

Member States, including those who have not ratified either the Revised European Social Charter or the European Social Charter or have signed or ratified one of the mentioned international treaties. The Committee of Ministers has developed the principles for the participation of authorities of these countries in amendments made to the Revised European Social Charter.[15] Decisions made by the Committee are preceded by consultations with the Parliamentary Assembly. After confirming the final text of the amendment, the Committee of Ministers presents it to Member States, Parties to the Revised European Social Charter by way of acceptance. Each amendment to Parts I and II of the Charter comes into force in the country party to the Charter, which decides to accept it, on the first day of the following month, a month after the day on which a third Member State, party to the Charter, informs the Secretary General that it accepts the amendment. With reference to the fourth Member State and the following, amendments come into force on the first day of the following month, after one month has passed from the day in which a country, a signatory to the Charter, informs the Secretary General of its acceptance.

Amendments to Parts III, IV, V, and VI of the Charter come into force on the first day of the following month, after one month has passed, in which all the countries, Parties to the Charter, inform the Secretary General of their acceptance.

Part VI of this Charter includes decisions based on decisions made in other international treaties accepted by the Committee of Ministers. The Revised European Social Charter is open to be signed by all Member States of the Council of Europe. Like all other international treaties, it is subject to ratification, acceptance or approval. Ratification documents are filed with the Secretary General of the Council of Europe. As already mentioned, the Charter came into force on 1 July 1999 after the first three Member States filed ratifying documents. It is not possible to indicate the first three Member States, as documents by five Member States were all filed on the same day, being 7 May 1999 (in alphabetical order): France, Italy, Norway, Romania and Slovenia. In reference to the subsequent countries which consented at a later date, the Charter came into force on the first day of the month following the expiration of one month passing after the day ratifying documents were filed or when it was accepted or approved (Article K).

Similarly, as in the European Social Charter, the Additional Protocol and their Amendments, the Revised European Social Charter also has a provision for territorial application (Article L). This provision states the Charter shall apply to the metropolitan territory of each party. The provision authorises each signatory of the Charter to declare by notification to the Secretary General of the Council of Europe that the Charter shall extend to non-metropolitan territories. This declaration should be made during the same time as the signing or the filing of the ratifying documents for the Charter. The declarations of a country ratifying the Charter should specify the non-metropolitan territories for whose international relations it is responsible or assumes international responsibility for, which will be bound by the Charter. The Charter will be in force on the specified territories as declared, from the first day of the month following the period of one month after the date the Secretary General of

15. *Ibid.*, p. 180.

the Council of Europe accepts the notification. It is also possible to notify the Secretary General of the Council of Europe of accepting as binding any article or paragraph in respect of a non-metropolitan territory which it has not already accepted in respect of the specified territory. The provisions, which are later accepted, are regarded as the integral element of the initial declaration concerning a given non-metropolitan territory. They come into legal force from the first day of the month following the period of one month after the date the Secretary General has accepted the notification (Article L).

Article M regulates the denunciatory procedures of the Revised European Social Charter. This provision allows that each Member State, a party to the Charter, can denounce the Charter no earlier than five years from the date the Charter came into force after being ratified by the given country. It is also possible to denounce the Charter at the end of any subsequent period of two years. In each case, an essential condition of the denouncing procedure is to give the Secretary General of the Council of Europe six months' notice. The Secretary General informs all other Parties accordingly about the denunciation of the Member State party to the Charter. Each party which has ratified the Charter may, in accordance with the aforesaid provisions, denounce any article or paragraph of Part II of the Charter, provided that the number of articles or paragraphs by which it is bound is 16 or 63, respectively. These must include at least six out of nine binding provisions: Articles 1, 5, 6, 7, 12, 13, 19 and 20. Any Member State has the right to denounce the Charter or any of its articles or paragraphs of Part II of the Charter, in respect of any territory to which the Charter is applicable, by virtue of Article L §2.

The actions undertaken by Member States, including the signing of the Charter, filing ratifying documents, accepting or approving the Charter, entering the Charter into force, declarations and amendments concerning the Charter, denunciations or amendment made to the Charter, or any other act dealing with the Charter, are by the Secretary General notified to all Member States and to the Director General of the International Labour Office (Article O).

The Revised European Social Charter has an appendix in which some significant provisions are clarified.

34. In the third edition of the monograph, the conclusions of the European Committee of Social Rights adopted at the end of 2016 are included. The European Committee of Social Rights conclusions published at the beginning of 2017 in respect of thirty-four Member States (Andorra, Armenia, Austria, Azerbaijan, Belgium, Bosnia and Herzegovina, Bulgaria, Denmark, Estonia, Finland, France, Georgia, Germany, Greece, Hungary, Iceland, Ireland, Italy, Latvia, Lithuania, Malta, the Republic of Moldova, Montenegro, Poland, Portugal, Romania, the Russian Federation, Serbia, the Slovak Republic, Spain, 'the former Yugoslav Republic of Macedonia (now North Macedonia)', Turkey, Ukraine and the United Kingdom) on the articles of the Charter relating to 'employment, training and equal opportunities'. The rights under review were: the right to work; the rights to vocational guidance and training; the right of persons with disabilities to independence, social integration and participation in the life of the community; the right to engage in a gainful occupation in the territory of other parties; the right to equal opportunities between women and men; the right to protection in cases of termination of employment; and the right of workers to the protection of their claims in the event of the insolvency of their employer.

The Committee found 166 cases of non-conformity with the Charter and 262 situations of conformity out of 513 conclusions on the rights examined in 2016. There were eighty-five cases where the Committee was unable to assess the situation due to a lack of information.

As a result, it was possible to identify several problems that a large number of states parties encounter when applying the Charter, for instance, insufficient protection against discrimination in employment on different grounds such as gender and sexual orientation, insufficient integration of persons with disabilities in mainstream education, the labour market and society in general and insufficient guarantee of equal rights between men and women in particular as regards equal pay. In some cases, the efforts to combat unemployment and encourage job creation remain inadequate.

Nevertheless, the Committee welcomes several positive developments, such as the adoption of anti-discrimination legislation in some countries, in particular in respect of persons with disabilities. The Committee also notes that vocational guidance and training systems are well-established in the majority of the states examined.

The next report on the accepted provisions was due before 31 October 2016 and concerned exclusively social issues: health, social security and social protection: Articles 3, 11–14, 23 and 30. The Committee returned to examine the Council of Europe labour standards in 2017 and publish its conclusions on those matters in 2018.

The years 2017 and 2018 have been recognised by the European Committee of Social Rights as 'difficult years'. The Committee was unable to finalise the evaluation of the Member States 'national reports on workers' rights on time. Thus, exceptionally, no decisions on compliance or non-compliance with European standards of legal regulations in the field of labour law and employment relations in individual Member States were agreed upon within the prescribed period. The consequence of the above-mentioned failure was the failure to publish the results of the – Committee's activities in the above-mentioned cases within the usual time limit. The situation in 2018 was better than the one in 2017. According to the report printed in 2018, 'the Committee was not able to produce and publish its traditional Activity Report relating to 2017 activities'.[16] In these two years (2017 and 2018), the number of collective complaints lodged with the Committee decreased. Compared to 2016, which saw twenty new complaints filed by authorised national and international trade unions and non-profit organisations, in 2017, eighteen collective complaints were entered into the Committee's register, and in 2018 only fifteen such complaints.[17] Only a few of these complaints can be included in the category of

16. Introduction by Giuseppe Palmisano, President of the European Committee of Social Rights, Activity Report 2018, p. 5.
17. *Ibid.*, p. 8.

employee cases and rights.[18] In 2018 and 2019, these were cases of violation of the provisions of Article 5 (strike) and Article 6 (collective bargaining and collective agreements), and in 2019 one case concerned remuneration for additional work.[19] On 31 October 2017, the deadline for presenting to the Committee thirty-eight reports from the Member States that ratified the provisions of both Charters, the 'old' (18 October 1961) and 'new' – revised (3 May 1996) ones, guaranteeing protection of workers' rights from 1 January 2013 by 31 December 2016. Thirty-five Member States submitted such reports on time.[20] Two countries did not submit complete reports on time.[21] One state party did not submit its report at all.[22] The reports concerned compliance with labour law standards regulated by the following provisions of the above-mentioned provisions: Article 2 (the right to just conditions work); Article 4 (the right to fair remuneration); Article 5 (the right to organised); Article 6 (the right to bargain collectively); Article 21 (the right to information and consultation); Article 22 (the right to take part in the determination and improvement of working conditions); Article 26 (the right to dignity at work); Article 28 (the right of workers' representatives to protection in the undertaking; Article 29 (the right to information and consultation in collective redundancy procedures). During the delayed plenary session in 2019, the Committee issued 580 conclusions, almost half of which (206) contain negative assessments of the national labour law provisions.

Negative conclusions are presented in the relevant parts of the fourth edition of this monograph. In part concerning individual employment rights, these are the following provisions: Article 4 §1, which guarantees employees and their family members a fair remuneration, and Article 26, on the employee's right to protection of his or her dignity. In the first case, the authorities of some Member States[23] have forgotten that the ratio between the minimum and average remuneration for work is decisive for meeting the standard of decent remuneration. The situation of fair remuneration occurs when the net remuneration exceeds 60% of the average remuneration for work. On the other hand, respect for the dignity of the employee in the

18. The decision on admissibility and the merits in European Organisation of Military Associations (EUROMIL); The decision on the merits in *Matica Hrvatskih Sindikata v. Croatia*, Complaint No. 116/2015, became public on 27 Aug. 2018; The decision on the merits in *Confédération Générale du Travail Force Ouvrière (CGT-FO) v. France*, Complaint No. 118/2015, became public on 26 Nov. 2018.
19. Article 5 – Complaint No. 112/2014, publication on 12 Feb. 2018; Complaint No 116/2015, published on 27 Aug. 2018; Art. 6 – Complaint No. 118/2015, publication on 26 Nov. 2018; Arts 5 and 6 §1, 2 and 4 – Complaint No. 140/2016, published 7 Jun. 2019. Art. 4 §2 – Complaint 154/2017 became public on 15 Mar. 2019.
20. Andorra, Armenia, Austria, Azerbaijan, Bosnia-Herzegovina, Croatia, Czech Republic, Denmark, Estonia, Georgia, Germany, Iceland, Latvia, Lithuania, Luxembourg (in part), Malta, Republic of Moldova, Montenegro, the Netherlands, the Netherlands in respect of Aruba, the Netherlands in respect of Curaçao, North Macedonia, Norway, Poland, Romania, Russian Federation, Serbia, Slovak Republic, Spain, Sweden, Turkey, Ukraine and United Kingdom. Conclusions 2018 of the European Committee of Social Rights: HUDOC Database https://hudoc.esc.coe.int/eng#{«ESCCycle»:[«year2018»,»XXI-3»,»2018»],»ESCDcType»:[«Conclusion»]}.
21. Luxembourg (part related to Art. 6), Hungary.
22. Albania.
23. Andorra, Austria, Azerbaijan, Germany, Iceland, Lithuania, Luxembourg, Malta, the Netherlands, Romania, Serbia, Spain, Sweden and the United Kingdom.

employment relationship may be written when the national labour laws of individual Member States provide adequate protection to the harassed employees. Negative conclusions were made both in cases after the Committee found that the above requirement was not respected by states or when other Member States had not provided information on compliance with the basic principle of protection against sexual and/or moral abuse in employment relationships. Each Member State should establish and require employers to apply appropriate preventive and repressive measures. Employers should be liable for mobbing or harassment on the premises of their workplaces or in employment relationships. Victims, on the other hand, must be guaranteed the right to seek compensation on a privileged basis in an independent judicial body.

In part on collective labour law (Part III, 'The Supervision of Complying with the Laws of the European Social Charter', Chapter 2, 'Adjudicating Collective Complaints' of the monograph), the negative conclusions concern the provisions of Article 5, which guarantees the right to associate in trade unions,[24] participate in legal strikes (Article 6 §4). Article 6 of the Charter on the rights of self-employed workers concludes collective labour agreements.[25]

In addition to the presented selected negative conclusions and opinions expressed in collective complaints, in 2018, the Committee took up and made public a statement of interpretation of Article 4 §4 establishing the right of all workers to a reasonable period of notice for termination of employment by the employer. The Committee considered that such a period is only a notice period, the length of which depends solely on the length of service in a given workplace. According to the Committee, 'a reasonable notice period is one which takes an account of the employees "length of service", the need not to deprive them abruptly of their means of subsistence and the need to inform them of the termination in good time to enable them to seek a new job, and during which employees are entitled to their regular remuneration'. In the event of a divergence of views between the Committee assessing the compliance of national regulations of the notice period with European standards and the authorities of individual Member States, the Committee imposed on the Member States an obligation to demonstrate that the notice period established could be considered acceptable. Thus, the Committee sent a message to the general public of the employed that it had regard to their legal situation during work in insecure, atypical employment relationships.

The second statement of interpretation concerning the provisions of labour law was presented in the next cycle of 2019, in which the Committee assessed the reports of the Member States on matters concerning the protection of the rights of working women (the right of employed women to protection of maternity – night work and dangerous and unhealthy work). Interpreting Articles 8 §4 and §5 of the 'old' and 'new' Charter, the Committee adopted the following statement of interpretation: 'grounds of gender, employed women during the protected period may not

24. Armenia, Azerbaijan, the Czech Republic, Georgia and the Republic of Moldova – police, personnel and members of the armed forces do not enjoy the right to join trade unions or restrictions on this right are excessive.
25. *See*, *ICTU v. Ireland*, Complaint No. 123/2016, decision on the merits of 12 Sep. 2018, §§37–40.

be placed in a less advantageous situation, if an adjustment of their working conditions is necessary in order to ensure the required level of the protection of health. It follows that, in the case a woman cannot be employed in her workplace due to health and safety concerns and as a result, she is transferred to another post or, should such transfer not be possible, she is granted leave instead. States Parties must ensure that during the protected period, she is entitled to her average previous pay or provided with a social security benefit corresponding to 100% of her previous average pay. Further, she should have the right to return to her previous post'.[26]

The year 2019 was recognised by the Committee as a breakthrough year, both for reasons related to the replacement of its four members and for the change of working methods. States Parties to the European Social Charter are invited to report on health, social security and social protection by 31 December 2020. The reports cover the period from 1 January 2014 until 31 December 2017. In 2020, the Committee recommended that Member State authorities focus in their 2020 reports on strategic issues closely related, in particular, to matters relating to the effective implementation of national labour law systems. The Committee recommended that the Member States focus on these kinds of issues in the matters set out in Part II, 'Labour Human Rights' of the monograph, Chapter 1 of 'Regulation of Individual Labour Human Rights'. Moreover, the Committee initiated 'a process to reinforce the quality and effectiveness of the collective complaints procedure'.[27] Instead of focusing on the general assessment of the state of the rule of law in labour relations, the Committee decided on two – in its opinion –most important legal and social aspects, enabling the Council of Europe to supervise the compliance of Member States with European standards in the most important issues concerning labour law and social policy systems. The first one covers subjective and objective grounds for examining a collective complaint. The second one refers to the follow-up of the substantive decision made by the Committee. The seeds of this kind of thinking were tested in 2018. It was then that the Committee began to wonder whether the authorities of the Member State, which reached the negative conclusion, immediately took steps to bring the state of the national labour law criticised by the Committee in line with the European model. On 19 September 2019, a seminar, 'Reinforcing Social Rights Protection in Europe: To Achieve Greater Unity and Equality', was organised. The results of this seminar were partially tested in two Committee sessions at the end of 2019. The Member States which ratified the collective complaints procedures became the beneficiaries of the above reform.[28] They were exempted from reporting on the compliance of their national regulations with European standards. In place of the current universal obligation, these states were invited to provide information on the follow-up given to decisions on the merit of collective complaints in which the Committee found a violation. The Committee examined thirty-seven national reports and made nine conclusions on Member States' compliance

26. Activity Report 2019, p. 28.
27. Activity Report 2019, *supra*, pp. 5–6.
28. Croatia, Cyprus, Czech Republic, the Netherlands, Norway, Slovenia and Sweden. Spain signs the Additional Protocol to the European Social Charter on collective complaints 7–11/09/2020 Strasbourg, France.

with the standards set out in the 'old' Charter[29] and twenty-nine conclusions on countries that ratified the 'new', revised Charter.[30] The provisions of both Charter included provisions belonging to the thematic group 'Children, families and migrants'. These were the norms of Article 7 (the right of children and young persons to protection), Article 8 (the right of employed women to protection of maternity), and Article 27 (the right of workers with family responsibilities to equal opportunities and equal treatment).

At the end of the first quarter of 2020, ECSR announced the results of its 2020 monitoring for employment, training and equal opportunities (group No. 1, Conclusions 2020).[31] The monitoring carried out by the ECSR consists of two components: Examination of: (1) national reports on the first thematic group of provisions of the Charter relating to 'Employment, training and equal opportunities' and (2) information on follow-up to collective complaints. The published report of 24 March 2020 included the following provisions of ECSR and RECSR: the right to work (Article 1); the right to vocational guidance[32] (Article 9); the right to vocational training (Article 10); the right to equal opportunities and equal treatment in matters of employment and occupation without discrimination on the grounds of sex (Article 20); the right to protection in cases of termination of employment (Article 24); the right of workers to the protection of their claims in the event of the insolvency of their employers (Article 25). The following thirty-three countries were examined: Albania, Andorra, Armenia, Austria, Azerbaijan, Bosnia and Herzegovina, Croatia, Cyprus, the Czech Republic, Denmark, Estonia, Georgia, Germany, Hungary, Iceland, Latvia, Lithuania, Luxembourg, Malta, Montenegro, the Netherlands in respect to Kingdom in Europe, Curaçao and Saint Maarten,[33] North Macedonia, Poland, Romania, the Russian Federation, Serbia, the Slovak Republic, Slovenia, Spain, Sweden, Turkey, Ukraine, the United Kingdom. No report was received from two Member States: the Republic of Moldova and Norway. The reports covered the reference period from 1 January 2015 to 31 December 2018. The ECSR adopted 349 conclusions. A significant part, almost a half (44%), were conclusions about the compliance of the above-mentioned national regulations with the EKPS and ZEKPS standards.[34] The remaining 56% of the conclusions were divided into two 28% parts equally between the conclusions stating the national law of the CoE Member States assessed by the Committee (152 situations in conformity and 100 deferrals due to the lack of information).

---

29. Denmark, Germany, Iceland, Luxembourg, the Netherlands Curaçao, Poland, Spain, the United Kingdom.
30. Albania, Andorra, Armenia, Austria, Azerbaijan, Belgium, Bosnia and Herzegovina, Bulgaria, Estonia, Finland, France, Georgia, Greece, Hungary, Ireland, Italy, Latvia, Lithuania, Malta, the Republic of Moldova, Montenegro, North Macedonia, Portugal, Romania, the Russian Federation, Serbia, the Slovak Republic, Turkey, Ukraine.
31. The European Committee of Social Rights, 24 Mar. 2021, www.coe.int>web>european-soci.
32. No questions were asked under this provision in cycle 2020. Member States were only obligated to report if there was a previous conclusion of non-conformity or deferral.
33. The conclusions related to the Netherland in respect of: Curaçao concern 4 conclusions of non-conformity: Art. 1§1, 1 §2, 1 §3 and Article of the Additional Protocol; Sint Maarten concern 2 conclusions of non-conformity: Art. 1 §1 and Art. 1 of the Additional Protocol.
34. European Social Charter, Social Rights Monitoring 2020: Employment, training and equal opportunities. www.coe.int>web>european-soci....

Compared to the decisions taken by the Committee on the basis of the reports of the Member States presented in the last quarter of 2015 in the first group, 'Employment, training and equal opportunities', the conclusions in 2020 have seen an improvement in the cases concerning Article 1 §1 and §2, Article 10 §1 and Article 20. In respect of Article 1 §1 in Germany, the chance of achieving full employment for young people aged 12–26 has increased.[35] School education has been integrated with professional practice. In Lithuania, more than half of the elderly, long-term unemployed, have been allowed to return to the labour market.[36] In Slovakia, regional differences in access to the labour market have been reduced, and nearly 50,000 new jobs have been created. In Sweden, the 'Job and Development Guarantee' programme was launched in which almost 400,000 long-term unemployed participated.[37] Under Article 1 §2 of the Charter, an act of law was passed in Andorra requiring the respect of equal treatment and non-discrimination on the labour market on grounds of race, ethnic origin, sexual orientation, religion, age, and political beliefs.[38] In Latvia, the burden of proof in administrative and court proceedings has changed. The labour law was amended to include a provision on the shift in the burden of proof in alleged discrimination cases on grounds of language.[39] Vocational education and technical training have been reformed in Slovakia and Slovenia.[40] A new, dual education system allows young people to acquire theoretical knowledge at school, which is put into practice during workplace training in companies.[41] The chosen mechanism enables apprentices, who have student status, to spend at least two days a week at school and three days with his/her employer.[42]

The most significant changes were made to the application by the Member States of Article 20 of the RESC. Albania made amendments to its Labour Code.[43] The burden of proof has been shifted to the employer, where the plaintiff is able to provide evidence enabling the court to presume that the employee has engaged in discriminatory conduct. The Committee understands that the legislation reverses the burden of proof in cases of wage discrimination on the grounds of gender. Notwithstanding the positive change, however, the Committee assessed that the situation in Albania is not in conformity with Article 20 (c) of RESC on the ground that the legislation explicitly covers only certain elements of pay for the purpose of equal pay principle.[44] Andorra passed the Equal Treatment and Non-discrimination Act No.

35. Conclusions 2020. Appendix II: Positive Developments. Examples of progress in the application of the European Social Charter relating to 'Employment, training and equal opportunities'.
36. *Ibid.*
37. *Ibid.*
38. *Ibid.*
39. *Ibid.*
40. *Ibid.*
41. Slovak Republic.
42. Slovenia.
43. The Law No. 136/2015 of 5 Dec. 2015 (which came into force in June 2016); Code of Administrative Procedure (Law No. 44/2015, 30 Apr. 2015, which came into force on 28 May 2016).
44. The gender gap is highest among machinery and equipment installation workers (at 28.4%) and lowest among armed forces personnel (at practically zero).

13/2019 of 15 February 2019.[45] It defines the principle of equal treatment regardless of the employee's gender. That principle entails an obligation to provide the same remuneration, whatever the nature of this remuneration, for work and equal value, without any form of discrimination against women regarding the elements or conditions of the work in question. The above act applies to both sectors of the economy, private and public. A similar situation is in Montenegro. The Labour Code enacted on 30 December 2019[46] provides that every worker is entitled to equal pay for equal work or work of equal value. In Romania, the reformed Agency for Equal Opportunities between Women and Men was established.[47] Subordinated to the Minister of Labour and Social Protection, it promotes the principle of equal treatment of women and men. Its mission is to eliminate any kind of discrimination in national policies and all programmes.[48]

The ECSR also made public its 'Findings 2020' in the framework of follow-up collective complaints decisions with respect to eight Member States: Belgium, Bulgaria, Finland, France, Greece, Ireland, Italy and Portugal. These Member States were exempted from reporting in 2020. However, they were required to provide EKSR with information on the follow-up to decisions on merits in the framework of collective complaints in which the Committee found a violation.

The country reports relating to conclusions 2016, 2017, 2018, 2019 and 2020 are available on the Charter's HUDOC database, social charter@coe.int, www.coe.int/social charter@socialcharter, https://www.coe.int/en/web/european-social-charter/national-reports.

§5. Reform of the European Social Charter System

35. On 27 September 2022, the Committee of Ministers adopted a reform package aimed at modernising the European Social Charter system (CM(2022)114-final). The ultimate goal is to assist States Parties in ensuring respect for social rights in line with their commitments. For this purpose, emphasis is placed on the need for enhanced dialogue between the Charter organs (European Committee of Social Rights and the Governmental Committee) and States Parties, as well as all relevant stakeholders (national human rights institutions, national equality bodies, trade unions and other civil society organisations).

In operational terms, several aspects of the monitoring process are evolving with a view to increasing the effectiveness of the European Social Charter system as a whole.

In the *reporting procedure*, the provisions on which States Parties are required to report are now to be divided into two groups, with a report on one group to be

45. Enter into force on 21 Mar. 2019.
46. In force since 8 Jan. 2020.
47. The Law No. 229/2015.
48. Conclusions 2020. Appendix II: Positive Developments. Examples of progress in the application of the European Social Charter relating to 'Employment, training and equal opportunities'.

submitted every two years. This means that all accepted Charter provisions are to be examined for each State every four years (see Reporting Table below [as found in CM dec]).

First Group

36. A total of fifty provisions: Article 1, Article 2, Article 3, Article 4, Article 5, Article 6, Article 8, Article 9, Article 10, Article 18, Article 19, Article 20, Article 21, Article 22, Article 24, Article, 25, Article 28 and Article 29.

Second Group

37. A total of forty-eight provisions: Article 7, Article 11, Article 12, Article 13, Article 14, Article 15, Article 16, Article 17, Article 23, Article 26, Article 27, Article 30 and Article 31.

In order to bring further focus to the reporting by States Parties and subsequent assessments by the European Committee of Social Rights and, at the same time, to lighten the reporting burden on States, *targeted questions* are to be drawn up by the European Committee of Social Rights and the Governmental Committee.

For States Parties bound by the *collective complaints procedure*, reporting on the two groups of provisions takes place every four years, which means that all accepted Charter provisions are examined for each of these States every eight years.[49] The required reporting will take into account decisions on collective complaints pertaining to the relevant provisions.

Moreover, the Governmental Committee will *strengthen the follow-up given to conclusions* adopted by the European Committee of Social Rights by proposing reasoned recommendations for adoption by the Committee of Ministers with a view to triggering changes at the national level and bringing situations in line with the European Social Charter.

When new or critical issues arise with a broad or transversal scope or of a pan-European nature, States Parties may be asked to submit an ad hoc *report* for examination by the European Committee of Social Rights. The subject and timing of ad hoc reports will be decided by the European Committee of Social Rights and the Governmental Committee. Follow-up should involve dialogue among the States Parties (within the framework of the Governmental Committee), associating relevant stakeholders (including the social partners and civil society).

With respect to reporting on *follow-up activities from collective complaints*, certain procedural adjustments have been made. In particular, in cases where the Committee of Ministers addressed recommendations to States Parties after the European Committee of Social Rights found that the Charter had not been applied in a satisfactory manner, States Parties will be asked to submit a single report on the follow-up undertaken two years after the recommendation. The European Committee of Social Rights' assessment of the follow-up reports will then be transmitted to the Committee of Ministers. Depending on this assessment, the Committee of Ministers may (1) close the case with a resolution, (2) renew the recommendation, or (3) before renewing the recommendation, it may refer the case to the Governmental

49. *See* Reporting Table below [as found in CM dec].

Committee for further consultation. In light of the outcome of these consultations, the Committee of Ministers will decide whether to close the procedure or renew the recommendation.

Dialogue is encouraged between the Charter's monitoring bodies (the European Committee of Social Rights, the Governmental Committee and, ultimately, the Committee of Ministers) and the competent authorities of each State Party, whichever procedure under the Charter system is involved (reporting, collective complaints or their respective follow-up). In certain cases, this may involve a group of States Parties seeking to address problematic issues that are common to them or sharing examples of good practice. Social partners and civil society organisations at the European and national levels should be involved in such dialogue.

Dialogue, whether requested by a State Party or at the initiative of one of the organs of the Charter, can involve requests for information, exchanges of letters or meetings. A State Party may also request a country visit. Conducted in a constructive spirit, dialogue is a tool to reach a common understanding of problematic issues and may identify possible solutions to such issues which are suitable for and acceptable to the State Party concerned. It may also serve as a means of facilitating technical assistance.

Year	*Submission of Report*	*ECSR Conclusions*[50]
2023	Possible ad hoc report[51]	
2024	27 states submit reports on the First Group of provisions	Possible ECSR analysis of ad hoc reports[52]
2025	16 states that accept collective complaints submit reports on the First Group of provisions	ECSR conclusions for 27 States (First Group of provisions)
2026	27 states submit reports on the Second Group of provisions	ECSR conclusions for 16 states (First Group of provisions)
2027	Possible ad hoc report	ECSR conclusions for 27 states (Second Group of provisions)
2028	27 states submit reports on the First Group of provisions	Possible ECSR analysis of ad hoc reports
2029	16 states that accept collective complaints submit reports on the Second Group of provisions	ECSR conclusions for 27 states (First Group of provisions)

50. In 2023, the ECSR is to examine the last reports submitted under the existing system.
51. In order to manage the transition from the current reporting arrangements to the new ones and avoid two consecutive years reporting on the same provisions, it could be envisaged to start in 2023 with a possible ad hoc report instead of a statutory report.
52. GC consideration in the following year, followed by transmission to the CM. This applies to each year.

Year	*Submission of Report*	*ECSR Conclusions*[50]
2030	27 states submit reports on the Second Group of provisions	ECSR conclusions for 16 states (Second Group of provisions)
2031	Possible ad hoc report	ECSR conclusions for 27 states (Second Group of provisions)
2032	27 states submit reports on First Group of provisions	Possible ECSR analysis of ad hoc reports
2033	16 states that accept collective complaints submit reports on the First Group of provisions	ECSR conclusions for 27 states (First Group of provisions)
2034	27 states submit reports on the Second Group of provisions	ECSR conclusions for 16 states (First Group of provisions)
2035	Possible ad hoc report	ECSR conclusions for 27 states (Second Group of provisions)
2036	27 states submit reports on the First Group of provisions	Possible ECSR analysis of ad hoc reports
2037	16 states that accept collective complaints submit reports on the Second Group of provisions	ECSR conclusions for 27 states (First Group of provisions)
2038	27 states submit reports on the Second Group of provisions	ECSR conclusions for 16 states (Second Group of provisions)

In 2022, in the framework of the reporting procedure, the European Committee of Social Rights examined national reports submitted by thirty-three States Parties on the Articles of the Charter relating to the thematic group 'Labour rights':

(1) The right to just conditions of work (Article 2)
(2) The right to fair remuneration (Article 4)
(3) The right to organise (Article 5)
(4) The right to bargain collectively (Article 6)
(5) The right to information and consultation (Article 21/Article 2 of the Additional Protocol)
(6) The right to take part in the determination and improvement of the working conditions and working environment (Article 22/Article 3 of the Additional Protocol)
(7) The right to dignity at work (Article 26)
(8) The right of worker's representatives to protection in the undertaking and facilities to be accorded to them (Article 28)

(9) The right to information and consultation in collective redundancy procedures (Article 29)

The national reports cover the period from January 2017 to 31 December 2020 (Conclusions 2022). The following countries were examined: Albania, Andorra, Armenia, Austria, Azerbaijan, Belgium, Bosnia and Hercegovina, Bulgaria, Estonia, Finland, Georgia, Greece, Hungary, Ireland, Italy, Latvia, Lithuania, Malta, Moldova, Montenegro, North Macedonia, Portugal, Romania, Serbia, Slovakia and Türkiye.[53]

53. Conclusions 2022, *Press Briefing Elements*, a document prepared by the Secretariat of the European Committee of Social Rights, 22 Mar. 2023.

Part II. Labour Human Rights

Introduction: Categories of Labour Human Rights Connected with Work and Methods of Their Protection

38. Labour rights guaranteed under the Charter apply to all individuals in their everyday lives. Depending on the criteria, they can be divided into a few categories. Looking at the various protected spheres, the following elements are employment and work, legal and social protection, as well as protection against discrimination and freedom of movement. For this reason, the most important part of the monograph concerning the legal protection of labour human rights was divided into chapters, explaining the labour rights being protected under individual and collective labour law.

The Committee controls whether authorities of Member States fulfil their aforesaid obligations. Because some provisions of the Charter require the fulfilment of the above obligations depending upon specified needs (e.g., Articles 9 and 10 RESC), the Committee researches whether a given situation in a Member State needs an organisation of appropriate services as well as to see whether a Member State has fulfilled the obligations which it has undertaken. The Committee assesses the reports filed by the Member States as well as analyses the complaints made against a country where Charter obligations are accused of not being met. The Committee makes decisions accordingly as to whether the behaviour of a Member State complies with the standards set in the Charter. The Committee does not have the basis to take into consideration the economic situation or the financial capabilities of a Member State which has undertaken to provide social services set out by the Charter. There is no provision in the Charter which takes into consideration, when fulfilling set obligations, the adequacy of a Member State's financial wealth. No provision in the Charter excuses a Member State from not fulfilling the obligations it has undertaken voluntarily.

39. Other types of obligations set by the Charter are provisions fulfilled by Member States that commit Member States to undertake systematic actions. During the first supervisory cycle dealing with whether obligations of the European Social Charter were being met by Member States, such provisions were mentioned and were classified into the 'dynamic norms' category.[54] 'In the opinion of the Committee of Independent Experts, some Charter provisions are dynamic in their character:

---

54. Conclusions 1969–1970, Council of Europe Press, Strasbourg 1995, p 9.

they place obligations to accept given behaviours in certain timeframes in order to gain desirable results.'[55] Member States that have bound themselves to abide by the above-mentioned provisions have the responsibility to inform the Committee of any changes which may take place during periods between supervisory cycles. The responsibility of the given Member States is to execute a presentation of the changes that have taken place between supervisory cycles so that the Committee can assess whether progress has been made in adapting domestic laws concerned with the protection of labour rights with those of the changing standards accepted by the Charter. The Committee stipulated as examples the following provisions of the European Social Charter, which are 'dynamic' in character:

- Article 1 §1 orders Member States to achieve and maintain the most stable and highest level of employment with an aim to reach full employment;
- Article 2 §1, standard obliging Member States to progressively reduce the working week to the extent that the increase in productivity and other relevant factors permit.

The Committee does not automatically employ international standards when supervising Member States. Interpreting certain provisions of the Charter while supervising Member States, it takes into consideration economic and social factors. It proceeds according to the classic Aristotelian principles, which criticise the identical treatment of all subjects functioning within a given society. Currently, these are countries coming into the makeup of the international organisation, the Council of Europe, having decided to abide by the international treaties chosen for them by their authorities. Accepting Article 4 §1 of the Charter as a measuring stick in the supervisory process (provisions which allocate workers the right to decent remuneration, provisions which deduce automatic equality ignoring the varying standards of living among Member States, means the Committee would be forced to establish uniform standards of wages and across Europe. This is not possible due to the vast range of living standards among workers and their families.

40. Some provisions of the Charter leave a margin of liberty for Member States that are bound by them. Interpreting those provisions of the Charter which order particular undertakings such as: promoting voluntary negotiations between stakeholders (Article 6 §2 RESC), ensuring the right to vocational guidance (Article 9 RESC), vocational training (Article 10 §1 RESC), training for adults (Article 10 §3 RESC), when it is 'necessary and proper' or when such necessities eventuate, then the Committee depends upon the assessment of particular state authorities. It is these assessments which are the deciding factor as regards the necessity of fulfilling the obligations established by the above-mentioned provisions of the Charter. This is because the Committee does not construct frameworks of rights protection appropriate to each country. It rather only assesses the frameworks provided by Member States and considers them as either sufficient, unnecessary, unsuitable or insufficient.

55. *Ibid.*

Chapter 1. Regulation of Individual Labour Human Rights

§1. The Right to Work

41. Article 1 of the Charter ensures the right to work belongs to the category of strict obligatory Charter provisions. Despite the popular definition of 'the right to work', this provision does not force authorities of Member States to provide those seeking employment or wanting employment with work. Those Member States that have bound themselves to abide by this provision are required to fulfil the demands set in three paragraphs of Article 1. Article 1 of the Charter establishes the principles of the right to work and regulates, most importantly, the legal measures which can implement the above principles. The above principles are designed for: full employment (§1), the ability to freely enter employment (§2), free employment services (§3), vocational guidance, training and rehabilitation (§4).

I. Full Employment

42. Countries which have ratified this provision are obliged to accept and maintain the highest and most stable level of employment possible, with a view to the attainment of full employment. Article 1 of the Charter is considered by legal practitioners to be part of the category of 'dynamic' provisions. Ratifying this provision means those Member States that have bound themselves to attain a level of full employment are bound to present information regarding the level of unemployment. Special consideration has to be taken towards measures to remedy long-term unemployment and prevent unemployment among young workers.[56] The Committee first assesses the level of unemployment, and then during the following supervisory cycles, it ascertains whether unemployment levels have increased or decreased compared to the levels given at previous supervisory cycles. The reports submitted by Member States should be prepared according to the form accepted by the Committee of Ministers during its 689th sitting on 24 November 1999 and modified during its 737th sitting on 17 January 2001.[57] In assessing the actions undertaken by Member States to achieve the goals of reaching full employment, questions are asked regarding the realisation of social-political issues in order to achieve and maintain full employment or at least to reduce the level of unemployment. Member States have the responsibility to present social programmes initiated and offered, conducted with the view of stabilising the level of employment. The Committee expects Member States to incorporate active techniques to fight against unemployment, addressing them to those social groups which are particularly at risk

56. The Committee concluded that the situation in Romania was not in conformity with Art. 1 §1 of the RESC on the grounds that the measures taken to remedy long-term unemployment and youth unemployment were inadequate for achieving substantial improvement of the situation. Conclusions 2008, vol. 2, p. 719.
57. Form for the reports submitted in pursuance of the European Social Charter, *Collected Texts*, *supra*, pp. 247 et seq.

of losing their jobs or to those social categories who have great difficulties in attaining a first job or are trying to re-enter the workforce: young people in the age group 15–24 years, women, older persons, those seeking employment for more than one year, the disabled, immigrants, ethnic minority members. In order to conduct comparisons of the labour markets between Member States, statistical information as well as definitions must be presented in the national reports in written format.[58] These national reports should include the number of people who are encompassed by these programmes as well as an introductory assessment concerning the effectiveness of these programmes. The presentation of these programmes should also include details which illustrate the trends accordingly to the national, regional and local labour markets, within all trade sectors,[59] so that the Committee will be able to assess the details concerning the number of people in active occupation, employed (in full-time employment based on a work agreement irrespective of a time frame, based on temporary work agreements, in part-time employment), or conducting their own business. The unemployment numbers should be presented with the same amount of detail, including periods of unemployment, their distribution, as well as the amount and types of positions vacant.

In the case of Denmark, the Committee was unable to judge whether the authorities of this country were obeying the provisions stipulated under Article 1 §1 of the Charter, even though the information presented in the second report indicated an unusual reduction in an already low unemployment level. This was due to a lack of information presented in the report, which would enable the Committee to conclude that the Danish authorities were executing previously planned employment measures.[60] Similar views were held during the same supervisory cycle concerning the United Kingdom's report. The authorities of this country did not present the Committee with the information to enable it to form an opinion on matters concerning employment policies in Northern Ireland and short-term goals relating to social measures of fighting against unemployment.

The Committee was able to hand down a decision indicating its negative position towards the United Kingdom's stance and declared that it was unable to decide whether the country fulfilled its obligations according to Article 1 §1 of the Charter. The Committee strives to find out whether authorities of Member States have drawn up short-term, mid-term and long-term plans counteracting unemployment. It pays close attention to structural or economic types of unemployment,[61] the standard of unemployment within regions of particular countries,[62] and necessary undertakings in reducing the scale of unemployment among women and young persons between the ages of 20 and 29 years[63] and among older persons. It considers that particular measures should be taken in order to improve employment chances for women,

58. Conclusions XIV-1, vol. 1, pp. 34–35.
59. In the case of Cyprus, the Committee in its second supervisory cycle was interested in the scale of hidden employment in the agricultural sector. Conclusions II, p. 179.
60. Conclusions II, 1971, Council of Europe Press, Strasbourg 1995, p. 3.
61. Conclusions IV 1975, Council of Europe Press, Strasbourg 1995, p. 5 (Sweden).
62. In the case of the United Kingdom – Northern England, Scotland, Northern Ireland, Conclusions IV, *supra*, p. 5.
63. Austria, Conclusions IV, *supra*, p. 3; Romania, Conclusions 2006, vol. 2, p. 735 and Conclusions 2008, vol. 2, p. 719.

young and older persons, as their loss of employment is at a higher risk.[64] It also pays close attention to measures undertaken by Member States to even out the regional disproportions of unemployment levels.[65] In principle, it did not limit itself to the information concerning the reduction of unemployment presented to it by Member State authorities.[66] It viewed that reducing the scale of unemployment alone is not a sufficient factor in attaining the goal of full employment, as 5% of people who are in the active age group able to and willing to work remain without jobs.[67] Mostly the Committee looks to actions taken by authorities of Member States in reducing the level of unemployment. If Member States can indicate in their report to the Committee that measures are intended and are being taken to rectify the issue of a sudden rise in unemployment during a supervisory cycle, the Committee will not automatically rule negatively, claiming that obligations were not met under Article 1 §2 of the Charter.[68] If the level of unemployment is retained at the same level for a period of time longer than one year, the Committee will view this as a dangerous indication, meaning the constant number of unemployed increases the risk of marginalisation leading to a negative occurrence of social exclusion.[69] The Committee, in its general report concluding the first part of the fourteenth supervisory cycle, stated that in the reporting period (1995–1996), there were 22–23 million unemployed persons within Member States.

43. In accordance with existing practices, the Committee refrained from indicating during subsequent supervisory cycles what methods should be used to reach the goals of achieving full employment. This also meant fulfilling obligations in accordance with Article 1 §1 of the Charter. The Committee is of the view that making any sort of suggestions concerning methods to be incorporated to achieve unemployment reduction (and to reach a standard of full employment) would be an imposition on the sovereignty of a given Member State. In the introduction of a report drawn up during the first supervisory cycle, the Committee stated that all policies of economic growth which are assumed to keep the unemployment rate at a stable level would be considered in violation of the above-mentioned regulation of the Charter.[70] This opinion was also repeated in the XIVth supervisory cycle report. The Committee concluded that the coexistence of a high economic growth index and a significant and stable unemployment rate in periods of mid- and long-term economic growth was a phenomenon that could not be accepted legally under Article 1 §1 of the Charter.[71] According to the Committee, the analysed regulation of Article 1 §1 of the Charter obliges Member States to thoughtfully conduct themselves by

64. Conclusions IV, *supra*, p. XIV.
65. Denmark, Conclusions IV, *supra*, p. 4.
66. In its fourth supervisory cycle, the Committee decided based on the information provided by Cyprus, without any additional information, that the country did not fulfil its obligations under Art. 1 §2 of the Charter, Conclusions IV, *supra*, p. 3.
67. Introduction of the Committee to the third supervisory cycle. Conclusions III, p. 3, Conclusions XIX-1 (2008), p. 429 (FYROM).
68. *Ibid*.
69. Romania, Conclusions 2006, vol. 2, p. 735.
70. Conclusions I, *supra*, p. 14.
71. Addendum to Conclusions XV-2 (Slovakia), European Social Charter, Council of Europe Publishing, Strasbourg 2001, p. 133.

not imposing the goal of a 0% unemployment rate. Supervising Member States to ensure they abide by this regulation, the Committee analyses social programmes and grants funds for this purpose as well as for results accomplished.

44. During the last cycle, 1 January 2011 to 31 December 2014, at the end of which the conclusions were presented in 2016, the Committee declared that a full employment policy in a number of countries did not conform with Article 1 §1 of the Charter on the basis that employment policy efforts were inadequate to combat unemployment and promote job creation. According to the reports, overall employment remained at an alarmingly low level in Bosnia and Herzegovina, at 31.9% (2011) – 31.7% (2014), with the unemployment rate standing at 27.5% (2014) and youth unemployment increasing even further from 56.4% (2011) to 61.0% (2014). The same development was observed with respect to the long-term unemployment rate, which increased from 22.3% in 2011 to 23.4% in 2014.[72] In Italy, the unemployment rate increased considerably from 8.4% in 2011 to 12.7% in 2014, which was above the EU average of 10.2%. Youth unemployment increased from 29.2% (2011) to 42.7% (2014). The same trend could be observed with respect to the long-term unemployment rate, which increased from 4.3% in 2011 to 7.8% in 2014. The Committee report notes that the Government of Italy was pursuing the EU 2020 strategy aimed at increasing employment for male and female workers. The most recent labour law initiative is the 'Jobs Act' project adopted in 2014. It creates additional incentives to increase the number of long-term unemployment. The 'Jobs Act' foresees the setting up of the Unique Agency Active Policies. This Agency has a central role in the coordination of regional action on the matter. However, these labour market programmes have not been sufficient to have an impact on employment rates.[73] In the 'Former Yugoslav Republic of Macedonia, now North Macedonia', overall employment slightly increased during the reference period from 23.9% in 2011 to 46.9% in 2014. However, the rate was 18% below the average EU rate of 64.9% in 2014. Male employment increased from 52.8% in 2009 to 56.1% in 2014, yet the rate was 14% below the EU 28 average rate, which stood at 70.1% in 2014. The female employment rate increased from 33.5% (2009) to 37.4% (2014) but remained significantly below the EU 28 average rate of 59.6%. The unemployment rate decreased slightly from 31.4% in 2011 to 28.6% in 2013, which was considerably higher than the EU 28 average rate of 10.2%. The youth unemployment rate stayed at a very high level despite decreasing slightly from 55.3% (2011) to 53.9% (2012). The Committee notes from the report show that employment policies are regulated in strategic governmental documents such as the 2015 National Employment Strategy, the National Employment Action Plan 2014–2015, the 2015 Youth Employment Action Plan, as well as the Annuals Operative Plans for Active Employment Programmes and Measures. Regardless of those instruments, the Committee concludes that the situation in the 'Former Yugoslav Republic of, now North Macedonia' is not in conformity with Article 1 §1 of the Charter on the basis that employment policy efforts have been inadequate in combating unemployment and

72. Conclusions 2016, pp. 3–4.
73. Conclusions 2016, pp. 146–147.

promoting job creation.[74] From time to time, the Committee deplores the fact that the report provides very little information on the matter examined under Article 1 §1 of the Charter. As the report contains no information on these matters, the Committee considers employment policies to have been inadequate in tackling unemployment and fostering job creation. The Committee uses other sources – the National Statistics Office and Eurostat.

In the case of Georgia, the Committee notes that according to the National Statistics Office, the GDP growth rate decreased from 6.7% in 2012 to 1.7% in 2014. According to Eurostat, the overall employment rate increased during the reference period from 59.3% in 2011 to 62.2% in 2014. On these matters, the Committee considers that employment policies have not been adequate in tackling unemployment and promoting job creation.[75] The very same conclusion is reached in the case of Moldova. According to a national report, specific plans contained measures to support a number of vulnerable groups such as young persons, the Roma population or people with disabilities. However, the information provided by the Government is not supported by relevant statistical data. Therefore, the Committee notes that labour market policies in Moldova have not succeeded in reducing unemployment and creating jobs.[76] A similar conclusion was reached in the case of Armenia. The Committee concluded that the country report fails to provide the requested data on the overall action rate as well as information on the evaluation of the applied employment policies. According to Eurostat, the overall employment rate remained virtually stable during the reference period (53.3% in 2011; 53.7% in 2014). Therefore, the Committee concluded that the situation in Armenia does not conform with Article 1 §1 of the Charter.[77] A negative conclusion was also reached in the case of Ukraine. This country report does not indicate what active labour market measures are available in general to job seekers. It also fails to provide complete information on the number of beneficiaries in the different types of active measures and on the overall action rate – the average number of participants in active measures as a percentage of the total number of unemployed. However, the report contains data in regard to expenditure on active labour market policies as a percentage of GDP. The figure stood at 0.04% in 2014, which is very low by international standards. The Committee states that it has not been established whether employment policy efforts have been adequate in combating unemployment and promoting job creation in the case of Ukraine.[78]

The Committee revealed that Bulgaria is gradually emerging from the economic crisis but with no prospects for a broad-based recovery. The male employment rate decreased from 66.9% in 2009 to 63.9% in 2014. The female employment rate remained virtually stable: 2009 – 58.3%, 2014 – 58.2% and was still below the EU 28 average of 59.6%. The unemployment rate remained relatively stable, increasing by 0.1% from 11.3% in 2011 to 11.4% in 2014, which was still higher than the EU 28 average of 10.2%. The youth unemployment rate remained at a high level,

74. Conclusions 2016, pp. 201–201.
75. Conclusions 2016, p. 253.
76. Conclusions 2016, p. 254.
77. Conclusions 2016, p. 268.
78. Conclusion 2016, p. 271.

although it decreased from 25.0% in 2011 to 23.8% in 2014. Concerning Active Labour Market Policies, only 12.1% of the registered unemployed took part in relevant programmes. According to Eurostat, public expenditure on active labour market policies amounted to 0.57% of GDP in 2011, below the EU 28 average, where spending that year was 1.8%. Therefore, the Committee concluded that the situation in Bulgaria is not in conformity with Article 1 §1 of the Charter. According to the report presented by Serbia, public expenditure on labour market policies amounted to 0.015% of the GDP in 2014, which was very low when compared with the EU 28 average. The male employment rate increased during the reference period (52.5% in 2009; 56.3% in 2014). However, the rate is still far below the EU average, which stood at 70.1% in 2014. The unemployment rate decreased slightly from 24.4% in 2011 to 21.2% in 2014, which was considerably higher than the EU average rate of 10.2%. The youth unemployment rate remained at a very high level (51.9% in 2011; 52.8% in 2014), whereas the long-term unemployed rate as a percentage of the active population aged 15–74 amounted to 14.1% in 2014. Taking into consideration that the economic situation in Serbia is rather fragile in the field of employment, the Committee concludes that it is not in conformity with Article 1 §1 of the Charter.[79]

In Montenegro, the Committee notes that several action measures that had been taken as far as employment policy is concerned have as yet turned out to be ineffective. The unemployment rate fell from 19.5% in December 2013 to 16.4% in December 2014. The youth unemployment rate reached 48.4% in December 2013. The employment rate stood in December 2014 at 44.0%, falling from 47.6% in 2010. The percentage of unemployed persons entitled to financial compensation amounted to 36.7%. The Committee concludes that it has not been established that employment policy efforts have been adequate in combating unemployment and promoting job creation.[80]

Two EU countries, Spain and Greece, were particularly badly hit by the consequences of the economic crisis. While the economy grew again in 2014, this growth had no impact on the employment situation in the XXI-1 reference period. The burden of this difficult situation was felt particularly by young people, with a worrying unemployment rate of 53.2% in 2014 in Spain. The Committee asked for an evaluation of the impact of the comprehensive reform of the Spanish labour market undertaken in 2012. According to the Spanish report, a key element of the reform was the priority given to collective bargaining agreements at the company level over those at the regional level and the greater possibility given to firms to opt out of a collective agreement to adopt internal flexibility measures to limit job destruction. In addition, the extension of collective bargaining agreements beyond their projected end date, if no new agreement is reached, was limited to a maximum period of one year. Dismissal regulations were also modified, redefining the conditions for fair dismissal, reducing monetary compensation in the case of unfair dismissal and eliminating the requirements of administrative authorisation in the case of collective redundancies. Moreover, a new permanent contract for full-time employees in small firms was introduced with an extended trial period of one year. According to

79. Conclusions 2016, pp. 274–275.
80. *Ibid.*, p. 276.

the report, the reform promoted the internal flexibility of employers while reducing dismissal costs for permanent workers. The reform led to significant wage moderation, and this contributed to increased hiring rates on permanent contracts. The Committee noted that activation in Spain, according to Eurostat, that is, the number of persons taking part in active measures as a percentage of those employed, was 23.3% in 2013, dropping dramatically from 55.2% in 2009. However, public expenditure on active labour market policies in Spain amounted to 3.6% of GDP in 2011, which was twice the EU 28 average (1.8%). The Committee notes that this important labour market reform has been inadequate and without any positive impact on the employment figures. Indeed, all employment figures show a negative trend, with youth employment hitting a record high of 53.2%. For those reasons, the Committee concluded that the situation in Spain is not in conformity with Article 1 §1 of the 1961 Charter on the basis that employment policy efforts have not been sufficient to combat unemployment and foster job creation.[81]

Greece is a similar case, where the male employment rate decreased sharply from 73.0% in 2009 to 58.0% in 2014. This rate was considerably below the EU 28 average of 70.1% in 2014. The female employment rate also decreased from 48.9% in 2009 to 41.1% in 2014. This rate was well below the EU 28 average rate of 59.6%. The employment rate of older workers also decreased from 42.2% in 2009 to 34.0% in 2014, more than 15% below the EU 28 average rate of 51.8%. The Committee notes from the report that a series of policy measures were undertaken aimed at containing unemployment, retaining existing jobs, creating new ones, integrating young persons and vulnerable groups in the labour market, undertaking entrepreneurial initiatives and supporting industries particularly affected by the impact of financial crisis. But those measures were not enough to counter the difficult employment situation in the country, and, therefore, the Committee decided that the situation did not conform with Article 1 §1 of the Charter.[82]

In 2020, the Committee announced that, after analysing thirty-five reports on measures taken by Member States to achieve full employment, it was found that slightly more than a quarter of the reports were assessed negatively (25.7%). Article 1, paragraph 1 of the Charter has been infringed by the following Member States: Albania,[83] Armenia,[84] Bosnia and Herzegovina,[85] Georgia,[86] Montenegro, the Netherlands in respect of Curaçao and Sint Maarten, North Macedonia,[87] Spain and Ukraine.[88] Public authorities in these countries did not make enough efforts to create new jobs, organise vocational training for job seekers and provide them with help in entering labour markets. Therefore it has not been demonstrated that their

81. Conclusions XXI-1 – Spain, pp. 297–298.
82. Conclusions XXI-1 – Greece, pp. 321–322.
83. The situation is not in conformity with Art. 1 §1 of the Charter on the grant that employment policy efforts have not been adequate in combatting unemployment and promoting job creation. Conclusions 2020.
84. *Ibid.*
85. *Ibid.*
86. *Ibid.*
87. *Ibid.*
88. *Ibid.*

efforts in terms of job creation, training and assistance to the unemployed are sufficient in view of the economic situation and the level of unemployment.

II. Freedom of Work

45. The Charter introduced a provision which ensures the effective protection of workers' rights to earn their living in an occupation which has been freely entered upon. During its first supervisory cycle, the Committee became convinced that Article 1 §2 of the Charter was strictly associated with the prohibition of forced employment as well as with removing any form of discrimination within employment.[89] This view of the Committee was upheld during the second and third supervisory cycles.[90]

A. Prohibition of Forced Labour

46. Forced labour is also considered to be the case when work has been voluntarily accepted but continued against the will of the worker who is unable to terminate it on legal terms.[91] Accepting the above basis for the definition of forced labour, the Committee analysed further such instances included in the presented reports of Member States. The Committee used the definition of forced or compulsory labour as defined by Article 2(1) of the above convention.

The Committee analysed the following instances in reports presented by the authorities of Member States and regarded them as contravening obligations set by Article 1 §2 of the Charter: forcing to report slave labour;[92] the possibility of penalty sanctions for people who remain without resources needed for living;[93] allocating unemployment benefits on the condition employment is actively being sought;[94] suspending all inspections related to entrepreneurial activity until 1 January 2021 is barriers to the mandate of labour inspection;[95] it has not been established that the national authorities have fulfilled their obligations to prevent forced labour and labour exploitation, to protect victims, to effectively investigate the offences committed, and punish those responsible for forced labour offences;[96] penalty sanctions for members of crews of merchant ships or fishing vessels in cases whereby work discipline is violated for:

89. Conclusions I, *supra*, p. 15.
90. Conclusions II, *supra*, pp. 4–5; Conclusions III, p. 5.
91. Conclusions III, p. 5.
92. No reports presented by Member States have given any indication regarding such labour existing in Europe. In the opinion of J. Darcy & D. Harris, *The European Social Charter* 44 (The Procedural Aspects of International Law Book Series, vol. 25, Ardsley, 2d ed., 2001), case 57 – there was a case exposing slave labour in reports prepared by Dutch authorities, which presented such a situation in the Dutch Antilles. The Committee's analysis of reports during the conclusion of the tenth supervisory cycle did not conclude that slave labour was present. Conclusions X-1, p. 36.
93. Conclusions XIII-1, pp. 45–46 (Denmark).
94. Conclusions XIV-1, p. 293 (Germany).
95. Conclusions 2020 (Azerbaijan).
96. Conclusions 2020 (Azerbaijan)

- the infringement of work responsibilities, which threaten the safety of the vessel but do not threaten the life or the health of the persons found on the vessel.[97] The Committee found previously that the situation in Portugal did not conform with Article 1 §2 of the Revised Charter because Articles 132 and 133 of the Merchants Navy Criminal and Disciplinary Code provided for criminal sanctions – prison sentences – against seafarers who abandoned their posts. In 2016, the report stated that no measures had been taken to bring the situation in Portugal in line with the article. The report refers to the information provided by the representative of Portugal during the 127th meeting of the Governmental Committee on May 2013 to the effect that the bill to repeal the Code was still pending. Bearing in mind that the Portuguese authorities had undertaken to bring the situation into conformity with the Charter with regard to the prohibition of forced labour since the previous cycle, the Committee upheld its finding of non-conformity in this respect;[98]
- authorising the suspension or transfer of local government officials and employees on the grounds that their employment constituted a threat to security in general, to the law and public order or safety, or because it was unnecessary. The Committee was of the view that, because of the imprecise manner in which it was described, these circumstances could not be considered to fall within the scope of Article G of the Charter because the national legislation does not adequately protect local government officials and employees;[99]
- abandoning one's work post or refusing to carry out a work task;[100]
- refusing to report to work,[101] particularly due to strike action,[102] the refusal of employees taking part in legal strike action to assume basic services;[103]
- placing penalty sanctions on government employees who abandon their work posts in an attempt to disorganise the functioning of government office;[104]
- making it the responsibility of the employees to gain the approval of a director of an administrative or regional employment body to terminate a work agreement;[105]
- establishing an inability to resign from duty for professional soldiers before reaching the national retirement age[106] or before completing national service requirements;[107]

---

97. Conclusions XIII-4, p. 330; Conclusions XIV-1, p. 104; Conclusions XV-1, pp. 71–72 (Belgium), p. 237 (France), pp. 294–295 (Greece); Conclusions 2006, vol. 1 (Italy), p. 426.
98. Conclusions 2016, pp. 48–49.
99. Conclusions 2016 (Turkey), pp. 194, 196.
100. Conclusions XV-1, p. 356 (Italy), Conclusions 2008, vol. 1, p. 405 (Italy). Also includes aviation employees. Conclusions XIV-1, pp. 467, 650 (Portugal), Conclusions 2006, vol. 1, p. 426 (Italy), Conclusions XIII-3, pp. 74–75 (Spain), Conclusions 2008, vol. 1, p. 405 (Italy).
101. Conclusions XIII-3, p. 238; Conclusions XIV-1, p. 762; Conclusions XV-1, s. 592 (Turkey).
102. Conclusions XV-1, p. 626 (United Kingdom).
103. At p. 356 (Italy).
104. Conclusions XIV-1, pp. 649–650 (Portugal).
105. Conclusions X1, p. 37; XIII-3, p. 71; Addendum to Conclusions XV-1, s. 83 (The Netherlands).
106. Conclusions XIV-1, p. 409 (Ireland).
107. Conclusions XIII-3, p. 64, Case of Greece, allowing for soldiers to resign from professional military service upon the completion of specialist courses after twenty-five years. Conclusions 2020,

- the Committee previously found Ireland to not be in compliance with Article 1 §2 of the Charter on the grounds that army officers could not seek the termination of their commissions unless they repaid at least part of the cost of their education and training to the state and the decision to grant early retirement was left to the discretion of the Minister of Defence. This reason for non-conformity has remained unchanged since 1998.[108] The Committee notes that at the meeting of the Governmental Committee in 2013, the representative of Ireland confirmed that there had been no change with respect to the requirements relating to the retirement of Commissioned Officers from the Permanent Defence Forces of Ireland since the finding of non-conformity. Ireland's arguments for not being in a position to change the situation centre on the need to maintain a minimum level of services in a country where the number of military personnel is small compared to other states. Nevertheless, the Department of Defence confirmed to the Committee that no officer of the Permanent Defence Force had, since 1992, made an application to retire which had been refused by the Minister. Regardless of this explanation, the Committee decided to uphold its finding of non-conformity on this point.[109] The Committee, in its conclusions from 2012,[110] pointed out that any minimum period of service in the armed forces had to be of a reasonable duration and, in cases of longer minimum periods, it had to be proportionate to the duration of the education and training. Likewise, any fees (costs) to be repaid on early termination of service needed to be proportionate. As the country report does not provide for such situations in this respect, the Committee asked for up-to-date information on the subject in the next report. In the meantime, the Committee concluded that the prohibition of forced labour is not properly guaranteed.[111] Consequently, the Committee repeated the request for relevant information in the next report on matters raised in the Statement of Interpretation of Article 1 §2 in the General Introduction to the Conclusions of 2012, which drew attention to the existence of forced labour in the domestic environment and in family businesses, as well as the prohibition of the forced labour of prisoners. In the absence of any relevant information on the various issues relating to forced labour, the Committee considers that the situation is not in conformity with the Charter because the fact that the rights of workers are properly protected in this respect has not been established;
- prolonging compulsory military service for those who refuse it. Persons, who refused to serve the compulsory twelve months of military service in Greece, were under the obligation to undertake alternative employment of thirty months

---

Case of Cyprus, on the ground that the duration of alternative military service amounting to almost three years is excessive and constitutes a disproportionate restriction on the right to earn a living freely entered upon.

108. Conclusion XIV-1.
109. Conclusion 2016, pp. 171–172.
110. Conclusions 2012 (Georgia).
111. Conclusions 2016 (Georgia), p. 205.

advised by governmental administration.[112] In the decision handed down in the matter of *Quaker Council for European Affairs v. Greece*,[113] the committee declared that the alternative form of employment specified for a period significantly longer than the military service was a violation of the provision of Article 2 §1 of the Charter. The decision of the Committee was adopted by the Resolution of the Committee of Ministers on 6 March 2002, claiming that Greece was in breach of Article 2 §1 of the Charter, which prohibits forced labour.[114] The Committee claims increasing twofold the period of alternative employment to that of the compulsory military service is against the principle of freely choosing your employment protected by Article 2 §1 of the Charter;[115]

– prohibiting private entrepreneurs from being able to employ prisoners without prior consent from the interested employees. Prisoners' labour should be regulated by the state. Governmental employers may employ prisoners. Private employers may employ prisoners, after receiving consent, on the same grounds as employing other workers.[116]

47. The Committee analyses cases in which state authorities invoke the provisions allowing for the temporary exclusion from the provision of freedom to choose employment in circumstances of threat, where legislating statutes allowing the authorities to introduce the obligation to work, as well as prohibiting protest actions, mostly the organisation of strikes.[117] The Committee's stance concerning the conformity or non-conformity of such provisions with Article 1 §2 of the Charter is dependent upon the reasons for which the provision in question was temporarily excluded.

In the case of Cyprus, the Committee came to the conclusion, after listening to the representing authorities, that the constructions which guarantee the freedom to work are too general. However, procedural guarantees – such as the ability to appeal against the legislation, which repeals freedom of work, placing an obligation on citizens to carry out work in particular instances, are not sufficient, as they do not guarantee protection for citizens against administrative orders to undertake employment. The definition incorporated in the Constitution of Cyprus, which prohibited obligations being placed on citizens to undertake employment with the exception of circumstances related to the endangering of life and health of the citizens, was termed as too general and seen as a possible opening for the authorities of the country to

112. Conclusions XVII-1, p. 239, Conclusions XIX-1 (2008), p. 182. In case of Romania the Committee concluded that the length of alternative service to compulsory military service is excessive. Conclusions 2006, vol. 2, p. 738, same in Conclusions 2008, vol. 1, p. 188 (Cyprus), p. 231 (Estonia), vol. 2, p. 535 (Moldova), p. 668 (Portugal), p. 723 (Romania).
113. Complaint No. 8/2000.
114. ResChS (2003) 3 *See* European Social Charter, *Collected Texts*, *supra*, p. 499.
115. Conclusions XVII-1, p. 239 (Greece). For the very same ground the Committee reached negative conclusions in 2008 against Cyprus (Conclusions, vol. 1, p. 188), Estonia (*ibid.*, p. 231), Moldova (Conclusions, vol. 2, p. 535), Romania (*ibid.*, p. 723).
116. Digest of the case law of the ECSR, European Social Charter, Strasbourg 2004, p. 10.
117. Case of Cyprus, Conclusions XIII-3, pp. 59–60.

suspend the right to freedom of work. The crucial element is the definition of endangerment, which justifies temporary suspension of obligations to abide by the freedom to choose employment provision. Assessing the case of Finland, which defined its terms in greater detail than Cyprus, referring to extraordinary circumstances which allow for the temporary suspension of abiding by Article 1 §2 of the Charter, the Committee concluded that the existing provisions within the country referring to extraordinary circumstance placed on its citizens are deemed to be in accordance with Article 1 §2 of the Charter.

These provisions were seen to be detailed enough in their definition of circumstances regarded as extraordinary. These are war, life-threatening disasters, as well as a great threat to the lives and the economy of the country. The seriousness of the above-mentioned threats, the last of which appears to be lacking in precision, are all meant to indicate a lack of the possibility to control the circumstances by the authorities of the state.

The Committee of Labour Rights was convinced by these arguments; however, it did oblige the authorities of Finland to present detailed information referring to the last incident when such legal possibilities of suspending the right to freedom of employment were utilised, as well as recommended that every such instance be reported to the Council of Europe by the authorities of the state.[118]

When analysing whether the Member States comply with the principle laid down in Article 1, paragraph 2 of the Charter, according to which the rights of employed persons to earn a living in a freely chosen job should be effectively protected, the Committee concluded that six assessed Member States[119] accept that work is carried out in the framework of 'electronic employment technologies'. The Committee found that the failure of Member States to take action against employment platforms, gig economy and unpaid work performed by home workers[120] violated the fundamental principle of freedom of choice of forms of employment. It also ruled that some of the forms of alternative work previously practised and negatively assessed by the Committee must be considered too serious restrictions on an employee's right to earn a living by freely chosen work.[121] The Committee also concluded that 'it has not been established that civil servants are sufficiently protected against arbitrary suspensions of transfers'.[122] It has also not been established that the national authorities have fulfilled their obligations to prevent forced labour and labour exploitation, to protect victims, to effectively investigate the offences committed, and to punish those responsible for forced labour offences.[123]

118. Conclusions XIV-1, pp. 209–210.
119. Albania, Azerbaijan, Bosnia and Herzegovina, Croatia, Montenegro and Serbia. Conclusions 2020.
120. Romania. Conclusions 2020.
121. 'The duration of alternative civil service amounts to an excessive restriction of the right to earn one's living in an occupation freely entered upon' (Armenia, Cyprus). Conclusions 2020.
122. Conclusions 2020 (Turkey).
123. Conclusions 2020 (Albania, Croatia).

B. Eliminating Forms of Discrimination in Employment

48. A Member State which allows for discrimination in the field of employment or carrying out employment does not guarantee sufficient protection of workers' rights to undertake freely chosen employment to support a standard of living.[124] In the preamble to the European Social Charter of 1961, the law was passed to utilise labour rights protected by the Charter without any discrimination on the basis of race, skin colour, sex, religion, political views,[125] or national[126] or social origin. Not fulfilling the principles of equal treatment and equal opportunity in the field of employment is regarded as contravening the obligations set under Article 1 §2 of the Charter. The Committee analysing national reports paid particular attention to legal and practical regulations which lead to discrimination against people who are applying for employment, as well as workers according to differentiating criteria that are legally prohibited. Among the above-mentioned prohibited circumstances differentiating between workers, the Committee paid close attention to gender and a worker's family situation as well as work candidates. Based on Article 1 §2 of the Charter, the Committee ensured the protection of workers' rights, particularly those employed in private and public sectors.

The Committee declared a violation of freedom of employment rights in Ireland, where married women had been not allowed to take up positions in civil service,[127] and in the United Kingdom, where men had not been allowed to work as midwives.[128]

49. However, the Committee did accept restrictions on the employment of women, including a total ban on women employed in hard physical labour, as well as in combat positions within the military.[129] It emphasised the need for regulations protecting against discrimination within the workplace based on gender in both private and public-sector workplaces.[130] It required Member State authorities to undertake efforts to efficiently execute equal treatment and regulations forbidding discrimination within the workplace. It did not indicate a manner of conduct for the above-mentioned propositions to be carried out; however, it obliged Member States

124. Conclusions 2008, vol. 2, p. 314 (France).
125. Previous involvement in security services is also included. The Committee concludes that the situation in Lithuania is not in conformity with Art. 1 §2 of the RESC on the grounds that the Act on the evaluation of the USSR State Security Committee (NKVD, NKGB, MGB, KGB) and the present activities of former permanent employees of the organisation entails restrictions which go beyond the scope of Art. G of the RESC. Conclusions 2008, vol. 2, p. 450.
126. The Committee concludes that in number of states foreign nationals' citizens of the Member States, access to employment in both public and private sectors is excessively restricted and constitutes discrimination on grounds of nationality. Conclusions 2008, vol. 1, p. 188 (Cyprus), p. 405 (Italy), vol. 2, p. 490 (Malta), Conclusions XIX-1 (2008), p. 182 (Greece), p. 255 (Iceland), p. 330 (Poland), p. 357 (Slovakia), p. 436 (FYROM) In number of Member States foreigners redundant first (p. 24, Austria).
127. Conclusions 1, p. 166.
128. Conclusions VIII, p. 33, Conclusions IX-1, p. 24.
129. Conclusions II, p. 4 (Sweden).
130. Conclusions XIII-5, p. 254.

to undertake all possible measures in order to ensure equal opportunity in the workplace and equal treatment of male and female workers.[131] According to the Committee, Article 1 §2 of the Charter did not create enough of a legal basis to commence litigation against employers who did not abide by the regulations concerning the equal treatment of men and women within the workplace, prohibiting discrimination of the workers according to their gender. The Committee approved a controlling function for national authorities, analysing collective agreements and other normative agreements in order to conclude whether they consisted of any clauses discriminating against workers according to prohibited criteria, especially gender.[132]

50. The Committee prioritised the regulation of discrimination against workers based on gender. It made a great effort to analyse issues of equal treatment of women's access to employment, their relations within the workplace and their possibility of partaking in vocational training.[133] After discovering significant disproportions in the utility of vocational training options, the Committee appealed for the equalisation of the existing disproportions in accessing vocational training by women, which was considered a necessary precondition for the execution of equal treatment of men and women in accessing employment and within the workplace. In order for this to be achieved, the Committee paid heed to the idea of the preferential treatment of women within the workplace.[134] Utilising the principles of the *acquis communautaire,* the Committee considered the policy of the preferential treatment of women within the workplace as allowable but not obligatory under Article 1 §2 of the Charter.[135] The Committee did not change its conservative approach to the above-mentioned issue, even though the supervisory process indicated no changes were being implemented.

The Committee declared that police force authorities in Greece fixed a limit as to the number of women allowed into police school academies at 20% and to academies training higher-ranked police officers and 15%.[136]

51. The Committee was interested in such practical aspects as well as the processes involved in the protection of rights against the discrimination of workers based on their sex, taking into consideration a balance of evidential material concerning discrimination,[137] the amount of compensation for the victims of discrimination,[138] as well as matters concerning the harassment and sexual harassment of workers.[139]

131. Conclusions VIII, p. 29 (Austria). Ceiling on compensation for discrimination is not accepted. Conclusions 2008, vol. 1, p. 270 (Finland).
132. Conclusions XIII-3, pp. 71–72 (the Netherlands).
133. Conclusions XIV-1, p. 148 (Cyprus).
134. Conclusions XIII-5, p. 254.
135. Darcy & Harris, *supra*, p. 50.
136. Conclusions XIV-1, p. 293.
137. Conclusions XIII-1, p. 49 (Iceland).
138. Conclusions XIV-1, p. 68 (Austria), Conclusions 2008, vol. 1, p. 270 (Finland).
139. Conclusions XIII-3, p. 61 (France).

Besides being concerned with the issues of discrimination within the workforce based on gender, the Committee was also concerned with the issue of discrimination based on trade union membership or its lack.[140] Ultimately it came to a conclusion, considering the format of the appendix to the Charter, which in part relates to Article 1 §2, that the above provision cannot be regarded as a norm permitting or forbidding the introduction of union security clauses forcing workers to join certain union organisations, an obligation to treat all workers equally regardless whether they are members of a trade union or not, as well as a prohibition of discriminating against workers who are members of a trade union or are active in it, and that the legal state, as well as national practices in these matters, should be carried out in accordance with Article 5 of the Charter.[141]

52. The Committee was concerned with the protection of labour rights in matters of discrimination based on religious and political premises in Northern Ireland,[142] religious premises in Greece,[143] Denmark and Norway,[144] as well as political premises in Germany.[145] Accepting the right of a religious faction to be excluded from the regulation of equal treatment in relation to religious beliefs, which carries the same connotations as some cases of discrimination based on denomination approved by law, the Committee decided that the above-mentioned exclusions were not applicable to the state as an employer.

In the last case, the Committee recognised as far-reaching the demand to keep loyalty to the provisions of the Constitution of the Federal Republic of Germany, which imposes a condition of neutrality when it comes to matters of denomination on civil servants, with respect to applicants seeking physical jobs in the following governmental employment sectors: drivers, postmen and gardeners.

The Charter assures general protection against discrimination based on illegal criteria, which differentiate workers as well as those seeking employment. It is applicable to those employed in the private or public sector, to individuals in small-scale workplaces,[146] and to those who are self-employed.[147] The addressees of the Charter are the authorities of Member States, which are responsible for eliminating various obstacles in attaining employment, for those who are regarded as part of a minority, separated due to illegal criteria, which differentiates during the employment process.

53. During the 2016 cycle, the Committee found eighteen cases of non-conformity with Article 1 §2 of the Charter in the matter of the prohibition of discrimination in employment. The most common restrictions on the access of foreign nationals of state parties to the European Social Charter, other than the European Economic Area and the Swiss Confederation, to civil service posts, are excessive

140. Conclusions XIII-1, p. 57, Conclusions XIII-3, p. 77 (United Kingdom).
141. Conclusions XIX-1, p. 454 (United Kingdom).
142. Conclusions XIV-1, p. 793 (United Kingdom).
143. Conclusions XIII-1, p. 48; Conclusions XIV-1, pp. 348–349.
144. Conclusions XIV-1, p. 174 (Denmark); p. 606 (Norway).
145. Conclusions V, p. 7.
146. Conclusions IX-1, p. 25 (United Kingdom).
147. Conclusions I, p. 8.

and therefore constitute discrimination on the grounds of nationality.[148] In its previous conclusion, the Committee asked whether (and if so) what categories of employment are closed to non-nationals.[149] The reports presented in the cycle (2016) indicate that a civil servant may be a person who is a Bulgarian citizen or a citizen of another state party to the Agreement on the European Economic Area or the Swiss Confederation.[150] A foreign national or a stateless person may enter employment within the state authority body as a state employee under the conditions stipulated by separate laws and international conventions. This right is not extended to a foreigner with temporary residence.[151] According to the legislation of the Russian Federation, the foreign citizen has no right to be employed either in the municipal or the state service. Foreigners cannot be a ship's master, chief officer, chief engineer or radio officer in the crew of a vessel sailing under the flag of the Russian Federation, nor can they be members of a warship crew of the Russian Federation or any other ship, state aircraft or experimental means of aviation which is exploited for commercial purposes. Until recently, foreigners were not allowed to be captains of civilian aircraft. They could not work at facilities and organisations whose activities are related to the security of the Russian Federation. Because of the total ban on foreign nationals being employed in the municipal and state services, the Committee considers that the situation is not in conformity with Article 1 §2 of the Charter on the basis that the restrictions on the access to employment for nationals of other state parties to the Charter are excessive, constituting discrimination based on nationality.[152] The Committee notes in the other conclusion that the list of jobs reserved for Spanish nationals is too long and that only nationals of EU Member States have access to other public jobs which are not included in the list. The Committee therefore reiterates its finding as to the non-conformity on this point.[153] The Committee recalls that, under Article 1 §2 of the Charter, while it is possible for states to make foreign nationals' access to employment on their territory subject to possession of a work permit, they cannot ban the nationals of the states which are party to the Charter, in general, from occupying jobs for reasons other than those set out in Article G. Restrictions on the right guaranteed by the Charter are admitted only if they are prescribed by law, serve a legitimate purpose and are necessary in a democratic society for the protection of the rights and freedoms of others or the protection of public interest, national security, public health or morals. The only jobs which foreigners may be banned from, therefore, are those that are inherently connected with the protection of the public interest or national security and involve the exercise of public authority.[154] Even if exceptions may be made for other foreign nationals in special circumstances, the Committee concludes that the situation

148. Conclusions 2016, pp. 8–10 (Bulgaria); (FYROM), pp. 83–84; (Ireland), p. 169; (Montenegro), p. 180; Russian (Federation), pp. 188–189; (Turkey), p. 193; (Moldova), p. 209; (Azerbaijan), pp. 213–214; (Belgium), pp. 244–245. Conclusions XXI-1 (Iceland), pp. 302–303); (Greece), p. 312; (Spain), p. 317.
149. Conclusions 2002.
150. Conclusions 2016 (Bulgaria).
151. Conclusions 2016 (Montenegro).
152. Conclusions 2016 (Russian Federation).
153. Conclusions 2016 (Spain), p. 318.
154. Conclusions 2012 (Albania).

is not in conformity with Article 1 §2 of the Charter on the basis that the legislation prohibiting discrimination in employment on grounds other than sex is inadequate.[155] The legal changes made in Belgium in order to allow non-European citizens access to public service jobs, namely a revision of the Constitution in order to allow non-citizens access to civil jobs, and the fact that the revision process is now underway, has not stopped the Committee from concluding that the situation in Belgium is not in conformity with Article 1 §2 of the Charter on the grounds that restrictions to the access of foreign nationals other than EEA to civil posts are excessive and that this constitutes discrimination on the grounds of nationality.[156] The Committee only asks for up-to-date information on the plans to amend the Constitution while maintaining its decision on non-conformity in this respect.

54. With regard to advocates, the Committee had previously concluded that the restriction imposed on non-citizens from becoming advocates was not in conformity with the Charter.[157] The Latvian national report reiterates that in order to become a 'sworn advocate' or an assistant to a sworn advocate in Latvia, according to its Advocacy Law, an individual must possess Latvian nationality. Citizens of other EU and EEA Member States may practice as advocates in Latvia under certain conditions. The report adds that according to the information provided by the Latvian Council of Sworn Advocates, there 'is no precedent when citizens of non-European Member States would have requested the Council to practice as sworn advocates in Latvia'. The Committee noted that the restrictions imposed on non-EEA nationals who wished to become advocates were excessive and have not changed, constituting discrimination on the grounds of nationality. The situation is similar in France, with the French report stating that the profession of advocate is only open to French citizens, those of the EU and Member States of the European Economic Area, refugees and stateless persons and nationals of any state that grants the reciprocal treatment of French advocates. It adds that any Member State of the World Trade Organisation, and thus of the General Agreement on Trade of Services (GATS), which covered 161 countries in 2015, is considered to fulfil this reciprocity condition. The Committee considers that the restriction on access to the profession of advocate, which is applicable to non-EEA nationals, is excessive, constituting discrimination based on nationality. It asks for information in the next report on positive measures (actions) taken to combat all forms of discrimination in employment.[158]

55. From the information provided in the reports, the Committee notes that discrimination on the grounds of sexual orientation is not prohibited in employment.[159] The Russian report does not provide any information on the employment situation of LGBT persons. It does not clarify what the legal basis for the prohibition of discrimination on the grounds of sexual orientation mentioned in the

155. Conclusions 2016 (Iceland), pp. 302, 305.
156. Conclusions 2016 (Belgium), pp. 245, 247.
157. Conclusions XX-I, 2012 (Latvia).
158. Conclusions 2016 (France), pp. 20–21.
159. Conclusions 2016 (Armenia, Russian Federation, Turkey).

Ombudsman report in 2014 attached to the national report is.[160] The Russian Federation is regularly criticised by the European human rights community. LGBT people who have lost their jobs have told Human Rights Watch that their dismissal or forced resignation was preceded by a public campaign by groups of citizens allegedly concerned by the morals and well-being of their children.[161] The Committee takes note that in its opinion, the Venice Commission expressed concerns and considered that the statutory provisions prohibiting 'propaganda of homosexuality' are incompatible with the ECHR and international human rights standards.[162]

The Turkish report indicates that there is no specific legislation for the prohibition of discrimination on the grounds of sexual orientation. The Committee takes note from other sources that there is widespread discrimination against LGBT people in employment. It notes from the European Commission reports that 'there were cases of police officers, teachers and bank personnel dismissed from their jobs due to the disclosure of the sexual identity'.[163] The Committee noted in 2012 that there was a ban on LGBT persons from serving in the armed forces and asked for the government's comments on that issue.[164] The information provided in the last report does not suggest that the restrictions have been removed.

Since none of the three above-mentioned country reports provides information that discrimination on the grounds of sexual orientation in employment is not expressly prohibited by national laws, the Community concludes that the situation in Armenia, the Russian Federation and Turkey is not in conformity with Article 1 §2 of the Charter.

56. Certain reports do not specify whether employers are required to make reasonable accommodations for persons with disabilities,[165] the treatment of aged workers,[166] or forms of discrimination other than gender[167] as well as the question of indirect discrimination in employment.[168] The Committee concludes that the situation is not in conformity with Article 1 §2 of the Charter on the grounds that the state legislation does not prohibit discrimination in employment on the grounds of age and disability; indirect discrimination is not expressly prohibited by law; there is adequate protection against all forms of discrimination in employment. The most spectacular list of charges was formulated in the Committee's conclusion in the case of Armenia. The Committee notes, among other things, that: (1) indirect discrimination is not defined and prohibited by the state legislation; (2) discrimination is not prohibited in connection with recruitment in employment; (3) there is no protection against discrimination in employment on the grounds of sexual orientation; (4) there

160. Conclusions 2016 (Russian Federation), p. 187.
161. Human Rights Watch Report, Russia: Anti-LGBT Law a Tool for Discrimination, 29 Jun. 2014, at: https://www.hrw.org/news/2014/06/29/russia-anti-lgbt-law-tool-discrimination.
162. Venice Commission, Opinion on the Issue of the Prohibition of the So-called 'Propaganda of Homosexuality', CDL-AD(2013)022.
163. European Commission, Turkey 2013 Progress Report, SWD (2013) 417 final, p. 59.
164. Conclusions 2012 (Turkey).
165. Conclusions 2016 (Bosnia and Herzegovina), pp. 156, 159; Azerbaijan, p. 216.
166. Conclusions 2016 (Bosnia and Herzegovina), pp. 156, 159.
167. Conclusions 2016 (Georgia), p. 205.
168. Conclusions 2016 (Russian Federation), pp. 186–187; (Armenia), pp. 277–278.

is no clear and comprehensive definition of the prohibition of direct and indirect discrimination[169] covering all aspects of employment and occupation, including recruitment; (5) Armenia still does not have a comprehensive legal framework against discrimination; and (6) the anti-discrimination strategy which would help to make legislative steps more consistent remained a draft.[170]

In the recent 2020 cycle, the Committee found that indirect discrimination was not prohibited in some Member States[171] and that discrimination against employees on the basis of their sexual orientation, ethnic origin and political views was not prohibited.[172] As the most problematic issue, the Committee identified the use by a large group of Member States of the provisions on the protection of the public interest and national security as a pretext to prevent citizens of other European Member States from entering national labour markets on the European continent.[173]

57. With regard to the compensation granted to victims of discrimination, the Committee concluded that the situation is not in conformity with Article 1 §2 of the Charter since there is an upper limit on the compensation awarded to employees who have suffered discrimination which may preclude damages from making good the loss suffered and from being sufficiently dissuasive. The Committee considered that compensation to a maximum amount of twelve months' average salary,[174] up to four months' wages plus claims for other benefits of which employees have been deprived, three times the wages for the term of office, between four and eight months' wages[175] or even 104 times the amount of the claimant's weekly remuneration (i.e., two years pay, or EUR 40,000)[176] is not accepted by the Committee. The Committee recalls that remedies available to victims of discrimination must be adequate, proportionate and dissuasive.[177] Any ceiling on compensation is proscribed.[178] Therefore, the upper limits on the amount of compensation that may be

169. The Committee states with regard to the definition of indirect discrimination, the Russian Federation report indicates that the definition of discrimination is not complete, in particular there is a lack of a clear distinction between direct and indirect discrimination. The Committee recalls that under Art. 1 §2 of the Charter, legislation should cover both direct and indirect discrimination (Conclusions XVIII-I, 2006, Austria). As regards indirect discrimination, the Committee recalls that it has stated that in the context of Art. E of the Revised Charter: 'such indirect discrimination may arise by failing to take due and positive account of all relevant differences or by failing to take adequate steps to ensure that the rights and collective advantages that are open to all are genuinely accessible by all and to all' (*Autism Europe v. France*, Collective Complaint No. 13/2000, decision on merits of 4 Nov. 2003, §52).
170. European Commission, Country Progress Report 2014, SWD(2015)63 final.
171. Armenia. Conclusion 2020.
172. Armenia Azerbaijan, Turkey. Conclusions 2020.
173. Albania, Armenia (e.g., all posts in the civil service are reserved to Armenian citizens), Bosnia and Herzegovina (nationals of other State Parties do not have access to civil service jobs), Croatia, Latvia, Montenegro, North Macedonia, Turkey, Serbia. Conclusions 2020.
174. Conclusions 2016 (Armenia), p. 278.
175. Conclusions 2016 (Turkey), p. 193.
176. Conclusions 2016 (Ireland), p. 169.
177. Conclusion 2020 (Azerbaijan).
178. Conclusions 2012 (Andorra).

awarded in discrimination cases (with the exception of gender discrimination cases) are considered by the Committee as insufficient protection against discrimination in employment.

In the 2020 cycle, the Committee monitored whether the Member States had introduced and applied effective legal measures to protect against discrimination, which would not only compensate discriminated persons but also use appropriate legal sanctions to limit the social pathology of discrimination in employment. In particular, the Committee was interested in whether the victims of discrimination were beneficiaries of their right to seek restitution for the unlawful termination of their employment and whether they benefited from the presumption of truthfulness of the allegation of discrimination and the appropriate adjustment of the burden of proof in court proceedings. The Committee found that the Member States listed below did not comply with the above recommendations.[179] Some Member States have not made any efforts to demonstrate that effective measures to protect workers from discrimination are put in place in practice. Others, on the other hand, have set low limits on compensation in cases of discrimination. Therefore, it could not be expected that the above legal sanctions would discourage employers from taking illegal actions. A favourable change in the distribution of the burden of evidence in court proceedings, consisting of demonstrating by the employer that he is not guilty of using legally prohibited activities, was not introduced to court proceedings by a relatively large proportion of the Member States audited in the 2020 cycle. There are reasons to believe that the situation in these cases in the thirty-five Member States audited in this cycle is not good. Only Denmark has been assessed by the Committee as a country that complies with the legal requirements set out in Article 1 paragraph 1 of the Charter. The remaining thirty-four countries were recognised as failing to meet European standards of effective protection of workers to earn a living by freely chosen work. The basis for the above statement is a high percentage of negative decisions or the lack of documentation of compliance with Article 1 paragraph 1 of the Charter.

Despite the Committee's actions, the situation in Eastern Europe is deteriorating. Reports from the Member States prove this. The Committee recalls that domestic law should provide for a shift in the burden of proof in favour of the plaintiff in discrimination cases.[180] Meanwhile, some national reports indicate there is no shift in the burden of proof in discrimination in employment cases.[181] Under the provisions of Civil Codes or Civil Procedure Codes, each party to the proceedings should provide evidence of their claims and objections. In its notes, the Committee concludes that the situation in Armenia,[182] Azerbaijan,[183] the Russian Federation,[184] and Ukraine is not in conformity with Article 1 §2 of the Charter. Other cases of discrimination against employees identified in the 2020 conclusions include the following: (1) it has not been established that the prohibition of discrimination in

179. Armenia, Azerbaijan, the Russian Federation, Serbia, Ukraine. Conclusions 2020.

180. *Syndicat de Défense des fonctionnaires v. France*, Complaint No. 73/2011, Decision on merits of 13 Sep. 2012, §59.

181. Armenia, Azerbaijan, Russian Federation, Ukraine.

182. Conclusions 2016, pp. 278, 281.

183. Conclusions 2016, pp. 214,216.

184. Conclusions 2016, pp. 187, 191.

employment is effectively implemented in practice; (2) the restriction on access of nationals of other State Parties to civil service is excessive, which constitutes a discrimination on the grounds of nationality; (3) legislation does not provide for a shift in the burden of proof in discrimination cases (Azerbaijan, Ukraine, Russian Federation); (4) the restrictions imposed on non-EU nationals to become advocates are excessive, which constitutes discrimination on the grounds of nationality (Latvia); (5) indirect discrimination is not expressly prohibited by law; (6) discrimination on grounds of sexual orientation in employment is not expressly prohibited by law (Azerbaijan, Russian Federation); (7) foreign nationals cannot be employed in the municipal and state service which constitutes a discrimination on grounds of nationality (Russian Federation); (8) the list of jobs which are barred to foreign nationals, in particular those from other State Parties than the members of the EU, is too broad (Croatia); (9) it has been established that employers are required to make reasonable accommodation for person with disabilities; (10) the suspension of all inspections related to entrepreneurial activity until 1 January 2021 is a barrier to the mandate of labour inspection services in preventing forced labour and labour exploitation.

III. To Establish and Maintain the Function of General Access to Free Employment Services

58. Member States that ratified Article 1 §3 of the Charter are obliged to establish or maintain free employment services for all workers. According to the provision in question, employment agencies are to provide services for workers. Article 1 §3 of the Charter uses the definition of a 'worker' as a person seeking employment in the scope of labour relations. People taking advantage of employment services are those who have remained without employment, are capable of employment and are willing to undertake employment. The definition of 'worker' in this analysed provision is a guideline, as employment agencies will not provide services for obtaining employment for those who are self-employed.[185]

The employment service sector is concerned with providing an individual who is seeking employment with a job. This is equivalent to providing employers with candidates for employment. Employment services are, therefore, agencies through which employment is found. They inform those seeking employment of vacant positions and provide employers with the details of possible candidates.[186] Under Article 1 §3 of the Charter, by definition, they are not responsible for providing vocational training services. Employment agencies and the services they provide may be done so through private or public employment services.[187] The Charter does not place an obligation on Member States to supervise the effectiveness of such agencies in how jobs are allocated to those seeking or candidates provided for employers. The Committee pays attention to the research on the effectiveness of activity of these services. It demands from authorities of Member States information regarding whether

185. Conclusions I, p. 8.
186. Conclusions I, p. 167 (Ireland).
187. Conclusions III, p. 9 (Austria).

and how governmental administration bodies monitor private employment agencies.[188] It considers that employment agencies should be supervised by governmental administration bodies together with stakeholders[189] on a local and national level.[190] It obliges authorities of Member States to present within the national reports information regarding the number of employment agencies and their methods of organising. It demands information concerning the number of people who are using these services, including their age, gender, and professional qualifications. The Committee seeks to establish the number of people who are registered in the employment agencies seeking employment as well as the number of positions that have been filled by those who have sought employment. It wants to know whether national regulations place obligations on employers to provide employment agencies with information regarding vacant work positions. If such regulations are not in place, the Committee pursues to find out how employment agencies receive such information regarding vacant positions. When a state has both private and public employment services, the Committee is interested in familiarising itself with their coordination and the results of their conduct. Of interest for the Committee is especially the comparison between public and private employment agencies.[191] The Committee of European Communities reports that only 10.5% of those seeking employment take advantage of public employment services. Therefore the Committee concluded unless this rate drops down to 5%, the situation should be considered as serious.[192]

Clients of employment services should not be charged fees. These are not charitable organisations; therefore, the costs associated with their services must be paid for by governmental funds. Such costs entailed by employment service agencies (both private and public) must not be covered by the job seeker or by the employer.[193]

The United Kingdom, as noted by the Committee in its fourth supervisory cycle, was in breach of Article 1 §3 of the Charter when it allowed employers to pay for employment agency services. The Committee concluded that the situation in Italy and Romania was not in conformity with Article 1 §3 of the Charter on the grounds that it was unable to assess whether the right to free placement services was granted in practice.[194]

59. The Committee's ruling allows for such payments by the employer to be made when seeking to fill all positions, including academic and administrative staff,

188. Conclusions I, p. 167 (Ireland).
189. Conclusions I, p. 16.
190. Conclusions III, p. 9 (Austria); Conclusions XIV-1, p. 691 (Spain); Conclusions XIV-3, pp. 88–89 (United Kingdom).
191. Conclusions XIII-1, pp. 58 et seq.; 221–222; Conclusions XIII-2, pp. 235 et seq.; Conclusions XIII-3, pp. 78 et seq., 238 et seq.; Addendum to Conclusions XIII-3, pp. 19–20.
192. Conclusions XIV-1, vol. 1, p. 351 (Greece).
193. Conclusions IV, p. 10.
194. Conclusions 2006, vol. 1, p. 427 (Italy), vol. 2, p. 740 (Romania).

managers, highly specialised technicians and engineers, only when normal free-of-charge employment service channels are not available.[195] The position of the Committee has not changed over subsequent supervisory cycles.[196] In its annual report of the eighth supervisory cycle of the Charter, the Committee stated that free-of-charge employment agencies would be jeopardised should they apply their services only to employment demand, without taking into consideration the offer of supply by employers. Considering the fact that some job positions do not follow supply and demand patterns, the Committee has noted that filling such positions is outside the legal regulations of Article 1 §3 of the Charter. The Committee has modified its earlier position on a general free-of-charge approach for employers using employment agency services. Instead, it has stated there are certain situations when demands for payments from employers using such services can be made, such as the recruitment of top-level position managers.[197] The above-mentioned stance was maintained by a report concluding the twelfth supervisory cycle.[198] Article 1 §3 of the Charter is thus interpreted by the Committee as guaranteeing standard employment agencies services which are free of charge. A fee for finding candidates should be rare and applicable only to managerial positions. Fees paid to employment agencies compensate for professional conduct performed in order to appoint an appropriate candidate for a managerial position. The availability of a candidate to begin work cannot be seen as a reason for the employer to be charged.

Employment services should be freely available regardless of sex,[199] age,[200] trade and profession, including farming[201] and housework,[202] for all persons willing to enter into work relations. Entitlements to free-of-charge services of employment agencies should be equally accessible to citizens of a given state as well as to citizens of other Member States.[203] An individual's right to free placement services ought to be guaranteed.[204]

60. In order to assess the effectiveness and capacity of public employment services, updated information ought to be provided by the Member States. In the previous conclusion of 2012, several Central–Eastern Member States[205] and Spain did not provide all or, at best, provided insufficient information on the requirement of fully fledged free employment services. In the last cycle, the reports presented by the above-mentioned states do contain any information on the number of persons placed via public employment services during the reference period. The reports do

195. As above, pp. 10–12.
196. Conclusions V, p. 10; Conclusions VI, p. 10; Conclusions VII, p. 11. All former cases apply to the United Kingdom. Conclusions XIII-3, p. 241; Conclusions XIV-1, pp. 762–763 (Turkey).
197. Conclusions VIII, pp. 36–37 (United Kingdom).
198. Conclusions XII-1, p. 62 (Denmark).
199. Conclusions III p. 10 (Italy).
200. Conclusions III p. 10 (Denmark, Ireland); Conclusions IV p. 12 (Norway), Conclusions XIII-1 p. 222 (Turkey).
201. Conclusions III p. 10 (Italy).
202. Conclusions IV p. 12 (Italy).
203. Conclusions XIV-1 p. 72 (Austria), p. 105 (Belgium), p. 213 (Finland), p. 250 (France), Conclusions 2008, vol. 1, p. 116 (Belgium), vol. 2, p. 725 (Romania).
204. Conclusions XIX-1 (2008), p. 332 (Poland), p. 358 (Slovakia).
205. Armenia, Azerbaijan, Georgia, Romania, Ukraine, Slovak Republic.

not provide any information on the quantitative indicators used to assess the effectiveness of employment services. The Committee asks that the next report contain information on the following indicators: (a) total number of registered job seekers/ unemployed persons in the Public Employment Service (PES; (b) the number of vacancies the PES has been notified of; (c) the number of persons placed via PES; (d) the placement rate (percentage of placement compared to the number of notified vacancies; (e) placements by PES as a percentage of total employment in the labour market and the respective market shares of public and private services; (f) the proportion of the staff concerned with placement activities.[206] The Committee presents an opinion that the existence of fee-charging by private employment agencies is not contrary to Article 1 §3 of the Charter, provided that fully fledged free employment services exist in all occupational sectors and geographical areas.[207] The examined reports do not answer the Committee's questions. The Spanish report states that a single job portal was set to be used as a database for registering applications for and offers of employment throughout the country.[208] The Committee notes from this report that this portal is not able to provide information concerning the performance indicators of the employment service. The European Commission's 2015 report states that the single job portal has been operational since July 2014, although it seems that no improvements have been made to the posting of job vacancies since the launch stage.[209] The Slovak report only indicates that an important amendment of the Act on Employment Services has entered into force since 1 May 2013, improving the administrative capacity of the provided employment services. However, the Committee notes the critical assessment of the public employment services in the European Commission's 2015 country report[210] that, notwithstanding the legal amendments mentioned above, limited progress has been achieved in enhancing the capacity of public employment services, as the reform is ongoing with completion foreseen for 2020 only. From the Report on the Social Situation of the Population of the Slovak Republic for 2014, the Committee notes that, according to statistical reports, there were, on average, 385,661 registered job seekers in Slovakia in 2014. In comparison with 2013, the average monthly number of registered job seekers fell by 7.07%. In 2013, there was a monthly average of 416,006 registered job seekers. In 2014, a total of 16,046 job vacancies were available in the national economy on average. Compared to 2013, the number increased by 6.6%.[211] The Committee considers that the number of vacancies notified to the public service is particularly low in the Slovak Republic. From the European Commission Country Report for 2015, the Committee notes that unemployment rates in Slovakia remain above the EU average (12.5% versus 9.9%) in the EU-28 in December 2014 and are mostly structural and long-term in nature. The above-mentioned report

206. Conclusions 2016 (Armenia), p. 136; (Azerbaijan), p. 160; (Georgia), p. 24; (Ukraine), p. 73; (Spain), p. 299.
207. Conclusions 2016 (Azerbaijan), p. 160.
208. Conclusions 2016, p. 299.
209. http://ec.europa.eu/europe2020/pdf/csr2015/cr2015_spain_en.pdf.
210. *Ibid.*
211. https://www.employment.gov.sk/files/slovensky/ministerstvo/analitycke-centrum/englis-version_kvalita-tlac.pdf.

points out that public employment services have a limited capacity to provide personalised services, in particular to those furthest from the labour market, such as the long-term unemployed, the low-skilled, young people and Roma. The Committee notes that the number of job seekers is too high in relation to PES staff (one front-line officer to 600 job seekers), and the report does not indicate the ratio of placement staff to registered job seekers.[212] Therefore, the Committee recalls that services must operate effectively throughout the national territory and with respect to all sectors of the economy. The main function of such services is to place unemployed job seekers in employment as well as employed workers looking for another job. However, in the present situation, taking into account the low number of vacancies notified to the public employment services, as well as the limited capacity to provide personalised services, the Committee considers that public employment services do not operate in an efficient manner.

Since the last cycle, the situation in some countries[213] which, by ratifying Article 1 §3 of the Charter, undertook to establish or maintain free employment services for all workers has not improved. In 2020, the Committee decided that the situation in some Member States is not in conformity with that Charter on the grounds that it has not been established that free placement services operate in an efficient measure. The Committee notes that reports submitted by the three Member States mentioned above do not provide information on free placement services and just contain no replies to the questions asked in the Committee's previous conclusions. The Committee considers that given the lack of information concerning quantities indicators, it cannot be established that the free placement services in Armenia, Azerbaijan and Cyprus operate in an efficient manner.

IV. Vocational Guidance, Training and Rehabilitation

61. Tasks imposed on Member States by Article 1 §4 of the Charter involve providing or promoting appropriate vocational guidance, training and rehabilitation. Authorities are obliged to organise a system of vocational guidance and training and maintain its proper level, as well as a system supporting all those who intend to take up a new job requiring new skills and abilities by providing them with the necessary preparation. This task is of an alternative character – if a state has a private system of vocational guidance, training and rehabilitation and if, according to the authorities, it works properly, there is no need to organise an identical or similar public system. The authorities are, however, obliged to support private systems to make sure their services are in accordance with the rules set by the Committee.

A provision of Article 1 §4 of the Charter is commonly applicable. Its scope embraces not only employers but also persons running their own businesses (self-employed).[214] The above-mentioned regulation obliges Member States not only to organise and support institutions providing services of vocational guidance, training, and rehabilitation but also to impose on them equal access to services for all

212. Conclusions 2016, p. 141.
213. Armenia, Azerbaijan, Cyprus. Conclusions 2020.
214. Conclusions I, p. 8.

interested people.[215] The only case – with the exception of a number of situations mentioned above when there were obstacles in partaking in vocational guidance, training, and rehabilitation by foreigners residing in a country which ratified Article 1 §4 of the Charter – of a systematic neglect of duties formulated by the provision in question by a Member State concerned unequal territorial distribution of services of vocational guidance, training, and rehabilitation.[216]

A national report filed by Turkey stated that centres providing service of vocational guidance, training, and rehabilitation were located in 6 out of 73 state provinces.

The Committee also indicated the limited scope of spending in the field of vocational guidance, training, and rehabilitation. There is a linkage between Article 1 §4 and Articles 9 (right to vocational guidance), 10 §3 (right of workers to vocational training) and 15 §1 (right of persons with disabilities to vocational guidance, education and training. In case the situation with regard to one of the above-mentioned provisions of the RESC is not in conformity, the Committee concludes non-compliance with Article 1 §4 of the RESC.[217]

62. During the last cycle, 50% of Member States, seventeen countries out of the thirty-four examined, failed to achieve positive conclusions concerning the educational, vocational guidance, training, and rehabilitation of workers.[218] A majority of these Member States, ten out of the above-mentioned seventeen, received negative conclusions due to the fact that they accepted Article 9s, 10 §3 and 15 §1 of the Charter and did not comply with one or more of the above-mentioned provisions of the Charter for the very same reasons. Therefore, it has not been established that the right of persons with disabilities and/or the right of people with disabilities is guaranteed or effectively guaranteed with regard to vocational guidance, vocational training and retraining, and mainstream education.[219] The most typical negative declaration of the Committee concerning Article 1 §4 of the Charter in Conclusions 2016 reads as follows: Denmark, France, FYROM (now North Macedonia), Luxembourg, Malta, Montenegro, Romania, Russian Federation, Slovak Republic, Turkey, Ukraine have accepted Articles 9, 10 §3, 15 §1 of the Charter and if the Committee found out that the situation in all, some or even one provision of those articles was declared as being in non-compliance with the Charter, the Committee automatically declared that it had not been established that the right to vocational

215. Greece, Conclusions XI-1, p. 149, Conclusions, XII-1, p. 68.
216. Turkey. Conclusions XIII-1; Conclusions XIII-3, p. 243; Conclusions XIV-2, p. 739.
217. Conclusions 2007, vol. 1, p. 157 (Belgium), vol. 2, p. 583 (Ireland), p. 667, p. 667, p. 871 (Moldova), p. 907 (Norway), p. 949 (Romania), p. 993 (Slovenia), p. 1057 (Sweden), Conclusions 2008, vol. 1, p. 117 (Belgium), vol. 2, p. 726 (Romania), Conclusions XIX-1 (2008), p. 302 (Luxembourg), p. 332 (Poland), p. 358 (Slovakia), p. 395 (Spain).
218. Conclusions 2016: (Denmark), p. 310; (France), p. 112; (FYROM), pp. 133, 135; (Luxembourg), p. 326; (Malta), p. 130; (Montenegro), p. 131; (Romania), pp. 128–129; (Russian Federation), p. 13; (Slovak Republic), p. 125; (Turkey), p. 127; (Ukraine), p. 132.
219. Denmark, France, FYROM, Luxembourg, Malta, Montenegro, Romania, Russian Federation, Slovak Republic, Turkey, Ukraine.

guidance, training and retraining, people with disabilities to participate in mainstream education and training was guaranteed or effectively guaranteed in its conclusions issued under Article 1 §4. This is made possible because Article 1 §4 of the Charter guarantees the right to vocational guidance and training for employed and unemployed persons and specialised guidance and training for persons with disabilities. This provision of the Charter is complemented by Articles 9 (right to vocational guidance), 10 §3 (right of adult workers to vocational training) and 15 §1 (right of persons with disabilities to vocational guidance and training), which contain more specific rights to vocational guidance and training. Accordingly, with a negative decision under one of the above-mentioned provisions accepted by the Member States, the Committee considers that the situation is not in conformity with Article 1 §4 on the same basis.

63. When the particular country has not accepted certain of the above-mentioned provisions of the Charter, the Committee assesses under Article 1 §4 the conformity of the situation relating to the right of adult workers to vocational training and/or the right of persons with disabilities to vocational guidance and training. In cases where no information was provided or indicated in the national report, the Committee concluded that the situation in a given country was not in conformity with Article 1 §4 of the Charter on the basis that it had been established that the right to vocational guidance, training, or retraining within the education system of a particular labour market is granted.[220] The Committee was obliged to establish itself the fact according to which the negative conclusion is declared. The reason for a negative decision concerning the lack of the right to vocational guidance in the education system and the labour market in Moldova is: (1) information presented to the Governmental[221] Committee that the number of workers in continuing vocational training increased in recent years from only 10% to 12%. There is also a lack of legislation explicitly prohibiting discrimination in training on the grounds of disability;[222] (2) a low number of persons with disabilities attending vocational training;[223] (3) no information concerning the operational details of the counselling service run by the Social Service Agency;[224] (4) a total lack of information concerning the right of an employed person to individual leave for training;[225] (5) no information in matters related to specialised guidance and training for persons with disabilities.[226] In the last case, the Committee asked the Georgian government to provide updated information on the implementation of the state programme on professional training and retraining, as well as the qualification raising of job seekers and reiterated its request for information on what type of vocational training and education are available in the labour market, the overall participation rate in such training, what percentage of companies provide in-house training or other types of

220. Conclusions Bosnia and Herzegovina, pp. 116–117.
221. Governmental Committee Report concerning Conclusions 2012, Conclusions 2016 (Moldova), p. 124.
222. Conclusions XXI-I (Iceland), p. 309; (Azerbaijan), p. 284.
223. Conclusions 2016 (Azerbaijan), p. 284.
224. Conclusion 2016 (Georgia), p. 119.
225. Conclusions 2016 (Serbia), p. 126.
226. Conclusions 2016 (Georgia), p. 119.

vocational training to employees, and under what conditions. In the meantime, the Committee considers that the right to continuing vocational training for workers is not guaranteed.

64. When it comes to guaranteeing job seekers adequate career guidance, proper training and re-adaptation, the situation is not good in 2020 for five Member States: Azerbaijan, Georgia, Lithuania, the Russian Federation and Ukraine. Malta is the sixth country at risk from the emerging maladjustment of education policy to the needs and requirements of the modern labour market. It is characteristic that all the countries mentioned were assessed equally negatively by the Committee. They did not allow the Committee to assess whether the right protected by Article 1 §4 of the Charter has a chance to be provided to those unemployed people who are able to work and seek work because they want to be professionally active. In each case, the Committee repeated the traditional formula six times: 'it has not been established that the right to vocational guidance within the education system and in the labour market is guaranteed'. With the exception of two cases – Lithuania and Malta, where the Committee had no further reservations regarding the right to vocational guidance, training and vocational re-adaptation vis-à-vis the remaining four eastern European countries, the Committee made additional reservations regarding education and employment policy. These are the following additional circumstances that make it difficult to enter the labour markets of these countries and – in the case of Maltese citizens – also to the common EU labour market. It has not been established that the right to vocational guidance is guaranteed to: persons with disabilities (Azerbaijan, Georgia) and nationals of other State Parties (Russian Federation) and the legislation does not provide for individual leave for training for all employed persons (Ukraine, Malta).

§2. The Right of Nationals to Engage in Gainful Occupation in the Territories of Other Countries

I. Introduction

65. The expansion of the EU has had a direct impact on the meaning of the provision in question. Article 18 of the Charter is applicable solely to matters associated with gainful employment by citizens of one Member State employed on the territory of another state that is a member of the Council of Europe. The free flow of workers between EU Member States means that Article 18 of the Charter is of greater importance for citizens who are employed within the EU yet who are citizens of states who do not belong to the EU or the European Economic Area. The article in question is also applicable to cases in which the citizens of the Member States that form the EU, as well as the three additional states form the EEA together with the EU, undertake employment in states which form the Council of Europe yet do not belong to the EU. The right to engage in gainful employment or self-employment guaranteed by Article 18 of the Charter obliges Member States to do the following:

- to apply existing regulations of employment of citizens of other Member States in a spirit of liberty (§1);
- to simplify the existing formalities and to reduce or abolish chancery dues and other charges (administrative and others) payable by foreign workers attempting to gain employment or by their employers (§2);
- to liberalise the regulations governing the employment of foreign workers (§3);
- to recognise the right of their nationals to leave the country to engage in a gainful occupation in the territories of other Member States (§4)

66. The Committee is of the opinion that the right to engage in gainful employment in the territory of another Member State party to the Charter is solely applicable to citizens of Member States which are party to the Charter.[227] The provision in question does not ensure the protection of the right to enter the territory of another Member State which is party to the Charter. It encompasses the protection of the right to seek gainful employment within a different country. The term 'a different Member State' is understood by the Committee to be the territory of that state as well as its structures which are located beyond the territorial waters being the property of that given Member State, such as oil rig platforms on the North Sea.

Article 18 §1 of the Charter is part of the dynamic category.[228] It obliges the authorities of Member States to achieve the following goals: to liberally apply existing regulations (§1); to simplify existing formalities and reduce or abolish charges payable (§2); liberalise the regulations governing the employment of foreign workers (§3) The dynamic nature of the provision has its boundaries. It has its goals specified that should be met thanks to the adaptation of domestic practices (§1) and domestic regulations (§2-3) to the international standards protecting human rights established by Article 18 §1-3 of the Charter. Full compliance of domestic legal systems with the international standards stipulated under Article 18 of the Charter will be reached if foreigners, citizens of other Member States, and parties to the Charter are treated equally to nationals (of the country in which they are employed) by the authorities of the Member State in which they are working. Article 18 of the Charter does not contain a thesis about an obligatory treatment of migrant workers likened to the treatment of the state's own nationals. The Committee did however base the above standards on section 18 of Part I of the Charter. In the social policy declaration in section 18 of the Charter, there is a clear statement that a citizen from each party has the right to carry out an occupation within the territory of another Member State 'according to the principles of equality with the nationals of the latter'. The Committee is of the opinion that the above statement of section 18 of the Charter is the 'letter and the spirit' of the provision.[229] The dynamism of the provision in question is also evident in its interpretation. The Committee's stance is that the authorities of Member States, parties to the Charter, have an obligation to take

227. Conclusions I, p. 79.
228. Conclusions II, p. 59.
229. Conclusions II, p. 60.

measures to gradually bring closer the legal positions of foreign nationals with their own citizens so that the rights of the former are more like the rights attained by the citizens of the given state.[230]

Allowing for differentiation between the rights of foreign nationals and a state's own citizens due to 'serious economic and social reasons' cannot be solely applied to foreigners, citizens of other Member States, or parties to the Charter.

The Committee ruled that Ireland and the United Kingdom did not adapt to the international standards of protecting the right to freely carry out gainful occupation in another Member State because the domestic legislation favoured British and Commonwealth citizens, who were largely not members of the Council of Europe, parties to the Charter.[231]

67. The provision in question, Article 18 of the Charter, does not permit the Committee to tolerate regional relationships, even when they extend beyond European boundaries. Limiting the liberal policies and employment regulations of foreigners cannot be solely applicable to citizens of other Member States that are applying for work and residency permits within the territory of another Member State which is party to the Charter. As mentioned earlier, Article 18 of the Charter does not regulate entry permits. For these reasons, the limitations placed on the liberal approaches to the citizens of other Member States wanting residency and work permits are in contradiction to the right to undertake employment in a different Member State.[232]

The Committee reserves itself the right to examine whether the exclusion due to serious economic and social reasons based on Article 31 §1 ESC or Article G §1 RESC is valid. Leaving margins of appreciation for the authorities of Member States, the Committee is able to examine such reasons and the scope of the exclusions.

The Committee does not view, referring to the above indicators, that economic and social reasons justify the exclusion of international standards for citizens of small Member States, e.g., Austria and Cyprus.[233]

68. Examining the reports filed by Member States concerning the fulfilment of the obligations stipulated by the ratified provision Article 18 of the Charter, the Committee demanded further information concerning the following: the legal and factual criteria used for making decisions about granting permission or refusing the right to employment based on a work agreement or being in self-employment; the number of applications filed for the above and the number of decisions made granting permission; the number of applications filed by citizens of Member States and

230. As above.

231. Conclusions III, p. 85 (Ireland); p. 86 (United Kingdom); Conclusions IV, p. 111 (United Kingdom). An analogical case occurred in Scandinavian countries. Citizens of these countries forming the 'Nordic labour market' were treated in a way more favourable that the citizens of the remaining members states. *See* case of Denmark: Conclusions XII-1, pp. 225–227.

232. Conclusions XIII-1, p. 204 (Sweden); Conclusions XIII-2, pp. 371–372 (Germany); Conclusions XIII-4, pp. 319–320 (Sweden).

233. Case of Denmark, which according to serious economic and social reasons introduced limitations against citizens of Cyprus and Austria. Conclusions IV, p. 108; Conclusions XII-1, p. 226.

the number of foreigners, citizens of other Member States, permitted to carry out gainful employment in another Member State; the number citizens of other Member States and the number of citizens of countries that are not members of the Charter, who have received permission to work within the territory of a given Member State; details concerning formalities preceding a decision in the matter of granting permission to carry out gainful occupation within a given Member State; the period of validity of such a permission as well as information about the situation of the individual, who has had his/her permission expire.[234] Furthermore, the Committee was interested in receiving information about whether it was possible to file applications and receive permission while abroad and further information about the procedure of extending the work permit once it is granted.[235] The Committee also attempted to establish if there is a connecting interdependency between the granting of permission to stay within a given Member State and carrying out gainful employment within that state. The Committee is of the view that the most influential in matters of work permits is the administrative body dealing with the rights of residency within a given state. Losing the right to remain within a given Member State has adverse effects on being able to take advantage of the right to carry out gainful employment. Losing the right to gainful employment usually leads to the withdrawal of the right to remain within a given Member State.[236] Taking into consideration the above, the Committee demanded further information from the authorities of Member States concerning the procedures dealing with the above practices.

II. An Obligation to Apply the Existing Regulations in a Spirit of Liberty

69. Article 18 §1 of the Charter obliges institutions which function according to domestic legislation to do so according to a liberal interpretation. The provision in question does not establish obligations for Member States to liberalise their domestic legal systems. Such an obligation was established by Article 18 §3 of the Charter. The Committee is of the view that Article 18 §1 of the Charter is a standard which holds more importance for administrative practices than for the position of the law. Even rigorous legislation interpreted according to the directives of the article in question does not give the Committee the legal basis to issue decisions about the non-compliance of Member States with the standards stipulated under Article 18 §1 of the Charter.

The case of the United Kingdom, where permission for undertaking occupation was granted for a strict period of time to carry out solely the occupation specified in the permission for a given employer, who cannot employ British citizens, and every change of employment required a further permission grant, exemplified that such rigorous regulations are non-compliant with the standards established under Article 18 §3 of the Charter.

234. Conclusions II, pp. 61–62.
235. Conclusions V, p. 118; Conclusions VIII, p. 197.
236. Conclusions XIII-2, p. 168.

70. Yet such a case does not provide the Committee with the grounds to voice its complaints since British administrative bodies dealing with employment were granted the right to liberally apply the existing regulations, and the permission to continue the work thus far was renewed without difficulty. After four years, foreign nationals were excused from renewing their permission grants for working and living in the United Kingdom.[237] A similar decision was rendered in the case of Greece.[238] Allowing administrative bodies that apply domestic regulations a large margin of interpretation means that the subject of examination for the Committee is how these state bodies deal with the power they are granted. The Committee compares the decisions to grant permission to carry out gainful employment with the number of applications filed.[239] It takes into consideration the above factors to evaluate whether the administrative state bodies apply the required regulations in accordance with Article 18 §1 of the Charter and thus liberally.[240] A systematic refusal to grant permission to work to a citizen of a Member State, who is filing the application for an extension of time as he is abroad in another Member State, is considered by the Committee as a restrictive interpretation of regulations.[241] Legalising migrant workers' stays residing within the territory of a given state for the purposes of employment is an example of a liberalised interpretation of domestic regulations.[242]

Turkey prohibits foreigners from being employed in more than twenty different types of professions and trades. The authorities of Turkey do not leave administrative bodies the freedom to interpret employment of foreign national regulations, which is a violation of Article 18 §1 of the Charter.[243]

The Committee had doubts about whether Member States function in accordance with international standards and therefore adjourned its decision and sought further information, which could prove whether administrative bodies interpret domestic regulations liberally.[244]

---

237. Conclusions III, p. 86.
238. Conclusions X-1, p. 137.
239. Conclusions VIII, p. 197; Conclusions XII-2, p. 210; Conclusions XIII-1, p. 263 (Turkey); Conclusions XIII-2, p. 369 (Belgium).
240. Conclusions IV, p. 109 (Austria); pp. 110–111 (United Kingdom); p. 112 (Ireland); Conclusions VII, p. 94 (France); Conclusions VIII, p. 194 (Germany); p. 197 (Ireland); p. 200 (United Kingdom); Conclusions IX-1, p. 101 (Sweden); Conclusions XII-1, p. 220 (Denmark); 221 (Iceland); Conclusions XIII-3, p. 393 (Finland). In the decision rendered during the 2003 supervisory cycle, the Committee analysed the Swedish report, which claimed that in 2001 there were 6,542 applications filed for a permission to work, out of which 4,684 were granted. The Committee claimed Sweden functioned in accordance with the standards established under Art. 18 §1 of the Charter. Conclusions 2003, vol. 2, p. 621. In the Conclusions 2008 the Committee flatly stated that the existing regulations were not being applied in a spirit of liberality by the following countries: Belgium (vol. 1, p. 140), Finland (vol. 1, p. 290), France (vol. 1, p. 342), Italy (vol. 1, p. 426), Slovenia (vol. 1, p. 779), Conclusions XIX-1 (2008), p. 412 (Spain).
241. Conclusions VI, p. 114 (Sweden).
242. Conclusions XII-2, p. 210 (Italy).
243. Conclusions XIII-3, p. 397.
244. Conclusions XV-2, p. 114 (Belgium); pp. 226–227 (France); p. 319 (Italy); pp. 370–371 (the Netherlands); pp. 570–571 (Sweden); Addendum to Conclusions XV-2, p. 37 (Ireland); Conclusions 2003, vol. 1, p. 180 (France); p. 305 (Italy); Conclusions 2003, vol. 2, pp. 517–519, Conclusions 2007, vol. 1, p. 232 (Belgium), vol. 2, p. 744 (Italy).

III. Simplifying Existing Formalities and Reducing or Abolishing Administrative Fees

71. Article 18 §2 of the Charter orders the authorities of Member States to simplify the existing formalities, while Article 18 §3 of the Charter obliges the authorities of these states to liberalise the regulations. The Committee supervising whether the above provisions are being abided by came to a conclusion that the range of these provisions overlaps, despite the fact that they establish different obligations. Simplifying the existing formalities is usually an indicator of an earlier completed liberalisation of regulations.[245] It is possible to deduce from the above argument there is a cause-and-effect dependency between the obligations stipulated under Article 18 §2 and 3 of the Charter. A liberalisation of the regulations provides the basis for simplifying formalities. There is, however, a possibility to simplify formalities which should be liberalised. In cases where Member States have ratified both comparable provisions, there is no difficulty in monitoring whether they are obeying the provisions. The border between formalities that should be simplified and regulations that should be liberalised no longer exists. Problems arise in situations when Member States ratify just one of the two standards.

This has occurred in Moldova, Romania and Slovenia. These countries ratified Article 18 §2 RESC but did not ratify Article 18 §3 of this Charter. In terms of the European Social Charter, Austria, the Czech Republic, Malta, Poland and Slovakia ratified Article 18 §2 ESC but did not ratify Article 18 §3.

In such cases, it is important to exactly and precisely divide up the obligations taken up by the authorities of the above countries, which have ratified one out of the two named provisions – obliging themselves to simplify the existing formalities dealing with the employment of foreign nationals (i.e., Article 18 §2 of the Charter), citizens of other Member States. They did not bind themselves to liberalise the domestic regulations dealing with the employment of foreigners within their own country. It is therefore possible to deduce that the obligation specified under Article 18 §2 of the Charter is easier to fulfil. The Committee did not concern itself with the essential differentiation between the ranges of obligations established by the two provisions. Based on the decisions rendered by the Committee, it is possible to form the opinion that Article 18 §2 of the Charter concerns itself with the procedural requirements carried out before making a decision permitting foreign nationals to undertake employment (e.g., concerning the obligation of documenting all decisions, whether they be ones of refusal or permission), while Article 18 §3 of the Charter deals with property rights regulations (e.g., the reasons for refusing or granting permission to undertake gainful employment).[246] Steps taken to simplify the existing formalities encompass the following: abolishing entry visas;[247] extending the validity period of permits from one year to four[248] or five[249] years; issuing permits for employment based on the conclusion of the employer or (if already applied)

245. Conclusions III, p. 83.
246. *See* Darcy & Harris, *supra*, p. 208.
247. Conclusions IX-1, p. 99 (Iceland).
248. Conclusions XII-1, p. 225 (United Kingdom).
249. Conclusions X-2, p. 142 (Spain).

based on the interested worker;[250] no longer require reports to be filed by prospective employers wanting to employ foreigners, citizens of Member States.[251]

72. Member States that required foreign workers to annually hand in their work permits or forced foreigners to leave the given Member State and terminate their work agreements for reasons not associated with themselves were regarded as not complying with the standards established by Article 18 §2 of the Charter.[252,253] Non-compliance was also evident when Member States made the issuing of work permits dependent on the presentation of documents showing no criminal record, financial independence, state of health, scope of insurance, residence permit[254] or being in possession of property.[255] Member States obliging foreigners wanting to open up their own businesses to file applications through the diplomatic departments of the country in which the business will function and further grant permission for such ventures depending on the assent of three ministries (ministry of foreign affairs, ministry of the interior as well as the trade ministry)[256] was also non-compliant with the established standards. The Committee generally handed down decisions about the non-compliance of domestic regulations with the international standards when the procedure carried out prior to granting permission was deemed to be too difficult while the permit to carry out gainful employment was seen as restrictive (i.e., concerned a particular employer, place of employment, type of work, is valid for a particular period and getting such a permit is made dependent upon the supply and demand of the labour market).[257]

73. Article 18 §2 of the Charter also obliges Member States to reduce or abolish administrative fees and other charges placed on migrant workers or their employers. The provision does not specify which charges and fees should be abolished or reduced. The practices of the Committee indicate that the charges concern the issuing of permits and also the taxes imposed by Member States on those wanting to open their own businesses within the territory of another Member State. It is not possible to deduce from Article 18 §2 of the Charter alone that the abolishment of all charges is necessary. From the decisions handed down by the Committee, it is evident that small charges for administrative purposes to grant work permits are in accordance with Article 18 §2 of the Charter. The Committee also accepts fees taken by employers or deposits taken by administrative authorities, which are low enough to allow a foreign worker arriving from another Member State (usually placed geographically distant from the place of the gainful employment) to cover the costs of

250. Conclusions XII-2, pp. 211–212 (Germany).
251. Conclusions XII-1, p. 224 (Sweden).
252. Case of Germany: Conclusions X-2, p. 141; Conclusions XIII-2, pp. 371–372; Conclusions XIII-4, p. 436. In the opinion of the Committee, repeating the identical procedure for renewing work permits is not necessary.
253. Conclusions XII-1, p. 223 (Iceland).
254. Conclusions XIX-1 (2008), p. 480 (Turkey).
255. Conclusions XVI-2, vol. 2, pp. 810–811 (Slovakia), Conclusions 2008, vol. 2, p. 779 (Slovenia).
256. Case of Italy: Conclusions XV-2, p. 320; Conclusions 2003, vol. 1, pp. 306–307.
257. Conclusions XIII-2, pp. 174–175 (Greece).

a return trip home.[258] The Committee negatively concluded on the charging of fees by authorities of Member States for administrative purposes from applications filed to receive permission to carry out gainful employment.[259]

IV. Liberalisation of Regulations

74. Article 18 §3 of the Charter is a standard which obliges the authorities of Member States to take measures and systematically continue them in order to substitute the existing regulations with provisions that are less restrictive with regard to the employment of foreign nationals. The dynamic nature of the provision in question also has its limits. Achieving the said goals means that further liberalisation of the regulations is no longer possible. The obligation of the authorities of Member States that have reached such goals is to sustain them.[260] Until the ideal state is reached, the Committee has instructed domestic regulations either to be solved by elimination or to be changed. Such regulations include the following: the prohibition of changing employment rules because permitting work amounts to the carrying out of certain actions for the purposes of the employer specified in the permit;[261] prohibiting the change of an employer within the first year of work abroad;[262] demanding a work permit prior to the entry onto the territory of the other Member State;[263] retaining the demand for a citizen of another Member State who has been granted a work permit, to abide by the same legal requirements as were made during his/her first employment;[264] granting a work permit depending on whether the foreign national interested in working abroad once granted such a permit creates an interest for the citizens of the given Member State in which he/she will be working;[265] the validity of the work permit.[266] The regulations requiring changes are as follows: those implementing a complete ban on employing foreign nationals of other Member States;[267] those limiting the rights of migrant workers and citizens of other Member States from changing employers as well as the workplace;[268] make the granting of a work permit for a citizen of another Member State

258. Conclusions IV, pp. 107–108 (Austria); Addendum to Conclusions XIII-3, pp. 89 et seq. (Luxembourg).
259. Conclusions XV-2, p. 72 (Austria); p. 175 (Finland).
260. Conclusions II, pp. 60–61; Conclusions III, p. 84 (Ireland).
261. Conclusions II, p. 60; Conclusions III, p. 84 (Ireland); Conclusions V, p. 117 (Denmark); p. 119 (Germany); Conclusions X-1, p. 141 (Denmark); Conclusions XIII-2, pp. 174–179 (Greece); Conclusions XIII-3, p. 403 (Turkey); Addendum to Conclusions XIII-3, pp 91–92 (Luxembourg), Conclusions 2007, vol. 2, pp. 638–639 (Ireland), p. 747 (Italy).
262. Conclusions II, p. 85 (Sweden); Conclusions III, p. 84 (Denmark); Conclusions XII-1, pp. 223 et seq. (Iceland); Addendum to Conclusions XIII-3, pp. 91–92 (Luxembourg).
263. Case of Denmark: Conclusions V, p. 117; Conclusions VI, p. 110; Conclusions X-1, p. 141; Conclusions VI, p. 114 (Sweden).
264. Conclusions III, p. 86 (United Kingdom); Conclusions X-2, pp. 140–141 (Germany), Conclusions XIX-1 (2008), p. 168 (Germany), p. 418 (Spain).
265. Conclusions V, p. 117; Conclusions VI, p. 110 (Denmark); Conclusions VIII, p. 198 (Spain).
266. Conclusions X-1, p. 141 (Denmark).
267. Conclusions VI, p. 111 (France); p. 112 (Germany).
268. Conclusions V, p. 119 (Germany).

based upon the 'valid professional reasons',[269] character references,[270] or on a specified amount of money invested.[271] Generally, the Committee in 2008 stated that the formalities governing the access of foreign workers to the national labour market were not simplified (liberalised)[272] or were too restrictive.[273]

75. Article 18 §3 of the Charter does not oblige the authorities of Member States to completely abolish regulations limiting citizens of other Member States but to gradually limit them. It recommends acting according to the rules: the longer the period of stay of a foreign national or citizen of another Member State, the less restrictions in extending his/her work and residency permit.[274] Cases of positive decisions handed down by the Committee in terms of actions taken by the authorities of Member States to liberalise regulations concerning the employment of foreign nationals encompass the following: granting work permits to family members of a migrant worker;[275] extending the validity of a work permit for a period of five years;[276] taking measures to assimilate migrant workers into the local society;[277] permitting a migrant worker to look for employment elsewhere when he/she finds themselves unemployed;[278] excusing young workers who are undertaking their first employment from certain formal requirements prior to the granting of a work permit.[279] The provision in question, Article 18 §3 of the Charter, obliges Member States to take measures ensuring 'to such a point as it is possible' that the situation of the migrant worker is as comparable to that of the Member State's own citizen.[280]

§3. The Right to Just Conditions of Work

76. Article 2 of the Charter does not compile a definition of the term 'conditions of work'. This term is vague and only encompasses what work the workers are involved in and its conditions. The Committee classified this provision already in its first supervisory cycle. From the very beginning of its functioning, Article 2 of the Charter was treated as an accepted norm, ensuring workers safe and hygienic working conditions. The Committee regarded that if workers are working above the

269. Conclusions XII-1, p. 225 (Denmark).
270. Case of Ireland: Conclusions XIII-4, p. 319; Addendum to Conclusions XV-2, pp. 41–42.
271. GBP 200,000 in Great Britain. Conclusions XIII-4, p. 320; Conclusions XV-2, pp. 621–622.
272. Conclusions 2008, vol. 1, p. 294 (Finland), p. 594, vol. 2, p. 781 (Slovenia), Conclusions XIX-1 (2008), p. 127 (Denmark).
273. Conclusions 2008, vol. 2, p. 778 (Netherlands), p. 823 (Sweden), Conclusions XIX-1 (2008), p. 482 (Turkey).
274. Conclusions II, p. 60.
275. Conclusions VIII, p. 196 (France).
276. Conclusions X-2, p. 143 (Spain).
277. Conclusions XI-1, p. 154 (United Kingdom).
278. Conclusions IX-1, p. 154 (United Kingdom).
279. Conclusions XI-2, p. 140 (Austria).
280. The Committee concludes that Ireland does not comply with that obligation due to the absence of measures to liberalise the regulations governing of foreign workers. Conclusions 2007, vol. 2, pp. 640–641.

daily and weekly standards of working hours, devoid of the right to daily, weekly and annual rest, then they are at a greater risk of having accidents at work.[281] Therefore, the practice of Article 2 of the Charter by the Committee is regarded as being part of the category of provisions which protects the health of workers. This provision, therefore, completes Article 3 of the Charter dealing with safe and hygienic conditions at work.

Article 2 of the Charter encompasses solely workers who are under a standard and non-standard work agreement (those employed for a specific period of time in an incomplete timeframe).[282] It does not offer any protection for the self-employed.[283] It does, however, protect family members who are employed as co-workers in an independently run agricultural business.[284]

In addition to Article 3 §1 ESC and Article I §2 RESC, the responsibilities defined in Article 2 of the Charter are regarded as fulfilled in situations when all provisions of Article 2 ESC, as well as Article 2 §1-5 and 7 RESC, encompass the majority[285] of interested workers.

I. The Definition of Reasonable Daily and Weekly Working Hours

77. Article 2 §1 of the Charter is a norm categorised as a 'dynamic' provision. It demands the authorities of Member States establish what reasonable daily and weekly working hours are, and then shorten the number of weekly working hours according to productivity growth as well as other factors associated with it. The provision in question therefore does not aim at establishing daily and weekly working-hour targets, and the Committee has not fixed any such standards. It took the position that the employment standards existing within Member States (eight hours daily and forty hours weekly)[286] are responsible for certain social problems, such as the organisation of free time.[287] The Committee, however, did not specify any particular regulations for Member States in terms of reducing working hours. It did not leave total freedom in setting weekly and monthly working-hour standards but gave sensible guidelines. Determining such weekly and monthly working hours should take into consideration many factors, especially those which are economic and economic-related. Other factors connected with work efficiency, according to the Committee, can be listed as follows: work environment, processes and factors harmful to the health and life of a worker.[288] The Committee thus took the position that weekly and monthly working-hour standards will be different in different Member

281. Conclusions XIV-2, vol. 1, pp. 364–365.
282. Conclusions XII-2, p. 61 (Malta); Conclusions XIV-2, vol. 1, p. 34; Conclusions XIII-3, p. 249 (Portugal).
283. Conclusions I, p. 8; Conclusions XIII-5, p. 47 (Finland).
284. Conclusions III, p. 12 (Ireland).
285. The Committee in the Charter defines the principle of 'majority' as 80% of workers.
286. On-call periods where no effective work is performed cannot be assimilated to rest periods. Conclusions 2010, vol. 1, p. 246 (France).
287. Conclusions I, p. 18.
288. Conclusions XIV-2, p. 32.

States.[289] According to the Committee authorities, the unemployment rate should be taken into consideration during the process of setting working-hour standards. A high unemployment rate justifies the shortening of working hours, as it maintains the number of employed at the same level.[290] Shortening working hours leads to a decrease in remuneration.

The case of Ireland is somewhat peculiar. The average Irish working hours at the beginning of the 1990s were 61–62 hours. An agreement made by stakeholders and Irish authorities assuming gradual shortening of weekly working hours by an hour within the next three years placed special duties on the country. Irish authorities were trying to fulfil duties under Article 2 §1 of the Charter by granting employees longer paid leave.

The Committee criticised this practice. It stated that these policies were in breach of Article 2 §1 of the Charter, which imposes on Member States a duty of gradual shortening of weekly working hours and does not allow substituting this regulation by different techniques, especially based on prolonging paid leave.

78. As a rule, daily and weekly working hours are longer in countries where efficiency of work is at a lower level. However, the correlation between working-hour standards and the level of work efficiency is not obvious. The case of France relying on a thirty-five-hour long working week proves that setting working-hour standards is often influenced by employer representatives and is not necessarily directly related to the level of work efficiency.

The questionnaire to Article 2 §1 of the Charter compiles a number of questions, allowing the Committee's familiarisation with daily and weekly working-hour standards, periods of rest and plans of shortening weekly working hours. According to its practice, the Committee does not recommend a number of hours described by Article 2 §1 as 'reasonable daily and weekly working hours'. Daily and weekly working-hour standards are understood as the time when an employee is available for his employer. Working-hour standards apply then in the case of work on a regular basis as well as in the case of extra hours.[291] It shows cases when daily and weekly working-hour standards can be regarded as 'reasonable'. National labour law violates the provision in question when it allows employing workers fourteen or sixteen hours a day and/or sixty hours a week.[292] The Committee demanded an additional explanation from authorities of Member States, which allowed exceeding a forty-eight-hour working week protected under Directive No. 104 of 1993 on aspects of work time organisation.[293] It reproved Member States that the postulate

289. Conclusions I, p. 18, Conclusions XIV-2, p. 32.
290. Conclusions I, p. 18; Conclusions II p. 7, Conclusions XIII-1 p. 70; last two cases concerning Ireland.
291. Conclusions XIV-2, p. 32.
292. Conclusions XIV-2, p. 32, Conclusions 2007 vol. 1, p. 357 (Estonia)), p. 414 (Finland), vol. 2, p. 803 (Lithuania), pp. 908–909 (Norway), Conclusions 2010, vol. 1, p. 20 (Albania), p. 83 (Armenia), p. 218 (Estonia), p. 246 (France), p. 278 (Georgia), p. 311 (Italy), vol. 2, p. 464 (Norway). Conclusions XIX-3, p. 32 (Croatia), p. 54 (Czech Republic), p. 134 (Iceland), p. 167 (Poland), p. 185 (Slovak Republic), p. 210 (Spain).
293. Conclusions XII-1, p. 70 (Iceland), p. 71 (The Netherlands); Conclusions XIII-1, p. 68 (Greece); Conclusions XIII-3, pp. 245–246 (Portugal).

of a 'reasonable' number of working hours should separately apply to daily and weekly standards. Not exceeding the accepted weekly standards does not guarantee a positive Committee ruling when daily standards are not met. Setting high weekly average standards automatically causes prolonging of daily standards beyond the limits approved by the Committee. No later than during the first two supervisory cycles the Committee declared Irish[294] and Italian[295] weekly working-hour standards of sixty-four hours as not in accordance with Article 2 §1 of the Charter. The Committee recalled that the daily working time ought in no circumstances – except for extraordinary situations – to exceed sixteen hours, even if, in compensation, it entailed a limitation on the weekly working time. The Committee found out that Article 139(4) of the Armenian Labour Code, as amended, provides that the daily working time of specific categories of workers may amount to twenty-four hours a day, provided that the weekly working hours do not exceed forty-eight hours. The Committee took note of Decision No. 1223-N of the Armenian Government of 11 August 2005, which approved the list of occupations, containing thirty-six different professions for whom a twenty-four-hour long working day is permitted. In its previous conclusion (2010), the Committee observed that the Labour Code permits exceptions to the limits on daily working time in the case of special categories of employee (health care, child care institutions, specialist electricity and gas companies, specialist communication services and specialist services for the elimination of the effects of accidents and others), who may work up to twenty-four hours per day. Due to the fact that the above-mentioned situation had not been changed, the Committee decided that Armenia was not in conformity with Article 2 §1 of the Charter.[296] The case of Armenia serves as a good example of the Committee's firm policy, according to which daily and/or weekly extensions of working time beyond the strict limits adopted by the Committee are considered to be clear-cut cases meriting a decision of non-conformity with Article 2 §1 of the Charter.[297] In 2019, the Committee found that certain categories of workers employed in the health sectors, supervising the operation of automatic machinery and ensuring the safety of the workplace, work above the sixty-hour maximum weekly working time.[298] Their standard working hours per week are seventy-two hours[299] or even seventy-six hours.[300] The above-mentioned working time management practice was found by the Committee to be inconsistent with the standards set out in Article 2 §1 of both Charters.

An employer may ask an employee to work more than an average of forty-eight hours per week. However, in such a case, written consent is required from the employee concerned. If an employee does not agree to work overtime, the employer can neither force nor victimise that particular employee as a consequence of their

294. Conclusions II, p. 7, Conclusions 2007, vol. 2, p. 585.
295. Conclusions I, p. 18, Conclusions 2007, vol. 2, p. 669.
296. Conclusions 2014.
297. Conclusion 2014 (Armenia – daily working time of some categories of workers can be extended to twenty-four hours, Norway and Slovakia up to sixteen hours daily, Turkey up to sixty-six hours weekly).
298. Spain, Cyprus, Norway, the Netherlands and Turkey. Activity Report 2018, p. 33.
299. Estonia, Island, *ibid.*
300. Czech Republic, Norway, *ibid.*

refusal. Where consent is given, the employer must ensure compliance with the daily and weekly rest periods established by law. All workers are entitled to a minimum daily rest period of eleven consecutive hours per twenty-four-hour period and to a minimum uninterrupted weekly rest period of twenty-four hours, in addition to the daily rest period of eleven hours for each seven-day period. Moreover, with respect to reference periods, the Committee considers that their duration should in general not exceed six months and may only be extended to a maximum of one year in exceptional consequences if it is justified by objective or technical reasons or reasons concerning the organisation of work.[301] The report presented during the last cycle by Malta, states that in certain sectors of the economy such as manufacturing and tourism, the reference period is one year.[302] The Committee also notes that where the worker gives his/her consent to work longer hours in Malta, there are absolute limits on working hours in individual weeks other than the statutory daily rest and weekly rest periods as long as the maximum average is respected over the reference period as a whole. In the Committee's opinion, this means that working weeks of more than sixty hours are possible in principle. The Committee considers that such hours are unreasonably long and although certain safeguards are in place as regards giving consent by the worker, the Committee recalls that working overtime must not be left to the discretion of the employer or the worker in view of the overriding aim of Article 2 §1 of the Charter which should protect the health and safety of workers.[303] Therefore, the Committee concludes that the situation in Malta is not in conformity with Article 2 §1 of the Charter on the basis that the law does not guarantee the right to reasonable weekly working hours.

The analysed Article 2 §1 of the Charter imposes a gradual shortening of weekly working-hour standards. However, this provision should not be interpreted as obliging Member States to a strict reduction of working-hour standards in all weeks of the year, quarters or months. The Committee approves of employers' flexible policies in terms of time management.[304] It allows extending working-hour standards in one week of a pay period on the condition that shortening these standards in another week of the same period. The Committee establishes certain requirements of time management policies in the workplace. The legality of these policies depends on the level of fulfilling the above-mentioned requirements. The Committee imposes setting a maximum number of working hours in weekly periods.[305] It prohibits exceeding the maximum working-hour standards set at the level of fifty hours. In its previous conclusion (2010) the Committee found that the situation in Estonia was not in conformity on two grounds: (1) shifts of up to twenty-four hours were authorised for security guards, health care professionals, welfare workers, fire and rescue workers; (2) the authorised working hours of crew members on vessels engaged in short sea shipping could rise to seventy-two hours per seven-day period. Currently,

301. Conclusions 2010 (Spain).
302. Conclusions 2016, p. 197.
303. Statement of interpretation on Art. 2 §1, Conclusions XIV-2 (1998).
304. However, it does not accept regulation which permits as a general rule to set reference periods up to or even beyond twelve months for the calculation of average working hours. Conclusions 2010, vol. 2, p. 410 (Moldova). Conclusions XIX-3, p. 92 (Germany), p. 210 (Spain).
305. Conclusions XIV-2, pp. 111 et seq. (Belgium), p. 329 (Greece).

the Committee observes that the situation regarding the second ground for non-conformity remains unchanged. The Ministry of Social Affairs has been negotiating with social partners to amend the labour legislation so that the weekly maximum working time of crew members shall be replaced with weekly minimum rest time regulation. Therefore, the Committee concludes that the situation in Estonia is not in conformity with Article 2 §1 of the Charter.[306] The very same situation has been uncovered in Ireland, and in Italy. In the previous (2007, 2010) conclusions,[307] as well as in the most up-to-date ones, the Committee concludes that the situation in Ireland is not in conformity with Article 2 §1 of the Charter, on the grounds that the working hours in the merchant shipping sector are allowed to rise to seventy-two hours per week.[308] The daily rest period cannot be reduced to seven hours for some categories of workers. An employer and an employee representative can agree on a temporary shorter daily rest period within the relevant employee's consent if the practical organisation of work so requires. Daily rest periods can also be shortened when working hours are flexible and employees decide on the time their work begins and ends. During the last reporting procedure (2018), the Committee concluded that the situation in Spain and Turkey was inconsistent with what is accepted by Article 2 §1 standards of daily and weekly working time. Flexibility in the working time standards can be accepted in the light of the powers guaranteed in Article 2 §1 and the criteria established by the Committee. These prohibit employers from hiring workers above the standards established in the Committee's jurisprudence.[309] The daily period must be at least seven hours. Even an on-call period during which no effective work is undertaken is regarded by the Committee as a violation of Article 2 §1 of the Charter.[310] The Committee argues that the absence of effective work determined *a posteriori* for a period of time that the employee *a priori* did not have at his or her disposal, cannot constitute an adequate criterion for regarding such a period as a rest period.[311] The Committee holds that the treating of an on-call period as equivalent, in its entirety, to a rest period, constitutes a violation of the right to reasonable working hours, both for stand-by duty at the employer's premises and for time spent on-call at home.[312] The Committee declares that on-call periods during which no effective work is undertaken cannot be assimilated to rest periods.[313] In its previous conclusion (2010), the Committee found that the hours spent in readiness by a medical officer cannot be considered a form of work when no effective work is undertaken. Therefore, the Committee concludes that the hours spent in preparedness for work of medical staff cannot be regarded as a period of rest.[314] This principle applies to all workers. In the event that there are no daily or weekly working time limits applying to certain categories of employees, such as

306. Conclusions 2014.
307. The report submitted by Ireland, registered on 11 Oct. 2010, and on 1 Dec. 2010, was not examined by the Committee because of its late submission.
308. Conclusions 2014.
309. Activity Report 2018, p. 33.
310. Conclusion 2014 (Finland, France).
311. Cases of Iceland, Poland, Serbia and Slovenia (2018). Activity Report 2018, p. 33.
312. Conclusions 2014 (Finland).
313. Conclusions 2014 (France, Hungary, Iceland, Lithuania, Slovenia).
314. Conclusion 2014 (FYROM).

sports professionals, scientists, performing artists, military personnel and police, as well as workers whose wages are more than three times the gross minimum wage,[315] the absence of any statutory limit to daily and weekly working hours serves as a legal basis for the Committee's non-conformity conclusion, on the ground of the exclusion of certain categories of workers from statutory protection against unreasonable working hours.[316] Continued lack of reaction on the part of any state government to repeated questioning by the Committee about the accepted limits of working hours, including overtime in any individual week, serves as the ground for concluding that the situation is not in conformity with Article 2 §1 of the Charter, on the grounds that it has not been established that the legislation guarantees the right to reasonable weekly working hours.[317]

The Committee allows for the introduction of four- and six-month-long wage-payment periods. In special cases, it also accepts extending this period to twelve months. It requires a special conduct from bodies authorised to regulate working hours in cases of extending working hours in some weeks of the pay period. It obliges employers to inform their employees about all changes in the work schedule.[318] It supervises the work of inspectors who monitor abiding work hour standards by employers.

79. The authorities of Member States are the addressees of Article 2 §1 of the Charter. However, it does not mean an obligation to pass regulations on work hour standards and rules of their reduction. Fulfilling the obligation regulated by the provision in question also takes place in cases of normative agreement by which stakeholders set reasonable weekly and daily working hours. The Committee accepts customs and ways of conduct which directly influence the working schedule. In cases when working-hour standards are regulated in a non-legal way, the relevant authorities must ensure the supervision of these standards. The Committee does not specify what bodies are responsible for controlling working-hour standards but work inspectors usually perform this function. The Committee, however, recalls that under Article 2 §1 of the Charter, an independent appropriate authority must supervise the observance of daily and weekly limits in order to ensure that the limits are respected in practice. In the case of Georgia, the Committee has recently noted that no such supervision is taking place, and therefore considers that there is no independent appropriate authority supervising the daily and weekly working limits, so the situation is not in conformity with the Charter.[319]

80. The last procedure for the third group of Member States required to submit normal and simplified reports for the period 1 January 2017 to 31 December 2020 (Group 3 Labour rights, Article 2, 4, 5, 6, 21,* 22,* 26, 28 and 29) was completed. The national reports cover the period from January 2017 until December 2020.[320]

315. Conclusions 2014 (the case of the Netherlands).
316. Conclusions 2014 (the Netherlands).
317. Conclusions (Malta).
318. As above, p. 34.
319. Conclusions 2014 (Georgia).
320. Conclusions 2022, *Press Briefing Elements*, European Committee of Social Rights, a document prepared by the Secretariat of the European Social Charter, 22 Mar. 2023.

81. The results of the work of the European Committee of Social Rights were presented to the general public on 23 March 2023. The above information is intended to make the readers of this edition of this book aware of the level of respect for social rights in the third and final thematic group, entitled 'Labour Rights'. The author's intention is to present all cases of negative decisions which indicate non-compliance by the Member States of the Council of Europe with the standards set out in both Charters of Social Rights: the first European Charter of Social Rights adopted on 18 October 1961 and its additional and amending protocols and the second, Revised European Charter of Social Rights of 3 May 1996. The negative conclusions of the European Committee of Social Rights will be presented in the last subsections of the arguments on labour rights, which are universally granted the status of human rights on a global scale. Very recent results of the effects of the control operation of the ECSR were presented to the general public on 22 March 2023.[321] At the first session of 2023, which took place on 23 January, the Committee issued 611 decisions (conclusions), including 245 positive decisions, 245 negative decisions and 111 cases in which it was impossible to issue either a positive or a negative decision. The European Committee of Social Rights examined national reports submitted by thirty-three States Parties.[322] Thirty-four national reports on labour law were assessed by the members of the Committee in 2022. In this edition of this monograph, I begin to complete the missing jurisprudence on labour law standards (individual and collective) with an analysis of the first paragraph of Article 2 of the European Social Charter. I conclude with the provisions of both above-mentioned Charters to the third group, the assessment of which was presented in Strasbourg on 23 March 2023 by the European Committee of Social Rights. I am also significantly expanding cases on collective labour disputes resolved by the European Committee of Social Rights from 2018 to 2022. The obligation of the authorities of the Council of Europe Member States was disregarded by several countries that ratified Article 2 §1 of the Charter in the last reference period, 2017–2020, assessed in 2022. Despite negative decisions in 2018, employers maintained extended standards for daily working time, from eight up to nineteen or twenty-four hours in one working day. They increased the weekly hours from forty hours, accepted by Council of Europe law, to fifty-two hours, and even to sixty or seventy-two hours a week. They did it not only in flexible periods of time, enabling employees to perform remote work, without the possibility for the employer to exercise direct supervision over the work performed by the employees. The ECSR considered cases in which the national labour law standards did not guarantee reasonable periods of work for all employees, but only for some of them, to be non-compliant with the standards regulated in the Charter. Employers' use of moderately long working time standards accepted by the Council of Europe law has been recognised by the ECSR in those cases where Member State reports showed that employers did not comply with reasonable working time standards. A certain

321. *See Degree of Compliance with Provisions of the Charter on Labour Rights, European Social Charter Social Rights Monitoring 2022: Labour Rights, 2022 Conclusions of the European Committee of Social Rights*, Council of Europe, Strasbourg 2023.

322. Conclusions 2022, *Press Briefing Elements*, a document prepared by the Secretariat of the ECSR, 23 Mar. 2023.

novelty, definitely recognised by the ECSR as incompatible with the provisions of Article 2 §1 of the Charter, was employers' recognition of employees who were obligated to remain ready to perform work at the employer's request. France and Serbia did not recognise as part of the work period the times when employees are on call at the employer's request outside of the workplace. This attitude towards employment relations resulted in the above-mentioned Member States being found not in compliance with the provisions of Article 2 §1 of the Charter. According to representatives of the Irish Human Rights and Equality Commission, cases of extending working time for employees who do not work at the workplace but work remotely are a natural phenomenon due to the blurring of boundaries between work and the private lives of professionally active people. This reasoning did not fully convince the ECSR. A similar situation occurred in the case of Italy. The ECSR was interested in whether reasonable daily and weekly working hours were being respected during the COVID-19 pandemic. The Italian report limited itself to stating that remote work is widely used during the pandemic, although it was rarely used by employers before. Law no. 81/2017 of the Italian labour code regulates the norms of daily and weekly work. The ambiguity of the above answer made the ECSR postpone the issuance of a decision on Italy's compliance or non-compliance with Article 21 §1 of the Charter. Georgia was treated differently, as in its conclusions adopted in 2018 the country disclosed in its report on compliance with Article 2 §1 of the Charter that its labour inspectors have the right to supervise and punish employers who do not comply with the obligations set out in this provision of the Charter only from 1 January 2021. Therefore, in part of the period under assessment, they had no right to apply administrative penalties. The ECSR considered that if a Member State lacks the legal competence to supervise employers' application of the provisions of the Charter, it does not constitute unlawful conduct by the authorities of the Member State.

II. Public Holidays with Pay (Article 2 §2)

82. The obligation of ensuring employees paid holidays embraces only these days which otherwise would be working days. Therefore it does not include holidays falling on free-from-work days such as Sundays. The provision in question does not determine the number of paid holidays in a year nor does the Committee. The authorities of a Member State should then guarantee paid holidays as the sum of bank holidays and religious holidays accepted by national regulations as free-from-work days.[323] These holidays are free-from-work days according to national labour law regulations, and additional wages should be paid as if they were working days.[324]

323. No guarantee of public holidays with pay in Moldova. Conclusions 2010, vol. 2, p. 410. Same, Conclusions XIX-3, p. 33 (Croatia), p. 249 (United Kingdom).

324. No compensation for work performed on a public holiday at a sufficiently high level in Albania. Conclusions 2010, vol. 1, p. 20. Same, Conclusions XIX-3, p. 112 (Greece), p. 186 (Slovak Republic).

Employing this principle the Committee regarded states guaranteeing six paid holidays a year (the United Kingdom[325]) as equally abiding by this provision as states guaranteeing seventeen holidays (Italy).[326]

83. The exemption from duty of work on holidays with guaranteed pay is not absolute. Depending on the type of work, employees may be obliged to work on holidays. However, work can be carried out on public holidays under specific circumstances set by the law or collective agreement. Work performed on public holidays entails a constraint on the part of the workers who should be compensated. Concerning the different approaches adopted in different European countries in relation to the forms and levels of such compensation and the lack of convergence between the Member States in this regard, state parties enjoy a margin of appreciation on this issue, subject to the requirement that all employees are entitled to adequate compensation provided for in the form of increased salaries and/or compensatory time off under the law or the various collective agreements in force, in addition to the regular wages paid on a public holiday, be calculated on a daily, weekly or monthly basis.[327] The Maltese report provides information on pay rates performed during public holidays in a large number of sectors of the economy and certain industries. The Committee notes that the general principle seems to be that work performed during public holidays is compensated at the rate of 'double-time', an increase of 100% of the regular wage in most sectors and industries and for most categories of workers. However, there are significant exceptions to that rule. In the beverages industries, outside workers and shift workers are only paid 'time-and-a-half', an increase of 50% for work performed during public holidays in period Monday to Friday.[328] The Committee asks that the next report contain information on the situation in practice, including examples of the level of the increased pay rate in different sectors and branches, both public and private. It declared the situation according to which parties can also agree to the compensation of work on public holidays by means of additional time off to not be in conformity with Article 2 §2.[329]

The duty of work embraces especially all employed in enterprises functioning in a constant cycle.[330] By working during a holiday, an employee acquires the right to an extra day off.[331] Accounting holiday wages are done on an hourly basis. Employees working full time during a holiday, obtain a whole free day. Employees working fewer hours during a holiday obtain as many off-work hours as to what they worked during a holiday.[332] It is not permissible for an employer to grant less

325. The Committee considered in 2018 the case of the UK as 'notable exception (...) where there is no specific entitlement to leave on public holidays'. Activity Report 2018, p. 33.
326. Conclusions I, p. 19.
327. Conclusions 2014 (Andorra, France).
328. Conclusions 2016 (Malta), p. 32.
329. Conclusions 2016 (Georgia), p. 207.
330. Conclusions XII-1, p. 72 (Greece).
331. The case of Greece. Conclusions XII-1, p. 72, XII-3, p. 205, XIV-2, pp. 329–330.
332. Conclusions XII-2 p. 61 (Malta) Employees employed for less than fourteen hours a week did not obtain an extra day off.

off-work time than what has been worked during a holiday.[333] Alternatively, holiday work may be additionally remunerated when a particular employee agrees to it.[334]

However, this is regarded as an exception from the rule of recompensing holiday work by an extra day off. The Committee believes additional pay for holiday work would violate the rule of not forcing any employee to work on holidays.

84. The ECSR announced on 22 March 2023 that eight Member States had failed to ensure that employees working on public holidays were being adequately compensated for their work. Article 2 §2 of the Charter does not state that work on public holidays should be compensated. It can therefore be assumed that due to the insufficiently defined concept of 'paid holidays', the authorities of individual Member States of the CoE enjoy full discretion in matters relating to the types of holidays (public or private). The employer's obligation is to provide salary on a day off paid. A public holiday recognised by the authorities of a particular Member State requires payment which is higher than the normal remuneration for working on a weekday. It is therefore one of the provisions of the European labour law system, in which the legislature transferred to the European institution the obligation to specify the general concept of 'payment'. It is difficult to determine the characteristics of this concept. Remuneration is not due for work of a particular type or due to the unusual nature of the work performed, but due to the external conditions in which it is performed. As a result of the unclear definition of what individual Member States consider work performed on holidays, there are differences in the understanding of the term 'holidays'. Therefore, from the very beginning, we are dealing with a vague justification of the ECSR's decision, taken not on the basis of the construction of standards of conduct accepted or not accepted by the legislature, but on the majority of views and opinions created by ECSR members. Everything I have written about so far forces the ECSR to apply a uniform formula of the decision, which is only somewhat carefully justified. The standard is the statement that is also used in the latest unified conclusion under analysis, which indicates the complete perception and observance by the authorities of the Council of Europe Member States of the labour rights protection standards formulated by the ECSR and presented to the general public on 22 March 2023. It is the uniform phrase that the 'situation is not in conformity with Article 2 §2 of the Charter on the grounds that work performed on a public holiday is not adequately compensated'. One thing is clear from it: theoretical employee rights are vested only in all persons employed without exception on days off from work falling on calendar days of all public holidays. Various examples of negative decisions due to various solutions to the problem of pay rates for work during holidays on a public holiday can be found in the decisions in the latest conclusions regarding the state of affairs on the last day of 2020. The following Member States received a negative conclusion:

- Bosnia and Herzegovina compensates the payment on a public holiday with a 40% bonus on top of basic and part-time pay.

333. Conclusions XIV-2, p. 631 (Portugal).
334. Conclusions XIV-2, p. 220 (Finland).

- France's authorities take the position that only one public holiday (1 May) does not justify the application of double remuneration for work performed. However, according to the French state authorities, this does not mean that the social partners – employers and employees – cannot supplement the state-mandated compensation for this public holiday. The French Labour Code[335] provides for 11 public holidays per year, while the only compulsory public holiday is 1 May.[336] Work carried out on this day in establishments and services which cannot interrupt their work because of the nature of their activity is paid at double the normal rate. It is also noted that this payment may not be replaced by compensatory time off, even when a collective agreement providing for this possibility has been negotiated. For other public holidays, the ECSR notes that the law provides solely that 'resting on public holidays may not result in loss of salary for any employee with three months or more of service in a company or establishment. These provisions do not apply to employees working at home, seasonal workers, intermittent employees or temporary workers'.[337] The ECSR considered that no compulsory salary increase was granted for work carried out on a public holiday other than 1 May, although the social partners could introduce one. It asked for clarification on the levels of compensation provided for in the form of increased salaries and/or compensatory time off under the various collective agreements in force, in addition to the regular wage paid for a public holiday. The current French report does not contain any information on this subject. Consequently, the ECSR finds that it has not been established that work performed on a public holiday is equally compensated.
- Georgia received a clear signal from the ECSR as to the pay rate for work on non-working days for public reasons. Work performed on these days must be honoured with at least equivalent remuneration in the amount of the working day payable to the employee.
- For Greece, a 75% supplement to the regular remuneration for work on days off for the occasion of a public holiday, which is used in the private sector, was found to be inconsistent with the legal norm of Article 2 §2 of the Charter. More or less the same applies to people employed in the Greek public sector. The difference between employees employed in these sectors is significant because civil servants are entitled to only one day off for working on a public holiday. However, this is not additional compensation because the Greek state authorities follow the principle that 'one day worked equals one day off'.
- The case of Portugal confirms the current practice. Remuneration compensating for work performed by an employee on a public holiday may in no way be supplemented (apart from the normal amount of remuneration for work performed) only by a 50% allowance for working on a public holiday. The ECSR found that the Portuguese authorities did not comply with the general requirements of Article 2 §2 of the Charter, despite the express permission amended to

335. Article 31–33.
336. *See* the previous Conclusions 2014 (France).
337. Article L. 31–33 of the French Labour Code.

the Labour Code in 2019. The amendment enabled the social partners to pay a higher allowance for work to supplement employees working on a public holiday.

- The case of Italy consolidated the ECSR's belief that 'work carried out may also be provided as compensatory time off, in which case it should be at least double the days worked'.
- The last report submitted by Moldova was not for substantive reasons, but formal ones. A previous audit in 2018 found that work performed on a public holiday was not sufficiently remunerated. One can only guess that the above statement refers to the same cases that were noticed by the ECSR in 2020. On this basis, without mentioning the legitimacy of the legal and factual assessment, the ECSR ruled that 'the report does not contain any information on this point'.

III. Two Weeks' Annual Holiday with Pay

85. Article 2 §3 of the Charter guarantees all employees annual holiday with pay, regardless of the basis of employment and the type of contract.[338] In 2018, the Committee concluded that not all workers employed in Cyprus, Luxembourg, the Netherlands and Spain are entitled to take at least of uninterrupted holiday during the year. The Committee found this situation incompatible with Article 2 §3 of both Charters.[339] The Charter sets a minimum period for this leave. The European Social Charter guarantees the right of at least two weeks of paid leave while the Revised European Social Charter guarantees at least four weeks of annual holiday with pay. Annual holiday with pay is the right of every employee. An employee cannot be deprived of this entitlement or pass it on to another person.[340] As early as during the first supervisory cycle, the Committee concluded that a voluntary act of passing this entitlement back to an employer in exchange for additional remuneration (a holiday 'sale') stands in breach of this regulation.[341] The above opinion was repeated in subsequent supervisory cycles and those Member States practising holiday 'sales' for additional remuneration were considered to be violators of Article 2 §3 of the Charter.[342] Article 2 §3 of the Charter does not determine the factors for acquiring the rights to employee holiday with pay. Therefore, it is permissible to acquire the right to four weeks of holiday with pay depending on the period of employment within one workplace assumed by labour law regulations.

During the first supervisory cycle, the Committee determined a twelve-month employment period as the maximum amount of time needed to acquire full holiday with pay.[343] Not fulfilling this requirement by an employee enables an employer to reduce the number of paid holidays accordingly to the period of employment.[344]

338. It has not been established that the right to annual holiday with pay is guaranteed in Moldova. Conclusions 2010, vol. 2, p. 411.
339. Activity Report 2018, p. 34.
340. Conclusions 2010, p. 21 (Albania).
341. Conclusions I, p. 170, Conclusions 2007, vol. 1, p. 30 (Albania).
342. Conclusions XII-2, p. 62 (Cyprus); Conclusions XIV-2, p. 222 (Finland); XIV-2, p. 503 (Malta).
343. Conclusions I, p. 20.
344. Conclusions VII, p. 14 (Ireland).

86. The Committee in its early supervisory cycles opted for a proportional amount of holiday with pay, depending on the period of employment. It may be assumed that each month of employment grants an employee a one-twelfth proportion of the yearly amount of holiday with pay. The Committee also accepted the separation of holiday entitlements from periods of employment in that it approved periods with paid remuneration and not periods of pure employment as the correct basis to calculate the number of days of holiday with pay.[345] The latter allowed for unpaid leave to be disregarded in periods of employment.

The ban on holiday 'sale' does not deprive an employee of the right to obtain money equivalent for holidays not utilised.[346] Only in cases of resignation may an employer implement the above solution, when he is not able to grant holidays with pay at a future date. The above case embraces situations when the period of notice is shorter than paid holidays or when it is not possible for a holidaying employee to obtain a rise, which results in paying him only part of his deserved remuneration.

87. Article 2 §3 of the Charter does not impose an obligation on Member States to grant continuous holidays with pay.

During the third supervisory cycle, the Committee addressed a query to Austria, asking what types of employees may be obliged to part with their annual holiday with pay. It expressed hope for a response in regard to this question as well as with matters of the employee's right to give up holidays with pay in exchange for additional remuneration.[347] The Austrian authorities during the following supervisory cycle (the fourth) provided a positive answer to one of the addressed questions referring to the rights of an employee to 'sell' his/her holiday to the employer. The Committee reminded Austria of the decisions undertaken in the first supervisory cycle and concluded Austria to be in breach of Article 2 §3 of the Charter.[348] It did not re-analyse the problem of employees being allowed to divide their holidays into parts or being forced to utilise holidays in parts.

The Committee is of the view that the reason for the existence of a holiday is to allow for the regeneration of physical and mental strength, weakened by labour. In accordance with the above principle, a conviction is formulated that paid holidays are not to be utilised by workers unable to work due to illness. The Committee raised this foregoing problem during the first supervisory cycle. It analysed how a worker utilised his holiday when falling ill during the holiday.[349]

88. By the twelfth supervisory cycle, when referring to the impossibility of forgoing a holiday, the Committee declared the above effect of forbidding such an activity, entitling the worker who is unable to utilise his/her holiday due to illness to seek the possibility of being able to use the holiday at a later date. Those utilising the above entitlements are workers who have been unable to take holidays, regardless of when the illness took place, which inhibited the utilisation of the holiday

345. Conclusions VII, p. 13 (Sweden).
346. Conclusions I, p. 170; Conclusions V, p. 14 (Austria).
347. Conclusions III, p. 13.
348. Conclusions IV, p. 16.
349. Conclusions I, p. 20.

either in whole or in part during a planned period, both before and during the holiday.[350] From this supervisory cycle, the Committee included a standard question in the form addressing the authorities of Member States that are obliged to file reports referring to the legal implications of the impossibility of a worker utilising his/her holiday due to the inability to carry out work caused by illness or an accident at work.[351] The Committee demanded all Member States answer the above question during all supervisory cycles in order to be in accordance with Article 2 §3 of the Charter.[352] During the thirteenth supervisory cycle, the Committee claimed that according to Danish,[353] Spanish[354] and United Kingdom[355] labour law regulations, workers do not have the right to demand the utilisation of holidays on a different day, if unused, as prescribed due to illness.

According to the reports of Spanish authorities, the above regulation is a consequence of an agreement between stakeholders who during collective bargaining agreements establish rigid periods for when holidays may be used according to given years. This above case is evident with regard to workers who are employed in production employment fields that close down for a given period of time (in accordance with the arrangements made with stakeholders), allocating holidays to all workers involved in the employment. Spanish courts refused those workers who sought to utilise holidays at a different date, due to illness, who were employed in such production fields of employment. The Committee expressed a concern regarding the inability to move one's holiday to a different period as to the one allocated by the employer and asked questions about whether the above practice was a general one, and in relation to it, whether it was possible to introduce a motion concerning the impossibility of moving an unutilised holiday to a later period.[356] The Spanish authorities informed the Committee that the decisions handed down by the labour law courts, forbidding workers to utilise holidays at a differing period to what was allocated, were sporadic in their nature, seen as controversial, and were appealed to the Supreme Court. The Committee once again during the following two supervisory cycles (the 13th and 14th) sought details concerning the number of workers, who due to illness during the agreed by stakeholders' holiday periods, lost their opportunity of utilising their holidays, as well as sought information about the

350. Conclusions XII-2, p. 62.
351. Form of the report submitted in pursuance of the Revised European Social Charter in European Social Charter, *Collected Texts, supra*, p. 307.
352. Conclusions XIII-1, p. 76; Conclusions XIV-2, p. 424 (Italy); Conclusions XIII-2, p. 242; Conclusions XIV-2, p. 117 (Belgium); Conclusions XIII-2, pp. 242–243; Conclusions XIV-2, p. 295 (Germany); Conclusions XIII-3, p. 248 (Finland); XIII-3, p. 250 (Portugal); Addendum to Conclusions XIII-3, p. 24 (Luxembourg); Conclusions XIV-2, p. 182 (Denmark); XIV-2, p. 330 (Greece); XIV-2, p. 365 (Iceland); XIV-2, p. 503 (Malta); XIV-2, p. 759 (United Kingdom); Conclusions XVI-2, p. 130 (Czech Republic); XVI-2, p. 196 (Denmark); XVI-2, p. 288 (Germany); XVI-2, p. 328 (Greece); XVI-2, p. 396 (Hungary); XVI-2, pp. 481–482 (Malta); XVI-2, p. 515 (the Netherlands); XVI-2, p. 719 (Slovakia); XVI-2, p. 833 (Spain); Addendum to Conclusions XVI-2, p. 19 (Ireland).
353. Conclusions XIX-3, p. 74.
354. Conclusions XIX-3, p. 211.
355. Conclusions XIX-3, p. 250.
356. Conclusions XIII-2, p. 64.

Supreme Court's stance on the matter.[357] During the sixteenth supervisory cycle, the Spanish authorities declared no changes concerning holidays had taken place in the regulations. The Committee therefore recognised, that the inability to move a holiday period, to which workers are entitled, to a different time frame from what was earlier decided, was a breach of Article 2 §3 of the Charter.[358]

Those workers who due to illness or accident are unable to utilise the whole or in part of the holiday should have the guarantee of being able to utilise it at a later date in a capacity of at least two weeks in the yearly calendar. The obligation of authorities of Member States is to enable workers to utilise holidays to the minimum extent of what is described by Article 2 §3 of the ESC or Article 2 §3 of the RESC, when workers due to illness or accident, are unable to do so in the period prescribed to them by the employer. The Committee underlined this during the fourteenth supervisory cycle.

Looking at Norwegian legislation, which allows workers to utilise holiday periods at a later date when unable to take holidays during a prescribed period due to illness or accident lasting for at least six days, the Committee saw this as being in accordance with Article 2 §3 of the Charter because Norwegian holiday rights guarantee workers twenty-five days' holiday. Therefore a loss of six days of holiday due to illness allows workers to utilise a minimum period of holidays, enforced by Article 2 §3 of the ESC.[359]

89. The position of the Committee would be different if Member States ratified Article 2 §3 of the RESC, which guarantees a four-week holiday period within the year. The obligation to ensure workers the possibility of utilising their holidays within the minimum standards guaranteed by the Charter (two or four weeks), encompasses all workers employed in full or part-time employment, regardless of the weekly and daily working-hour standards.[360] The Committee was particularly interested in the holiday structures of atypical workers. It demanded information concerning the regulations of their holidays, the means of allocating holidays as well as the possibility of moving an unutilised holiday to a later period.[361] Sporadically, the Committee encountered obstacles in the evaluation of information concerning the possibility of shifting a paid holiday, which cannot be utilised by an employee due to sickness or accident.

The case of Malta may be presented as an example where falling ill during a holiday with pay neither automatically extends the holiday nor entitles an employee to break this holiday to utilise it afterwards. According to Maltese regulations, an employee who is taken ill during a holiday with pay is treated exactly the same as a healthy person having a holiday. He is only entitled to continue his sick leave when the holiday period is finished. The Maltese law uses a double legal fiction.

357. Conclusions XIII-1, p. 77; Conclusions XIV-2, p. 670.
358. Conclusions XVI-2, p. 833.
359. Conclusions XIV-2, p. 580.
360. Conclusions XIV-2, p. 222 (Finland); XIV-2, p. 502 (Malta).
361. Conclusions XIII-1, p. 74 (Austria); Conclusions XIII-3, p. 249 (Finland); Conclusions XIV-2, p. 365 (Iceland); Addendum to Conclusions XIII-1, p. 77 (United Kingdom).

First, it recognises an ill employee as a healthy person who can utilise holiday with pay, and second, it allows an employee to remain on sick leave having already regained work abilities.

This is why the Committee concluded that the Maltese labour law regulations do not guarantee employers unable to work due to illness or accident the right to utilise the entitled holiday at other times.[362]

90. In matters relating to annual leave, the provisions of Article 2 §2 of both Charters of Social Rights, those from 1961 and from 1996, the Council of Europe proved to be almost as fundamental and laconic as it was in the previous, second paragraph of the analysed Article 2. Regardless of which version of the Charter is analysed, the minimum period of uninterrupted paid annual leave due to an employee – two or four weeks – is known. In neither version did the legislature deal with matters such as the possibility of exchanging the holiday leave due to an employee for a separately paid, uninterrupted continuation of work; not guaranteeing an employee's uninterrupted use of their holiday leave; granting the employee less than the minimum two- or four-week leave; or deducting from leave any days which an employee on leave could not use all or part of their holiday leave, for reasons beyond their control, particularly illness. These issues will be discussed in this part of the arguments on the Charter of Social Rights because – despite not being mentioned in Article 2 §3 of the Charter – they were recognised by the ECSR as the basic core of considerations on the standards of rights at work for professionally active people. With two exceptions for political reasons concerning Belarus and the Russian Federation, the other Member States have voluntarily committed themselves to comply with European labour law norms in matters relating to the protection of work carried out in any Member State of the Council of Europe located on the European continent. Member States have chosen to provide employees with paid annual leave. However, several countries have come to the conclusion that will not conflict with the requirements of the ECSR:

– Albania and Greece[363] have decided to 'sell' employees their holiday entitlements to employers in exchange for continued, uninterrupted continuation of their current work. The essence of the problem is considered as a 'sale' on resignation from holiday leave to an employee who, in exchange for a higher salary, resigns from using the time off work granted by the employer. The term 'leave sale' is used to emphasise the willingness to continue working during time off work. In a conceptual shorthand, the word 'resignation' means that the employer does not withdraw the leave previously granted to the employee. During this leave, the employee agrees not to use the time off granted by the employer for a period of two or four weeks a year and signs a contract with this employer, establishing a new employment relationship – in fact, the same or a different one than performed before the leave granted to him. In light of the provisions of the labour law, an employee who does not take leave during their time off from work establishes a second legal relationship with the same employer. The payment by the

362. Conclusions XVI-2, pp. 481–482.
363. Conclusions 2022 (Albania), (Greece).

employer of two salaries in the same month or two weeks during which the employee continues the current work performed before and after the leave is only possible if the employee decides to do so with the same employer. No provisions of law prohibit an employee who is on leave granted by a current employer from taking up employment with another employer during the leave. There is no official obstacle preventing the 'selling' of the leave of employer X due and granted to the employee on leave by employer Y.

– In Bosnia and Herzegovina,[364] the four-week holiday leave should be granted in full, counted in working days. Therefore, full annual leave cannot be approved when an employer, as did one in the district of the federation in question, grants eighteen days of annual leave in a single month. The ECSR has ruled that twenty days of leave is equal to one month. Thus, the monthly leave to which a police officer is entitled may not be less than the minimum of twenty days.
– In Hungary, a twelve-day holiday may not be interrupted without the consent of the worker concerned. 'The Committee recalls that an employee must take at least two weeks uninterrupted annual holidays during the year the holidays were due and that annual holidays exceeding two weeks may be postponed in particular circumstances defined by domestic law, the nature of which should justify the postponement.'[365] For this reason, the ECSR ruled that the 'situation in Hungary is not in conformity with Article 2 §2 of the Charter on the ground that the employees' right to take at least two weeks of uninterrupted holiday during the year in respect of which the holidays were due is not sufficiently guaranteed.' The same position was taken by the ECSR in the case of Albania discussed above.[366]
– Ireland allows employers to carry over the annual leave that employees accrue in a given calendar year, subject to limitations and objectively justified reasons. Without giving any reasons, the ECSR ruled that this solution was incompatible with Article 2 §3 of the Charter.[367] This procedure is possible due to the illness granted to the employee who is unable to take this leave.[368] Such an employee should therefore be able to exercise their unfulfilled entitlement in whole or in part at a different time.[369]

IV. The Duty to Eliminate Risks for Workers in Dangerous or Unhealthy Occupations and Provide Them with Additional Paid Holidays or Reduced Working Hours when Possible

91. As is declared in the European Social Charter, Article 2 §4 obliges the authorities of Member States to ensure employees in certain dangerous and unhealthy occupations have additional paid holidays or reduced working hours.[370]

364. Conclusions 2022 (Bosnia, Herzegovina).
365. Conclusions 2022 (Hungary).
366. Conclusions 2022 (Albania).
367. Conclusions 2022 (Ireland).
368. Conclusions 2022 (Greece).
369. Conclusions 2022 (Ireland).
370. No steps have been taken to eliminate or reduce the risks associated with dangerous or unhealthy work in Moldova and Portugal. Conclusions 2010, vol. 2, p. 413 (Moldova), p. 493 (Portugal).

This regulation gives authorities the choice in determining which occupations are considered dangerous and unhealthy. The Committee evaluates the lists of dangerous and unhealthy occupations presented by Member States and in cases of omitting occupations commonly believed as such, makes a ruling of the non-conformity of domestic regulations with Article 2 §4 of the Charter.[371] The provision in question is strictly connected with Article 3 of the Charter, ensuring employees have the right to work in safe and hygienic conditions. In the supervisory process of abiding by Article 2 §3 of the Charter, the Committee often referred to arrangements and conclusions based on Article 3 of the Charter.[372] Reasoning in the two above-mentioned articles of the Charter, the Committee classified as dangerous all work that is in contact with radioactive and toxic substances, connected with the risk of being subject to lead, asbestos, high pressure, noise, high or low temperatures, explosives, works carried out underground, in steelworks, shipyards, and in front of monitors due to radiation.[373] The Committee utilises the above-mentioned standards in the supervisory cycle process of abiding by the Charter's regulations by Member States. The above-mentioned standards have no exceptions. A register of work dangerous and harmful to health should be systematically completed. The Committee advises authorities of Member States to provide information concerning protection against hazards caused by particular factors which were omitted from registers presented by particular countries.[374] Work which is dangerous and hazardous to health and undertaken by workers cannot be compensated by any other means other than those directed in Article 2 §4 of the ESC. In particular, it is impossible to hire personnel in such conditions for higher wages without reducing daily working hours.[375] The first stipulated requirement concerning workers employed in dangerous and hazardous work is the entitlement to longer leave. Further down the list is the reduction of working hours for such employees. Reducing the exposure of the body to physical, chemical and biological factors which occur in dangerous or hazardous labour, reduces the threat.[376] Longer periods of leave allow for the regeneration of the worker's body. Both above-mentioned techniques of protecting the health and life of workers exposed to such risks may be implemented simultaneously. Despite the obligation placed on Member States by the usage of the term 'longer paid holidays or limited working hours', Member States may, or rather should, take advantage of the above-mentioned measures to protect the life and health of workers, irrespectively of each other. According to the Committee, it is permissible to undertake all measures limiting the risks of being subject to factors listed by Article 2 §4 of the ESC.[377] In the earlier supervisory cycle, the Committee

371. Conclusions II, p. 9.
372. Conclusions IV, p. 18, Conclusions III-1, p. 80 (The Netherlands).
373. Conclusions V, p. 17 (Italy); Conclusions XII-1, pp. 74–75 (Greece, the Netherlands); Conclusions XIII-1, p. 80 (Norway).
374. During the fourteenth supervisory cycle, Germany became obliged to provide information concerning protection against hazards, such as industrial noise, high temperatures, and radiation. Conclusions IV-2, p. 296 (Germany).
375. Conclusions III, p. 14 (Austria), Conclusions XIX-3, p. 20 (Austria), p. 115 (Greece).
376. It has not been established that such measures are provided in the United Kingdom. Conclusions XIX-3, p. 251.
377. Conclusions III, p. 15 (Ireland).

anticipated the changes introduced by the Revised European Social Charter, which, as a priority, obliges Member States to remove the threatening elements associated with dangerous and hazardous for health and, only when it is impossible to remove or sufficiently reduce such threats, to ensure the cutting down of working hours or provide additional paid holidays. Measures taken to protect the health and life of a worker exposed to the threats of dangerous and hazardous work should complement one another. It is not enough to temporarily restrict the exposure of the worker to dangerous or hazardous factors.[378] In the fifth supervisory cycle, the Committee was convinced that the constant improvement of safety and hygiene in the workplace as well as the protection of the worker's health against threats caused by processes, conditions and the work environment, should be in line with the reduction of daily and weekly working hours as well as with the increase of paid holidays.[379] The Committee underlined that the responsibility of reducing work hours and increasing holidays is especially important when there is the existence of danger within the working environment.[380] The goal, for which Article 2 §4 of the Charter was analysed, will be in constant activation mode, unless all dangers for the life and health of workers brought about by work, by the factors and conditions of work as well as the working environment, are eliminated. Utilising the appropriate measures allocated to the authorities of Member States, employers are to eliminate and, if impossible, to reduce as much as it is possible, the level of risk workers are exposed to, and to factors which are dangerous and hazardous to life and health.[381]

92. The Revised European Social Charter logically associating Article 2 §4 with Article 3 of the Charter, places paramount importance on the obligation of Member States, stakeholders as well as employers, the duty to remove the risks affiliated with work that is dangerous or hazardous to the health. The underlined that the analysed provision is a standard, which heightens the effects of undertaking measures in an attempt to guarantee workers safe and hygienic working conditions. Arguments provided by authorities of Member States concerning the undertakings of particular measures to protect the lives and health of workers employed in dangerous or hazardous conditions were not accepted by the Committee as there was no improvement in working conditions post the utilisation of these measures. It paid heed to the fact that the obligation to reduce working hours or the increasing of holidays, in these particular situations, when prevention policies at their root did not ensure removal or a significant reduction of threats against health or life.[382] The obligation to reduce the working-hour standards for workers employed in dangerous or hazardous to health employment is a point of reference for the working-hour standards existing within a given country.

The Committee, therefore, rejected Austria's arguments claiming it fulfilled its obligations under Article 2 §4 of the Charter, as it introduced 40 working-hour

378. Conclusions XIII-2, p. 244 (Belgium).
379. Conclusions V, pp. 15–16.
380. Conclusions VIII, p. 45 (Ireland).
381. Addendum to Conclusions XIII-3, p. 24 (Luxembourg); Conclusions XIII-4, p. 339 (Belgium); XIV-2, pp. 117–118 (Belgium); XIV-2, p. 386 (Ireland); XIV-2, p. 467 (Luxembourg).
382. Conclusions XIII-1, pp. 79–80; XIII-4, p. 202 (the Netherlands).

weeks and four weeks of paid holidays. The Committee underlined that the provisions Articles 1-3 of the Charter place on Member States obligations of introducing working-hour standards as well as minimum paid holidays of four weeks. Article 2 §4 of the Charter is the standard in terms of provisions 1–3 which is why it requires for workers employed in dangerous or hazardous to health working conditions, shorter than ordinary obligatory daily and weekly working hours as well as longer than the minimum paid holidays.[383] As of 2014, the Committee recalled that Article 2 §4 of the Charter requires states to ensure that some form of compensation is received by workers exposed to risks where it has not yet been possible to eliminate or sufficiently reduce these risks in spite of the application of preventive measures or in the absence of their application. Member States enjoy certain discretion to determine the activities and risks concerned, but the Committee monitors their decisions. They must at least consider sectors and occupations that are manifestly dangerous or unhealthy, such as mining, quarrying, steel-making and shipbuilding, and occupations exposing employees to ionising radiation, extreme temperatures and noise. The aim of the compensation must be to offer those concerned sufficient and regular time to recover from the associated stress and fatigue and thus maintain their vigilance in the workplace.[384]

The Committee found that the situation was not in conformity in the following states: Portugal, Greece, Luxembourg and the United Kingdom. In Portugal, public workers exposed to dangerous or unhealthy activities are not entitled to additional annual holidays or shorter working hours. The report submitted by Portugal also indicates that, out of a sample group of 13 collective agreements, only 7 (covering 4,355 workers) provide for shorter working times and longer annual holidays. The Committee does not consider that the effectiveness of the preventive measures implemented in Portugal and aimed at eliminating or reducing risks is such that all residual risks are sufficiently covered. As not all the workers exposed to residual risks are entitled to adequate and compensatory measures (reduced working hours, additional leave), the Committee considers that the situation in Portugal remains in non-conformity with Article 2 §4 of the Charter.[385] The Committee notes that in a report presented by Greece, the payment of an unhealthy work allowance was introduced in a new Collective Labour Agreement on Mines for workers in metal mines, lignite mines and quarries. The Committee points out in this respect that under no circumstances can financial compensation be considered an appropriate response compliant with Article 2 §4 of the Charter. It also considers that the additional measures provided for in the collective agreement – one additional day of public holidays and the setting of the weekly period of work at forty hours – do not adequately correspond to the aim of offering workers exposed to risks regular and sufficient time to recover from associated stress and fatigue, and thus maintain their vigilance in the workplace. The Committee does not consider that the measure introduced in Greece is relevant and appropriate to achieving the aims of Article 2 §4.[386] In the

383. Conclusions V, p. 17; XII-2, p. 65; XIII-1, p. 78; XIII-3, pp. 199–200, Conclusions 2010, vol. 1, p. 22 (Albania).
384. Conclusions 2014 (Portugal).
385. *Ibid.*
386. Conclusions XX-3 (Greece).

absence of specific rules creating an obligation to compensate workers dealing with residual risks, the non-binding guidance (the Managing Shift Work Guidance or Good Practice Guidelines) does not allow one to judge that the situation is in conformity with Article 2 §4 of the Charter.[387] Specific regulations applying to identified risks focus on prevention rather than on measures compensating for the risks that persist in spite of the preventive arrangements implemented. Failure to present examples and relevant statistical data in the application as required by Article 2 §4 of the Charter, for such measures as the reduction of working hours, or extra holidays, is adjudicated by the Committee as constituting a ground for a negative conclusion, to the effect that it has not been established that workers exposed to occupational risks are entitled to appropriate compensation measures.[388] A report provided by a Member State ought to give details of the sections concerned and supply the legal basis guaranteeing the practical application of specific compensation measures relating to working time (management of work patterns as regards daily, weekly and annual rest and holiday periods).

In the 2016 cycle, the Committee recalls that Article 2 §4 of the Charter mentions two forms of compensation for workers exposed to residual risks that cannot be or have not yet been eliminated or sufficiently reduced: reduced working hours and additional holidays. In view of the emphasis exposure time may also ensure conformity with the Charter. At the European level, the relevance and adequacy of such measures are assessed on a case-by-case basis.[389] However, it does not mean that the labour law in Member States may not specify the methods of the elimination of risks or the form of compensation. In particular, neither the state nor the social partners are entitled to leave the choice to be made on the basis of case-by-case assessment.[390] The Committee also states that the most current approach taken by the report submitted by the United Kingdom is explicitly focused on reducing exposure to occupational health risks in line with a set of principles enshrined in legislation. The approach adopted by the United Kingdom presents the potential for a higher level of risk control than simply focusing on reducing the time of exposure to the risk and providing additional leave once workers have been exposed to risks to their safety or health at work. Taking into consideration that only one form of compensation leads to the conclusion that not only is the United Kingdom not in conformity with Article 2 §4 of the Charter[391] but that it is also the case with Luxembourg.[392] In the latter case, the Committee took into consideration that Luxembourg has submitted no new information on Article 2 §4 and the Committee therefore only reiterates its previous conclusion according to which it had not been established that workers exposed to occupational risks, despite the existing risk elimination policy, were entitled to appropriate compensatory measures. In the 2018 cycle, the Committee found that two Member States, Armenia, and Bosnia and

387. Conclusions XX-3 (United Kingdom).
388. Conclusions XX-3 (Luxembourg).
389. Conclusions XX-3 (Germany).
390. Conclusions 2016 (Italy), p. 206.
391. Conclusions XXI-1, p. 325.
392. Conclusions XXI-1, p. 306.

Herzegovina, do not have an appropriate preventive policy to avoid risks in hazardous or unhealthy work.[393] In addition, the Committee stated that even if such a preventive policy was implemented, in some countries, not all workers exposed to residual risks have the right to use appropriate protective measures, such as: reduced working hours or additional paid leave.[394]

93. Article 2 §4 of the European Social Charter introduces the obligation to remove hazards related to work that is dangerous or harmful. Where this is not possible, the authorities of the Member States are obliged to introduce and apply shortened standards for working time and to grant employees performing such work additional holiday leave. In the six cases where the ECSR adjudicated on the compliance or non-compliance of the authorities of Member States in the last impact assessment concerning the elimination of hazardous and harmful work, all negative decisions had one common opinion: the Member States' authorities were unable to provide employees with appropriate means and tools to protect their body from hazards caused by working in unsafe and unhygienic conditions. This conclusion is surprising in that it does not apply to less developed, less wealthy countries which were relatively recently admitted to the Council of Europe. The negative opinions were expressed not only about countries such as Serbia, Bosnia and Herzegovina and Moldova but also about France, Greece, Italy and Portugal. A lack of interest in the protection of workers' health is evidenced by the statements made in the ECSR's negative conclusions.

France did not furnish the information requested by the ECSR on the dangerous and unhealthy conditions in which employees work. In the previous cycle of examining harmful employment conditions, the ECSR ordered the French authorities to limit the work duties and the time during which such work must be carried out. Nothing has changed. In its latest negative conclusion, the ECSR reiterates its appeal to the French authorities to allow all workers exposed to harmful working conditions to make use of reduced working hours and additional holidays.[395] The same was repeated by ECSR auditors for Greece, Italy and Portugal.[396] In the ECSR's conclusions, there are specific proposals in addition to the general wording, such as granting employees an additional fifteen days of rest from work and a 15% increase in property benefits from social security.[397] Not all workers employed in harmful and unhealthy work, as stated by the ECSR, are able to continue their work, as it is very dangerous for humans. The main purpose of these compensatory measures should be to provide those concerned with sufficient, regular time to recover from the stress and fatigue caused by their unhealthy and very hard work.

393. Activity Report, p. 34.
394. Luxembourg, the Netherlands, UK, *ibid.*
395. Conclusions 2022 (France).
396. Conclusions 2022 (Greece), (Italy), (Portugal).
397. Conclusions 2022 (Portugal).

V. To Ensure a Weekly Rest Period

94. Article 2 §5 imposes on the authorities of Member States another obligation by placing two types of responsibilities on them. First, it compels them to ensure one day of rest from work per week.[398] The working week, therefore, wherein workers are obliged to attend to their working responsibilities, is comprised of five working days. The sixth day of the weekly calendar is regarded as a day free from work and allocated for rest.[399] The obligation is fulfilled if the majority of workers (i.e., at least 80%) take advantage of this one day free from work.[400] The above responsibility is regarded as being a strict one, and the Charter does not accept any exceptions to this provision. Second, authorities of Member States should ensure that the day free from work in each calendar week for workers coincides with the day recognised by tradition or custom in the particular country as a day of rest.[401] In the majority of Member States, the day free from work within the week is Sunday, recognised by tradition or custom in the particular country or region. This regulation, however, is not strictly binding since, depending on the nature of the business run by a particular employer (the hospitality sector) or the specificity of a given branch (medical services), the employer may establish that the day free from work may be the day that does not coincide with the traditional rest day (Sunday or any other day considered to be free from work).[402] However, it does not have the right to make decisions in arbitrary matters. Authorities of Member States have the responsibility to monitor why such decisions have been made. In situations where it has been established that major groups of workers are employed on a Sunday and utilise their day free from work on another day of the week, the Committee has the basis for deciding that there has been a breach of Article 2 §5 of the Charter by a given country.[403] The above provision did not place any obligations on the authorities of Member States in matters concerning which day should be free from work. National labour laws leave this matter to stakeholders or employers. They are entitled to appoint a day free from work 'coinciding with' the day traditionally or customarily regarded as a day free from work and have their duties fulfilled if they decide to make the preceding (Saturday) or the following (Monday) a day free from work or any other day commonly regarded as a day free from work according to the tradition or customs within a country or a region. The Committee takes the position that the rules utilised in interpreting Article 2 §3 of the Charter, particularly the provision obliging Member States to guarantee a minimum of four weeks (according to

398. It has not been established that the right to weekly rest period is guaranteed in Moldova. Conclusions 2010, vol. 2, p. 413.
399. The weekly rest cannot be postponed by either collective agreement or an individual contract. Conclusions XIX, p. 57 (Czech Republic), p. 92 (Germany), p. 252 (United Kingdom).
400. Conclusions I, p. 20. In Albania, Art. 2 §5 of the RESC does not apply to the great majority of the workers concerned. Conclusions 2010, vol. 1, p. 23.
401. Conclusions XI, p. 55; Conclusions XIII-3, pp. 203–204; analysing the report filed by the Netherlands, the Committee demanded further information, as it was concerned that too many workers were employed on Sunday. Conclusions XIV-2, p. 539.
402. Conclusions XIV-2, p. 239 (the Netherlands).
403. Such instances took place during the fourteenth supervisory cycle. Conclusions XIV-2, p. 386 (Ireland – 36% employed on Sundays); p. 761 (United Kingdom – 40% employed on Sundays).

RESC) or two weeks (according to ESC) of holiday with pay, also apply to the interpretation of the Article in question. An employee cannot either voluntarily relinquish[404] or 'sell' to a third party[405] his one day free from work within a week. The Committee points out that to be in conformity with the Charter, it must not be possible for the worker to renounce his/her rest – not even in exchange for remuneration. The rest period may, however, be deferred to the following week as long as no worker works more than twelve days consecutively before being granted a two-day rest period.[406] In 2018, the Committee discovered that in seven Member States,[407] there were no adequate guarantees preventing workers from taking a week's rest after working twelve consecutive working days. The Committee asks for confirmation that weekly rest periods may not be replaced by financial compensation,[408] that employees may not forfeit their rest, and that, in cases of the postponement of the weekly rest period for justified reasons, no worker may be made to work more than twelve days in succession before being granted a two-day rest period.[409] It also asserts that an arrangement as described above, under which the weekly rest period may be postponed beyond twelve consecutive days, can only be acceptable in exceptional cases and is subject to strict safeguards. The Committee always asks what the exact circumstances are and whether there are any specific safeguards in addition to the approval of the collective agreement by the Labour Court: for example, obtaining prior authorisation from the Labour Inspectorate.[410] Therefore, the Committee concludes that in the case of the Czech Republic, the situation is not in conformity with Article 2 §5 of the Charter on the grounds that agricultural workers may, pursuant to a collective agreement or individual contract, postpone weekly rest, resulting in excessive numbers of consecutive working days.[411] Other negative conclusions were issued as of 2014 against Armenia, Georgia and Ireland on the grounds that it had not been established that the right to a weekly rest period was sufficiently guaranteed, could not be forfeited or replaced by financial compensation, or that adequate safeguards existed to ensure that workers could not work more than twelve consecutive days without a rest period. In the case of Finland, the Committee has concluded that the situation is not in conformity with the Charter because

404. Conclusions I, p. 172 (Ireland).
405. As seen: Conclusions XIII-3, p. 253; XIV-2, p. 223 (Finland); XIV-2, p. 503 (Malta).
406. Conclusions 2014 (Georgia).
407. Czech Republic, Georgia, the Netherlands, Russian Federation, North Macedonia, United Kingdom, Ukraine. Activity Report 2018, p. 34.
408. Conclusions 2016 (Georgia), p. 25. The national report submitted by Georgia states that under the Labour Code, provision of rest time is an essential feature of a labour agreement but the conditions of rest time may by defined according to preferences of the parties. The Committee considers that the question of the weekly rest period cannot be left to 'the preferences of the parties' and, while noting the information on the daily rest period, concludes that the situation in Georgia is not in conformity with Art. 2 §5 of the Charter.
409. Conclusions 2014 (Armenia, Finland).
410. Conclusions 2014 (Ireland).
411. Conclusions 2014 (Czech Republic).

workers can work more than twelve consecutive days without a rest period and might, in certain cases, give up their right to compensatory time off in exchange for an indemnification.[412]

Deferring holidays with pay-in-time stands is in accordance with standards established by Article 2 §5 of the Charter. According to the Committee, this practice is permissible in cases strictly regulated by national labour law. Furthermore, deferring a paid holiday in time cannot exceed twelve following months. In such a case, an employer is obliged to grant an employee two days free from work respectively.[413] Any employment exceeding twelve consecutive days means when considering daily working-hour standards, an extension of weekly working hours beyond the permissible international limits. Referring to the interpretation of the Committee on Article 2 §1 of the Charter, infringing on sixty hours of work per week, deferring in time the utilisation of a day free from work in the week by the worker, is sufficient basis to regard the matter as a breach of Article 2 §5 of the Charter by a Member State.[414] When accepting the deference of a day free from work to the next week, the Committee takes into consideration the sector the worker is employed in. The Committee treats Article 2 §5 of the Charter as a legal basis assisting in the protection of the right to work in safe and hygienic conditions. It attempts to establish whether, for example, reporting to work by an employee for nine consecutive calendar days without the allocation of a rest day during a 60-hour week, which is the practice in the Netherlands, creates a threat to the health of the worker.[415]

The right to a day free from work within the week is utilised by all workers, those employed in full or part-time employment. Based on Article 33 ESC and Article I §2 RESC, authorities of particular Member States have the right to exclude some categories of employment, for example, agricultural or forest workers.[416]

95. The six-day working week protected by Article 2 §5 of the Charter requires the authorities of the Member States to provide employers with one day off work per week. This day should, as far as possible, be coordinated with another day traditionally recognised as a non-working day in the various Member States of the Council of Europe. Therefore, employers may not require employees to work every week or give them days off every other week or even once a month. All of these cases took place in Member States. The cases in France and Hungary are the most interesting.[417]

In the French labour law system, workers were generally considered not to work on Sundays. The problem was that some employees – doctors, for example – were on call on Sundays. Contrary to the legal standards of the Council of Europe, a state

412. Under s. 31 of the Working Hours Act, 'The weekly rest period can be arranged so that it averages 35 hours within a 14-day period, provided that the worker at least enjoys a rest of 24 hours each week. Derogation can be made from the provision of this section if the regular working hours are less than 3 hours per day, when caring for farm animals, and in urgent sowing and harvesting work.'
413. Conclusions XIV-2, p. 387 (Ireland); XIV-2, p. 672 (Spain).
414. Conclusions XIV-2, pp. 668–669 (Spain).
415. Conclusions XIV-2, p. 539.
416. But not domestic staff and seamen. Conclusions XIX, p. 115 (Greece).
417. Conclusions 2022 (France), (Hungary).

of emergency was not regarded as performing work and not a rest from the obligation to perform work. Two collective complaints[418, 419] brought by French trade union organisations against the country's state authorities, made it clear that workers' readiness to work had nothing to do with leisure. For this reason, in the conclusions from 2014, the ECSR clearly stated that from the position of the state authorities and employers, France violated the provisions of Article 2 §1 and §5 of the Charter. Despite the ECSR's clear interpretation of these provisions, the French authorities ignored the ECSR's requests regarding Article 2 §5 of the Charter. For this reason, two trade union centres, the *Confédération générale du travail* (CDT) and the Confédération française de l'encadrement, brought a collective complaint to the ECSR, accusing the French authorities of refusing to amend the provisions of the Labour Code (Articles L.3121-5 and 3121-6). The ECSR therefore considered that the situation remained essentially unchanged and held that there was a violation of Article 2 §5 of the Charter on the ground that on-call periods that are assimilated to rest periods can occur on Sundays.

In the case of Hungary, the ECSR had stated prior to the 2019 report that the employment relations in that country were generally in line with the standards set out in Article 2 §5 of the Charter. The Hungarian state authorities did not inform the ECSR about possible cases in which employees may continue to work for more than twelve days without a day off. There was basically no problem before 1 January 2019. The amended provisions of the Hungarian Labour Code entered into force on this day. Since this change, in cases of non-typical employment, i.e., performing irregular work, employment in continuous systems, consecutive work shifts and seasonal work, employees enjoy one day of rest per month, regardless of the period of work. Shift workers in the metal, automotive, chemical and pharmaceutical industries regularly have to work 18–20 consecutive days without a single day of rest. On this basis, the Committee concluded that the situation in Hungary is not in conformity with Article 2 §5 of the Charter. Therefore, 'there are insufficient safeguards to prevent workers from working for more than twelve consecutive days before being granted a rest period'.

Bosnia and Herzegovina and Slovakia[420] were found to be in non-compliance with Article 2 §5 of the Charter due to protection measures that do not allow employees to take breaks after twelve hours of continuous employment. Workers in North Macedonia[421] were in a similar situation: the weekly breaks could be postponed for more than twelve successive working days. Domestic workers in Greece are in the worst situation as they are not entitled to any breaks at work.[422]

418. Collective Complaint No. 55/2009.
419. Collective Complaint No. 149/2017.
420. Conclusions 2022 (Bosnia and Herzegovina), (Greece), (Slovakia).
421. Conclusions 2022 (North Macedonia).
422. *Ibid.*

VI. To Ensure Workers Are Informed in Writing of the Aspects of the Work Agreement

96. Article 2 §6 of the Charter places the responsibility of providing information in written form on the essential aspects of the work agreement or the working relationship with the employer. The Committee recalls that, under Article 2 §6 of the Charter, workers must be provided with written information covering at least the following essential aspects of employment relations or contracts when starting employment: the identities of the parties; the place of work; the date of commencement of the contractual relationship; in the case of a temporary contract of employment, the expected duration thereof; the periods of notice required in the event of the termination of the contract of employment or the employment relationship; the remuneration; the length of the employee's normal working day or week; where appropriate, a reference to the collective agreements governing the employee's conditions of work.[423] When it does not appear from the report that all essential aspects of the employment or contract, as provided by Article 2 §6 of the Charter, have been presented in writing to the employees, the Committee is compelled to reiterate the question and, in the meantime, finds that the right to information about the employment contract has not been established.[424] The Committee considers that the absence of the required information amounts to a breach of the reporting obligation entered upon by the Member State under the terms of the Charter.[425] The government consequently has an obligation to provide the requested information in the next report on this provision. The provision analysed here does not define these aspects. In the formula dictating the preparation of national reports, the Committee obliges Member States to provide information regarding the source of a country's labour law by which the above obligation has been introduced to the domestic laws of a given Member State.[426] It instructs them to present the content and manner by which the above provision is defined and how it is utilised and practised. The responsibility of providing a worker with the information mentioned in Article 2 §6 of the Charter rests on all employers, both those in the public and in the private sector. There is no exemption from the provision for those employers who have signed a written work agreement with employees. Fulfilling the above-mentioned duty can only be done by Member States that apply administrative penalties and place fines on employers who do not abide by this public and legal obligation.

The appendix to the Revised European Social Charter authorises Member State authorities to exclude employees contracted via atypical work agreements from the legal application of Article 2 §6 of the Charter. Parties can decide upon extinguishing Article 2 §6 of the Charter in cases of provisional employees when the total contracting time does not exceed one month. It is also possible to make such exclusions when employment does not exceed eight hours per week, regardless of whether the

423. Conclusions 2014 (Armenia, Turkey).
424. Conclusions 2014 (Turkey). During the 2018 circle the Committee established that Bosnia and Herzegovina is the last country in Europe that does not require employers to inform employees about this type of obligation under the Charter and national Labour Code. Activity Report 2018, p. 34.
425. Conclusions 2014 (Armenia).
426. Form for the reports in: European Social Charter, *supra*, pp. 308–309.

agreement is made for specified or unspecified periods of time. Exclusions of Article 2 §6 of the Charter concerning the above-mentioned cases need to be approved by the authorities of a given Member State. Objective reasons can justify the exclusions of Article 2 §6 of the Charter in cases of seasonal and irregular workers. Neither the practice of the Committee nor the scant literature on the provision in question allows for examples to be given in any cases of exclusion by Member States or parties to the Revised European Social Charter.[427]

In the last period of the Group 3 (Labour rights), from 1 January 2017 to 21 December 2020, the ECSR examined how high the property benefits (paid leave) are and how much termination of the concluded contract for employees is to be made redundant by employers.[428] The lack of information about such documents, as well as some other unspecified judgments issued in cases concerning employment, justifies the legal groundlessness of some of the employer's activities. According to the ECSR, expressed in the opinion of 2020 issued on the basis of Article 2 §6 of the Charter, therefore, they cannot be accepted as employer's conduct contrary to the Council of Europe law.[429]

VII. Protection of Workers Employed in Night Work

97. Article 2 §7 of the Charter broadens the scope of the application of protection in comparison with the assurance given under Article 8 §4(a) ESC. It obliges Member States to ensure protection for all workers employed in night work, not only for women (as did Article 8 §4(a) ESC). Article 2 §7 extends the protection to men working at night. The original version of this provision (Article 8 §4(a) ESC) was applicable only to female workers employed in industrial occupations at night. Article 2 §7 applies to all workers, regardless of their sex and employer.

Article 2 §7 does not give a legal definition of the period of night. The Charter leaves this matter to be regulated by Member States. Therefore a night period is regarded by Article 2 §7 of the Charter as night-time as determined by national labour law regulations. The Committee recalls that Article 2 §7 guarantees compensatory measures for persons performing night work. National law or practice must define 'night' within the context of this provision. Measures which take account of the special nature of the night work must at least include the following: regular medical examinations, including a check prior to employment in night work; the provision of possibilities for transfer to daytime work; continuous consultation with workers' representatives on the introduction of night work, on night work conditions and on measures taken to reconcile the needs of workers with the special

427. However, in 2010 the Committee concludes that the situation in Moldova is not in conformity with Art. 2 §6 of the RESC on the grounds that it has not been established that the right to information on the employment contract is guaranteed in Moldova. Conclusions 2010, vol. 2, p. 415.
428. Conclusions 2022 (Armenia).
429. Conclusions 2022 (Serbia).

nature of night work. For all of the above-mentioned reasons, as of 2014, the Committee considered that the situation in Ukraine was not in conformity with the Charter.[430] Three other countries, Andorra, Bosnia and Herzegovina, and Georgia, face problems with the obligation to perform a medical check-up of night workers. The Committee notes that there is no provision in the domestic laws for workers assigned to night work to be given a medical check-up prior to taking up their duties or regular check-ups thereafter.[431] According to the Committee, failure to comply with the obligation to conduct systematic medical examinations of workers employed at night is a basic premise for non-compliance by a Member State which ratified Article 2 §7.[432] The Committee has asked whether night work is deemed to systematically require preliminary and periodical medical examinations and whether regular examinations are carried out in practice.[433] The Community has also asked whether the law provides for continuous consultation with workers' representatives about the introduction of night work, about night work conditions, and about measures taken to reconcile the needs of workers with the special nature of night work.[434] Since it has not been established that night workers are effectively subject to compulsory regular medical examining of all workers about to take up night jobs, with regard to night work conditions and the measures taken to reconcile the needs of workers with the special nature of night work, the Committee concludes that the situation in all of the above-mentioned Member States is not in conformity with Article 2 §7 of the Charter. Assuming that work during nighttime involves an extra burden for workers, Article 2 §7 obliges Member States to ensure all those working at night to have proper resources according to the nature of work carried out during night hours. In a form drawn up by the Committee, which is used by Member States for the preparation of reports on abiding Charter regulations, there are examples of measures that can be used in order to minimise the burden of nighttime work. These are as follows: additional breaks, additional holidays with

---

430. Conclusions 2014. The report submitted in 2016 provides no new information but describes the operation of shift work which includes night shifts. The Committee considers that there must also be the possibility to transferring to daytime work on a more permanent basis and since no such possibilities appear to be provided for, it holds that the situation in Ukraine is in breach with the Charter.
431. Conclusions 2014 (Andorra).
432. Andorra, Bosnia and Herzegovina, Georgia, Republic of Moldova, Serbia, Ukraine. Activity Report, p. 34.
433. Conclusions 2014 (Georgia, Bosnia and Herzegovina). The Georgian next report refers to the regulation of night work, in particular Art. 18 of the Labour Code on obligatory periodical medical examination at the cost of the employer. The report once again does not indicate whether and to what extent night workers are subject to regular medical examination. Conclusions 2016, p. 285.
434. Conclusions 2014 (Georgia). With respect to continuous consultation with worker representatives on night work conditions and measures taken to reconcile the needs for workers with the special nature of night work, the Ukrainian report examined in 2016 merely states that national legislation does not define night workers as a separate category. In this basis the Committee's understands that there is no provision for regular and systematic consultation with workers' representatives on night work-related questions at the situation is therefore in breach of the Charter.

pay, frequent medical check-ups,[435] possibility of utilising facilities such as rooms for resting used during breaks and conditions allowing nighttime work to be done during day hours.[436]

In several cases mentioned by the ECSC on 22 March 20023, during the public presentation and interpretation of the Council of Europe's standards in labour matters, attention was paid to the protection of work performed at night by both women and men. Employers are obliged to define night and day work, to make job candidates and employees aware of the different conditions of each and to present their advantages and disadvantages.[437] All night workers – regardless of gender or the employer – should be able to request, for any reason, particularly health reasons, a transfer from night work to day work.[438] All employees are subject to medical examinations, while night workers are subject to specific mandatory medical examinations.[439] Individuals who work at night are obliged to undergo regular medical examinations organised at the workplace.[440] These tests should be performed regularly. A certain novelty is the legal regulations, according to which employers are obliged to consult with social representatives of employees on all issues related to the conditions of employment at night. This requirement was introduced in order to meet the needs of employees and with a view to determining the specific requirements that should be reported to the employer in order to protect the interests of all persons working at night.[441] The consultations should be carried out regularly by the social partners, i.e., representatives of the employees and their trade unions, as well as the employers themselves. If the consultations do not take place, the ECSR is authorised to issue a decision of non-compliance with the standards set out in Article 2 §7 of the Charter.[442]

§4. The Right to Safe and Healthy Working Conditions

98. Member States have been obliged to undertake all measures in order to protect the health and lives of employees. Article 3 of the Charter ensures all persons employed in work, regardless of whether it is a work agreement or self-employment,[443] have the right to physical and psychological integrity at work.[444] The Committee accepted a broader definition of the 'worker'. The European Social Charter obliges Member States to legislate provisions concerning safe and healthy working conditions, to ensure means of control and to consult stakeholders in order to improve the level of health and safety in the workplace. As early as during the

435. There is no provision in the national labour legislation for a compulsory medical examination for persons about to take up night work in Ukraine. Conclusions 2010, vol. 2, p. 621.
436. Form for the reports in European Social Charter, *supra*, p. 311.
437. Conclusions 2022 (Bosnia and Herzegovina).
438. Conclusions 2022 (Albania), (Serbia).
439. Conclusions 2022 (Albania), (Andorra).
440. Conclusions 2022 (Albania), (Bosnia and Herzegovina).
441. Conclusions 2022 (Albania), (Georgia), (Serbia).
442. Conclusions 2022 (Ireland), (Italy), (North Macedonia).
443. Conclusions I, p. 8; Conclusions XIV-2, p. 38.
444. Conclusions XIV-2, p. 36.

first supervisory cycle of the abiding Charter regulations by Member States, the Committee stated that a country which committed itself to follow requirements of Article 3 ESC should prove it had legislated provisions concerning health and safety in the workplace. The application of these provisions is of a general nature and relates to all sectors of the economy, trade, services and others[445] where entrepreneurs employ workers. Government work inspectors execute such provisions effectively. They are authorised to sanction accordingly through the legal civil code and to administer penalties. State authorities initiate and lead consultations with workers' representatives and workers' organisations concerning the protection of workers' health within the workplace.[446] Fulfilling the three obligations named in Article 3 of the Charter means ensuring that work conditions are safe and hygienic for the worker. Under Article 3 §1 of the Charter, the Committee examines: (1) the general objectives of an occupational health and safety policy; (2) the organisation of occupational risk prevention; (3) the improvement of occupational safety and health; (4) consultations with employers' and workers' organisations. Paragraph 2 of this article requires that Member States issue health and safety regulations providing for preventive and protective measures against most of the risks recognised by specialists and laid down in EU and international regulations and standards. These regulations have to be specific in that they must set out rules in sufficient detail for them to be applied properly and efficiently.[447] They must also cover the majority of the risks listed in Conclusions XIV-2.[448] All workers, all places of work, and all sectors of activity must be covered by the applicable legislation and regulations on health and safety at work.[449] The Committee concludes that the situation in Albania and in the Republic of Moldova is not in conformity with Article 3 §2 of the Charter on the grounds that the health and safety legislation and regulations do not specifically cover the majority of the risks related to hazardous substances and agents: in particular, asbestos and ionising radiation.[450] It also concludes that self-employed workers (entrepreneurs, farmers, craft workers on construction sites), temporary workers, domestic workers, and workers on fixed-term contracts are not adequately protected.[451] Preventive measures ought to protect employees, workers and the self-employed against industrial injury and occupational diseases. In 2013, it was noted that no data had been provided in the Greek report and that important problems of under-reporting exist in this domain. The Committee notes that the report does not provide pertinent figures or statistics on the number of occupational diseases involved. It, therefore, considers that during the reference period, occupational diseases were not adequately monitored.

445. Conclusions II, p. 12.
446. Conclusions I, p. 22.
447. Conclusions XIV-2 (Norway).
448. Statement of interpretation on Art. 3 §1, p. 36–43.
449. Conclusions II, Observations on Art. 3, p. 12.
450. Conclusions 2013 (Albania, Republic of Moldova, Ukraine).
451. Conclusions 2013: Andorra, Austria, France (workers which do not work under an employer's authority), Hungary, Republic of Moldova, Ukraine (self-employed workers); Slovak Republic (temporary workers); Hungary, Romania (domestic workers).

I. According to the European Social Charter

A. *The Responsibility to Issue Regulations Dealing with Health and Safety at Work*

99. The scope of the above provision is general. It encompasses the following economic spheres: industry, mines (mining industry),[452] trade, transport (road,[453] rail, sea[454] and air), and agriculture.[455] Authorities of Member States have the obligation to regulate, according to law, safety and health matters within the workplace in the above-mentioned sectors. Article 3 §1 ESC is not of a standard which is considered as 'dynamic'. The Charter does not oblige Member States to regulate safety and health at work to a higher or more effective level. It does not dictate raising the level of protection of health. Considering the constant threats against the safety and health of workers, the Committee came to the conclusion that the process of regulating safety and health at work according to the law is a continuous process. The authorities of Member States are obliged to systematically review provisions concerning the protection of workers' health, as well as upgrade them. During supervisory cycles, Member State authorities should meet the obligation of proving that domestic regulations on health and safety issues are kept up to date.[456] The Committee, when evaluating whether this obligation is met, will demand statistical data concerning work accidents and occupational diseases. It is up to the Member State to establish that there is an occupational health and safety policy in conformity with the Charter. The Committee demands that reports provide information on the policy's content and goals: in particular, the extent to which it is consistent with the EU strategy on health and safety at work and whether it is intended to foster and preserve a culture of prevention in the occupational health and safety field. It also wishes to know whether the Member State re-appraises the existing policies in light of new risks. The Committee demands that reports contain information on the organisation of the assessment of work-related risks, the determination of appropriate preventive measures (taking account of the nature of risks concerned), and the provision of information and training of employees within the workplace. It also asks that reports contain information on the labour inspectorate's role in developing an occupational health and safety culture among employers and employees and in the sharing of any knowledge about occupational hazards and prevention it acquires during inspection activities in the form of practical instructions, prevention measures and advice.

Cases violating Article 3 §1 discovered by the Committee concern no adequate protection for domestic workers,[457] agricultural workers and their families,[458]

452. Oil rig platforms on the sea. Conclusions XII-1, p. 81 (United Kingdom).
453. Conclusions III, p. 18 (Ireland).
454. Conclusions XI-2, p. 61 (Italy).
455. Conclusions I, p. 22.
456. Conclusions III, p. 17.
457. Cyprus – Conclusions 2007, vol. 1, p. 324, Conclusions 2009, p. 188; Romania – Conclusions 2007, vol. 2, p. 960, Conclusions 2009, vol. 2, p. 686, Conclusions XIX-2 (2009), p. 244 (Hungary).
458. Addendum to Conclusions XI-2, p. 14.

self-employed persons and temporary workers,[459] and cottage industry workers.[460] The Committee is unable to conclude that there is an occupational health and safety policy in conformity with the EU standards. It notes the existence of a system for gathering and managing data on occupational accidents and diseases as well as protection and monitoring plans in certain sectors (agricultural and construction). However, it also notes that the system for licensing undertakings in occupational health and safety matters and standardised procedures for assessing specific risks in undertakings with less than ten employees were not in force during the reference period.[461] It requests that examples be given of the practical application of risk-assessment measures, preventive measures geared to the nature of risks, and training and information measures for agricultural sector workers. It also asks for details about how many committees on occupational health and safety have been set up in practice, how often external protection and prevention services have been used, and the conditions in which employers themselves perform the tasks of the protection and prevention services. It also would like to know the number of employers involved in drawing up annual safety plans in practice.[462] The Committee notes Albania's efforts to establish and implement a national policy on occupational health and safety. In view of the recent adoption of legislation on health and safety at work, the Committee considers that it will be possible to assess the impact and trend of general policy only during the next cycle and asks for information in the next report on any new developments which occur during the reference period. It also requests additional information on the way the general policy is updated in light of changing risks.[463] The Committee concludes that the situation in Italy, Armenia, and Malta is not in conformity with Article 3 §1 of the Charter on the grounds that there is no appropriate occupational safety and health policy.[464]

As far as organisation and occupational risk prevention are concerned, the Committee concludes that there is no adequate system for organising occupational risk prevention in Italy or the Republic of Moldova.[465]

Conclusions 2017 of the European Committee of Social Rights were adopted in 2017[466] in twenty-five Member States. Out of the twenty-five Member States that ratified Article 3 of the Charter, only two (Finland and FYROM, now North Macedonia) did not receive a negative conclusion. One ought to remember that the right to work in a safe and hygienic environment is one of the most important human

459. Conclusions XIII-3, pp. 205–206 (Italy); XIII-3, pp. 206–207 (The Netherlands); XIV-2, pp. 429–430 (Italy); XIII-4, p. 342 (Belgium); XIV-2, pp. 333 et seq. (Greece). Conclusions 2007, vol. 1, p. 364 (Estonia), vol. 2, p. 677 (Italy), p. 811 (Lithuania), p. 960 (Romania); Conclusions 2009, vol. 1, p. 24 (Albania), p. 294 (France); Conclusions 2009, vol. 2, p. 529 (Moldova), p. 686 (Romania). Conclusions XIX-2 (2009), p. 24 (Austria), p. 170 (Germany), p. 416 (Spain).
460. Conclusions XIV-2. p. 123–124.
461. Conclusions 2013 (Italy).
462. Conclusions 2013 (Republic of Moldova).
463. Conclusions 2013 (Albania).
464. Conclusions 2013 (Italy, Armenia, Malta).
465. Conclusions 2013 (Italy, Republic of Moldova).
466. Albania, Andorra, Armenia, Austria, Azerbaijan, Belgium, Bosnia and Herzegovina, Bulgaria, Estonia, Finland, France, Georgia, Hungary, Ireland, Italy, Latvia, Lithuania, Malta, the Republic of Moldova, Montenegro, Portugal, Romania, Russian Federation, Serbia, Slovak Republic, Slovenia, 'the former Yugoslav Republic of Macedonia', now North Macedonia, Turkey and Ukraine.

rights. It is analysed in the thematic group on the right to social security. In 2017, in the above group of countries, the Committee found 175 cases of violations of health protection, safety of employees and social protection. Article 3 §1 ESC = Article 3§2 RESC – Safety and health regulations. The main criteria used by the ECSR to assess compliance with Article 3 §2 of the Charter, which also applies to Article 3 §1 of the 1961 Charter, are as follows.[467]

The right of every worker to a safe and healthy working environment is a 'widely recognised principle, stemming directly from the right to personal integrity, one of the fundamental principles of human rights'. The purpose of Article 3 is thus directly related to that of Article 2 of the ECHR, which recognises the right to life. It applies to the whole economy, covering both the public and private sectors. With regard to Article 3 §2 of the Charter (3§1 of the 1961 Charter), the determination and implementation of an occupational safety and health policy must be based on a precise legal framework. Risks must be covered by the legal framework. States Parties' first obligation under Article 3 is to ensure the right to safe and healthy working standards of the highest possible level. Under §2, this obligation entails issuing safety and health regulations providing for preventive and protective measures against workplace risks recognised by the scientific and lay communities. The Charter does not actually define the risks to be regulated. Supervision takes an indirect form, referring to international technical occupational health and safety standards such as the ILO Conventions and EU Directives on health and safety at work. Domestic law must include framework legislation – often the Labour Code – setting out employers' responsibilities and the workers' rights and duties, as well as specific regulations. In view of the particularly variable nature of the subject matter in light of technological, ergonomic and medical advances, existing regulations must be geared to new circumstances where the rules prove to be out of keeping with the situation.

During its examination, the ECSR is based on the catalogue of risks which contains four groups of risks: (1) Psychosocial risks. The legal framework should cover work-related stress, aggression and violence. (2) Establishment, alteration and upkeep of workplaces – work equipment – workplaces and equipment, particularly the protection of machines, manual handling of loads, work with display screen equipment; hygiene (shops and offices); maximum weight; air pollution, noise and vibration; personal protective equipment; safety and/or health signs at work. (3) Hazardous agents and substances – chemical, physical and biological agents, particularly carcinogens, including white lead (in paint), benzene, asbestos, vinyl chloride monomer, metallic lead and its ionic compounds and ionising radiation; control of major accident hazards involving dangerous substances. (4) Sectoral risks – indication of weight on packages to be transported by boat; protection of dockers against accidents; dock handling; building safety rules, temporary or mobile construction sites; mines, extractive industries using drilling and opencast or underground mining; ships and fishing vessels; prevention of major industrial accidents; agriculture; transport. The ECSR also examines levels of prevention and protection.

467. Strasbourg, 31 Jan. 2019, GC(2018)24, European Social Charter Governmental Committee Report Concerning Conclusions 2017 of the European Social Charter (revised), GC (2018)24, pp. 33 ff.

Limits must be aligned with those adopted in the above-mentioned international reference standards. A state party has satisfied this general requirement if it has transposed most of the *acquis communautaire* on occupational safety and health into its domestic legislation. In sectors of activity in which the acquis is incomplete, e.g., in shipping or fishing, main international standards are offered by the ILO conventions.

The Secretariat of the European Social Charter recalls that States Parties are required to pay particular attention with regard to asbestos and ionising radiation, producing evidence that workers are protected up to a level at least equivalent to that set by international reference standards.

With regard to protection against asbestos, the international reference standards, which determine minimum exposure limit values to be implemented at national level, are ILO Asbestos Convention No. 162 (1986), Rotterdam Convention (2004) and Council Directive 83/477/EEC of 19 September 1983 on the protection of workers from the risks related to exposure to asbestos at work, but since it was repelled, Directive 2009/148/EC of the Parliament and the Council of 30 November 2009 that fixes a single limit value for all fibres, reduced to 0.1 fibres/cm^3. The exposure limit values must be reviewed and updated in light of technological progress and development in technical and scientific knowledge.

As for the protection against ionising radiations, national standards must take account of Recommendation No. 103 made in 2007 by the International Commission on Radiological Protection (ICRP, Publication No. 103), relating in particular to maximum doses of exposure in the workplace but also to persons who, although not directly assigned to work in a radioactive environment, may be exposed to radiation occasionally. The transposition into domestic law of Council Directive 2013/59/Euratom of 5 December 2013, laying down basic safety standards for protection against the dangers arising from exposure to ionising radiation, and repealing some Directives is sufficient as this Directive takes up the ICRP's recommendations. Where applicable, the transposition of legislation complementing Council Directive 2013/59/Euratom in some sectors of activity or some situations, i.e., Council Directive 2006/117/Euratom of 20 November 2006 on the supervision and control of shipments of radioactive waste and spent fuel and Council Directive 2009/71/Euratom of 25 June 2009 establishing a Community framework for the nuclear safety of nuclear installations are also examined.

With regard to the personal scope of laws and regulations, the ESCR stressed that all workers, all workplaces and all sectors of activity must be covered by occupational safety and health regulations.

The term ‘workers’ used in Article 3 covers both employed and self-employed persons, especially as the latter are often employed in high-risk sectors. The aim is to ensure that the working environment is safe and healthy for all operators, where necessary, by adopting rules adapted to the operators’ specific situation.

The protection of interim, temporary, seasonal workers and those on fixed-term contracts, without necessarily being specific, must take the exposure to dangerous agents and substances accumulated with several successive employments into account in order to avoid any discrimination in respect of occupational safety and health with permanent workers. If needed, regulations must prohibit the hiring of temporary workers for some particularly dangerous activities. In this regard, the implementation of international reference standards in the field is examined: ILO Fee-charging Employment Agencies Convention No. 96 (1949) and Private Employment Agencies Convention No. 181 (1997); and some EU directives. The ESCR also examines obligations under regulations benefitting temporary workers on medical checks, information and training in occupational safety and health matters upon recruitment, transfer or the introduction of new technology, as well as the representation of these workers in occupational safety and health matters, and even measures adopted to reduce the high incidence of occupational accidents suffered by these workers.

The Secretariat of the European Social Charter specified that all economic sectors must be covered by the regulations. It is not necessary for a specific text to be adopted for each activity or sector, but the wording of texts should be sufficiently precise to allow their effective application in all sectors, taking particular account of the scale of or degree of danger in each sector. Sectors must be covered in their entirety, and all companies must be covered regardless of the number of employees. No workplace can be 'exempted' from the application of health and safety rules. Workers employed on residential premises, i.e., domestic staff and home workers, must therefore be covered, but the rules may be adapted to the type of activity and the relatively risk-free nature of these workers' occupations and be worded in general terms.

Independent workers who intervene in several workplaces must suffer no discrimination in occupational safety and health matters, as compared to wage-earning workers or civil servants, and hence must also be covered by the regulations. The duty to provide for regulations goes beyond the prevention, training and medical supervision policies advocated by Council Recommendation No. 2003/134/EC of 18 February 2003. High figures on independent workers may be a factor to be taken into account.

To comply with the provisions of Article 3 §2, States Parties must specifically cover most of the risks listed and examine measures taken by public authorities to protect workers against work-related stress, aggression and violence specific to work performed under atypical working relationships in examining the personal scope of occupational safety and health regulations.

The Secretariat of the European Committee of Social Rights also recalled that regulations must be drawn up in consultation with employers' and workers' organisations. Consultation goes beyond mere tripartite – public authorities, employers' and workers' organisations – cooperation in the search for ways to improve the working conditions and environment in general, and includes the coordination of their actions and the cooperation in the drafting of laws and regulations at all levels and in all sectors. In this fragment of deliberations on the protection of the rights of employees and self-employed persons to work in safe and hygienic conditions, the cases collected by the Secretariat of the Committee of the European Social Charter and the negative conclusions of the members of this Committee were used.[468] In the latter case, the content of the conclusions is not quoted in this monograph; only their meaning is quoted because, in many cases, the above conclusions were repeated in terms of their content.

468. *Ibid*., pp. 141 ff.

B. Obligation to Provide for the Enforcement of Such Regulations by Measures of Supervision

100. The above provision of the Charter obliges Member States to organise a system of supervision and control, as well as the enforcement of the regulations of the Charter. The Committee assumed that violating provisions of Article 3 §1 of the Charter, namely not fulfilling the duty of issuing safety and health regulations, automatically leads to violating the duty of Article 3 §2 ESC. This is logical because it is impossible to control employers abiding by non-existing safety and health regulations. Fulfilling the duty of Article 3 §1 ESC can be legally deduced by checking whether the provision of Article 3 §2 ESC was enforced by applying the relevant civil, administrative and penalty sanctions.[469] The relation between the provisions of Article 3 §1 and §2 ESC can be seen in the obligation to ensure a means of control over health and safety regulations that should be legislated under Article 3 §1 of the Charter. Article 3 §2 uses the term 'such regulations' (*ces règlements*). This expression refers to the health and safety regulations listed in Article 3 §1 of the Charter.[470] The responsibility of the governmental work inspections is the supervising of employers and whether they are meeting safety and health regulations. It is therefore not possible to accept the Committee's stance, which during the fourteenth supervisory cycle came to the conclusion that there is no direct link between Article 3 §1 and §2 of the Charter supporting the decisions that are handed down according to the provisions and that each section of the provision makes its own demands which should be undertaken irrespectively of each other.[471] Article 3 §2 of the Charter places on Member States the obligation to develop a sound national policy on health and safety,[472] to maintain controlling mechanisms with strict labour law regulations, to enforce the protection of health, and to guarantee safety and hygiene at the workplace.[473] In order to establish the level of the effectiveness of such control mechanisms, the Committee demands authorities of Member States provide information concerning the number of workplaces, the number of work inspectors, the frequency of governmental work inspections being carried out dealing with the safety and health of the working conditions within the workplace, the number of safety and health regulation violations taking place, the amount and type of penalties being enforced on employers not abiding by the said provisions.[474]

In the case of Portugal from 1996, governmental work inspectors undertook the supervision of a workplace in which only 6% of the workforce was employed; it was decided that there was a breach of Article 3 §2 of the Charter by Portugal.[475] A negative ruling was also made against Ireland, where there was desistence of

469. Conclusions I, p. 23.
470. Conclusions XII-1, p. 83, Conclusions XIII-3, p. 209 (Greece), XIII-3, p. 212 (The Netherlands).
471. Conclusions XIV-2, p. 43.
472. Lack of such policy was detected by the Committee in Albania, Italy and Romania. Conclusions 2009, vol. 1, p. 23 (Albania), pp. 399–400, pp. 683–684 (Romania).
473. Conclusions XX-2 and 2013 (Moldova).
474. Conclusions VIII, pp. 54–55.
475. Conclusions XIV-2, pp. 641–642.

supervision, meaning to monitor compliance with safety and health regulations within the agricultural production sector and only sporadic monitoring of small places of work.[476]

The number of controls taking place and the number of workers employed in sectors monitored by work inspectors, along with the number of workers of governmental inspectors, allows the Committee to establish the effectiveness of such control monitoring safety and health regulations.

101. The objective criteria in analysing the effectiveness of abiding by safety and health regulations by Member States are mentioned earlier by the number of accidents or work-related illnesses taking place.[477] The Committee notes the accident rate, as indicated by the number of accidents per 100 workers. It utilises the statistics entailed in the national reports as well as ILO information regarding accidents within the workplace and information provided by the EU.[478]

Analysing the reports filed during the fourteenth supervisory cycle by the Portuguese authorities, the Committee claimed that compared to the previous year, in 1996, the number of accidents occurring within the workplace increased. The rate of accidents also increased (from 3.5 per 100 workers in 1995 to 4.8 per 100 workers in 1996). In the mid-1990s, in Portugal, there was an increase in work-related accidents as opposed to the normal trend of a decrease.[479] The Committee demanded of the Portuguese authorities additional information concerning the reasons for the increase in accidents. Analysing the situation from an EU perspective, the Committee claimed that the highest number of work-related accidents per 100,000 inhabitants was in Portugal.[480] It, therefore, pointed out to the Portuguese authorities that the ratification of Article 3 of the Charter meant the acceptance of an obligation to ensure safe and healthy working conditions. The above-mentioned obligation should be fulfilled by utilising well-organised work safety and health services.

102. The obligation of authorities of Member States is to organise and support governmental (labour) work inspections, an institution called to supervise whether employers are following the safety and health regulations within the workplace across all the sectors of the economy. The Committee placed an obligation on the authorities of Member States to provide the Committee with regular information

476. Conclusions X-2, p. 56.
477. Due to the high number of occupational accidents the Committee concluded that the situation in France, Ireland and in Slovenia is not in conformity with Art. 3 §3 of the RESC. Conclusions 2007, vol. 1, p. 534 (France), vol. 2, p. 599 (Ireland), p. 1004 (Ireland). In 2009 manifestly high number of fatal occupational accidents was detected in: Bulgaria, Moldova, Portugal, and Slovenia. Conclusions 2009, vol. 1, p. 157 (Bulgaria), vol. 531 (Moldova), p. 644 (Portugal), p. 721 (Slovenia). In Romania, statistics on occupational accidents were considered 'not reliable'. Conclusions 2009, vol. 2, p. 689.
478. Eurostat, Accidents at work in European Union in 1994, Statistics in focus, Population and Social Conditions, 1998; *ILO Yearbook of Labour Statistics*, 1997.
479. In 1990, the rate of accidents was 6.4 per 100 workers. By 1995, it was 3.5.
480. The average of the highest number of accidents at work in Europe was 7,361, whereas the average in Portugal was 4,539. Conclusions XIV-2, pp. 639–640.

concerning the structure of governmental work inspections, the number of inspectors employed, as well as information concerning their competence. Testing the competency of work inspectors across particular Member States, the Committee decided that inspectors have been qualified to directly enforce the following within the majority of national labour law systems: fines, placing administrative penalties, temporarily stopping the work of a business if the work is being carried out against the safety and health regulations, and closing down a place of work.[481] In the mind of the Committee, the supervisory monitoring of whether safety and health regulations within the workplace are being met should be effective. It was not the case in the following Member States: Albania, Italy, Malta, Moldova, and Ukraine.[482]

In 2013, the Committee concluded that labour inspectors should share their knowledge of risk and risk prevention gained in light of their inspection experience and as part of their preventive activities. It noted the involvement of public authorities in the improvement of occupational health and safety through awareness-raising activities, publications and seminars. It asked for information on the training of qualified professionals, the design of training modules and existing certification schemes. It also requested the involvement of scientific institutions in research, applied research and technical knowledge pertaining to occupational health and safety issues.[483] In 2017, the Committee found the following shortcomings in compliance with the standards set by the European Committee of Social Rights by the following Member States which ratified the provisions of Article 3 §1 and §2 of the revised European Social Charter: **Article 3 §1 RESC** ***Armeni**a*: there is no clearly defined policy on occupational health and safety. Slovak Republic: (1) it has not been established that there is an adequate occupational health and safety policy; (2) it has not been established that occupational risk prevention is organised at company level, work-related risk is assessed, and preventive measures geared to the nature of risks are adopted; (3) it has not been established that the national policy on health and safety includes training, information, quality assurance and research in a satisfactory manner. **Article 3 §2 RESC:**

Albania: (1) public authorities are not involved in research relating to occupational health and safety; (2) employers' and employees' organisations are not being consulted by public authorities in practice.

Andorra: (1) the health and safety legislation and regulations do not specifically cover a majority of risks; (2) the level of protection against asbestos and ionising radiation is insufficient; (3) self-employed workers are not adequately protected.

France: certain categories of self-employed workers are not sufficiently covered by occupational health and safety regulations.

Hungary: self-employed and domestic workers, as well as other categories of workers, are not protected by occupational health and safety regulations.

Montenegro: (1) it has not been established that levels of protection required by the legislation and regulations in relation to the establishment, alteration and upkeep of workplaces are in line with the level set up by international reference standards;

481. Conclusions XIII-1, pp. 92–93.
482. Conclusions 2009, vol. 1, p. 25 (Albania), p. 404 (Italy), vol. 2, p. 490 (Malta), p. 531 (Moldova).
483. Conclusions 2013 (Malta).

(2) it has not been established that levels of protection against asbestos and ionising radiation are adequate; (3) domestic workers are not protected by occupational health and safety regulations.

Republic of Moldova: (1) it has not been established that levels of prevention and protection required by the legislation and regulations in relation to the establishment, alteration and upkeep of workplaces are in line with the level set by international reference standards; (2) self-employed workers are not covered by occupational health and safety legislation.

Ukraine: the coverage of occupational hazards by specific occupational health and safety legislation and regulations is insufficient.

Romania: domestic workers are not covered by occupational health and safety regulations.

Serbia: (1) it has been established that the level of protection against ionising radiation is adequate; (2) domestic workers are not covered by occupational health and safety.

C. *To Ensure Consultation with Stakeholders in Matters of Industrial Health and Safety*

103. Authorities of Member States have an obligation to provide consultations with workers‘ and employers‘ organisations on measures intended to improve industrial health and safety. Consultations should be provided ‘when necessary’. The above provision encompasses the regulation of rights, principles and procedures of consultations in matters of the health and life protection of the workers. It obliges the authorities of Member States to initiate consultations as well as to take note of the reported conclusions provided by workers’ and employers’ organisations interested in undertaking such consultations.[484] Independent authorities of Member States do not, therefore, decide on the necessity of such consultations. The analysed provision requires the authorities of Member States to participate in such consultations, but stakeholders do not have this obligation. However, with technological processes, when such decisions are being made concerning the improvement of industrial health and safety, stakeholders should really take part in the process. For this reason, the Committee requires that information from the authorities of Member States should encompass the scope and frequency of such consultations taking place between state authorities and stakeholders.[485] Consultations in such matters should be regularly carried out[486] at a national level within particular workplaces.[487] The Committee did not demand information be provided dealing with regional consultations. Consultations dealing with the improvement of industrial safety and health should reach the majority of workplaces. The Committee takes

484. Conclusions I, p. 24.
485. Conclusions V, p. 23; Addendum to Conclusions XI-2, p. 15 (Ireland); Conclusions XIII-1, p. 103 (Ireland); XIII-1, p. 259 (Portugal); Addendum to Conclusions XIII-3, p. 29 (Luxembourg).
486. Addendum to Conclusions XI-2, p. 15 (Ireland).
487. Conclusions XIV-2, pp. 46 et seq.

into consideration that, according to some national labour law systems, appointing workers' representatives is dependent on the number of workers employed.

If the minimum standard of employment is established at too high a level, as it occurred in Greece, where workers' committees for industrial health and safety (EYAE) were only to be called upon from industries where at least 150 workers were employed, the responsibility of leading such consultations with stakeholders may be conducted within certain industries.[488]

The Committee, during its fourteenth supervisory cycle, addressed the Member States of the EU and of the European Economic Area, abiding by Article 3 of the Charter (Denmark, Finland, the Netherlands, Norway, Sweden, Italy) a question regarding changes brought about by implementing into domestic legal regulations the obligation of consultancy with workers' representatives with regard to measures employed to improve the level of health and safety standards.[489] During the following supervisory cycles, the Committee did not recognise any violation of the obligation to consult with workers' representatives with regard to measures employed to improve the level of health and safety standards by Member States. Ensuring this obligation, which does not require employers to allow workers' representatives into a decision-making process on a partner level, creates no obstacles for Member States. The scope of rights for workers' representatives to obtain information on matters of health and safety within the workplace has been broadened by Article 2 §3 of the Additional Protocol (currently Articles 21 and 22 of the Revised European Social Charter). The Committee considers that the information provided by the Member States on the role of the Occupational Health and Safety Commission within the National Labour Council in promoting cooperation at all levels and on the actions thereof establishes the setting up of health and safety committees within undertakings, these being consultative guides purporting to convene employers and workers for the evaluation and prevention of occupational hazards, which employers are required to consult at regular intervals. It considers that such information does not suffice to establish that the social partners are consulted by public authorities in practice. It asks that detailed information on the matter of consultation (bodies, jurisdiction, participants, frequency of meetings, subject dealt with) be provided. It also demands information on the setup and the consultation of health and safety committees in practice.[490] It concludes that it has not been established that employers' and employees' organisations are being consulted by public authorities.

II. According to the Revised European Social Charter

104. The Revised European Social Charter broadens the scope of consultation that Member State authorities should carry out with stakeholders. Subject to these, consultations cannot be limited to improving the level of health and safety (Article 3 §3 ESC), but they should also deal with all actions undertaken in order to ensure

488. *Ibid.*, p. 48.
489. Conclusions XIV-2, pp. 48–49.
490. Conclusions 2013 (Albania).

the efficient execution of the right to healthy and safe working conditions. Countries parties to the Revised European Social Charter, in consultation with stakeholders, commit themselves to:

(a) determining, executing and inspecting national policies concerning safety, workers' health and work environment. These policies should set their most important goal at improving occupational safety and health as well as preventing work accidents and health hazards resulting from work, related to work or occurring in the workplace. It should be implemented first of all by minimising the reasons for workers' health and life threats deriving from the work environment;
(b) legislating provisions concerning occupational health and safety;
(c) ensuring enforcement of these provisions;
(d) supporting of gradual development of occupational health services accessible for all employed persons.[491] They are meant to provide employees with advisory and preventive services.

The Committee recalls that State Parties have a duty to provide precise information on developments in respect of occupational accidents and that when assessing respect for the rights enshrined in Article 3 §3 of the Charter, the number and frequency of occupational accidents and their trends are decisive factors. It asks that the next report explain the disparity between the number of accidents indicated in the reports and those published by other international and European sources (ILOSTAT, EUROSTAT).[492] It examines the legal context and the function of the Labour Inspectorates and notes that the reports provide no updated information on activities and resources of the labour inspection during the reference period.[493] It asks that the new report provide detailed information (competence, number of inspection staff, enforcement powers, imposed penalties of the state inspection, internal bodies of supervision, central and regional authorities and local self-government bodies, specialist authority of supervision, occupational safety services, occupational safety commissions, trade unions). It also asks for figures, year by year and limited to offences pertaining to occupational health and safety legislation and regulations, on the number of workers covered by labour inspections, the overall budget of the state labour inspectorates, their overall staff, and any administrative penalties other than fines.[494] Recalling that the report must provide full, up-to-date information on changes in the legislation and regulations during the reference period, the Committee asks that information be provided about the labour inspection system, its activity and resources, the public authorities vested with labour inspection powers, its development, and how these public authorities coordinate in practice to make labour inspection effective.[495] The Committee remarks that due to the low level of material and human resources in the labour inspectorate,

491. Conclusions XX-2 and 2013 (Albania, Belgium, Netherlands, Ukraine).
492. Conclusions 2013 (Bulgaria, Lithuania, Luxembourg, Russian Federation).
493. Conclusions 2013 (Bulgaria, Russian Federation, Ukraine).
494. Conclusions 2013 (Russian Federation).
495. Conclusions 2013 (Bulgaria).

the fact that the law entrusts the investigation of most occupational accidents to employees, and the low level of administrative fines, it cannot be concluded that the labour inspection system is efficient. The Committee asks that the next report provide information on the following points: (1) any change in the general framework of labour inspection activities during the reference period; (2) the number, while distinguishing clearly between administrative staff and inspection staff, of inspectors assigned to supervising the application of the legislation and regulations on occupational health and safety; (3) the number of general, thematic and unscheduled inspection visits assigned solely to the occupational health and safety legislation and regulations; (4) the regulations of the labour inspectorate, and their application in practice, through the country; (5) details, by category, of administrative measures that labour inspectors are entitled to take and, for each category, the number of such measures actually taken; (6) the outcome of cases referred to the prosecution authorities with a view to initiating criminal proceedings; (7) figures for each year of the reference period.[496] In several countries, the Committee notes that the figures for the number of fatal accidents are either manifestly high[497] or extremely low compared to other state parties.[498] In both cases, it takes it as a sign that the measures to reduce the excessive rate of fatal accidents are inadequate. In the second case, the Committee also imposes on the Member State an obligation to provide detailed information, in its next report, about obligations to report occupational accidents and about any measures taken to counter potential under-reporting in practice. It further asks for a standardised rate of fatal accidents. In the event of the information required being lacking, this amounts to breach of the reporting system entered into by the Member State under the Charter. In two additional cases, the Committee concludes that the situation is not in conformity with Article 3 §3 of the Charter on the grounds that measures to reduce the excessive rate of fatal accidents are inadequate.[499] The Revised European Social Charter has given Article 3 a new significance. Member States have been obliged to work out policies of work protection and to enforce their postulates. Provisions of occupational health and safety and their execution are meant to ensure the abiding of intentions of these policies. Preparing priorities of health protection, drafting guidelines for work protection policies and bringing about social programmes in order to improve occupational health and safety to avoid work accidents and dangerous factors and processes workers are subject to in the work environment may be considered important new elements of this document. In 2017, the Committee found that a large proportion of the Member States that ratified Article 3 §3 of the revised Charter of Social Rights did not comply with this provision. These are the following Member States: *Bulgaria*: on the grounds that measures to reduce the number of fatal accidents are inadequate; **Estonia:** labour inspection system, insofar as it concerns occupational health and safety, is inefficient; **France, Latvia, Lithuania:** measures taken to reduce the number of accidents at work are insufficient or inadequate; **Malta**: (1) measures taken to reduce the number of accidents at work is insufficient; (2) it has

496. Conclusions 2013 (Republic of Moldova).
497. Conclusions 2013 (Portugal).
498. Conclusions 2013 (Turkey).
499. Conclusions 2013 (Romania, Ukraine).

not been established that the labour inspection system is inefficient; **Montenegro**: it has not been established that accidents at work and occupational diseases are monitored efficiently; **Portugal**: on the grounds that: (1) measures taken to reduce the number of accidents at work are insufficient; (2) the labour inspection system does not have sufficient human resources to adequately monitor compliance with occupational health and safety legislation; **the Republic of Moldova**: the labour inspection system is inefficient; **Romania**: measures to reduce the excessive rate of fatal accidents are inadequate; **Russian Federation, Turkey**: (1) measures to reduce the excessive rate of fatal accidents are inadequate; (2) the labour inspection is so understaffed it cannot be considered as efficient; **Ukraine**: the labour inspection system, insofar as it concerns occupational health and safety, is inefficient.

A. *Policies of Occupational Safety and Health*

105. A new obligation was introduced by a new element in Article 3 §4 RESC. This regulation obliges Member States to support the development of occupational health services.

106. According to the requirements regulated by Article 3 §4, RESC Member State authorities are obliged to develop a strategy allowing for the evaluation of the types and the level of threats to employees' health and life. Policies of work protection should be regarded as an integral part of social policies. Within the confines of social policies, Member State authorities should analyse risks, evaluate threats in the work environment, employ preventative actions, monitor protective measures, organise periodic occupational health and safety training for workers, and ensure professional treatment for victims of work accidents. The obligation of Member State authorities is to constantly and methodically supervise the execution of social programmes. The authorities are also obliged to periodically evaluate national social policies in terms of work protection.

B. *Occupational Health Services*

107. The above provision demands authorities of Member States undertake measures to promote the progressive development of occupational health services. Occupational health services should be structured according to the French concept of *medicine du travail*, with preventative and advisory functions. In the appendix to Article 3 §4 RESC, it was decided that the definition of functions, organisation and the conditions of such occupational health services are matters which should be left to the authorities of Member States. The authorities of such states also make decisions regarding the legal regulations and their functioning, such as acts, executory provisions, collective bargaining agreements or any other legal matters concerned within that country. With the exception of Slovenia where the Committee concludes that it has not been established that there are adequate occupational health services,[500] the situation is in compliance with Article 3 §4 of the RESC. In 2013 and 2015, the Committee recalled that under Article 3 §4, RESC states must promote, in consultation with employers' and workers' organisations, the progressive development of occupational health services for all workers with essentially preventive and advisory functions. These services may be run jointly by several companies. The services must be efficient and should be able to identify, measure and prevent work-related stress, aggression and violence.[501] It further recalls that if occupational health services are not established for all enterprises, the authorities must develop a strategy, in consultation with employers' and employees' organisations, for that purpose. Thus, Member States must take measures that will allow them to achieve the objectives of the Charter within a reasonable time, with measurable progress and to an extent consistent with the maximum use of available resources.[502] In 2015, the Committee concluded that the situation in Ireland was not in conformity with Article 3 §4 of the Charter on the grounds that there was no strategy for developing occupational services for all workers. The Irish government states there is no statutory requirement in Ireland for employers to provide access to occupational health services and no statutory plans to establish such services. Larger organisations in both the public and private sectors may provide some occupational health services for employees. These services are provided on a full or part-time basis, depending on the number of employees and the employment sector. The services provided would include rehabilitation, absence management and health promotion. Small and micro-scale enterprises rarely provide occupational health services due to the cost involved. The Committee noted that the government was not in a position to give an accurate estimate of the number of companies or the proportion of employees still not having access to occupational services. The government said that 'it is highly likely that the majority do not'. The Committee further noted that there was no plan put in place by the government, its agencies or private enterprise to improve the provision of such services for small and micro-scale enterprises.[503]

The very same conclusions, but for different various reasons, were arrived at in 2013 with respect to the following Member States: (1) Albania (whose law requires all organisations employing more than fifteen persons to have an occupational doctor); (2) Ireland (information on Article 3 §4 of the Charter not provided); (3) Malta (the report indicated that in practice a number of workers were not covered by medical examination and had no access to a workers' health and safety representative); (4) the Netherlands (while the government helped to establish a supported centre for risk identification and to develop more user-friendly digital assessment tools, the report did not follow up, either on the strategies for assisting small and medium-sized concerns, or on providing the information requested by the Committee); (5) Turkey (no information on how the progressive development of occupational health

500. Conclusions 2009, vol. 2, p. 722.
501. Conclusions 2013, Statement of interpretation of Art. 3 §4.
502. Conclusions 2003 (Bulgaria); Conclusions 2009 (Albania).
503. Conclusions (Ireland).

services has been promoted, and failure to establish the existence, during the reference period, of a strategy for instituting occupational health services for all enterprises in all sectors of the economy); (6) Ukraine (it is unclear whether occupational health services are available for all workers in all branches and sectors of the economy, public or private, and, if not, whether there is any national strategy for bringing about such access).[504] In 2017, it has not been established that in the Russian Federation, there is a strategy to progressively provide access to occupational health services for all workers in all sectors of the economy.

§5. The Right to Fair Remuneration

108. Already, during its first supervisory cycle, the Committee was convinced that the right to fair remuneration should be treated as a right ensured by labour rights regulated by three provisions of the Charter: the right to work, the right to appropriate work conditions, the right to safe and healthy working conditions.[505] The above three provisions would be breached if the right to fair remuneration was not ensured. The right to appropriate work conditions in safe and healthy working conditions would lose its significance were there to be no fair remuneration.[506] The text of Article 4 of the Charter does not indicate a significant character to the above standard. The provision in question provides no indication of how these standards could be connected to the other three provisions of the regulations in Part II of the Charter. Legal practitioners specialising in labour law consider that the necessary distinguishing element in carrying out work is its remuneration. Remuneration compensates for the type of work carried out, the amount and quality of work services provided, as well as the qualifications and occupational skills of the worker. Remuneration varies according to whether the work undertaken is completed as part of relations under civil law or under economic relations regulated by contract law provisions.[507] In this context, it is important to note the Committee's view stipulating that remuneration for work should be treated as a guarantee of the realisation of the right to work in appropriately safe and healthy working conditions.

Analysing the employment cases in terms of administrative responsibilities resting on the citizens, i.e., the reserve army, work by prisoners (as part of a prison sentence) – the Committee did not regard this as part of the compulsory work category, as considered by Article 1 of the Charter, but rather work that is not remunerated for even in part, as provided for by Article 4 of the Charter. These matters are considered further below. Matters analysed here refer to the basic problem of the definition of 'fair (decent) remuneration'. In the introduction to the considerations on the level and factors for determining fair wages, an important observation was announced in 2018. Only a few Member States (Austria, Iceland, Luxembourg and

504. Conclusions 2013 (Albania, Ireland, Malta, the Netherlands, Turkey, Ukraine).
505. Conclusions I, p. 25.
506. As above.
507. The personal nature of the work and the worker complying to the employer are both elements which can separate work from employment not regulated by labour law provisions.

Sweden)[508] meet the requirements laid down in the Committee's case law on the concept of a decent standard of living. In the other Member States that have ratified Article 4 of both Charters, the minimum wage cannot be compared with the average wage at all[509] or is too low in relation to the average wage.[510] In some Member States, only salaries subsidised by the state[511] or paid to senior government officials[512] can be compared with the average salary in the private sector.

I. Decent Remuneration

109. Member States, which ratified Article 4 §1 of the Charter, are obliged to ensure workers are remunerated in a way that will give them and their families a decent standard of living. The Committee, from its first supervisory cycle, was aware of the ambiguity of terms used within Article 4 of the Charter. As early as the second supervisory cycle, the Committee addressed an important message to Member States who are parties to the Charter. The term fair (decent) remuneration has different meanings. All Member States can understand it accordingly. Understanding of this term is directly related to the level of economic development of a particular state.[513]

The Committee sees all Member States as one entity and does not accept diversity in cases of given states.[514] Fair (decent) remuneration is a social policy category applicable in the exact same manner to all Member States. The rulings of the Committee on defining fair (decent) remuneration have had two phases. In both cases, the point of reference for defining the term fair (decent) remuneration was the average national remuneration. Initially, the Committee believed remuneration did not differ significantly from the average wage and would be regarded as fair (decent).[515] However, this attempt to define fair (decent) remuneration was not precise enough. It lacked a percentage relation between remuneration paid for a certain job and the average remuneration for this type of job in a given country. The Committee familiarised itself with the studies during the fifth supervisory cycle and utilised them to draft a more precise definition of fair (decent) remuneration.[516] In a study prepared for the Council of Europe, it was suggested that 68% might be regarded as measurable criteria of fair (decent) remuneration, determining a relation between the remuneration in question and the average remuneration in all of the Member States of the Council of Europe. Therefore remuneration above the 68% rate was considered to be meeting requirements for fair (decent) remuneration formulated under Article 4 §1 of the Charter. Any remuneration below this level

508. Activity Report 2018, p. 35.
509. Andorra, Azerbaijan, Lithuania, Malta, the Netherlands, Romania, Serbia, Spain and the United Kingdom. *Ibid.*
510. Germany, *ibid.*
511. The Netherlands, the United Kingdom, *ibid.*
512. Spain, *ibid.*
513. Conclusions II, p. 16.
514. Conclusions IV, p. 31 (United Kingdom).
515. Conclusions V, pp. 25–26.
516. *Ibid.*, p. 25.

cannot be qualified as fair (decent). The Committee decided upon utilising the rate, which allows for distinguishing remunerations into two categories: fair (decent) remuneration and not fair (decent) remuneration ('decency threshold' approach). Making an attempt to determine measurable criteria of fair (decent) remuneration, the Committee took into consideration not only a nominal value of money paid for work (remuneration) but also other benefits employees are provided with by their employer. The Committee considered this only in cases where the real amount of remuneration received was lower than the 68% rate mentioned above. Authorities of Member States had the responsibility to provide a fair (decent) rate of remuneration. They had to provide the Committee with details with which the rate was calculated: realistic remuneration amounts as well as the average remuneration. They were instructed that in cases when the latter rate was lower than the 68% rate, they should also provide details concerning the material value of various types of social benefits allocated to workers, to the insured as well as to their family members. Among these various social benefits named, were family benefits, benefits covering part of training/ educational courses, and low levels of tax or exemptions from it for those earning the lowest wage. Article 4 §1 of the Charter tells authorities of Member States to recognise such legal remuneration (fair – decent) that will ensure workers and members of their families a decent standard of living. Being supported by such guidelines, the Committee prepared separate techniques measuring the rate of remuneration, which were meant to satisfy the material needs of single individuals, married couples, single parents raising one or two or more children, and married couples with children. It measured the value of social benefits and other benefits utilised by families, especially non-nuclear families as well as families with multiple children, to see whether such benefits supplemented the difference between the remuneration received and the average remuneration. Lower wages than the 68% remuneration rate, defining fair (decent) remuneration, frequently appeared in reports provided by authorities of Member States. In the Committee's experience, there were cases where economically developed nations did not guarantee to keep fair (decent) remuneration standards, even when considering the definition as understood by Article 4 §1 of the Charter not only incorporating the nominal amount of the pay but also the material value of social benefits.[517]

110. The first intentions of the Committee, to construct objective, measurable rates of remuneration to assist in assessing the standard of living of a worker and his/her family, were not realised. During the thirteenth supervisory cycle, the Committee abandoned the technique of measuring fair (decent) remuneration. Because it did not create an alternate method of measuring the standard of living of a worker and his/her family in that supervisory cycle, it did not attempt to assess the national labour law standards in matters of remuneration, social benefits ensured by national social security schemes as well as social policies carried out by particular authorities of Member States to create the possibility for the fair remuneration of workers and to provide them with a decent standard of living.[518]

517. Conclusions XII-1, pp. 92 et seq. (United Kingdom).
518. Conclusions XIII-3, pp. 215 et seq.

The method incorporated by the Committee during the next fourteenth supervisory cycle is based on a percentage rate used for differentiating the categories of fair (decent) remuneration from remuneration which does not ensure workers and their families with a decency threshold approach (an appropriate standard of living).[519] The difference between the new and the former technique establishing the level of remuneration is based on the lowering from 68% to 60% rate as well as constructing a broad definition of remuneration. Currently, remuneration encompasses all cash and non-cash benefits provided to workers by their employers. The level of remuneration comparable to the average rate is the net payable after the worker makes tax and other insurance payments. To this cash remuneration, with the added non-cash benefits provided by the employer for the worker for work carried out, there are also added benefits from national social security schemes. A comparison basis with the average wage is the payment and value of social security benefits calculated according to the different techniques. The important *novum* when comparing real wages to the average remuneration in a given Member State is the abandonment of calculating the profits per family member. The Committee analyses whether the remuneration is fair (decent) based purely on the remuneration received by one family member in employment. It is of no importance how many people within the family are employed and how many family members there are. The basis for this new method of analysing the level of remuneration is the net wage, non-cash benefits and the value of social benefits. If the remuneration of one family member, usually the main breadwinner, crosses 60% of the average domestic remuneration, the Committee claims that the given Member State is fulfilling its obligations under Article 4 §1 of the Charter.

111. Even if the remuneration is less than 60% of the average domestic remuneration, authorities of Member States may prove that the real wages earned enable workers and their families to fulfil their requirements and provide a decent standard of living. Free education, free medical services, discounts for public transport use and other benefits associated with payable non-cash benefits provided by the employer for workers are all taken into consideration by the Committee in the supervisory process of fulfilling obligations under Article 4 §1 of the Charter.[520] If the material value of the above-mentioned benefits supplements the real wages earned, which is less than 60% of the average remuneration within a given country, the Committee is of the view the authorities should fulfil the obligations set by the Charter.[521]

519. Conclusions XIV-2, pp. 49 et seq.

520. Conclusions XIV-2, p. 52.

521. The Committee concluded that it has not been established that a decent standard of living is guaranteed for a single worker earning the minimum wage. Conclusions 2007, vol. 2, p. 602 (Ireland), p. 683 (Italy), p. 917 (Norway), p. 964 (Romania), p. 1067 (Sweden). The Committee concludes that either the minimum age is manifestly unfair or too low and does not guarantee a decent standard of living. Conclusions 2010, vol. 1, p. 25 (Albania), p. 111 (Azerbaijan), p. 317 (Italy), vol. 2, p. 446 (Netherlands), p. 495 (Portugal), p. 524 (Romania), p. 556 (Slovenia). Conclusions XIX-3, p. 96 (Germany), p. 137 (Iceland), p. 189 (Slovakia), p. 214 (Spain), p. 253 (United Kingdom).

The most reliable evidence for fulfilling obligations under Article 4 §1 of the Charter is the establishment of a minimum wage.[522]

The following Member States did just that: France, the United Kingdom, Ireland, Luxembourg, Malta, the Netherlands, Poland, Portugal, and Spain. This method enabled the comparison of the level of minimum wages (net) with the average wage (net) of a given country. If the minimum wage is 40% of the average wage, the Committee claims the Member State in question is not fulfilling its obligations under Article 4 §1 of the Charter. A 20% difference between a minimum wage and an average may be supplemented by the material value of benefits and services provided by the employer for the worker. As of 2014, the Committee points out that, in order to ensure a decent standard of living within the meaning of Article 4 §1 of the Charter, wages must not be lower than the minimum threshold, which is set at 50% of the net average. This is the case when the net minimum wage is more than 60% of the net average wage.[523] When the net minimum wage is between 50% and 60% of the net average wage, it is for the state party to establish whether this wage is sufficient to ensure a decent standard of living.[524] The Committee noted that in the cycle for 2014,[525] the situation in the following countries was considered not in conformity with Article 4 §1 of the Charter due to the fact that the minimum inter-professional wage does not ensure a decent standard of living: Andorra (47.5%), Azerbaijan (50%),[526] Austria (50%), Belgium (50% of wages of young workers under the age of 21), Germany (20.60% of workers in establishments with ten or more employees earning less than 66.67% of the national gross median wage,[527] Ireland (adult workers in their first employment and those following a course of studies were below the minimum threshold),[528] the Netherlands (45.50% for 18-year-olds, and 52.50% for 19-year-olds),[529] Romania (34.20%),[530] Slovak Republic (45.60%).[531]

The Committee further concluded that the situation in the following countries (Greece, Lithuania, Luxembourg, Portugal, Spain, United Kingdom) was not in conformity with Article 4 §1 of the Charter on the grounds that the minimum wage applied to private-sector workers does not ensure a decent standard of living.[532] In addition, the Committee concluded that in Greece and Spain, the minimum wage applicable to contractual staff in the civil service is also not sufficient and does not guarantee a decent standard of living.[533]

522. Harris & Darcy, *supra*, p. 76.
523. Conclusions 2014 (Ireland).
524. Conclusions XIV-2, 1998. Statement of Interpretation of Art. 4 §1.
525. Conclusions 2014.
526. The Committee notes that the monthly minimum wage (MMW) net of social contributions and trade union dues is lower than the minimum thresholds, and hence does not amount to a decent remuneration within the meaning of Art. 4 §1 of the Charter. Conclusions 2014.
527. Conclusions XX-3.
528. Conclusions 2014.
529. *Ibid.*
530. *Ibid.*
531. *Ibid.*
532. *Ibid.*
533. *Ibid.*

112. The above standard obliges Member States to fulfil the requirements provided by this provision of the Charter either when completing agreements concerning collective bargaining are being made with stakeholders or when legally deciding upon the work contracts in accordance with domestic regulations. Minimum wages established by the authority of a Member State is one of three above-mentioned techniques to standardise domestic labour law regulations with Article 4 §1 of the Charter. When establishing the minimum wage, authorities of Member States take into consideration the costs involved in satisfying basic needs. Identifying a minimum wage with a fair wage, which ensures a decent standard of living, creates uncertainty and questions the Committee's technique in analysing remuneration within Member States. It is possible to view that the method utilised by the Committee in assessing remuneration has been accepted by those bodies taking part in the process of abiding by the Charter, namely the Governmental Committee and the Committee of Ministers. The Council of Europe has failed to provide a decisive critique authorised to partake in the supervisory process of fulfilling obligations under the Charter. During the debates of the Governmental Committee, two major points were considered: to reduce the real wages rate from 68% to 60% which is comparable to the average pay and to move away from the earlier applicable notion of measuring the level of remuneration according to the requirements of a family, and not just the breadwinner. It was also pointed out that the newly reduced remuneration rate of 60%, similar to the 68% rate, is arbitrary in its nature.[534] The approval of the new technique is undoubtedly caused by the fact that the majority of Member States fulfil the obligations under Article 4 §1 of the Charter because they recognise workers' rights to minimum wages.

113. The special case of non-compliance with the obligation to guarantee the right to fair remuneration is Austria. In 2014, the Committee took note of the information submitted by Austria in response to the conclusion that it had not been established that the lowest wage paid was sufficient to ensure a decent standard of living.[535] The Austrian report analysed in 2016 refers to the net value of the average wage of manual workers, which was EUR 22,484 in 2013 and increased to EUR 22,777 in 2014. The report does not provide explicit information on the monthly average wage, but the aforementioned 2014 annual amount for all dependent workers. The report provides little information on the lowest wages paid in the labour market. It reiterates information already noted by the Committee, according to which approximately 98% Austrian employees are covered by collective agreements, and indicates that the lowest wage rate foreseen by these agreements ranges between EUR 1,200 and EUR 1,400 as of March 2015. The Committee notes that a gross monthly wage of EUR 1,200 corresponds to only about 51% of the net average monthly wage based on micro-census data and to 47% net average monthly wage based on social security data. On the basis of the information at its disposal, the Committee considers that the lowest wages are too low to meet the requirements of the Charter.

534. Governmental Committee XIV-2, pp. 220 et seq.
535. Conclusions 2014.

The Committee takes note of the explanation regarding Article of the General Civil Code, which provides for 'appropriate remuneration' where the employer is not bound by an existing collective agreement. In such cases, an appropriate wage has to be determined on the basis of collective agreements for comparable activities, with factors such as wage level in the geographical area being considered. The Committee considers the *modus operandi* which is reasonable under Article 4 §1 of the Charter; however, it requires a proper assessment of the situation in the next report in order to receive information on the lowest wages actually paid to full-time workers not covered by collective agreements. It concludes that the situation in Austria is not in conformity with Article 4 §1 of the Charter on the basis that the lowest wage paid is too low to ensure a decent standard of living for all workers.

Finally, on 22 March 2023, the ECSR presented a new concept for the protection of employee rights regulated in the provisions of Article 4 of the Charter. It will be presented in the final paragraphs dealing with this article. Article 4 §1 of the Charter[536] guarantees the right to remuneration that will give workers and their families a decent standard of living.[537] In order to ensure a decent standard of living, the minimum net wage or the lowest net wages paid must be above the threshold of 50% of the net average wage. Although the Committee found that some Member States had made progress by raising their minimum statutory wages, its conclusion was that there was non-compliance. In the case of eleven out of the nineteen Member States that it examined in this reporting cycle, the Committee found that:

- the right to increased remuneration for overtime work is not guaranteed to all workers,
- public officials are not guaranteed an increased period of time off in lieu of remuneration for overtime,
- increased remuneration or an increased compensatory period of time off for overtime work is not guaranteed,
- overtime work performed by ordinary members of the supervision and enforcement corps of the police is not remunerated at a higher rate and
- the increased command bonus for senior managers only compensates for a very small number of overtime hours, while compensatory time off provided at the statutory minimum wage or the lowest wages fixed by collective agreements was too low in comparison with the average wage and therefore did not ensure a decent standard of living.

The Committee considered that the national reports did not provide enough information to establish that the minimum wage was fair. The Committee also addressed targeted questions to Member States in relation to workers in non-typical employment, such as those working in the gig economy or platform economy who are incorrectly classified as self-employed and therefore do not have the applicable

536. Conclusions 2022, *Press Briefing Elements*, European Committee of Social Rights, 22 Mar. 2023, pp. 10–11.

537. Conclusions 2022 (Albania), (France), (Ireland), (Italy), (North Macedonia), (Poland), (Spain), (Türkiye), (United Kingdom).

labour and social protection rights. As a result of the misclassification, these workers cannot enjoy the rights and protection to which they are entitled, including the right to a minimum wage.

II. Additional Remuneration for Overtime Work

114. Overtime work should have additional remuneration. Article 4 §2 of the Charter deals with the workers‘ right to an increased rate of remuneration for overtime work. The Committee did not define work as overtime. It claimed that work above the standard of working hours (it did not provide those standards; therefore, there is a basis to believe that it deals with the hours above the daily standard) is work carried out outside the normal working hours or in addition to normal working hours.[538] Overtime work, according to the understanding of Article 4 §2 of the Charter, is work carried out at night. According to the Committee, carrying out such work requires additional effort from the workers who should be additionally remunerated.

Article 4 §2 of the Charter is generally applicable.[539] It is applicable to workers in full-time employment based on a work agreement not defined by a period as well as to workers in temporary/ periodical employment in an unidentifiable period of time. Additional work for this last category of workers is work carried out beyond the shortened daily and working-hour standards. To fulfil the obligation of increased remuneration for overtime work, there is no actual place for the carrying out of such work. The right to additional remuneration for overtime hours is with workers who are carrying out work outside the workplace of the employer. The above argument refers to people working from home.[540] The obligation to additional remuneration is applicable to persons employed in agriculture,[541] the public sector,[542] and domestic services hired by individuals.[543]

115. Member States are allowed to adopt a general approach to the obligations set in Article 4 §2 of the Charter. The legal basis for this is to be found in this provision. It is applicable in certain cases which the Charter does not specify. In 2014, the Committee concluded that an exception to the right to increased remuneration could apply to senior officials and managerial executives.[544] The exceptions refer to situations other than those specified in Article 33 ESC. The Committee takes care

538. Conclusions XIV-2, p. 35.

539. In Malta, all time worked as overtime must be paid. The Committee recalls that overtime must not only be paid but also paid at an increased rate and it asks again for information on how and to what extent this is guaranteed to all workers, whether by statute, collective agreement, individual employment contract and/or any other means. In the absence of such information, the Committee concludes that the situation in Malta is not in conformity with Art. 4 §2 of the Charter on the basis that it has not been established that the right to increased remuneration for overtime work is guaranteed to all workers.

540. Conclusions XIII-5, p. 54 (Finland).

541. Conclusions XIV-2, p. 479 (Luxembourg).

542. Conclusions 2007, vol. 1, p. 172 (Belgium).

543. Conclusions XIII-5, p. 168 (Portugal).

544. Conclusions 2014 (Lithuania).

so the authorities of Member States do not use the rights provided in Article 4 §2 of the Charter *in fine* excessively. The Committee has accepted in practice excluding additional remuneration paid for overtime to those employed in managerial positions from the obligations[545] as well as those employed in executive organisational units of power and national administration.[546] For the 2014 cycle, however, the Committee concluded that the situation in some countries (France, Portugal and Turkey) was not in conformity with Article 4 §2 of the Charter on the following grounds: (1) the flat-rate compensation for overtime work performed by ordinary members of the supervision and enforcement corps of the police did not guarantee an increased rate of remuneration; (2) the increase in the command bonus could only compensate for a very small number of overtime hours, and compensatory time off provided to senior police officers working overtime when performing certain duties was equivalent in length to the overtime worked;[547] (3) police officers on active prevention and shift duties did not receive increased remuneration as required, nor even remuneration equivalent to their basic hourly pay;[548] (4) civil servants were not entitled to increased time off in lieu of remuneration for overtime hours.[549] In 2016, the Committee concluded that the situation in Lithuania is not in conformity with Article 4 §2 of the Charter on the basis that it has not been established that the exception to the right to increased remuneration only applies to senior officials and management executives.[550] Article 4 §2 of the Charter does not define methods for introducing this provision into the domestic labour law system. The regulation within the last paragraph of Article 4 of the Charter instructs Member States as to how to fulfil their obligations under Article 4 §1-5 of the Charter and is applicable to all of the five regulations and paragraphs which are part of the provision in question. Carrying out the obligations of additional remuneration for overtime work should be guaranteed either during collective bargaining agreements or through other legal means of establishing remuneration (e.g., statutes, decrees, regulations) or with the help of other sources in accordance with domestic conditions.

In the United Kingdom, the usual custom is to establish all obligations according to standard processes. The Committee analysed a report filed by the British authorities, which compiled in its part concerning the implementation of Article 4 §2 of the Charter a notion of 'very widespread expectations among workers that additional work will be remunerated with the higher rates', and concluded that a custom could be regarded as a source of workers' entitlement to additional remuneration for additional work, creating, as a consequence, enough legal grounds to impose on

545. Conclusions IX-1, p. 41 (Netherlands).
546. Conclusions XIV-2, pp. 479–480 (Luxembourg).
547. Conclusions 2014 (France).
548. Conclusions (Portugal).
549. Conclusions 2014 (Turkey).
550. Conclusions 2016, p. 217. The Committee examined the new draft Labour Code which proposes a narrowing of the special cases where overtime is not reimbursed. The special cases would henceforth apply to senior managers such as heads of companies and managers of branches and executive offices.

employers a duty of greater remunerating for the extra hours of work, on the condition that custom law embraces all employed and their employers and that state authorities efficiently supervise abiding of the obligation determined by a customary standard.[551]

Notions used in the report presented by British authorities do not create enough legal basis to admit that 'widespread expectations among workers', interpreted by the Committee lawyers as expectations, do not legally enable workers to litigate for additional remuneration for extra hours of work.

In connection with the above, the Committee concluded that British authorities did not fulfil the obligation formulated in Article 4 §2 of the Charter.

116. The notion of 'other measures adequate to national conditions', which can be used in order to grant workers employed for extra time greater remuneration, also embraces work agreements. Work agreements are considered to be sources of mutual obligations between the parties in an individual working relationship. Work agreements can regulate the rendering of work done at extra time, beyond the common daily or weekly standards, work during night hours as well as employer's obligation of paying remuneration calculated at higher rates for additional work. The obligations of one party in a work relation answer the entitlements of the other. The worker's right to carry out work in extra time answers the employer's right to employ workers in extra time. The employer's obligation of paying remuneration calculated on higher rates for additional work answers the worker's right to demand to be paid additional (greater) remuneration for the work done. A freedom of work agreement guaranteed by labour law cannot be utilised to regulate rules of additional employment other than those prescribed under Article 4 §2 of the Charter. If the content of a work agreement makes it stand against labour law regulations or makes an employee's situation less advantageous than predicted by labour law regulations, such an agreement has no legal force. The rule of employee's privilege commonly accepted by Member States orders the regulation of matters of additional employment according to a greater rate and forbids parties to work relations from making exceptions to this rule in work agreements.

This is why the Committee regarded the conduct of Spanish authorities as violating Article 4 §2 of the Charter when Spain decided to depart from the rules of remunerating workers employed in extra time and leaving this issue for the interested parties of a work relation. The Committee concluded that such conduct is evidence of not abiding by regulations set by Article 4 §2 of the Charter by Spanish authorities, even though the changed provisions of Spanish labour law compiled clauses guaranteeing that work in extra time should not be remunerated according to lower rates than the ones used for accounting wages of workers employed full time on a regular basis.[552]

117. The Committee claims that Article 4 §2 allows Member States to regulate the rules of remunerating additional work in an adequate way, according to the practices in a given country. Despite the fact that Member State authorities may allow

551. Conclusions XIV-2, p. 773.
552. Conclusions XIV-2, p. 682.

the regulation of the rules of remuneration for workers employed above daily and weekly standards by stakeholders in collective agreements or parties to individual work relations guaranteed by work agreements, the authorities are still responsible for any non-fulfilment of the obligations stipulated under Article 4 of the Charter. They may also leave the regulations of the above-mentioned issues to be dealt with in other ways by all interested parties mutually abiding by commonly accepted customs, but this does not ameliorate the responsibility of the authorities. (stakeholders and parties to individual work relations), Member States are not excused in cases of the non-fulfilment of the obligations resulting from the ratified provisions of the Charter, even when the specific nature of the domestic labour law regulations excludes the interference of state authorities in issues left for the regulation of stakeholders.

The Nordic countries may serve as a good example as the issue of workers‘ remuneration is regulated by collective work agreements, whereby stakeholders draft the provisions. Authorities of these countries evade responsibility for not abiding by regulations of the Charter concerning remunerating workers and deducting wages, arguing that the above sphere was passed onto stakeholders and is regulated by social dialogue. As stakeholders are not international entities of labour law, social security law or social policy, the whole responsibility for not abiding by the regulations and standards set by the Council of Europe must be seen as a Member State‘s responsibility, i.e., a party to the Charter.

Article 4 §2 of the Charter recognises the right of workers employed in extra time to an ‘increased rate of remuneration’. The above provision does not compile any guidelines as to the rates of remuneration and how they may be regarded as ‘increased’. The basis for comparison is based on a standard rate of remuneration, which is paid to a worker by an employer for work in regular working hours, namely for work according to the commonly accepted daily and weekly standards of work time. From the textual interpretation of this provision, it can be concluded that any rate surpassing the standard rate paid to workers employed according to daily and weekly standards meets the requirements of Article 4 §2 of the Charter and should be regarded as ‘increased’. As it has been mentioned several times before, the Committee does not create models, which should be implemented into provisions of domestic labour law by Member States. The Committee only evaluates domestic regulations in terms of their conformity with the standards set by the Charter. This is why analysing the obligation of increased remuneration for workers employed in extra time, is sensible. Rulings of the Committee state domestic regulations, according to which workers employed above the daily and weekly standards of work time, obtain remuneration increased by 25%, 50% or 100% stand in line with the requirements of Article 4 §2 of the Charter.[553]

553. Conclusions II, p. 18 (Germany). Neither increased remuneration nor a sufficient longer period in compensation for overtime is guaranteed in Member States listed by the Committee. Conclusions 2010, vol. 1, p. 88 (Armenia), p. 150 (Belgium), p. 176 (Bulgaria), p. 254 (France), p. 280 (Georgia), p. 318 (Italy), vol. 2, p. 526 (Romania). Conclusions XIX-3, p. 77 (Denmark), p. 170 (Poland), p. 190 (Slovakia), p. 215 (Spain), p. 254 (United Kingdom).

The Committee accepted a legal solution in Belgium where additional remuneration for civil service clerks working in extra time was 6.8% higher than the standard, on the basis of which it was calculated.[554] The employee may be provided with paid time off, to be taken in compensation for overtime, or to be added to their annual leave. However, the rest time provided in place of overtime work must correspond to the duration of the overtime worked. Therefore, the Committee concluded as of 2014 that the situation in Armenia, Belgium, Estonia, the Czech Republic, Finland, Malta, the Netherlands, Poland, Russian Federation, the Slovak Republic, Spain and the United Kingdom was not in conformity with Article 4 §2 of the Charter, on the grounds that: (1) the legislation did not guarantee increased time off in lieu of remuneration of overtime;[555] (2) in the public sector, the compensatory time off for overtime hours was not sufficient[556] or adequate;[557] (3) workers in both public and private sectors did not have a right to increased compensatory time off for overtime hours.[558] The same view was presented in 2018. The Committee concluded that ten Member States would not guarantee workers an additional, fair payment for overtime work.[559] The Committee noted from the country report that in Ireland the remuneration paid for overtime was not subject to statutory regulation, but was determined through negotiation and agreement between the parties at the same level at which basic pay and conditions of employment are normally settled. Most collective agreements contain provisions in relation to remuneration for overtime work. In its previous conclusion (2010), the Committee had asked the government to provide more detailed information about remuneration for overtime work being guaranteed to workers. The current report does not provide this information. Therefore, the Committee considers that it has not been established that the right to increased remuneration for overtime work is guaranteed to all workers.[560]

118. Article 4 §2 does not mention anything about the rules of calculating the additional remuneration for work in terms of extra time. The above-mentioned provision orders Member States to accept the workers' right to an increased rate of remuneration for work in extra time. Therefore, a rate of remuneration higher than the rate paid for work carried out according to daily and weekly standards of work time meets the requirements of Article 4 §2 of the Charter. The Committee requires that the national report contain the requested details on remuneration as agreed in collective agreements covering a significant part of the labour market.[561] Analysing the jurisdiction of the Committee so far, there has not been a case of the obligations

554. Conclusions XIV-2, p. 134.
555. Conclusions 2014 (Armenia, Czech Republic, Estonia, Malta, the Netherlands, Russian Federation, Spain).
556. Conclusions 2014 (Belgium, Slovak Republic).
557. Conclusions 2014 (United Kingdom).
558. Conclusions 2014 (Poland).
559. Armenia, Czech Republic, Estonia, the Netherlands, North Macedonia, Poland, Slovak Republic, Spain, Turkey, United Kingdom. Activity report 2018, p. 35.
560. Conclusions 2014 (Ireland).
561. Therefore, the Committee concludes that the situation in Ireland is not in conformity with Art. 4 §2 of the Charter on the ground that it has not been established that the right to increased remuneration for overtime work is guaranteed to all workers. Conclusions 2016 (Ireland), p. 30.

formulated in Article 4 §2 of the Charter not being fulfilled by any Member State. Even minimal increases in the rate of remuneration for additional work have been regarded, at least up to now, as meeting the requirements formulated in the Charter.

The Committee claims that the increased rate of remuneration mentioned in Article 4 §2 of the Charter also encompasses cases of granting time free from work in exchange for additional work overtime. It is important to ensure time free from work granted in exchange for additional work is longer than the nominal standard of work in extra time.

For this reason, France and Belgium were regarded as states not abiding by the obligations stipulated under Article 4 §2 of the Charter because France did not determine a conversion rate between time free from work and additional work[562] and Belgium‘s civil service clerks employed in extra time obtained in exchange the amount of time free from work equal to the amount of time they had worked.[563]

By accepting Article 4 §2,[564] Member States recognised the right of workers to an increased rate of remuneration for overtime work, subject to exceptions in particular cases.

With regard to COVID-19, Member States were to explain the impact of the COVID-19 crisis on the right to fair overtime remuneration and to detail the measures taken to protect and fulfil this right. The ECSR asked for specific information on the enjoyment of the right to fair overtime compensation for medical staff during the pandemic and for an explanation of how the matter of overtime and working hours was addressed in respect of teleworking. Of the 28 conclusions under Article 4 §2, the Committee considered that thirteen cases were in conformity with the requirements of the provision.[565] The ECSR deferred its conclusion for eight countries,[566] and in seven cases, it considered that the situation was not in conformity with this provision.[567] The grounds of non-conformity were as follows:

- the right to increased remuneration for overtime work is not guaranteed to all workers,
- increased remuneration or an increased compensatory period of time off for overtime work is not guaranteed,
- overtime work performed by ordinary members of the supervision and enforcement corps of the police is not remunerated at an increased rate, and
- the increase in the command bonus for senior managers only compensates for a very small number of overtime hours while compensatory time off provided to the senior police officers working overtime when performing certain duties is only equivalent in length to the overtime worked.

562. Conclusions X-2, p. 62.
563. Conclusions XIV, p. 134.
564. Conclusions 2022, *Press Briefing Elements*, European Committee of Social Rights, 22 Mar. 2023, pp. 11–12.
565. Conclusions 2022 (Andorra), (Armenia), (Austria), (Bulgaria), (Estonia), (Germany), (Italy), (Lithuania), (Luxembourg), (Montenegro), (Portugal), (Romania), (Slovakia).
566. Conclusions 2022 (Albania), (Belgium), (Finland), (Georgia), (Greece), (Latvia), (Malta), (Serbia).
567. Conclusions 2022 (France), (Ireland), (North Macedonia), (Poland), (Spain), (Türkiye), (United Kingdom).

III. The Right of Men and Women to Equal Remuneration for Work of Equal Value

119. Article 4 §3 of the Charter orders Member States to recognise the right of men and women to equal remuneration for work of equal value. As regards statistics for equal pay, the Committee notes that in 2009, across all economic activities, the average wages of women amounted to 58.6% of that of men and 46.2% of that of men in 2012.[568] The Committee considers that the unadjusted pay gap is manifestly too high and finds the situation not to be in conformity with the Charter. As regards statistics for equal pay in Estonia, the Committee notes that across all economic activities, the average pay gap amounted to 24.6% in 2012. The Committee further notes from EUROSTAT that the unadjusted pay gap stood at 30% in 2012 and 27.3% in 2011. The wage gap between men and women performing identical or comparable work is growing. In 2018, the Committee concluded that the gender gap is larger, to the disadvantage of female workers, and it is over 25%.[569] The above observation proves the ineffectiveness of the provision of Article 4 §3 of both Charters ('old' and 'new') of Social Rights.[570] The Committee notes that this indicator is substantially higher than the EU 27 average and is the highest of all EU countries. Therefore, the Committee considers that, despite the measures taken to narrow the gap, the unjust pay gap remains manifestly high, and the situation is therefore not in conformity with the Charter.[571] From the first supervisory cycle, the Committee emphasised that the execution of this rule needs to be determined by Member States' objective criteria for determining the work carried out by men and women, and the respecting of these criteria by employers while making decisions about remuneration rates.[572] According to the Committee, determining Member States' adherence to the above rule depends on the pursuit of systematic studies analysing different factors that can have a legal and practical impact on the work carried out by men and women.[573] When examining work-evaluation techniques and remuneration paid to men and women for work of equal value, the Committee pays attention to the equality of wages regardless of sex, as well as to the conduct of Member State authorities in cases violating this rule, which is supposed to bring about an ongoing convergence of domestic regulations and practices with the requirements of Article 4 §3 of the Charter.[574] The rule of the equal remuneration of men and women for work of equal value can be put into force differently in different Member States. Implementation of this rule may be passed by Member State authorities onto stakeholders, and employers or left for the judiciary. According to the Committee, however, the only subject responsible for implementing this rule is the state.[575] The rule of equal remuneration for men and women is one of the few regulations of labour law which, according to the Committee, requires the involvement of Member

568. Conclusions 2014 (Azerbaijan).
569. Armenia, Azerbaijan, Estonia, Activity Report 2018, p. 36.
570. *Ibid.*
571. Conclusions (Estonia).
572. Conclusions I, p. 9.
573. Conclusions II, p. 19.
574. Conclusions III, p. 26.
575. Conclusions I, p. 28.

States,[576] possibly at the legislative, and definitely in the supervisory phase. The Committee emphasises the necessity of applying this rule de jure and de facto.[577] The right of men and women to 'equal pay for work of equal value' must be expressly provided for in legislation.[578] As of 2014, the Committee observes that in Georgian legislation there is no express statutory guarantee of the right of men and women to equal pay for work of equal value. Therefore, it considers that the situation is not in conformity with the Charter.[579]

Article 4 §3 of the Charter orders the equal remuneration of workers regardless of their gender for work of equal value. The above rule is not limited to equal remuneration for men and women for the same, like or identical work. This means that different work having the same value should be remunerated equally, regardless of whether it was a man or a woman who completed it. The basic task of the supervision, therefore, monitoring whether this rule is being abided by the Member States, is the evaluation of the remuneration rate criteria and their differences. The Committee claims that criteria used by employers to estimate work should be objective.[580] It is interested in familiarising itself with ways employed by Member States authorities in determining objective indicators of different works having the same value.[581] During a session on the methods used by Member States in the process of work estimation, the Committee reflected upon introducing a uniform technique allowing all states to make estimations regardless of the sector of the economy in which workers are employed and whose work was to be estimated. It concluded it is impossible to find such a universal technique which could be used for estimating different types of work.[582] It authorised particular employees discriminated on the basis of sex (women) to file claims for their work to be estimated in order to compare the latter with the estimation of work carried out by better-remunerated male employees. The Committee as a rule took the position that the processes of work estimation should be restricted to one particular workplace. The rule of equal remuneration for work of equal value had a limited influence, as it did not take into consideration the sector of the economy of a particular workplace.[583] It agreed to the exceptions to the above rule only in cases of workplaces where the proportion of employed women was high, making it difficult to compare the remuneration of men and women in certain positions.[584] In the Statement of Interpretation of Article 20, the Committee considered that equal treatment between women and men includes

576. Conclusions V, p. 31; Conclusions VII, p. xvi.
577. Conclusions II, p. 19; Conclusions III, p. xiii; Conclusions VI, p. xv; Conclusions VIII, pp. 67 et seq.; Conclusions X-1, pp. 60–61; Conclusions XI-2, pp. 69 et seq.; Conclusions XIII-2, p. 262 (Germany); Conclusions XIII-4, p. 351; Conclusions XIII-4, p. 350 (Belgium); Addendum to Conclusions XIII-3, p. 32 (Luxembourg).
578. Conclusions XV-2 2001 (Slovak Republic).
579. Conclusions 2014 (Georgia).
580. Conclusions I, p. 28.
581. Conclusions IV, pp. 34–35 (Germany, Italy, Sweden); Conclusions V, pp. 32–33; Conclusions X-2, pp. 63–64 (Austria, Spain); Conclusions XII-1, p. 98; Conclusions XIII-1, p. 117 (Greece); Conclusions XIV-2, p. 480 (Luxembourg).
582. Conclusions I, pp. 10–11 (United Kingdom).
583. Conclusions XII-1, p. 102 (Norway, The Netherlands).
584. Conclusions XIII-1, p. 120 (The Netherlands); *supra*, p. 121 (Norway).

the issue of equal pay for work of equal value.[585] Usually, pay comparisons are made between persons within the same concern/company. However, there may be situations in which, in order to be meaningful, this comparison can only be made across concerns/companies. Therefore, the Committee requires that it be possible to make pay comparisons across companies. It notes that, at the very least, legislation should require pay comparison across companies in one or more of the following situations: (1) cases in which statutory rules apply to the working and pay conditions in more than one company; (2) cases in which several companies are covered by a collective agreement or regulations governing the terms and conditions of employment; (3) cases in which the terms and conditions of employment are laid down centrally for more than one company within a holding or conglomerate. As of 2014, the Committee concludes that the situation in Norway is not in conformity with Article 4 §3 of the Charter, on the grounds that in equal pay litigation cases, pay comparison cannot be made with companies other than the company directly concerned.[586] The Committee took a similar position in 2013 in the Moldova case. The regulations in force in this country do not allow the comparison of remuneration for work performed in the private sector in different workplaces, even those that are part of the same holding company.[587]

During the first six supervisory cycles (monitoring whether the obligations of Article 4 §3 of the Charter were being met by the Member States), the Committee became convinced that none of the Member States had determined objective criteria of work evaluation, which resulted in a ruling stating that none of the Member States followed the regulations under Article 4 §3 of the Charter. It was not until the seventh supervisory cycle that the Committee noted a significant improvement in these issues within Member States. Changes were seen due to legislating regulations guaranteeing equal remuneration for men and women based on objective indicators of work estimation, remuneration rates as well as due to the broadening of competences of the national supervisory systems controlling employers and stakeholders in terms of following the above rules of remuneration.[588]

Supervising the usage of objective criteria of work evaluation by Member States the Committee intended to eliminate workers‘ discrimination based on sex in the process of remuneration. It underlined cases of direct discrimination where workers were performing the same, like or comparable jobs and were differently remunerated, with men earning more than women. It examined whether seemingly neutral criteria of work evaluation resulting in the amount of remuneration for men and women did not lead to indirect discrimination. Greater availability, readiness to work extra hours, work at night and bonuses for work connected with physical effort are circumstances that, according to the Committee,[589] lead to indirect discrimination as they create preferences for higher amounts of remuneration for workers accepting work conditions proposed by employers. These workers are mostly men.

585. Conclusions 2012.
586. Conclusions 2014.
587. Activity Report 2018, p. 35.
588. L. Samuel, *supra*, p. 93.
589. Conclusions XIII-1, p. 126 (Norway); Conclusions IX-1, p. 42 (Denmark).

120. Article 4 §3 of the Charter prescribes the equal remuneration of work of equal value. Applying this rule solely to the same and like work can be considered a violation of this regulation of the Charter.[590] Member States who did not distinguish these categories were judged negatively and obliged to introduce changes into their labour law regulations, replacing provisions guaranteeing equal rates of remuneration for the same and like work with provisions imposing the duty on employers to ensure equal rates of remuneration for men and women for work of equal value. The terms 'the same' or 'the like' and 'of the same value' differ significantly.

Evaluating a report presented by the Turkish authorities based on efficiency as understood as the relation between labour inputs and the achieved effect, arguing it was the main reason for differentiating between the remunerations, the Committee took the position that the above criteria of differentiating between the remuneration rates did not take into consideration the important factors such as the scope of responsibility, occupational preparation, skills, physical and psychological effort, working conditions, etc.

As a consequence, the Committee concluded that work efficiency could not be the only criterion for differentiating between work remuneration.[591]

During the eight supervisory cycles, the Committee formulated a rule, according to which Member State authorities are obliged to issue provisions commanding employers to remunerate workers equally for work of equal value.[592] In order to enforce the above rule it obligated Member State authorities to declare that all clauses violating this rule listed in collective work agreements and work agreements lose their legal power, having no legal consequences.[593] In cases of not abiding by the above rule by employers, national labour law regulations should allow for litigation, which once decided, should cease legal power of all agreements standing in conflict with the rule of equal remuneration for workers doing work of equal value.[594] This ruling should result in *erga omnes* consequences.

Norwegian labour law regulations were regarded as being in violation of Article 4 §3 of the Charter on several occasions, as labour court jurisdictions invalidated the regulations, only in the cases of the person filing the claim.[595]

121. In order to declare the invalidity of the agreements during such proceedings, trade unions should have the right to represent workers. Procedural provisions should allow for class actions by all interested workers. Additionally, the Committee suggested that Member States introduce preventive measures in order to avoid applying, consciously or unconsciously, any invalid legal acts bearing no force.[596] Ensuring the rule of equal remuneration for workers regardless of sex should be effective. In doing so, the authorities of Member States should employ adequate

590. Conclusions VIII, p. 67; Conclusions XI-1, p. 42 (Denmark).
591. Conclusions XIV-2, p. 741.
592. Conclusions VIII, p. 66.
593. As above.
594. Conclusions XI-1, p. 72 (Norway).
595. Conclusions XII-1, pp. 102–103; XIII-1, p. 121; XIII-3, pp. 219–220.
596. Conclusions XIII-5, p. 255; Conclusions XIV-2, p. 593 (Norway).

legal measures.[597] Among these measures, the Committee suggested first and foremost using litigation based on the rights of aggrieved workers to file claims for the payment of the due amount of money not paid by an employer violating the rule of equal remuneration for work of equal value regardless of who carried it out, whether it was a man or a woman. The procedure for appealing to a superior court serves the same goal.[598] It should be based on the provisions and references to labour law that the above-mentioned guarantee of the enforcement of proper efficient measures employed by Member States in order to monitor whether the rule of equal remuneration for work of equal value is being abided by, does not have a legal foundation in Article 4 §3 of the Charter.[599] The Committee is pushing for the provision of the Charter to be efficiently executed.

Reinstating a worker who obtained the proper amount of remuneration but was made redundant by an employer is considered the most adequate measure.[600] As of 2014, the Committee concludes that the situation in Iceland is not in conformity with Article 4 of the Charter, on the grounds that the law does not provide for reinstatement in cases in which an employee is dismissed in retaliation for bringing an equal pay claim.[601] The situation did not change, as in 2018, the Committee found that it was not possible for female workers to request a reactivation of their employment relationship, complaining of discrimination in pay for their work.[602] As an exception, the Committee accepts an alternative solution, namely compensation for the unlawful termination of a work agreement with a woman worker demanding the proper amount of remuneration. This is the case when work relations cannot be efficiently reactivated or a worker is not interested in regaining a lost work position.[603] An obstacle in efficiently demanding the reactivation of work relations can be the employer‘s conduct claiming denial of a legally binding judicial decree for the reinstatement of a worker.[604] In the opinion of the Committee regarding unlawful termination of work relations, this significantly weakens the rule presented above, according to which a worker discriminated in matters of remuneration in a case of unlawful termination of his work agreement should regain not only his work position but also due remuneration according to the amount of the work carried out. A worker should be convinced that the court, in a case where his argument is accepted, is to be reinstated to his previous position. Otherwise, a worker will have no motivation to pursue litigation for his due remuneration.[605] The threat of losing one‘s job emerges as a serious obstacle to the pursuit of pending remuneration entitlements for workers discriminated against on the basis of sex.[606]

597. Conclusions VIII, p. 66.
598. Conclusions IX-1, p. 13; Conclusions IX-2, pp. 10–11.
599. Harris & Darcy, *supra*, p. 82.
600. Conclusions XIII-5, p. 524.
601. Conclusions 2014.
602. Activity Report 2018, p. 35.
603. As above, p. 525.
604. Conclusions XII-1, pp. 96–97 (Denmark).
605. Conclusions VII, pp. 26–27 (Denmark).
606. Conclusions IX-1, p. 13.

In such cases where an employer has terminated a work agreement breaching the contract, the court may make a ruling for damages in favour of the worker, instead of having the worker resume his job. Paying damages has to serve the purpose of compensation and be a deterrent.

Analysing the case of Denmark, which established a limit of compensation for a worker having been made redundant to be worth twenty-six weeks of pay, the Committee came to the conclusion the Danish legislation does not meet the requirements stipulated in Article 4 §3 of the Charter.[607] It did not alter its position even when Danish authorities increased the payment of redundancy to thirty-nine weeks.[608] A similar statement was made in the conclusion issued in 2018 on Armenia. The Committee found situations of non-conformity in Armenia, 'where there is an upper limit on the amount of compensation that may be awarded in gender discrimination cases'.[609] Analysing Sweden's report the Committee concluded that damages paid at unlimited levels are seen as appropriate compensation for a worker who has been discriminated against, whose legal due process allocates him rights, only when the court is unable to make a ruling due to domestic legislative limitations of reinstating the worker into his former employment. The possibility of such a case existing may occur when the defendant is a private employer who has the right to appeal the court's verdict.[610] As of 2014 and 2018, the Committee concludes that the situation in Bulgaria, Germany, Finland and Armenia is not in conformity with Article 4 §3 of the Charter, on the grounds that there is a ceiling on compensation in reappraisal litigation.[611] A predominant upper limit on compensation for employees who are dismissed as a result of gender discrimination may prevent damages from making good the losses suffered or serve as an adequate deterrent.[612] The Committee recalls that in the event of retaliatory dismissal, the remedy should in principle be reinstatement in the same job or a job with similar duties. Only when reinstatement is not possible, or the employee has no desire to be reinstated, should damages be paid instead.[613]

122. The Charter should ensure effective legal protection for workers against discrimination based on sex. It is for this reason that in the following supervisory cycles, the Committee underlined the necessity of introducing into domestic labour law legislation a prohibition of terminating work agreements with workers whose legal due course allocates them a right to fair remuneration comparable to the value of work carried out. As an exception, the Committee accepted verdicts of compensation instead of re-employment in cases when work agreements were terminated illegally. It underlined nonetheless, that the level of compensation should fulfil the two above-mentioned requirements, first, it is to deter private employers from unlawfully terminating work contracts, and second to provide compensation for the

607. Conclusions VII, pp. 26–27.
608. Conclusions IX-1, p. 13; Conclusions X-1, p. 60; Conclusions XI-1, p. 68; Conclusions XII-1, pp. 96–97.
609. Activity Report 2018, p. 35.
610. Conclusions IX-1, p. 44.
611. Conclusion 2014 (Germany).
612. Conclusions 2014 Bulgaria).
613. Conclusions (Finland).

damages entailed by the worker.[614] It is therefore of no surprise to note the Committee's negative stance concerning Turkey, which has limited the amount of compensation paid to twenty-four weeks of pay.[615] The Committee concludes that the situation is not in conformity, on the grounds that no severance pay in lieu of a notice period applies to dismissals in the private sector, or to the termination of employment duties or contracts in the public sector.[616]

A necessary element of effective protection against discrimination based on sex is the appropriate spreading of the burden of proof of behaviour when a worker with whom the employer terminated a work agreement in retaliation for demanding equal treatment concerning remuneration is claiming compensation or re-employment. Domestic law should provide for a shift of the burden of proof in favour of the plaintiff in discrimination cases.[617] The Charter does not oblige Member States to describe the reasons for giving notice at work. It is unlikely for an employer when terminating a work agreement with a worker who is demanding equal treatment in matters concerning remuneration, to inform of the real reason for the termination. A worker demanding his/her rights, when faced with the prospect of litigation, has many obstacles to overcome. A worker is unable to prove that the termination of a work agreement by the employer was done due to their earlier actions – such as demands made for equal pay, and not to be discriminated against due to sex.[618] The burden of proof, normally lying with the party suing for damages, is seen by the Committee as having little use in matters concerning the protection of workers' rights demanding equal treatment.[619] The situation changed in 2018. The cases of the Russian Federation and Ukraine prove that the legal structure of the 'shift of the burden of proof' has been accepted by the Committee. Presumption of the truthfulness of the injured person's substantiated assertion is treated as the claimant's privilege in cases of discrimination based on sex.[620] It obliged Member States to introduce information in their reports dealing with the abidance of Article 4 §3 of the Charter, concerning the spreading of the burden of proof referring to the actions undertaken at earlier stages by workers accusing their employers of discrimination based on sex in matters of employment and pay.[621]

In a similar manner as terminating a work agreement with workers who are demanding equal pay for equal work, the Committee looked at other sources undertaken by employers in retaliation to the actions taken by the workers discriminated

---

614. Conclusions XIII-5, pp. 254–255; Conclusions XIV-2, p. 374 (Iceland); XIV-2, p. 480 (Luxembourg). Conclusions 2014 (Andorra). Conclusions XX-3 (Greece).
615. Conclusions XIII-3, pp. 265–266.
616. Conclusions 2014 (Republic of Moldova, Armenia).
617. The Committee concludes that the situation in Azerbaijan is not in conformity with Art. 4 §3 of the Charter, on the ground that there is no shift in the burden of proof in discrimination cases. Conclusions 2014.
618. Conclusions IX-2, p. 39 (Austria).
619. Conclusions XII-1, p. 100 (Iceland).
620. Activity Report 2018, p. 35.
621. Conclusions XIII-1, p. 118; Conclusions XIII-3, p. 219; Conclusions XIII-5, p. 256; Conclusions XIV-2, p. 274 (France).

against due to sex: changing the terms of resignation, temporarily placements into different positions, decreasing wages, making changes in working conditions.[622]

Article 4 §3 guarantees the right to equal pay without discrimination on grounds of gender.[623] As a result, the case law under Article 20 also applies to Article 4 §3. In a targeted question the Committee requested information on the impact of the COVID-19 pandemic on the right of women and men to equal pay for work of equal value. In addition, it examined the situation in Member States for which there was a previous finding of non-conformity, deferral or conformity pending receipt of requested information. The Committee examined thirty countries under this article[624] and considered that four cases were in conformity with the requirements of this provision.[625] In respect of one country (Lithuania), conformity is pending receipt of requested information. The ECSR deferred its conclusions for four countries,[626] and it released twenty-one conclusions of non-conformity.[627] The main grounds for non-conformity were as follows:

- comparisons of pay are not possible across companies,
- there is no explicit guarantee of equal pay for work of equal value,
- there is no shift in the burden of proof in pay discrimination cases,
- the obligation to ensure pay transparency is not guaranteed, and
- there is a predetermined upper limit on compensation for employees who are dismissed as a result of gender discrimination.

IV. The Right of All Workers to a Reasonable Period of Notice for Termination of Employment

123. An employer has a right to terminate employment with a worker giving a reasonable period of notice for such termination.[628] The above right of the employer was regulated under Article 4 §4 of the Charter due to the legal consequences.[629] During the period of notice, workers have a right to remuneration. The goal of Article 4 §4 of the Charter is therefore to guarantee workers a right to remuneration during the period of notice. The remuneration paid to a worker during the period of

622. Conclusions XI-1, p. 43 (the Netherlands); Conclusions XIII-3, pp. 219–220 (Norway); Conclusions XIII-5, p. 270 (Norway).
623. Conclusions 2022, *Press Briefing Elements*, European Committee of Social Rights, 22 March 2023, p. 43.
624. Conclusions 2022 (Albania), (Andorra), (Armenia), (Austria), (Azerbaijan), (Belgium), (Bulgaria), (Bosnia and Herzegovina), (Germany), (Spain), (Estonia), (Finland), (France), (Georgia), (Greece), (Ireland), (Italy), (Lithuania), (Latvia), (Luxembourg), (Moldova), (North Macedonia), (Malta), (Montenegro), (Poland), (Portugal), (Romania), (Serbia), (Slovakia), (Türkiye).
625. Conclusions 2022 (Austria), (France), (Portugal), (Spain).
626. Conclusions 2022 (Albania), (Estonia), (Latvia), (Slovakia).
627. Conclusions 2022 (Andorra), (Armenia), (Azerbaijan), (Belgium), (Bulgaria), (Bosnia and Herzegovina), (Germany), (Finland), (Georgia), (Greece), (Ireland), (Italy), (Luxembourg), (Moldova), (North Macedonia), (Malta), (Montenegro), (Poland), (Romania), (Serbia), (Türkiye).
628. With exception of Georgia where the Labour Code does not specify any period of notice for termination of employment. Conclusions 2010, vol. 1, pp. 282–283.
629. *See* Statement of interpretation of Art. 4 §4, Activity Report 2018, Published in point 34 b of that monograph.

notice should also be paid to the worker during the period preceding the period of notice being given by the employer. Article 4 §4 of the Charter is applicable to all work agreements, regardless of whether they are standard or non-standard contracts.[630] As of 2014, the Committee concludes that the situation in Estonia is not in conformity with Article 4 §4 of the Charter, on the grounds that the wages due to the ending of a temporary contract may be withdrawn in the event of early termination, on grounds other than economic ones.[631]

Poland[632] and Spain[633] were regarded as a country not fulfilling their obligations under Article 4 §4 because temporary work agreements for periods longer than a year were terminated regardless of their length, giving only fifteen days' notice.

It was applicable to workers employed on a trial basis.

Analysing Portugal's report, the Committee was of the view that in cases of employment on a trial basis, where the period of employment may be extended to 240 days for employees in managerial positions, the period of notice when terminating a work agreement is dependent upon the agreement made by both individual parties to the contract.[634] There is no, however, obligation to regulate the period of giving notice in cases of self-employment.[635] As of 2014, the Committee concludes that the situation in Portugal is not in conformity with Article 4 §4 of the Charter on the grounds that: (1) the notice periods applicable to probationary periods in the private sector are insufficient below four months of service; (2) the notice periods applicable to probationary periods for fixed-term, seasonal or show contracts in the private sector are insufficient; (3) no provision is made for notice of termination of duties during probationary periods for tenured civil servants; (4) the conditions governing the termination of the duties of tenured civil servants are left to the discretion of the parties.[636]

124. Article 4 §4 of the Charter does not place an obligation on the authorities of Member States to make the periods of giving notice uniform for all workers. Differences are acceptable in the period of giving notice for various categories of workers, on the condition that the variety of periods of giving notice for all the various work categories are regarded as 'reasonable', according to the definition of Article 4 §4 of the Charter.[637] As of 2014, the Committee concludes that notice periods are

---

630. Conclusions XIII-1, p. 124 (Iceland), p. 126 (United Kingdom).
631. Conclusions 2014 (Estonia).
632. Conclusions XIX-3, pp. 172–173. Conclusions 2014 (the notice period which applies in the event of early termination of fixed-term contracts is not reasonable).
633. Conclusions XIV-2, pp. 684–685. Conclusions XIX-3, p. 254. Conclusions 2014 (the notice period that applies to permanent and fixed-term employment contracts under the following circumstances is not reasonable: (1) dismissal when an employment contract expires or when its objectives are realised; (2) termination of employment contracts based on the death or retirement of the employer, who is a natural person, or based on the winding up of an employer that is a legal person, beyond three years of service; (3) termination of employment contracts for objective reasons, beyond six months of service).
634. Conclusions XIV-2, p. 648.
635. Conclusions I, p. 8.
636. Conclusions 2104 (Portugal).
637. Conclusions I, p. 8. The Committee concludes that in the 2014 cycle, the situation in the Netherlands is not in conformity with Art. 4 §4, on the grounds that 'notice periods are reasonable'.

not reasonable or sufficient in the following circumstances: (1) termination of employment for refusal to agree to a transfer when the concern relocates, or for refusal to accept essential changes in working conditions; dismissal as a result of changes in the organisation of production or labour or a reduction in staff numbers; dismissal due to unfitness for medical reasons, lack of qualification, withdrawal of access to top-secret information, or the reinstatement of a previous post-holder, after more than seven years of service;[638] dismissal with the application of the legal period of notice, after more than three years of service; dismissal in some cases of redundancy after more than five years of service; dismissal on grounds of long-term illness or incapacity for health reasons, after more than seven years of service; retirement, after between seven and ten years of service; dismissal in respect of additional jobs, after more than six months of service;[639] (2) termination of employment or dismissal on all other grounds, after more than two years of service.[640] Notice periods are not reasonable for employees with more than three years of service in the following circumstances: (1) dismissal in companies with ten employees or fewer, in accordance with some collective agreements; (2) receivership or liquidation; (3) ordinary dismissal for economic reasons.[641] (4) liquidation where no administrator has been appointed;[642] (5) in economic, technological or organisational circumstances requiring changes in the workforce;[643] (6) custody or arrest;[644] (7) a judicial decision preventing the performance of the work, a request from officials authorised by law, or unfitness for work certified by authorised bodies;[645] (8) in the food-processing and mechanical industries and in the textile industry, for employees in the seventh and eighth categories above, with more than fifteen years of service, as well as those in the second, third and fourth of the above categories.[646]

The Committee concludes that notice periods are not reasonable or sufficient in the following cases: (1) professional incompetence for employees with more than three years of service;[647] (2) physical or mental incapacity, professional inadequacy, or as a result of the abolition of the post;[648] (3) economic, health or any other grounds, beyond five years of service;[649] (4) general notice periods for workers with more than three years of service or with ten years of service who are younger than 60; (5) notice periods applicable to temporary workers with less than one year or more than three years of service; (6) notice periods applicable to civil servants with more than seven years of service;[650] (7) generally applied in the following cases: less than six months of service; between six months and two years of service;

638. Conclusions 2014 (Ukraine).
639. Conclusions 2014 (Bulgaria).
640. Conclusions 2014 (Ukraine)
641. Conclusions 2014 (Slovenia).
642. Conclusions 2014 (Slovenia).
643. Conclusions 2014 (Malta).
644. Conclusions 2014 (Turkey).
645. Conclusions 2014 (Lithuania).
646. Conclusions 2014 (Italy).
647. Conclusions 2014 (Serbia).
648. Conclusions 2014 (Romania).
649. Conclusions 2014 (Slovak Republic).
650. Conclusions 2014 (Norway)

between three and four years of service;[651] (8) dismissal on the grounds of liquidation of the undertaking or reduction in the number of staff, or termination of employment on account of a change in the terms and conditions of employment after more than seven years of service; termination of employment on account of being called up for military service or long-term illness or disability, after more than 5 years of service; dismissal during a probationary period;[652] (9) dismissal of employees with more than fifteen years of service following the dissolution of the organisation or reduction in staff numbers; dismissal of employees with more than six months of service for medical incapacity, call-up for military service, judicial or administrative reinstatement of the employee or refusal to be transferred when an employer relocates; dismissal during a probationary period, dismissal of an employee in additional employment with more than six months of service upon reinstatement of the principal post-holder; early termination of temporary contracts.[653] The Committee also concludes that the situation in France is not in conformity with Article 4 §4 of the Charter because the statutory notice periods for employees with seven to ten years of service are unreasonable.[654]

In general, the Committee accepts variations to the period of giving notice depending on the nature of the employment, whether it be physical or mental. It does not give consent, as specified by the dynamic approach of Article 4 §4 of the Charter, for the different periods of giving notice for employees in particular employment for less than twenty years (twenty-eight days‘ notice period) and above (fifty-six days‘ notice period).[655]

A 'reasonable' period of notice, a term used in Article 4 §4 of the Charter is neither a universal understanding nor an abstract one. It should be interpreted according to concrete cases analysed in the following supervisory cycles.[656] The Committee never attempted to judge whether an introduced labour law regulation of a notice period, by a Member State is considered to be reasonable. Referring to earlier arguments disallowing the establishing models of legal institutions by the Committee, during subsequent supervisory cycles monitoring whether obligations under the Charter are being met, the Committee pointed to cases where periods of notice were regulated by a state, which could not be regarded as reasonable according to the understanding of Article 4 §4 of the Charter. The Committee analysed whether the basis for differentiating periods of giving notice according to national labour law, form objective criteria. It is generally accepted that the objective criteria for establishing a period of giving notice are the number of years worked, either generally or in that particular employment.[657] Already by the fourth supervisory cycle the Committee came to the conclusion that the term 'reasonable' used in Article 4 §4 of the Charter referring to the period of giving notice is indicative of its dynamic nature and places on Member States an obligation of extending the period of giving notice according to the amount of time worked by the employee by

651. Conclusions 2014 (Malta)
652. Conclusions 2014 (Azerbaijan)
653. Conclusions 2014 (Russian Federation).
654. Conclusions 2014 (France).
655. Conclusions XIII-2, pp. 263–264 (Belgium).
656. As above, p. 29.
657. Conclusions IV, p. 35.

a specified employer.[658] Giving Article 4 §4 of the Charter a specific character means the Committee must step away from principles used during the supervisory process, which monitors whether Member States are following the obligations under the Charter, according to which determining the conformity of conduct within the previous supervisory cycles automatically gives the same conclusion in subsequent cycles, in cases where the situation had not changed. The period of giving notice regarded as reasonable in the earlier supervisory cycles could be regarded as 'unreasonable' in the subsequent cycles if the period did not lengthen along with the time of carried out employment for the same employer. The Committee regarded that the legal mechanism for lengthening the giving of notice period, whereby two weeks for a worker having worked two years for the same employer are given, by an additional one week for every year worked up to a maximum period of notice of twelve weeks, reflects the progressive nature of the obligations under Article 4 §4 of the Charter.[659] The fulfilment of obligations by Member States under Article 4 §4 of the Charter also has an influence on the labour market. The increase in unemployment and the decrease in opportunities for attaining a job should be taken into consideration by Member States when establishing the period of giving notice, which should be lengthened.[660] As of 2014, the Committee has also used the term 'insufficient notice'. It is concluded that general notice periods are either insufficient or unreasonable, being inadequate after more than[661] or below[662] three years of service.[663]

125. Accepting the connection between the periods of notice and the number of years worked for the same employer,[664] the Committee announced that it could not approve of the following national regulations concerning the period of giving notice:

- the period of giving notice of five days‘ notice with fewer than three months‘ service, even in the probationary period;[665]
- one week for six months of employment. A week of giving notice is regarded as 'reasonable' for the first couple of months of employment. During the thirteenth supervisory cycle, the Committee claimed, that Portugal had breached Article 4 §4 of the Charter, since an employer had the right to terminate a work agreement with a worker having worked for six months, having a one-week notice period.[666] More importantly, an 'unreasonable' period could not be a one-week period of notice for terminating employment for an employee having had worked from one month to two years;[667]

658. As above. Conclusions XIII-2, pp. 263–264 (Belgium); Conclusions XIII-3, p. 267 (Malta).
659. Conclusions XII-1, p. 107 (United Kingdom).
660. Conclusions XIV-2, pp. 274–275 (France).
661. Conclusions 2014 (Estonia).
662. Conclusion 2014 (United Kingdom).
663. Neither of the terms 'general notice' or 'inadequate notice' is explained in the conclusions cited.
664. No such connection exists in Armenia. Conclusions 2010, vol. 1, p. 89.
665. Conclusions 2007, vol. 1, p. 46 (Albania), Conclusions 2010, vol. 1, p. 29 (Albania).
666. Conclusions XIII-3, p. 267.
667. Conclusions 2010, p. 319 (Italy).

- fifteen days is not a reasonable period of notice for employees with six or more months of service under contract for additional work;[668] a two-week notice period was provided in the collective agreement applying to skilled construction and industrial workers;[669]
- a monthly period of notice for a worker having completed one year of employment.[670] One month (thirty days) is not a sufficient period of notice for workers with five or more years‘ service.[671] The Committee is of the view, that Article 4 §4 of the Charter is breached by countries which establish the following periods of notice: period of notice of five calendar days in the first year of employment, seven days within the second, fifteen days within the subsequent years up to the fifth year of employment, thirty days from five to ten years of employment;[672] six days of notice period for workers in less than five-year employment, nine days for workers in five to ten years employment, twelve days for workers in more than ten years employment;[673] a week of notice for workers up to one year of employment; two weeks in the next year and eight weeks for workers employed in the same employment for more than three[674] or five years;[675] a week for workers in up to two years of employment, two weeks for workers in two to five years of employment, four weeks for five to ten years employment, six weeks for ten to fifteen years employment and the minimum statutory notice[676] or eight weeks for workers employed for more than ten[677] or fifteen years;[678] fifteen days‘ notice for employees with less than one year‘s service, thirty days‘ notice for employees with one to five years‘ service, sixty days‘ notice for employees with five to ten years‘ service, seventy-five days‘ notice for employees with over ten years‘ service.[679]

The minimum length of established period of notice may be lengthened by collective bargaining agreements. The Committee takes into consideration the above possibility and gives it its approval. It does, however, concern itself with such a possibility that covers all workers.

---

668. Conclusions 2007, vo. 1, p. 283 (Bulgaria), vol. 2, p. 965 (Romania). Conclusions 2010, vol. 1, p. 177 (Bulgaria), vol. 2, p. 527 (Romania). Conclusions XIX-3, p. 141.
669. Conclusions XX-3 (Ireland).
670. Conclusions 2007, vol. 1, p. 104 (Armenia). The Committee concluded that two weeks’ notice for employees dismissed because of long-term incapacity who had one or more years’ service. Conclusions 2007, vol. 1, p. 369 (Estonia). Conclusions 2010, vol. 1, p. 223 (Estonia).
671. Conclusions 2007, vol. 1, p. 46 (Albania), p. 283 (Bulgaria), pp. 368–369 (Estonia), vol. 2, p. 1068 (Sweden). Conclusions 2010, vol. 2, p. 416 (Moldova), p. 448 (Netherlands). Conclusions 2010, vol. 2, p. 579 (Sweden).
672. Conclusions XII-1, p. 104 (Greece).
673. Conclusions I, p. 29 (Italy), Conclusions 2010, vol. 1, p. 319 (Italy).
674. Conclusions 2010, vol. 2, p. 597 (Turkey).
675. Conclusions XIV-2, pp. 513–514 (Malta), Conclusions 2010, vol. 2, p. 388 (Malta).
676. Conclusions 2007, vol. 1, p. 539 (France).
677. Conclusions 2010, vol. 2, p. 623 (Ukraine).
678. Case of Ireland. Conclusions I, pp. 177–178; Conclusions XIII-3, pp. 220–221; Conclusions XIV-2, pp. 397–398. Conclusions 2010, vol. 2, p. 416 (Moldova). Conclusions XIX-3, p. 59 (Czech Republic).
679. Conclusions 2010, vol. 2, p. 497 (Netherlands).

For this reason, the Committee viewed France's report negatively during the fourteenth supervisory cycle.[680] The generalising approach of collective bargaining should have a strictly obligatory standard. They may not be modified to worsen the position of the worker either by the stakeholders or by any individual side of the work agreement. The above requirements are not fulfilled by Swedish collective bargaining agreements. It is, for this reason, that the Committee came to the conclusion that the Swedish authorities are not fulfilling the requirements stipulated under Article 4 §4 of the Charter.[681]

The length of the period of notice cannot be dependent upon the age of the worker.

The Committee came to the conclusion that national labour law regulations in Sweden are not in accordance with the requirements set in Article 4 §4 of the Charter because based on the collective bargaining agreements for workers in the metal trade, the period of notice for workers who have not finished 30 years of age, regardless of the number of years worked, is one month.[682] The Committee took note that some of these workers had sixteen years of employment.

The Swedish government explained that the stakeholders who partook in collective bargaining agreements, consciously differentiated between the periods of notice according to the age of the worker and not the amount of employment. They believed that the chances for employment are proportionate according to the age of a worker.

The Committee in part divided its arguments. It agreed that the amount of employment and the age of a worker might be regarded as objective criteria for different periods of notice only when they are both included. As mentioned earlier, the number of years in employment may be regarded as an objective criterion for different periods of notice. However, according to the Committee, the age of the worker alone cannot be a stand-alone deciding criterion in establishing a period of notice.[683]

126. The period of notice commences from the day the employer informs the worker with an appropriate statement concerning an act of will. A reasonable period of notice, as treated by Article 4 §4 of the Charter, commences from the day the worker becomes familiarised with the employer's announced act of will. It is irrelevant whether the statement made by the employer deals with an individual matter, or whether it forms a part of a larger decision like group termination of contracts.[684] The above-mentioned period is not subjected to preceding periods to the period of notice to the worker, even when the national labour law regulations oblige the employer to inform them of work agreement termination (this mainly concerns group terminations) the trade unions, employment services or work inspectors.[685]

680. Conclusions XIV-2, p. 275.
681. Conclusions XIV-2, p. 715.
682. As above.
683. Conclusions XII-1, p. 106; Conclusions XIII-3, pp. 221–222; Conclusions XIV-2. pp. 715–716.
684. Conclusions XIV-2, p. 513 (Malta).
685. Conclusions IX-1, p. 45 (the Netherlands); Conclusions XI-1, p. 75 (Sweden); Conclusions XI-2, Addendum on Ireland, p. 17.

Periods of compulsory consultations preceding a decision with regard to the termination of a work agreement are not included in a notice period because an employer has not given the written act of terminating a work agreement. This is because the above-mentioned consultations can result in changing plans in terms of collective redundancy. Presenting the employee with the employer's notice for the termination of a work agreement is regarded as an announcement in legal terms as binding both parties in a particular work agreement. An employer warning a worker about the terminating work relation, which is to take effect on the last day of the period of notice is done so to allow a worker to engage in a new work relationship. The Committee takes the position that an employer is obliged to grant a worker some days free from work during the period of notice in order to help him/her seek new employment.[686] During the period of notice, a worker is obliged to carry out work as per usual with the same amount of hours and of the same value as prior to obtaining the notice of termination. However, the Committee claims that an employer has the right to excuse a worker from the above-mentioned duty. The Committee's opinion is that the point of the period of notice (warning a worker of a certain event which will eventuate in the near future and allowing him/her to find a new job) is achieved after informing a worker by writing about the termination of the work relation and excusing him/her from the obligation of carrying out the work. The essential condition for fulfilling the regulations imposed on employers by labour law provisions is the obligation to pay a worker an amount of money equal to the remuneration due, according to the period of notice.[687] The term 'amount' is mentioned and not 'remuneration' because an employer can shorten the period of notice which results in terminating the work relation before the end of the period of notice, yet an employer is still obliged to pay a worker the amount of compensation equal to the remuneration for the whole period of notice.

127. Article 4 §4 of the Charter does not prohibit employers from terminating work agreements without respecting the notice period. In the appendix to the Charter, it is explicitly stated that the obligation of introducing sensible periods of notice can be by no means interpreted as a standard prohibiting employers from terminating work agreements without respecting the period of notice if the reason for the immediate termination of employment is a serious violation. The appendix to the Charter does not contain a 'serious violation' definition, which gives reasons for the termination of a work relation without a period of notice. The Committee examines individual cases deciding upon whether there were reasons for the termination of a work relation without a period of notice[688] The Committee concludes that the situation in the Member State is not in conformity with Article 4 §4 of the Charter when it finds out that the notice period may be left to the discretion of the parties to an employment contract.[689] It also declares non-compliance with the Charter when no notice period is provided for in the following cases: (1) termination of employment

---

686. Conclusions XIII-1, p. 124 (Greece).
687. Conclusions XII-1, p. 104 (Greece).
688. Conclusions XIII-2, p. 264, p. 513 (Malta).
689. Conclusions XX-3 (Spain). Conclusions 2014 (Russia). In Russia, notice periods applicable to self-employed persons or religious organisations or to home workers are left to the discretion of the parties to the employment contract.

for enforcement of a prison sentence; (2) disqualification from the category or academic diploma required by the employment contract; (3) being struck off the list of a professional association; (4) existing incompatibilities of functions identified in the labour code; (5) proven conflict of interest within the meaning of the conflict-of-interest legislation;[690] (6) dismissal for professional incompetence or lack of qualifications; (7) termination of employment in the event of a change of ownership of the undertaking or after military service; (8) termination of employment on account of the withdrawal of the worker's driving licence or a ban on performing certain duties or activities; (9) termination of employment in the event of a disability recorded in a judicial decision;[691] (10) dismissal during a probationary period.[692]

128. In 2022, the Committee adopted several statements of interpretation on the right of all workers to a reasonable notice period for termination of employment under Article 4 §4 of the Charter, limits to deductions of wages under Article 4 §5 and online harassment related to work under Article 26 of the Charter.

129. From the interpretive statement in Article 4 §4,[693] the question of the reasonableness of the notice periods will no longer be addressed, except where the notice periods are manifestly unreasonable. The Committee will assess this question on the basis of the rules governing the setting of notice periods (or the level of compensation in lieu of notice):

- according to the source of the rule, namely the law, collective agreements, individual contracts and court judgments;
- during any probationary periods, including those in the public service;
- with regard to the treatment of workers in insecure jobs;
- in the event of termination of employment for reasons outside the parties' control; and
- including any circumstances in which workers can be dismissed without notice compensation.

The statements of interpretation for Article 4 §4: acknowledgement, by law, collective agreement or individual contract of length of service, whether with the same employer or where a worker has been successively employed in precarious forms of employment relations. The Committee considers that in the event of the death of an employer who is a natural person, there is no obligation to give a notice period. However, it asks if there is a mechanism to protect the interests of workers employed by an employer who is a natural person in the event of the employer's death (contractual or statutory compensation).

---

690. Conclusions 2014 (Bulgaria)
691. Conclusions 2014 (Azerbaijan, Slovenia in cases of expiry of work permits).
692. Conclusions 2014 (Ukraine, Turkey, Slovenia, Slovak Republic, the Netherlands, Romania, Georgia, Andorra).
693. *European Social Charter. Social Rights Monitoring: Labour Rights, 2022 Conclusions of the European Committee of Social Rights*, Council of Europe. (www.coe.int/socialcharter).

V. Deductions from Wages

130. The workers' right to just (decent) remuneration is protected by a provision prohibiting employers from making a deduction from wages for work completed without legal authorisation. An employee cannot be authorised to waive their right to deductions from wages limited by a state law.[694] Article 4 §5 of the Charter obliges Member States to regulate rules allowing employers to make a deduction from workers' wages. Member States grant permissions for making deductions from the remuneration for work. The above-mentioned permission and its scope are commonly accepted and seen as appropriate for particular Member States. The provision in question does not make any restrictions in this matter for Member State authorities. Conditions and the field of deductions can be regulated by provisions legislated by a given state, in work collective agreements made by social stakeholders, by arbitrary court decisions or in other ways determined by legal mechanisms of establishing work remuneration. They may also be regulated in a different way. Therefore, Article 4 §5 disallows making deductions from wages which are unauthorised in view of domestic labour law. Under the term 'unauthorised' one should understand deductions not regulated by domestic labour law. The Charter assumes the need to make deductions from remuneration for work. Looking at the rulings of the Committee, there was no case where a Member State would *expressis verbis* prohibit employers from making any deductions from workers' remuneration. A lack of regulations in terms of making a deduction from a worker's remuneration cannot be regarded as a ban on making a deduction at all. In light of the regulation of Article 4 §5 of the Charter, it may be perceived as granting permission to make unauthorised deductions. Therefore, the provision in question obligates Member State authorities to undertake relevant legislative initiatives. The legal regulations resulting from these actions should be clear. As of 2014, the Committee concludes that the situation in some Member States is not in conformity with Article 4 §5 of the Charter, on the grounds that the guarantees in place to prevent workers from waiving their rights to limitations in respect of wage deductions are insufficient.[695] In order to examine whether all the circumstances in which deductions from wages are permitted are set out in the legal instruments, the Committee asks that the country reports stipulate the 'other mandatory payments specified by law', and include supplementary information on any other circumstances (tax debts, a decline in activity, deductions for health expenses, etc.) that may lead to deductions from wages. It also requests information on the application of the 20%, 50% and 70% limits to workers receiving the monthly minimum wage (MMW) who consent to assign portions of their wages, or to those whose wages are paid partly in kind, in accordance with the provisions of the national laws.[696] A good example[697] is the Norwegian Act of 17 June 2005, as amended when it came into force on 1 January 2010, on the

694. Conclusions 2007, vol. 2, p. 605 (Italy), p. 918 (Norway).
695. Conclusions 2014 (Azerbaijan, Cyprus, Ireland, Norway, Portugal).
696. Conclusions 2014 (Azerbaijan).
697. A good example is the Portuguese legal system. The Labour Code of 29 Aug. 2012 stated that deductions permitted in the private sector listed in the Labour Code may not exceed one-sixth of the net workers' wage deductions made for the state or the social security service or in enforcement of judicial decisions or conciliation agreements. In the public sector, s. 219 of Law No. 59/2008 of

working environment, working hours and employment protection (WEA),[698] and the Regulations issued on 13 June 2014 by the Ministry of Children, Equality and Social Inclusion. Section 14-15 §2 of the WEA limits deductions from wages to the following grounds: (1) authorisation by the law; (2) contributions to pension schemes; (3) prior written individual agreement; (4) collective agreement providing for the deduction of trade union and similar dues; (5) reparation of loss or damage caused to the undertaking by employees in the course of their work, either intentionally or through serious negligence, liability for which they acknowledge themselves or has been established by a court, or loss or damage caused by an unlawful termination by the employee of the employment relationship; (6) reimbursement of advances on pay. The Committee concludes that the above-mentioned statutory acts do not afford workers and their dependents sufficient protection from being deprived of their measure of subsistence because they do not prevent workers from waiving their right to limits to deductions from wages.

A general rule listed in Article 36 of the Constitution of the Republic of Italy, says that employers have the right to remunerate workers according to the amount and quality of work carried out, ensuring a decent standard of living for an individual and his/her family.

The Committee regarded this as inadequate. The above-mentioned ruling was clarified by Italian authorities that argued under the above clause of the Constitution that the real scope of protection of workers‘ remuneration is left to the judiciary. The legal system in Italy is not based on precedence. Nevertheless, the Committee asked Italian authorities to provide information on the position of the courts regarding protection of work remuneration. Simultaneously the Committee presented a view that a more efficient and more likely to be socially accepted is remuneration, calculated according to the provisions legislated by the state, which is obliged to precisely determine the limits of deductions from remunerations made by employers in cases of employees not meeting employer obligations.[699]

Precise legal regulations are intended to protect wages. Lack of such regulations occurred due to negative conclusions of the Committee addressed to Member States in a few subsequent supervisory cycles.[700] The obligation of introducing a regulation concerning motives and the field of deductions from wages for work made by employers on a basis of either collective agreement or legislated law cannot be passed onto the involved parties of work agreements, to the subjects of a work relation.[701] The Committee considers that the absence of adequate limits to the deductions that may be made to wages paid at the level of the national minimum wage

11 Sep. 2008, establishing civil service employment contracts, rules out deductions from the salaries of tenured civil servants or contractual staff, except under conditions provided by law, at the workers' express request or on execution of judicial decisions. The Committee concludes that the situation in Portugal is not in conformity with Art. 4 §5 of the Charter on the grounds that guarantees in place to prevent tenured civil servants and civil service contracted staff from waiving their light to the limitation of deductions from wages are insufficient.

698. No. 62/2005, quoted in Conclusions 2014 (Norway).

699. Conclusions X-2, p. 66.

700. Conclusions XI-2, p. 72; Conclusions XII-2, p. 94; Conclusions XIII-1, p. 124; Conclusions XIII-3, pp. 222–223; Conclusions XIV-3, p. 438.

701. Conclusions XIV-2, p. 399 (Ireland); XIV-2, p. 774 (United Kingdom).

(deductions related to penalties, advance of wages, purchase of shares or securities, accidental overpayment) is contrary to the Charter as it may result in depriving workers and the dependants of their means of subsistence).[702] The Charter ensures workers' protection of their remuneration. The Committee points out that the goal of Article 4 §of the Charter is to guarantee that workers protected by this provision are not deprived of their means of subsistence.[703] Therefore, workers should have the option to utilise legal measures in order to check the legitimacy of the employer's decision about the deductions from their wages that are due.

131. The Charter guarantees workers the right to obtain the earned remuneration in full. Neither the Charter nor the Committee determines the allowable field of deductions. The above responsibility is given to Member State authorities or may be passed on by the authorities to the stakeholders. The Committee never analysed the grounds or the scope of permissible deductions from wages. It presented the view that social collections (taxes, social security premiums), workers' financial obligation in relation to their trade union membership (trade union fees), civil obligations (alimonies), deposits paid by employers to workers as well as employers' amounts due to damages committed by workers can be classified to a category that is regulated by domestic labour law. Additionally, the Committee stated that in regulating the rules and the field of deductions from wages, Member State authorities or stakeholders should take into consideration the protection of remuneration, which according to Article 4 §1 of the Charter should ensure workers and their families decent standards of living.[704] More recently, the Committee concluded that in practice the wages paid after any deductions ought to be still sufficient for workers to provide for themselves and their dependants.[705] In 2010, the Committee accepted a new formula. It concludes negatively on the grounds that it has not been established that deductions from wages will not deprive workers or their dependents of their very means of subsistence.[706] As of 2014, the Committee has come to a negative conclusion, on the grounds that after all authorised deductions, the wages of workers with the lowest pay do not allow them to provide for themselves and their dependants.[707]

---

702. Conclusions XXI-1 (United Kingdom), p. 316. Therefore, the Committee concludes that the situation in United Kingdom is not in conformity with Art. 4 §5 of the Charter on the ground that the absence of adequate limits on deduction from wages equivalent to the National Minimum Wage may result in depriving workers and their dependants of their means of subsistence.
703. Conclusions XVIII-2, 2007 (Poland).
704. Conclusions XII-1, pp. 108–109 (Greece); Conclusions XII-1, pp. 127–128 (Norway); Conclusions XIII-3, p. 270 (Turkey); Addendum to Conclusions XIII-3, pp. 33–34 (Luxembourg); Conclusions XIV-2, p. 230 (Finland); XIV-2, p. 399 (Ireland); XIV-2, pp. 481–482 (Luxembourg); XIV-2, pp. 514–515 (Malta); XIV-2, pp. 594–595 (Norway); XIV-2, p. 743 (Norway); XIX-2, pp. 774–775 (United Kingdom).
705. Conclusions 2007, vol. 2, p. 605 (Ireland), p. 688 (Italy), p. 818 (Lithuania), p. 885 (Moldova), p. 966 (Romania). Conclusions XX-3 (Iceland, Poland).
706. Conclusions 2010, vol. 1, p. 30 (Albania), p. 90 (Armenia), p. 320 (Italy), vol. 2, pp. 354–355 (Lithuania), p. 388 (Malta), p. 528 (Romania), p. 600 (Turkey). Conclusions XIX-3, p. 173 (Poland), p. 192 (Slovakia).
707. Conclusions 2014 (Armenia, Azerbaijan, Bulgaria, Estonia, Russian Federation, Finland, Ireland, Italy, Lithuania, Republic of Moldova, Romania, Ukraine).

132. Article 4 §5 of the Charter is commonly applied, encompassing workers employed by both public and private sectors, being parties to typical and atypical work relations.[708] The analysed protection standard is not applied to persons running their own businesses (self-employed).[709]

A motion made by the United Kingdom resulted in a regulation based on a legal fiction listed in the appendix to the Charter. According to this regulation, Member State authorities meet requirements set by Article 4 §5 of the Charter when domestic labour law regulations ensure protection for wage deductions for the majority of workers.

It is difficult to determine reasons why this regulation was introduced in the appendix to the Charter. The clause listed in the appendix gave the same effect as applying the clauses listed in Article 33 §2 ESC and Article 1 §2 RESC. As far as protection against unauthorised deductions from wages by domestic labour law regulations is concerned, workers seem to be the interested party. Therefore, it is sensible to use the same rules of interpretation while interpreting the content of Article 4 §5 of the Charter as the one used to analyse Article 33 §2 ESC and Article 1 §2 RESC. This means that in the light of Article 4 §5 of the Charter, a 'significant majority' of workers occurs when there are 80% of persons in work relations in a given country. The above basis for the calculation of the category of workers used by the appendix to the Charter should be deducted from persons whose legal situation is not defined by national labour law regulations, collective work agreements, or the courts' arbitrary decisions. In the appendix to the Charter, in the part containing an explanation of the content of Article 4 §5 of the Charter the notion 'persons' was used for describing a group of subjects (workers), out of which the significant majority should be protected against deductions from wages made by employers. Article 4 §5 of the Charter is a standard, which applies solely to employees. Some of them may be excluded from the scope of application of collective agreements or courts' arbitrary decisions. Occupational entitlements and rights of this group of workers are subject to domestic labour law regulations legislated by a particular state. Therefore a 'significant majority' is a term that should be related to all 'persons', also the ones regarded by the final part of the appendix to Article 4 §5 of the Charter, as exceptions not encompassed by the law and rulings listed in the appendix.

Statement of interpretation of Article 4 §5 of the Charter:

> The Committee recalls that the deductions envisaged in Article 4 §5[710] of the Charter can only be authorised in certain circumstances, which must be well-defined in a legal instrument (for instance, a law, regulation, collective agreement or arbitration award). The Committee further recalls that deductions from wages must be subject to reasonable limits and should not per se result in depriving workers and their dependents of their means of subsistence.

---

708. Conclusions XII-2, pp. 94–95; Conclusions XIII-1, pp. 227–228 (Turkey); Conclusions XII-2, p. 267 (Malta); Conclusions XIII-3, p. 270 (Turkey); Conclusions XIII-3, p. 269 (Portugal).
709. Conclusions I, p. 8.
710. Conclusions 2022, *Press Briefing Elements*, 22 March 2023, p. 4.

With a view to making an in-depth assessment of national situations, the Committee has considered it necessary to change its approach. Therefore, the Committee asks States Parties to provide the following information in their next reports:

- a description of the legal framework regarding wage deductions, including the amount of protected (unattachable) wage;
- information on the national subsistence level, how it is calculated and how the calculation of that minimum subsistence level ensures that workers can provide for their own and their dependents' subsistence needs;
- information establishing that the disposable income of a worker earning the minimum wage after all deductions (including for child maintenance) is enough to guarantee the means of subsistence (i.e., to ensure that workers can provide for their own and their dependents' subsistence needs); and a description of safeguards that prevent workers from waiving their right to the restriction on deductions from wages.

§6. The Right of Children and Young Persons to Protection

I. Introduction

133. Legal protection guaranteed by Article 7 of the Charter encompasses the following: those at the minimum age of admission to employment (children and young persons); the maximum standards of work time; ban of employment for some types of work and for all work carried out during night hours; the right to just remuneration for the allowed work; annual paid holiday; regular medical examination and special protection against physical and moral dangers. The article in question protects children and young people under the age of 18 from direct or indirect dangers resulting from the workplace. Additionally, Article 7 §10 of the Charter protects children and young persons from other factors associated with carrying out the work or the working environment, and from the physical or moral dangers that children or young persons may be subjected to. Supervising whether the obligations set by this provision are being met by Member States, the Committee also demands from the authorities of such states a requisition of information concerning clear prohibitions of employing children, legally permissible hours of employment for young persons, types of jobs where young persons are able to be employed in, regulated principles of employing young persons and the number of employable young persons allowed in domestic duties and family businesses. The Committee requires information concerning the controlling mechanisms undertaken by Member States in terms of monitoring the employment of young workers.[711]

II. A Ban on Employing Children under the Age of 15 Years

134. The Charter prohibits the employment of children and young persons under the age of 15 years. Despite this prohibition, the situation in practice is very

711. Conclusions XIII-2, p. 77.

problematic in many Member States. In the opinion of the Committee, this means that the competent public authorities (labour inspection) do not sufficiently effectively monitor compliance with the ban on employment of children and young people under the age of 15.[712] It refers to all types of employment, paid or unpaid, in all sectors of the economy, in agriculture and in the service sector.[713] It also encompasses jobs organised by individuals as well as the relatives of the young person. The prohibition of family relatives employing children or young persons is broad in its scope. It encompasses a wide range of 'help' labour allocated to children by adults necessary in running the family business. It is also applicable to job activities carried out by young persons.[714] The Charter does allow for the employment of those children and young persons who are not 15 years of age, only in specific light categories of work, without harming the health and morality of those carrying out such work, and if it does not inhibit their schooling responsibilities. The exception in Article 7 §1 of the Charter places on the authorities of Member States the responsibility of drawing up and publishing such categories of light work, accessible to those who have not yet completed the age of 15 years. The authorities of Member States do not have a responsibility to state what types of jobs these are. A lack of such statements means that a particular Member State does not permit exemption from the general rule concerning the employment of young persons under the age of 15 years. Light work is defined as work which is not harmful to health and which does not interfere with the education process, carried out in free time from studies.[715] It is claimed that it should not be possible to allow for a general rule allowing the employment of young persons under the age of 15. It is also impermissible generally to employ young persons under the age of 15 in light labour without prior specificity of such jobs as 'light' being established by the authorities of Member States.[716] Some Member State authorities allow children and adolescents to perform 'light' work several hours a day. For this reason, the Committee believes that light work performed genuinely in excess must be regarded as prohibited by the provisions of both Charter.[717] There are no jobs that may be categorised as light. In particular, all jobs associated with the service sector are run by family businesses (hotels, restaurants, farming).[718] For this reason, the employment of children and young persons in positions organised by family relatives, without being

712. Albania, Armenia, Azerbaijan, Bosnia and Herzegovina, Georgia, the Republic of Moldova, Romania, Serbia, Turkey and Ukraine. Activity Report 2019, p. 30.
713. Complaint No. 1/1998 *International Commission of Jurists v. Portugal;* Conclusions XII-1, p. 133 (Greece); Conclusions XIII-4, p. 291 (France); XIII-4, p. 293 (Italy), Conclusions 2006, vol. 1, p. 105 (Bulgaria), p. 149 (Cyprus), p. 190 (Estonia).
714. Conclusions XIII-4, p. 291 (France).
715. Conclusions (Ukraine). The Committee concludes that the situation in Ukraine, the Republic of Moldova work is not sufficiently precise.
716. Conclusions I, p. 42; Conclusions II, p. 30; Conclusions III, p. 39; Conclusions IV, p. 53; Conclusions V, p. 56; Conclusions VI, p. 44; Conclusions VII, p. 41; Conclusions VIII, p. 101; Conclusions X-2, p. 80; Conclusions XI-2, p. 82; Conclusions XII-2, p. 119; Conclusions XIII-2, p. 78; Conclusions XIII-4, p. 293; Conclusions XV-2, p. 292, Conclusions 2011, vol. 3, p. 1153 (Turkey), p. 1222 (Ukraine).
717. Armenia, Estonia, Georgia, Greece, Lithuania, Malta, Portugal, Activity Report 2019, p. 30.
718. Conclusions I, p. 42. Conclusions 2011, vol. 1, p. 34 (Albania), p. 115 (Armenia), p. 306 (Cyprus), vol. 2, p. 548 (Ireland), p. 598 (Italy), p. 753 (Moldova), vol. 3, p. 971 (Romania), p. 1010 (Slovakia).

safeguarded by Article 7 §1 of the Charter is impermissible.[719] Banning such employment encompasses various jobs, regardless of the type of work agreements signed, whether they be work contracts or work experience.[720]

135. The type of employment of young persons as an exception, under the age of 15 years, should be specified on registers prepared by the authorities of Member States. They should, in reality, be very light labour indeed. They cannot be of harm encroaching on the physical, moral and educational well-being of the young person.[721] The Committee evaluates the type of jobs where persons under the age of 15 may be employed. Whether such jobs really do belong in the category of light labour is decided by factors such as the number of hours worked in the given job, the time of day in which the work is carried out (whether it be before school, after school hours, on the weekend or during holiday periods) as well as the amount of time spent on rest.[722] In the opinion of the Committee, it is impossible to include in the category of light labour work the transportation and/or delivery of heavy goods using physically powered vehicles (such as bicycles).[723] Depending on the nature of the duties carried out in the light labour category, it is impossible to include all work carried out on a farm, work in forests cutting down and bringing in timber, or breeding pigs.[724] The Committee analysed the type and the nature of specified duties, allowing for the possibility of employing young persons under the age of 15 years. It is permissible to employ children and young persons in the artistic field, such as working as models or in advertising agencies. When the Committee found out that the report submitted by Cyprus indicates that no child can participate in cultural, or artistic activities for more than seven hours and fifteen minutes per day or more than thirty-six hours per week, it concluded that the situation in Cyprus was not in conformity with Article 7 §1 of the Charter, on the grounds that the duration of light work during non-school days was excessive.[725] The Committee demanded as a necessary requirement for such employment that the employer receives permission for employing such individuals who are not normally employable.[726] It accepted the type of employment which enriched the practical work experience of the young person, especially when it is directly associated with an apprenticeship or vocational training. The Committee insisted that the register of light labour allowing for the employment of children under the age of 15 years be completely precise. It was of a lesser importance how it was drawn up. Publishing such a register by the competent authoritative governmental bodies, administratively or in a format of a collective list prepared on the basis of court or administrative decisions, fulfils the

719. Conclusions VI, p. 44 (France); Conclusions VII, p. 41 (France). Conclusions 2011, vol. 1, p. 306 (Cyprus).

720. First report on certain provisions of the Charter which have not been accepted, p. 17.

721. Conclusions V, p. 55.

722. Conclusions VIII, pp. 101–102 (France, Netherlands).

723. Conclusions XIII-3, p. 285 (Portugal).

724. Conclusions III, p. 39 (Italy); Conclusions XII-1, p. 133 (Greece).

725. Conclusions (Cyprus).

726. Conclusions XII-2, p. 118 (France); Conclusions XIII-2, pp. 285–286 (Belgium); Conclusions XIII-3, p. 283 (Finland); Conclusions XIII-3 Addendum on Luxembourg, p. 40; Conclusions XIII-4, p. 292 (Sweden).

function as specified under Article 7 §1 of the Charter, on the condition that the chosen method by the Member State authorities of preparing such registers is subject to control, and the decisions establishing what light labour may be, are not made in an arbitrary fashion.[727]

136. Employed in light labour, young persons who have not completed 15 years of age, may not be employed in before-school hours. Work time should be made reasonable. The employment of seven hours daily five times a week, making it thirty-five hours per week is considered to be excessive.[728] Young persons under the age of 15 years should utilise one day free from work. They should also be free from work responsibilities at least for half of their holidays.[729] The Committee considers that children under the age of 15, and those who are subject to compulsory schooling, should not perform light work during school holidays for more than six hours per day or thirty hours per week, in order to avoid risks that the performance of such work might have for their health, moral welfare, development or education.[730] The Committee concludes that daily or weekly work for children under the age of 15 measuring more than six hours per day or thirty hours per week is excessive and therefore cannot qualify as light work.[731]

In particular, the Committee applied pressure on the necessity of obeying the regulations prohibiting the employment of children and young persons under the age of 15 years.[732] It paid heed to the category creating the highest level of harm, i.e., children whose work responsibility caused the ending of their education before completing 15 years of age.[733] According to the Committee, the authorities of Member States are obliged to undertake vigorous enforcement measures to obey the prohibition of employing children and young persons under the age of 15 years.[734] Children's absence at school was not regarded to be among these measures.[735] In a form used by the Committee as well as Member State authorities in preparations of reports concerning the obligations under Article 7 §1 of the Charter, were included questions referring to the activities carried out by state labour inspectors monitoring and supervising the ban of employing children and young persons under the age of 15 years. The Member State authorities were obliged to provide information about the number of confirmed violations employing children under the age of 15 years as

727. Conclusions XIII-3, p. 285 (Portugal).
728. As above. Conclusions 2011, vol. 1, p. 115 (Armenia). Conclusions (Armenia, Cyprus, Estonia, Georgia, Lithuania, Norway, Sweden).
729. Conclusions VI, p. 43 (France); Conclusions VIII, p. 103 (Sweden); Conclusions X-2, p. 81.
730. General Introduction, Conclusion.
731. Conclusions (Armenia, Cyprus, Estonia, Georgia, Lithuania, Norway, Sweden). The Committee notes from the Governmental Committee Report concerning Conclusions 2011 that, according to s. 36 of the Law on Occupational Safety and Health, during holidays, young persons in Lithuania under 15 years of age may work up to seven hours per day and thirty-five hours per week, and young persons who have reached the age of 15 may work up to eight hours per day and forty hours per week. Conclusions 2015 (Lithuania).
732. Conclusions XIX-4 (2011), p. 184 (Greece). Conclusions (Georgia, Malta, Romania, Turkey).
733. In the opinion of the Committee the most fragile group is children between the ages of 14 and 15 years. Conclusions X-2, p. 80 (Sweden); Conclusions XIII-1, p. 229 (Turkey); Conclusions XIII-2, p. 78 (Italy); Conclusions XIII-5, p. 185 (Portugal).
734. Conclusions XI-2, p. 82 (Spain); Conclusions XIII-3, p. 286 (Portugal).
735. Conclusions X-2, p. 79 (France).

well as the penalties involved in failing to obey the provision, the level of such employment of children and the measures and intentions undertaken in rectifying this problem.[736]

III. A Prohibition of Employing Persons under the Age of 18 Years in Employment Dangerous or Harmful to Health

137. The Charter provides for a minimum age of admission to employment, 18 years of age, with respect to prescribed occupations regarded as dangerous or unhealthy. Article 7 §2 of the ESC orders Member States to set a minimum age requirement for employment. The minimum age set by Article 7 §1 of the Charter, is 15 years of age.[737] The Committee claimed that establishing such limits is dependent upon the type and conditions of work to be undertaken. It ordered Member State authorities to set such minimum ages as are required for any employment requiring jobs to be undertaken by young persons.[738] This provision was changed by the Revised European Social Charter, which sets a minimum age of 18, required for employment in particular occupations and dangerous or unhealthy jobs.[739] Analysing the report prepared by the Italian authorities, the Committee was of the view that in the following provisions concerning obligations of equal treatment of workers of men and women, the age of 18 was lowered to 16 years as a minimum age for women employed in jobs where there is a danger of harming the body by means of benzol poisoning or by products containing benzol.[740]

It, therefore, questioned the Italian authorities regarding whether the domestic labour law regulations were congruous with Article 11 (2) of the above convention, which prohibits the employment of young persons under the age of 18 years from being employed in jobs where they may be exposed to dangers caused by benzol or benzol products. Without waiting for a reply, the Committee came to a conclusion the Italian authorities decreasing the minimum age limit required for employment in work associated with exposure to dangerous substances were simply doing so in order to guarantee equal treatment in the workplace for both men and women. The Italian authorities[741] were in breach of Article 7 §2 of the Charter. Prior to the amendment by the Revised European Social Charter, the Committee, supported by Article 7 §2 ESC, decided that 18 years of age is the permissible borderline age for the employment of young persons in dangerous or unhealthy jobs.

736. Conclusions XV-2, p. 235, 515.
737. Conclusions I, p. 186.
738. Conclusions XIII-2, p. 81 (Italy).
739. In 2011 the Committee declares lack of implementation of that provision by Albania and France. Conclusions 2011, vol. 1, p. 36 (Albania), p. 434 (France).
740. Conclusions X-2, p. 82.
741. Conclusions XIII-2, pp. 81–82. Also the Turkish authorities, which do not ensure effective protection against employment under the age of 18 for dangerous or unhealthy activities. Conclusions 2011, vol. 3, p. 1155 (Turkey).

138. Article 7 §2 of the Charter obliges Member State authorities to produce a list of dangerous or unhealthy work for young persons.[742] The Committee is of the opinion that dangerous or unhealthy work for young persons may exist within all sectors of the economy, not just in heavy industries.

During the 3rd supervisory cycle, the Committee did not accept the arguments presented by Germany, which claimed there were no such jobs in question in trade, transport, hospitality, or gastronomy services. The Committee was of the view that within such sectors, undoubtedly, were in existence jobs dangerous or unhealthy for young persons.[743] Accepting the above proposition, the Committee turned to other Member State authorities for their input, whether on their lists of prohibited employment for young persons were jobs outside heavy industry, in agriculture, or family-run businesses. The Committee claimed that these sectors of the economy consist of some work demanding heavy lifting, which is carried out in conditions where a worker is subject to factors harmful to health (vibration, noise, chemicals).[744]

As an exception to the rule disallowing young persons below the age of 18 to enter employment, which is dangerous and harmful to the health, the appendix to Article 7 §2 of the RESC allows Member States to employ young persons in such occupations when it is necessary for their vocational training. This is allowable on the condition that an employer undertakes special measures of safety and health protection. The authorities of Member States should determine these measures in advance.

Analogically, like in cases of supervision whereby Article 7 §1 of the Charter is being abided by Member States, the Committee demands from Member States the presentation of data on the efficiency of conduct of work inspectors.[745] An indicator of such efficiency is the information on the number of work-related accidents and occupational diseases among young workers.[746]

IV. The Banning of Employment of Children of School Age in Work Affecting Their Education

139. Article 7 §3 of the Charter complements Article 7 §1. It is applicable to children and young persons who must attend school despite being over 15. Member

742. French labour law does not provide, except in vocational training, for general prohibition of employment under the age of 18 for dangerous jobs. Therefore, the Committee in 2006 concluded that the situation in France is not in conformity with Art. 7 §2 of the RESC. Conclusions 2006, vol. 1, p. 313. As of 2015 the Committee concludes that the situation in Bosnia and Herzegovina is not in conformity with Art. 7 §2 of the Charter on the grounds that the legislation does not define or provide a list of dangerous or unhealthy activities prohibited to young workers under 18. Conclusions (Bosnia and Herzegovina).

743. Conclusions III, p. 39.

744. Conclusions XII-2, p. 120; Conclusions XII-2, p. 287 (Malta); Conclusions, XIII-3, p. 289 (Portugal).

745. Conclusions XIII-5, pp. 66–67 (Finland); Conclusions XIII-5, p. 124 (Luxembourg). As of 2015, the Committee concluded that the situation in Georgia was not in conformity with Art. 7 §2 of the Charter on the grounds that during the reference period there was no labour inspection to supervise how the regulations regarding the prohibition of employment of young persons under 18 for dangerous or unhealthy activities were being implemented in practice.

746. Conclusions XV-2, p. 37 (Austria); XV-2, p. 78 (Belgium); XV-2, p. 234 (Greece); XV-2, p. 292 (Italy); XV-2, p. 337 (The Netherlands); XV-2, p. 516 (Spain).

States are obliged to prohibit the employment of children and young persons below the age of 15 in light labour, which is harmful to their health, morals or education. The notion of light work for children ought to be defined.[747] In cases of young persons over the age of 15, the above ban only applies to work which may conflict with their compulsory education. Keeping in mind the contradicting scopes of the application of the provisions in question, Member States who did not ratify Article 7 §1 of the Charter can be regarded as violating obligations determined by Article 7 §3 of the Charter also in cases when they allow employers to employ children and persons under 15 years of age in light labour, making it difficult for them to fully benefit from a compulsory system of education.[748] The goal of Article 7 §3 of the Charter is to limit the daily work standards for young people attending schools within a compulsory education system.[749] The analysed provision creates a legal basis for determining the maximum daily limits for the employment of young persons on days when they have educational duties.[750] This provision caused the Committee to determine at what appropriate times young persons can be employed on days when they have educational commitments. The Committee ruled out the possibility of employing young persons before they undertake tasks connected with their education.

It made a ruling against the case of the Netherlands and Norway, whose national labour laws allowed children to be employed as newspaper distributors from 6 o'clock in the morning.[751] It allowed for the employment of young persons after school hours on condition that this did not have a negative impact on their education.[752]

140. According to the Committee, employment of four hours per day prevents a young person from fully benefiting from an educational programme.[753] Similar reservations were submitted in cases of the employment of young persons for twenty-five or twenty-seven hours per week during the school year.[754] The Committee considered any employment engaging young persons for forty-nine hours as excessive, involving time they should spend on studying during the school year.[755] During school holidays, it was regarded as unacceptable to employ children below the age of 15 for seven hours per day and thirty-five hours per week and young persons

747. Conclusions 2006, vol 2, p. 760 (Romania). Conclusions 2010, vol. 3, p. 1012 (Slovakia).
748. Conclusions XIII-2, pp. 83–84 (Austria). Conclusions 2010, vol. 3, p. 1157 (Turkey). Conclusions XIX-4 (2011), p. 185 (Greece).
749. Conclusions I, p. 43. The majority of the Member States do not guarantee reasonable working time. Conclusions 2011 (Albania, Armenia, Cyprus, Estonia, Italy, Lithuania, Moldova, Netherlands, Norway, Portugal Romania, Slovakia). The Committee concludes that the situation in the following Member States is not in conformity with the Charter, on the grounds that the duration of working time for young persons subject to compulsory education is excessive, and therefore cannot be qualified as light work: Armenia, Estonia, Romania, Ukraine, the former Yugoslav Republic of Macedonia. Conclusions 2015.
750. Conclusions III, p. 40. Conclusions 2011, vol. 2, p. 600 (Italy), p. 754 (Moldova).
751. Conclusions XII-2, p. 85; Conclusions XIII-4, p. 298. Conclusions 2011, vol. 2, p. 790. Conclusions 2015 (Netherlands). Conclusions 2015 (Norway)
752. Conclusions XI-2, p. 85 (Italy).
753. Addendum to Conclusions XV-2, p. 102 (Malta). Conclusions 2010, vol. 3, p. 975 (Romania).
754. Conclusions XV-2, p. 586 (United Kingdom).
755. Conclusions XV-2, p. 382 (Norway).

over the age of 15 for eight hours per day and forty hours weekly.[756] Analysing the employment of young persons over the age of 15 during periods free from classes (holidays, school breaks, seasonal holidays), the Committee emphasised that young children subject to compulsory education should rest at least half of the time they are free from school (vacation time).[757] The German regulation allowing for the employment of young persons under the age of 15 for four weeks per year was considered contrary to the obligation imposed by Article 7 §3 of the Charter. The Committee argued that the summer holiday lasts for six weeks, and therefore provisions allowing for the employment of young persons for 75% of their holiday time conflict with the protection standards of children and young persons guaranteed by the Charter.[758] The point of holidays is to guarantee young persons a rest after a year of studying in order to allow them to fully benefit from their education during the next school year.[759] Therefore, the Committee concludes that the situation in Azerbaijan, the Netherlands, Norway, and the Republic of Moldova is not in conformity with Article 7 §3 of the Charter on the grounds that children aged 15 who are still subject to compulsory education are not guaranteed an uninterrupted rest period of at least two weeks during the summer holiday.[760] The Committee concluded that the situation in Bosnia and Herzegovina is not in conformity with Article 7 §3 of the Charter on the ground that it has not been established that the effective protection against employment of children subject to compulsory education is ensured in practice.[761]

141. The ban on employing young persons under the age of 15 in work, which deprives them of educational possibilities, should be clear in its layout. Therefore, it is not enough to simply refer to the ratification of ILO conventions by a Member State, one prescribing a ban on children's employment,[762] the other imposing on Member States the obligation of controlling those persons who have the responsibility of educational duty and whether this expectation is being met.[763] Regular class attendance and achieving good grades by a young person who is also working is not regarded as enough evidence that the job is not a negative influence on their education as it is impossible to tell whether such employment does or does not prevent young persons from fully benefiting from compulsory education.[764]

756. Conclusions XV-2, p. 549 (Sweden), Conclusions 2011, vol. 1, p. 37 (Albania), p. 119 (Armenia), vol. 2, p. 308 (Cyprus), p. 340 (Estonia), p. 603 (Italy), p. 669 (Lithuania), p. 755 (Moldova), p. 790 (the Netherlands).
757. Conclusions XV-2, p. 382 (Norway); XV-2, p. 587 (United Kingdom), Conclusions 2006, vol. 2, p. 869 (Sweden), vol. 3, p. 913 (Portugal). The Committee concludes that the situation in Cyprus, Lithuania, Slovenia, Sweden, and Turkey is not in conformity with Art. 7 §3 of the Charter, on the grounds that during school holidays the daily and weekly working time for children subject to compulsory education is excessive and therefore cannot be qualified as light work. Conclusions 2015.
758. Addendum to Conclusions XV-2, p. 38.
759. Conclusions XI-1, p. 92; Conclusions XII-1, p. 136, Conclusions 2006, vol. 2, p. 632 (Italy).
760. Conclusions 2015 (Azerbaijan, the Netherlands, Norway, Republic of Moldova).
761. Conclusions 2015 relating to conclusions of on-conformity due to a repeated lack of information in conclusions 2015.
762. For instance, ILO convention of 25 Oct. 1921 concerning the admission age for work in agriculture.
763. Conclusions VIII, p. 106 (Austria).
764. Conclusions XI-2, p. 85 (Italy).

The ban formulated by Article 7 §3 of the Charter is of a common nature. It applies to all types of work, including farming work[765] and work carried out within a household.[766] Any exclusion from applying to this provision must be regarded by the Committee as conflicting with the standards of the Charter.

Turkey, which allowed for the exclusion from the list of prohibited work for those studying below the age of 15, work in farming, crafts, construction and work involving domestic services for individuals. This was judged negatively, and the decisions stated the approach to be conflicting in its nature of national labour law regulations and Article 7 §3 of the Charter.[767]

The ban on studying young persons below the age of 15 to be allowed to work is applicable to all work regardless of the legal basis of the employment and the relation between the young persons and the persons commissioning the work.[768]

The Committee declared Spain in violation of Article 7 §3 of the Charter, which allowed young persons at the age of 16 who were still subject to the duty of education to undertake work for their relatives within their own businesses.[769]

The structure of the ban introduced by Article 7 §3 of the Charter can be described as:

- determining a limit of age, which would excuse a young person from the duty of education. The above limit has to be calculated with consideration of a particular age when a young person subject to the duty of education comes of age. Turning that age takes away the status from a young person, thus is not protected by Article 7 §3 of the Charter;
- determining maximum daily and weekly standards of work time in periods of education and during holidays.[770]

Summing up the Committee's rulings in matters concerning the abiding of Article 7 §3 of the Charter, it has to be noted that it is forbidden to employ young persons at nighttime, in the morning hours before school,[771] not for more than a half of a daily standard, during public holidays and seasonal holidays as well as for a period longer than half the time of the annual holiday or school break.[772] Labour inspections should monitor the conditions of work of children who are still in compulsory education.[773]

---

765. Case of France: Conclusions XIII-2. p. 84; XIII-4, p. 296; XV-2, p. 192; Case of Austria: Conclusions XIII-2, pp. 83–84; XIII-4, pp. 295–296.
766. Conclusions XII-2, p. 83, Austria, Conclusions 2006, vol. 1, p. 151 (Cyprus), p. 193 (Estonia), p. 376 (Ireland), vol. 2, p. 760 (Romania).
767. Conclusions XIII-1, pp. 229–230; XIII-3, p. 293; Addendum to Conclusions XV-2, pp. 249–250.
768. Conclusions XIII-4, p. 299; Conclusions XV-2, p. 516.
769. Conclusions XIII-2; p. 86; XIII-4, p. 299; XV-2, p. 516.
770. Conclusions XIII-2. p. 83 (Austria).
771. Conclusions 2010, vol. 3, p. 859 (Norway).
772. Conclusions VIII, p. 108.
773. The Committee concludes that the situation is not in conformity with Art. 7 §3 of the Charter, on the grounds that it has been established that effective protection against employment of children subject to compulsory education is not ensured in practice (Conclusions, Bosnia and Herzegovina), or that during the reference period there was no labour inspection to monitor the conditions of work of children who are still subject to compulsory education (Conclusions 2015, Georgia). It has been not established that children who are still subject to compulsory education are guaranteed at least

V. Time of Work for Young Workers

142. The working hours of young workers should be shortened. A 'young person' is understood as someone under the age of 16 years, according to the definition in Article 7 §4 ESC. The same provision in the Revised European Social Charter raises this age definition to young persons under the age of 18. Article 7 §4 of the Charter is applied to young workers who are under no schooling obligations. This analysed provision regulates the working-hour standards of young persons who do not have the responsibility of attending school. It is not applicable to those young persons who are continuing their education without any legal requirement to do so. Young people who are not encompassed by the scope of the provisions of the European Social Charter are those who have finished their compulsory schooling before the age of 16. They are neither protected by Article 7 §3 nor by Article 7 §4 of the Charter. The Committee came to the conclusion that there is undoubtedly room for legal error in the Charter provisions protecting the rights of children and young people.[774] By analogy, according to the provisions of Article 7 §4 of the Charter, there should be a standard protecting young persons under the age of 16 who do not have educational responsibilities. Normally, this responsibility of education ends at the age of 18. Before reaching this age of maturity, people tend to finish their education at the level of primary and secondary school. They fulfil the educational requirements set by the state. Mimicking the views expressed by Article 7 §4 ESC towards young workers under the age of 18 who completed compulsory education would lead to a faultless opinion concerning the application of Article 7 §4 RESC in cases where young persons have undertaken employment after having completed their compulsory education but prior to coming of age.

143. The analysed provision takes into consideration the protection of young workers. The shortening of working hours, in the case of employment of young persons who are no longer in compulsory education, is required for their mental and physical development. They are particularly necessary for their vocational training needs. Ceasing his/her education at the level that is compulsory does not deprive the young person of continuing their vocational education or training. Primary as well as secondary school does not provide a young person with job qualifications. It is for this reason that the usual practice of employing young persons is connected with a work agreement that is based on apprenticeship training or on the preparation for particular employment. This, in turn, places an obligation on the young worker to gain qualifications and knowledge connected with the job. Therefore, shorter working hours should help in achieving such goals. A point of reference to see whether Member States are following the obligations set by Article 7 §4 of the Charter is the basic work day (eight hours) and the working week (forty hours).[775]

---

two consecutive weeks of rest during summer holidays (Republic of Moldova). Conclusions 2017 on conclusions of non-conformity for repeated lack of information in Conclusions 2015.

774. Second report on certain provisions of the Charter which have not been accepted, 1982, Supervision relating to reports submitted under Art. 22 of the European Social Charter (1961), European Social Charter, *supra*, pp. 491–494.

775. The following states did not comply with Art. 7 §4 of the Charter: Bulgaria, Estonia, Ireland, Italy, Romania, Turkey due to ineffective application of the legislation or lack of coverage of young

The Committee ruled that the Member States which are in breach of the provision set by the Charter are those who permit young workers to be employed in eight-hour working days and forty-hour working weeks[776] or longer.[777]

144. The responsibility towards young workers and the shortening of their weekly and daily hours have a general scope of application. It does not mean, however, that all young workers are beneficiaries of this standard. Article 33 §3 ESC and Article I §2 RESC are applicable to Article 7 §4 of the Charter, creating the basis of admitting that Member States comply with the duties established by the Charter when Article 7 §4 of the Charter applied to a significant majority (80%) of interested workers. To form an opinion as to whether the obligation of shortening daily working hours is being met, the Committee turned to Member State authorities for information concerning the working-hour standards, as well as the number of young workers to whom shortening of working-hour standards apply.

VI. Remuneration for Young Workers

145. Remuneration for young workers should be fair, and other allowances paid to apprentices should be appropriate.[778] The analysed provision regulates the principles of remuneration in terms of two categories of young workers: those who are employed after signing a work agreement and persons who are employed under a contract preparing them for a future profession, apprentices for whom the job is part of the training undertaken in their vocational education. Article 7 §5 of the Charter completes Article 4 §1 of the Charter. The Charter protects all those who are employed from exploitation, regardless of their age or the work contract that they may have signed. However, most importantly, the Charter protects young workers due to the fact that this group is at higher risk level of being exploited by employers.[779] Taking into account the level of remuneration and other allowances paid to young workers, the Committee uses the net salary[780] of workers who have come of age in their first year of work as a point of reference. The Committee recalls the young worker's wage must be less than the adult starting wage, but any difference must be reasonable, and the gap must close quickly. For 15/16-year-olds, a wage

people employed as domestic staff. Conclusions 2006, vol. 1, p. 109 (Bulgaria), p. 193 (Estonia), p. 376 (Ireland), p. 441 (Italy), vol. 2, p. 760 (Romania), vol. 3, p. 1153 (Turkey).

776. Case of Italy: Conclusions XIII-2, p. 88; Conclusions XIII-4, p. 301; Conclusions XIV-2, pp. 293–294. (Luxembourg); Conclusions XIII-5, p. 124; Addendum to Conclusions XV-2, p. 70. Conclusions XIX-4 (2011), p. 69 (Croatia), p. 99 (Czech Republic).

777. The Committee claimed, that the average weekly working hours in Turkey were: for workers between 12 to 14 years – 40 to 49 hours; for workers between 15 to 19 years – 47 to 48 hours. Conclusions XIII-1, p. 230; XIII-3, p. 296; Addendum to Conclusions XV-2, pp. 250–251. Conclusions 2011, vol. 1, p. 232 (Bosnia and Herzegovina), vol. 2, p. 603 (Ireland), p. 756 (Moldova).

778. In the last cycle – 2011 – the Committee declared compliance with Art. 7 §5 of the RESC on the part of only three Member States: Albania, Finland and France. In the case of ten states (Azerbaijan, Belgium, Bulgaria, Croatia, Ireland, Lithuania, Moldova, Netherlands, Norway, Romania and Slovakia, its conclusions were negative – 'the minimum wage of young workers is unfair'.

779. Conclusions XV-2, pp. 340–341 (the Netherlands).

780. Conclusions XV-2, p. 294 (Italy).

30% lower than the adult starting wage is acceptable. For 16/18-year-olds, the difference may not exceed 20%. The adult reference wage is too low; even a young worker's wage, which respects these percentage differentials, cannot be considered fair.[781] It makes sure that employers will not lower the salary used as a reference point when analysing the remuneration and allowances of young workers.[782] It does not accept excuses such as that giving lower wages to workers who undertake their first employment revitalises the economy and allows for the introduction of a larger number of people into the labour market who were, up to that point, unemployed. The Committee considers this matter according to the perspective of Article 4 §1 of the Charter[783] and its standards, which dictate that all workers, regardless of what category they may fall into and regardless of whether it be their first job or not, have a right to fair remuneration.[784] The obligation of Member State authorities is to provide the Committee with reports containing information about the level of remuneration for workers who are of age having commenced their first employment as well as the minimum wage paid in specified branches of the economy. Apart from this, Member State authorities are obliged to present information concerning the level of wages paid to young workers as well as to inform about the type and the value of additional allowances utilised by young workers during their apprenticeships.[785] As of 2015, it is determined that the situation in the following Member States is not in conformity with Article 7 §5 of the Charter on the grounds that young workers' wages are not fair: Andorra, Armenia,[786] Azerbaijan,[787] Bosnia and Herzegovina,[788] Czech Republic,[789] Georgia[790] Germany,[791] the Netherlands,[792] Romania,[793] the Slovak Republic,[794] Spain,[795] the United Kingdom,[796] and the

781. Conclusions 2015 (Bosnia and Herzegovina).
782. Conclusions XI-1, p. 28; Conclusions.
783. The adult reference wage must in all cases be sufficient to comply with Art. 4 §1 of the Charter. Conclusions 2015 (Andorra).
784. Case of Spain: Conclusions XIV-2, p. 771; Conclusions XV-2, pp. 589–590.
785. Conclusions I, p. 44; Conclusions VI, p. 52 (France).
786. The monthly minimum wage corresponds to only 30% of the average wage, which is too low to secure a decent standard of living. Conclusions 2015.
787. For 15–16-year-olds, a wage 30% lower than the adult starting wage is acceptable. For 16–18-year-olds, the difference may not exceed 20%. Conclusions 2015.
788. For 15–16-year-olds, a wage of 30% lower than the adult starting wage is acceptable. The MMW corresponds to less than 50% of the average wage. Therefore, the Committee considers that the right to fair pay of young workers is not guaranteed since the reference wage itself (the minimum wage of adult workers) is too low to secure a decent standard of living. Conclusions 2015.
789. The net minimum wage corresponds to only 39% of the net average wage. Therefore, even if young workers are paid at least 80% of the minimum statutory wage, the right to fair pay of young workers is not guaranteed, since the reference wage is too low to secure a decent standard of living. Conclusions 2015.
790. It has not been established that the minimum wage paid to young workers is fair. Conclusions relating to conclusions of non-conformity due to a repeated lack of information in conclusions 2015.
791. The German report does not provide any information on minimum wages paid to young workers who are not covered by the collective agreement. Conclusions 2015.
792. For 15/16-year-olds, a wage of 30% lower than the adult starting wage is acceptable. For 16/17-year-olds, the difference may not exceed 20%. Conclusions 2015.
793. The monthly minimum wage does not ensure a decent standard of living, as it amounts to only 34.32% of the net average wage, in contrast with the 60% of the net average wage considered a satisfactory threshold under Art. 4 §1 of the Charter. Conclusions 2015.

Ukraine.[797] Since then, the situation of adolescent 'workers' has not changed significantly. The 2019 conclusion lists almost the same number of Member States that do not comply with the obligation to fairly reward young people for the work they do.[798]

Apprentices do not remain in the employ of the employer training them. During practical training, jobs that are undertaken for the purpose of the apprenticeship, having a certain value, are advantageous for the employer, who prepares such vocational training, therefore, the apprentices have the right to attain appropriate allowances, not to be classified by the state as remuneration. Such allowances, at times referred to as 'scholarships', should be left alone in relation to the wages that are paid to workers who have come of age and are working in their first job. Depending on the wages paid to workers who have come of age, to the young workers and the appropriate allowances are paid to apprentices as follows: taking as a reference point 100% of net remuneration paid by an employer of given trade to workers undertaking their first job, remuneration for young workers should be calculated at the level of 75%–80% of that amount, whereas young apprentices should obtain from one-third to two-thirds of the remuneration accepted as a basis of comparison for wages and financial benefits. Evaluating national reports, the Committee clearly stated that remuneration lower by 30%, 34% and 40% from the amount of net remuneration paid by an employer to workers of an age entering into the work market is in conflict with the standards established under Article 7 §5 of the Charter.[799] Wage differences between a net remuneration obtained by a worker of age who is employed for the first time in his/her career and remunerations of young workers as well as allowances paid to young apprentices by an employer providing training, depend on the professional experience of young workers. In case of young workers, the difference in the net amount of remuneration should decrease with age and through gaining professional experience. The Committee accepts a 20% difference between the remuneration of workers of age and young workers aged from 16 to 18

794. The net minimum wage represents 46% of the net average, which does not meet the requirements of Art. 7 §5 of the Charter. Conclusions 2015.
795. The gross minimum wage corresponds to 75% of the thresholds required under Art. 4 §1 of the Charter. Therefore, the Committee considers that the right to fair pay for young workers is not guaranteed. Conclusions 2015.
796. The difference between adults' minimum wage and that of young workers aged 16–18 is 26% and 41% respectively (referring to the two values of the adult minimum wage indicated above), which is higher than the maximum of 26% considered acceptable for 16–18-year-olds under Art. 7 §5 of the Charter. Conclusions 2015.
797. The minimum wage corresponds to only 34.44% of the net average wage, which is too low to secure a decent standard of living for young workers. Conclusions 2015.
798. Albania, Andorra, Armenia, Azerbaijan, Belgium, Georgia, Germany, Serbia, Spain, Romania, the United Kingdom and Ukraine, Activity Report 2019, p. 30.
799. Case of the Netherlands: Conclusions XIII-1, p. 167; Conclusions XIII-2, p. 91; Conclusions XIII-4, p. 303; Conclusions XV-2, p. 340–341; Case of Luxembourg: Addendum to Conclusions XIII-3, p. 42; Conclusions XIII-5, p. 125; Addendum to Conclusions XV-2, p. 71; Case of Belgium: Conclusions XV-2, pp. 80–81; Case of Ireland: Conclusions XIII-4, pp. 302–303; Addendum to Conclusions XIV-2, pp. 16–17; Case of Spain: XIII-2, p. 92; Conclusions XV-2, pp. 517–518. Conclusions XIX-4 (2011), p. 70 (Croatia), p. 147 (Germany), p. 330 (Spain), p. 399 (United Kingdom).

years. It also approves of a 5% increase in this difference in the case of remunerating young workers under the age of 16.[800]

146. In the case of young apprentices, the differences in the level of remuneration paid by employers organising vocational training in comparison to wages obtained by workers of age undertaking their first job should not be greater than one-third in the first year of training and not larger than two-thirds of the remuneration obtained by workers of age in the second year of training. The Committee is of the view that the maximum length of a training cycle should not exceed two or three years. The period of fostering the professional skills and efficiency of young persons serving their apprenticeships is lower than those of workers who have already been trained. The above disproportion decreases in the course of the training. Establishing the amount of remuneration paid out to young persons benefiting from vocational training organised by an employer should include the value of this training. There are mutual links between the value of knowledge and practical skills provided for young persons in the process of vocational training and the amount of remuneration (scholarships) they are entitled to obtain from an employer organising the vocational training. The value of professional skills acquired during the training should then automatically relate to the amounts of remuneration obtained by young persons in subsequent stages of training. This is why the difference in the remuneration of young apprentices and the initial remuneration of workers should not exceed one-third in the first stage and two-thirds in the final phase of training. The apprentices' allowances were considered inadequate in the following countries: Andorra, the Czech Republic, Georgia and Turkey. This was due to the fact that the reports of the Member States examined did not provide any information about apprentices.[801]

147. Practice can be examined after comparing the remuneration of young workers and allowances for young apprentices with net remunerations of workers who are beginning their professional careers. This net remuneration cannot be lower than the minimum wage in a particular country. The Committee concluded that the right of young workers and apprentices to a fair wage and other appropriate allowances is not guaranteed due to the ineffective enforcement of the legislation in Bulgaria, Ireland, Italy and Romania.[802]

Article 7 §5 of the Charter does not provide us with guidelines on how to establish remuneration for young workers and appropriate allowances for young apprentices. It can occur both by provisions legislated by the state or by collective work agreements entered into by stakeholders.[803] As collective work agreements usually

800. Conclusions V, p. 63.
801. Conclusions 2015 (Andorra, Czech Republic, Georgia, Turkey).
802. Conclusions 2006, vol. 1, p. 110 (Bulgaria), p. 377 (Ireland), p. 442 (Italy), vol. 2, p. 762 (Romania). In Romania young people employed as domestic staff are not covered by the labour legislation.
803. Third report on certain provisions of the Charter which have not been accepted, 1989, Supervision relating to reports submitted under Art. 22 of the European Social Charter (1961), European Social Charter, *supra*, pp. 484 et seq.

regulate the conditions of individual work agreements, the amount of remuneration for young apprentices in a period of vocational training is usually specified by provisions legislated by the Member States.

VII. Time of Vocational Training

148. Employers must treat the time spent in vocational training by young persons as forming part of their working day. Article 7 §6 of the Charter applies to young workers and apprentices employed on the basis of work agreements specifying that the above employment has been undertaken in order to partake in vocational training and professional preparation.[804] Considering the time spent by young persons in vocational training and forming part of the working day means that young persons obtain remuneration for time spent in training equal to the amount of remuneration they would be entitled to if they carried out work. They are by no means obliged to catch up on the time spent in vocational training, the time employers have been obliged to pay for, by carrying out extra work.[805] Article 7 §6 of the Charter established a rule explicitly expressed by the following citation: 'time spent by young persons in vocational training during normal working hours should be remunerated not recuperated'.[806] It can be concluded from Article 7 §6 of the Charter that the necessary condition of judging time spent in vocational training among regular time of work is done by the employer's consent. The Committee declared that the above regulation could not be interpreted as though an employer's consent is considered *conditio sine qua non* of granting a young person by an employer the right to remuneration for time spent in vocational training without the obligation of catching up on it. During the fifth supervisory cycle, the Committee concluded that Article 7 §6 of the Charter does not provide employers with the imperative rights with regard to making a decision about including or not including time spent by a young person in vocational training into the total amount of working time which is binding for this person. Including the time spent by a young person in vocational training into a standard of working time occurs automatically, at the employer's will.[807] The analysed provision is interpreted by the Committee as a legal standard allowing employers to determine the time and conditions of utilising the right of vocational training by a young person and, in turn, the right to have the time spent in vocational training included in a daily standard of working time.[808] As of 2015, the Committee concludes that the situation in Bosnia and Herzegovina, Georgia, the Netherlands, Romania and Turkey is not in conformity with Article 7 §6 of the Charter on the grounds that the time spent in vocational training is not included in

804. Conclusions VIII, p. 116; Conclusions IX-1, p. 63 (Norway).
805. Conclusions V, p. 67.
806. Samuel, *supra*, s. 195.
807. In principle, young workers are not entitled to have their training time paid as working hours in Bulgaria, Norway and Romania. Conclusions 2006, vol. 1, p. 110 (Bulgaria), vol. 2, p. 434 (Norway), p. 763 (Romania). The list of Member States which had negative conclusions considerably expanded in 2011. It covers Albania, Belgium, Bosnia and Herzegovina, Croatia, Netherlands, Norway, Romania, Slovakia, Slovenia and Turkey. Conclusions 2011, vol. 1, 2 and 3.
808. Conclusions V. p. 67.

the normal working time and remunerated as such for all employees,[809] or the majority of workers,[810] or that it has not been established that the right to have the time spent on vocational training included in the normal working time and remunerated is guaranteed in practice,[811] or that the legislative framework does not provide for time spent at the training with the consent of employer to be included in normal working time and remunerated as such.[812]

VIII. Annual Holiday for Young Persons

149. Young workers employed on the basis of a work agreement are entitled to an annual holiday with pay. The European Social Charter sets the length of this holiday at three weeks, while the Revised European Social Charter extends this period to four weeks. Holidays are calculated by working days. Its length is directly proportional to the amount of working time. Young workers employed full time are entitled to three or four weeks of paid holidays per year. Young workers employed part-time acquire a decreased number of holidays.[813] Young workers whose holiday entitlements are regulated by the European Social Charter employed six days per week are entitled to eighteen days of holidays calculated by working days. Young workers employed five days per week are entitled to fifteen days of holidays.[814] In the case of minimum holidays (four weeks), six-day-a-week employment ensures a worker the entitlement to twenty-four working days of holiday. In that case, five-day-a-week employment entitles a young worker to twenty working days of holiday within a calendar year.[815]

Accepting the rule *pro rata temporis* by the Charter makes it difficult to enforce the proposition formulated by Belgian labour law regulations prescribing young workers to utilise the right of at least three consecutive weeks of holiday between 1 May and 31 October.[816]

The Revised European Social Charter introduced the same holiday period for both young workers and workers that have come of age. In the European Social Charter, holidays for young workers are longer by one week than those for workers who have come of age (Article 2 §3). The rules for acquiring holidays for both young and of age workers are similar. The pattern of legal regulation concerning holidays for young workers may be allocated according to the period of employment, subjected to the regulations of the national labour laws. A young worker having completed a twelve-month period of employment is entitled, according to the

809. Conclusions 2015 (Georgia). The report indicates that the labour relationship is suspended during vocational training, professional retraining or education which does not exceed thirty calendar days per year.
810. Conclusions 2015 (the Netherlands). The report states that although time spent in vocational training is deemed to be working time, this does not necessarily mean it should also be remunerated as such.
811. Conclusions 2015 (Romania, Turkey).
812. Conclusions 2015 (Bosnia and Herzegovina).
813. Conclusions I, p. 45.
814. Samuel, *supra,* s. 196.
815. Conclusions XV-2, pp. 81–82 (Belgium).
816. As above, p. 82.

Committee, to have a legal right to a holiday.[817] The Committee emphasised, to a greater extent than it does to workers who are of age, the importance of a holiday for the sake of physical and mental health for young workers.[818] For this reason, a young worker is unable to voluntarily transfer his/her holiday to another worker, even if for the receivership of a payment.[819] Young workers should utilise their holidays according to the regulations. If the worker is unable to attend work due to illness, which takes place during the worker's holiday period, the holiday period is suspended and utilised at a later date when the worker has recovered.[820] Young workers are allowed to waive their right to annual leave in return for increased remuneration. One report submitted in 2015 by Azerbaijan states that the employees are paid compensation in the established amount and manner for unused holidays during the relevant employment year. The Committee considers that the option of giving up one's annual holiday for financial compensation is not in conformity with Article 7 §7 of the Charter.[821]

150. Article 7 §7 of the Charter is general in its scope,[822] although the most applicable principles are found in Article 33 §2 ESC and in Article I §2 RESC. An indication that a Member State abides by the obligations set by this provision is when annual paid leave, as prescribed by the regulation set in the Charter, is utilised by at least 80% of young workers.[823] An apprentice or a young worker undertaking vocational training is entitled to uninterrupted rest. Because such workers do not remain in employment, such rest from vocational training responsibilities is not referred to as paid leave. This type of rest, however, does have the same point as leave.[824]

IX. Banning the Employment of Young Persons in Night Employment

151. Member State authorities have the obligation to set regulations prohibiting the employment of young persons under the age of 18 years to carry out employment during night hours. This prohibition has a general scope. It is applicable to all young workers regardless of their sex.[825] It encompasses all sectors of the economy

817. Conclusions I, p. 20.
818. The Committee concluded that Bulgaria and Romania do not cope with that obligation. Conclusions 2006, vol. 1, p. 111 (Bulgaria), vol. 2, p. 763 (Romania).
819. Conclusions I, p. 70. The Committee found out that this prohibition is not accepted in Albania, Armenia, Moldova or Romania. Conclusions 2011, vol. 1, p. 41 (Albania), p. 122 (Armenia), vol. 2, p. 756 (Moldova), vol. 3, p. 978 (Romania).
820. Conclusions XV-1, p. 519; Addendum to Conclusions XV-2, p. 176.
821. Conclusions 2015 (Azerbaijan).
822. Young workers also have the right to annual paid leave when employed in businesses that are run by family members. Addendum to Conclusions XV-2, p. 176 (Slovakia). In France, young workers incapacitated by accident or illness during all or part of their annual leave are not entitled to extended or additional leave. Conclusions 2006, vol. 1, p. 316.
823. Conclusions XIII-5, p. 70 (Finland).
824. Addendum to Conclusions XV-2, p. 176 (Slovakia).
825. Conclusions XII-2, p. 130 (Malta).

and cannot be limited to employment in heavy industry,[826] other industrial undertakings,[827] or some economic sectors.[828] Turkey is considered to have breached its obligations under Article 7 §8 of the Charter, as the prohibition of the employment of young persons during night hours does not encompass the farming or service sectors.[829]

This prohibition on the employment of young persons in night work should encompass the majority of young persons. The appendix to Article 7 §8 of the Charter decided that a state fulfils its obligations stipulated by this provision if 'it adapts itself to the spirit of this obligation' and if it ensures in its domestic labour regulations that a significant majority of persons under the age of 18 years will not be employed during night hours. In accordance with the regulation, as part of the appendix, Member State authorities are obligated to produce information concerning whether Article 7 §8 of the Charter is being followed. Not fulfilling this above provision means there is an injunction on the decision being handed down by the Committee with regard to whether domestic labour law regulations practices exist in accordance with Article 7 §8 of the Charter.[830] Member States, when completing the requirements stipulated by the provision in question, should establish what nighttime is and ensure a clear ban on employing young persons within this timeframe. A necessary requirement for fulfilling the obligation of this provision is to provide in written format the regulations of the domestic labour laws, which establish what night hours are and what the above-mentioned prohibition is, as well as include information about how employers are abiding by such a prohibition.[831] Article 7 §8 does not have any guidelines regarding the definition of what 'night hours' may be. The Committee does not demand Member States to incorporate both definitions of this period, i.e., one period required for young persons, the other for mature workers. The regulation prohibiting young people from working during what the Committee regards as 'night', a period in which mature workers receive overtime wages, is seen as having fulfilled the obligations of the Charter. Member States have the right to define the 'night' period depending upon the possibility of paying the worker who is able to work during the night, additional remuneration, and the prohibition of employing young persons under the age of 16 or 18 years. The time frame ban for employing young persons is considered an appropriate prohibition, for persons under 16 years being the hours between 7 pm and 6 am, and for persons under the age of 18 years to be between 10 pm and 5 am.[832] State legislation, which forbids the employment of young persons between the hours of 11 pm and 6 am, is

826. Conclusions XIII-2, pp. 96–97 (Cyprus); Conclusions XIII-5, p. 191 (Portugal). It is obeyed by Belgium, Ireland, Malta, Moldova, Norway and Turkey. Conclusions 2011, vol. 1, p. 193 (Belgium), vol. 2, p. 554 (Ireland), p. 726 (Malta), p. 755 (Moldova), vol. 3, p. 863 (Norway), p. 1162 (Turkey).
827. Conclusions 2015 (Turkey).
828. Conclusions 2015 (Malta)
829. Conclusions XIII-3, p. 305; Addendum to Conclusions XV-2, pp. 252–253.
830. Conclusions XV-2, p. 82 (Belgium); Conclusions XV-2, pp. 236–237 (Greece); Conclusions XV-2, p. 519 (Spain).
831. Bulgaria, Ireland and Romania do not comply with that obligations. Conclusions 2006, vol. 1, p. 111 (Bulgaria), p. 380 (Ireland), vol. 2, p. 764 (Romania).
832. Conclusions XIII-2, pp. 96–97 (Cyprus); Conclusions XIII-5, p. 191 (Portugal).

considered to fulfil the obligations set by the Charter.[833] The prohibition of employing young persons during night hours is not absolute in its nature. Article 7 §8 of the Charter authorises Member States to allow for the employment during night hours of young persons who have not completed 18 years of age in certain occupations recognised by the state's legislation. The necessary exceptions to the prohibition of night work in some sectors occur for the sake of the proper functioning of these sectors, but only on condition that the number of young workers concerned is not too high.[834] In Malta, it has not been established that the exceptions to the prohibition of night work in some economic sectors are necessary for the proper functioning of these sectors and that the number of young workers concerned is not high.[835] The Committee recalls that the satisfactory application of Article 7 §8 of the Charter cannot be ensured solely by the operation of legislation if this is not effectively supervised. The situation in practice should be regularly monitored, and labour inspections play a decisive role in effectively implementing Article 7 of the Charter.[836] As of 2015, the Committee concludes that the situation in Bosnia and Herzegovina and Georgia is not in conformity with Article 7 §8 of the Charter on the grounds that during the reference period, there was no labour inspection to monitor how the regulations regarding prohibition of night work of young persons under 18 years of age were implemented in practice,[837] or it had not been established that the regulations regarding prohibition of night work for young persons under 18 years of age were being implemented in practice.[838]

The Committee, during its supervisory process monitoring whether the provision decided upon by a Member State is being met, does not consider the jobs which are the exceptions to the prohibition of employing young persons during the night period. It requires presenting information on occupations and types of work in which young persons can be employed during nighttime, the scope of exceptions from this rule concerning the age of young persons who can be employed during nighttime and the number of hours during which the above work is allowed to be carried out.[839] Having this data, the Committee is able to control whether the rule of the majority listed in the appendix to Article 7 §8 was violated or not.

X. Regular Medical Supervision of Young Persons

152. Member States are obliged to make provisions concerning the health protection of young persons. The above-mentioned provisions should introduce the obligation of regular medical control for young persons under the age of 18 who are

833. Conclusions XII-2, p. 130 (Malta).
834. Conclusions 2015 (Malta).
835. Conclusions relating to conclusions of non-conformity due to the repeated lack of information in conclusions 2015.
836. *International Commission of Jurists (CIJ) v. Portugal*, Complaint No. 1/1998, Decision on the merits of 9 Sep. 1999, §32).
837. Conclusions 2015 (Georgia).
838. Conclusions relating to conclusions of non-conformity due to a repeated lack of information in conclusions 2015 (Bosnia and Herzegovina).
839. Conclusion I, p. 46.

employed in certain occupations. As of 2015, the Committee stated that employers should provide general mandatory/compulsory medical examinations for young workers at regular and frequent intervals. The Committee concludes that the situation is not in conformity with Article 7 §9 of the Charter, on the grounds that: (1) legislation does not provide for compulsory regular medical examinations;[840] (2) medical examinations for young workers are not frequent enough;[841] (3) it has been not established that there is an initial medical check-up at recruitment and regular medical checks-up thereafter of young workers under 18 years of age employed in occupations specified by national laws and regulations;[842] (4) there is in practice no general mandatory medical examinations of workers under 18 years of age.[843]

The obligation of regular medical control of young persons encompasses young workers, young persons running their own businesses,[844] going through professional preparation, attending vocational training, and carrying out work free of charge by helping out in the running of a family business.[845] The rule concerns young persons carrying out work that is listed in the domestic labour law regulations. The Charter leaves the drafting of such a list of these occupations and types of work to Member States. The Committee familiarises itself with registers drawn up by Member States and evaluates them in terms of the number of occupations and types of work listed in the register and also in terms of availability of out-of-work medical services or a place where learning of trade, professional preparation or vocational training takes place.[846] The Committee finds it important that regular medical control is performed for the largest possible number of young workers, and not only restricted to young persons employed in work exposing them to dangerous substances[847] or in selected occupations or types of work. The Committee demands from Member States not only to present information on some medical examinations but also to provide information on all examinations performed in occupations and types of work listed by the domestic labour law regulations.[848] There is no reason for the organisation of medical control in some sectors of the economy or services. Article 7 §9 of the Charter imposes on Member States the obligation of preparing registers of occupations where regular medical control of young employees is necessary. Occupations and types of work encompassed by the obligation of regular medical control are located in different sectors. Therefore, there is not enough

840. Conclusions 2015 (Bosnia and Herzegovina, the Netherlands, Sweden).
841. Conclusions 2015 (Estonia, Former Yugoslav Republic of Macedonia, now North Macedonia) and in the Netherlands – Conclusions 2017. The Committee notes that the minimum interval between medical check-ups is two years which it considers to be excessive.
842. Conclusions 2015 (Georgia).
843. Conclusions 2015 (the Netherlands, the former Yugoslav Republic of Macedonia, now North Macedonia)
844. Conclusions XIII-2, pp. 99–100 (Spain).
845. As above; Conclusions XIII-4, p. 3120; Conclusions XV-2, pp. 519–520.
846. Conclusions VI, p. 58 (United Kingdom).
847. Conclusions III, p. 46 (Germany).
848. Conclusions VI, p. 58 (United Kingdom).

ground to exclude particular sectors of the economy from the above-mentioned obligation. Regular medical control should also apply to young persons employed in particular types of work in agriculture, craft and trade.[849]

153. Medical checks should be performed very regularly.[850] Performing a medical examination before making a decision about the employment of a young person and conducting further medical control a year from the date of signing a work agreement or agreement of learning a trade only, does not meet requirements set by Article 7 §9 of the Charter.[851] Medical examinations of young people should be performed at regular intervals of time, for example annually.[852] Organising medical controls at longer intervals, for instance, medical controls of young sailors which are performed once every two years, was considered by the Committee as not fulfilling the obligation established by Article 7 §9 of the Charter.[853] Performing regular medical controls of young persons is an obligation that can be substituted by means of consultations. Regulations existing in one of the Member States leaving the decision as to whether they want to go through a medical examination or not to young persons was regarded by the Committee as conflicting with the standards established by the Charter. Medical control of young persons is an important aspect of the social protection of young persons and the decision to carry them out cannot be left to the goodwill of the interested parties.[854]

Sweden was considered a state that did not meet the requirements formulated in Article 7 §9 of the Charter because its national report does not explicitly state whether medical examinations of young persons are performed systematically and are obligatory in certain intervals of time or solely precede making a decision by an employer upon employing a young person.[855] The authorities of Member States are obliged to provide information proving that regular medical controls of young persons' health are performed as a practice.

The Charter does not impose on Member States the obligation of organising a separate health service system, accessible only for young persons. Existing health service units, as referred to in Article 7 §9 of the Charter, can carry out regular medical controls.[856] The Committee demands however that doctors are informed who is performing such controls and that the young persons are their patients, as well as to provide doctors with detailed instructions on performing such examinations.[857] The

849. Case of Turkey: Conclusions XIII-1, pp. 232–233; Conclusions XIII-3, pp. 306–307; Addendum to Conclusions XV-2, p. 254.
850. Conclusions II, p. 37.
851. Conclusions VI, p. 57 (Germany).
852. Conclusions XIII-2, p. 99 (Italy).
853. Conclusions X-1, p. 89 (Sweden).
854. Conclusions VI, p. 99; Conclusions XV-2, p. 551 (Sweden).
855. Conclusions XV-2, pp. 550–551.
856. Conclusions VIII-2, p. 119.
857. As above, pp. 120–121.

Committee concluded that the right of young workers to regular medical examinations is not guaranteed due to ineffective enforcement of the legislation.[858] In some countries, the medical examinations for young workers are irregular[859] or not frequent enough.[860]

XI. Special Protection of Children and Young Persons against Physical and Moral Dangers

154. The objective scope of Article 7 §10 of the Charter is significantly broader than the objective scope of the nine described provisions. As early as during the first supervisory cycle, the Committee declared that the goal of Article 7 §1-9 of the Charter is to ensure the protection of children and young people from the dangers created by work, work factors and processes and work environment.[861] Article 7 §10 of the Charter takes it a step further, imposing on Member States the obligation of guaranteeing children and young people legal protection against all dangers of a physical and moral nature, which they can be subject to not only in the workplace but also in all aspects of life.[862] Member States are obliged to ensure protection for children and young people against dangers resulting directly or indirectly from the work carried out. Because such protection against these dangers is ensured for children and young persons by other provisions of the Charter (Article 7 §1-9), the Committee demands the authorities of Member States provide the broadest range of information on physical and moral dangers in families, schools, local communities and in the work environment from the day children start their education to the moment of coming of age.[863] As of 2015, the Committee concludes that Armenia, Austria, Azerbaijan, Estonia, Turkey, Ukraine, the United Kingdom, and the former Yugoslav Republic of Macedonia are not in conformity with Article 7 §10 of the Charter, on the grounds that it has not been established that all children are protected against all forms of sexual exploitation, or that all forms of corporal punishment are prohibited in the home and institutions.[864] In 2019, it was found that national law does not provide effective protection for children against sexual harassment[865] and economic exploitation.[866]

858. Conclusions 2006, vol. 1, p. 112 (Bulgaria), vol. 2, p. 763 (Romania).
859. Conclusions 2006, vol. 2, p. 822 Slovenia), p. 870 (Sweden). Conclusions 2011, vol. 1, p. 236 (Bosnia and Herzegovina), p. 277 (Bulgaria), p. 344 (Estonia), vol. 2, p. 758 (Moldova), p. 795 (Netherlands), vol. 3, p. 1113 (Sweden).
860. Conclusions 2006, vol. 1, p. 196 (Estonia).
861. Conclusions I, p. 41.
862. Conclusions XII-1, p. 31.
863. Conclusions V, p. 73.
864. Conclusions 2015.
865. Bosnia and Herzegovina, Georgia, the Russian Federation, Turkey and Ukraine, Activity Report 2019, p. 30.
866. Albania Georgia, *ibid.*

§7. The Right of Employed Women to Protection

155. The aim of this provision is to allow women workers to efficiently fulfil their maternity duties without fear of losing employment. During the first supervisory cycle on whether Article 8 of the Charter is being abided by, the Committee stated that the provision in question guarantees a women worker protection in the period of maternity and protects a woman's body against dangers deriving from work factors and processes and the work environment.[867] In matters concerning maternity protection Article 8 of the Charter guarantees pregnant women workers maternity leave and financial entitlements during this leave (§1), deems it unlawful for an employer to give a woman notice of dismissal during the period from the time she notifies she is pregnant (§2), ensures nursing mothers who are working the right to take time off during work for this purpose (§3), regulates the employment in night work of pregnant women, women who have recently given birth and women nursing their infants (§4), prohibits the employment of pregnant women, women who have recently given birth and women nursing their infants in underground mines as well as in all dangerous, unhealthy and arduous work, imposes on Member States the obligation of undertaking appropriate measures to ensure the protection of rights in terms of employment for this group of women (§5). The provision of Article 8 is of a complex nature. It consists of standards belonging to the category of individual labour law (protection of work relation stability, protection of women workers) and to the category of provisions of social security law (maternity leave and financial entitlements obtained by women during such leave)

156. Article 8 of the Charter shapes the situation of women being parties to work relations.[868] Its legal protection encompasses all women employed on the basis of work agreements for both defined and undefined amounts of time,[869] full time or part time.[870] It applies to women workers employed in household work,[871] even if they are employer's relatives.[872] It applies to women employed in the public service, on the sea[873] regardless of being a citizen of a Member State. The Charter imposes on Member States the obligation of the equal treatment of other Member States citizens, parties to the Charter, legally residing on the territories of other states. Foreigners legally employed on the territory of Member States have the standard workers' rights and entitlements. The above-mentioned rule applies to women workers during the period of maternity.[874] Women running their own businesses are

867. Conclusions I, p. 49.
868. Conclusions *I*, p. 53.
869. Conclusions XIII-4, p. 73.
870. For example, employment for 3 days a week. Conclusions XIII-4, pp. 85–86 (The Netherlands); Conclusions XV-2, p. 345; Conclusions XIII-1, pp. 174–175 (Ireland).
871. Conclusions XIII-4, pp. 85–86 (The Netherlands); Conclusions XIII-4, pp. 93–94 (Austria); Conclusions XIII-4, pp. 96–97 (Italy); Conclusions XV-2, p. 345 (The Netherlands).
872. Case of Malta: Conclusions XIII-2, p. 304; Addendum to Conclusions XV-2, pp. 108–109.
873. Case of Greece: Conclusions XIII-1, p. 178; Conclusions XIII-4, p. 96.
874. Case of Greece: Conclusions XI-1, p. 103; Conclusions XII-1, p. 148; Cases of Malta: Conclusions XII-2, p. 137; Conclusions XIII-2, pp. 306–307; Conclusions XIII-4, pp. 84–85; Addendum to Conclusions XV-2, p. 110.

excluded from the range of protection guaranteed by the provision in question. During the first supervisory cycle, the Committee considered ensuring protection for women who were not parties to work relations. However, it concluded that the content of Article 8 of the Charter gives no reason for a broadening of the interpretation of this provision resulting in protection for women active in professional life albeit not parties to work relations. Article 8 §1 of the Charter imposes on Member States an obligation to guarantee legal protection for 'employees'. Section 2 of Article 8 prohibits 'employers' from handing women a 'notice of dismissal'. It uses terms of clear content for labour law specialists. They are used only while analysing legal relations regulated by provisions of labour law – work relations.[875]

I. Maternity Leave

157. Member States are obliged to ensure women workers' maternity leave. The Committee interprets this obligation as an obligation to regulate the right to maternity leave by provisions legislated by a Member State.[876] Despite the fact that in some Member States where systems of labour law and social security law are based on precedence, the Committee takes the position that the provision in question of Article 8 §1 of the Charter does not excuse the authorities of these states from legislating provisions establishing the obligation of ensuring women workers the right to maternity leave and confirming the right of women workers to take advantage such leave.[877] A Member State that regulates maternity leave by collective work agreements or by custom does not fulfil the obligation established by the analysed provision.[878]

The Committee did not accept reasons presented by Irish authorities arguing that Article 8 §1 of the Charter does not give women workers a subjective right to maternity leave but only orders Member States to provide women workers utilising such a leave with financial entitlements. According to the Committee Article 8 §1 of the Charter obliges to guarantee women workers paid maternity leave or leave, during which a woman worker would have the right to obtain benefits either from social security (maternity benefits) or from public funds. Article 8 §1 of the Charter ensures women workers the right to stop carrying out work when pregnant and giving birth, and guarantees reinstating a worker with all her professional duties after the period of maternity. Ireland, who did not guarantee women workers the right to be reinstated into previous positions after maternity leave, was regarded as a state not adhering to Article 8 §1 of the Charter.[879]

Article 8 §1 ESC orders to guarantee pregnant workers the right to maternity leave for at least twelve weeks. The same provision of the Revised European Social Charter imposes on Member States the obligation to treat women workers with fourteen weeks of maternity leave. The length of maternity leave cannot be shortened in

875. Conclusions I, pp. 49–50.
876. Conclusions II, p. 39 (United Kingdom).
877. Conclusions III, p. 49 (United Kingdom).
878. Case of United Kingdom: Conclusions III, p. 48; Conclusions IV, p. 66; Cases of Ireland: Conclusions V, p. 76.
879. Conclusions V, p. 76.

cases when an employee does not inform her employer about her intention of taking maternity leave.[880] Giving birth to a stillborn does not influence the length of maternity leave. The Committee declared that a Member State limiting the length of maternity leave to one month in the case of a stillbirth violates Article 8 §1 of the Charter.[881] The same applies to a premature birth.

Granting a woman worker less than twelve weeks of maternity leave guaranteed by Article 8 §1 ESC in the case of premature delivery created grounds for the Committee to make a negative ruling against the Netherlands.[882]

158. Maternity leave should be utilised in periods preceding the giving of birth to a child and directly following this event. Member States have been obliged to ensure women workers the right to maternity leave 'before and after giving birth'. Analysing the above provision, the Committee considered whether Member States should divide this break into two periods, one to be utilised by workers before birth, and the other to be utilised afterwards. It also debated on the scope of workers' entitlements to utilise maternity leave. During the first four supervisory cycles, the Committee claimed maternity leave is an entitlement for a worker who can decide upon its utilisation.[883] The above view was presented based on the information on inadequate financial benefits obtained by workers utilising maternity leave. According to the Committee, workers who are in difficult material situations should have the right to resign from a significant part of maternity leave and come back to work quicker or the right not to utilise maternity leave at all. However, maternity leave helps to achieve three socially important goals: it allows for a woman's preparation for childbirth, enables them to establish a psychological bond with a child, and makes it possible for a woman's system to regenerate (mentally and physically). Total or partial resignation from the right to utilise maternity leave is contradictory to the goals that maternity leave is meant to achieve. For this very reason, during the fifth supervisory cycle, the Committee declared that maternity leave should be obligatory at least throughout a part of the minimum twelve-week period.[884] The above ruling created a problem for Member States, as the Committee did not precisely determine the part of maternity leave that is obligatory, and which part the worker can reject.

Sweden introducing parental leaves by provisions legislated in 1976 gave the Committee the reason for inquiry that took place during the sixth supervisory cycle. The Committee asked Swedish authorities about the following: the nature of this leave, the mother's right to pass a part of the leave onto a man and the plausible obligation of utilising maternity leave by a woman who does not take personal care

880. Conclusions XIII-2, p. 104; Addendum to Conclusions XV-2, pp. 108–109 Malta. The Committee stated that maternity leave is too short in Bosnia and Herzegovina and Ireland. Conclusions 2011, vol. 1, p. 242 (Bosnia and Herzegovina), vol. 2, p. 558 (Ireland).
881. Case of Greece: Conclusions XII-1, p. 148; Conclusions XIII-1, p. 173
882. Conclusions XII-1, p. 149.
883. Conclusions I, p. 50; Conclusions IV, p. 66 (United Kingdom).
884. Conclusions V, p. 76 (Sweden). The above view was presented in accordance with Art. 8 §1 ESC. It has relevant application to reports on abiding of Art. 8 §1 RESC, with reservation that in such case, a woman worker is obliged to utilise a part of minimum fourteen weeks of maternity leave period.

for a child up to the 29th day post childbirth.[885] The questions were intended to determine the scope of plausibly utilising maternity leave by a woman worker entitled to maternity leave.

159. During the eighth supervisory cycle, it was decided that a worker who gave birth to a child should utilise at least six weeks of maternity leave she is entitled to.[886] Therefore maternity leave is a type of entitlement that can be taken advantage of by an interested woman worker. The above statement does not refer to six weeks of maternity leave, which a worker should utilise after childbirth and which must be granted by an employer.[887] There is no exclusion from the obligation of utilising a minimum of six weeks of maternity leave straight after childbirth.[888] Member States were obligated to introduce this rule into their domestic labour law regulations.[889]

Not complying with this obligation resulted in a negative ruling being passed by the Committee against Denmark,[890] Ireland,[891] and the United Kingdom.[892] As of 2015, the Committee concludes that the Ukrainian report does not provide evidence that there is a six-week compulsory postnatal leave that cannot be shortened (even at the employee's request), or that there are, in law or in practice, any adequate safeguards to protect employees from pressure to take less than six weeks‘ postnatal leave. Accordingly, the Committee finds that the situation is not in conformity with Article 8 §1 of the Charter, on the grounds that it has not been established that there are adequate safeguards to protect employees from undue pressure to take less than six weeks‘ post-natal leave.[893] The Committee recalls that, while national law may permit women to opt for a shorter period of maternity leave, in all cases there must be a compulsory period of postnatal leave of no less than six weeks, which may not be waived by the women concerned. If no such compulsory leave is provided for, legal safeguards must exist to avoid any undue pressure on employees to shorten their maternity leave, in specific legislation against discrimination at work based on gender and family responsibilities, an agreement between social partners protecting the freedom of choice of women concerned, or other guarantees enshrined in the general legal framework surrounding maternity – for instance, a parental-leave system whereby either parent can take paid leave at the end of maternity leave.[894]

The same consequences eventuated from granting women workers the right to shorter leave than the minimum of four or five weeks, which should be granted after childbirth.[895] The obligation of granting a woman worker at least six weeks of maternity leave is intended to protect the mother and the child. On the one hand, it makes it impossible for an employer to put pressure on a woman worker to come

885. Conclusions VI, p. 62.
886. Conclusions VIII, p. 123; Conclusions XII-1, pp. 253–254.
887. Conclusions XIII-5, p. 195 (Portugal).
888. Conclusions VIII, p. 125.
889. Conclusions XV-2, pp. 123–124 (Denmark); XV-2, p. 552 (Sweden); XV-2, p. 593 (United Kingdom).
890. Conclusions VIII, p. 124; Conclusions XIII-4, pp. 76–77.
891. Conclusions III, p. 48.
892. Conclusions III, p. 49; Conclusions IV, p. 66.
893. Conclusions 2015 (Ukraine).
894. Conclusions 2015 (Turkey).
895. Conclusions XIII-5, p. 194 (Portugal); Addendum to Conclusions XV-2, p. 108 (Malta).

back to work straight after giving birth, on the other hand, it opposes women workers interested in immediately returning to work and their decision upon ceasing to look after a baby. Among the following three options: the obligation of utilising maternity leave by a woman worker to its full length, utilising six weeks of maternity leave after giving birth and authorising a worker to decide what length of maternity leave she wants to utilise, the Committee decided upon accepting a solution, which reconciles conflicting interests of interested parties, i.e., women workers, newborn babies and employers. A woman worker must utilise six weeks of maternity leave straight after giving birth herself. She cannot renounce this part of maternity leave passing this entitlement on to a man – a father or a guardian, or on to another woman – a proper carer.

During maternity leave, a worker should obtain financial allowances. Article 8 §1 of the Charter imposes on Member States particular financial obligations. It prescribes that a worker on maternity leave should be obtaining remuneration for work (paid holiday), appropriate allowances from social security (maternity benefits) or from public funds. The Committee takes the position that the above regulation of financial obligation leaves the authorities of Member States the choice of the most adequate technique of funding financial allowances paid during maternity leave.[896] The authorities of Member States can choose one of the above-mentioned techniques presented in the analysed provision or create their own combinations of these techniques: combine the obligation of paying a part of the remuneration by an employer with maternity allowances, or supplementing the whole amount due to a worker.[897] The Charter does not determine the amount of allowances that should be paid out to employers during the period of maternity leave. It only mentions that allowances paid by social security or public funds should be 'adequate'.[898] The Charter does not specify the amount of remuneration paid to a woman worker during maternity leave, which creates a basis for the Committee to evaluate individual cases. In the above-mentioned first supervisory cycle dealing with the obligations of non-ratified provisions of the Charter, the Committee emphasised that Article 8 §1 of the Charter should be treated equally to regulations of labour law, guaranteeing a holiday with remuneration equal to the standard remuneration paid to a given worker during the carrying out of the work.[899] The Committee started evaluating financial allowances paid to women workers during maternity leave from the sixth supervisory cycle.

It stated that allowances equal to 40% of the weekly remuneration for work, giving the amount from IEP 14 to IEP 50 cannot be considered adequate.[900] Cases of allowances paid to women workers earning less than IEP 30 a week as well as allowances obtained by agriculture workers were treated the same.[901] As of 2015,

896. First report on certain provisions of the Charter which have not been accepted, 1981, Supervision relating to reports submitted under Art. 22 of the European Social Charter (1961), European Social Charter, *supra*, p. 480.
897. Conclusions VIII, p. 124 (Germany); Conclusions X-1, p. 93 (Greece).
898. Conclusions 2011, vol. 3, p. 1019 (Slovakia), p. 1170 (Turkey). Conclusions XIX-4 (2011), p. 404 (United Kingdom).
899. First report, *supra*.
900. Conclusions VI, p. 61.
901. Conclusions XIII-4, p. 82.

the Committee recalls that Article 8 §1 of the Charter requires maternity benefits to be equal to the salary or close to its value, i.e., at least equal to 70% of the employee's previous salary during the whole length of the compulsory maternity leave.[902] Therefore, the Committee concludes that the situation in Bosnia and Herzegovina,[903] Slovak Republic,[904] Turkey,[905] and the United Kingdom[906] is not in conformity with the Charter, on the grounds that the level of maternity benefits is not adequate. In 2019 several states[907] were found not be in conformity on the ground that: period of unemployment is not taken into account when calculating the qualifying period required to be entitled to maternity benefits;[908] it has been not established that: (1) there are in law and practice adequate safeguards to protect employees from pressure to take less than six weeks' postnatal leave;[909] (2) career breaks are taken into account when assessing the qualifying period required for a women to receive maternity benefits; (3) the period of 365 days for which employees are required to have contributed to the social security scheme before pregnancy in order to be entitled to maternity leave and maternity benefits is too long;[910] the amount of maternity benefit of employees in private sector is manifestly too low;[911] (4) pregnant women, female who have recently given birth and who are breastfeeding their infants are entitled to paid leave if it is impossible to transfer them to lighter duties; (5) in case of reassignment to a different post, the law guarantees the

902. With some exceptions for high salaries. Activity Report 2019, p. 31.
903. Conclusions 2015 (Bosnia and Herzegovina). The Committee found that some of the cantons of the Federation of Bosnia and Herzegovina do not provide maternity benefits, or that the benefit level was inadequate. The country report acknowledges that, while new legislation is being prepared to bring the situation into conformity with the Charter, no change has occurred yet. As a result, two cantons do not yet provide maternity benefits, while in some others the level of benefits is below 70% of the employee's salary or is based on the average salary in the canton, rather than the employee's salary. Conclusions 2019 (Bosnia and Herzegovina). The report does not contain any information on the level of maternity benefits compared to 50% of the equivalised median income.
904. Conclusions 2015 (Slovak Republic). During the reference period the level of maternity benefits was increase from 55% to 65% of the worker's salary. Despite the progress made, the Committee cannot consider the situation to be in conformity with Art. 8 §1 of the Charter.
905. Conclusions 2015 (Turkey). The Committee finds that the maternity benefits correspond only to 66% of the worker's earnings in the last three months. Conclusion 2019 on the ground that the amount of maternity benefits provided to women in the private sector is inadequate.
906. Conclusions 2015 (United Kingdom). The UK report indicates that women in receipt of the minimum wage would receive statutory maternity pay (SMP) worth 66% of their wages over a thirty-nine-week payment period. If a worker in receipt of the minimum wage receives maternity allowance (MA), then the MA could be worth 62% of her wages over a thirty-nine-week period. Therefore, the Committee concludes that the situation in the United Kingdom is not in conformity with Art. 8 §1 of the 1961 Charter, on the grounds that the standard rates of statutory maternity pay, after six weeks, and of maternity allowance, are inadequate. Conclusions 2019 on the ground that the standard weekly rate of Statutory Maternity Pay after six weeks and the maximum weekly rate of Maternity Allowance are inadequate.
907. Bosnia and Herzegovina, Ireland, the Republic of Moldova, Turkey, the Russian Federation and the United Kingdom. Activity Report 2019, p. 31.
908. Greece.
909. Ukraine.
910. Hungary, Albania.
911. Ireland, Russian Federation.

employees' right to return to their previous employment at the end of the maternity/nursing period;[912] the right to compulsory maternity leave is granted.[913]

160. Generally, the Committee declared that allowances paid during maternity leave which are at 80% of a standard remuneration meet the requirements established by the Charter. Lower allowances were not regarded as adequate unless they approached 100% of net remuneration or oscillated between 84% and 90% of the previous remuneration for work. The Committee took the position that allowances paid to women workers during maternity leave meet requirements set by the provisions of the Charter when they are as concurrent as possible with remuneration obtained by women workers in the period of employment.[914] The amount of financial allowances paid during maternity leave is dependent upon the basic amount regulated by the provisions of social security law. As a rule, this basic amount is subject to limitations. The national provisions of social security law set a limit above which remuneration is not taken into consideration while calculating allowances paid to women workers during their maternity leave. Using this technique of calculating allowances paid to women workers during their maternity leave, the Committee wanted to find out whether and in what ways the domestic provisions of labour and social security laws compensate women workers utilising maternity leave allowances calculated according to the lower basis than their standard work remuneration.[915] Comparing the amount of financial allowance paid to women workers utilising maternity leave to the amount of remuneration paid to these workers in the period of employment preceding the commencement of maternity leave, the Committee stated that the authorities of some Member States[916] established the maximum amount of allowances regardless of the basis of calculating of the above-mentioned allowances.

The Committee found out that maternity allowances in France did not exceed 58% of monthly wages paid to workers employed in managerial positions in workplaces.[917]

161. After making these statements concerning one Member State, the Committee became interested in the situation of other workers earning above the maximum limits as a basis used for calculating allowances paid to workers during maternity leave. It aimed at finding out the number of workers obtaining allowances not corresponding with the amount of their remuneration as well as the reason for the level of these allowances (the difference between the amount of standard remuneration and the amount of allowances obtained during the period of maternity leave).[918] As one of the three possibilities formulated in the analysed provision of the Charter

912. Moldova.
913. Azerbaijan.
914. Conclusions XIII-4, p. 72 (Denmark).
915. Conclusions XII-2, p. 134 (France).
916. Belgium, the Netherlands, Ireland. Conclusions XIII-1, p. 174; Conclusions XIII-2, p. 303.
917. Conclusions XII-2, p. 134.
918. Conclusions XIII-4, pp. 76 et seq.

relates to maternity benefits as to financial allowances paid by the system of social security, which is the most common way of regulating financial allowances paid to workers utilising maternity leave, the Committee was interested in familiarising itself with national provisions of social security law granting entitlements to the above-mentioned benefits such as the length of insurance policy[919] or the obligation of paying insurance premiums.[920]

The Committee declared the situation of acquiring entitlements to maternity allowances is dependent upon employment from two to five years before childbirth and paying insurance premiums in the period of 180 to 200 days two years prior to childbirth must be regarded as conflicting with the standards established by the Charter.[921]

A similar ruling was made against the requirement of employment with a particular employer for the period of two years as a condition of acquiring the right to maternity benefits[922] and the requirement of employment with a particular employer for the period of twelve months as a condition of obtaining entitlements to maternity leave.[923] Less firm requirements of acquiring entitlements of a woman worker who gave birth to a child, such as the requirement of employment with a particular employer for the period of six or twelve months as a condition of obtaining entitlements to the above allowances,[924] were not criticised by the Committee. The Committee examined premises by which domestic labour law regulations condition the acquirement of entitlements to maternity leave and benefits and insisted on Member States providing information on women workers who do not meet the above-mentioned requirements or obtain allowances of insufficient amounts. It especially insisted on presenting data on entitlements of such workers taking advantage of additional benefits of social security.[925] The Committee previously noted that, in order to be entitled to maternity benefits, the woman concerned (or her husband) should have paid contributions to the social insurance scheme during the six months preceding the request for maternity benefit, and asked whether periods of unemployment were included in the calculation of the required six months of contribution. As of 2015, the Committee concludes that the situation in the Republic of Moldova and Azerbaijan is not in conformity with Article 8 §1 of the Charter, on the grounds that it has not been established that interruptions in the employment record are included in the calculation of the qualifying period for maternity benefits.[926]

919. Conclusions XIII-1, p. 172.
920. Conclusions XV-2, p. 197.
921. Conclusions XV-2, pp. 239–240 (Greece); p. 522 (Spain).
922. Conclusions VI, p. 62 (United Kingdom).
923. Conclusions II, p. 39 (Sweden).
924. Conclusions XIII-5, p. 130 (Luxembourg). Conclusions 2011, vol. 1, p. 48 (Albania). Any unemployment periods ought to be included in the calculation of the qualifying period for maternity benefits. Conclusions 2011, vol. 1, p. 170 (Azerbaijan).
925. Addendum to Conclusions XV-2, p. 20 (Cyprus).
926. Conclusions 2015 (Republic of Moldova, Azerbaijan).

II. Prohibiting the Termination of a Work Agreement with a Pregnant Woman

162. The European Social Charter forbids employers from dismissing or terminating a work agreement during a female worker's absence due to maternity leave. It classifies a termination of a work agreement during this protective period as unlawful. The protective period embraces solely the period of maternity leave which a worker utilises. The Committee took the position that it would have been more advantageous for workers *de lege ferenda* if the special protection of work relations lasted throughout pregnancy and the period of maternity leave.[927] The above position was achieved by the Revised European Social Charter, which ensures the special protection of work relations from the day of informing an employer about the pregnancy up to the termination of the period of maternity. The Committee claims that a Member State meets the requirement imposed by Article 8 §2 of the Charter, even when maternity leave is shorter than the minimum period determined by Article 8 §2 of the Charter, which creates the legal basis for determining whether the latter provision is being abided by.[928] Not fulfilling the obligations set by Article 8 §1 of the Charter does not automatically mean non-fulfilment of obligations set by Article 8 §2 of the Charter. Special protection of work relations during the period defined by national labour law regulations should be ensured by Member States for all women workers. The rule of majority enlisted in Article 33 §2 ESC and Article I §2 RESC cannot be applied.[929]

Negative rulings made by the Committee concern cases when Member States exclude from the scope of protective regulations some categories of women workers those who are employed part-time,[930] as household service employed by individuals,[931] women workers from small workplaces where the total employment does not exceed twenty workers,[932] and workers employed on merchant ships.[933] The above-mentioned observation does not mean that Member States strictly comply with the prohibition of terminating employment contracts with workers legally protected on the grounds of maternity. In more than a quarter of cases of unlawful termination of employment with women in the protective period, the prohibitions on dismissal were violated. Also ignored by the national judicial authorities were the obligations to ensure that illegally dismissed workers receive appropriate redress or compensation.[934] In those countries where the applicable provisions of the labour law do not make it possible to reinstate the previously occupied position of an

927. First report on certain provisions of the Charter, which have been not accepted, *supra*.
928. Conclusions VI, p. 63 (Austria).
929. Conclusions IV, p. 67 (Austria); Addendum to Conclusions XV-2, p. 111 (Malta).
930. Conclusions XIII-4, p. 97 (Malta).
931. Conclusions I, p. 51 – Conclusions XIII-4, pp. 96–97 (Italy); Conclusions III, p. 49 – Conclusions XIII-4, pp. 93–94 (Austria); Conclusions XV-2, p. 523 (Spain).
932. Addendum to Conclusions XV-2, pp. 22–23 (Cyprus).
933. Case of Greece: Conclusions XIII-1, p. 178; Conclusions XIII-4, p. 96; Conclusions XV-2, p. 241.
934. Bosnia and Herzegovina, Ireland, the Slovak Republic, Spain and Turkey, Activity Report 2019, p. 31.

unlawfully dismissed employee who is under the protection period, the legal guarantees are even lower.[935] The Committee concludes that the situation in Bosnia and Herzegovina is in conformity with Article 8 §2 of the 1961 Charter on the ground that, in the Brčko District, compensation awarded in cases of unlawful dismissal during pregnancy or maternity leave is inadequate.[936] In Spain and Ireland, the reasons for dismissal of an employee during pregnancy or maternity leave go beyond the admissible exceptions. In Finland, the legislation does not provide for the reinstatement of women illegally dismissed during pregnancy or maternity leave in the private sector. In Bulgaria: (1) exceptions[937] to the prohibition of dismissal of pregnant women are excessively broad; (2) the compensation awarded in some circumstances is inadequate. In Turkey: (1) the reasons for dismissal of an employee during pregnancy or maternity leave go beyond the admissible exceptions; (2) it has not been established that adequate protection is provided for in cases of unlawful dismissal during pregnancy or maternity leave in the case of women employed in the public sector on temporary contracts; (3) not all employed women are entitled to reinstatement in case of unlawful dismissal during pregnancy or maternity leave; (4) it has not been established that legal remedies are available to employees on fixed-term contracts and civil servants in the case of unlawful dismissal based on pregnancy or maternity; (5) adequate compensation is not provided for in cases of unlawful dismissal during pregnancy or maternity. In Albania: (1) it has been established that there is adequate protection against unlawful dismissal during pregnancy; (2) the compensation awarded in the event of illegal dismissal during pregnancy or maternity leave is inadequate; and (3) reinstatement is not the rule in cases dismissals on the grounds of pregnancy or maternity leave in the private sector.

163. Prohibiting the giving of notice and terminating a work agreement during the protective period regulated by Article 8 §2 ESC was not absolute. Even though the appendix to the European Social Charter did not list cases excluded from the application of this provision, the Committee during all supervisory periods beginning from the first presented the view that domestic labour law regulations can introduce exceptions from the rule prohibiting termination of work agreements in the protective period. It allowed for the possibility of terminating a work agreement in the protective period in cases of behaviour or actions performed by a worker deemed offensive or inappropriate to the standards of the workplace and which justify terminating a legal bond by an employer; ceasing entrepreneurship by an employer, and termination of the period a work agreement was signed for.[938] The Committee stated that terminating a work relation in the protective period could be justified by 'sudden', 'objective' and 'serious' reasons.[939] The experiences of the

935. Albania, Finland Italy, Turkey. *Ibid.*

936. Conclusions relating to conclusions of non-conformity due to a repeated lack of information in Conclusions 2015.

937. Such as misconduct which justifies breaking off the employment relationship, and if the undertaking ceases to operate of if the period prescribed in the employment contract has expired.

938. Conclusions I, p. 51.

939. Conclusions XIII-1, p. 179 (the Netherlands); Conclusions XIII-2, pp. 215–216 (Spain); XIII-4, pp. 98 et seq.; Addendum to Conclusions XIII-3, p. 49 (Luxembourg). An exemption from the

Committee were taken into consideration by the Revised European Social Charter where its appendix stated that prohibiting the termination of a work relation with a woman worker whose work relation is encompassed by special protection of stability, is not of an absolute character.

As an example, it lists reasons for terminating a work agreement mentioned by the Committee in rulings made during previous supervisory cycles when debating the abidance of Article 8 §2 ESC by Member States.

Exceptions from the rule of special protection of stability of work relations should be interpreted strictly. The Committee concludes that in Lithuania, the exceptions to the prohibition of dismissal of employees during pregnancy or maternity leave are excessively broad.[940] Pursuant to Articles 132 and 136 of the Lithuanian Labour Code, which applies to the private and public sector, a pregnant woman may not be dismissed from the day she notified her employer of her pregnancy and until a month after the expiry of the maternity leave, except in the following cases: (1) following a court sentence passed on the employee which prevents him or her from continuing work; (2) when an employee is deprived of special rights to perform certain work in accordance with a procedure prescribed by law; (3) upon request of bodies or officials authorised by law; (4) when an employee is unable to perform his or her work given a medical conclusion or a conclusion of the Disability and Capacity for Work Establishment Office of the Ministry of Social Security and Labour; (5) upon the liquidation of an employer‘s activity. Similar situations exist in Latvia,[941] Romania[942] and Turkey.[943] In all those cases, the Commission

---

rule of no dismissal during pregnancy and maternity cannot be too broad. Conclusions 2011, vol. 1,
p. 129 (Armenia), vol. 2, p. 283 (Belgium), vol. 3, p. 1020 (Slovakia). Conclusions XIX-4, p. 107 (Czech Republic).

940. Conclusions 2015.
941. Conclusions 2015. Under Arts 101 and 109 of Latvian Labour Law exceptions to this rule exist when: (1) the employee has without justified cause significantly violated the employment contract or the specified working procedures; (2) the employee, when performing work, has acted illegally and therefore has lost the trust of the employer; (3) the employee, when performing work has acted contrary to moral principles and such action is incompatible with the continuation of employment legal relationships; (4) the employee, when performing work, is under the influence of alcohol, narcotic or toxic substances; (5) the employee has grossly violated labour protection regulations and has jeopardised the safety and health of other persons; (6) the employer – legal person or partnership – is being liquidated; (7) the employee has not performed any work due to temporary incapacity, for more than six months if the incapacity is interrupted, or for one year within three years, if the incapacity repeats with interruptions, excluding any prenatal and maternity leave in that period, as well as any period of incapacity, if the reason for the incapacity is an accident at work or an occupational disease.
942. Conclusions 2015. As an exception, dismissal can be allowed during pregnancy and maternity in cases of judicial reorganisation or bankruptcy of the employer.
943. Conclusions 2015. The Turkish report explains that dismissal is possible during pregnancy and maternity on the one hand for reasons related to economic, technological, structural and similar requirements of the enterprise, for example in the context of reorganisation, or with a view to increasing its productivity and competitiveness and, on the other hand, for reasons related to employee capacity or conduct, for example in cases of under-performance compared to other employees, or lack of skills and failure to develop them, frequent sickness, behaviour causing or potentially causing a prejudice to the employer, etc. The Committee furthermore notes that the Labour Act provides for dismissal without notice for employees with open-ended or fixed-term contracts. Therefore the Committee concludes that the situation in Turkey is not in conformity with

concludes that it has not been established that there is adequate protection against unlawful dismissal during pregnancy or maternity leave. According to the Committee, the policy of collective redundancy does not justify including into the group of dismissed employees women workers encompassed by special protection of stability of work relations. In cases of collective redundancy, the dismissal of pregnant workers is acceptable when the reason for this dismissal lies in the closing down of their workplace.[944] The case of taking over a workplace by another employer is treated analogically. The conversion within the employing party is not the same as liquidation, even though the employer passing on a workplace ceases entrepreneurship.[945]

164. The Committee regards Article 8 §2 of the Charter as a standard supplementing the provision of Article 8 §1 legislated in order to ensure the efficient protection of maternity for women workers. The aim of Article 8 §2 of the Charter is to guarantee financial stability for women workers and ensure the protection of a lasting work relation.[946] Prohibiting the giving of notice of the termination of a work agreement in the protective period includes filing acts of will by employers as well as legal consequences of the earlier acts of will informing on dismissal, received by women workers in the period preceding the commencement of the protective period. The above classification of acts of employers' will and their legal character in terms of terminating a work agreement requires a more detailed explanation. It is not clear whether the ban on giving notice in the protective period means that unlawful notice of an employer has no legal consequences or, despite its illegality, results in the termination of a work relation. The jurisdiction of the Committee concerning this issue is vague. On the one hand, the Committee presents the view that despite violating the ban on terminating work agreements in the protective period, termination of work relations eventuates. In that case, the necessary condition for reactivating an unlawfully terminated work relation is t the filing of court proceedings by the protected woman worker aimed at reinstating her to the previous position.[947] During the thirteenth supervisory cycle, the Committee made a ruling stating that a work agreement with a woman who is pregnant cannot be terminated during the protective period. Prohibiting the giving of notice of the termination of a work agreement at the will of the pregnant woman and prohibiting the termination of work agreements before the commencement of the protective period if the above notice would evoke legal consequences in the protective period, strengthen the provision of special protection of stabilising work relations. The Committee claims that an unlawful notice given by an employer results in suspending the course of the notice period

Art. 8 §2 of the Charter on three grounds. One of these is that there is no adequate protection in the Labour Act against unlawful dismissal during pregnancy or maternity leave. The other two could be cited in the part related to reinstatement and compensation provided for in cases of illegal dismissal during pregnancy and maternity leave.

944. Conclusions XIII-4, p. 99 (Spain); Conclusions XIII-5, p. 197 (Portugal).
945. Addendum to Conclusions XV-1, pp. 181–182.
946. Conclusions VII, p. 54.
947. Conclusions XII-2, p. 140 (Cyprus); Conclusions XIII-2, pp. 307–308 (Belgium); XIII-2, pp. 308–309 (Malta); Conclusions XIII-3, p. 314 (Finland); XIV-2, p. 157; XIV-2, p. 200 (France).

for the duration of the period of special protection of stability of the work relation.[948] Therefore, there are enough grounds to state that the employer actions which would have legal consequences in the protective period are not binding. Hence, it does not result in the consequences intended by an employer. Since the notice does not eventuate in terminating a work relation, there is no basis to present views on the necessity of reinstating an unlawfully dismissed woman worker to the previous position as an efficient way of resolving this issue. The Committee does not notice the emerging inconsistency. It takes the firm position that decisions upon reinstating a dismissed woman worker who is pregnant should be a general rule.[949] The exceptions to this rule can only be legislated by Member States in special circumstances. In these cases, the decision upon reinstating should be replaced by compensation.[950] The amount of this compensation should be as high as the trouble the employer has caused and compensate the woman worker for the loss of employment during the protective period.[951] The Committee claims that compensation should perform two functions: repressive and compensative. It gives a list of Member States who are not following this rule as they have not introduced the rule of reinstating women workers dismissed in the protective period: Belgium,[952] Bosnia and Herzegovina,[953] Cyprus,[954] France,[955] Greece,[956] Luxembourg,[957] Turkey,[958] and the former Yugoslav Republic of Macedonia, (now North Macedonia).[959] Some of them grant women workers compensation if they are unlawfully dismissed from work, something which was not regarded by the Committee as appropriate: Belgium – 6 months; Finland – 3 to 24 months,[960] Bosnia and Herzegovina – 18 salary payments.[961] The Committee declared that any ceiling on compensation that may preclude damages from being commensurate with the loss suffered and which are sufficiently dissuasive are proscribed, if there is such ceiling on compensation for

948. Conclusions XIII-4, pp. 92–93. The Committee negatively judged regulations of labour law in Slovakia where a protected woman worker can make a declaration upon not utilising the construction of suspending the period of notice. Addendum to Conclusions XV-1, pp. 181 et seq.
949. Conclusions 2011, vol. 1, p. 49 (Albania), vol. 1, p. 394 (Finland), vol. 2, p. 560 (Ireland), vol. 3, p. 1172 (Turkey), Conclusions 2015 (the former Yugoslav Republic of Macedonia).
950. Conclusions XIX-4 (2011), p. 263 (Luxembourg).
951. Compare the ruling invoked in footnote 709.
952. Conclusions XV-2, p. 89.
953. Conclusions 2015.
954. Addendum to Conclusions XV-2, pp. 22–23.
955. Conclusions XV-2, pp. 199–200.
956. Conclusions XIII-1, p. 178; Conclusions XIII-4, p. 96; Conclusions XV-2, p. 241.
957. Conclusions XIII-5, pp. 131 et seq. During the fifteenth supervisory cycle, the Committee stated that the situation of pregnant women had changed. Women workers were granted the right to litigate to be reinstated with the help of the head of the court of labour law in case of finding out that the notice of the agreement is legally invalid. All announcements made by employers stating termination of a work agreement with a pregnant woman are legally invalid. Addendum to Conclusions XV-2, p. 75.
958. Conclusions 2015.
959. Conclusions 2015.
960. Conclusions XV-2, pp. 156–157. The Committee decided in 2011 that the compensation should be adequate. Conclusions 2011, vol. 2, p. 560 (Ireland).
961. Conclusions 2015 (District of Brčko).

pecuniary damage through other legal avenues (e.g., anti-discrimination legislation), and the courts competent for awarding compensation for pecuniary and non-pecuniary damage must decide within reasonable time.[962] In light of this, the Committee finds that the situation is not in conformity with the Charter because adequate compensation is not provided for in cases of unlawful dismissal during pregnancy and maternity leave. If the report submitted by a Member State which ratified Article 8 §2 of the Charter does not provide any information in this respect, or answer any of the questions previously raised, the Committee reiterates them: (1) does the law provide for reinstatement of employees unlawfully dismissed during pregnancy or maternity leave? (2) Does it provide for adequate compensation of such employees, particularly when the reinstatement cannot take place? (3) Is there a ceiling on the amount that can be awarded as compensation to the employee? (4) If so, does this upper limit cover both pecuniary and non-pecuniary damage or can victims also seek unlimited non-pecuniary damage through other legal avenues (e.g., anti-discrimination legislation)? (5) Are both types of compensation awarded by the same courts? (6) How long does it take on average for courts to award compensation? (7) Does the same regime apply to women employed in the public sector? In the absence of this information, the Committee does not find it established that the situation is in conformity with Article 8 §2 of the Charter. In the case of Turkey, the Committee concludes that the situation in that Member State is not in conformity with Article 8 §2 of the Charter on the grounds not only of the lack of adequate protection against unlawful dismissal during pregnancy and maternity leave already mentioned but also of two additional grounds: (1) that not all employed women are entitled to reinstatement in cases of unlawful dismissal during pregnancy and maternity leave; (2) that it has not been established that adequate compensation is provided for in cases of unlawful dismissal during pregnancy and maternity leave.[963] Special protection of the stability of women's work relations does not change the character of the work agreement for the specified amount of time. While it is true that in the period pregnant women workers and women workers on maternity leave benefit from special protection of the stability of the work relation when a fixed agreement is in force, neither pregnancy nor maternity leave ensures protection against the termination of a work relation as a consequence of time passed which is subject to the agreement.[964]

III. Time Off Work for Mothers Nursing their Infants

165. Member States that ratified Article 8 §3 of the Charter are obliged to ensure that women workers nursing their infants have time off work. The above obligation is of a general nature. In 2019, the Committee concluded that France and Spain had failed to comply with the obligations set out in Article 8 §3 of both Charters.[965]

962. Conclusions 2011, Statement of interpretation of Art. 8 §2.
963. Conclusions 2015 (Turkey).
964. Conclusions XII-2, p. 139; XIII-2, pp. 213–214 (Austria); Addendum to Conclusions XIII-3, p. 49 (Luxembourg); Addendum to Conclusions XV-2, p. 22 (Cyprus), p. 111 (Malta).
965. Activity Report 2019, p. 31.

France is not in conformity for two reasons: (1) the remuneration of breastfeeding breaks is not guaranteed for employed women covered by the French Labour Code; (2) not all women working in the civil service are entitled to breastfeeding breaks and leave of absence is not provided. The situation in Spain is not in conformity on the ground that it has been not established that women working in the public sector are entitled to paid breastfeeding breaks. The Committee examines whether this entitlement to take breaks during work to nurse infants is organised for women workers employed in agriculture[966] and in household service by individuals[967] and in the civil service.[968] It allows for non-regulated breaks from work for women workers carrying out work in their own homes.[969] Its view is that, in the case of piecework jobs, women workers can independently decide upon the number and the length of breaks needed for nursing infants. The Committee emphasised that employers are obliged to pay women workers taking nursing breaks remuneration equal to what they would obtain for carrying out work. Breaks for nursing infants are treated by the Committee as part of the working day, during which women workers retain the right to remuneration equal to what they would obtain for carrying out the work.[970] Therefore, domestic labour law regulations allowing employers to demand women workers catch up for the time spent on breaks for nursing infants or regulations authorising employers to deduct a part of the remuneration paid for work that has not been carried out due to nursing infants' breaks, are in conflict with the standards established by the Charter.[971] The Committee states that Member States are obliged to introduce standards into their labour law regulations allowing women workers nursing infants to utilise paid time off during work. It is not enough, according to the Committee, to introduce the above obligation based on the argument of an employer taking care of his/her employees especially when there is a lack of specific legal regulations in establishing collective labour agreements.[972] Mothers nursing their infants should be entitled to utilise breaks for nursing during their working day.[973] The above obligation is not fulfilled by Member States that employ alternative measures, such as part-time employment, exemptions from the obligation of carrying out work without the right to remuneration.[974]

The Committee gave particular attention to the Swedish report of 1978 when instead of breaks for nursing infants, parental 'leave' of two hours a day was introduced.[975] This Swedish regulation is an intermediate solution between employing mothers raising small children part-time and entitling them to utilise parental leave.

966. Conclusions XIII-4, p. 101 (France), p. 103 (the Netherlands).
967. Conclusions IV, p. 67 (Italy). Conclusions 2011, vol. 2, p. 613 (Italy). Conclusions XIX-4, p. 338 (Spain).
968. Conclusions 2011, vol. 2, p. 446 (France).
969. Conclusions XV-2, p. 300 (Italy).
970. Conclusions I, p. 51 (Italy); Addendum to Conclusions XIII-3, p. 49 (Luxembourg); Conclusions XIII-4, p. 104 (Sweden); Conclusions XV-2, p. 200 (France).
971. Conclusions IX-1, pp. 71–72.
972. Case of the Netherlands: Conclusions X-1, p. 97; XI-1, p. 107; XIII-1, p. 180.
973. Conclusions XIII-4, p. 104 (Sweden).
974. Conclusions XIII-2, p. 309; Conclusions XIII-4, pp. 374–375; Conclusions XV-2, p. 89. Conclusions 2011, vol. 2, p. 446.
975. Conclusions XIII-4, p. 104; Conclusions XV-2, p. 554.

166. When taking breaks during the day, women workers were not guaranteed remuneration. Therefore, the Committee concluded that the above-mentioned regulation violated the standards set by the Charter and emphasised that the authorities of Member States should ensure paid breaks from work for all women workers, domestic workers and home workers included,[976] nursing infants.[977] Article 8 §3 of the Charter does not specify either the number or the length of time taken off work which is spent on nursing infants. Neither does it regulate the period of time when women workers are entitled to utilise the above breaks. The Committee requires information from the authorities of Member States concerning the above matters and states the obligation of the provision of the Charter in question is met by Member States that ensure two 30-minute breaks from work per day for working mothers. A necessary condition of compliance with the provisions of the Charter is providing a day nursery or some room where women workers can nurse their infants. In cases of not ensuring women workers have such a possibility in the workplace or in its proximity, employers are obliged to enable mothers to utilise two breaks from work, each one hour long.[978] Regulations, according to which workers nursing infants are entitled to two forty-five-minute-long breaks[979] and one one-hour-long break[980] were regarded as compliant with the international standards established by the Charter. Taking into consideration one of the cases, the Committee became convinced that an hour break from work for nursing infants could be divided into two equal parts or replaced by the thirty-minute-shorter working day.[981] Despite the accepted rule, there is still a need to evaluate domestic legal regulations on an individual basis. This was a ruling made by the Committee during the tenth supervisory cycle, drastically different for the interested disadvantaged parties (breastfeeding women and infants) from the standards approved during the first supervisory cycle. The right to utilise breaks from work for nursing infants by a worker lasts for nine months,[982] or no longer than past the age of one year of the baby.[983]

IV. Obligation to Regulate Rules of Employment Concerning Women Workers Employed at Nighttime in Industrial Occupations

167. The European Social Charter orders Member States to regulate the rules of employment concerning women workers employed at nighttime in industrial occupations. Article 8 §4 ESC includes the legal protection of all women, not only

976. Conclusions 2007, vol. 2, p. 690 (Italy).
977. Conclusions XIII-4, p. 104. Conclusions 2011, vol. 3, p. 1064 (Slovenia). Conclusions 2015 (Slovenia).
978. Conclusions I, p. 51 (Italy), p. 191 (Germany); Conclusions XIII-3, p. 315 (Portugal).
979. Addendum to Conclusions XIII-3, p. 49 (Luxembourg).
980. Conclusions V, p. 78 (France).
981. Addendum to Conclusions IX-2, p. 22 (Spain).
982. *Ibid.*
983. The Committee concludes that the situation in Belgium is not in conformity with Art. 8 §5 of the RESC on the grounds that breaks granted to women for the purpose of breastfeeding are only granted until the child reaches the age of seven months. Conclusions 2007, vol. 1, p. 178.

pregnant women and women on maternity leave. Regulating the rules of employment concerning women workers employed at nighttime in industrial occupations, Member States are obliged to consider whether establishing provisions for women's work protection will not be in conflict with the obligation of equal opportunities for all workers regardless of the sex and prohibition of discrimination in the field of employment.[984] Supervising the compliance of the above provision, the Committee remarked that Member States were not obliged to introduce the banning of women's work at nighttime but only to regulate the rules of such work in terms of law. Legal regulations of the employment at nighttime which is not defined by the Charter, may apply to all categories of workers regardless of sex. Provisions of domestic labour law should determine the rules of employment (concerning men and women) at nighttime and allow for carrying out work in industrial workplaces in cases justified by the requirements of production or the job organisation. In the case of employing women workers at nighttime in industrial workplaces, Member States should specify additional requirements, such as acceptance of work inspectors, breaks from work, days free from work at nighttime, and the obligation of shifting a woman worker to daily work in case of medical problems.[985] The aim of these regulations is to decrease the negative impact of employment at nighttime on a woman worker's body and her family life.[986] As of 2015, the Committee concludes that the situation in Armenia, Bosnia and Herzegovina, and Poland is not in conformity with Article 8 §4 of the Charter, on the grounds that regulations for night work do not offer sufficient/adequate protection for employment of those who are pregnant, have recently given birth or are nursing their infant.[987] In 2019, Bosnia and Herzegovina, Georgia, the Republic of Moldova and Poland were not in conformity with Article 8 §4.[988] The Committee concludes that in the situation of Bosnia and Herzegovina not in conformity with Article 8 §4 of the 1961 Charter on the ground that night work of pregnant women, women having recently given birth and women who are nursing their infants is not adequately regulated in the Brčko District. In Georgia, the rationale for the negative conclusion is almost identical. It has not been established that regulations on night work offer sufficient protection for employed women who are pregnant, have recently given birth or are nursing their infant. In Poland, the Committee concludes that the situation is not in conformity because work does not adequately protect women carrying out night work in industrial employment.

168. The range of protection for women's work at nighttime encompasses all industrial jobs. According to the Committee, the obligation of regulating the employment of women workers at night did not relate to jobs of a non-industrial nature carried out by women workers in industrial workplaces.[989] The Committee

984. Conclusions XII-1, pp. 22 et seq.
985. Conclusions XV-2, p. 242 (Greece), p. 349 (Austria), p. 436 (the Netherlands and Poland), p. 486 (Portugal).
986. Conclusions X-2, p. 97; Conclusions XII-1, pp. 22–23.
987. Conclusions 2015 (Armenia, Bosnia and Herzegovina) Conclusions XX-4 (Poland). Poland denounced sub-para. (b) of this provision in 2011.
988. Activity Report 2019, p. 31.
989. Conclusions I, p. 192.

paid special attention to examining the rules of employment of women workers at nighttime in cases of pregnant workers, workers who have recently given birth to a child or workers nursing infants.[990] It stated that international standards should force Member States to regulate the employment of women covered by special protection at nighttime or even to introduce the banning of employment of such women at nighttime.[991]

V. Duty to Regulate the Rules of Employment at Nighttime Concerning Pregnant Women, Women Who Have Recently Given Birth or Women Nursing Their Infants

169. Comparing the ranges of the analysed provision worded by the ESC and the Revised European Social Charter, it has to be noted that Article 8 §4 RESC provides protection for all women workers taking advantage of the special protection during the period of maternity, regardless of the place of their employment and the type of work they carry out. Article 8 §4 ESC applies to all women workers employed in industrial occupations.

In light of Article 8 §4 RESC protection is ensured for workers who inform an employer about the state of pregnancy, workers who have recently given birth to a child as well as workers nursing their infants. Labour law regulations in Member States compile legal definitions of these three categories. Legal limitations for including men to utilise the right to protection on the basis of Article 8 §4 of the Charter do not have a discriminative character. Women workers not benefiting from special protection in relation to the state of pregnancy, childbirth or breastfeeding an infant are comprised of protection guaranteed by Article 2 §7 RESC on equal grounds with men.

VI. Prohibiting the Employment of Women

170. Member States are obligated to legislate provisions prohibiting the employment of women in work in underground mining, as well as carrying out other jobs inappropriate for women because of their dangerous, unhealthy or arduous nature. The Committee debated whether the ban on the employment of women in underground mining is of a general nature. It concluded that women workers can be employed in underground mining in work, which is not considered inappropriate for women because of its dangerous, unhealthy or arduous nature, other than connected with the direct extraction of minerals.[992] Hence, there are no legal obstacles, moreover it is recommended – with regard to equal opportunities and the prohibition of discrimination on the basis of sex – to employ women workers underground in

990. Conclusions XII-2, p. 145 (France), p. 146 (Italy); Conclusions XIII-1, p. 181 (Greece); Conclusions XIII-2, p. 218 (Italy), p. 310 (Belgium), p. 312 (Malta); Conclusions XIII-4, p. 106 (France). Conclusions 2011, vol. 1, p. 130. (Armenia), p. 245 (Bosnia and Herzegovina).

991. Conclusions XIII-4, p. 107 (Greece), p. 109 (Italy); Conclusions XIII-5, p. 199 (Portugal). Conclusions XIX-4, p. 298 (Poland).

992. Conclusions X-2, p. 97 (Italy).

works of a medical, managerial or other nature, not connected with mining, as well as in mines where minerals are not excavated from under the ground.[993] Article 8 §4(b) ESC does not regulate the conditions of employment of women beyond the excavating industry.[994]

Examining national reports the Committee concluded that two of the Member States did not comply with the prohibition of employing women underground, namely Italy which overruled the ban of employment of women underground for women who were not pregnant[995] and Ireland.[996] In both cases, the Committee made negative rulings. It did not take into consideration explanations of the authorities of the two Member States that referred to international documents prescribing equal treatment of workers regardless of sex as well as the practical insignificance of the analysed issue.[997]

171. Article 8 §4(b) ESC prohibits employing women workers in all other work inappropriate for women because of its dangerous, unhealthy or arduous nature. Introducing the prohibition of employing women was left to be evaluated by the authorities of Member States. The Committee interprets the provision in question as a basis for legislating such bans on women's employment in work which is dangerous for a pregnant woman's health, *nasciturus* and infants.[998] Such dangers are created by work, which exposes a worker to the impact of chemical substances and factors (lead, asbestos, ionising radiation) or demands heavy lifting.[999] The Committee recalls that, under Article 8 §5 of the Charter, dangerous activities, such as those involving exposures to lead, benzene, ionising radiation, high temperatures, vibration or viral agents, must be prohibited or strictly regulated for pregnant women, women who have recently given birth and women nursing their infants, depending on the risks posed by the work.[1000] The Committee furthermore recalls that national law must make provisions for the reassignment of women who are pregnant or nursing their infant if their work is unsuitable for their condition, with no loss of pay. If that is not possible, such women should be entitled to paid leave and should retain their right to return to their previous employment.[1001] The Committee concludes that the situation in Azerbaijan, Bosnia and Herzegovina, Turkey and Ukraine is not in conformity with Article 8 §5 of the Charter, on the grounds that: (1) there are not adequate regulations on dangerous, unhealthy and arduous work in respect of protected female employees;[1002] (2) they are only entitled to

993. Conclusions XII-2, p. 147 (Malta); Conclusions XIII-1 (the Netherlands).
994. Conclusions XII-2, p. 147 (Malta); Conclusions XIII-1, p. 184 (the Netherlands).
995. Conclusions XIII-2, p. 217; XIII-4, pp. 110–111.
996. Conclusions III-1, p. 183; Addendum to Conclusions XV-2, p. 22.
997. Case of Italy where there was only one mine employing a few women. *See* Samuel, *supra*, p. 233.
998. Conclusions X-2, pp. 97–98.
999. L. Samuel, *Fundamental Social Rights: Case Law of the Committee*, 234–235 (Council of Europe Publishing, 2d ed., 2002).
1000. Conclusions 2015 (Ukraine).
1001. Conclusions (Azerbaijan).
1002. Conclusions 2015 (Azerbaijan, Bosnia and Herzegovina, Ukraine).

unpaid leave when such leave is granted because no other protective measures can be taken to protect them from exposure to risks inherent in their post.[1003]

VII. Prohibiting the Employment of Pregnant Women, Women Who have Recently Given Birth, or Who Are Nursing Their Infants, in Underground Mining and All Other Work of Dangerous, Unhealthy or Arduous Nature

172. Remarks of the Committee were utilised in the drafting of the new provision of Article 8 §5 RESC. This new standard orders Member States to establish the prohibitions against employment of women workers in underground mining and all other work considered to be of a dangerous, unhealthy or arduous nature during the protective period: in pregnancy, directly after giving birth and during breastfeeding. It imposes on Member States the obligation to undertake adequate actions in order to protect women workers employed in work that should not be carried out by them. Article 8 §5 RESC is a standard, which, during the special period, protects women workers against all types of risk brought by work, work factors and processes and conditions in which work is carried out, especially the work environment.[1004] The new obligation introduced by Article 8 §5 of the Charter commands Member States to legislate provisions ensuring women workers in their protective period who are employed in work they should not carry out, the entitlement to request to be relocated to another position with guaranteed remuneration for work of the same amount or – in the case of an impossibility of providing them with work in a different position – the entitlement to be excused from carrying out prohibited types of work. During the period of being excused from carrying out prohibited types of work, women workers utilising the right to special protection should be ensured entitlements guaranteeing adequate financial benefits, compensating for lost wages. The period of notice should be included in the work tenure, according to domestic labour law regulations. It is the basis for acquiring and retaining entitlements to workers' benefits and determining their scope in an individual case. In 2019 Azerbaijan, Bosnia and Herzegovina, Georgia, Hungary, the Republic of Moldova, Serbia, Turkey and Ukraine are not in conformity with Article 8 §5.[1005] The Committee concludes that the situation in Bosnia and Herzegovina is not in conformity with Article 8 §5 of the 1961 Charter on the ground that there are no adequate regulations and dangerous, unhealthy and arduous work in respect of pregnant women, women who have recently given birth or who are nursing their infants. In Hungary, the Committee concludes that, in the event of reassignment to a different post, the law does not guarantee the right of the women concerned to return to their previous jobs at the end of the protected period. In Ukraine, the law does not guarantee the

1003. Conclusions 2015 (Turkey).

1004. Conclusions 2003, vol. 2, pp. 385–386 (Romania). During this supervisory cycle the Committee postponed the decision in cases of: Bulgaria, Romania and Slovenia. In cases of France and Italy the Committee stated congruousness of the national labour law regulations with the standards established by Art. 8 §5 RESC. Conclusions 2011, vol. 1, p. 246 (Bosnia and Herzegovina).

1005. Activity Report 2019, p. 31. In cases of Georgia and Ukraine *see also* Conclusions relating to conclusions on non-conformity due to a repeated lack of information in conclusions 2015.

employees' right to return to their previous employment at the end of their maternity/nursing period. The situation in Azerbaijan is not in conformity with Article 8 §5 of the Charter on the ground that: (1) it has not been established that pregnant women, females who have recently given birth and women who are breastfeeding are entitled to paid leave if it is impossible to transfer them to lighter duties; (2) in case of reassignment to a different post, the law does not guarantee the right of the women concerned to return to their previous post at the end of the maternity/breastfeeding period.

§8. The Right to Vocational Guidance

173. Article 9 of the Charter is a dynamic provision. Member States are obliged to independently organise advisable services for all persons interested in choosing or changing his/her occupation or, alternatively, to support actions undertaken by public organisations in order to establish such services. The point of the analysed legal regulation finds expression in ensuring free-of-charge access to vocational guidance according to individual predispositions and characteristics of the labour market.[1006] Article 9 – the right to vocational guidance was included in the first thematic group – 'Employment, training and equal opportunities' assessed by the Committee in the 2020 cycle, therefore only a few questions were asked under this provision. States were only obliged to report if there was a previous conclusion of non-conformity or deferral.

174. The Committee previously noted that foreigners and stateless nationals enjoy access to vocational guidance on an equal footing to citizens of a given Member State.[1007] It asks the next report to clarify whether foreign nationals are included in the notion of 'citizen' and are accordingly also entitled to free guidance service both in the education system and in the labour market.[1008] Member States have full freedom in organising institutions carrying out vocational guidance. Domestic systems of vocational guidance can be organised within the confines of commonly accessible systems of education or of courses teaching particular qualifications or occupational skills, in order to acquire new skills, which will help enter the labour

1006. Conclusions IV, p. 69.

1007. Conclusions 2012.

1008. Conclusions 2016 (Azerbaijan), p. 98; (Bosnia and Herzegovina), p. 4 (Montenegro), p. 41 which is asked to clarify whether the holders of temporary residence titles have the same access as Montenegrin nationals to vocational services within the education system and labour market); (Serbia), p. 62 and (Ukraine), p. 75 should explain whether foreigners can have free access to vocational guidance services not related to unemployment status, in particular within the education system. In response to that Committee's question the Russian report indicates that free access to vocational guidance is provided without restrictions not only to Russian citizens but also to foreign nationals and stateless persons. The Committee, however, notes that only Russian citizens are entitled to services for unemployed people. Therefore, the Committee accordingly asks the next report to clarify which nationals of other states which are parties to the Charter are guaranteed access to free educational guidance provided by the Employment Service. Conclusions 2016, p. 16.

market.[1009] The important element is to ensure common access to institutions of vocational guidance.[1010] These services should be available for schoolchildren, university students and adults.[1011] First of all, institutions of vocational guidance should serve the disabled[1012] and other particular social categories (women, young persons, the unemployed, foreigners) whose needs are more difficult to satisfy.[1013]

Article 9 of the Charter is a standard obligating Member States to satisfy needs related to the organisation and promotion of vocational guidance 'as needed'. Therefore the objective scope of this duty is dictated by the situation of the national labour market. The interdependency between the situation of the national labour market and the duty of organisation and promotion of vocational guidance is direct. The higher the unemployment rate, the more serious the duty of organisation and promotion of institutions of vocational guidance.[1014] The above rule was used by the Committee in consecutive supervisory cycles. The increase in unemployment inspired the Committee to address the authorities of Member States' questions concerning expenses on vocational guidance and the number of institutions of vocational guidance advising persons intending to change their jobs or to undertake employment.[1015]

Article 9 of the Charter imposes on Member States the obligation of ensuring free-of-charge vocational guidance. The way of executing the above duty does not matter. It may be happening via public or private institutions. The services provided by these organisations, should not be financed by persons seeking employment or intending to acquire new occupational qualifications. The Committee took a firm position about the payment for vocational guidance. It ruled negatively against the Dutch legal regulations, according to which services of vocational guidance were delivered to the interested parties to an essential extent and with the possibility of charging for the services in 'hard cases'.[1016]

1009. Conclusions XIII-3, p. 31.
1010. The Committee concluded that the situation is not in conformity in Estonia where in practice access to vocational guidance is restricted to registered unemployed persons or those threatened with unemployment (Conclusions 2007, vol. 1, p. 373) and in Ireland where access to vocational guidance is not guaranteed for nationals of the other states party which are not members of the EU (Conclusions 2007, vol. 2, p. 608). In case of Belgium, Lithuania, Malta, Moldova and Romania the Committee concluded that it has been not established that the right to vocational guidance in the education system and in labour market is guaranteed to all nationals of State Parties. Conclusions 2008, vol. 1, p. 120 (Belgium), vol. 2, p. 455 (Lithuania), p. 494 (Malta), p. 542 (Moldova), p. 725 (Romania).
1011. Conclusions I, p. 53; Conclusions XIV-2, p. 55.
1012. No information had been provided concerning vocational guidance for persons with disabilities by the Azerbaijan government. Conclusion 2016, p. 99. The Committee also asks the next Bosnian and Herzegovina's report to provide any information, including relevant statistical data where available, showing that persons with disabilities are guaranteed free access to vocational guidance in the education system. It points out that the information requested should focus on guidance activities, not training, and should cover every part of the country. Conclusions 2016, p. 5.
1013. Conclusions XIII-2, p. 314 (Belgium); Conclusions XIII-3, p. 318 (Finland).
1014. Conclusions I, p. 53.
1015. Conclusions XIII-5, p. 77 (Finland).
1016. Conclusions XIV-2, p. 255.

175. The Committee demanded data from Member States on the organisation and conduct of such vocational guidance services.[1017] It was interested in familiarising itself with the organisational structure of these services, number of workers involved, their funds, and the number of persons to whom help was given.[1018] Taking into consideration the above data, the Committee made a negative ruling against Turkey as the small number of persons employed within the vocational guidance services, their uneven geographical distribution and inadequate financial measures did not guarantee general access to the services provided.[1019] According to the Committee services of vocational guidance should be organised in regions with the highest unemployment rate.[1020] The small number of workers employed in the vocational guidance services sector has a direct, negative impact on the evaluation of the obeying of the requirements of Article 9 of the Charter by a Member State.[1021] The Committee concludes that the majority of reports presented in 2016 do not provide the information previously requested[1022] concerning: (1) the budget allocated to vocational guidance; (2) expenditure on vocational guidance during reference period; (3) the number of staff involved in the provision of vocational guidance in labour market; (4) the number of beneficiaries of vocational guidance; (5) information tools (media, brochures, events) and measures taken to ensure dissemination of information on vocational guidance (interned websites and databases, information leaflets and publications, one-to-one and group sessions, career days, etc.). It also imprints negative consequences on the social perception of the activity of the above-mentioned services. It makes citizens of a given Member State, as well as citizens of other Member States which are parties to the Charter, notice that the authorities of a particular state do not fulfil the obligations formulated under Article 9 of the Charter.[1023] The authorities of Member States should try to prove in front of the Committee that they ensure or support the conduct of institutions dealing with vocational guidance for schoolchildren, young people and adults. Not fulfilling the above duty results in – in the case of not fulfilling the same duty as in previous supervisory cycles – a ruling stating that a given Member State does not abide by the standards regulated by the Charter.[1024]

In the last audit cycle – Conclusions 2020, the Committee issued two negative decisions proving that domestic legal systems did not comply with the provisions of Article 9 of the Charter. Bosnia and Herzegovina and Croatia have not proved that the right to vocational guidance within the education system and labour market is guaranteed. In the case of Bosnia, the lack of guarantees was not only of general

1017. Lack of sufficient information was taken as a ground for negative conclusion. Conclusions 2007, vol. 1, p. 183 (Belgium).
1018. *Ibid.*
1019. Conclusions XIII-1, pp. 234–235. In 2008 the Committee concludes that it has not been established that the right to vocational guidance in the education system in Turkey is guaranteed. Conclusions XIX-1 (2008), p. 470.
1020. Conclusions XIII-2, p. 219 (Italy).
1021. Conclusions XIII-3, p. 318 (Finland).
1022. Conclusions 2012.
1023. Conclusions XIX-1 (2008), p. 398 (Spain).
1024. Conclusions 2003, vol. 1, p. 265 (Italy). Conclusions 2016 (Azerbaijan), p. 100; Bosnia and Herzegovina, p. 7; (Moldova), p. 40; (Montenegro), p. 43; (Russian Federation), p. 18; (Serbia), p. 64; (Slovak Republic), p. 57; (Ukraine), p. 77.

application but especially for those persons with disabilities. However, in the case of Croatia, it had even greater scope. It concerned 'all of other States Parties'.

§9. The Right to Vocational Training

176. The provision of Article 10 ESC consists of four paragraphs. They impose on Member States the obligation to organise and/or support: common vocational and technical training, free access to higher technical and university education (§1); system of apprenticeship (§2); vocational training for adults (§3); access to utilising vocational training (§4) The Revised European Social Charter introduced additional obligations of ensuring and supporting special measures of training and reintegration of the long-term unemployed. This provision was marked as §4, while §4 ESC was marked as §5 RESC. In the 2020 cycle, some of the five paragraphs of Article 2010 were excluded from the control of the Committee in line with the adopted principle that 'the Committee notes that targeted questions were asked under this provision. As the previous conclusion found the situation to be in conformity there was no examination of the 'situation in 2020'.

The scope of obligation of providing and/or supporting vocational training on all levels including university courses has a general nature. It comprises citizens of Member States, migrants, citizens of other states, parties to the Charter,[1025] young persons and adults, educated and uneducated, non-working persons, unemployed persons, carrying out work according to work relation agreements as well as those running their own business.[1026] According to the Committee, some of the mentioned above social groups should utilise the right to vocational training according to preference rules. This concerns persons who experience above-average obstacles in finding employment: the disabled and immigrants. The opinion of the Committee is that the privileged treatment of these persons does not prompt the accusation of discrimination against the remaining beneficiaries of the right to vocational training.[1027] In the light of legal regulations introduced by Article 10 §4 RESC privileged treatment can also apply to the long-term unemployed.

177. Enforcement of the duty regulated by this provision is related to the needs of labour markets occurring in particular Member States. The Committee emphasises that the unemployment rate cannot be considered as a main or sole indicator of the executing of duties imposed on Member States by the analysed provision of the Charter. The unemployment rate is the most obvious indicator. Another important factor in determining the scope of provision and/or supporting vocational training on all levels is the demand for a particular type of work.[1028] The latter means that the authorities of Member States should organise and/or support vocational training on various levels and respond to the changing demand of labour market as

1025. Conclusions XIII-3, pp. 32 et seq.
1026. Conclusions XIV-2, p. 59.
1027. Conclusions I, p. 81.
1028. Conclusions XIII-3, p. 37.

well as to the expectations of different social groups in the age of professional activity. Under the term 'vocational training' used in Article 10 of the Charter the Committee understands the entirety of duties imposed on Members States related to enabling all persons interested in acquiring education, from primary school to university, increasing occupational qualifications and occupational reorientation. According to the Committee, the right to vocational training is the entitlement that should be available during the course of life for all social categories considered as potentially professional active groups: students, young persons, educated and uneducated, employed and unemployed.[1029] European societies are learning societies by their nature. The above classifications oblige Member States to undertake constant efforts in order to organise and/or support initiatives aimed at increasing the level of knowledge, skills, and occupational qualifications of all interested subjects. The execution of the above-mentioned duty is considered the most crucial and most efficient measure to prevent social exclusion.

I. The Obligation to Provide or Promote Technical and Vocational Training and Granting Facilities for Access to Higher Technical and University Education

178. Member States who ratified the above provision are obliged to provide all interested persons, including the disabled, with technical and vocational training and to grant facilities for access to higher technical and university education. It does not imply that the above training has to be organised by the state. Article 10 §1 of the Charter obliges the authorities of Member States that do not want to provide technical and vocational training themselves to support technical and vocational training provided by private institutions. In the case of higher technical and university education, Article 10 §1 of the Charter orders a Member State to grant facilities for access to higher technical and university education existing in a given state. During the first supervisory cycle, the Committee became convinced that the essence of the duties listed in the analysed provision comprises the following: providing, promoting and granting access to units and institutions providing technical and vocational training from the basic to the advanced level.[1030] Article 10 §1 has a common range. All citizens of a particular Member State and citizens of other states who ratified the Charter should be provided with vocational training.[1031] However, this entitlement is not of an absolute nature. Member States were obliged to provide or promote technical and vocational training 'as needed'. The 'need' in a particular Member State is determined by the authorities of that state. The Committee exists to verify the above evaluations. It demands information from the authorities of Member States concerning the undertaken actions in order to provide all interested persons with technical and vocational training. It orders the presentation of information concerning the number of persons who utilised the above option.[1032] The

1029. Conclusions XIV-2, p. 59.
1030. Conclusions I, p. 55.
1031. Conclusions XIX-1 (2008), p. 31 (Austria), p. 365 (Slovenia).
1032. Conclusions II, p. 42 (Denmark).

Committee particularly insists on delivering data on the number of immigrants coming from other Member States who are parties to the Charter and who have taken part in technical and vocational training.[1033] It is interested in the measures undertaken in order to prevent discrimination among immigrants in terms of technical and vocational training.[1034] Preferential treatment is acceptable in the case of disabled persons. Despite the fact that disabled persons should experience privileged treatment in matters concerning technical and vocational training as it is prescribed by the analysed provision, the Committee states that these preferences should be spread over all types of training, including higher, technical and university education, which is mentioned in the final part of the provision in question.[1035] Access to higher, technical and university education should be granted according to democratic rules, based solely on individual merit.[1036] Attending university and studying are enabled by scholarships and other measures of financial help. The Committee is interested in knowing about the benefits provided for interested persons by Member States for those undertaking higher, technical and university education.[1037] Familiarisation with domestic systems of vocational training obliges Member States to provide detailed information about the organisations, division of tasks between various educational bodies and institutions, conduct of these institutions and ways of financing them. The Committee demands this information be presented regularly.[1038]

179. Providing and/or supporting vocational training by a Member State should be performed in consultation with stakeholders. According to the Committee, this reservation does not imply passing the duties set by Article 10 §1 of the Charter onto tripartite committees, consisting of representatives of employers and workers, debating under the chairmanship of state authorities.[1039] Stakeholders should partake in the authorities' decisions regarding the planning of educational institutions and bodies and achieving the statutory goals set by these organisations.

In the case of the United Kingdom and Turkey, the Committee stated trade unions were incidentally involved in the planning of technical and vocational training happening within the conduct of governmental bodies.[1040] Institutions providing technical and vocational training should be evenly spread over the territory of a state, so all parties interested in utilising their services could have equal access. In the case of Germany after the unification, the Committee stated that there are significant differences between eastern and western provinces in terms of the density of training institutions.[1041] It obliged the German authorities to eliminate the above disproportion.

1033. Conclusions IV, p. 71 (Germany).
1034. Conclusions V, p. 81 (France), Conclusions 2007, vol. 2, p. 610 (Ireland), p. 1021 (Slovenia).
1035. Conclusions II, p. 43; Conclusions III, p. 54 (Norway).
1036. Conclusions I, pp. 55–56.
1037. Conclusions II, p. 42 (Denmark).
1038. Conclusions XIII-3, p. 33.
1039. Conclusions XII-1, p. 165 (United Kingdom).
1040. Conclusions XIV-2, p. 748 (Turkey); XIV–2, p. 779 (United Kingdom).
1041. Conclusions XIII-2, p. 319; XIII-4, p. 382.

Training institutions should be organised in order to ensure the maximum utilisation of their services by persons interested in undertaking technical or vocational training. The necessary condition for the execution of this rule is the proper proportion between learners and teachers. The increase of persons undertaking training accompanied by a stable number of teachers resulted in the Committee's reaction,[1042] examining the level of state expenses on technical and vocational training. The Committee considered the proportion of state expenses on technical and vocational training in the whole state budget as an important indicator of actions undertaken by state authorities in order to meet the obligations determined by Article 10 §1 of the Charter.[1043]

180. Article 10 §1 of the Charter orders Member States to organise recruitment procedures for higher, technical and university education as solely based on individual merit. The obligation to grant access to higher, technical and university education to all faculties,[1044] not only faculties leading to particular occupational qualifications such as law and medicine, orders Member State authorities to provide financial benefits (scholarships, allowances, loans) for persons studying as well as eliminating all barriers in accessing education. The requirement to obtain a work permit before entering into a vocational training agreement[1045] and the option of applying for a scholarship was regarded as acting as an obstacle. The Committee declared that the right to apply for financial assistance during education and training is treated as a necessary condition of ensuring persons the right guaranteed by Article 10 §1 of the Charter to utilise vocational training.[1046]

Evaluating the German report the Committee was obliged to state Article 10 §1 ESC does not impose on Member States the duty of granting financial aid to persons learning or studying. This obligation is derived from Article 10 §4.

The right to technical and vocational training as well as to higher, technical and university education should be equally utilised by citizens of a particular country and citizens of other Member States. Cases of unequal treatment of citizens of Member States and signatories of the Charter were detected by the Committee during these supervisory cycles when the Committee held the position that granting financial aid to persons learning or studying is a duty formulated in Article 10 §1 of the Charter.

The Committee stated that discriminatory practices concerning the granting of financial aid to persons learning or studying, which were employed by the Belgian authorities against citizens of Turkey as conflicting with Article 10 §1 of the Charter.[1047] The regulation of Finish authorities that introduced the requirement of two years of residency as the necessary condition for acquiring the right to financial aid for persons learning or studying was considered a manifestation of discrimination.[1048]

1042. Conclusions XIV-2, p. 234 (Finland).
1043. Conclusions XIV-2, p. 349 (Greece).
1044. Conclusions XIII-3, p. 37.
1045. Conclusions VII, p. 59 (Germany).
1046. Conclusions VIII, p. 136.
1047. Conclusions XIII-4, p. 382.
1048. Conclusions XIII-5, p. 81.

In the eleventh supervisory cycle, Greece was evaluated negatively by the Committee.

It was regarded as a state in violation of the provision as it made the right of foreigners to partake in vocational training dependent upon being born and being a permanent resident of the territory of Greece.[1049] It was not until the Greek regulations changed and Greece declared equal access to technical and vocational training as well as to higher, technical and university education for Greek citizens and for citizens of other Member States, parties to the Charter, when the Committee changed its jurisdiction towards this country.[1050] In 2003 and 2008 the Committee detected one case of national labour regulations conflicting Article 10 §1 RESC. Slovenia had not provided citizens of other Member States with equal access to vocational training. It conditioned the option of utilising vocational training on work permits for an unspecified period of time.[1051] The exception from the above rule was introduced for citizens of those Member States, parties to the Charter, which were bound with Slovenia by international multilateral agreements on facilitating vocational training. In the last cycle, in conformity with Article 10 §1 of the Charter on the grounds that it has not been established that: (1) the right to vocational training is effectively granted;[1052] (2) the system of secondary and higher education operates in an efficient manner.[1053] In the case of the Slovak Republic, the Committee notes that the educational attainment of youth does not translate into success in placement in the labour market. The unemployment of young people is higher than in the EU 28 at all education levels. There are reliable instruments for the anticipation of labour market needs. There is no institution or specialist focusing on the qualitative anticipation of skill needs. Ad hoc sectoral/regional data have been collected, without efforts to develop regular national instruments to be used periodically to monitor labour market supply and demand. In Montenegro, the Committee observes that insufficient measures were taken to match the skills acquired through vocational training with the labour market requirements and thus to bridge the gap between education and work. Therefore, the Committee concludes that the right to vocational training is not effectively guaranteed in practice as measures taken to make vocational education qualifications relevant from the perspective of professional integration in the job market have been insufficient.

In the case of Ukraine, the Committee recalls that under Article 10 §1 of the Charter, the Member States must introduce mechanisms for the recognition/validation of knowledge and experience required in the context of training/working activity in order to achieve qualifications or gain access to general, technical and university higher education. Moreover, the states are obliged to take measures to make secondary education and general higher education qualifications relevant from the perspective of professional integration in the job market. In the absence of information on these points, the Committee concludes that the system of secondary and higher education in Ukraine does not operate in an efficient manner.

1049. Conclusions XI-1, p. 112; Conclusions XII-1, pp. 161–162; Conclusions XIII-1, p. 185; Conclusions XIII-3, p. 155.
1050. Conclusions XIV-2, p. 349.
1051. Conclusions 2003, vol. 2, pp. 472–473, Conclusions 2008, vol. 2, p. 762.
1052. Conclusions 2016 (Slovakia), p. 92; (Montenegro), pp. 44–45.
1053. Conclusions 2016 (Ukraine), pp. 119–200.

In 2020, the Committee examined technical and vocational training and gave access to higher technical and university education in twenty-three Member States. It found out that, in some of them,[1054] the situation was not in conformity. The legal basis for issuing such a negative opinion in these cases is the Committee's enigmatic statement that it has not been established that the right to vocational education is effectively guaranteed. In the report, Cyprus stated that it had received technical assistance from the EU. However, it did not present what these programs were about. Therefore, the Committee concludes that it has not been established that the right to vocational education is effectively guaranteed.

The Polish authorities indicated that the provisions on access by foreigners to vocational training had been amended in 2013 following the incorporation of a European directive into national law. Under these provisions, persons holding work visas or temporary residence periods are entitled to labour market services except for grants, the reimbursement of training costs, loans to cover training costs and additional funding for postgraduate studies. However, the Committee notes that the law on employment promotion and labour market institutions does not provide for any specific instruments on vocational training or skill development for refugees. Therefore, the Committee concluded that the situation in Poland is not in conformity with Article 10 §1 of the 1961 Charter on the ground that there are no specific instruments deployed to integrate migrants and refugees into vocational education and training. In the case of Ukraine, the Committee repeated the content of the negative decision presented in the previous cycle in 2016 – 'it has been not established that the system of secondary and higher vocational education operates in an efficient manner'.

II. The Duty of Providing or Promoting a System of Apprenticeship for Young Persons

181. Member States that ratified the above regulation are obliged to provide or promote a system of apprenticeship for young persons (boys and girls) or to provide or promote other systematic arrangements for training young persons in their various employments.[1055] The Committee defined an apprenticeship during the first supervisory cycle as a mixed system of training, a combination of theoretical and practical aspects. An apprenticeship is not intended solely to acquire practical skills. It is a complex system based on full, coordinated and systematic vocational training.[1056] It may occur in a formalised legal form, according to which training is understood strictly in terms of vocational training. Vocational training can also be comprised of apprenticeships, served by older students of technical and academic faculties such as pedagogical science, medicine, dentistry, and law.[1057] The Committee evaluates whether systems of vocational training existing in Member States

1054. Cyprus, Poland and Ukraine. Conclusion 2020.
1055. No questions were asked under Art. 10 §2 in cycle 2020. States were only obliged to report if there was a previous conclusion of non-conformity or a deferral.
1056. Conclusions I, p. 57.
1057. Conclusions III, p. 55.

meet the requirements of the analysed provision of the Charter. It monitors the actions undertaken by the authorities of Member States in order to provide young people with systematic vocational training; the number of persons who can enrol for training;[1058] the number of persons who took part in vocational training;[1059] the type of vocational training offered; financial support for persons attending training;[1060] the number of persons who completed training taking into consideration their sex[1061] and geographical location.[1062] The Committee supervised the obeying of the rule of equal opportunities for the citizens of Member States.[1063] It continued to hand down negative rulings against states that restricted the entitlement of foreigners to utilise financial aid during apprenticeships,[1064] demanding the acquisition of a work permit or a certificate excusing from the above obligation.[1065] It did not accept the explanation from the authorities of Member States, which provided information on the results of the above protective actions intended for the future protection of national labour markets concerning a small minority, approximately 5% of the whole working population, hence smaller than the 20% accepted according to the rule of majority formulated in Article 33 §2 ESC and Article I §2 RESC. The Committee declared that excluding less than 5% of foreigners out of 100% of citizens who had been deprived of the entitlement to serve an apprenticeship is, in fact, excluding 100% of foreigners residing in the territory of another Member State. This is why the rule of majority cannot be applied to all members of a particular social category. Therefore, the regulations of domestic labour law were regarded by the Committee as conflicting with Article 10 §2 of the Charter, although the authorities of a given Member State treated work permits as a 'pure formality'.[1066]

Identical rulings were handed down in the case of Greece which also required a work permit from participants of vocational training,[1067] while Ireland,[1068] Malta and Slovenia privileged their own citizens in accessing vocational training.[1069]

During the last cycle, the Committee made a distinction between Member States in which there is either no well-functioning,[1070] functioning[1071] or effective[1072] system of apprenticeship. The efficiency of the apprenticeship is assessed on the basis of the following elements: length of the apprenticeship and division of time between

1058. Conclusions XIV-2, p. 97 (Austria); p. 200 (Denmark).
1059. Case of Spain: Conclusions XII-2, pp. 159–160; Conclusions XIII-3, p. 167.
1060. Conclusions I, pp. 56–57.
1061. Conclusions XIV-2, p. 749 (Turkey).
1062. Conclusions XIII-3, p. 240 (Turkey).
1063. Conclusions 2007, vol. 1, p. 1016 (Slovenia).
1064. Conclusions XIII-4, p. 386 (Germany).
1065. Case of Austria: Conclusions VIII, pp. 138–139; Conclusions XIII-3, p. 162; Conclusions XIV-2, pp. 97 et seq.
1066. Addendum to Conclusions on Luxembourg, pp. 56 et seq.; Conclusions XIV-2, p. 486 (Luxembourg).
1067. Conclusions XII-2, pp. 156–157; XIII-2, p. 220; XIII-3, p. 165; Addendum to Conclusions XIII-3, pp. 56 et seq.
1068. Conclusions XIV-2, p. 404.
1069. Conclusions XIII-2, p. 323; Conclusions XIII-3, pp. 165–166, Conclusions 2008, vol. 2, p. 498 (Malta), p. 762 (Slovenia), Conclusions XIX-1 (2008), p. 366 (Slovenia).
1070. Conclusions (Georgia), p. 26; (Slovak Republic), p. 59.
1071. Conclusions (Montenegro), p. 93.
1072. Conclusions 2016 (Ukraine), p. 79.

practical and theoretical learning. The main indicators of complicity are the existence of apprenticeship and other training arrangements for young people, the numbers controlled and the total spending, both public and private. The Committee asks for information on the selection of apprentices, the choice of training and instructors. It also tries to work out how many apprenticeship places are on offer, approximately how many young people take up apprentice-style training and how many of the apprentices completed training. The Committee noted that the reports mentioned above provided limited information, some information or no information at all regarding these points. Therefore, in the absence of necessary information in the reports concerning apprentices, the Committee concludes that it has not been established that there is a well-functioning, functioning or effective system of apprenticeship.

III. Vocational Training for Adult Workers

182. The duty of Member States is to guarantee or provide adequate training for adult workers. The Adult Education Strategy for the period 2015–2025 and the Adult Education Plan for the period 2015–2020 adopted by the government are enough to comply with the provision of Article 10 §3. The Committee wishes to receive information about the types of continuing vocational training and education available on the labour market for unemployed persons, the overall participation rate of persons in training and the total expenditure. It also asks about the activation rate, the ratio between the annual average number of unemployed persons and participants in active measures. It wishes to be informed of the sharing of the burden of the cost of vocational training among public bodies, unemployment insurance systems, enterprises and households with regard to continuing training. If the report does not provide information about the implementation of the strategy and adult education plan, the conclusion is negative.[1073] Special facilities for the retraining of adult workers which are needed as a consequence of technological development and new trends in employment, should be provided by Member States. The obligation stipulated under Article 10 §3 of the Charter has a relative nature. Providing or promoting vocational training and adequate training for adult workers should be organised as necessary. The Committee believes that the authorities of particular Member States decide themselves, whether the above necessity applies. During the early supervisory cycles, the Committee took the position that the margin of freedom for Member State authorities in terms of making decisions upon promoting and providing vocational training should be limited. It is usually determined by the unemployment rate existing in given Member States. According to the Committee, Article 10 §3 of the Charter imposes special duties on Member States where unemployment is high.[1074] The Committee made a negative ruling in the case of Italy which neglected to provide training for adult workers. According to the report presented by the Italian authorities, the percentage of unemployed utilising the option

1073. Conclusion 2016 (Montenegro), p. 47.
1074. Conclusions I, p. 58 (Italy, United Kingdom).

of vocational training was minimal.[1075] The situation in the aforementioned countries looked similar during the second supervisory cycle.[1076] Influenced by the negative rulings of the Committee, the British and Italian authorities changed the policy of vocational training for adult workers, which let them obtain positive decisions of the Committee in terms of abiding by regulations formulated in the analysed provision of the Charter during the following supervisory cycle. Gradually, the Committee became convinced there was no direct correlation between fulfilling the obligation of promoting and providing adequate training for adult workers and the unemployment rate. It concluded that what is protected by Article 10 §3 of the Charter is vocational training for adult workers as a virtue per se, which, generally analysing, plays an important role in the process of evaluating the chances of adult workers within the labour market, adult workers who want to work, who want to apply for jobs. The Committee ordered the authorities of Member States to prepare reports concerning the number and geographical location of public and private institutions of vocational training dealing with adult workers, especially those who are unemployed; permanent centres of upgrading skills for persons of particular occupations (doctors, dentists, lawyers, etc.) craftsmen, merchants, etc.; and actions undertaken by administrative bodies in order to promote these institutions.[1077] It observed a disproportion between the number of vocational training institutions and their localisation and the unemployment rate in particular Member States.[1078] On the one hand, vocational training contributed to the increased mobility of persons seeking employment and migrating for employment purposes,[1079] on the other hand, vocational training provided by employers enables workers to undertake new responsibilities, giving employers a reason for not leaving and extending their work relations with the same workers but those with higher professional qualifications.[1080] In the last two cycles (2016 and 2020), the Committee concluded that the situation in Malta is not in conformity with Article 10 §3 of the Charter on the ground that it has not been established that the legislation provides for individual leave for the training of employed persons.

183. The Committee paid special attention to Member States fulfilling the duty of providing or promoting actions aimed at vocational training for adult workers in social groups vulnerable to changes in the labour market: women, the unemployed, migrant workers, and citizens of other Member States. Evaluating the national reports, the Committee emphasised that in some countries the participation of women in programmes of vocational training is low, especially training with professional qualifications essential for carrying out work dominated by men. In relation to the above, the Committee emphasised the need for the privileged treatment

1075. *Ibid.*
1076. Conclusions II, p. 43 (Italy), p. 44 (United Kingdom).
1077. Conclusions V, p. 84 (France).
1078. Case of Turkey: Conclusions XIII-1, pp. 240–241; Conclusions XIV-2, p. 751.
1079. Conclusions XIII-3, pp. 34–35 (Denmark).
1080. As above, Ireland, Iceland.

of women applying for participation in vocational training, which, once accomplished, increased the chances of women carrying out work within occupations traditionally regarded as 'male'.[1081] Despite the previously certified lack of a direct correlation between professional training and the rate of unemployment, the Committee demanded the reasons why a significant part of the unemployed are not included in training from the authorities of Member States.[1082] It presented the opinion that unemployed persons, especially those who remain without employment for a period of one year, should be included in special programmes of vocational training and upgrading skills. It noted that in some countries such programmes had been drafted and were executed.[1083] The experience of the Committee was taken into consideration by Article 10 §4 RESC, a standard which orders Member States to undertake special measures for professional training and the reintegration of the long-term unemployed.

184. During each supervisory cycle, the Committee demanded information from the authorities of Member States concerning programmes of vocational training for adult workers and citizens of other Member States. The lack of such information resulted in postponing a ruling on the compliance of national regulations and practices with the requirements of the Charter.[1084] During its supervisory session, the Committee held the position that excluding or limiting the rights of foreigners and citizens of other Member States who are parties to the Charter because of their national identity is a case of discrimination and must be considered a violation of Article 10 §3 of the Charter.[1085] It pursued the goal of encouraging the authorities of Member States to apply the same requirements in accessing vocational training for adult workers as for their own citizens. Evaluating the case of Germany, which introduced the requirement of a particular work tenure for candidates for vocational training for adult workers (three years for qualified workers and six years for unqualified), the Committee made attempts in order to determine whether the work

1081. Cases of: Spain, Ireland, Portugal, Sweden and Turkey. General introduction to Conclusions XIII-3, p. 35.

1082. Conclusions XIV-2, p. 237 (Finland).

1083. Spain, Ireland, Portugal, Sweden, United Kingdom. General introduction to Conclusions XIII-3, p. 35.

1084. During five consecutive supervisory cycles: the eighth, the ninth the tenth, the eleventh and the twelfth, the Committee postponed making a ruling in case of Austria. Conclusions VIII, p. 142; Conclusions IX-2, p. 69; Conclusions X-2, pp. 106–107; Conclusions XI-2, p. 13, p. 105; Conclusions XII-2, p. 160. It demanded information on the possibility of participation of immigrants in training organised for Austrian citizens. The Committee opposed the policy of providing vocational training for own citizens and foreigners according to different rules. During the fourteenth supervisory cycle, the Committee postponed making a ruling in case of: Belgium (Conclusions XIV-2, pp. 144 et seq.); Denmark (XIV-2, pp. 200 et seq.); Finland (XIV-2, pp. 235 et seq.); Ireland (XIV-2, pp. 405 et seq.); Malta (XIV-2, p. 521); Portugal (XIV-2, pp. 655–656); Turkey (XIV-2, pp. 750 et seq.) and Italy (XIV-2, pp. 444–445) During the following supervisory cycle in 2003, the Committee postponed making a ruling in case of Italy (Conclusions 2003, vol. 1, p. 274).

1085. Conclusions 2003, vol. 2, p. 478 (Slovenia), Conclusions 2007, vol. 1, p. 191 (Belgium), vol. 2, p. 1018 (Slovenia).

tenure from different Member States is respected in this requirement. After a positive answer, the Committee declared that the requirements were not in conflict with the analysed provision of Article 10 §3 of the Charter.[1086]

The above position was repeated in the case of Denmark.[1087] It negatively evaluated the legal regulation existing in Austria which allowed for utilising vocational training for adult workers by foreigners from Member States, other than members of the European Economic Area according to the availability of places, not engaged by citizens of the privileged states.[1088]

It also stated that introducing the requirement of residency as the condition of accessing vocational training was not in accordance with the standards of the Charter.[1089] It took the identical position towards work permits,[1090] but when debating on a different case, the Committee concluded that the final legal evaluation of such a requirement depends on the conditions of obtaining a work permit in light of the national labour law regulations and the practice of applying this provision, namely on comparing the number of issued permits with the number of negative decisions. It also concluded that when the authorities of a Member State made a decision upon granting a work permit on the basis of objective criteria not having been guided by citizenship of candidates, and granted work permits to an adequate number of foreigners, there was no legal basis for the negative ruling to be made.[1091] It asks about the existence of legislation authorising individual leave for training and, if so, under what conditions and on whose initiative, how long it lasts and whether it is paid or unpaid. In the absence of any information regarding this issue, the Committee considers that it has not been established that the legislation provides for an individual leave of training for employed persons. In effect, the Committee concludes that the right of an employee to an individual leave of absence is not guaranteed due to the lack of information.[1092] In 2018, the Committee concluded that the situation in four Member States which ratified Article 10 §3 of the RESC (Belgium, Cyprus, Lithuania and Slovenia) was not in conformity with the above-mentioned provision due to the right of individual training leave for the purpose of vocational training and retraining of adult workers, lack of equal treatment of nationals of other State Parties and national minorities regarding access to continuing vocational training as well as a lack of effective guarantees of such training for the unemployed.[1093] During the supervision of the last cycle – Conclusions 2020, the Committee analysed the situation in twenty-three Member States related to vocational training of employees and special facilities, necessary due to technical progress or new trends in the labour market. In five countries, it found a breach of applicable laws. The authorities of the two countries[1094] did not grant employees the right to receive

1086. Conclusions V, p. 84; Conclusions VI, p. 73.
1087. Conclusions XIV-2, p. 202.
1088. Conclusions XIII-2, p. 221.
1089. Conclusions XIV-2, p. 103 (Ireland).
1090. Conclusions XIV-2, p. 521 (Malta).
1091. Conclusions XIV-2, p. 488 (Luxembourg).
1092. Conclusions 2016 (Malta), pp. 33–34; (Serbia), p. 185.
1093. Conclusions 2008, vol. 1, p. 123 (Belgium), p. 197 (Cyprus), vol. 2, p. 458 (Lithuania), p. 763 (Slovenia).
1094. Malta, Serbia, Ukraine. Conclusions 2020.

vocational training at all. On the other hand, in three other countries, a negative conclusion was issued due to the impossibility of using the individual right of the concerned employee to undergo training and vocational training.[1095]

IV. Special Measures for the Retraining and Reintegration of the Long-Term Unemployed

185. Because of the limited possibilities for the reintroduction of the long-term unemployed into the labour market, a new provision was added to the Charter, the provision that imposes on Member States the duty of providing or promoting special measures for the retraining and reintegration of the long-term unemployed.[1096] The supervision of this duty took place for the first time in 2003. Among six Member States who delivered their reports,[1097] two states[1098] did not ratify Article 10 §4 RESC. Therefore, the Committee supervised this provision in the four remaining Member States. In two cases[1099] it declared compliance of the national conduct with the standards established by the Charter.

Slovenia drafted seven employment programmes enabling the unemployed, especially persons under the age of 26, to acquire professional qualifications and employment. One of these programmes marked by the number '5000' is addressed to young persons who are missing professional preparation or obtained qualifications, which are not demanded by the labour market. 60% of the persons benefiting from this programme were women. The programme enabled them to obtain a secondary education. Due to acquired professional qualifications over 20% of persons previously regarded as long-term unemployed found employment.[1100] Better results of training programmes were ascertained in Sweden; 35% of persons taking part in the special programme 'Activity Guarantee' found employment.

The long-term unemployed are persons remaining without employment for a period longer than a year.

This definition of long-term unemployed is not applied by the Italian authorities. Three employment programmes for the long-term unemployed were addressed to workers from 16 to 32 years old, remaining without employment for at least twenty-four to thirty months. None of the programmes significantly reduced unemployment. The Committee emphasised that in Italy the percentage of long-term unemployed is the highest in Europe. For this reason, it declared that the Italian authorities did not fulfil the obligations formulated in Article 10 §4 RESC.[1101] The Committee critically evaluated the French report. Relating to independent sources,

1095. Montenegro, Spain. Conclusions 2020.
1096. Explanatory report to the revised European Social Charter, European Social Charter, *supra*, p. 166.
1097. Bulgaria, France, Romania, Slovenia, Sweden, Italy.
1098. Bulgaria and Romania.
1099. Slovenia, Sweden.
1100. Conclusions 2003, vol. 2, p. 480 (Slovenia).
1101. Conclusions 2003, vol. 2, pp. 275–276.

it prescribed the French authorities to undertake more efficient measures of professional elicitation of the long-term unemployed.[1102]

186. Non-conformities due to special measures for the retraining and reintegration of the long-term unemployed have not been effectively provided or promoted in some Members States.[1103] Also due to the lack of equal access, guaranteed to all interested workers, to vocational training and retraining of long-term unemployed persons who are nationals of other Member States, legally residing and employed in another European country, it was the basis for a negative opinion on countries obliged to comply with the standards set out in Article 10 paragraph 4 of the RESC.[1104]

V. The Duty of Encouraging Actions Facilitating Vocational Training

187. The analysed provisions list the duties imposed on Member States that ratified one of the paragraphs of Article 10 paragraph 5 a.– d. of the Charter.[1105] They are obliged to employ appropriate measures aimed at:

(a) reducing or abolishing any fees or charges for apprenticeships;
(b) granting financial assistance in appropriate cases for persons serving apprenticeships;
(c) including supplementary training during normal working hours. The Charter introduces two conditions for including the time of training in the time of work: first, undertaking training during the period of employment; second vocational training should be undertaken at the request of the employer;
(d) adequate supervision, in consultation with social stakeholders, over the efficiency of apprenticeship of young workers and adequate protection in general.

188. The above list is only an example as the Committee did not previously extend supervision over different cases not mentioned in the above list. In a form used in preparation of national reports by Member States, the set of questions relate directly to the benefits mentioned in (a)–(d) of the analysed provision.[1106] The Committee is interested in obtaining an answer as to whether fees for serving apprenticeship are charged in Member States, what the amount of these charges is and

1102. According to the information delivered in the French report, 40% of the long-term unemployed embraced by governmental programmes undertake the employment within the period of six months from the date of completion of the training. According to the data of EC Joint Employment Reports 1999–2001, the indicator of professional elicitation of the long-term unemployed came to 23%. Conclusions 2003, vol. 1, p. 142. The Committee postponed making a ruling until the above discrepancy was clarified.
1103. Georgia, Montenegro, Turkey, Ukraine. Conclusions 2020.
1104. Georgia, Montenegro, Slovak Republic, Ukraine. Conclusions 2020.
1105. No questions were asked under the provision of Art. 10 §4 – 1961 Charter and Art. 10 §5 – Revised Charter – 'Full use of facilities available' in cycle 2020. States were only obliged to report if there was a previous conclusion in non-conformity or a deferral.
1106. Form for the reports, *supra*, s. 335.

what actions are undertaken in order to reduce or resign from the charging of fees. It pursues the goal of obtaining information concerning the prevailing system of financial assistance for persons serving apprenticeships. It is interested in types of allowances (scholarships, loans, credits, others) and the nature of these allowances. It makes an attempt to determine the conditions for acquiring the entitlements of the above allowances, their amounts, and the period they are obtained in. It pays special attention to Member States abiding by the rule of the equal treatment of its own citizens and citizens of other Member States. It orders the authorities of Member States to deliver information concerning actions undertaken in order to include vocational training undertaken during the period of employment at the request of the employer, during normal working hours. The Committee recalls that under Article 10 §5 of the Charter, time spent on supplementary training at the request of the employer must be included in the normal working hours.[1107]

189. It also obliges the authorities of Member States to describe the supervisory techniques introduced in consultation with employers' and workers' organisations to ensure the workers' right to attend vocational training.

In the majority of cases, the Committee adjourned its decision with regard to whether the analysed provision in question is being followed by Member States.[1108] The reason for this adjournment was a lack of information provided about the introduction of measures by a given Member State dealing with a worker's vocational training.

190. Financial aid for those partaking in vocational training should be ensured in appropriate cases (Article 10(5)(b)). The Committee came to the conclusion that this definition encompasses cases whereby participation in vocational training would have been impossible had it not been for the financial assistance.[1109] The scope of this obligation refers to the various types of vocational training considered by Article 10 §1-3 of the Charter. In all cases referred to in these provisions, subjects authorised to make a decision upon granting financial assistance to persons serving apprenticeships utilised the freedom of the material evaluation of these persons. Article 10 §1-3 cannot be the basis of imposing the duty to grant financial assistance to all persons serving an apprenticeship upon Member States.[1110] The duty of providing persons serving apprenticeships with financial assistance is independent of the duty to reduce or abolish any fees or charges for apprenticeships.[1111] In relation to the evaluative language used twice in Article 10 of the Charter – once in Article 10 §1 'as necessary', and again in the analysed provisions of Article 10 §4 ESC and §5 RESC (b) 'in appropriate cases', the Committee decided that all matters concerning the provision of vocational training financed by Member States on

1107. Conclusions 2016 (Ukraine), p. 81.

1108. Conclusions XIII-1, pp. 241–242 (Turkey); Conclusions XIII-2, pp. 327–328 (Belgium); Conclusions XIII-3, pp. 337 et seq. (Finland, Portugal); Addendum to Conclusions XIII-3, pp. 60 et seq. (Luxembourg); Conclusions 2003, vol. 1, pp. 276–278 (Italy); Conclusions 2003, vol. 2, pp. 594–596.

1109. Conclusions XIII-1, p. 242 (Turkey).

1110. Conclusions XIV-2, p. 62.

1111. Conclusions XIII-3, p. 339.

all levels, from the basic training and apprenticeship to the higher, technical and university education will be analysed in the supervisory processes over Article 10 §4 ESC and §5 RESC.[1112] Financial assistance in the form of scholarships, grants, loans and credits should be utilised to account for the different expenses related to participation in vocational training, not vocational training fees. Participation in vocational training is an entitlement not an obligation and, therefore, the regulation of national labour law depriving the unemployed of benefits in case of not accepting the option of vocational training turns into a duty of a legal nature for this group. For this very reason, the Committee was interested in obtaining information on balancing the labour market with the individual expectations of the unemployed in matters of undertaking employment.[1113] The opinion of the Committee reflects the entitlement to undertaking employment according to the education, professional qualification and individual predispositions. Member States of the Council of Europe should attempt to provide the rules for freely choosing the place and type of work by those able to undertake employment, wanting or looking for employment. The threat of losing unemployment benefits due to a refusal to undertake employment offered by an employment agency or failing to carry out specified vocational training in order to attain certain trade qualifications that are at the time required within the domestic labour market is in contradiction to the principle of the freedom to work. Despite its doubts, the Committee did not conclude that British authorities were violating Article 10 §4 ESC. It concluded that the typical example of the violation of the standards established by the given provision of the Charter is evident in the discriminatory treatment of citizens of other Member States which are parties to the Charter.

Among the countries that do not meet the standards specified by the provision in question of the Charter Article 10 §§4–5, are 20 Member States: Andorra,[1114] Austria,[1115] Belgium,[1116] Denmark,[1117] Georgia,[1118] Greece,[1119] Finland,[1120] France,[1121]

1112. Conclusions XIV-2, p. 62.
1113. Case of United Kingdom: Conclusions XII-1, p. 172; Conclusions XIII-3, pp. 177–178.
1114. Conclusions 2016, p. 145 (as regards the equality of treatment of foreign nationals concerning access to financial aid and scholarships, the law sets a minimum residence period of three consecutive years for students to apply for financial aid). In 2020 the Committee concludes that the situation is not in conformity with Art. 10 §§4–5 of the Charter on the ground that: (1) there is a length of residence requirement of three years for eligibility for financial aid for vocational training (Andorra, Denmark, Georgia); (2) equal treatment of nationals of other State Parties residing or working lawfully was not guaranteed with regard to fees and to financial assistance for training (Austria, Croatia, Georgia, Luxembourg, Ukraine); special measures for retraining and reintegration of the long-term unemployed, including youth, have not been effectively provided or promoted (Ukraine). Conclusions 2020.
1115. Conclusions XIII-2, p. 221, Conclusions XIX-1 (2008), p. 35, Conclusions 2016, p. 256 (the length of residence requirements of five years for non-EEA nationals to be eligible for financial assistance for training). Equal treatment of nationals of other State Parties residing or working lawfully in Austria was not.
1116. Conclusions 2007, vol. 1, p. 194, Conclusions 2008, vol. 1, p. 126, Conclusions 2016, p. 2 (two years to be eligible for financial aid for education for non-EEA nationals).
1117. Conclusions XIX-1 (2008), p. 115, Conclusions 2016, pp. 323–324 (non-EEA nationals are subject to a length of residence requirement of two years).
1118. Conclusions 2016, p. 248 (no special measures for retraining of the long-term unemployed).
1119. Conclusions XI-1, p. 171; Conclusions XIII-3, p. 175.

Hungary,[1122] Malta,[1123] Montenegro,[1124] Norway,[1125] Portugal,[1126] Serbia,[1127] Slovakia,[1128] Spain,[1129] Slovenia,[1130] Sweden,[1131] Turkey[1132] and Ukraine.[1133]

191. None of the mentioned states[1134] ordered less favourable treatment of foreign nationals in matters concerning financial assistance for those wanting to undertake vocational training. All the mentioned states specified the requirement of residency within the territory of the given Member State for those attempting to undertake vocational training in order to be able to seek financial assistance.

Turkish citizens in Belgium under the age of 21 have to prove five-year residency within the territory of the said state as well as a five-year period of study within Belgium educational institutions.[1135] Finland demands from foreign nationals, with the exception of citizens of Member States of the EU and the European Economic Area, seeking financial grants and scholarships to reside within Finland for at least a period of two years continuously.[1136] France, in addition to the identical requirements, requires taxes to be paid within that same period of residency within its territory.[1137] Slovenia grants financial assistance to those undertaking vocational training based on being in possession of a work permit. Permits are granted to those residing in Slovenia for a period of eight years.[1138]

The Committee reminds the authorities of Member States that the introduction of residency requirements within the territory of a given Member State as a condition for being able to receive financial assistance for those wanting to undertake vocational training within the territory of another Member State is regarded as indirect

1120. Conclusions 2007, vol. 1, p. 435, Conclusions 2016, pp. 167–168 (two years to be eligible for financial aid for education for non-EEA nationals).
1121. Conclusions 2007, vol. 1, p. 551, Conclusions 2008, vol. 1, p. 326, Conclusions 2016, pp. 269–270 (There is a residence requirement of two years for non-EEA nationals to apply for scholarships granted on the basis of social criteria for higher education). The Committee also concludes that it has not being established that in France there is a mechanism to evaluate the efficiency of vocational education.
1122. Conclusions 2016, p. 258.
1123. Conclusions 2008, vol. 2, p. 501.
1124. Conclusions 2016, p. 143 (no special measures for retraining of the unemployed).
1125. Conclusions 2008, vol. 2, p. 642, Conclusions 2008, vol. 2, p. 643.
1126. Conclusions 2008, vol. 2, p. 676, Conclusions 2016, p. 182 (no special measures for the reintegration of long-term unemployed).
1127. Conclusions 2016, p. 87 (no special measures for the retraining of the long-term unemployed).
1128. Conclusions XIX-1 (2008), p. 369, Conclusion 2016, p. 61. (It has not been established that special measures for the retraining and reintegration of the long-term unemployed have effectively been provided or promoted.)
1129. Conclusions XIX-1 (2008), p. 404), Conclusions XX-1, p. 301.
1130. Conclusions 2007, vol. 2, p. 1021; Conclusions 2008, vol. 2, p. 765.
1131. Conclusions 2007, vol. 2, p. 1078; Conclusions 2008, vol. 2, p. 806.
1132. Conclusion 2016, p. 68 (no special measures for the retraining of the long-term unemployed).
1133. *Ibid.*
1134. With the exception of Belgium, which regards citizenship as a necessary condition for being able to receive financial assistance for those undertaking vocational training. Conclusions III-4, pp. 386–388; Conclusions XIV-2, pp. 146–147.
1135. *Ibid.*
1136. Conclusions XIII-5, pp. 84–85; Conclusions XIV-2, pp. 237–238.
1137. Conclusions 2003, vol. 1, p. 144.
1138. Conclusions 2003, vol. 2, p. 483.

discrimination. It is forbidden. Member States that have introduced such requirements are in violation of Article 10 of the Charter. In all the above-mentioned cases the Committee rendered decisions that the mentioned Member States violated the obligations stipulated under the provision in question of the Charter. In cases where Member States did not provide the relevant information dealing with foreign nationals of other Member States seeking financial assistance during vocational training, the Committee adjourned its decisions dealing with the legal situation of the said foreign nationals.[1139]

§10. The Right to Equal Opportunities and Equal Treatment in Matters of Employment Without Discrimination on the Grounds of Sex

192. Article 20 of the Charter obliges Member States to employ the rule of equal opportunities and equal treatment in matters of employment without discrimination based on sex towards workers and candidates for work. This provision orders the authorities of Member States to recognise the right to equal opportunities and equal treatment in matters of employment, to prohibit discrimination based on sex within the above-mentioned issues, and to undertake adequate measures to guarantee the enforcement of the above-mentioned provision in the following areas:

- accessing employment, protection against terminating a work agreement, professional reintegration;
- vocational training, upgrading professional skills, changing occupation, professional re-adaptation;
- working conditions, conditions of employment, including remuneration and insurance;
- path of professional career, including promotion.

193. The range of legal protection guaranteed by this provision is large.[1140] It encompasses nearly all categories of issues regulated by the labour law, including those previously described: Article 1 §2 (prohibiting the discrimination in work relations); Article 4 §3 (the right to the equal remuneration of men and women for work of equal value; Article 8 (the right of female workers to protection during maternity); Article 9 (the right to vocational guidance); Article 10 (the right to vocational training). Despite the fact that all the above-mentioned regulations of the Charter oblige the authorities of Member States to guarantee the above-mentioned rights without discrimination on the basis of sex, Article 20 of the Charter imposes on Member States additional duties.[1141] According to the Committee,[1142] a Member

1139. Conclusions XIV-2, pp. 352–353 (Greece); pp. 406–407 (Ireland); pp. 657–658 (Portugal); pp. 752–753 (Turkey); pp. 445–446 (Italy).
1140. Equality between men and women in the European Social Charter: study compiled on the basis of the case law of the Committee of Independent Experts, Council of Europe Publishing, Strasbourg 1999.
1141. Conclusions XIII-5, p. 253.
1142. Conclusions XIII-3, p. 429.

State that has ratified Article 20 is obliged to: introduce the rule of equal opportunities and equal treatment in matters of employment into its national labour law regulations as well as establish the prohibition of the discrimination of workers on the basis of sex; to undertake adequate measures in order to guarantee the efficient protection of workers' right to equal treatment; to prepare special programmes for the enforcement of the policy of equal treatment and to undertake proper actions in order to enact it.[1143] Similar duties are not imposed by the above-mentioned Articles of the Charter. Additionally, the Committee emphasised the different objective ranges of the provisions in question: Article 20 and Articles 1 §2, 4 §3, 8, 9 and 10.[1144] The provision of Article 1 §2 of the Charter disallows the differentiation of workers on the basis of unlawful criteria, not only on the basis of sex. The provision of Article 4 §3 applies to work of equal value. Therefore, the objective scope of Article 20 is significantly larger.[1145] The provision of Article 8 guarantees entitlements not accessible by all workers. The provisions of Articles 9 and 10 of the Charter order the equal treatment of 'all persons'. Article 20 is a special standard. It orders Member States to guarantee the equal treatment of workers regardless of sex within all categories regulated by the individual provisions of labour law as well as selected aspects of social policies, such as the policy of employment and the policy of promoting workers. The term 'conditions of work and employment' has many understandings. It relates to all rights and situations of persons benefiting from and within the confines of work relations, with the exception of social security and other benefits for the unemployed, pensioner allowances and allowances due to the death of the sole breadwinner in the family.[1146] These allowances can be excluded by Member States from the objective scope of this provision on the basis of the authorisation listed in the appendix to Article 20 of the Charter. The exclusion of applying Article 20 of the Charter in matters of social security is possible after filing a relevant notification at a proper time by a Member State. In the period until such a notification is filed, Member States are obliged to follow the rule of equal treatment in matters of social security.

On this basis, the Committee demanded that Sweden present data on the numbers of men and women employed part-time who were not entitled to obtain social security benefits such as the unemployed benefit, health pension and retirement pension.[1147]

After having familiarised itself with the information provided by the Swedish authorities the Committee concluded that the provisions of Swedish social security law discriminate against women indirectly because workers employed part-time, whose employment does not exceed three hours per day or seventeen hours per week are not covered by the insurance in case of losing the job. The significant

1143. Conclusions XIII-3, p. 429.
1144. Conclusions XIII-5, p. 253.
1145. Explanatory report to the 1988 Additional Protocol, European Social Charter, *supra*, p. 130.
1146. *Ibid.*
1147. Conclusions XV-2, pp. 575 et seq., Conclusions 2008, vol. 2, p. 784.

majority of workers employed part-time are women.[1148] Swedish regulations concerning benefits in case of unemployment are conditional on the entitlement of being covered by insurance on the employment of at least seventeen hours a week. Workers who do not meet this requirement are entitled to apply for financial assistance from social security if they were employed for at least seventy-five hours per month.[1149] The above differentiation of the insured men and women in their range of social benefit entitlements was recognised by the Committee as a case of discrimination on the basis of sex, which violates Article 20 of the Charter.

194. Legal measures that Member States are obliged to undertake under the provision in question include the authorisation of judicial bodies and labour courts to overrule or recognise as not binding all provisions of law and clauses of collective and individual work agreements violating the rule of equal treatment of workers regardless of the sex.[1150] In order to meet this obligation, the authorities of Member States should introduce special measures preventing discriminatory action against workers that may possibly be undertaken by the state, stakeholders or parties of individual work agreements. Among these measures the Committee lists: ruling upon the common invalidity (*erga omnes*) of provisions and clauses violating the rule of equal treatment of workers regardless of sex; the entitlements of trade union organisations to litigate on behalf of an individual worker, interfering into the ongoing proceedings initiated by the discriminated workers as well as registering class actions on behalf of workers interested in the court's verdict upon the invalidity of regulations violating the rule of the equal treatment of workers regardless of the sex.[1151]

Within the confines of enabling workers to utilise the right to equal opportunity and equal treatment in the matters of employment and professional occupation without discrimination on the basis of sex, Member States are obligated to ensure the adequate (material-legal and procedural) measures of workers' legal protection,[1152] for those workers who are the victims of discrimination on the basis of sex.[1153] The Committee demands that Member States introduce procedural facilities for the process of proving cases of discrimination being necessary to reinstate the rights of the discriminated workers that have been violated. The sued employer is obliged to give

1148. Conclusions 2004, vol. 2, p. 594. Conclusions 2006, vol. 2, p. 894. In 2000 77.3% of workers employed part time were women. Comparing the percentage of employed part time and full time, 36.3% employed part time were women, 10.9% were men. *See*: Conclusions 2002, p. 260.
1149. Conclusions XIII-5, p. 274; Conclusions 2002, p. 260.
1150. Conclusions XIII-3, p. 429.
1151. Conclusions XIII-5, p. 255.
1152. The Committee states that the burden of proof in discrimination cases must be shifted. The shift in the burden of proof consists of ensuring that where a person believes he or she suffered discrimination on the grounds of sex and establishes facts which make it reasonable to suppose that discrimination has occurred, the onus is on the defendant to prove that there has been no infringement of the principle of equal treatment. Conclusions XIII-5 (1997).
1153. Conclusions XIII-3, p. 429; Conclusions XIII-5, p. 255.

evidence that the rule of equal treatment of workers regardless of sex was not violated. The employer has to prove the said discrimination did not take place or that differentiating workers resulted from objective criteria, not on the basis of the worker's sex.[1154]

In the case of the termination of labour relations as a result of registering a complaint by a worker asserting the rule of equal treatment within labour relations had been violated or applying for benefits he or she is entitled to as a victim of discrimination, it should become a common practice to reinstate unlawfully terminated labour relation as well as granting the compensation for the period the worker remained without a job. Only when it is not possible to make a ruling upon reinstating a worker into the previous position does the Committee allow for the granting of compensation for unlawfully terminated labour relations. It notes this compensation should be adequate, meaning it will repair all losses caused by employer to illegally dismissed employee. It also should serve the repressive function for the employer to be aware of the financial consequences.[1155] The right to utilise adequate legal measures should encompass all aggrieved workers, regardless of the sector of employment (private or public) complaining about employers not abiding by the rule of equal treatment in labour relations and matters of professional occupation.[1156]

195. It distinguishes indirect and direct discrimination. It argues that the rule of the equal treatment of workers means a lack of any discrimination, direct as well as indirect, on the basis of sex in labour relations and matters of professional occupation. It gives the following example of indirect discrimination: less favourable conditions of employment (lower remuneration) for part-time workers among whom the majority represents one social category, distinguished on the grounds of sex (women).[1157] Indirect discrimination is the case when the employer does not remunerate part-time workers proportionally to the daily or weekly wages of full-time workers.

1154. Conclusions XIII-5, p. 256; Conclusions 2004, vol. 2, pp. 495–496 (Romania). In 2016 the Committee found that two reports indicate that there are no special provisions in the legislation with respect to the burden of proof in discrimination cases. Conclusions 2016 (Russian Federation), pp. 102, 104); (Ukraine), pp. 109, 111.
1155. Conclusions XIII-3, p. 429; Conclusions XIII-5, p. 256. In 2004, the Committee decided that Swedish employers who made redundant workers demanding the rule of equal treatment are obliged to pay a compensation of SEK 10,000 to SEK 60,000 (SEK 1,096–EUR 6,578). The Committee requested information whether apart from the compensation national regulations of labour law allow for cash penalties. Conclusions 2004, vol. 2, p. 594.
1156. Conclusions XIII-5, p. 266 (the Netherlands). Two reports indicate that in cases of discrimination in employment, employees may demand compensation up to four months' wages plus claims of other benefits of which they have been deprived. In cases of unlawful termination of an employment contract due to discrimination, the employee is entitled to compensation of between four and eight months' wages. The Committee decided that the limits imposed on compensatory awards in cases of discrimination based on sex may prevent such violations from being adequately remedied and effectively prevented. Conclusions 2016 (Turkey), pp. 120, 122. The second one adds compensation to a maximum amount of 12 months' average wage. Conclusions 2016 (Armenia), p. 105.
1157. Conclusions XIII-5, p. 274 (Sweden).

For example, he pays workers employed for half of the standard weekly norm 40% of what full-time workers obtain.

The excuse given by employers arguing that differentiating remuneration between workers employed full time and part time can be explained by the limited availability of the latter is regarded by the Committee as untrue should disproportion between men and women in the two above systems of work organisation be discovered. The obligation of assuring workers the protection against indirect discrimination in matters of employment and professional occupation imposes on the Committee the duty of supervising the observing of labour law regulations in Member States, as well as practices. In 2016, the Committee discovered that it has not been established that the right to equal treatment in employment without discrimination on grounds of sex is guaranteed in practice. The average monthly wages of women are lower than those of men.[1158] In the legislation, there is no express statutory guarantee of the right of men and women to equal pay for work of equal value. Therefore, the Committee considers that the situation is not in conformity with the Charter on this point.[1159] From the data provided in the report, the Committee notes that the number of inquiries concerning gender equality in employment has increased from sixteen (out of sixty inquiries concerning gender equality) in 2012 to sixty-one in 2014 (out of ninety-eight inquiries concerning gender equality).[1160] On the other hand, the Azerbaijan report indicates that, as noted in the previous reports, no cases of discrimination on the grounds of sex were found and subsequently no court cases regarding discrimination at work on the grounds of sex were identified.[1161] Taking into consideration that in some countries the main legislative provisions on equal pay expressly prohibit 'terms of payment' that are less favourable than those applied to an employee in the same work or work of equal value, on the basis of discriminatory payment, the Committee asks whether in equal pay litigation cases it is possible to make a comparison of the pay and jobs outside the company directly concerned. It considers no reaction to the repeated request for information as a sign that it has not been established that legislation allows a pay comparison to be made across companies in equal pay litigation cases.[1162] If the

1158. The Committee notes that in Armenia women earn 35.9% less than what men are paid. Diagnostic Study on Discrimination Against Women in Armenia 2015–2016, United Nations Population Fund. Conclusions 2016, p. 106. The Azerbaijan report indicates that the ratio of women's average monthly salary to men's is 47.5%. Conclusions 2016, p. 149. According to the information provided by the Government and State Statistics Service of Ukraine on average monthly wages and salaries of women and men, the gender wage gap was 22.8% in 2013 and 24% in the first quarter of 2014 (as compared to 23% in 2009). Data from 2013 also show a significant gap in the monthly wages of women and men in certain sectors of the economy, particularly in the manufacturing (30.3%), postal and courier services (35.5%) and sports, entertainment and recreation (37.8%). The government indicates that differences in wages are largely due to the system of the gender division of labour, with women being concentrated in sectors with relatively high education requirements, but lower wages, primarily in the public sector. Conclusions 2016, p. 111.
1159. Conclusions 2016 (Georgia), pp. 28–29.
1160. Conclusion 2016 (Estonia), p. 13.
1161. Conclusions 2016 (Azerbaijan), p. 148.
1162. Conclusions 2016 (Malta), p. 36; (Ukraine), pp. 110, 111.

country report does not provide any information on the gender pay gap, the Committee concludes that it has not been established that the right to equal treatment in employment without discrimination on the grounds of sex is guaranteed in practice.[1163]

Therefore the Committee requests the authorities of Member States to deliver detailed information on:

- the situation of men and women on the labour market; numbers of employment, part time and full time taking into consideration the criteria of sex; number of unemployed and self-employed within these two social categories (men and women) Member States are obliged to provide information on the number of men and women in active employment age. The above information is to allow the Committee to review national labour markets and establish the position in matters of equal treatment of workers regardless of sex;
- access to and participation in vocational training of men and women. The Committee is especially interested in obtaining data on the opportunity for women to acquire professional qualifications for jobs traditionally regarded as 'male';
- differences between the conditions of employment for men and women employed at identical, similar or comparable jobs existing in practice. First of all the Committee is interested in familiarising itself with the differences in the remuneration of men and women employed in identical, similar or comparable jobs. It obliges Member States to deliver information on the amount of basic and minimal remuneration, all other benefits paid by employers in cash, regularly or sporadically as well as material benefits and bonuses of the job that workers are entitled to.[1164] In order to enable the Committee to make the comparison of men and women in terms of remuneration for work all data mentioned above should take sex into consideration;
- practical differences in the 'path of career' for men and women employed in different sectors of the economy;
- social programmes introduced in order to ensure equal treatment for men and women in matters of employment and professional occupation;[1165]
- official prohibition of women from performing certain occupations.[1166]

1163. Conclusions 2016 (Serbia), p. 67.

1164. Explanatory report to the 1988 Additional Protocol, European Social Charter, *supra*, p. 130.

1165. Conclusions XIII-5, pp. 256–257.

1166. Reports indicate that women are prohibited from working underground in mining and construction of underground structures, cleaning pipes, furnaces and flues. They shall not work in a job position with prevailing hard physical labour, work under water or jobs involving tasks that can have detrimental effect on and increased risk to their health and life. Conclusions 2016 (Russian Federation, p. 101); (Montenegro), p. 52; (Moldova), p. 94; (Bosnia and Herzegovina), p. 1163. The Russian Labour Code excludes women from being employed in 456 occupations. It further indicates that the refusal by an employer to hire women to perform the kind of work listed is not discriminatory if the employer has not established a safe working environment and this is confirmed by a special assessment of the working conditions. Conclusions 2016, p. 101. The Turkish report indicates that administrative positions, trainees and positions that do not require physical effort are excluded with exception mining engineers who have been working in mines. Conclusions 2016 (Turkey), p. 120.

In the next scrutiny cycle in 2020 on the right to equal opportunities and treatment in matters of employment and occupation, without discrimination on the basis of gender, the Committee focused on the remuneration of women and men for work performed. The Committee examined 30 Member States. The obtained effects are shocking. Only in three countries the principle of equal treatment of employees was observed. The above shows that in 90% of the analysed Member States in 2020, the prohibition of discrimination against employees on the basis of gender was not respected. The reasons why the Committee was forced to issue a negative opinion about the non-compliance by the authorities of twenty-seven European Member States with the principle of equal treatment in employment relations and ignoring the prohibition of discrimination on the basis of sex are as follows:

(1) There is no explicit statutory guarantee of equal pay for women and men for equal work of equal value. The Committee observes that applicable law in the countries mentioned in the footnotes provides for equal pay for men and women for 'equal work' and for 'equivalent work' but not for 'work of equal or comparable value'. It takes note that this wording is narrower than the principle set out in the Charter. The Committee repeats this last sentence in all cases mentioned in the footnotes.[1167]
(2) The legislation explicitly covers only certain elements of remuneration for the purposes of equal pay principle. The Committee also observes that the gender gap is persistent and, although slightly below the EU average, it remains high. Segregation exists in the labour market and there is no clear trend for a lower gender pay gap, particularly in the private sector. The measures adopted by the Government have not achieved measurable progress in this respect.[1168]
(3) Women are not permitted to work in all professions (in particular when performing better-paid jobs) which constitutes discrimination based on sex. The above rule applies in cases where the professional qualifications of women are equal to or even higher than those of men performing more attractive jobs. Gender segregation persists on occupational level. While women are mostly professionals, service workers and shop and market sales assistants and technicians and associate professionals, men are mostly craft and related trades workers, plant and machine operators and assemblers and legislators, senior officials and managers. Although the gender pay gap has decreased during the present circle, it still remains very high.[1169]
(4) The upper limit on the amount of compensation that may be awarded in gender discrimination cases may preclude damages from making good the loss suffered and from being sufficiently dissuasive. Any ceiling on compensation that may preclude damages from being commensurate with the loss suffered and from being sufficiently dissuasive is contrary to the Charter.[1170] It has not been established that legislation provides for a shift in the burden of proof in gender pay discrimination cases. The report does not contain any information

1167. Armenia, Azerbaijan, Estonia, Georgia, Conclusions 2020.
1168. Albania, the Netherlands (Kingdom in Europe, Curaçao and Sint Maarten). Conclusions 2020.
1169. Azerbaijan, Bosnia and Herzegovina, Russian Federation. Conclusions 2020.
1170. Armenia. Conclusions 2020.

regarding the burden of proof in cases of gender pay discrimination. In its previous conclusions (2012 and 2016) the Committee noted that during judicial proceedings in discrimination cases there had been no shift in the burden of proof.[1171]

(5) Legislation does not provide for a shift in the burden of proof in gender pay discrimination cases.[1172]

(6) The obligation to ensure access to effective remedies in cases of pay discrimination has not been fulfilled. The Committee refers to its decision on the merits of 5 December 2019 (*University Women of Europe v. Belgium*, Complaint No. 126/20, §§134 to 145) in which is noted that in the light of the lack of information on the number of relevant cases on gender pay discrimination, the complexities in accessing the contents of case law, the current obstacles to assessing judicial proceedings, as well as the lack of shift of the burden of proof in practice in pay discrimination cases, the obligation to ensure access to effective remedies in case pay discrimination were not satisfied.[1173]

(7) It has not been established that the right to compensation is provided for in gender pay discrimination cases. In the course of a ten-year period, the gender pay gap in Denmark has not been significantly reduced and hence there has been measurable progress. Consequently, it finds out that the situation is not in conformity with Article 1 of the Additional Protocol to the 1961 Charter on the ground that the obligation to make measurable progress in reducing the gender gap has not been fulfilled.[1174]

(8) The obligation to ensure pay transparency has not been satisfied. With regard to pay transparency, the report indicates that no strategies or measures have been adopted to ensure pay transparency on the job market and there is no way for workers to obtain information on the levels of remuneration of other workers. Individual salaries are confidential and not transparent or accessible to the public.[1175]

(9) The obligation to make measurable progress in reducing the gender pay gap has not been fulfilled. The Committee finds that there is a significant wage gap between men and women in the Russian Federation that has not been greatly reduced during the reference period.[1176]

196. In cases when the authorities of Member States did not utilise the option created by the appendix to Article 20 of the Charter and did not exclude matters concerning social security from the range of this provision, the Committee

1171. *Ibid.*
1172. Azerbaijan, Russian Federation. Conclusions 2020.
1173. Croatia – Art. 1 of the Additional Protocol to the 1961 Charter. Conclusions 2020.
1174. Serbia. Conclusions 2020.
1175. Bosnia and Herzegovina, Croatia. Conclusions 2020.
1176. Andorra, Armenia, Austria, Azerbaijan, Bosnia and Herzegovina, Croatia, the Czech Republic – Art. 1 of the Additional Protocol of 1988 to the 1961 Charter, Denmark, Georgia, Malta, the Netherlands (Kingdom in Europe, Curaçao, Sint Maarten), North Macedonia, the Russian Federation. Conclusions 2020.

requested a presentation of the situation of men and women in terms of matters regulated by social security law as well.[1177]

The appendix to Article 20 of the Charter also gave the legal ground to create the two anti-types in national regulations of labour law. First, the appendix to Article 20 of the Charter does not consider the provision on the protection of a woman worker's body and labour relations during pregnancy and maternity leave as a case of discrimination in employment. Second, the obligation of equal treatment of workers and the prohibition of discriminating against them on the grounds of sex does not create a legal obstacle to undertaking measures leading to the decrease of the actual inequalities between men and women in labour relations. The appendix to Article 20 of the Charter authorises Member States to run the policy of privilege towards previously discriminated social categories distinguished on the grounds of sex.[1178] Member States have been authorised to exclude from the rule of equal treatment of workers regardless of sex particular types of jobs and occupations, which due to their character or conditions may be given only to persons of one sex. The authorities of Member States that utilise the above option are not obliged to enlist within binding regulations the list of occupations available for one sex. In cases when the authorities of Member States decide to prepare and publicly advertise the lists of jobs prohibited for women, the Committee requests to see such lists and postpones the ruling on conformity of national labour law regulations and Article 20 of the Charter to subsequent supervisory cycle.[1179]

197. Supervising whether Article 20 of the Charter has been obeyed by the Member State, the Committee considered national labour law regulations of the Netherlands,[1180] Norway,[1181] France,[1182] Ireland,[1183] Lithuania[1184] and Italy[1185] as being in accordance with the provision in question.

In the case of Italy, a positive ruling was subject to the provision of information on the elements of remuneration used as the basis of comparison of men's and women's wages as well as material-legal measures of protection of workers demanding equal treatment and registering complaints regarding discriminatory acts of employers.[1186] The Committee postponed a ruling in the case of Finland.[1187] It demanded information on actions undertaken in order to overrule the clauses of collective and individual work agreements contradicting the rule of equal treatment. It also asked about the possibility of obtaining a ruling on reactivating a labour relation with workers who were made redundant because of registering a complaint concerning discriminating treatment by an employer. It was interested in gathering information

1177. Conclusions XIII-5, p. 259 (Finland); XIII-5, pp. 266–267 (the Netherlands).
1178. Conclusions XIII-5, p. 256.
1179. Conclusions 2004, vol. 1, p. 197.
1180. Conclusions XV-2, pp. 376 et seq.
1181. Conclusions XV-2, pp. 401 et seq.; Conclusions 2004, vol. 2, pp. 440 et seq.
1182. Conclusions 2002, pp. 58 et seq.; Conclusions 2004, vol. 1, pp. 250 et seq.
1183. Conclusions 2004, vol. 1, pp. 293 et seq.
1184. Conclusions 2004, vol. 2, pp. 390 et seq.
1185. Conclusions 2002, pp. 103 et seq.; Conclusions 2004, vol. 2, pp. 325 et seq.
1186. Conclusions XIII-5, pp. 261 et seq.; Conclusions XIV-2, pp. 452–453; Conclusions XV-2, pp. 324 et seq.
1187. Conclusions XIII-5, pp. 257 et seq.; Conclusions XV-2, pp. 178 et seq.

on executing the rule of equal treatment of workers regardless of sex practised in all the fields listed in Article 20 of the Charter: first, access to employment, protection against redundancy and vocational reintegration; second, vocational guidance and training, re-qualification, professional re-adaptation; third, conditions of employment, working conditions, remuneration; fourthly, career, policy of promoting workers.[1188] It wanted to know the proportion of men and women employed part time and full time,[1189] and about the programmes of equalising professional chances of social categories previously discriminated on the labour market prepared by the national authorities,[1190] underground mines and all labour-intensive jobs.[1191] It enquired whether Member States introduced restrictions in accessing police and army services[1192] and dangerous work jobs.[1193] It demanded detailed and comprehensive answers. It wanted to familiarise itself with the results brought about by introducing programmes of equal treatment of workers by Member States. It postponed making a ruling in the case of Slovenia which informed about introducing three programmes introduced in order to promote the rule of equal treatment: 'positive programme' allowing for the active policy of preference employment for persons so far discriminated in matters of employment and professional occupation; 'encouraging programmes' aimed at employers to stimulate employment of persons of a particular sex; 'promoting programmes' emphasising the necessity of abiding by the rule of equality of employment prohibiting discrimination in matters of employment on the grounds of sex.[1194] Finally, the Committee concluded that the situation in Cyprus and Portugal was not in conformity with Article 20 of the RESC, on the grounds that under Portuguese labour law, the scope of the comparison of wages for determining equality or equal value is limited to the same enterprise.[1195]

The provision of Article 20 of the Charter is regarded by the Committee as a progressive standard obliging Member States to undertake systematic actions within the four fields listed in this regulation, the fields regulated by labour law and formed by social policy. In the case of not utilising the option delivered by the appendix to this provision, these actions should also include the introduction of maintenance and strengthening of the rule of equal treatment of workers regardless of sex in matters of social security.

§11. The Right to Protection in Cases of Termination of Employment

198. The Revised European Social Charter ensures workers' protection in cases when their employment is terminated (Article 24).

1188. Conclusions XV-1, pp. 172 et seq.
1189. Conclusions 2002, p. 160 (Romania).
1190. Conclusions 2002, pp. 219–220 (Slovenia).
1191. Conclusions 2008, vol. 1, p. 96 (Azerbaijan).
1192. Conclusions 2004, vol. 1, p. 123 (Cyprus).
1193. Conclusions 2004, vol. 1, p. 197 (Estonia).
1194. Conclusions 2004, vol. 2, p. 548.
1195. Conclusions 2008, vol. 1, p. 214 (Cyprus), Conclusions 2006, vol. 2, p. 726, Conclusions 2008, vol. 2, p. 700 (Portugal).

Article 24 RESC hopes to ensure workers with sufficient legal protection in cases where their agreements may be terminated. The preservation of the permanence of labour relations is protected by the following guarantees:

- the obligation to provide the worker with a valid reason for the termination of the employment. Such reasons validating the termination of a work agreement are connected with the conduct or the capacity of the worker (reasons concerning the worker) or reasons that are based on the operational requirements of the undertaking, the establishment or service (reasons concerning the employer);[1196]
- ensuring that all workers who have their employment terminated without a valid reason have a right to adequate compensation or other appropriate relief;[1197]
- the right of a worker to appeal to an impartial body, which will determine the reasons for the termination.

Despite the three separate obligations placed on Member States, Article 24 RESC is regarded as a standard, which should be abided by in its entirety by the Member States that ratified the RESC. The regulations stipulated under paragraphs (a) and (b) as well as the last unlettered paragraph of Article 24, are not separate in their nature and do not allow Member States to choose which of those paragraphs they would prefer to abide by, to fulfil the required quota of 16 out of 31 Articles or 63 out of 98 paragraphs of the RESC.

199. Article 24 RESC ensures the protection of workers' rights in cases of work agreement termination by the employer or due to the employer's initiative.[1198] Such legal protection ensured by the provision in question may also be utilised by workers who have terminated their work agreement by the consent of both parties, even if the termination was initiated by the employer. The Addendum to Article 24 fulfils a significant requirement, and that is how Article 24, i.e., a general standard, is not applicable to particular categories of workers specified in the Addendum. The Addendum authorises Member State authorities to wholly or partially exclude from legal protection during the termination of employment the following categories of workers: those employed on a temporary basis[1199] or on a contractual basis where the aim of the employment is to fulfil particular requirements of the job, those

1196. Retaliatory dismissal is prohibited. Conclusions 2020 (Albania).

1197. For that reason the Committee concludes that the situation in Cyprus in not in conformity with Art. 24 of the RESC on the grounds that employees who have not been employed with their employer for a continuum period of twenty-six weeks are not entitled to protection against dismissal regardless of their qualifications. Conclusions 2007, vol. 1, p. 345. The Committee also concludes that Italy does not comply with above-mentioned provision of the RESC because the categories of workers excluded from the protection against termination of employment (employees over the age of 60 years, professional athletes) are more extensive that provided by this provision. Conclusions 2007, vol. 2, p. 762.

1198. Addendum to the Revised European Social Charter.

1199. Case of Malta. The Committee concludes that the situation in Malta is not in conformity with Art. 24 the RESC on the grounds that employees are excluded from protection against dismissal during a six-month probationary period that might be extended until up to one year for certain categories of employee. Conclusions 2008, vol. 2, p. 520. The same position was taken by the Committee in the Conclusion announced in 2020.

employed on a probationary basis, as well as those employed on a casual basis. This list is exhaustive in its nature.[1200] Member State authorities do not have the right to expand upon this list in the Addendum to Article 24. The Committee notes from the various reports that some categories of employees are not covered by the protective provisions of the domestic employment law, such as: (1) employees with less than one year's continuous service; (2) employees on probation or undergoing training of up to one year's duration. In the case of apprentices, the state law does not apply if the dismissal takes place within six months after the commencement of the apprenticeship or within one month after its completion.[1201] It was argued by the government that the probationary period considers the protection of the common interests of both parties in the work relationship in order to verify the mutual suitability of the contract, therefore during the probation period, or at the end of it, each party can withdraw without notice or compensation.[1202] The Committee decides that the exclusion of employees from protection against dismissal for six months or 26 weeks in view of the probationary period is not reasonable if applied indiscriminately, regardless of the employee's qualifications.[1203] It concludes that all cases considered by the end of the latest cycle are not in conformity with Article 24 of the Charter regardless of the length of the probationary period, be it six months,[1204] or one year.[1205]

The Committee, a supervisory body monitoring the obligations under the European Social Charter of 1961 and the Revised European Social Charter of 1996, was of the view that Italian authorities were not abiding by the obligations set in Article 24, as the list of exclusions was expanded to the following categories of workers: those employed in senior positions in employment service agencies, domestic help, those employed in professional sports, employees who are aged 60 years or more and entitled to social security benefits in the case of old age, and those laid-off as part of a group.[1206] Some Member States[1207] specify that the law gives an employer the right to terminate an employee's employment relationship upon the employee's reaching the national retirement age but does not preclude the recruitment of a person of pensionable age. The Committee rejects that way of thinking and concludes that the situation in Malta is not in conformity with Article 24 of the Charter on the ground that termination of employment at the initiative of the employer on the sole

1200. The same reason was mentioned for Cyprus in the conclusion taken in 2020. The Committee found that the categories of person excluded from protection against unlawful dismissal go beyond what is allowed under the Appendix to the Charter. Moreover, in the case of Cyprus, the Committee considered employment under a contract for a trial period as an unjustified reason for dismissal of an employee.
1201. Conclusions 2016 (Ireland, Malta).
1202. Conclusions (Italy), p. 264.
1203. Conclusions 2005 (Cyprus).
1204. Conclusions 2016 (Bulgaria), p. 25; (Italy), p. 266.
1205. Conclusions 2016 (Ireland), p. 263; (Malta), p. 250.
1206. Conclusions 2003, vol. 1 (Bulgaria, France, Italy), Council of Europe Publishing, Strasbourg 2003, pp. 319 et seq., Conclusions 2008, vol. 2, p. 437 (Italy).
1207. Malta.

basis that the person has reached pensionable age permitted by law, is not reasonably justified.[1208] The Committee maintained its position on the reasons for the dismissal on the basis of age in the conclusion expressed in the last scrutiny cycle in 2020. Against Malta and the Netherlands (Kingdom in Europe) acting on behalf of Curaçao and Sint Maarten. It ruled that termination of employment at the initiative of employer on the sole ground that the person has reached the pensionable age cannot be considered to comply with the standard set out in Article 24 of the Charter. In the other cases, a similar conclusion was reached due to a lack of information on the real reason for termination of employment contract, different from the grounds connected with age but with the capacity, and conduct of the employee as well as those based on the operational requirements of the enterprise (economic reasons).[1209] The Committee concluded that the situation in Cyprus is not in conformity with Article 24 RESC, on the grounds that Cypriot labour law excludes from protection against dismissal employees who have not completed a continuous period of 26 weeks with their employer regardless of the employee's qualifications.[1210]

200. The Committee has undertaken efforts to decrease the categories of workers excluded from the protection of the law during the termination instigated by their employers.

In the report produced by Bulgaria, it is impossible to deduct information concerning those who are employed on a temporary basis and the level of legal protection received during the termination of their work agreements.

Because of this, the Committee decided not to pass judgment concerning Bulgaria's labour law compatibility with Article 24 RESC and instead obliged Bulgaria's authorities to respond to the questions produced regarding whether workers who are signed to atypical work agreements utilise from the same rights guaranteed to those workers who are employed in full-time employment without an established period of duration of the employment and whether a necessary requirement for receiving legal protection during termination, is that one completed in full their probationary period.[1211] Establishing the above criteria is necessary for the Committee when deciding whether Bulgarian labour law is in accordance with the standards stipulated under Article 24 RESC. At the same time, the Committee points out the necessity to the authorities of Bulgaria for equal treatment of all workers regardless of the basis of employment (typical or atypical work agreements)

201. The Committee draws the attention of Member State authorities to provisions in both Social Charters of the Council of Europe, which demand the enforcement of increased worker rights protection and forbid the termination of work agreements based on the following reasons: participating in trade union activities (Article 5) as well as partaking in worker representative organisations (Article 28),

1208. Conclusions 2016 (Malta), p. 250.
1209. Conclusions 2016 (Armenia), pp. 218–229; (Montenegro), p. 223.
1210. Conclusions 2005, vol. 1 (Bulgaria, Cyprus, Estonia, France, Ireland, Italy, Lithuania), p. 111, Conclusions 2008, vol. 2, p. 217 (Cyprus).
1211. Conclusions vol. 1, *supra,* p. 81.

taking part in legal strike actions (Article 6 §4), maternity leave (Article 8 §2), family responsibilities (Article 27). Some of the provisions in the Social Charters (namely Article 1 §2, Article 4 §3) forbid the discrimination of workers and especially the termination of work agreements based on legally prohibited criteria (Article 1 §2, Article 4 §3, Article 20).[1212] The Revised European Social Charter also additionally supports the Committee's stance. In paragraph 3 to Article 24 of the Addendum to this Charter, there are six reasons which do not constitute validity when terminating a work agreement. They are: (a) trade union membership or participating in trade union activities outside working hours or with the consent of the employer within working hours; (b) seeking office as a workers' representative undertaking responsibilities (either acting or having acted in) in such a body; (c) the filing of complaints or the participation in proceedings against an employer involving alleged violations of labour law regulations; (d) illegal premises of discriminating against, i.e., race, colour, sex, marital status, family responsibilities, pregnancy, religion, political opinion, national extraction or social origin; (e) maternity or paternity leave; (f) temporary absence from work due to illness or injury. These specified reasons, which do not validate the termination of a work agreement, are only examples. This is indicated by the term 'in particular' in the Addendum to Article 24 RESC.[1213] Utilising the above-mentioned possibilities, the Committee sought information from the Romanian authorities as to whether there were labour law regulations in existence within the country that would ensure workers protection from the termination of work agreements for such reasons as exercising their civil liberties.[1214]

Member States regulate their own grounds for terminating work agreements. Member States usually utilise one of two legislative methods: standard contractual clauses or expressed terms. In the first supervisory cycle monitoring whether Member States were abiding by the obligations of Article 24 RESC in 2003, The Committee was of the view,[1215] that the first technique of protecting the right to work out of the above provisions, was administered by French legislation. The French labour law code authorises employers to terminate a work agreement in cases where there are objective and serious reasons (section L 122-14-3).[1216] The second legislative technique is applied by Romania's labour law code, which stipulates 12 valid reasons for terminating a work agreement[1217] and by Bulgaria's labour law code, in which the valid reasons for terminating a work agreement are divided into three categories.

202. Analysing the general clause, as well as the specifically defined cases which according to national labour law regulations validate the termination of work

1212. As above, p. 423 (Romania); p. 533 (Slovenia).
1213. *Ibid.* Harris and Darcy, *supra*, p. 273.
1214. Conclusions vol. 1, *supra*, p. 424.
1215. The reasons for the above-mentioned provisions were not part of the report prepared by French authorities, rather they were discussed in a labour law textbook by J. Pellissier, J. Supiot & A. Jeammaud, *Droit de travail*, (Dalloz 20th ed., 2000).
1216. Conclusions vol. 1, *supra*, pp. 190 et seq. (France).
1217. Committee, Revised European Social Charter. Conclusions 2003 – vol. 2 (Romania, Slovenia, Sweden), Council of Europe Publishing, Strasbourg 2003, pp. 421–422 (Romania).

agreements by employers, the Committee aims to familiarise itself with the litigation process of applying these provisions. Its view is dependent on the compliance or non-compliance of the above legislative techniques with the standard of workers' rights protection established by Article 24 RESC.

As in the cases of France, Romania and Bulgaria, the Committee did not provide a ruling, withholding its decision until the filing of the next reports in the following supervisory cycle (in 2007) by the Member State authorities in question, concerning the information of applying the provisions regarding the protection of workers from the termination of work agreements.

In cases where there is a termination of a work agreement without a valid or serious reason, Article 24(b) RESC pressures Member State authorities of the Council of Europe to oblige employers to compensate the worker or provide him or her with other appropriate relief.[1218] As is made obvious by the Addendum to Article 24 RESC the legal basis for compensation to which a worker is entitled when there is no valid reason for the termination of a work agreement, may be regulated by national labour law provisions, such as acts and statutes depending on their jurisdiction, by collective agreements or by other measures acceptable by the given country. Article 24 RESC is another provision of the Social Charters, which establishes the principles associated with compensation for damages protected by the legal regulations of the European Social Charters. The Committee has worked on its position with regard to this issue during its supervisory cycles which monitor whether Member States to the Council of Europe are abiding by the obligations of equal treatment, forbidding discrimination based on sex at the workplace, regulated by legislation. According to the opinion of the Committee, national legislation dealing with labour rights should ensure that the injured has the possibility to regain his/her employment. In cases where the termination of the work agreement has not been sufficiently validated, there should be a possibility of being reinstated to the previous work position as well as compensation for the various financial damages entailed during the unsubstantiated lay-off period.[1219] Only in cases where it is impossible to reinstate the worker to the same position, other forms of compensation for damages are permissible. Insufficient compensation for loss of job cannot be considered adequate compensation within the meaning of Article 24b of the RESC.[1220] It is the basis for the recognition of dismissal not in accordance with the standards set out in the Charter. The same applies when the provisions of labour law do not guarantee the dismissed employee the right to be reinstated.[1221] Compensation received instead of being reinstated into a former position, should fore mostly deter an employer from breaching labour law regulations protecting workers, and second should compensate the worker for losing his/her employment. National legislation may also introduce further sanctions for employers who are guilty of

1218. *See* D. Harris & J. Darcy, *European Social Charter*, The Procedural Aspects of International Law Monograph Series, Vol. 25, 273 (Transnational Publishers Inc., 2001).
1219. Conclusions XIII-5, p. 256.
1220. Case of Turkey. Conclusions 2020.
1221. Case of Albania. Conclusions 2020.

violating workers' labour rights.[1222] In cases where there has been unequal treatment of workers and discrimination against them, the Committee advises the introduction of supplementary sanctions.

In one case in Bulgaria, the Committee ruled Article 24 was violated, as the maximum amount of compensation that may not exceed a six-month remuneration amount, cannot be seen as an adequate method in calculating damages for an unwarranted termination of a work agreement.[1223] The Finnish legislation did not provide for the possibility of reinstatement in a case of unlawful dismissal, although Article 24 required that such a possibility must be guaranteed by legislation.[1224] The Committee in the last cycle notes from the Governmental Committee report[1225] that the new Employment Contracts Act does not include a provision on the alternative compensation the employer had to pay in cases of reinstatement. In cases of the illegal termination of an employment contract, the employee's financial status is secured by a compensation set by the law. The Finnish government considers that the employment contract is a contractual relationship (private law) between employer and employee. Thus, a legal obligation of reinstatement in cases of unlawful dismissal will poorly suit the Finnish legal system as it would create an impossible and impractical situation for both the employee and the employer. For the reinstatement of a service relationship (public law), termination is regulated in the Civil Service Act, with identical grounds to those in the Employment Contracts Act. Civil service being a contractual relationship, if the termination is found to be groundless, the service relationship continues uninterrupted and the authority that has terminated the relationship may (before the end of the notice and upon the civil servant's acceptance) cancel the termination. The Committee finds that this obligation cannot be regarded as a substitute for reinstatement as it has a limited scope of application and does not have as its purpose for reinstatement of workers unlawfully dismissed. Therefore, the Committee reiterates its previous conclusion of non-conformity. The Committee also finds the Tort Liability Act does not provide an adequate alternative legal measure for the victims of unlawful dismissal not linked to discrimination. It considers that the upper limit to compensation provided for by the Employment Contracts Act may result in situations where the compensation awarded is not commensurate with the loss suffered. Therefore, the Committee considers that the situation is not in conformity with the Charter.[1226]

203. The Committee repeated its conclusion in 2008.[1227] It is of the opinion[1228] that one year's wages is also not an adequate compensation for breaches of Article 24 of the RESC. Moreover, it establishes a general principle according to which a

---

1222. *Ibid.*, p. 256.
1223. Conclusions 2003, vol. 1, *supra*, p. 82, Conclusions 2007, vol. 1, p. 296.
1224. Therefore, the Committee considered that the situation was contrary to the Charter. Conclusions 2012.
1225. GC(2013)25.
1226. Conclusions 2016 (Finland), pp. 220–221.
1227. Conclusions 2008, vol. 1, p. 175 (Bulgaria).
1228. Conclusions 2008, vol. 1, p. 33 (Albania).

ceiling (upper limit) on compensation for the unlawful termination of an employment relationship is contrary to Article 24 of the RESC.[1229]

A non-typical method of regulation in the Lithuanian labour law code, accepted under Article 297 §4, obliges the court to make a ruling in cases of unwarranted work agreement termination, in favour of compensation in an amount equal to the normal remuneration for which a worker would be entitled to, if he/she remained in the employment from the day of the contract termination to the day of the court ruling. This poses many problems for the Committee. The amount of compensation is obviously dependent upon the speed with which litigation may be carried out. On the one hand, paying compensation for the entire period, the worker is left unemployed if an efficient deterring mechanism is sanctioning the employer, if the compensation is a high amount, for breaching regulations governing work agreements. On the other hand, efficient running of the court system has a direct influence on lowering the amount of compensation paid. Taking note of the latter point, the Committee will seek information from Lithuanian authorities concerning the amount of compensation calculated by the courts for workers who have lost their employment due to unwarranted work agreement terminations. Depending on the details or lack of provided to the Committee, it would hand down a ruling during the following supervisory cycle, which may be one against the Lithuanian authorities due to the predicted lack of specific information, which would help in analysing the pros and cons of such compensation. A ruling of the Committee is on the way to ensuring protection for workers who have had their work agreements terminated without valid reasons, to help them regain employment as well as guaranteeing them compensation calculated from the day of the illegal termination of the work agreement until a decision is passed down by the court or some other body, concerning the reactivation of the work contract. If there is an exception and work may not be reinstated, compensation may be paid to cover the damages, and should, as specified by the Committee, prove to be as onerous to the employer who is paying it, as it is beneficial to the worker, who has been discriminated against at the workplace and lost his/her wages. It is therefore a necessity the compensation be of a higher amount than the remuneration, calculated from the day the work agreement is illegally terminated to the day of the judgment being passed.

204. A worker who has had his/her work agreement terminated by a breach of the provisions protecting against such termination has a right to appeal to an impartial body. Neither Article 24 RESC nor the Addendum names such impartial bodies authorised to deal with appeals concerning unwarranted work agreement terminations. Such bodies in particular are courts, arbitration tribunals or commissions. National labour law regulations determine the statute of limitations in which a worker who has had his/her work agreement terminated may file an appeal to an impartial body. Verifying the position of the supervisory bodies monitoring administrative and quasi-administrative institutions, the Committee attempts to analyse the manner in which members of such bodies are appointed and the length of their candidature and also researches the level of independence of such bodies from

1229. Conclusions 2008, vol. 1, p. 217 (Cyprus), p. 299 (Finland).

national administration.[1230] In cases where such bodies show they cannot fulfil the required conditions to establish their independence based on the collected data concerning the above preliminaries, the Committee then must turn to state authorities seeking additional information with regard to control procedures applicable to administrative bodies existing within the given country and analysing the country's reports concerning the obligations under the Social Charter. The Committee regards the rulings handed down by supervisory bodies monitoring the decisions of administrative and quasi-administrative institutions in matters of registration of employee and employer organisations (trade unions and other representative organisations), decisions made with regard to the refusal or the allocation of social and medical benefits, as rulings which should be handed down by a truly independent body. If such rulings are made by administrative and quasi-administrative institutions, they may be appealed on accusations based on merit, and the judiciary and the arbitration tribunal have the jurisdiction to deal with such matters substantively and look over the content of the supervisory body's decisions. It is obliged to function according to rigid provisions and cannot hand down an arbitrary decision concerning the rulings made by such supervisory bodies. There is a basis for concluding the impartiality and the independence of such supervision over decisions made by employers who terminate work agreements.[1231] According to the Committee, the burden of proof between employee and employer in proceedings relating to dismissal should not rest entirely on the complainants.[1232]

§12. The Right of Workers to the Protection of Their Claims in the Event of the Insolvency of Their Employer

205. The Revised European Social Charter ensures worker protection in cases of the insolvency of employers (Article 25). The Committee notes that no targeted questions were asked in the Circle 2020 under this provision. As the previous conclusion found the situation to be in conformity there was no examination of the situation in 2020. The above observation applies to the following Member States: Austria, Latvia, Lithuania, Malta and the Netherlands (Kingdom in Europe, Curaçao, Sint Maarten). Article 25 RESC obliges the authorities of Member States to ensure the protection of workers' claims which have resulted out of a work agreement or from insecure labour relations due to employer insolvency. The goal of this provision is to ensure protection for workers and their claims in cases of the insolvency of their employer. The European Social Charter does not define insolvency. In the appendix, RESC authorities of Member States became authorised to define their meaning of insolvency. They may do so independently or put the matter into practice (Article 25(2)).

Looking at the Member State reports dealing with Article 25 RESC, the Committee took note of Slovenia's report, which protects workers' claims that are not settled by employers who have commenced bankruptcy proceedings or are legally

1230. Conclusions XIII-4, p. 55.
1231. Conclusions XIII-4, *supra*, p. 56.
1232. Conclusions 2016 (Slovak Republic), p. 287.

bound to undergo economic restructuring of the bankrupted company. The Committee questioned Slovenia's authorities whether the settling of property claims encompasses cases where the employer ceased business activities prior to commencing bankruptcy proceedings.[1233] The Committee adopted the above-mentioned wide definition of insolvency in the process of assessing Slovenia‘s report and adjourned its decision in the matter of whether the national laws of the country are or are not in accordance with Article 25 RESC.

Article 25 RESC does not oblige authorities of Member States that have ratified the article and the standards for choosing any out-of-the-familiar techniques of protecting the solvency of asset and property claims of workers by an insolvent employer. It leaves for Member State authorities the choice of familiar techniques, such as calling upon insurance institutions, which guarantee to cover workers' claims in cases of employer insolvency, or to choose alternate efficient methods of protecting such claims.

According to the jurisdiction of the Committee, the technique of protecting workers' claims against insolvent employers is of minor importance. The Committee emphasises however the legal protection of these claims should be efficient regardless of the technique employed.[1234]

The case of Bulgaria indicates the protection of workers' claims needs to be adequate. Bulgarian insolvency law states that workers' claims are fulfilled as fourth in priority. First three positions on the list of debts of an insolvent employer are three other claimants, which emerged during the insolvency procedures. In reality, therefore, workers' claims are listed in the first position before the insolvency proceedings begin. Evaluating this system the Committee concluded workers' claims could not be characterised as being in a privileged position in comparison with other claimants of the insolvent employer. According to the Committee, the Bulgarian legislation does not meet the standards established by Article 25 RESC.[1235]

This does not mean that the introduction of a privileged system of fulfilling workers' claims by an insolvent employer is, as a rule (treated by the Committee as inadequate, thus contrary to Article 25 RESC), a technique of assuring a worker's claim. The Committee concluded in a recent cycle that the situation in Albania is not in conformity with Article 25 of the Charter on the ground 'that workers' claims are not effectively protected in case of insolvency of the employer under the privilege system'. In the opinion of the Committee, only a privileged system supplemented by an alternative mechanism effectively guarantees the satisfaction of pecuniary claims of those employed by entrepreneurs who do not own any assets.[1236]

At the same time, the Council of Europe allows the authorities of Member States to apply other measures of protection of workers' claims on the grounds of work agreement or labour relations not fulfilled by insolvent employers, aside from the technique verified by the EU of fulfilling worker's material claims not fulfilled by insolvent employers by the assuring institution, whose assets are independent of the capital of entrepreneurs. The Committee evaluates the efficiency of these measures.

1233. Conclusions 2003, vol. 2, *supra,* pp. 535–536.
1234. Conclusions 2003, vol. 1, *supra,* p. 83 (Bulgaria).
1235. As above, p. 84.
1236. Conclusions 2020.

In order to demonstrate the efficiency and adequacy in the practice of the protection of workers' claims in the event of the insolvency of their employees, Member States must provide information, *inter alia*, on the average duration of the period from when a claim is lodged until the worker is paid and on the overall proportion of worker claims which are satisfied by the guaranteeing institution and/or the privilege system. The 2012 Belgium report stated that the average time that elapses between the filing of the claim and the payment of any sums owned was eleven months. The Committee considered that was excessive and therefore considered the situation to not be in conformity with the Charter.[1237] The 2016 report provides an explanation of the lengths of the procedure for worker claims in case of the insolvency of the employer. The report states that before the claim is transmitted to the business closing fund, it must be accepted by the Trustee. This acceptance takes place in the context of the bankruptcy proceedings in the Commercial Court and this procedure can be lengthy. In addition, the report states that the management of these claims is based on many prerequisites (surveys) which are often required to verify in particular the certainty of those claims. The report points out again that these procedures can take time, especially in the context of bankruptcy. The Committee notes that there have been no changes to the situation which it has previously found to not be in conformity with the Charter.[1238] The very same decision is taken in the case of Portugal. The Portuguese report indicates that in the last reference period, the average time that elapsed between the filing of the claim and payment increased from 221 days in 2011 to 314 days in 2014, as well as the number of cases concluded, which increased from 22,741 to 41, 939. The Committee considers that the average period for completing the overall procedure of 11–12 months is excessive and therefore the situation is not in conformity with Article 25 of the Charter.[1239]

The appendix to RESC (Article 25 §1) authorises the authorities of Member States to exclude particular groups of workers from the protection guaranteed by Article 25 of the Charter. This authorisation is addressed to the 'proper authorities'. This term should be understood as governmental bodies relevant in regulating the legal conditions of particular occupations. Depending on the scale of the regulation this authorisation applies to legislative bodies, able to regulate legal conditions of workers in the whole of the country or bodies of governmental administration in charge of certain occupations and professions only. The authorisation was granted to the 'proper authority'. Interpreting Article 25 §1 the appendix to RESC states this term should also include stakeholders entitled to shape conditions of employment and remuneration for particular occupations within the collective work agreements or other normative documents. The exclusion from the force of provisions ensuring workers' material claims on the grounds of labour relations not fulfilled by insolvent employers cannot be a common practice. It may encompass only particular groups of employees. Categories of workers, whom Article 25 RESC can protect, can also be overruled due to the nature of the labour relation. Working papers enlist, workers of public administration as well as workers of small workplaces employed

1237. Conclusions 2012.
1238. Conclusions 2016 (Belgium), p. 151.
1239. Conclusions 2016 (Portugal), p. 153.

in managerial positions as categories of workers authorities of Member States ratifying Article 25 RESC can exclude from legal protection of claims made by workers in cases of insolvency of employer.[1240] According to the rule of majority applied during the supervisory cycle over abiding by the provisions of the European Social Charter by Member States and also employed by the Committee, provisions of the Charter ratified by the authorities of particular states should be applied at least to 80% of workers employed within the given state. Before making a decision upon restricting the application of Article 25 RESC the authorities of a Member State are obliged to run consultations with stakeholders, i.e., organisations of workers and employers. The employers for workers of public administrations are particular on the state agendas. Allowing for the exclusion of this category of workers from the protection given by Article 25 RESC the Charter expresses trust to the state as the employer assuming it is not going to declare insolvency. In cases of workers of small workplaces employed in managerial positions, the reason for their exclusion is the conviction that workers employed in managerial positions are, because of their positions implying the proper proportion of remuneration, in possession of allocated savings, which guarantee covering of their expenses in the case of employer's insolvency. The Committee regarded the above exclusions as being in accordance with the standards of legal protection established by Article 25 RESC.

Taking advantage of the possibility of the above exclusion Sweden broadened categories beyond the guaranteed protection of workers to co-owners of a workplace being a part of the insolvent's assets.[1241] The necessary condition of not applying Article 25 RESC is the initial date of entering into the ownership, not exceeding six months from the date of declaring insolvency, individually or being a member of the closest family a significant part of the property being a part of the insolvent‘s assets. Guarantees determined under Article 25 RESC do not apply, in Sweden or elsewhere, to members of the family of the insolvent entrepreneur.[1242]

206. The appendix to the Revised European Social Charter lists three categories of workers‘ material claims which should be fulfilled in cases of employer insolvency (Article 25 §3). The order is random and can be explicitly concluded from the statement of Article 25 §2, which simply says that workers' claims being the main subject of Article 25 of the Charter, it must include at least:

(a) workers‘ claims on the ground of remunerations for work for a given period of time before insolvency was declared or – depending on legal regulations of the particular state – from the day the labour relation was terminated if the above-mentioned event took place in the period preceding insolvency. The length of this period cannot be shorter than three months in the system where the technique of fulfilling workers' material claims in the first order before other outstanding claimants of the insolvent is in force. In the case of employing the technique of protection of workers‘ material claims by the assuring institution, material benefits cannot be lower than the worker‘s remuneration paid in the

1240. As above, p. 275.
1241. Conclusions 2003, vol. 2, p. 632.
1242. *Ibid.*

period of 8 weeks before insolvency was declared or from termination of labour relation in the period preceding insolvency (Article 25 §2). In its previous conclusions from 2012, the Committee asked whether the worker's claims other than the monthly wage are also covered by the Grand Fund established in Turkey. This question was asked due to the fact that in the Regulation on Wage Guarantee Fund, the unpaid wage is defined as 'the claims concerning maximum three months basic wage prior to insolvency arising from the employee's working relationship and due to the employer's going bankrupt', and that the claims other than monthly wage are not evaluated within this scope. Therefore, the Committee holds that the situation is not in conformity with Article 25 of the Charter on the basis that holiday pay due, which shall not be less than three months under the privilege system and eight weeks under the guarantee system, is not covered by Turkish legislation.[1243]

(b) workers' claims on the ground of paid holidays workers are entitled to on the basis of employment in the year when insolvency took place or labour relations terminated (Article 25 (2);

(c) workers' claims on the grounds of liabilities not fulfilled by the employer in the periods of employment listed in the appendix to Article 25 §1 RESC.

207. The appendix to Article 25 RESC allows authorities of Member States of the Council of Europe to limit workers' material claims included in either one or another system of assurance: protected within the privilege or ensured by the assurance institutions (Article 25 §4). Limitation is only possible by the legal standards legislated by the state, normative acts being at the rank of bills or executive provisions. It is not acceptable for stakeholders to introduce such limitations. The appendix to Article 25 RESC does not directly describe the extent to which Member States can restrict the range of the guarantee of material claims not fulfilled by insolvent employers. However, it gives an important guideline, according to which the extent of guaranteed protection of the material claims in the system of privilege or of the institution of guarantee should be set to the 'socially accepted' extent (Article 25 §4). The provision in question establishes the legal ground for the Committee to evaluate the range of protection in particular Member States. The Committee's practices give no guidelines as to what reasons should be taken into consideration while analysing the extent of the guaranteed compensation when they are lower than the remuneration or other financial liabilities listed in the appendix to Article 25 RESC due to three-month or eight-week periods preceding the employer's insolvency or the termination of labour relations before the date of insolvency being declared.

There was only one case when the Committee ruled the Swedish system of limiting the benefits compensating the worker's material claims not fulfilled by the insolvent employers, established at the level of SEK 100,000 (equivalent of EUR 10,966) was sufficient. It guarantees workers protection at the adequate level, meeting, therefore, requirements established in the appendix to Article 25 §4 RESC.[1244]

1243. Conclusions 2016 (Turkey), p. 251.
1244. Conclusions 2003, vol. 2, p. 632.

Swedish regulations guarantee the protection of workers' material claims by privilege. They do not create any restrictions in terms of the amount of the compensation, which is paid before other claimants of the insolvent employer. Having in mind the protection of the state's financial system and in order to prevent possible abuse, the Swedish authorities introduced the above-mentioned limit within the guaranteed workers' compensation if not fulfilled by the insolvent employer. As the Swedish report did not compile the information on the periods when the claims were protected by the privilege, the Committee having stated the conformity of Swedish regulations with the standards established by Article 25 RESC, requested for the presentation of this data during the subsequent cycle.[1245]

208. The appendix to Article 25 §3 RESC does not determine the amount of workers' material claims on the basis of labour relations protected by privilege or by the assurance institution. The authorities of Member States of the Council of Europe present a range of guarantees in their reports. It can be concluded from the report delivered by Slovenia that three legal acts legislated between 1997 and 2000[1246] determine the obligation of the guarantee fund to compensate worker's material claims not fulfilled by the insolvent employer in the period of three months before the labour relation terminated in the amount not exceeding the three minimum state-guaranteed monthly remunerations. The financial equivalent for paid leave, which has not been utilised in the calendar year in which the insolvency took place, is also paid by the above-mentioned fund, being the amount not exceeding half of the minimum state-guaranteed monthly remuneration. When severance pay for those workers having had their work agreements terminated for reasons concerning the workplace is not paid out by the insolvent employer, it is compensated for by the state assurance fund to the amount of one state-assured minimum monthly wage.[1247] The Committee takes the position that the range of material benefits not paid out by the insolvent employers in Slovenia is in accordance with the requirements set in Article 25 RESC. Accepting the above-mentioned national legal regulations, the Committee requested confirmation from the Slovenian authorities of their own approach to the legal situation in terms of protecting workers' material claims in cases of employer insolvency.[1248]

France is a state where the system of labour law employs the two techniques of guaranteeing the protection of workers' claims not fulfilled by insolvent employers. The remuneration for the last sixty days not exceeding the double monthly basis of the insurance premium not paid by insolvent employers is prioritised in the process of paying out the claims of insolvent employers out of their assets. The labour code imposes on employers the obligation to ensure responsibility for unfulfilled workers' material claims. The range of responsibility of the insurance company for covering liabilities of insolvent employers, based upon the binding regulations, collective as well as individual work agreements, cannot exceed the amount of 13

1245. *Ibid.*
1246. No. 25/1997; No. 80-3784/1999; No. 22/2000; No. 103-4344/2000; *ibid.*, p. 535.
1247. *Ibid.*, p. 536.
1248. *Ibid.* In addition, the basic obstacle of the Committee work has to be brought to attention being the vague editing of reports on abiding the ratified provisions of the Revised European Social Charter by Member States.

times the monthly basis of the insurance premium in cases of unemployment (*plafond 13*). The range of responsibility of the insurer for fulfilling other entitlements of workers on behalf of the insolvent employer cannot exceed the amount of 4 times the monthly basis of the insurance premium in case of unemployment (*plafond 4*).[1249] The Committee stated conformity of the national system of labour law in France with the requirements listed in Article 25 RESC. It obliged the French authorities to explain the relation between the material benefits compensated by the insurer within the two above-mentioned programmes 13 and 4.[1250]

§13. THE RIGHT TO DIGNITY AT WORK

209. Article 26 protects the dignity of workers. It was formed in order to counteract harassment, sexual harassment and mobbing in workplaces. Article 26 does not produce a legal definition of sexual harassment. The Committee defines sexual harassment as behaviour violating the sphere of privacy, mental balance, defaming the dignity of workers, interrupting the carrying out of the duties of the job and contradicting socially accepted patterns of conduct within labour relations.[1251] Sexual harassment in light of this provision would be behaviour based on sex or on sexual connotations which is not accepted and violates the dignity of the person that this conduct is addressed at. Classifying a given behaviour as an act of sexual harassment, whether the behaviour is performed by a superior or by a work colleague, makes no difference.[1252] The Committee has broadened the above definition. It pays attention to actions violating the sphere of privacy which is unwanted and disapproved of by the victim of the prohibited conduct. The basic characteristic of such sexual harassment is that the prohibited behaviour is felt as undesired by the person it is addressed to. Sexual interest becomes sexual harassment when a person being the addressee of such behaviour regards it as insulting. The undesirable nature of such behaviour is a very important characteristic allowing sexual harassment to be distinguished from friendly behaviour which is welcome and reciprocated. The necessary condition of classifying given behaviour as an act of sexual harassment is not utilising the work position by a person harassed, higher ranked within the workplace hierarchy than the victim. Sexual harassment is not directly connected with using power to achieve a goal, which is not forbidden in itself. Cases of sexual harassment also take place when the initiators of the undesirable behaviour of a sexual nature are other workers with no labour ties with a victim and third parties not entering into a labour relation with a victim (clients, representatives of other workplaces). In the appendix to Article 26 RESC, it was decided that fulfilling the obligations determined by this provision does not impose on Member States the

1249. Conclusions, vol. 1, *supra*, pp. 199–201.
1250. As above, p. 200.
1251. Conclusions 2003, vol. 1, p. 85 (Bulgaria).
1252. Explanatory report to the revised European Social Charter, European Social Charter, *supra* , p. 171.

obligation for the legal regulation of harassment and sexual harassment. Supervising the reports delivered by Member States, the Committee was also interested in obtaining information concerning whether national labour law regulations give legal definitions of sexual harassment.[1253]

210. Article 26 §1 RESC obliges authorities of Member States to take appropriate measures to promote awareness of the harm sexual harassment may cause in the workplace. Authorities of these Member States should support and promote information and prevention. They should also undertake all appropriate measures to protect workers from sexual harassment. This obligation is interpreted by the Committee as a basis upon which the Committee can demand annual reports from Member State authorities concerning the introduction of domestic legislation protecting workers against sexual harassment.

The Committee concludes that the situation in Moldova is not in conformity with Article 26 §1 RESC, as neither Moldovan legislation nor any other regulatory or administrative measures provide for the necessary preventive and reparatory means to protect individual workers against harassment directed against them at the workplace and there is no indication in the Moldavian report of any practical application of the existing laws by public authorities or courts that would provide such protection.[1254] As of 2014, the Committee concludes that the situation in Georgia and Turkey is not in conformity with Article 26 §1 of RESC, on the grounds that there are no preventive or reparatory means to effectively protect employees against sexual harassment. In both cases, the Committee in its previous conclusions had requested information on measures taken (information, awareness-raising and prevention campaigns in the workplace or in relation to work) in order to combat sexual harassment. As the report does not answer this question, the Committee reiterates it and refers to its findings on non-conformity as regards the lack of preventive measures against sexual harassment.[1255] Turkey, in response to the Committee's request for information, states that there is no regulation concerning preventive measures yet.[1256]

During the first supervisory cycle dealing with the compliance of Article 26 §1 RESC, the Committee concluded that Member States were utilising one of the two models of protection of the rights of workers from sexual harassment. Member States were seen to either render separate regulations prohibiting harassment or analyse the act of sexual harassment in other widely defined categories of dealing with prohibition. The former model is utilised by French and Swedish authorities.

In France, victims of sexual harassment within the workplace have the right to take part in mediation or to file criminal charges. The perpetrator of the act may be sentenced to a period of one-year imprisonment and be subjected to a fine. The injured party has a right to seek compensation as well as demand to be reinstated to

1253. Conclusions 2003, vol. 1, p. 85 (Bulgaria).
1254. Conclusions 2005 (Moldova, Norway, Romania, Slovenia, Sweden), vol. 2, p. 496, Conclusions 2007, vol. 1, pp. 896–897.
1255. Conclusions 2014 (Georgia).
1256. Conclusions 2014, Conclusions 2016, p. 231 (Turkey).

their former employment position.[1257] Swedish employers are forbidden from harassing their employees and are obligated to develop guidelines for the procedures required should sexual harassment charges be laid. Victims of sexual harassment may directly file claims against their offenders as well as their employers in labour courts as well as in criminal jurisdictions. They may also benefit from the assistance provided by the ombudsman in matters of equal treatment in labour relations and in trade unions.[1258]

211. A different method, using the already existing regulations, which treat sexual harassment as a civil law matter as well as an act forbidden by the criminal code protecting the personal inviolability of the worker, is used in Bulgaria, Italy and Slovenia. Using the already existing regulations to counter sexual harassment means the Committee is interested in the various types of legal sanctions which may be used to examine its effectiveness.[1259] States which introduced separate legal measures to counteract sexual harassment within the workplace gained the approval of the Committee, which considered such measures to be in compliance with Article 26 §1 of RESC. Those states which have been making use of the legal implementations already in existence to combat sexual harassment, have to provide the Committee with complete information while the Committee postpones handing down any decisions.

The Committee does not regard a sexual harassment act within labour relations as an act discriminating against gender in itself. In the opinion of the Committee sexual harassment is regarded as an act violating the principles of equal treatment of workers. This is because it creates more or less favourable grounds for the treatment of workers, straying from the acceptable norm. The Committee therefore monitors whether authorities of Member States are fulfilling the set obligations of informing and preventing sexual harassment. Good examples of fulfilling such obligations by the authorities of Member States are widespread information and advertising campaigns and the preparation and distribution of publications dealing with the harm caused by sexual harassment. The Committee considers that sexual harassment in the workplace covers a much broader range of discriminatory behaviour and practice than what is covered by the Criminal Code alone. Apart from the right to break the contract, the victim can file a request for adoption of prevention and remedial measures. In the absence of sufficient indications of the employee's liability, the effectiveness of the procedures and the existence of guarantees against retaliation, the Committee does not consider it established that employees are given appropriate and effective protection against sexual harassment in the workplace or in relation to work.[1260] The Committee recalls that, in order to allow effective protection of employees, a shift in the burden of proof is required, making it possible for a court to find in favour of the victim on the basis of sufficient prima facie evidence and the contribution of the judge. The civil procedure requires a shift in the burden

1257. Conclusions 2003, vol. 1, pp. 202–203.
1258. Conclusions 2003, vol. 2, pp. 633–634.
1259. Conclusions 2003, vol. 1, p. 86 (Bulgaria); pp. 324–325 (Italy); Conclusions 2003, vol. 2, pp. 537–538 (Slovenia).
1260. Conclusions 2014 (Turkey).

of proof. This does not apply to sexual harassment cases in Azerbaijan and Turkey. Therefore, the Committee considers that the situation in both countries mentioned above is not in conformity with Article 26 §1 of RESC.

Article 26 §2 of RESC orders Member States to undertake actions informing and preventing harassment of workers, which is not sexual in its nature. Authorities of Member States have the obligation to counteract other forms of harassment and mobbing.

This obligation was introduced thanks to an application made by Sweden. The point of this regulation is to protect workers from hostile, insulting and offensive behaviour by their superiors or by other workers, which violates the recipient's dignity, within or in connection to the workplace. Examples of such behaviour include: a systematic exclusion of workers from discussions dealing with labour organisations in which other workers are involved, provoked by the employer's dislike or hatred; and refusal to inform the worker about the duties involved in his/her position.[1261] State parties are required to take all necessary preventive and compensatory measures to protect individual workers against recurrent reprehensible or distinctly negative and offensive action directed against them at the workplace or in relation to their work since these acts constitute humiliating behaviour. Harassment creating a hostile working environment characterised by the adoption towards one or more persons of persistent behaviours which may undermine their dignity or harm their career shall be prohibited and repressed in the same way as acts of discrimination.[1262] In these circumstances, it does regard merely posting the rules on equal opportunities as appropriate and sufficient prevention measures under Article 26 §2 of the Charter to combat psychological harassment in the workplace.[1263] The Committee recalls that workers must be afforded effective protection against harassment. The Committee asks Member States to provide information on the prevention measures undertaken during the reference period in order to specifically inform workers about the nature of moral harassment and the available remedies to combat it. The Committee furthermore asks to indicate and what extent the social partners are involved in the adoption and implementation of such measures.[1264] As some reports and their addendums do not provide answers to the Committee's request for such information, the Committee reiterates its question and, in the meantime, finds that it has not been established that appropriate prevention measures apply.[1265]

The Committee considers that the civil and criminal provisions mentioned do not adequately cover the phenomenon of moral harassment at work, although they can be relevant in certain cases. It recalls that workers must be afforded effective protection against harassment by domestic norms, irrespective of whether this is a general anti-discrimination act or a specific law against harassment.[1266] This protection

1261. Explanatory reports, *supra*, p. 172.
1262. Conclusions 2014 (Azerbaijan).
1263. Conclusions 2014 (Republic of Moldova).
1264. Conclusions 2014 (Lithuania).
1265. Conclusions 2014 (Azerbaijan, Georgia, Lithuania, Republic Moldova, the Netherlands, Turkey).
1266. The Georgian report states that moral harassment is covered by the Criminal Code in Arts 144 (torture), 150 (coercion) and 151 (intimidation). The Committee asks the next report to provide examples of case law showing that the provisions referred to have been used in the context of moral harassment in the workplace. Conclusions 2014 (Georgia). During the next reference

must include the right to appeal to an independent body in the event of harassment and the right not to be retaliated against for upholding these rights.[1267] The Committee asks for clarification on how moral harassment is defined and prohibited.[1268] It asks in particular what legal remedies (judicial and non-judicial),[1269] if any, are available to victims of harassment. It also asks for specific information on any specialist bodies that register and investigate complaints of harassment, such as mediation services and advice centres.[1270] The report must provide information on the burden of proof in moral harassment cases. When examining natural persons' or legal entities' complaints, applications, requests, reports or claims of discrimination on the ground of age, sexual orientation, social status, disability, race or ethnic origin, religion, convictions or beliefs, in courts or other competent bodies, the defendant has to prove that the principal of equal treatment has not been violated.[1271] Under Article 26 §2 of RESC, victims of harassment must have effective judicial remedies for seeking reparation for pecuniary and non-pecuniary damage. These

---

period, the Committee declared that the report fails to provide information on several issues (effective judicial protection against harassment, judicial remedies to seek reparation for pecuniary and non-pecuniary damage) which leads to the conclusion that the employees were given appropriate and effective protection against moral (psychological) harassment in the work place or in relation to work. Conclusions 2016 (Georgia), p. 232; (Ukraine), p. 236. The Dutch report on psychological harassment. The Committee has asked the next report provide information on remedies for victims of moral harassment while concluding that the situation in the Netherlands is not in conformity with Art. 26 §2 of the Charter on the grounds that it has not been established that employees are effectively protected, in law and in practice, against moral harassment Conclusions 2016 (Netherland), p. 235. The report submitted by Azerbaijan confirms that victims of moral/psychological harassment may claim damages, however no further information is provided. The Turkish report provides detailed information on legal rules prohibiting moral harassment at work as well as information on new initiatives taken by the Turkish government to prevent such behaviour and provide support to victims. However, it provides no information on any relevant case law. The Lithuanian report provides information on the draft Labour Code which contains explicit provisions on mobbing. The Committee decided to examine these when the draft Code enters into force. In the meantime, the Committee concludes that the situation in Azerbaijan, Turkey and Lithuania is not in conformity with the Charter. Conclusions 2016 (Azerbaijan), p. 260; (Turkey), p. 234; (Lithuania), p. 233.

1267. Conclusions 2014 (the Netherlands, Lithuania and Azerbaijan): the employer's liability may be incurred if employees are subjected to harassment in the work place or in relation to their work by third parties (entrepreneurs, self-employed, visitors, clients, patience, etc.), or if such third parties are victims of harassment by an employee. The Committee concludes that the situation in Finland is not in conformity with Art. 26 §2 of RESC, on the grounds that employers cannot be held liable in cases of harassment involving employees under their responsibility, or on premises under their responsibility, when a person not employed by them is the perpetrator. Conclusions 2014 (Finland). As regards the procedures available, the Turkish report states that, apart from the right to break the contract of employment, the victim of harassment can file a penal complaint and request adoption of prevention and remedial measures. The Committee asks that the next report clarify what procedures conducted before an independent body, other than criminal ones, are available to victims of harassment in the workplace, in the light of relevant case examples. Conclusions 2014 (Turkey).

1268. Conclusions 2014 (Turkey). This definition is not included in the Turkish Labour Code, which only considers harassment as discrimination rather implicitly, and prohibits it, no matter whether it occurs on grounds of language, sex, political opinion, philosophical belief, religion and confession, or other similar reasons (Art. 5).

1269. Conclusions 2014 (Azerbaijan).

1270. Conclusions 2014 (the Netherlands).

1271. Conclusions 2014 (Georgia).

remedies must allow for appropriate compensation and for an amount sufficient to make good the victim's pecuniary and non-pecuniary damage and act as a deterrent to the employee.[1272] In addition, the persons concerned must have a right to be reinstated in their post when they have been unfairly dismissed or forced to resign for reasons linked to moral harassment. Pointing out that the effectiveness of legal protection against moral harassment depends on how the domestic courts interpret the law as it stands, the Committee repeats its request for relevant examples of case law in the field of moral harassment.[1273] In the case of Turkey, the Committee noted that a worker who quits his/her job on account of harassment is entitled to severance pay, on condition that he/she served for at least one year, to discrimination compensation of up to four month's wages and the restoration of his/her rights.[1274] The Committee concludes that the situation in Turkey is not in conformity with Article 26 §2 of RESC, on the grounds that it has not been established that employees are given appropriate and effective protection against more harassment in the workplace or in relation to work. The very same decision was rendered in the other Member States: Azerbaijan, Georgia, the Netherlands and the Republic of Moldova.[1275] In 2018, the Committee considered that, in several countries, employees did not enjoy adequate protection from sexual harassment (Azerbaijan, Georgia, Lithuania, Ukraine) or from moral harassment (Azerbaijan, Georgia, Lithuania, Malta, Ukraine). In most cases, however, this finding was based on the lack of relevant information in response to the questions previously raised.[1276]

212. The Committee interprets Article 26 §2 of the Charter as a standard which obliges Member States to create 'friendly' working environments.[1277] In fulfilling the above obligation, some states introduced particular regulations, despite the fact that the appendix to Article 26 RESC did not demand the banning of the psychological harassment of workers (this definition encompasses certain actions undertaken or tolerated by employers), which may result in the marginalisation of the employee discriminated against.[1278] The effect of such psychological harassment is worsened by the conditions of work, exerting negativity on the rights and dignity of the workers. This causes the deterioration of health as well as threatens the worker's future within the place of employment.[1279] Workers who are the victims of psychological harassment should use those legal measures which are available to victims of sexual harassment within the workplace.

1272. Conclusions 2014 (the Netherlands, Republic of Moldova).
1273. Conclusions 2014 (Azerbaijan).
1274. Conclusions 2014 (Turkey).
1275. Conclusion 2014.
1276. Activity Report 2018, p. 28.
1277. The Committee concludes that situation in Albania and Moldova is not in conformity with Art. 26 §2 of the RESC on the grounds that neither legislation nor any other regulatory or administrative measures in those countries provides for the necessary measures to protect individual workers against harassment other than sexual harassment directed against them. Conclusions 2007, vol. 1, pp. 78–79 (Albania), vol. 2, p. 898 (Moldova).
1278. Conclusions 2003, vol. 2, p. 635 (Sweden).
1279. Conclusions 2003, vol. 1, p. 204 (France).

213. During the inspection of compliance with Article 26 of the Charter, the ECSR obliged the Member States to pay particular attention to the protection of dignity at work for all employees. In both provisions of paragraphs 1 and 2 of Article 26 of the Charter, the Committee drew attention to the urgent need for action by the Member States to sensitise, inform and prevent illegal activities by state authorities and businesses, both in the workplace and in connection with work. The Committee was not only concerned with maintaining the culture of the workplace and the working environment but also preventing employees and employers from committing punishable or formally legal but clearly hostile offensive acts in the workplace and beyond. The key role in protecting the rights of employees against two types of mobbing and/or harassment is played by the concept of the employee's 'relationship' with the work they perform. During the pandemic, the ECSR asked the Member States of the Council of Europe whose public authorities had ratified one or both paragraphs of Article 26 to identify categories of employees who were potentially primarily at risk of illegal activities in matters strictly prohibited by Article 26 §1 and §2, and people employed in jobs such as night work, work carried out at the employer's home, work in shops and warehouses and other similar types of work that the ECSR calls 'front work'. In 2022, the Committee decided in twenty-three cases on compliance or non-compliance with the standards of the Council of Europe and the Revised European Social Charter adopted by it.[1280] This is because so many Member States have ratified Article 26 of the Charter. In ten Member States, the ECSR found non-compliance with the law by the authorities of those countries because they tolerate mobbing and harassment.[1281] In six cases, the Committee postponed a negative assessment due to doubts as to whether the work carried out in these countries could be regarded as complying or not complying with the standards laid down in the Charter.[1282] The bias of seven other countries was found to be legal. This was the attitude of the state authorities of Andorra, Austria, Belgium, Bulgaria, Latvia, North Macedonia and Moldova in cases against mobbing and sexual harassment in the place, environment and time of work and in connection with work. In accordance with the established tradition of the previous four editions of the book *Labour Law: Council of Europe*, the reader's attention is drawn to the unlawful cases established by the Council of Europe in the Revised European Charter of Social Rights at various stages of development of the rights of economically active people working in Europe.

In 2022 Article 26 §1 of the Charter, the grounds of non-conformity were as follows:

(1) It has not been established that there is adequate prevention of sexual harassment in relation to work (Azerbaijan, Serbia and Türkiye). For the monitoring cycle, the Committee welcomed information on awareness-raising and prevention campaigns as well as on education taken to ensure that the right to dignity at work is fully respected in practice. Azerbaijan's report provides no

1280. Conclusions 2022, *Press Briefing Elements*, pp. 18–19.

1281. Conclusions 2022 (Albania), (Azerbaijan), (Finland), (Georgia), (Lithuania), (Malta), (Montenegro), (Serbia), (Slovakia), (Türkiye).

1282. Conclusions 2022 (Estonia), (France), (Greece), (Ireland), (Italy), (Portugal).

information in response to the Committee's questions. Given the lack of information, the Committee concludes that the situation is not in conformity with Article 26 §1 of the Charter. Serbia's report provides no information in response to the above-mentioned questions. Given the absence of information, the Committee concludes negatively. No information is provided on awareness-raising activities and prevention measures for sexual harassment. The Committee also notes that in comments the Human Rights Association states that there are no policy documents on combating sexual harassment, except for a very limited number of private-sector workplaces.

(2) It has not been established that employers' and workers' organisations were consulted in the promotion of awareness, information and prevention of sexual harassment in the workplace or in relation to work (Türkiye). No prevention is provided on sexual harassment specially, whether taken by the TIHEK of government institutions. The Committee also notes in the comments that the Human Rights Association states that there are no policy documents on combating sexual harassment.

(3) The legislative framework does not provide for a shift in the burden of proof in cases of sexual harassment (Azerbaijan). The Labour Code does not provide for a shift in the burden of proof in sexual harassment cases.

(4) The existing framework in respect of employers' liability does provide for sufficient and effective remedies in cases of sexual harassment when third parties are involved (Finland, Georgia and Azerbaijan). The Committee notes that the report provides an example of a specific situation of a 'shared workplace' where one employer exercises the main authority. Finland's report does describe legislation that defines the employer's responsibility in situations of sexual harassment where the victims or perpetrators are persons not employed by them, such as visitors, clients or independent contractors.

(5) It has not been established that, in relation to employee protection, there are sufficient and effective remedies against sexual harassment in the workplace or in relation to work (Albania and Azerbaijan). The current report provides no information on cases in response to the Committee's previous request. Albania's report mentions that difficulties are encountered by employees when denouncing/reporting cases of sexual harassment at work and when proving such cases because most facts are verbal and difficult to document. The report further states that only a few claims have been filed.

(6) Victims of sexual harassment are not guaranteed sufficient and effective remedies against sexual harassment in relation to work (Slovakia). The government did not respond to the comments of the National Centre for Human Rights (NCHR), given to the concluding observations on the third periodic review of Slovakia adopted in 2019, which expressed its concern about the high incidence of violence against women, including sexual harassment and domestic violence. The (NCHR) made a series of recommendations to Slovakia, such as developing specific legislation that would address violence against women, ensuring full protection to victims and improving their access to justice, ensuring systematic collection of disaggregated data on violence against women and ratifying the Istanbul Convention. Slovakia signed the Istanbul Convention but did not pursue the ratification process in 2019.

(7) The existing framework in respect of employers' liability does not provide for sufficient and effective remedies against sexual harassment in relation to work (Lithuania). In its previous conclusion, the Committee noted that the report did not clarify whether any liability of the employers applies under the Equal Opportunities Act when a third party is a victim of harassment by a person under the employer's responsibility. The current report does not clarify the situation. The Committee, therefore, reiterates its request for clarification. Meanwhile, it concludes that the situation is in conformity with Article 26 §1 of the Charter on the grounds that the existing framework with respect to an employer's liability does not provide for sufficient and effective remedies against sexual harassment in relation to work.

(8) It has not been established that appropriate and effective remedies (compensation and reinstatement) are guaranteed in cases of sexual harassment (Azerbaijan, Malta, Montenegro, Serbia and Slovakia). The report does not provide the information requested in both the previous conclusion and the targeted question. Given this absence of information, the Committee concludes that the situation in Malta is not in conformity with Article 26 §1 of the Charter. Montenegro's report provides information on cases of harassment reported by the Labour Inspectorates during the reference period (twenty-one reported cases in 2017, of which six were by women, fourteen reported cases in 2018, of which five were by women, thirteen reported cases in 2019, of which six were by women and eight reported cases in 2020, of which four were by women). No information is provided on the outcome of these cases or the compensation awarded to victims.

(9) The law does not guarantee the right of reinstatement to employees who have been unfairly dismissed or have been pressurised to resign for reasons related to sexual harassment (Finland). The report does not provide any information on relevant case law or on damages awarded. The Committee notes from the *Country Report on Gender Quality 2021* of the European network of legal experts in the field of gender equality and non-discrimination that there is no upper limit to compensation under the Act on Equality. It reiterates its request for information on the case law on sexual harassment and on amounts actually awarded as compensation in such cases.

The Committee considered that five of the twenty-one situations examined in 2020 with respect to Article 26 §2 were not in conformity with the requirements of the provision (Estonia, France, Ireland, Italy and Portugal). The ECSR deferred its conclusions in respect of eight countries (Andorra, Belgium, Bulgaria, Greece, Latvia, North Macedonia, Moldova and Türkiye). In another eight cases (Albania, Azerbaijan, Finland, Georgia, Lithuania, Malta, Serbia and Slovakia), the ECSR considered that the situation was not in conformity with the provisions of the Charter. The grounds of non-conformity were as follows:

(1) It has been established that there is adequate prevention of moral (psychological) harassment in relation to work (Albania, Azerbaijan and Slovakia). For this monitoring cycle, the Committee welcomed information on awareness-raising and prevention campaigns as well as on actions to ensure that the right

to dignity at work is fully respected in practice. Albania's report provides no information on this point. The Committee concludes that the situation in Albania is not in conformity with Article 26 §2 of the Charter. The situation is identical in Azerbaijan and Slovakia. No information was provided about initiatives aimed at promoting awareness and preventing moral (psychological) harassment in the workplace.

(2) It has been established that in relation to the employers' responsibility, there are sufficient and effective remedies against moral (psychological) harassment in the workplace or in relation to work (Malta). The report includes information on the awareness-raising and prevention activities undertaken by the National Commission for the Promotion of Equality (NCP) during the reference period, such as social media posts, participation in TV and radio programmes, articles and press releases. It also includes an awards ceremony organized for both public and private sector organizations and an Equality Sign Ceremony.

(3) The existing framework with respect to employers' liability does not provide for sufficient and effective remedies against moral (psychological) harassment in relation to work (Lithuania). In its previous conclusion, the Committee noted that under the Equal Opportunities Act employers or their representatives are only directly responsible for acts of discrimination committed by them; no liability applies in cases of harassment between colleagues or involving third parties. The Committee asked that the next report clarify this point (2008). The current report does not clarify the situation. The Committee therefore reiterates its request for clarification. Meanwhile, it concludes that the situation is not in conformity with Article 26 §2 of the Charter on the grounds that the existing framework in respect of employers' liability does not provide for sufficient and effective remedies against moral (psychological) harassment in relation to work.

(4) The Labour Code does not provide for a shift in the burden of proof in cases of moral (psychological) harassment (Azerbaijan). With regard to the burden of proof, the Committee considered in its previous conclusion that the situation was not in conformity with the Charter on the grounds that no shift in the burden of proof applies in moral (psychological) harassment cases (Conclusion 2008). As the report does not indicate any change in the situation during the reference period, the Committee reiterates its previous conclusion of non-conformity on this point.

(5) It has not been established that in relation to employers' protection, there are sufficient and effective remedies in cases of moral (psychological) harassment when third parties are involved (Azerbaijan). The report does not provide the requested information as regards employers' liability for sexual harassment involving third parties. The Committee considers that the situation is not in conformity with Article 26 §2 of the Charter on the grounds that the existing framework for employers' liability does not provide sufficient and effective measures of moral (psychological) harassment in relation to work when a third party is involved.

(6) The existing framework for employers' liability does not provide for sufficient and effective remedies in cases of moral (psychological) harassment (Finland,

Georgia and Azerbaijan). In its previous conclusion, the Committee stated that the situation in Finland was not in conformity on the grounds that employers cannot be held liable in cases of harassment involving employees under their responsibility, or on premises under their responsibility when a person not employed by them is the victim or the perpetrator. The Committee notes in the current cycle that the information provided in the report does not demonstrate that the situation has been remedied with regard to the liability of employers in cases of harassment when persons not employed by them are the victims. In Georgia, sanctions were provided by the legislative amendments of 2020 for violations of the principle of non-discrimination by employers. It was established that such violations should result in a warning or a fine in the amount of three times the fine prescribed by law. The report does not provide information with respect to the liability of employers in cases of moral (psychological) harassment when a third party is involved. As Azerbaijan's report does not indicate any change to the situation during the reference period, the Committee reiterates its previous conclusion on non-conformity.

(7) It has not been established that appropriate and effective redress (compensation and reinstatement) is guaranteed in cases of moral (psychological) harassment (Malta, Serbia and Slovakia). In a targeted conclusion, the Committee asked the government whether any limits apply to compensation that might be awarded to a victim of harassment for moral and material damages. The current report does not provide any information in response to the conclusion of non-conformity or in response to the targeted questions or those in the previous conclusion. Meanwhile, the Committee concludes that the situation is not in conformity with Article 26 §2 of the Charter on the grounds that appropriate and effective redress (compensation and reinstatement) is not guaranteed in cases of moral (psychological) harassment in relation to work. Given the absence in Serbia's report of rules and examples of case law regarding compensation in cases of moral harassment, the Committee considers that the situation is not in conformity with Article 26 §1 of the Charter on the grounds that the existence of appropriate and effective redress (compensation and reinstatement) in such cases has not been established. As regards the right to reinstatement, the Committee noted previously that Article 79 of the Labour Code guarantees this right to all victims of unfair dismissals whatever the reason.[1283] The Committee asked Slovakia if this also applies when the person has not been formally dismissed but is pressurised to resign in the context of moral (psychological) harassment.[1284] In reply to this question, the report states that such a person may initiate a lawsuit and claim their rights and that the court could order the employer to reinstate that person.

(8) Appropriate and effective redress (compensation and reinstatement is not guaranteed in cases of moral [psychological] harassment in relation to work (Azerbaijan). The report does not provide the requested information; it only indicates that during the reference period the State Labour Inspection Service, under the Ministry of Labour and Social Protection of the Population, did not

1283. Conclusions 2018.
1284. Conclusion 2018.

receive any complaints about the moral harassment of employees. The Committee considers that the situation is not in conformity with Article 26 §2 of the Charter on the grounds that appropriate and effective redress is not guaranteed in such cases.

(9) The law does not guarantee the right of reinstatement to employees who have been unfairly dismissed or pressurised to resign for reasons related to moral (psychological) harassment (Finland). The Committee considers that the situation is not in conformity with Article 26 §2 of the Charter on the grounds that the law does not guarantee the right of reinstatement to such employees.

Moreover, in both paragraphs of Article 26 of the Charter, the Committee asked for information on specific measures taken during the pandemic to protect the right to dignity in the workplace, notably as regards moral (psychological) harassment. The Committee welcomed specific information about categories of workers at a higher risk, such as night workers, home and domestic workers, store workers, medical staff and other frontline workers. The report indicates that no practical changes were made during the pandemic with regard to the risk of harassment at work. Therefore, harassment issues were dealt with the same way as before the pandemic.

In addition to the cases mentioned above, the Committee decided to enact a Statement of interpretation[1285] on online harassment related to work, stressing that the rights and obligations deriving from Article 26 of the Charter apply to incidents of online harassment. The Committee notes that the Charter applies to harassment in all places and circumstances related to work, including a worker's usual workplace as well as situations in which a worker is working remotely (including at home) or where the worker works at client's or contractor's workplace or home. It also applies to situations where a worker is engaged in work-related activities such as conferences, training, work trips and work-related corporate events or activities. The Committee considers that the rights and obligations deriving from Article 26 of the Charter apply to incidents of online harassment. Online harassment may occur through a range of different media, including digital technologies/information and communication technologies ('ICT'), such as emails, text messages, chats/instant messages as well as video conferencing and social media platforms and virtual spaces. Online harassment may result in very speedy propagation of information, mass dissemination and long-term availability of information. The Committee recalls that Article 26 of the Charter imposes passive obligations on States Parties to take appropriate preventive measures against online harassment and to take all appropriate measures to protect workers from such conduct. In particular, States Parties should – after consulting employers' and workers' organisations – provide information and carry out awareness-raising and training programmes in order to help workers identify, understand and be aware of online work-related harassment and its manifestation and effects, as well as their rights and responsibilities in this regard. Furthermore, information should be provided to workers on how to report and respond to online harassment (such as by reporting the harassment to their

1285. *Press Briefing ...* , *supra*, pp. 4–5.

employers, the line platform, the labour inspectorate or police or by blocking/ closing accounts). Moreover, workers should be informed about the procedure to follow and the available remedies. There must be protection from retaliation where workers report incidents of online harassment.

Furthermore, Article 26 of the Charter requires that victims enjoy effective protection in the law and in practice against online harassment. This protection should include the right to challenge offensive behaviour before an independent body, the right to obtain adequate compensation and the right to not be retaliated against for having pursued the respect of these rights. Victims of online harassment must have effective judicial remedies to seek reparation for pecuniary and non-pecuniary damages. In addition, the right to reinstatement should be guaranteed to workers who have been dismissed or pressurised to resign for reasons linked to online harassment.

Finally, responsible persons should be held accountable with a view to preventing the recurrence of online harassment. It must be possible for employers to be held liable when online harassment occurs in relation to work. States Parties shall ensure that the employer is under a formal obligation to report alleged incidents of online harassment to the competent investigating authorities.

§14. The Right of Workers with Family Responsibilities to Equal Opportunities and Equal Treatment

214. The goal of Article 27 RESC is to protect against discrimination based on sex and to ensure the equal treatment of both men and women carrying out family responsibilities with those who do not. The appendix to Article 27 RESC defines workers 'having family responsibilities' as workers of both sexes with family responsibilities in relation to their dependent children as well in relation to other members of their immediate family who clearly need their care or support. The Committee found that the situation in Lithuania is not in conformity with Article 27 §1 of RESC, on the grounds that fathers who are not single are discriminated against with regard to part-time work.

Article 46 of the Lithuanian Act on Safety and Health at Work states that a part-time schedule must be agreed to by an employer only upon request of a pregnant female, a nursing mother, a woman or a single parent raising a child or children under 14 years of age or a disabled child under 16 years of age, or a person nursing a sick family member.

The Committee noted that there is no legal obligation to agree to part-time work for a father who is not single.[1286] The Charter obliges authorities of Member States to clearly define, within the domestic legislation, the persons who are encompassed by the regulations (dependent children or other members of the immediate family), and to undertake measures aimed at creating equal treatment and opportunity within employment for those persons executing child rearing responsibilities. Those who

1286. Conclusions 2005, vol. 1, pp. 397–398.

are caring for dependent children as well as other members of their immediate family, who clearly need their care or support, should have their right to equal opportunity in employment ensured by the bound Member States. Those who are preparing for, entering, participating in or advancing in economic activity and are restricted by family responsibilities, also should have these rights of equal treatment ensured. Article 27 RESC is comprised of three paragraphs. Paragraph 1 obliges Member States to undertake the following measures in an attempt to:

(a) enable workers with family responsibilities to enter and remain in employment, as well as to re-enter employment after an absence due to those responsibilities, including measures in the field of vocational guidance and training;[1287]
(b) take account of their needs in terms of conditions of employment and social security;[1288]
(c) develop or promote services, public or private, in particular child day-care services and other childcare arrangements.[1289]

215. Supervising compliance with Article 27 RESC, the Committee is particularly concerned about Member States fulfilling the obligations stipulated under Article 1 §1 and 3 as well as Article 10 §4 of the Charter. Not fulfilling at all or inappropriately fulfilling the obligations specified in the provisions in question renders a judgment of non-compliance with Article 27 §1 RESC. During the first supervisory cycle, Member States did not pay heed to the differences evident between Article 27 §1 RESC and Articles 1 §1 and 3 as well as Article 10 §4 RESC. It was, for this reason, that the Committee obliged Member States to provide information regarding techniques that were actively appropriated in employment policies, which could be introduced to the labour market and enable equal employment for those who have family responsibilities. Member States are obliged to ensure particular assistance to workers with family responsibilities in gaining employment. Because of the responsibilities having to be met, such workers have difficulties in establishing good labour relations, as the breaks in employment caused by family and care

1287. As of 2015, it has not been established that in Georgia there are employment services providing vocational guidance, training and retraining of workers with family responsibilities. It also has not been established that the legislation provides for any facilitation in respect of reconciling working and private life for persons with family responsibilities. Conclusions 2014 (Georgia).

1288. Conclusions 2011, vol. 2, p. 588 (Ireland). In its previous conclusion the Committee asked Georgia and Turkey whether workers are entitled to social security benefits under the different schemes, in particular health care, during periods of childcare leave. The Committee notes that reports do not provide this information. Therefore the Committee considers that it has been established that workers on parental leave are entitled to social security benefits. Conclusion 2015 (Georgia, Turkey).

1289. In the previous conclusion, the Committee asked whether there was sufficient provision of childcare facilities, which would be affordable and of high quality. Given the absence of such information from reports submitted by two Member States, Armenia and Azerbaijan, the Committee concludes that the situation is not in conformity with Art. 27 §1 of RESC, on the grounds that it has not been established that childcare services are adequate in Armenia or in Azerbaijan. Conclusions 2015 (Armenia, Azerbaijan).

responsibilities usually lead to the worker falling behind with the latest technological developments. Workers who have family responsibilities do not have the ability to keep up with the advances occurring within their field of employment.[1290]

One of the techniques that is implemented to help workers with family responsibilities carry out their work duties on equal grounds with other employees is flexible working hours (working part-time or working from home). Authorities of Member States are obliged to inform workers with family responsibilities of such employment possibilities. In the Committee's view, Article 27 RESC is not a standard, which orders Member States to take into consideration the particular requirements certain workers with family responsibilities may have. The provision in question obliges Member States to grant those workers with family responsibilities the right to make demands regarding the betterment of their employment conditions in a manner comparable to the conditions of other employees.[1291] In 2019, the Committee found that the situation is not in conformity with Article 27 §1 RESC (participation in working life) only in one case on the ground that the legislation does not specifically provide for facilitation of reconciliation of working and private life for persons with family responsibilities.[1292] In previous conclusions (2017 and 2015), the Committee found that workers on parental leave maintain their social security rights. The Committee demanded information on the provision of places in preschool institutions, and on the healthcare services by workers on leave owing to family responsibilities. It also wanted to know whether periods of absence were taken into account for determining the right to pension and for calculating the amount of pension. As Georgian state authorities did not provide any information on these matters the Committee concludes in the last three cycles that the situation in Georgia is not in conformity with Article 27 §1 of the RESC on the grounds that it has not been established that: (1) there are employment services providing vocational guidance, training and retraining of workers with family responsibilities; (2) the legislation provides for facilitation of reconciliation of working and private life for a person with family responsibilities; (3) workers on parental leave maintain the social security rights.

Article 27 §2 RESC obliges Member States to issue regulations concerning parental leave.[1293] The entitlement to such leave should be allocated to the parents of a child. The point of such parental leave is to enable working parents to care for their children without having to terminate a working agreement. During parental leave, workers are exempt from work duties. The loss of remuneration is fully covered by social security benefits. The measure of parental leave and the circumstances with which one acquires such leave is regulated by the Member States. During the first supervisory cycle monitoring compliance with Article 27 §2 of the Charter, the Committee claimed all the regulations of all the Member States are in

1290. Conclusions 2003, vol. 2, p. 637 (Sweden).
1291. Conclusions 2003, vol. 1, p. 328.
1292. Georgia, Activity Report 2019, pp. 35–36.
1293. No parental leave for fathers in Turkey. Conclusions 2011, vol. 3, p. 1203. In 2015, the Committee concludes that the situation in Azerbaijan is not in conformity with Art. 27 §2 RESC, on the grounds that it has not been established that the legislation provides for an individual non-transferable right to parental leave for each parent who is not single. The level of social leave benefit is inadequate. Conclusions 2015 (Azerbaijan).

compliance with the standards established by the Charter. This decision was handed down based on various legal systems. In accordance with the standards established by the Charter, domestic regulations were recognised as ensuring paid parental leave as an entitlement for parents until their child reaches the age of two,[1294] for a period of one year until the child turns 3,[1295] or entitled to leave for ten months until their child reaches the age of 8.[1296] In some cases, parental leave may be renewed. The maximum period for parental leave cannot exceed three years.[1297] A necessary requirement to acquire parental leave is to remain with the same employer for a period of one year[1298] or to be covered by the general insurance and superannuation fund for a period of six months during the last twelve months, or for a period of twelve months during the last twenty-four months.[1299] The Member States shall ensure that any employed parent is adequately compensated for his/her loss of earnings during the period of parental leave. The modality of compensation is within the margin of appreciation of state parties and may be either paid leave (continued payment of wages by the employer), a social security benefit, any alternative benefit from public funds or a combination of such forms of compensation. Regardless of the modality of payment, the level shall be adequate.[1300] In 2019, the Committee stated that, from the point of view of Article 27 §2 of the Charter, it is crucial for the state to ensure adequate compensation for the employee or employees caring for a child during parental leave. In several cases, the Committee found that such compensation had not been provided because the level of the pecuniary benefit was inadequate (Armenia, Azerbaijan and Ukraine), and in some cases, no compensation or remuneration was granted to those parents taking such leave (Ireland, Malta and Turkey). The above-mentioned breach was the reason for taking a negative conclusion towards the above-mentioned Member States which ratified Article 27 §2 RESC. Under that provision, Member States will provide for the possibility for each parent to be given parental leave. The Committee considers it important that national regulations should entitle men and women to an individual right to parental leave following birth or adoption of a child. In order to promote equal opportunities and equal treatment between men and women, leave should be provided on a non-transferable basis to each parent. The Committee reiterates its findings on non-conformity with Article 27 §2 of RESC that there must be a guarantee of an individual, non-transferable right to parental leave (Ukraine and Montenegro).

The Committee treats Article 27 §3 RESC as a standard forbidding the termination of a work agreement by an employer with his/her employee based on the utilisation of parental leave.[1301] The Committee demands information from Member States regarding the termination of employment with workers who have family

1294. Conclusions 2003, vol. 1, p. 89 (Bulgaria); Conclusions 2003, vol. 2, p. 427 (Romania).
1295. *Ibid.* (France).
1296. Conclusions 2003, vol. 1, p. 329 (Italy).
1297. Conclusions 2003, vol. 1, p. 206 (France).
1298. *Ibid.*
1299. Conclusions 2003, vol. 2, p. 427.
1300. Statement of Interpretation of Art. 27 §2 of RESC, Conclusions 2015. The level of social leave benefit (the amount of AZN 30, equivalent to EUR 25, paid until the child is 1.5 years old, and a monthly benefit of AZN 15 (EUR 12), is inadequate. Conclusions 2015 (Azerbaijan).
1301. Conclusions 2003, vol. 2003, p. 542 (Slovenia).

responsibilities.[1302] Article 27 §2 RESC is a standard that compliments the prohibition of terminating employment without a valid reason, citing Article 24 RESC. This provision, however, may not be regarded as *superfluum*.[1303] Article 24 (a) RESC established the prohibition of terminating employment without valid reason as being connected with the worker's capacity or conduct. Article 27 §2 RESC strengthens this prohibition. It demands from Member States a guarantee that family responsibilities alone will not stand as a valid reason for terminating a work agreement.[1304] This is an indication of the obligation which Member States entered into after ratifying the above provision, which forbids the termination of employment of a worker by an employer for carrying out family responsibilities. Unlawfully terminated employees ought to be efficiently protected by the law. The Committee declares that the situation in the Member State is in conformity with Article 27 §3 of the RESC if legislation makes no provision for the reinstatement of workers unlawfully dismissed on grounds of their family responsibilities[1305] or the compensation to be awarded to such employee is subject to a ceiling.[1306] During parental leave, an employee taking such leave should be subject to special legal protection against termination of employment by the employer. However, some Member States (Bulgaria, Italy and Turkey) have not granted such protection. In cases of Bulgaria and Italy, the Labour Codes do not specially protect workers with family responsibilities against dismissal. In Turkey workers in companies with less than 30 employees are not protected against dismissal based on family responsibilities. The Committee also took into account that in Turkey and Italy, adequate compensation is not provided for in cases of illegal termination of employment contracts on grounds of family responsibilities if the worker concerned does not wish to be reinstated. In Finland, the relevant legislation did not provide the possibility for reinstatement of workers unlawfully dismissed on grounds of their family responsibilities.

1302. Conclusions 2003, vol. 1, p. 207 (France).
1303. Distinguished without valid reason, and irrelevant. Harris & Darcy, *supra*, p. 278.
1304. The Committee concludes that the situation in Turkey is not in conformity with Art. 27 §3 of RESC, on the grounds that workers in companies with less thirty employees are not protected against dismissal due to family responsibilities. Conclusions 2015 (Turkey).
1305. Conclusions 2007, vol. 1, p. 496 (Finland). *See* Conclusions 2015 (Cyprus), where the courts can only reinstate an unlawfully dismissed employee in cases where the enterprise concerned has more than twenty employees.
1306. Conclusions 2007, vol. 2, p. 653 (Ireland). Conclusions 2011, vol. 1, p. 153 (Armenia), p. 300 (Bulgaria), p. 330 (Cyprus), p. 417 (Finland). *See* Conclusions 2015 (Armenia, Turkey), where it has not been established that adequate compensation is provided in cases of unlawful dismissal due to family responsibilities.

Chapter 2. The Regulation of Collective Labour Rights

§1. The Right to Organise

216. Article 5 of the Charter obliges Member States to not impair the freedom of workers and employers to organise. The Committee interprets Article 5 of the Charter as a standard placing positive obligation on Member States. The law should protect the right to form coalitions, which encompasses the freedom to associate and organise, of workers within a trade union as well as employees within an organisation. Authorities of Member States are therefore obligated to pass legislation ensuring full freedom of association.[1307] In Article 5 of the Charter, two obligations are specified, both negative and positive. The addressees of these obligations are Member States. The negative obligation applies to Member States not to violate or restrict freedom of association. This means governmental administrative bodies may not issue actions that may infringe on the freedoms in question.[1308] State governmental and administrative bodies should neither forbid nor order workers to form trade unions and join already existing union organisations. Member States cannot determine the demands which need to be fulfilled to form an organisation. Trade unions and employers' organisations should take advantage of their autonomy. A Member State and its bodies should refrain from interfering in the internal issues of an organisation representing the economic and social interests of the parties to labour relations (collective and individual).[1309] In the below-mentioned decisions handed down by the Committee, there are cases mentioning behaviour that is compliant and non-compliant with the standards established by Article 5 of the Charter. The mentioned cases do not cover the whole array of instances. The essence of such instances is reflected by Member States forbidding the disruption of workers who are utilising the right to associate in trade unions.[1310]

The positive obligation is implicated in the necessity of a Member State to undertake actions, especially in issuing appropriate legislation, which will ensure workers the full possibility of associating with trade unions as well as ensuring such organisations' freedom to act and to be protected from employers.[1311]

Member States have the right to restrict the freedom of association in trade unions, through the power of the police. The Charter gives the right to exclude from Article 5 provision professional soldiers (members of armed forces). The freedom to associate as stipulated under Article 5 of the Charter remains in force. Article 5 of the Charter grants the extent of the guarantees provided for police officers wishing to organise and having the right to do so, to Member States.[1312]

1307. Conclusions XI-1, p. 78 (Iceland).
1308. Conclusions I, p. 31.
1309. *The Right to Organise and to Bargain Collectively* 12 (Council of Europe Publishing, 2d ed. 2001).
1310. Conclusion XII-1, p. 116.
1311. Conclusions I, p. 31; Conclusions XIII-3, p. 108. Conclusions 2010, vol. 1, p. 33 (Albania).
1312. The obligation of police officers to adhere to the National Police Association in Romania was used by the Committee as one of the legal grounds for negative conclusion in 2006. Conclusions 2006, vol. 2, p. 744.

217. In the last stage of the third group audit (01/01/2017–31/12/2020) carried out by the European Committee of Social Rights, which was aimed at determining whether the authorities of the Member States respect the rights of all professionally active people, mainly employed persons and not just employees, to associate in all national organisations operating in democratic Member States, it turned out that in fourteen Member States (Albania, Armenia, Azerbaijan, Denmark, France, Ireland, Italy, Lithuania, Moldova, Poland, Serbia and the UK) the authorities do not comply with the legal standards laid down in Article 5 governing the right to organise. Generally, the shortcomings concern police officers and professional soldiers serving in the state armed forces of individual Member States. It should be noted that professional soldiers do not have the status of either employee, engaged or hired in the national collective labour law systems of European countries. Their legal relation with the army is governed by the provisions of administrative law. In the system of European law, soldiers are presented as professionally active persons in military spheres, performing military service for the state and its citizens in various types of military units. This means that they are directly and fully affiliated with the army. However, this fact does not allow military personnel to associate during military service with organisations that do not represent the service interests of professional soldiers. Members of the armed forces may establish organisations capable of meeting the needs of life and may join associations established by military institutions of existing organisations operating in Member States. A necessary condition for military personnel to exercise the right of association is the position of state authorities. The right of association and the resulting freedom of association depend on the position of state authorities competent to issue permits for which - the state and its citizens - soldiers perform professional military service. Interpretation of Article 5 of the Charter holds that the state has no right to decide whether the subject of the protection of the right of association which professional soldiers wish to enjoy is fully dependent on the decision of the state authorities. The state and its public and political authorities have no right to decide whether professional soldiers may establish or join existing military organisations. The principle concerning the enjoyment of the right of association by members of the armed forces is indisputable. No one, including state authorities, can undermine it. The right of professional soldiers to organise, created by state legislation, cannot be subjected to any limits determining the exercise of a right undisputed in public relations. However, state authorities have a certain power to set limits on the exercise of powers vested in military and police institutions. Police officers were treated in a similar way by the European legislature. In order to distinguish these two professional groups – the army and the police – which maintain societal peace in the internal and external relations of each Member State, from the remaining, much larger group of citizens engaged in employment, legal relations should be used under which work is provided by people performing various professions. Non-military workers perform work, are self-employed and employ others; therefore, they are employers and entrepreneurs of people considered professionally active. In Article 5 of the Charter, the right to associate of all these persons (military, police officers, employees, self-employed people and entrepreneurs) is limited by the type and nature of the activities performed within the power to organise in order to protect their interests. The ECSR analysed and published the reasons underlying its findings of non-compliance with Council of Europe standards of preventing association among professional military personnel (Armenia, France, Italy, Latvia, Lithuania and the UK), police officers (Albania, Armenia and Moldova) and a large body of civil servants (Albania and Poland). In addition, it pointed out that employees' right of association, which was not subject to assessment, was limited and made dependent on the views of the state authorities (Armenia, Latvia and Serbia). The most popular are bans on establishing organisations that represent and protect the interests of professional soldiers, police officers and other paramilitary units. This prohibition has been applied despite the ECSR's clear indication of illegality for some time now.

In the critical report of France, the Committee pointed to the forfeiture that took place in the case between the European Council of Trade Unions (CESP) and France.[1313] It is an open ban on creating such organisations of professional soldiers. In another, slightly later case, *Confederazione Generale Italiana del Lavoro (CGIL) v. Italy*, it was stated in the report[1314] that 'the complete suppression of the right to organize is not a measure which is necessary in a democratic society for protection of, *inter alia*, national security'. This type of argument is invoked in almost all reports negatively assessed by the ECSR in 2022. In Italy, this argumentation was cited by the ECSR in its latest report on the unequal treatment of military personnel. The ECSR gave two reasons for the negative conclusions regarding Italy: it ruled that the situation 'in Italy is not in conformity with Article 5 of the Charter on the grounds that: the restriction on the right to organize of members of the Guardia di Finanza is excessive; there is absolute prohibition of Guardia di Finanza from joining other trade unions'. The last statement, 'prohibited joining other trade unions', was quoted in extenso in the Irish report. Listing the views of state authorities of some European Member States as inaccurate, harsh and inconsistent with the standards of Article 5 of the Charter, the ECSR listed military organisations, also including state security institutions.[1315] In the broadest and most accurate way, which does not reflect well on the state authorities criticised by the ECSR, the ECSR listed in the edition included the army, police officers, and self-employed. people, freelancers and others employed in the so-called black zone of the economy.[1316] Regardless of the occupational categories and groups of professionally active people presented above, it is important to point out the elderly, their professional position and their importance in the national systems of individual Member States of the Council of Europe. It is precisely these elements of power exercised by senior civil servants that prevent them from organizing and joining trade unions.[1317]

1313. Complaint No. 101/2013, decision on the merits of 27 Jan. 2017, point 84.
1314. Conclusions 2022 (Italy).
1315. Conclusions 2022 (Latvia).
1316. Conclusions 2022 (Armenia).
1317. Conclusions 2022 (Albania).

I. Forming Trade Unions

218. The right to form trade unions is assured to workers regardless of the labour relations,[1318] type of employer[1319] and whether one is self-employed or not.[1320] This right is also applicable to civil servants.[1321] Membership of a civil service,[1322] or a citizen of another Member State legally inhabiting the territory of a different Member State, or being a migrant worker, cannot be a valid reason to avoid the above provision.[1323] With regard to restrictions being introduced by Member States on the general availability of the freedom to organise by workers, the issue is discussed in the last point raised in the paragraph. It is necessary to point out that the restrictions on the freedom to organise specified elsewhere than in Article 5 of the Charter, may be introduced by a Member State through the general principles stipulated under Article 31 (1) ESC or under Article G (1) RESC. The range available, therefore, is crucial for a democratic society to protect the rights and freedoms of others or to protect public order, national security, public health and good customs. Workers take advantage of forming trade unions and joining organisations. This is an indication of workers' independence in deciding what type of trade union to form or to which organisation to belong.[1324] The obligation of Member States is to issue legislation ensuring such freedom of choice in deciding the above, as well as inhibiting other

1318. Conclusions XIX, p. 175 (Poland). Conclusions (Armenia, Poland). The Committee concludes that persons carrying out work under a civil-law contract, home workers (Poland), and self-employed workers, those working in liberal professions and the informal sector workers (Armenia), do not have the right to set up or join a trade union.

1319. Conclusions 2010, vol. 1, p. 119 (Azerbaijan). Conclusions 2014 (Azerbaijan) – it has not been established that, in practice, the free exercise of the right to form trade unions is ensured in multinational companies. The Committee previously noted from the observation made by the ILO Committee Experts on the Application of Conventions and Recommendations those trade union activities in multinational companies are often hampered in practice. In 2016, the Committee noted that in its report the government of Azerbaijan indicates that as result to the activity of the Confederation of Trade Unions of Azerbaijan, trade unions have been established in twenty-eight multinational companies. Regardless of that information, the Committee concludes that the situation in Azerbaijan is not in conformity with Art. 5 of the Charter on the grounds that it has been not established that, in practice, the free exercise of the right to form trade unions is ensured in multinational companies. Conclusions 2016 (Azerbaijan), pp. 291–292.

1320. Conclusions I, p. 8.

1321. *Ibid.*, p. 31; Conclusions II, p. 184; Conclusions VI, p. 29 (Cyprus). Conclusions 2010, vol. 1, p. 33 (Albania). Conclusions 2014 (Armenia, Georgia, Poland, Ukraine). The following categories of employee and civil servant cannot form or join a trade union of their own choosing: the staff of law enforcement bodies (Armenia, Georgia), some categories of civil servant (Poland), and civilians employed by the police (Armenia).

1322. The Committee concludes that it has not been established that the right to organise applies to staff of law enforcement bodies of the prosecutor's office. Conclusion 2016 (Georgia), p. 294.

1323. Conclusions I, p. 79, Conclusions 2006, vol. 2, p. 744 (Romania), Conclusions 2014 (Bulgaria). No restrictions for foreigners concerning the setting up of trade unions or participation in their activities are provided by the Bulgarian Labour Code. Ordinance No. 1 of 15 Aug. 2002, which regulates professional activities, requires prior authorisation for foreigners. Therefore, the Committee concludes that the situation in Bulgaria is not in conformity with Art. 5 of the Charter, on the grounds that foreign workers' right to form or to participate in the formation of trade unions is subject to prior authorisation.

1324. Conclusions II, p. 184. Conclusions 2010, vol. 1, p. 287 (Georgia).

entities (such as state authorities, or trade unions themselves) from influencing workers in their decision-making process.

This issue is exemplified by the case of Denmark, in which the domestic legislation restricts the right of trade unions to negotiate collective work agreements within the maritime sector representing workers who are citizens of Denmark and are employed on ocean vessels, which are registered in Denmark.[1325] The legislation on the International Ship Register provides that collective agreements on wages and working conditions concluded by trade unions are only applicable to seafarers resident in Denmark. Seafarers who are not resident in Denmark, but who work on board ships entered in the Register, are entitled to be members of several trade unions: that is, both a Danish trade union and a trade union in their country.[1326]

219. According to the Committee, granting trade unions the right to negotiate collective work agreements for their members is one of the major reasons for association. The refusal to grant such rights to particular organisations causes workers to allocate their membership elsewhere. Restricting such activities of trade unions is in contradiction to the freedom to form and join organisations.[1327]

Authorities of Member States, citing domestic labour legislation, are obliged to make demands of workers, who are committee members of trade organisations. Such demands may be twofold. On the one hand domestic labour legislation may require workers to join trade unions based on a membership criterion of a particular category of employment.

The labour law regulations in Cyprus, which restricted the freedom of association of workers (for example those employed in specific workplaces), were regarded as non-compliant with Article 5 of the Charter, ensuring freedom to organise.[1328] Workers do not have the obligation to join already existing trade organisations within their workplace. A legal requirement for civil servants to be members of a particular trade union, associating exclusively with public civil servants, was deemed in violation of Article 5 of the Charter.[1329] They may take advantage of the freedom to form different trade unions.[1330]

The Committee is of the view, that the pluralism within trade organisations is a legal and organisational after-effect of the organisations' freedoms ensured by Article 5 of the Charter. It accepts trade union pluralism. It does not consider that the existence of many trade organisations within the workplace inhibits trade union movements.[1331] Taking advantage of such freedom by workers, who have the right

1325. Conclusions XX-3 (Denmark).
1326. The number of Danish nationals not residing in Denmark and working on board ships entered in the Register is very limited in comparison with the number on non-Danish seafarers engaged on vessels entered in the Register not having residence in Denmark. Conclusions XX-3 2014 (Denmark).
1327. Conclusions XII-1, p. 111; Conclusions XVII-1, vol. 1, p. 126.
1328. Conclusions XI-2, p. 74.
1329. Conclusions II, p. 184 (Cyprus).
1330. Conclusions XII-2, p. 97.
1331. Conclusions VII, p. 31.

to choose between joining an already existing trade union within the workplace or forming a new one, cannot be regarded as non-compliant with the standards established under Article 5 of the Charter.[1332]

Member States may elect to establish formal demands which should be fulfilled by workers forming a new trade union. Such demands include registration fees as well as a minimum number of members. The minimum requirement for the number of founding members of a trade union organisation cannot be too high. Otherwise, it prevents the freedom of employees from associating with trade unions.[1333] The Committee regards some of these requirements as in compliance with the standards established under Article 5 of the Charter. Some, however, are seen as excessive.[1334] Settling such discrepancies between domestic collective labour law and international standards and deciding whether there is compliance or non-compliance on behalf of the domestic legislation, is dependent upon the scope and the definition of the demands made by Member States. A trade union should accept a defined number of members, workers, the self-employed or the unemployed. Article 5 of the Charter does not define a minimum number of members necessary for a trade union to form and be able to protect the economic and social interests of its members. The Committee does not indicate how many members should be associated in an organisation for it to be regarded as a trade union. It renders judgments concerning the compliance and non-compliance of domestic demands with Article 5 of the Charter regarding the number of members within a trade organisation.

Considering the reports filed by Member State authorities, the Committee claimed Polish legislation requiring a minimum of 10 members for a trade union formed by workers to be recognised, is in compliance with international standards.[1335] It is not compliant, however, with such standards, to make demands for the number of workers in a trade union to be 30,[1336] 50,[1337] 100,[1338] 500,[1339] 2000,[1340] or any other excessive number of employees.[1341]

Negative judgments were handed down in respect of the demands concerning the number of members in worker and employer organisations regarding membership in its hundreds compared to the overall number of those having the right to join a

---

1332. Conclusions XIII-1, pp. 129–130.
1333. Activity Report 2018, p. 36. Armenia, Latvia, Serbia.
1334. Section 17 of the Law on the Employers' Organisations lays down the documentation which is required to be submitted to the Ministry of Justice for the registration of employers' organisations. These include: two copies of the statute, the minutes of the founding assembly of the employers' organisation, a list of the founders, a document providing the address of the employers' organisation, and a bank receipt proving that the registration fee has been paid. Therefore, the Committee concludes that it has not been established that national law is applied in such a way that it does not impair the freedom to register a trade union. Conclusions 2014 (Moldova).
1335. Addendum to Conclusions XV-1, pp. 108–109.
1336. Conclusions 2004, vol. 2, p. 342. Conclusions 2010, vol. 2, p. 356 (Lithuania).
1337. Conclusions XIX, p. 152 (Latvia). The Committee concluded that the situation in Latvia is not in conformity with Art. 5 of The Charter, on the grounds that a minimum of fifty members or at least one-quarter of the employees of an undertaking are required to form a trade union, which is an excessive restriction on the right to organise. Conclusions XX-3 2014 (Latvia).
1338. Conclusions 2014 (Georgia).
1339. Conclusions III, p. 31 (Ireland).
1340. Conclusions XIII-3, p. 272 (Portugal).
1341. Conclusions 2010, vol. 1, p. 287 (Georgia).

trade union. This refers to the precondition for a trade organisation to have 10% membership,[1342] an employers' organisation 25% membership,[1343] and a federation of workers' organisations with 30% membership.[1344] As of 2015, the Committee notes that pursuant to section 4(1) and (2) of the Law on Employers' Organisations in Armenia, the number of employers required to form an employers' organisation is as follows: (1) at the national level – over half of the employers' organisations operating at the sectoral and territorial levels; (2) at sectoral level – half of the employers' organisations operating at the territorial level; (3) at territorial level – the majority of employers in a particular administrative territory consisting of employers' organisations from different sectors of that administrative territory. In Serbia, in order to form an employers' organisation, the founding members must employ no less than 5% of the total number of employees in a given branch of industry, group, sub-group, or line of business or in the territory of a given territorial unit (section 216 of the Labour Code). Therefore, the Committee concludes that the situation in Armenia and Serbia is not in conformity with Article 5 of the Charter, on the grounds that the minimum membership requirements set for forming employers' organisations are too high and constitute an obstacle to the freedom to organise.[1345] The Committee made one exception to this rule. Setting excessive minimum member counts as a condition of registering either workers' or employers' organisations does not breach Article 5 of the Charter standards, as a registering body cannot refuse registration based on an insufficient number of members.[1346] In reality, therefore, it is possible to set a required minimum number of members as a condition of registering a trade union, on the condition that it is not a requirement upon which the existence of the trade union depends.

The obligation of registering an organisation is in compliance with Article 5 of the Charter, as long as domestic labour law ensures such an organisation sufficient protection (administrative and legal) during the registration process.[1347] In accordance with the standards based on Article 5 of the Charter, fees upon registration are payable by workers' and employers' organisations on the condition the fees are not too exorbitant. The fees must also be validated objectively and cover the registration costs.[1348]

In some states' legal systems, a registered trade union may carry out certain functions for which they were created. These include negotiating collective labour agreements after the organisation attains representative status. It is possible to achieve such a status after concluding the following step concerning the granting of a licence to carry out negotiations on behalf of the workers in matters dealing with

1342. Conclusions XIV-1, pp. 654–655 (Portugal).
1343. Conclusions XIII-3, p. 272 (Portugal); Conclusions XIV-1, vol. 2, pp. 654–655; Conclusions XV-1, vol. 2, p. 469.
1344. Conclusions XIII-5, p. 172.
1345. Conclusions 2014 (Armenia, Serbia). *See*, the same situation in 2018.
1346. Conclusions XIV-1, pp. 654–655.
1347. Conclusions II, p. 184.
1348. Conclusions IV, pp. 40–41; Conclusions XII-2, p. 99; Conclusions XV-1, vol. 2, p. 629. Conclusions XX-3, 2014 (Ireland).

employment conditions and ages as well as reaching collective labour agreements.[1349] If a condition of registering a trade union is the requirement of a minimum of 1000 members as well as paying significant fees (IEP 20,000–IEP 60,000), the Committee recognises the above requirements as restrictions and deems such domestic collective labour law as violating international standards stipulated under Article 5 of the Charter.[1350] In Ukraine, the Committee notes that employers' organisations have to pay registration fees amounting to between 2.5 and 10 times the non-taxable minimum income.[1351] The Committee concludes that the amount of the fee, and the procedure for collection for state registration established by the Cabinet of Ministers of Ukraine, are not reasonable.[1352]

II. The Freedom of Trade Unions to Regulate Their Internal Organisational Affairs

220. Trade unions have broad autonomy. Interference in the autonomy of trade unions was a problem in the United Kingdom.[1353] The Committee usually regards the authorities of Member States that interfere in the internal organisational matters of trade unions as being in breach of Article 5 of the Charter.[1354] The Committee is of the opinion that a state which restricts the freedom of a union organisation in terms of its internal organisational structure determines its membership, disciplinary methods (of members) or denies membership is non-compliant with the standards stipulated under Article 5 of the Charter.[1355] The freedom of trade unions to regulate their internal organisational affairs may in certain cases collide with state regulations that deal with equal treatment, anti-discrimination and the protection of

1349. In 2016 the Committee concludes that it has not been established that the condition regarding the representativeness of trade unions are not detrimental to the right to organise in Georgia (Conclusions 2016, p. 294); Armenia (Conclusions 2016, pp. 288–289) to have access to workplaces to carry out their responsibilities and Ukraine (Conclusions 2016, p. 296). In the last country, the Committee concludes that it has been not established that the criteria used to determine representativeness are open to judicial review.

1350. Case of Ireland: Conclusions III, p. 31; Conclusions XIV-1, vol. 2, pp. 654–655; Conclusions 2004, vol. 1, p. 263.

1351. Conclusions 2010.

1352. Conclusions 2014 (Ukraine).

1353. Activity Report 2018, p. 36.

1354. Conclusions II, p. 23. Conclusions 2014 (Moldova) – trade unions not operating nationwide are required to belong to a national, sectoral or inter-sectoral trade union in order to acquire a legal personality.

1355. Case of United Kingdom: Conclusions XII-1, p. 115; Conclusions XIII-3, p. 109; Conclusions XIV-1, vol. 2, p. 797; Conclusions XV-1, vol. 2, p. 629; Conclusions XVII-1, vol. 1, p. 513. Conclusions XIX, p. 259. Conclusions 2014 (Georgia). The Committee notes in observations that the ILO Committee on the Applications of Conventions and Recommendations (ILO-CEACR) of 2012, regarding implementation of ILO Convention No. 98 by Georgia, refers to numerous allegations of employers' interference in internal trade union affairs, in private and public sectors, including the prohibition of collection of trade union dues, and harassment pressurising trade union members to leave their respective union. Therefore, the Committee concludes that it has not been established that trade unions are entitled to perform, and indeed perform, their activities without interference from authorities and/or employers.

rights. It may, therefore, seem that state intervention is justified in matters concerning the treatment of members by the authorities of the trade union, ensuring trade union members the right to sue in court against violations made which breach the obligatory regulations of such a union. Nonetheless, a trade union's autonomy stands against such interference. The institutions which are entitled to supervise the actions of a trade union are other overriding trade unions. Therefore, the regulations established by Member States should be treated as a threat to the autonomy of a trade union as should the interference into internal organisational affairs of a trade union.[1356] In its previous conclusions, the Committee concluded that the United Kingdom was not in conformity with Article 5 of the Charter.[1357] The grounds for these conclusions were that sections 15 and 65 of the Trade Union and Labour Relations Consolidation Act (TULRCA) represent unjustified incursions into the autonomy of trade unions. Section 15 of this Act severely restricts the grounds on which trade unions may lawfully discipline members, while Section 65 makes it unlawful for trade unions to indemnify an individual union member for a penalty imposed for an offence or contempt of court. As regards the previously found nonconformity, the Government again takes the view that these provisions do not breach Article 5 of the Charter and are necessary in a democratic society for the protection of the rights and freedoms of others. The Committee concludes that the situation in the United Kingdom is not in conformity with Article 5 of the Charter, on the grounds that legislation which makes it unlawful for a trade union to indemnify an individual union member for a penalty imposed for an offence or contempt of court, and which severely restricts the grounds on which a trade union may lawfully discipline members, represents an unjustified incursion into the autonomy of trade unions.[1358] In such legal systems where the actions of a trade union do not require the supervision of the lower trade union structures, the state may include legal guarantees for members of union organisations in its regulations. State legislation protecting members of trade unions from potential violations of their rights by the authorities of such unions is seen by the Committee as excessive and therefore disallows state interference in the internal organisational affairs of a trade union.[1359]

221. Trade unions have the right to specify the ways and means by which they elect their representatives. For this reason, it is deemed to be a contravention of Article 5 of the Charter if a state regulation stipulating the election of trade union officials is available only to those who are at that moment employed within the given workplace, sector or undertaking.[1360] On the other hand, it is seen as a violation of international standards for trade unions to introduce demands calling for the filling of positions associated with the representation of the trade union to be comprised of citizens of a given Member State only, or at least from a Member State chosen by the trade union,[1361] making such positions to be held by foreign nationals

1356. Conclusions XIII-1, pp. 137–138.
1357. Conclusions XVI-1 (2002), XVII-1 (2004), XVIII-1 (2006) (United Kingdom).
1358. XX-3 2014 (United Kingdom).
1359. Conclusions XVII-1, vol. 1, p. 512 (United Kingdom). Conclusions 2014 (Georgia).
1360. Case of Cyprus: Conclusions XII-2, p. 96; Conclusions XIII-1, p. 127.
1361. Case of Finland: the positions of trade union representatives within industry sectors were reserved for citizens of that country, or citizens of other Nordic countries. Conclusions XIV-1, vol. 1, p.

be dependent upon the period of their stay and employment within the given country,[1362] as well as specifying the limit of such positions which may be filled by foreign nationals.[1363] The Committee did not accept arguments made by the authorities of Member States which stated that filling such positions with foreign nationals would mean the citizens of other Member States would become acquainted with the labour relations of that given country in which they would be carrying out trade union functions. In countries where the above restrictions concerning the election process for foreigners are established by trade unions, such citizens of the EU have non-restricted rights to be able to carry out trade union functions.[1364]

222. Authorities of trade unions have the right to fully administer the property of the union organisation.[1365] This also applies to the ability to accumulate trade union funds. Granting employers leave not to deduct union fees from workers' wages (who are members of trade unions), may be regarded as restricting the income of trade organisations.[1366] Fines, however, do not have the same application when administered by competent authorities or administrative bodies, implemented when trade unions breach regulations concerning the organisation of strikes and protests. The Committee does not regard monetary penalties and asset liability imposed for illegal strikes that are organised by trade unions as a way of reducing the property of trade unions.[1367]

Member States have the right to establish some demands, which in a democratic fashion, have in mind the protection of rights and freedoms of others and serve as protection of public order. Based on this, the Committee decided that in accordance with Article 5 of the Charter, regulations are imposed by Member States, which demand trade unions to observe confidentiality requirements during elections of representative officials, to make resolutions in strike matters and manage collective actions as well as develop 'political funds' out of trade union budgets.[1368]

Trade unions have the freedom to start federations or confederations of unions as well as centralised international unions. The Committee regards the various forms of restricting this right by Member States as contravening Article 5 of the Charter.

The case of Cyprus is an example in which the authorities issued regulations restricting joining already existing trade union federations or confederations as well as indicated a criterion to which trade unions had to refer when selecting to start trade union federations or confederations.

The Committee was of the opinion that trade unions have the right to form superior trade union structures, which they deem appropriate. It also pointed out trade

215; Conclusions XV-1, pp. 198–199; Conclusions XX-3 2014 (Luxembourg). The national legislation does not enable trade unions to choose their candidates for joint works council elections freely, regardless of nationality. For that reason the Committee concludes that the situation is in not conformity with Art. 5 of the Charter.

1362. Conclusions VI, p. 30 (France). Conclusions 2010, vol. 2, p. 532 (Romania).

1363. *Ibid.*

1364. Conclusions XIV-1, p. 74 (Austria); Conclusions XIV-1, p. 492 (Luxembourg); Conclusions XIII-1, p. 131 (Denmark).

1365. Conclusions XIV-1, vol. 2, p. 796.

1366. Conclusions XIII-1, p. 137 (United Kingdom).

1367. Conclusions X-2, p. 68 (France); Conclusions XV-1, vol. 2, p. 629.

1368. Conclusions X-1, p. 68 (United Kingdom).

unions have the freedom of selecting the trade union federations or confederations to which they want to join. Authorities of Member States do not have the right to define the ways (trade, territorial or professional) by which certain trade unions form their organisational structures (federations or confederations).[1369]

III. The Right of Workers to Join a Trade Union or Elect Not To

223. Member States are obliged to issue regulations to establish the protection of workers' rights to elect whether they will or will not join a trade union.[1370] The Committee examines whether Member States fulfil such obligations. If such rights are sufficiently declared, the Committee sees to it that such regulations are in force.

A. The Right to Join a Trade Union

224. Workers have the right to join trade unions freely elected by themselves. A union organisation may not be included in this, as a worker must seek permission to join. Therefore, Article 5 of the Charter guarantees workers expecting to join a trade union the right to choose such an organisation – one of which they would like to be members. This provision is not to be treated as a standard ensuring such rights. Trade unions take advantage of autonomy, and thanks to it may regulate the intake of members. The right to join a trade union is therefore understood by the Committee as a right prohibiting Member States from establishing the conditions a person must fulfil before joining a given union. At first, the Committee was of the opinion that Member States could not make the above right dependent upon the workplace of a person wanting to join a particular trade union or to demand this person to be of particular employment.[1371] In subsequent supervisory cycles, the Committee came to the conclusion that authorities of Member States have the right to establish the rules upon which workers will base their Charter rights of having the freedom to select the trade union they wish to join. Determining the rules of workers' associations in trade unions by Member States cannot restrict the workers' rights to freely elect the trade union.[1372] Evaluating the legality of the actions of Member State authorities which have decided to determine through their labour law criteria (according to which trade unions may be formed) depends on the union plurality within the confines of the work, trade or profession. A necessary requirement to execute the right of an unconstrained choice of union organisation by a worker in a situation where the state has determined a set of criteria for forming trade unions (industrial, trade, territorial or professional) is the existence within the undertaking

1369. Case of Cyprus: Conclusions II, p. 184; Conclusions III, p. 31; Conclusions XII-2, p. 97; Conclusions XIII-1, pp. 129, 133.
1370. Case of Ireland: Conclusions XIII-1, p. 133; Conclusions XIII-3, p. 100.
1371. Conclusions XI-2, p. 74 (Cyprus).
1372. Conclusions XII-2, p. 97; Conclusions XIII-1, p. 129.

of at least two union organisations, from which workers may elect to join one. During the supervisory process, the Committee concluded Article 5 of the Charter is breached if the following occurs:

- the legislator approves the introduction of a clause into individual work relations disallowing a worker employed in the position of a foreman to enter into a trade union where his subordinates are also members;[1373]
- an advantageous position of higher earnings for workers who are not members of a given union organisation or a trade union[1374] or to a trade union which is authorised to negotiate collective labour agreements.[1375]

B. The Right Not to Join a Trade Union

225. Article 5 of the Charter does not prevent trade unions from forming agreements with employers concerning the sole employment of members of a given union organisation. However, during the first supervisory cycle, the Committee handed down the judgment that Article 5 of the Charter is a provision which also encompasses the 'negative' aspect of union freedom and protects workers from the obligation of joining a trade union. The Committee also stated that all cases of requirements for workers to form an association with trade unions which have been forced or imposed by the state labour regulations or negotiated by stakeholders should be regarded as non-compliant with the international standards stipulated under Article 5 of the Charter.[1376]

Despite the above unambiguous position of being against domestic collective labour law which makes employment dependent upon trade union pre-entry or post-entry closed shop, the Committee initially was unable to take up such a position on the compliance or non-compliance of Article 5 of the Charter of British statutes concerning trade unions and labour relations in 1974, containing the regulations that the termination of a work agreement by the employer with a worker is validated if the worker has failed to join a trade union.

The legal basis for the Committee's doubt was the appendix to Article 1 §2 ESC, a standard seeking the neutral interpretation of Article 1 §2 ESC, a provision which demanded that Member States protect the right of the worker to earn a living in an employment freely selected by him or her. In the appendix to the European Social

1373. Conclusions II, p. 23 (Sweden); Conclusions 2014 (Georgia). The Committee notes that the representative of Georgia in the Governmental Committee declared that the rights which can be limited in the employment contract refer to the 'interests and powers' of both parties (the employer and the employee) and not to fundamental rights, such as the right to organise. The Committee concludes that it has not been established that the situation in Georgia is not in conformity with Art. 5 of the Charter, on the grounds that the legal framework allowing restrictions on the right to organise that may be included in employment contracts is not detrimental to the right to organise.

1374. Case of United Kingdom: Conclusions XIII-3, p. 108; Conclusions XIV-1, p. 798; Conclusions XV-1, p. 631.

1375. Case of Denmark: Conclusions XII-1, p. 111; Conclusions XIII-1, p. 131; Conclusions XIII-3, p. 97; Conclusions XIV-1, p. 178; Conclusions XV-1, pp. 144–145; Conclusions XVII-1, vol. 1, p. 128.

1376. Conclusions I, p. 31.

Charter, an obligation was stipulated not to interpret Article 1 ESC as a prohibiting or as an allowing provision for the introduction of a union security clause.[1377] It should be pointed out that in the appendix to Article 5 of the Charter, a similar clause was also introduced. The Committee took the decision rendered by the European Tribunal of Human Rights in the case of Young, James and Webster into consideration during its seventh supervisory cycle.[1378] The Committee stated that the obligation of trade union membership always collides with the 'spirit' of Article 5 of the Charter. Placing the two aspects of trade union freedom (negative and positive) was heralded as a ruling made by the Committee in the following, eighth supervisory cycle. As for this ruling, the Committee did not refer to the 'spirit' of Article 5 of the Charter. It stated explicitly, as the language of this provision leaves no doubt that the negligence in terms of regulating the workers' right to make a free decision upon joining or refraining from joining a trade union or establishing any legal sanction in relation to this on the site of Member States should be regarded as violating the freedom of trade unions. There are not enough grounds to analyse the clause of 'closed shop' in the context of Article 5 of the Charter.[1379]

The British authorities reported on adjusting their regulations to the international standards established by the Committee, which allowed the Committee assembled on its ninth supervisory cycle to make a ruling stating the conformity of the British regulations with the provision of Article 5 of the Charter.[1380]

The Committee, however, reserved the right to change this verdict, should cases of employees who were made redundant due to the refusal to join trade unions be discovered. Because in the following tenth supervisory cycle, there were cases of employment termination, which were included in the category of not being in accordance with British labour law, the Committee postponed its ruling and demanded from British authorities additional information concerning the reasons for such terminations.[1381]

The case of the United Kingdom exemplifies how much the Committee pays attention to the scope of Article 5 of the Charter, a provision ensuring workers union freedom in both negative and positive aspects. Under the influence of the decisive position of the Committee British authorities altered their regulations and introduced a record of employers who terminate work agreements with their employees based on the fact they are or are not members of a trade union.[1382] The Committee has considered that the situation in Ireland is not in conformity with the Charter, on the grounds that although Article 40 of the Constitution guarantees freedom of association, pre-entry closed shops exist in Ireland.[1383] In its previous conclusion, the Committee noted from the report that the Irish courts have held that post-entry closed shops are unconstitutional when they apply to workers who were in their jobs

1377. *Ibid.*
1378. Conclusions VII, pp. 32–33.
1379. As above, p. 230.
1380. Conclusions IX-1, pp. 48–49.
1381. Conclusions X-1, p. 69.
1382. *Ibid.*, p. 79.
1383. Conclusions XIII-1 (1990–1991).

before the closed shop was agreed on or introduced.[1384] The courts have not, however, definitely ruled on the constitutionality of either pre-entry or post-entry closed shops when they apply to newly recruited employees since the courts have not had occasion to settle the issue. The Committee recalls that any form of legally compulsory trade unionism is incompatible with Article 5 of the Charter.[1385] The freedom guaranteed by Article 5 is the result of a choice, and such decisions must not be taken under the influence of constraints that rule out the exercise of this freedom.[1386] To secure this freedom, domestic law must clearly prohibit all pre-entry or post-entry closed-shop clauses and all union security clauses (automatic deduction from the wages of all workers, whether union members or not, to finance the trade union acting with the company). Clauses in collective agreements or legally authorised arrangements whereby jobs are reserved in practice for members of a specific trade union are in breach of the freedom guaranteed by Article 5 of the Charter.[1387] As of 2014, the Committee concludes that the Irish report does not provide any information on this point. As the situation in Ireland has not improved during the reference period, the Committee maintains its conclusion of non-conformity on the grounds that certain closed-shop practices are authorised by law.[1388]

From this moment on, the Committee has been of the solid view that 'negative' freedom of association may take advantage of the protection of Article 5 of the Charter. Such a lack of protection of workers not joining a trade union by a Member State cannot be seen as compliant with Article 5 of the Charter.[1389] Accepting the standpoint as an entry point into the interpretation of Article 5 of the Charter, the Committee views those Member States that have not implemented legislation protecting such workers as in contravention of international standards.

In particular, the Committee passed a decision of non-compliance with Article 5 of the Charter in respect of Danish labour law, which allows termination of a work agreement with a worker who has refused to join a given union organisation even though, when the work agreement was being signed, the worker knew that trade union membership was a crucial element for continuance of the employment.[1390] In 2018, the Committee concluded that the right not to associate with trade unions was not adequately protected in Iceland.[1391]

The Committee claims that making demands for a worker to join a particular trade union is a breach of Article 5 of the Charter. Not in accordance with international standards, based on the provision of Article 5 of the Charter, are cases whereby stakeholders were allowed to give their opinion in matters concerning the termination of employment of workers who had decided not to take up trade union

1384. Conclusions (2006).
1385. Conclusions III (1973), Statement of Interpretation of Art. 5.
1386. *Confederation of Swedish Enterprise v. Sweden*, Complaint No. 12/220, decision of 15 May 2003, §29.
1387. Conclusions XIX-3 (2010) Iceland.
1388. Conclusions 2014 (Ireland).
1389. Conclusions XI-1, p. 78.
1390. Conclusions XI-1, p. 77; Conclusions XII-1, p. 110; Conclusions XIII-1, p. 130; Conclusions XIV-1, vol. 1, p. 177; Conclusions XV-1, vol. 1, pp. 142–143.
1391. Activity Report 2018, p. 36.

membership.[1392] The history of closed-shop clauses has not come to its completion. During the last supervisory cycles, the Committee handed down a series of decisions about the non-compliance of domestic labour law regulations with Article 5 of the Charter in Denmark,[1393] France,[1394] the Netherlands,[1395] Iceland,[1396] Ireland,[1397] and Sweden[1398] due to their inclusion of such a clause.

In the case of France, the Committee handed down a decision about the non-compliance of domestic labour law regulations with international standards for implementing forbidden practices of employing members of the CGT trade union in the printing industry.[1399]

Other cases of violating the 'negative' trade union freedom are evident where the right to financial benefits, if there is a loss of employment (unemployment benefits), is dependent upon whether the worker was a trade union member or not,[1400] when there are obligatory membership limits established for a given trade organisation,[1401] and when a trade union is authorised to act as an employment agency.[1402] In this last situation, the closed-shop clause is a basis for one of the major collective complaints, which was filed in 2002 by the Workers Confederation to the Committee against Sweden.[1403]

After conducting a public hearing on 31 March 2003 the Committee handed down a decision against Sweden for not applying the international standards of Article 5 of the Charter, for approving stakeholder practices that allow for pre-entry closed-shop clauses in collective work agreements. On the basis of this decision of the Committee, the Committee of Ministers on 26 September 2003 passed the resolution[1404] confirming Sweden's non-compliant behaviour with the international standards.

The obligation for workers who are not associated with an organisation to contribute membership fee payments equal to those paid by actual members is also non-compliant with Article 5 of the Charter. The Committee regards this obligation as a substitute for the closed-shop clause.[1405] A trade union, however, does have the right

1392. Conclusions XI-1, pp. 78, 133; Conclusions XIII-3, pp. 97, 99, 107; Conclusions XV-1, pp. 240–241, 325–326, 413, Addendum to Conclusions XV-1, p. 23. Conclusions 2010, vol. 1, p. 259 (France).
1393. Conclusions XVII-1, vol. 1, p. 128.
1394. In the book sector, Conclusions 2006, vol. 1, p. 303. Conclusions 2010, vol. 1, p. 259.
1395. Conclusions XVII-1, vol. 2, p. 314.
1396. Conclusions XIX, p. 143. Conclusions XX-3 2014 (Iceland).
1397. Conclusions 2004, vol. 1, p. 263; Conclusions 2006, vol. 1, p. 368.
1398. Conclusions 2002, p. 233; Conclusions 2004, vol. 2, p. 564; Conclusions 2006, vol. 2, p. 863.
1399. Conclusions XIII-1, p. 131; Conclusions XIII-3, pp. 97–98; Conclusions 2002, p. 31; Conclusions 2004, vol. 1, p. 217.
1400. Conclusions XI-1, p. 78.
1401. Case of Belgium: Conclusions XIII-2, p. 268; Conclusions XIV-1, vol. 1, p. 106; Conclusions XV-1, vol. 1, p. 74.
1402. Case of Sweden: Conclusions XIII-3, p. 107; Conclusions XIV-1, vol. 2, pp. 730 et seq.; Conclusions XVI-1, vol. 2, p. 559.
1403. Complaint No. 12/2002: *Confederation of Swedish Enterprise v. Sweden*. List of registered collective complaints (as from 1 Jan. 2005), European Social Charter. *Collected Texts* 513 (Council of Europe Publishing, 5th ed., 2005).
1404. ResChS (2003) 1, as above.
1405. Conclusions 2002, p. 131 (Romania).

to charge fees from workers who are not members of a trade organisation for services rendered, such as monitoring whether employers are making wage payments in accordance with the collective agreement.[1406]

IV. The Freedom to Carry Out Trade Union Activities

226. Workers join trade unions in order to have their economic and market interests represented and protected. A workers' organisation which has the features of a trade union should be able to carry out such functions. The freedom of trade union activities requires the utility of the right to negotiate collective labour agreements which determine working conditions and wages for its members and non-members; to carry out trade union activities within the territory of the workplace; and to hold meetings. Guaranteeing the right of association and the right to freely carry out trade union activities by statute are provisions forbidding employers from discriminating against workers who are trade union members, and are engaged in trade union activities as well as provisions which forbid employers from ordering workers to carry out duties that are not being completed by other employees who are on strike. These issues are connected with the rights which are ensured by Article 6 of the Charter. The Committee decided to deal with these issues during the supervisory cycle which monitored compliance with Article 5 of the Charter. It concluded that the right of trade unions to negotiate in collective labour agreements is a crucial basis for ensuring trade union freedom regulated by Article 5 of the Charter.

A. Negotiating Collective Labour Agreements

227. The Committee emphasises that the right of workers to organise in trade unions is not a complete right in itself. Workers form trade unions or join already existing ones because they want their interests to be protected and have available negotiators ready to talk terms about the collective labour agreements, work and wage conditions.[1407] In such circumstances where domestic labour law regulations restrict the rights of trade organisations to negotiate collective labour agreements, it may be deduced that the fundamental basis of labour law is being violated, as there is a breach of the freedom to join a trade union.[1408] The interconnection between collective labour law foundations and Article 5 of the Charter should be obvious. In order to comply with international standards, which stipulate the limits of trade unions' freedom, under Article 5 of the Charter, a necessary requirement of conducting dialogue with stakeholders has to be met (as is stipulated under Article 6 §2 of the Charter).[1409] Member States have the right to make demands, on which the

1406. Complaint No. 12/2002, Collective complaints, *supra*.
1407. Conclusions I, p. 31.
1408. Conclusions IV, p. 39; Addendum to Conclusions XI-2, p. 19 (the Netherlands).
1409. Conclusions VI, p. 36.

negotiating rights (collective labour agreements) of a trade union depend.[1410] The Committee viewed the issuing of a licence by a state for a trade union to be able to carry out negotiating activities (in collective labour agreements) only if it fulfils a minimum membership requirement (at least 500 or 1,000 members), as non-compliant with the right of trade union freedom.[1411]

The same view was appropriated for the increase of administration fees payable for a licence (IEP 20,000–IEP 60,000)[1412] or the payment of an amount that is dependent upon the number of members (IEP 5,000 for 20,000 members; IEP 15,000 for more than 39,000 members).[1413] The Irish authorities attempted to protect their domestic regulations. They pointed out that such high demands are implemented to increase a trade union's position when acting prior to a collective work agreement being signed. The authorities argued that due to the increased number of existing trade unions, some organisations were too weak and therefore unable to evoke sufficient pressure during work and wage conditions as well as in collective labour agreements negotiations. The Committee did not accept such arguments. It claimed that trade union pluralism was a typical phenomenon of the Irish union movement.

228. An increased number of trade unions does not weaken unions as long as they continue to have the right to develop horizontal or vertical structures.[1414] Regional, national, federal and confederate trade unions, as well as trade unions representing the interests of the undertakings themselves, constitute unions of trade unions. The Committee was not against the introduction of licences for negotiating purposes and establishing fees for administrative costs and services. It considers standards of collective labour relations are being complied with if every trade organisation seeking a negotiating licence actually receives one unless public security is against it (*l'ordre public*). Administrative fees taken from trade organisations seeking permission to undertake negotiating activities involving employers and establishing collective labour agreements are permissible if they cover the costs involved in issuing the licence.[1415] The Committee is of the view that negotiating licences should be issued automatically to all trade unions. Depriving a trade union of a licence for negotiating purposes in collective labour agreements because domestic labour regulations which demand confidentiality during given resolutions

---

1410. According to Law No. 62/2011 on social dialogue (Law on Social Dialogue), in companies with no representative trade unions, collective bargaining shall be conducted as follows: (1) if there is a trade union at company level affiliated to a representative sectoral federation, the negotiations will be carried out by the federation to which the existing trade union belongs, together with the elected representatives of the employees; (2) if there is no trade union, or the trade union is not affiliated to a representative federation, the collective bargaining and the workers' representation will be carried out by representatives of the employees (Art. 135, Law on Social Dialogue). The Committee concludes that the situation in Romania is not in conformity with Art. 5 of the Charter, on the grounds that the right of the non-representative trade unions to exercise key trade union prerogatives (to carry on the negotiations) is restricted. Conclusions 2014 (Romania).
1411. Conclusions III, p. 30 (Ireland).
1412. *Ibid.*
1413. Conclusions II, p. 22 (Ireland).
1414. Conclusions VII, p. 31; Addendum to Conclusions XIII-3, p. 100.
1415. Conclusions IV, p. 39.

are not met, and this is in breach of Article 5 of the Charter.[1416] A lack of negotiating rights in collective labour agreements undermines the existence of a trade union. For this reason, the Committee decided that the Irish labour law regulations which only granted negotiating licences to trade unions if there was disclosure concerning the number of members, while eliminating those unions having less than the required amount, was in breach of Article 5 of the Charter.[1417] The same was applied to the increase of administrative fees for trade unions with regard to the number of members. The Committee is of the view that the introduction of an obligatory negotiating licence to reach collective labour agreements, and collecting administrative fees for issuing permission to enable social dialogue (which is one of the stakeholders' responsibilities), is superfluous. It violates the basis of the freedom to associate in trade unions. It is therefore in contravention to Article 5 of the Charter.[1418]

Contravening to Article 5 of the Charter was the Danish regulation registering sea vessels, forbidding maritime trade unions to negotiate work and wage conditions for the workers who were neither citizens of Denmark nor permanently residing in Denmark. The Committee decided the exclusion of such workers who are members of the trade union, from the scope of collective labour relations creates a serious violation of the right to associate as it deprives trade unions of the right to represent and protect the interests of their members.[1419]

The Committee recognised British labour regulations, which permitted employers to offer advantageous employment conditions for workers who would not form trade unions or join already existing ones, as non-compliant with union freedom.[1420] An identical view was appropriated to restrictions imposed on stakeholders who sought arbitrary processes during collective labour disputes.

According to collective labour laws in Malta, a minister representing one of the two stakeholders in leading the negotiating process had the right to present before the industrial tribunal dispute issues. These dispute issues were binding in their nature, forbidding stakeholders from negotiating this problem for a year.[1421]

229. The Committee's position with regard to such restrictions being placed on stakeholders during negotiating collective labour agreements and leading collective labour disputes is in conflict with competent trade organisations and undermines the freedom of association for workers in a trade union. They are in breach of Article 5 of the Charter. This decision was handed down during the Committee's supervision over the compliance of Member States of Articles 6 §2 and 3 of the Charter. This indicates a dependency between those regulations and Article 5 of the Charter.

1416. Case of Ireland: Conclusions XIII-1, p. 133; Conclusions XIII-3, p. 100.
1417. Conclusions IV, p. 40.
1418. Addendum to Conclusions XI-2, p. 19; Conclusions XIII-3, p. 100; Conclusions XIV-1, p. 23; Addendum to Conclusions XV-1, vol. 1, p. 14.
1419. Conclusions XII-1, p. 119; Conclusions XIII-1, p. 131; Conclusions XIV-1, pp. 177–178. Conclusions XX-3 (Denmark).
1420. Conclusions XIII-3, pp. 108–109; Conclusions XIV-1, vol. 2, p. 798; Conclusions XV-1, vol. 2, pp. 630–631.
1421. Conclusions XIII-2, p. 270; Conclusions XIII-3, p. 102; Conclusions XV-1, vol. 1. p. 402.

The Committee also declared that restrictions placed on one stakeholder during collective negotiations by Member States, are to be considered as violating trade union freedom.

In the above-mentioned decisions, it is not possible however to conclude that there is non-compliance of domestic collective labour regulations with Article 5 of the Charter, which creates criteria for establishing representative status of a trade union. During the sixth supervisory cycle, the Committee decided that Member States introduce objective criteria for evaluating whether their trade organisation may be regarded as a representative one, which cannot be seen as a breach of Article 5 of the Charter.[1422] Representative status, according to the Committee, is dependent upon fulfilling the required and verifiable criteria. It obliged the authorities of Member States to present such criteria.[1423] During the individual supervisory cycles, it examined whether the criteria were known earlier by the trade organisation, whether they were subject to control of an independent body or whether such control was systematically carried out.[1424] The Committee aspired to establish whether a trade union, which does not have representative status, was not devoid of certain competencies with regard to the interests and protection of rights of its members.[1425]

B. Carrying Out Trade Union Activities in the Territory of the Workplace

230. A necessary requirement for carrying out statutory activities by a trade union is the possibility to enter the grounds of the undertaking, employing members of the given trade organisations.

Examining a report filed by German authorities during the eleventh supervisory cycle, the Committee claimed trade unionists who were no longer employed by the employer (who employed other members of the trade union) had no right to enter the grounds of the plant.[1426] The Committee demanded clarification from the German authorities. In the following supervisory cycle the information was presented indicating that the trade unionists took advantage of a restricting right to enter the

1422. Conclusions VI, p. 29.
1423. The Committee concludes that the situation in Portugal is not in conformity with Art. 5 of the Charter, on the grounds that the criteria used to determine representativeness are not adequate. Conclusions 2014 (Portugal). In its previous conclusion, following an individual observation of the ILO Committee of Experts on the Application of Conventions and Recommendations (CEACR), the Committee asked whether criteria of representativeness or other criteria were used to create a distinction between trade unions (Conclusions 2010). In reply, the Portuguese government indicated that: (1) the President of the Economic and Social Council had taken the initiative of launching a general discussion on the composition of the Economic and Social Council, with the cooperation of members; (2) it was impossible to forecast the outcome of these discussions or the proposals and recommendations which the President might make. Given such information, as of 2014 the Committee concludes that the criteria used to determine representativeness are not adequate (Conclusions 2014).
1424. Conclusions XIV-1, vol. 1, p. 43; Conclusions XV-1, vol. 1, p. 40 (Austria); p. 79 (Belgium); p. 144 (Denmark); p. 198 (Finland); pp. 247–248 (France).
1425. Conclusions XV-1, vol. 1, p. 79 (Belgium); p. 144 (Denmark); p. 248 (France).
1426. Conclusions XI-2, pp. 75, 98.

grounds of the plant, in which other members were employed. The ruling from 1972 *Betriebsverfassungsgesetz* mentions cases in which trade unionists were granted permission to enter the grounds of a workplace where at least one member of the given trade union is an employee. A taxing amount of such cases does not encompass the issues, in which trade unions are most interested in, i.e., the issue of recruiting non-member workers into the trade organisation and the issues of information and advice. In those places of work where there are no members of a trade union employed, unionists would be able to apply for the right of entry. The Constitutional Tribunal in the above-mentioned decision made the above rights dependent upon coming into force in appropriate legal regulations. It did not exclude that the above rights may be accepted in the future exclusively for trade unions with representative status.[1427]

Because this cited Act from 1972 was not applicable to workplaces employing less than five workers, to minority religious organisations and to charitable institutions, the Committee demanded information from the German authorities regarding the practices of the regulations concerning trade unionists' access to work grounds. German authorities refused to provide such information, as the above matter could not be considered based on Article 5 of the Charter. The Committee declared and justified a different approach for considering this issue. It concluded that Article 5 of the Charter ensures workers the right to form trade unions and to join existing trade organisations, as well as giving them the right to refrain from participating in union activities. This cited provision also encompasses trade unions to carry out their statutory requirements and tasks. Allowing trade unionists to enter the grounds of a workplace, a workplace employing the trade union members and those who are not is an important point from the point of protecting the economic and social interests of the workers.[1428] Voicing its opinion about access for trade unionists to workplace grounds the Committee concluded that in performing this right trade union activists should take into consideration the employers' rights and interests such as the necessity to keep a fully functioning workplace, abide by security and health regulations in the workplace and not to disclose information regarded as confidential.[1429]

The Committee incorporated the judgment of the Federal German Labour Court handing down a decision on 25 March 1992, that the representatives of 'representative' trade unions take advantage of the right to enter the grounds of that workplace. Whether the trade union is 'represented' within the workplace is a deciding factor if in the given workplace there should be at least one member of the trade organisation that is employed within that workplace. Basing its argument on this, the Committee decided that German labour law is responsible for the standards stipulated under Article 5 of the Charter and demanded information from German authorities concerning the practices of applying the Act of 1972.[1430]

1427. Conclusions XII-2, p. 98.
1428. As above. Conclusions XIX, p. 217 (Spain).
1429. *Ibid.*
1430. Conclusions XIII-4, pp. 355–356; Addendum to Conclusions XV-1, p. 22.

231. The problem of allowing access to trade unionists onto workplace territory and having access to the workers is an issue which authorities of Member States should explain in their annual reports presented before the Committee dealing with the fulfilment of the obligations stipulated under Article 5 of the Charter.[1431] Only on two occasions (the fourteenth and fifteenth supervisory cycles) did the Committee demand information from Member States concerning the right of trade unionists to have access to the grounds of the workplace.[1432] In its Conclusions 2010, the Committee asked whether trade union representatives have access to workplaces to carry out their union responsibilities and whether union members are entitled to hold meetings in the workplace.[1433] The report presented by the Armenian government in 2015 does not provide answers in this respect. The Committee therefore concludes that the situation is not in conformity with the Charter on the grounds that it has not been established that the trade union representatives have access to workplaces in order to carry out their responsibilities.[1434]

In a strict connection with the right of trade union representatives to enter the grounds of the workplace is the right to organise meeting by the trade union with worker and member participation. Despite the information provided by the authorities of Member States, the Committee did not conclude there were violations of international standards based on Article 5 of the Charter and instead had doubts about the possibility of police officers making use of this right[1435] and about the rights of state administrative bodies to suspend the availability of this right.[1436] The Committee did not further occupy itself with the details of situations where trade unions had the right to organise meetings on the grounds of a workplace.

It rendered one opinion concerning the fulfilment of obligations by Finland stipulated under Article 5 of the Charter. It exemplified how Finnish authorities demand employers employing at least ten workers to make available (entailing no costs) an area within the workplace for purposes of holding trade union meetings after working hours.[1437]

V. Legal Guarantees Allowing Workers to Freely Associate in Trade Unions

A. *Prohibiting Discrimination of Workers Based on Their Trade Union Membership and Participation in Trade Union Activities*

232. Article 5 of the Charter is interpreted by the Committee as a standard obliging Member States to ensure legal protection against employer discrimination against workers based on trade union membership and/or participation in trade

1431. Question D, Form for the Reports Submitted in Pursuance of the Revised European Social Charter (1996), European Social Charter. *Collected Texts*, 325 (Council of Europe Publishing, 5th ed., 2005).
1432. Conclusions XIV-1, pp. 295–296; Conclusions XV-1.
1433. Conclusions 2010 (Armenia).
1434. Conclusions 2014 (Armenia).
1435. Case of Cyprus; Conclusions X-2, p. 67; Conclusions XI-2, p. 74.
1436. Conclusions III, p. 30 (Austria).
1437. Conclusions XIV-1, p. vol. 1, p. 215.

union activities. Such a prohibition of discrimination is regarded by the Committee as an assurance for workers to freely associate in trade unions, and the scope of this protection should be applied generally. Austria's labour laws therefore cannot be seen as compliant with the international standards, as they exclude workers in small workplaces where employment is less than five workers from such protection.[1438] Issuing regulations forbidding employers to discriminate against workers for reasons of trade union membership is not a valid reason for concluding compliance with domestic labour laws of Member States with international standards.[1439] As of 2014, the Committee concluded that the national legislation in Ireland does not protect all workers against dismissal on grounds of membership of trade unions or involvement in trade union activity.[1440] The Committee notes from the European Industrial Relations Observatory On-Line (Ireland: Industrial Relations Profile) that one problem facing trade unions is that the growth in employment legislation providing rights for individual employees has coincided with a decline in union density, which was 34% in 2009. Trade unions are not present in many workplaces, especially not in the private sector. That same source indicates that procedures introduced in the Industrial Relations Act 2001–2004 have meant that trade unions could seek legally binding determinations of pay and terms and conditions of employment through the Labour Court – in the event that the voluntary process failed – for members in companies that do not recognise a trade union for the purposes of any collective bargaining process. However, this legislation was rendered redundant by the Irish Supreme Court.[1441] The Committee concludes that the situation in Ireland is not in conformity with Article 5 of the Charter, on the grounds that the national legislation does not protect all workers against dismissal on grounds of membership of a trade union or involvement in trade union activities. In 2016, the Committee concluded that it has not been established that domestic labour law in Ukraine provides effective sanctions and remedies in case of discrimination and reprisals based on trade union membership and its activities and in particular it has been established that domestic labour law provides for compensation that is adequate and proportionate to the harm suffered by the victim.[1442] Lack of adequate protection was detected in 2016 in Armenia. The Committee noted that the report did not indicate whether there is any protection against harmful consequences of discrimination for employees who are trade union members or engage in trade union activities, nor whether the compensation provided for that is sufficient.[1443]

233. In the case of Georgia, the Committee notes from another source (the ITUC Survey of Violations of Trade-Union Rights) that: (1) owners of privatised hospitals and policlinics have refused to negotiate with unions, and actively intimidate any

1438. Addendum to Conclusions XV-1, pp. 14–15.
1439. The Committee concluded that the situation in Ireland is not in conformity with Art. 5 of RESC due to the fact that national legislation does not protect all the workers against dismissal on the grounds of membership of a trade union or involvement in trade union activities. Conclusions 2006, vol. 1, p. 368.
1440. Conclusions 2014 (Ireland).
1441. Conclusions 2014 (Ireland).
1442. Conclusions 2016, pp. 295–296.
1443. Conclusions 2016, pp. 289–290.

staff cooperating with trade unionism. Many medical workers have withdrawn from trade unions because of the fear of dismissal; 45% of trade union organisations have ceased to exist, and membership has fallen by 41%; (2) union members who had recently organised unions at the municipal level were forced to sign forms resigning from the union, under threat of dismissal, resulting in the loss of hundreds of members. Fourteen cities and district-level organisations of the Public Servants Union ceased to exist – amounting to the loss of 2,350 members; (3) although anti-union discrimination is prohibited under Georgian legislation, the courts do not apply this legislation. Article 23 of the Trade Union Act, which states that employers can dismiss employees elected as chairpersons of trade union organisations only with the consent of the union, is ignored in practice. For these reasons, the Committee concludes that the protection against discrimination based on trade union membership in the context of recruitment and dismissal is insufficient.[1444] In the case of Ukraine, the Committee concludes that it has not been established that domestic law provides effective sanctions and remedies in cases of discrimination and reprisals based on trade union membership and activities.[1445] The Committee asks whether such prohibited behaviour by an employer under Article 5 of the Charter, should entail a penalty. The Committee is interested in whether discriminatory behaviour of employers violating such workers' rights has met with a response or whether the injured worker received compensation. It heightens the fact that the authorities of Member States which have ratified Article 5 of the Charter, are obliged to undertake measures to reinstate the initial rights or ensure compensation for the injured discriminated against workers.[1446] According to the Committee, Member States should ensure compensation equal to the amount of remuneration to workers who are discriminated against due to their trade union membership or participation, from the period of terminating the work agreement until the labour court renders a judgment about the reinstatement of the worker to his/her previous position. Because Bulgarian and Irish labour law regulations do not ensure legal protection against such discrimination, the Committee decided that these countries do not fulfil the obligations under Article 5 of the Charter.[1447] As of 2014, the Committee concludes that Azerbaijan, Bulgaria, the Republic of Moldova and Ukraine are not in conformity with Article 5 of the Charter, on the grounds that either it has not been established that there is adequate and proportionate compensation for the harm suffered by a worker discriminated against for having joined a trade union,[1448] or the legislation does not provide for adequate compensation suffered by the victims of discriminatory dismissal based on involvement in trade union activities.[1449] Employers do not have the right to demand lists of members from trade unions. In cases of a trade union providing an employer with such a list or when an employer gains such information, the Committee demands assurances from the authorities of Member States that the workers who were found on that list did not experience

1444. Conclusions 2014 (Georgia).
1445. Conclusions 2014 (Ukraine).
1446. Case of Austria: Conclusions XX-2, p. 101; Conclusions XIII-2, p. 271; Conclusions XV-1, vol. 1, p. 39.
1447. Conclusions 2004, vol. 1, pp. 34, 37–38 (Bulgaria); p. 263 (Ireland).
1448. Conclusions 2014 (Azerbaijan, the Republic of Moldova, Ukraine).
1449. Conclusions 2014 (Bulgaria).

repressive actions by their employers.[1450] Examining the Finnish reports, the Committee questioned whether there was a case of discrimination in the carried-out actions that were beyond labour law regulations.

The report showed that in Finland, a council worker for a period of carrying out the responsibilities of a trade union representative within the workplace had his/her right to take part in council elections suspended. Taking into consideration the potential conflict of interests, the Committee was convinced this prohibition of being able to carry out both functions is not in accordance with Article 5 of the Charter.[1451]

Article 5 of the Charter ensures the protection of the rights of workers who are members and non-members of trade unions. The provision obliges Member States to issue appropriate regulations and carry out suitable measures in an attempt to protect workers who have not joined a trade union or those who joined a trade organisation without having representative status, against discrimination.[1452]

B. *Prohibition of Allocating Workers Duties, Which Are Not Being Fulfilled by Workers Participating in a Legal Strike Action*

234. The compliance of domestic collective labour regulations with international standards is monitored by the Committee when analysing the reports concerning the fulfilment of obligations stipulated under Articles 5 and 6 of the Charter. In situations of collective action carried out by stakeholders, the point of reference for establishing legislation and practices is Article 6 §4 of the Charter. The Committee also indicated the importance of obligation stipulated under Articles 5 and 6 of the Charter. Workers form trade unions and join such unions to have their economic and social interests protected. A strike is a last resort option used to protect interests regulated by collective labour law. Similarly, cases of restricting trade union rights to carry out negotiations in achieving collective labour agreements as well as employers undertaking actions restricting the after-effects of a strike are also treated by the Committee as non-compliant with the trade union freedoms protected under Article 5 of the Charter.

These conclusions were appropriated in the case of Germany, which allowed council employers to employ council clerks to carry out duties which were not being fulfilled by workers taking part in a legal strike (including manual labour workers) Employing ‘strike-breaker’ clerks, council employers limit trade union freedom for the workers who are striking. An additional circumstance in support of disallowing employer interference in the workers’ right to associate in trade unions was that the council clerks and those workers who were legally striking were all members of the same trade union.[1453] Because the right to employ ‘strike-breakers’ is in accordance

1450. Conclusions XIII-1, p. 136 (Great Britain); Case of France: Conclusions XIV-1, vol. 1, pp. 254–255; Conclusions XV-1, vol. 1, p. 243.
1451. Conclusions XX-1, pp. 197–198.
1452. Addendum to Conclusions XI-2, p. 19 (Ireland); Conclusions XIV-1, vol. 1, p. 414 Conclusions 2010, vol. 1, p. 155 (Belgium), p. 181 (Bulgaria), vol. 2, p. 390 (Malta), p. 420 (Moldova).
1453. Conclusions XII-2, p. 99.

with trade union freedom in Germany according to its Constitutional Tribunal, the Committee adjourned its judgment. In the following supervisory cycle, it took note of the decision handed down by the German Constitutional Tribunal, which claimed non-compliance of the practices not regulated by the existing legislation with constitutional principles of trade union freedoms.[1454]

Because this case at first instance concerns the principles of undertaking collective actions by trade unions, especially in reference to organising strikes, the Committee concluded that such instances would be analysed during the supervisory processes, according to Article 6 §4 of the Charter and its compliance by Member States.

VI. Union Freedom and the Right to Associate in Trade Unions for Certain Categories of Worker

235. The Committee pays particular attention to the way domestic labour laws are regulated as well as the practices used when attempting to administer the international standards established by Article 5 of the Charter to the following workers: civil servants, police officers, professional soldiers and foreigners who are citizens of a Member State. As mentioned earlier, Article 5 of the Charter creates a legal basis for restricting trade union freedoms for two categories of the employed: police officers and professional militia. In the latter category, Article 5 of the Charter even allows the complete exclusion of the right to associate with employers of the armed forces. The large number of judgments handed down by the Committee in such matters is indicative of the fact that Member States are expanding their restrictions and excluding trade union freedoms which may be regulated by domestic collective labour laws as different categories of employment, such as civil servants and migrant workers (citizens of Member States parties to the Charter)

A. *Trade Union Freedom for Civil Servants*

236. With the exception of police officers and professional military personnel, the remainder of the employment categories can take advantage of unrestricted rights of association in trade unions.[1455] These rights are also applicable to civil servants.[1456] The Committee is of the view that the various restrictions imposed on the freedom of trade unions in the case of civil servants are in breach of Article 5 of the Charter. This view related particularly to Member State demands from civil servants to form or join trade organisations, which were compiled strictly of employers in the civil sector.[1457] Because of the unique nature of the employers (state organisational units) and the nature of the employment duties (collecting information, preparing and handing down decisions to state authorities and administrative

1454. Conclusions XIII-2, p. 269.
1455. Conclusions I, p. 31.
1456. Conclusions II, p. 184.
1457. *Ibid.*

bodies), the Committee permitted the implementation of a few restrictions based on Article 31 §1 ESC, on the trade union freedom of civil servants. Of particular note is the unique nature of the decision rendered in the case of the UK Government Communications Headquarters (GCHQ) in Cheltenham.

The Committee received information that British authorities deprived more than 7000 civil servants working in connection with a military centre of communication, of the right to association in trade unions.[1458] From the details presented by the UK British authorities, it may be deduced the given centre of communication was carrying out duties concerning public security.

The Committee agreed, citing Article 31 §1 ESC, that such restrictions on the right to form and join trade unions were permissible in such particular cases. It adjourned its decision.[1459] UK authorities permitted the workers in question to form a staff federation, which was registered as a trade union whose members were civil servants and employees of GCHQ. The federation was authorised to negotiate the conditions and wages of its members. Taking into consideration the above circumstances as well as the fact that these employees did not have the obligation to join a trade union, the Committee concluded that restrictions implemented on this category of workers were not a violation of Article 31 §1 of the Charter.[1460] It claimed that there was a lack of legal grounds to conclude the domestic labour laws were non-compliant with Article 5 of the Charter. The Charter does not permit Member States to exclude or limit trade union freedoms of all civil servants. It also allows for the exclusion of rights of association for judges and civil servants in managerial positions.[1461] It is against depriving civil servants of their rights to take part in trade union functions.[1462] Because of the need to protect public order and national security within democratic societies, the Committee accepted the restrictions on trade union freedoms for some civil servants, especially those who are part of the authority and administrative hierarchy in political decision-making positions.[1463] The only basis for allowing such restrictions and depriving certain civil servants of their right to organise are Article 31 §1 ESC and Article E §1 RESC.

B. The Right of Police Officers to Organise

237. Member States are capable of introducing restrictions for police officers and their right to organise in trade unions. The restrictions established by the members cannot be too severe. The statement by the Committee that a Member State completely forbids policemen to form trade unions and join such trade unions justifies the Committee's negative conclusion.[1464] Member States cannot, however,

1458. Conclusions IX-1, p. 49.
1459. Conclusions X-1, pp. 68–69.
1460. As above, p. 80.
1461. Conclusions 2004, vol. 2, pp. 455–456 (Romania).
1462. Conclusions XVII-1, vol. 2, pp. 376, 378 (Poland).
1463. The restrictions on the right to organise of senior civil servants and official holding management positions or high public office cannot be too general. Conclusions 2006, vol. 2, p. 744.
1464. Activity Report 2018, p. 36, Armenia, Azerbaijan, the Czech Republic, Georgia and the Republic of Moldova.

deprive police officers of the right to form trade unions or to become members.[1465] Depriving police officers of their right to organise is a breach of Article 5 of the Charter.[1466] The Committee supervises Member States and whether they are compliant with Article 5 of the Charter in terms of allowing police officers to organise. In the second supervisory cycle, the Committee decided that domestic labour laws which forbid the police to form their own trade unions or forbid the police to join organisations of their own choosing, are not in accordance with Article 5 of the Charter. A breach of Article 5 by domestic labour laws is also apparent when such regulations force police officers to join trade unions that are chosen by the state.[1467] This is a violation of trade union freedom. The above approach by the Committee was undertaken in subsequent supervisory cycles.[1468] Limitations on trade union freedom are not reduced even when those trade unions which are chosen by the state for police officers to join have the right to negotiate the work and wage conditions of the workers. The Committee is of the opinion that the assurance of the chosen trade union rights is not determined simply because it has the power to negotiate collective labour agreements.[1469] In the case of police officers, restricting trade union freedoms may cause domestic labour legislation to include regulations for trade organisations formed by the police only to have other police officers as members.[1470] The above trade union freedom limitations are caused by the particular duties police officers are obliged to carry out. The limitations placed on the police and their right to associate in trade unions is the restriction on associating in national and international trade unions (federations and confederations).[1471] Member States have the right to stop police trade unions from joining other trade organisation structures which have other workers as members.[1472] The Committee accepted Member State regulations which allowed police officers to form and join professional associations and federations only accepting police officers as members rather than a trade union.[1473] A necessary requirement for fulfilling the obligations under Article 5 of the Charter is for the police to form trade unions. Appointing representatives authorised to represent the interests of police officers (even according to democratic procedures), was considered by the Committee as non-compliant with international standards. The community of police officers does not fulfil legal expectations simply by being regarded as a professional association or federation.[1474] A necessary condition for the existence of an association is the voluntariness with which one can

1465. Conclusions I, p. 31.
1466. Conclusions II, p. 22; Conclusions III, p. 30. Conclusions 2010, vol. 1, p. 61 (Czech Republic).
1467. Conclusions II, p. 22.
1468. Conclusions III, p. 30; Conclusions XII-2, p. 100 (Malta); Conclusions XIII-2, p. 268 (Belgium). Conclusions 2010, vol. 2, p. 390 (Malta).
1469. Conclusions II, p. 22.
1470. Conclusions X-2, pp. 68–69; Conclusions XIII-3, p. 106 (Spain).
1471. Conclusions VIII, p. 80 (Italy); Conclusions IX-1, p. 49 (United Kingdom); Conclusions XIII-3, p. 106 (Spain), Conclusions 2006, vol. 2, p. 744 (Romania). Conclusions XX-3 (Ireland – police representative associations are prohibited from joining national employees' organisations).
1472. Conclusions XV-1, vol. 2, p. 359 (Italy).
1473. Conclusions II, p. 23.
1474. Conclusions VI, p. 31 (Italy).

make a decision to join a trade union or organisation. The Committee was against cases in which trade union membership for police officers was obligatory.[1475]

Professional associations of police officers may be regarded as quasi trade unions, as they fulfil some of the fundamental functions of a trade organisation such as holding meetings as well as having the right to negotiate with the police employers about employment and salary conditions.[1476] Limitations on trade union freedom for workers and the police call for Member States to have the necessary rights of regulating the conditions of association for the police into trade organisations to which police officers have the right to join, substituting the professional associations. All cases of non-compliance with Article 5 of the Charter therefore are those where the state excludes police officers the right to associate in trade organisations or forcing membership to take place.[1477] Due to lack of compliance with Article 5 of the Charter, the social and economic interests of the police are not protected by professional organisations or trade unions.[1478]

C. Union Freedom for Professional Militia

238. Professional soldiers are not considered to be workers by labour law. They are tied to the army through administrative (official) relations However, the law does not exclude professional militia from taking advantage of the assurance established by Article 5. It may be concluded from the said provision that the international guarantees of union freedom apply to professional soldiers if the scope of application of Article 5 in relation to professional soldiers is determined in national labour law or if there is a legislated regulation stating the said provision does not apply to professional militia at all. The situation appears analogical to that of the police force. The Committee stated: 'the third sentence of Article 5 allows a Member State to limit or entirely deprive professional militia of union freedom'.[1479] The position of the Committee expressed during the supervisory process of abiding by Article 5 of the Charter was repeated in rulings made by the Committee acting as a quasi-judicial body dealing with collective complaints[1480] in the cases *European Federation of Employees in Public Services v. France*,[1481] *European Federation of*

1475. Conclusions X-1, p. 68; Addendum to Conclusions XI-2, p. 20 (Ireland)

1476. Conclusions X-2, p. 67; Conclusions XIII-3, p. 237 (Portugal).

1477. Conclusions 2014 (in Armenia, police officers are prohibited from joining trade unions; in Malta, it has not been established that there are adequate remedies against refusals to register police trade unions).

1478. Conclusions 2014 (Azerbaijan).

1479. Conclusions I, p. 31; Conclusions III, p. 30; Conclusions XIII-2, p. 268.

1480. A. Świątkowski, 'Quasi jurysdykcyjna funkcja Komitetu Praw Społecznych Rady Europy' ('Quasi-judicial function of the Committee of the Council of Europe'), Państwo i Prawo (State and Law), No. 9, 2004, pp. 46 et seq.

1481. Complaint No. 2/1999. The complaint was registered on 13 Aug. 1999 and concerned violating the Arts 5 and 6 in relation to professional militia. The Committee accepted the complaint to recognition on 10 Feb. 2000 and on 12 Dec. 2000 made a ruling stating France did not violate Arts 5 and 6 of the Charter. The Committee of Ministers of the Council of Europe approved of the above verdict on 7 Feb. 2001 ResChS (2001)2.

Employees in Public Services v. Italy,[1482] *European Federation of Employees in Public Services v. Portugal.*[1483]

The applicant, the international federation of trade unions (EFEPS) argued that the authorities of three Member States, France, Italy and Portugal, violated Articles 5 and 6 of the Charter because they did not guarantee their professional militia the right to associate in trade unions as well as the right to negotiate in collective work agreements.

The Committee referred to the rulings made during the following supervisory cycles monitoring the abiding of Article 5 of the Charter, stating that the third sentence of Article 5 allows the authorities of Member States to entirely deprive professional militia of the right to associate in trade unions. It emphasised the international federation of trade unions registering the collective complaints against three Member States had not provided arguments that could have changed the Committee's position towards the freedom of union of professional militia.

The only contentious issues within the interpretation of Article 5 concerning professional militia were those dealing with the background of the right of the authorities of Member States to deprive persons employed in paramilitary organisations, of the right to associate in trade unions, e.g., gendarmes in France,[1484] officers of civil guard in Spain,[1485] and Security of Internal Affairs and the Intelligence Agency in Poland.

The Committee was interested in the legal status of the above-listed organisations. Regarding them as military organisations automatically excused the deprivation of the right to associate in trade unions imposed on the officers of these organisations.

D. The Right of Migrant Workers, Citizens of a Member State, to Organise

239. Citizens of Member States which are parties to the Charter take advantage of the right to organise in a trade union in a manner permissible to them by the regulations specified by the given country that are applicable to its own citizens (Article 19 (4)(b) of the Charter). The Committee sought information from Member States concerning the regulations dealing with the equal treatment of Member State citizens in issues regarding trade union membership.[1486] Further, during the fourteenth supervisory cycle, the Committee took an interest in what kind of approaches were taken by foreigners (citizens of a Member State) within trade unions legally employed and living on the territory of another Member State.[1487] A questionnaire

1482. Complaint No. 4/1999. The complaint was registered on 13 Aug. 1999. The Committee accepted it to recognition on 10 Feb. 2000. The Committee's ruling on 12 Dec. 2000, approved by the Committee of Ministers on 7 Feb. 2001 ResChS (2001)3. The content of the verdict as in the case No. 2/1999.
1483. Complaint No. 5/1999. The content and the dates of decisions as in the cases Complaint No. 2/1999 and Complaint No. 4/1999.
1484. Conclusions XV-1, vol. 1, p. 249.
1485. Conclusions XV-1, vol. 2, p. 512.
1486. Conclusions XV-1, vol. 2, p. 512.
1487. Conclusions XIV-1, vol. 1, p. 45.

addressed to Member States included a question concerning the rights of foreigners, and members of another Member State, to form trade unions, join already existing trade organisations, and carry out trade union functions.[1488] From the reports filed by the authorities of Member States, it may be concluded, that in some Member States the citizens of other Member States (with the exception of the contracting parties of the European Economic Area EEA), do not take advantage of the right to stand for election in representative body elections within the workplace,[1489] or in bodies recognising the wage-claim disputes of workers, or in matters of social security.[1490] The Committee decided that depriving foreigners of the right to stand for elections, who are legally employed within the given Member State, is in breach of Article 5 of the Charter. It did not however claim there is non-compliance in cases of depriving foreigners of the right to sit representatives in recognising wage-claim disputes and as representatives of workers' interests. Establishing equality within workplace relations is part of the state's responsibility, which is capable of restricting the scope of persons authorised to deal with equality within the field of its own citizens.[1491]

The following domestic labour laws have been considered by the Committee as non-compliant with Article 5 of the Charter: prohibiting citizens of other Member States from forming trade unions in the country where they are legally employed;[1492] making the right to stand elections be dependent upon a period of 5 years employment within the given country;[1493] allowing citizens of other Member States not to take up more than one-third of the managerial positions with a trade organisation. In the opinion of the Committee, legally binding restrictions upon the number of foreigners permitted to function in managerial positions within trade unions create doubts about the representation of the trade union. In certain cases, this inhibits the process of forming trade organisations within the workplace and in industrial sectors employing migrant workers.[1494]

E. *Aftermath – A prelude to what is happening today*

240. Obstacles and bans on the formation of trade unions and business organisations were introduced through requirements that are difficult to meet, such as limiting it to those workplaces where a significant part of the employees have expressed their approval for the idea of establishing trade unions in the enterprise,[1495] requiring that founders of trade union organisations receive support for this idea from at

1488. Form for the reports submitted in pursuance of the Revised European Social Charter, European Social Charter, *supra*, pp. 317–318.
1489. Case of Austria: Conclusions XIII-3, p. 96; Conclusions XIV-1, vol. 1, p. 74; Conclusions XV-1, vol. 1, p. 42. Case of Luxembourg: Conclusions XIV-1, vol. 2, p. 492; Addendum to Conclusions XV-1, p. 45.
1490. Conclusions XV-1, vol. 1, p. 249 (France); Addendum to Conclusions XV-1, p. 23 (Germany), Conclusion 2006, vol. 2, p. 745 (Romania).
1491. Conclusions XIX-3, p. 79 (Denmark). The right to organise, *supra*, p. 45.
1492. Case of Turkey: Conclusions XIII-3, p. 414; Conclusions XIV-1, vol. 2, p. 780.
1493. Conclusions VI, pp. 30, 121.
1494. As above, p. 30.
1495. Conclusions 2022 (Armenia).

least 25% of the employees or requiring 50 employees among the founding teams of trade union organisations.[1496] People employed in corporations and employees from neighbouring Council of Europe Member States, employed on the common market of the EU or entering national labour markets from other Member States[1497] were against introducing trade union organisations in enterprises and other workplaces. The labour law norms of some European countries were constructed in a manner that is inconsistent with European standards. A classic example is the phenomenon described by the American term 'a closed shop'. Its legal and factual structure makes it impossible for foreigners coming from another Member State[1498] to enter national labour markets. The provisions of labour law applicable in some Member States did not protect professionally active people who did not support the formation of trade union organisations.[1499] The provisions of these labour law systems support the anti-European practice of discriminating against job applicants who are in favour of establishing trade union organisations, as well as persons who are the only employers in a limited, narrow group of 'small' entrepreneurs. 'Protection against anti-union discrimination and interference is not effectively insured'.[1500]

§2. The Right to Bargain Collectively

I. Introduction

241. The exercise of the right to bargain collectively and the right to collective action laid down by Article 6 ESC represents an essential basis for the fulfilment of other fundamental rights guaranteed by the Charter.[1501] Article 6 of the Charter promotes social dialogue between stakeholders: representatives of workers and employers. Four paragraphs of the regulation govern various aspects of the legal relations between stakeholders. The first three paragraphs cover the relations between stakeholders in times of social peace: consultations, negotiation of normative agreements, primarily collective agreements; and resolving collective labour disputes by means of peaceful methods: conciliation and voluntary arbitration.[1502] The last and fourth paragraph of Article 6 of the Charter specifies the techniques for conducting collective actions by stakeholders who are parties to collective labour disputes. Article 6 §4 of the Charter is the first legal standard of international labour law that guarantees the right to strike.[1503]

Similarly to Article 5 of the Charter, Article 6 applies to foreigners and citizens of Member States to the Council of Europe legally residing and employed in other Member States. Contrary to Article 5 of the Charter, Article 6 has not introduced

1496. Conclusions 2022 (Latvia)
1497. (Azerbaijan).
1498. Conclusions 2022 (Ireland).
1499. Conclusions 2022 (Bulgaria), (Ireland).
1500. Conclusions 2022 (Moldova).
1501. Activity Report 2018, p. 36.
1502. Conclusions I, p. 34.
1503. *Ibid.*

any limitations or exceptions with respect to exercising the stakeholders' right to bargain collectively. Certain limitations in taking collective actions are admissible for the sake of protecting public order, national security, public health or good practice.

II. Joint Consultations Between Workers and Employers

242. Article 6 §1 imposes on Member States the obligation to promote joint consultations between workers and employers. The analysed provision does not grant stakeholders 'the right to consultations'.[1504] It obliges authorities of Member States to promote such consultations. This obligation is absolute in its nature. It is not dependent upon the opinion expressed by the authorities of individual Member States as in the case of being obliged to promote, where necessary and appropriate, voluntary negotiations with a view to regulate the terms and conditions of employment by means of collective labour agreements. The Committee has a broad interpretation of such consultations. Joint (*paritaire*) consultations with stakeholders cover a variety of relations between such stakeholders that are based on the principles of equality.[1505] In accordance with the analysed provision, the authorities of Member States are obliged to encourage stakeholders to initiate mutual relations and communicate on all the issues within the area of their interest. In 2018, the Committee revealed that in seven Member States, the idea of negotiating and concluding provisions binding collective labour parties is not sufficiently promoted. The Committee issued seven negative conclusions. It also found that in one country (Spain) the situation is incompatible with Article 6 §2 of the Charter of 1961, as national labour law allows employers not to comply with the provisions of collective agreements. In this case, the Committee gave a negative opinion on the state of collective bargaining in Spain.[1506] The consultations may be conducted directly by the interested parties or they may involve representatives of Member State authorities. Consultations conducted within the framework of the so-called trilateral commissions by stakeholders and organised by the authorities of the Member States, headed by competent ministers of labour and social policy meet the requirements arising from 6 §1 of the Charter.[1507]

243. Member States are obliged to promote joint consultations. This obligation signifies that some specific, positive steps should be taken when a stakeholder fails to initiate mutual relations independently.[1508] When stakeholders show an initiative and take a voluntary and independent step to encourage negotiations on all matters falling within the scope of their interest, the authorities of the Member States should refrain from taking any actions that could discourage stakeholders from such social dialogue. The principle of tripartism should not replace the principle of the

1504. *See* judgment of the European Human Rights Tribunal on: *National Union of Belgium Police*, 279 ECtHR (ser. A) (1975).
1505. Conclusions IV, p. 43.
1506. Activity Report 2018, p. 36.
1507. Conclusions V, p. 41; Conclusions XVII-1, vol. 2, p. 355 (Aruba).
1508. Conclusions 2004, vol. 2, p. 457 (Romania).

autonomy of workers' organisations and employers (or their organisations) in collective bargaining over conditions of employment.[1509] In order to be in conformity with Article 6 §1 of the Charter, representativeness criteria should be prescribed by law, be objective and reasonable, and be subject to judicial review, which offers appropriate protection against arbitrary refusals.[1510] In cases where minimum membership requirements excessively limit the possibility of trade unions participating effectively in consultations, the situation is judged by the Committee to be contrary to the Charter.[1511] Article 6 §1 of the Charter leaves the authorities of Member States relatively large freedom of evaluation of the relations between stakeholders. Nevertheless, the approach to such freedom adopted by the authorities of Member States is subject to the control of the Committee. The Committee does not accept explanations of Member State authorities outlining that some appropriate actions were undertaken in order to prompt stakeholders towards mutual relations and social dialogue if such efforts did not bring about a positive result due to a lack of interest on the part of the parties in question or due to an aggressive attitude on the part of the representatives of trade unions.[1512] The Committee stressed that Article 6 §1 of the Charter introduces an absolute obligation to take appropriate measures with a view to promoting joint consultations of stakeholders.[1513] In reality, therefore, Article 6 §1 of the Charter is interpreted by the Committee as standard which obligates Member States to ascertain particular results. Postponing a judgment with relation to the compliance of a Member State to the obligations arising from Article 6 §1 of the Charter is the best-case scenario in justifying situations where efforts have been made towards prompting stakeholders to enter into direct relations and run joint consultations presented by Member States.[1514] In accordance with the practice followed so far, the Committee is interested in reading the regulations underlying joint consultations of stakeholders and how they are applied practically.[1515] A particular practice which is of some interest to the Committee are cases when joint consultations of stakeholders are not based on the legal regulations introduced by the state.[1516]

244. Article 6 §1 of the Charter does not identify any entities authorised to conduct the consultations. Joint consultations should be conducted 'between workers and employers'. In the consultations, workers are typically represented by trade unions.[1517] However, the provision analysed herein should not be approached as a

1509. Conclusions 2014 (Azerbaijan). Therefore, the Committee concludes that the situation in Azerbaijan is not in conformity with Art. 6 §1 of the Charter, on the grounds that it has not been established that the promotion of joint consultation between workers and employers on most matters of mutual interest covered by Art. 6 §1 of the Charter is ensured.
1510. Conclusions 2006 (Albania),
1511. Conclusions 2014 (Armenia).
1512. Conclusions I, p. 35 (Italy, United Kingdom); Conclusions III, p. 33 (Italy); Conclusions IV, p. 44 (Italy); Addendum to Conclusions XV-1, p. 115.
1513. Addendum to Conclusions XI-2, pp. 22–23 (Ireland).
1514. Addendum to Conclusions XV-1, p. 24.
1515. Conclusions XIII-3, p. 113 (Ireland), p. 114 (Malta), p. 274 (Portugal).
1516. The case of the United Kingdom: Conclusions XIII-1, p. 141; Conclusions XIII-2, p. 275; Conclusions XIII-3, pp. 116–117; Conclusions XIV-1, p. 801; of Malta: Conclusions XV-1, p. 405.
1517. Conclusions 2010, vol. 1, p. 119 (Belgium). Conclusions XIX, p. 34 (Albania).

legal standard granting a monopoly on conducting consultations with employers to trade unions. The Committee does not investigate whether other representative bodies, apart from trade unions, have been authorised to represent workers. However, it is interested to learn what bodies representing workers take part in the consultations with employers and the entities where trade unions do not operate.[1518] The Committee notes, from individual observations of the ILO Committee on the Application of Conventions and Recommendation (ILO-CEACR),[1519] that it has requested that the government, in consultation with the most representative organisations of employers and workers, work out and lay down objective, precise and predetermined criteria to evaluate the representativeness and independence of employers' and workers' organisations. On the basis of that observation, the Committee concludes that the situation in Portugal is not in conformity with Article 6 §1 of the Charter, on the grounds that the criteria used to determine representativeness with respect to joint consultation are not adequate.[1520] The Committee advised the authorities of Ireland that the Joint Labour Committees formed in some sectors, primarily in the agricultural sector, do not allow for the participation of workers' representatives in joint consultations in the manner described in Article 6 §1 of the Charter, although they are competent in matters of the regulation of remuneration.[1521]

Furthermore, the Committee raised some doubts whether regulations authorising workers to express suggestions on the matters connected with managing establishments to their employers conform with the requirements towards consultations as construed by the provisions of 6 §1 of the Charter.[1522]

245. The scope of the matters subject to joint consultations covers all issues of interest to stakeholders: work efficiency, work safety and hygiene, conditions of employment, working hours, vocational training, any matters in connection with organisation of work and management of establishments and social security of workers.[1523] The above specification of the matters indicated for the joint consultation of stakeholders is presented by way of example. As stakeholders enjoy equal status during their joint consultations, the consultations should be conducted on any economic, professional and social matters within the scope of their mutual interests.

246. Joint consultations should be conducted at all levels: national, regional and in-house level. As of 2015, the Committee concludes that the situation in Georgia is

1518. The case of the United Kingdom: Conclusions XIII-1, p. 141; Conclusions XIV-1, p. 801; Conclusions XIII-2, p. 273 (Belgium); Conclusions XIII-3, p. 274 (Finland).
1519. Observation CEACR adopted 2012, Publisher by 102nd session 2013 – Right to Organise and Collective Bargaining Convention, 1949 (No. 98) – Portugal (ratification: 1964).
1520. Conclusions 2014 (Portugal).
1521. Conclusions II, p. 25; Addendum to Conclusions XI-2; Conclusions XIII-3, p. 113.
1522. Conclusions XVII-1, vol. 2, p. 286 (Malta).
1523. Conclusions I, pp. 34–35; Conclusions IV, p. 43; Conclusions V, p. 42; Conclusions VII, pp. 35–36; Addendum to Conclusions XI-2, pp. 22–23 (Ireland). Conclusions XIX, p. 38 (Croatia).

not in conformity with Article 6 §1 of the Charter, on the grounds that joint consultation does not place on several levels.[1524] In its previous conclusions, the Committee found that The Tripartite Social Partnership Commission's (TSPC) regulation and composition was established in 2010 to ensure good communication and create a platform for exchanging views on labour relations issues.[1525] However, the ILO Committee on the Application of Conventions and Recommendations (ILO-CEACR) noted 'that TSPC remains very ineffective, and that over two and a half years of its existence, the body has not resolved one single issue and not one of its decisions and recommendations has been acted upon'.[1526] Therefore, as of 2015, the Committee reiterates its question about whether employers' and employees' organisations have the opportunity for joint consultation on a bipartite basis. In this respect, it recalls that if adequate consultation exists, there is no need for the state to intervene.[1527] In smaller countries, the Committee did not require stakeholders to conduct consultations at a regional level.[1528] However it heightened the importance of such consultations within the workplace,[1529] both in the public[1530] and private sectors. In such cases, the obligation to conduct joint consultations is deemed fulfilled when representatives of workers employed on the basis other than employment contracts have the right to express their opinion at the stage preceding the issuance of regulations governing any formal work relations and in the process of application of these regulations by employers.[1531] Any work relations initiated on the basis of employment contracts in offices and other public-sector workplaces are governed by the same rules applicable to private entrepreneurs. Because of the unique nature of joint consultations in public-sector workplaces, the Committee requested that Member States provide it with information on the techniques used in the consulting process used by stakeholders in state offices and other public-sector workplaces.[1532] It is not enough to refer to the public institutions such as the Council for Safety and Health at Work and its expert/consultative functions.[1533] The EC Progress Report notes that there is no effective social dialogue in the public sector in North Macedonia and that collective agreements are not respected. The Committee concludes that as regards joint consultation in the public sector that it has not been established that the situation is in conformity with Article 6 §1 of the Charter.[1534] Consultations should be conducted in all sectors, including agricultural

1524. Conclusions 2014 (Georgia).
1525. Conclusions 2010 (Georgia).
1526. Observations of ILO-CEACR adopted in 2012, published by 102nd ILC session (2013).
1527. Conclusions 2014.
1528. The case of Malta: Conclusions XIII-2, p. 274; Conclusions XIV-1, p. 528.
1529. Consultation XII-2, p. 104 (Malta); Consultation XIII-3, p. 274 (Finland); Conclusions XIV-1, vol. 1, p. 153 (Cyprus), p. 179 (Denmark); Conclusions 2002, p. 132 (Romania).
1530. No joint consultation in public sector in Albania, Bulgaria, Moldova. Conclusions 2010, vol. 1, p. 34 (Albania), p. 183 (Bulgaria), vol. 2, p. 424 (Moldova). Conclusions 2014 (Bulgaria).
1531. Conclusions III, p. 33 (Germany).
1532. Conclusions V, p. 42 (France); Conclusions XI-2, p. 77 (Spain); Conclusions XIII-3, p. 114 (Malta); Conclusions XIII-3, p. 275 (Portugal); Conclusions XIII-5, p. 59 (Finland); Conclusions XIV-1, vol. 1, s. 418 (Ireland); Conclusions XV-1, vol. 2, p. 635 (United Kingdom); Conclusions XVII-1, vol. 2, p. 355 (Aruba).
1533. Conclusions 2014 (Macedonia).
1534. *Ibid.*

sectors,[1535] and involve all workers. In the case of Article 6 §1 of the Charter, the principle of 'the great majority' is introduced by the provisions of Article 33 §1 ESC and Article I §2 RESC. The self-employed have been excluded from the scope of obligations to promote joint consultations.

247. Joint consultation of the social partners, employees and employers, is rightly considered to be the essence of exercising the right to collective bargaining. The consultative community in labour relations guarantees the maintenance of social peace, during which neither takes steps to force the other partner to act: employees in the form of a strike and employers through the threat of a lockout. An analysis of 32 cases of monitoring by the ECSR during the conclusions 2022 review cycle showed that a quarter of the Member States of the Council of Europe carry out almost no activities regarding cooperation between entities with disparate expectations and requirements. Most of the findings of non-conformity concerned the absence of joint consultative bodies in the public sector.[1536] This phenomenon concerned both the public sector and, less surprisingly, the private sector. Thus, there was a lack of institutions in the public sector authorised by the state authorities to conduct consultations.[1537] State authorities do not use appropriate criteria for selecting employee representatives in order to properly select negotiators in cases concerning the interests of both parties to the dispute: employers and employees. Meanwhile, the opposing sides should be interested in conducting peaceful negotiations on cooperation.[1538] In Georgia, for example, the trade union organisation the Georgian Confederation of Trade Unions is not just treated as a proper negotiation forum with employers' representatives.[1539] The provisions of the Labour Code which establish the rules for the exchange of information (Articles 70–73) were ignored. In assessing the legal and factual situation, the ECSR clearly noted the 'complete lack of promotion' of joint consultations between social partners.[1540] The country's reports did not contain information on bilateral and tripartite consultations on matters of common economic and social interest.[1541] In one of the three constituent parts of this country's federation – the Republic of Srpska[1542] – the presented report, which should be treated as a positive exception from the other reports laconically states that consultations 'are taking place'. The ECSR noted that European Member States' refusal to grant any trade union organisation a status that authorises it to represent the interests of workers to trade unions is not subject to judicial review.[1543] This means that at present, joint consultations of employees and employers have no chance of promotion as referred to in Article 6 §1 of the Charter.

1535. Conclusions II, p. 25 (Ireland); Conclusions 2004, vol. 1, p. 144 (Estonia).
1536. Conclusions 2022 (Albania), (Armenia), (Georgia), (Malta). *See* Conclusions 2022, *Press Briefing Elements*, *supra*, pp. 14–15.
1537. Conclusions 2022 (Albania).
1538. Conclusions 2022 (Portugal).
1539. Conclusions 2022 (Georgia)
1540. Conclusions 2022 (Malta).
1541. Conclusions 2022 (Bosnia and Herzegovina).
1542. *Ibid.*
1543. Conclusions 2022 (Albania, Malta)).

III. Collective Labour Agreements

248. Article 6 §2 of the Charter is a standard which has a voluntary nature as far as collective bargaining and collective labour agreements are concerned.[1544] It not only imposes on Member States the obligation of accepting negotiations of stakeholders in collective labour agreements but also obliges state authorities to actively promote negotiations of employment, remuneration conditions and entering into collective labour agreements.[1545] Therefore, the obligation stipulated in Article 6 §2 of the Charter is composed of two sections. The first one imposes an obligation upon the legal framework of any Member State, allowing for the participation of employees in the public sector in determining their working conditions.[1546] The second section of the obligation, i.e., an active promotion of negotiation of collective labour agreements, applies when stakeholders do not make an independent and spontaneous agreement as to the negotiation techniques applicable when entering into collective labour agreements.[1547] Member States are obliged to provide detailed information on the procedures applied in the process of negotiating collective labour agreements as well as on their effects,[1548] number of finalised collective labour agreements, number of workers covered by collective labour agreements and the number and type of organisations authorised to represent interest of workers and employers when negotiating collective labour agreements.[1549] Supervising Member States' conformity with the provisions of Article 6 §2 of the Charter, the Committee made conclusive remarks in cases where the authorities of these states intervened, thus restricting the freedom to negotiate collective labour agreements enjoyed by stakeholders. The right to negotiate conditions of employment and salaries and the freedom to enter into collective labour agreements is inherent in the freedom to associate enjoyed by workers. For this reason, any of the above-mentioned cases of violating the freedom to form trade unions, guaranteed by the provisions of Article 5 of the Charter, are deemed conflicting with the provisions of Article 6 §2 of the Charter. Issuing a judgment on the non-compliance of national regulations with the provisions of Article 5 of the Charter is equal to the non-compliance with the provisions of Article 6 §2 of the Charter. It is worth remembering the judgment of non-compliance of requirements to issue permissions to bargain collectively and to enter into collective labour agreements with the provisions of Article 5 of the Charter.[1550]

1544. The judgment of the European Court of Human Rights on *Swedish Engine Drivers Union*, 20 ECtHR (ser A) (1976).
1545. Conclusions I, p. 35.
1546. As of 2014, the Committee concludes that the situation in Ireland is not in conformity with Art. 6 §2 of the Charter on the grounds that the legislation and practice fail to ensure the sufficient access on the part of police representative associations to pay agreement decisions (Ireland). In the case of Georgia, it has not been established that public employees may participate in collective negotiations concerning the determination of their working conditions.
1547. *Ibid.*
1548. The Committee concludes that it has not been established that an employer may unilaterally disregard a collective agreement. Conclusions 2016 (Georgia), p. 290.
1549. As above; Conclusions III, p. 34 (Austria, Cyprus, Denmark); Conclusions XIV-1, vol. 1, p. 384 (Iceland); Conclusions XV-1, p. 146.
1550. Conclusions III, s. 35 (Ireland); Conclusions XIV-1, p. 179 (Denmark), p. 419 (Ireland), p. 530 (Malta).

Similarly, the Committee automatically concluded that any requirements towards candidates or workers (the 'closed-shop' clauses) that violate the freedom to associate in trade unions arising from legal regulations or provisions of collective labour agreements were in breach of Article 6 §2 of the Charter.[1551] The closed-shop clause, which is in conflict with Article 5 of the Charter, does not constitute an automatic breach of the provision of Article 6 §2 of the Charter if trade unions associate all workers employed in a workplace in accordance with the principle of common obligation, enjoy the freedom to negotiate conditions of employment, remuneration and entering into collective labour agreements. However, the situation differs when trade unions enjoy the right to negotiate collective labour agreements for some workers employed by a given employer.

In the case of Denmark, which prohibited citizens of other Member States (except for the citizens of the members of the European Economic Area), employed in sea navigation from accessing trade unions and prohibited trade unions from negotiating conditions of work and pay for the workers, indicates a direct dependence between the freedom to associate in trade unions and the freedom to negotiate collective labour agreements.[1552] The conclusion on breaching the provisions of Article 5 of the Charter by Denmark automatically justifies the Committee's conclusion on the non-compliance of national labour law regulations with Article 6 §2 of the Charter.[1553] However, the Committee has a very decisive and consistent view on a bilateral dependency between the freedom of association in trade unions and the freedom to negotiate collective labour agreements. In the Committee's opinion, any breach of the provisions of Article 5 of the Charter may automatically serve as the basis for issuing a judgment on non-compliance of a Member State with the standards established in Article 6 §2 of the Charter.[1554]

249. Member States are obliged to promote, whenever required and appropriate, negotiations between stakeholders on collective labour agreements.[1555] Article 6 §2 of the Charter empowers the authorities of Member States to assess the need for

1551. Conclusions XIV-1, p. 257 (France); Conclusions 2004, vol. 1, pp. 264–265 (Ireland).

1552. Conclusions XX-3 2014 (Denmark). The latest Danish International Register of Shipping Framework Agreement from 2013 states that seafarers who are not resident in Denmark, but who work on board of Danish ships, are entitled to be members of several trade unions (i.e., both a Danish trade union and a trade union in their home country). This enables seafarers' organisations to represent and assist seafarers not domiciled in Denmark or foreign trade unions in matters related to Danish legislation and in dealings with the Danish public authorities. Therefore, the Committee concludes that the situation in Denmark is not in conformity with Art. 6 §2 of the Charter on the grounds that the right to collective bargaining of non-resident seafarers engaged on vessels entered in the International Shipping Register is restricted.

1553. Conclusions XI-1, p. 72. Conclusions XIX, p. 80.

1554. The case of Denmark: Conclusions XIII-1, pp. 142–143; Conclusions XIII-3, p. 118; The case of Malta: Conclusions XIII-1, pp. 142–143; Conclusions XIII-3, p. 118; The case of the United Kingdom: Conclusions VI, p. 36; Conclusions XIII-1, p. 145; Conclusions XIII-2, p. 277.

1555. Conclusions 2010, vol. 1, p. 185 (Bulgaria), p. 292 (Georgia), vol. p. 424 (Moldova). Conclusions XIX, p. 155 (Latvia). As of 2014 (Conclusions 2014), the Committee concludes that the situation in the following Member States is not in conformity with Art. 6 §2 of the Charter, on the grounds that there is no adequate promotion of voluntary negotiation between employers or employers' organisations and workers' organisations: Azerbaijan – the report does not mention measures aiming at promoting voluntary negotiations between social partners; Bulgaria – the report does not

negotiating collective labour agreements. Collective bargaining is largely a matter for individual employers, their employees and their trade unions. Therefore, the situation where public authorities decree extensions to collective agreements subject to tripartite analysis of the consequences would have a significant impact on the sector to which it applies. Hence, the Committee concludes that the situation in the following Member States is not in conformity with the Charter on the basis that voluntary negotiations are sufficiently promoted in practice in the following countries: Latvia – if the members of the organisation of employers, or an association of organisations of employers, employ more than 50% of the employees in a given sector or the turnover related to their business represents more than 60% in that sector, they will be obliged to apply a general agreement signed between the above-mentioned organisation or association and a trade union or trade union's association, to all employers and their employees within the sector;[1556] Spain – the Royal Decree No. 718/2005 of 20 June 2005 regulates the extension of collective agreements and affects the right to bargain collectively, without consultation of trade unions and employers' organisations.[1557] This is not relevant to the United Kingdom. In keeping with the UK's voluntarist approach to collective bargaining, it is largely a matter for individual employers to decide whether they wish to recognise a trade union for collective bargaining purposes. The British government takes the view that the current state of domestic law relating to collective bargaining gives sufficient protection to the rights of workers and trade unions under Article 6 of the Charter. In particular, it considers that Article 6 §2 of the Charter does not guarantee a right for co-workers or trade unions to bring proceedings regarding offers to induce the surrender of union rights. The Committee does not share such a legal opinion. It concludes that the situation in the United Kingdom is not in conformity with Article 6 §2 of the Charter on the grounds that workers and trade unions do not have the right to bring legal proceedings in the event that employers offer financial incentives to induce workers to exclude themselves from collective bargaining.[1558] Moreover, the Committee concludes that the situation is not in conformity with the Charter if the statutory legislation allows employers to unitarily not apply (i.e., disregard) conditions agreed in a collective agreement.[1559]

---

indicate the concrete positive measures taken by the government in order to facilitate and encourage the conclusion of collective agreements; Estonia – the promotion of collective bargaining is not sufficient; Hungary – no promotion measures have been taken, even though the coverage of workers by collective agreements in manifestly low; Lithuania – it has been not established that the machinery for voluntary negotiations has been efficiently promoted; Moldova – in the public sector the negotiations reflect budgetary ceilings which significantly limit the basis for the negotiations; Slovak Republic – that, instead of negotiation, the extension of the collective agreements is possible without the consent of the employer affected by the extension; Sweden – foreign companies which conduct their economic activities in Sweden are not obliged to create a branch office with independent management in Sweden, if the economic activity is made subject to the provisions on free movement of goods and services in EU and EEA; therefore, the statutory framework on posted workers does not promote the development of suitable machinery for voluntary negotiations between employers and workers' organisations with a view to the regulation of terms and conditions of employment by means of collective agreements.

1556. Conclusions XX-3 (Latvia).
1557. Conclusions XX-3 (Spain).
1558. Conclusions XX-3 (United Kingdom).
1559. Conclusions XX-3 (Spain). Conclusions 2014 (Georgia).

Workers' conditions of employment may be regulated in a manner other than through collective labour agreements. The Committee assesses whether any departures from the principle of entering into collective labour agreements are justified. Undoubtedly, conditions of employment offered to the workers employed by the private sector should be negotiated by stakeholders and introduced in collective labour agreements they enter into. A prohibition against negotiating collective labour agreements,[1560] regulating more favourable conditions of employment and pay on an individual basis for the workers, who refuse to be represented by trade unions negotiating collective labour agreements on behalf of their employer, is considered not in compliance with the standards set by the provisions of Article 6 §2 of the Charter.[1561] In the opinion of the Committee, any restriction of the freedom to negotiate collective labour agreements by the organisations representing workers employed by private employers is not in compliance with the provisions of Article 6 §2 of the Charter. Some exceptions from the aforementioned rule may be introduced on the basis of Article 31 of the Charter.[1562] The Committee arrived at the conclusion that the authorities of Member States had the right to impose certain restrictions on the right to negotiate collective labour agreements by stakeholders, in particular in matters connected with pay rises, especially in grave economic circumstances.[1563] However, the above-mentioned restriction of the freedom to negotiate in collective labour agreements may be imposed by a Member State authority after in-depth consultations with all interested entities, trade unions and employers in particular. The reasons underlying the imposition of the above-mentioned restrictions should be presented to stakeholders and be of extraordinary nature. The authorities of Member States do not have the right to increase remuneration limits for workers who are covered under collective labour agreements.[1564] The authorities of Member States should convince stakeholders because of exceptional circumstances restricting the freedom to negotiate in social agreements is necessary, as the situations cannot be rectified otherwise.[1565] The restrictions may be imposed in a precisely determined period, required for the re-establishment of regular conditions, where collective labour agreements serve as the basis for regulating work and pay conditions of workers.[1566]

1560. Conclusions XII-1, pp. 120–121; Conclusions XIV-1, vol. 1, pp. 384–385.
1561. Conclusions XIII-3, pp. 127–129; Conclusions XVII-1, vol. 2, p. 516 (United Kingdom). Conclusions XIX, p. 260 (United Kingdom). The Committee referred to the judgement of the European Count of Human Rights of 2 Jul. 2002, the case: *Wilson and the National Union of Journalists, Palmer, Wyeth and the NURMTW, Doolan and others v. United Kingdom*. In the judgment, the Court adjudicated that permitting an employer to use the means of financial motivation in relation to employees in exchange for their resignation from representation of their interests during negotiations of collective labour agreements is in conflict with Art. 11 of the European Convention on Human Rights Protection.
1562. Conclusions X-1, p. 72; Conclusions XII-1, p. 123.
1563. General Introduction to Conclusions VIII, p. 11; Conclusions IX-1, p. 53; Conclusions XIV-1, vol. 2, pp. 734–735.
1564. Conclusions VIII, p. 11.
1565. Conclusions IX-1, p. 53.
1566. Conclusions X-1, p. 72; Conclusions XII-1, p. 123.

In the case of the Netherlands, where the authorities had restricted the freedom to negotiate collective agreements for a period of six months, the Committee concluded there was compliance of the above regulation introduced with the domestic legislation, conditional to the authorities taking appropriate steps towards ensuring workers an appropriate standard of living.[1567] Although in its conclusion on Ireland, where the authorities limited the pay of workers employed in navigation of ferries by 10% as a result of a strike announced in 1993, the Committee established there was non-compliance by the former intervention in the freedom to negotiate collective labour agreements[1568] and in the same decision, it concluded that the decision of the state authorities suspending the freedom to negotiate collective labour agreements and the freedom to set wages by the state authorities equipped with appropriate legislative powers falls into the margin of the power enjoyed by the state authorities authorised to make decisions on the basis of Article 31 §1 ESC and Article I §2 RESC introducing restrictions in the enjoyment of the rights ensured by the Charter aimed at protecting the rights and freedom of other persons and the public order.[1569] The Committee issued its negative conclusions in the case of Denmark, where the authorities, acting in accordance with special regulations issued solely for the purpose of ending collective labour disputes in 1985 and 1987, extended the validity period of collective labour agreements.

250. The Committee concluded that the above-mentioned interventions prevented stakeholders from freely negotiating in collective labour agreements, and a breach of the provisions of Article 6 §2 of the Charter was established.[1570] The prohibition of any interference in the freedom to negotiate collective labour agreements in the private sector for the authorities of Member States also applies to the generalisation of collective agreements. This term is commonly used in collective labour law for extending a collective labour agreement to the employers who are not covered by the agreement by the bodies of a Member State competent in labour law matters.

Reading the report presented by the Dutch authorities, the Committee concluded that the generalisation of a collective labour agreement by virtue of an administrative decision of a competent minister (of social affairs) represented the intervention of Member State authorities in the freedom to negotiate collective labour agreements violating Article 6 §2 of the Charter.[1571] The report presented by the Dutch authorities in the subsequent supervisory cycle informed that an employer, who enters into a collective labour agreement, has the right to request for his exclusion from the obligation to follow the provisions of a sectoral or nationwide collective labour agreement, where the validity and effectiveness of the agreement have been extended by virtue of a regulation issued by a competent minister of labour.

The Committee concluded that the above-mentioned case did not constitute a breach of the standards of the freedom to negotiate in collective labour agreements

1567. Conclusions XII-1, pp. 122–123.
1568. Conclusions XIV-1, pp. 385 et seq.
1569. Conclusions XV-1, vol. 1, p. 333.
1570. Conclusions X-1, p. 72; Conclusions XII-1, p. 118.
1571. Conclusions XVI-1, vol. 2, p. 444.

established on the basis of Article 6 §2 of the Charter.[1572] The Netherlands does not respect the division of trade unions into representative trade unions, i.e., trade unions empowered to negotiate collective labour agreements and other trade unions not empowered to enter into collective agreements. As collective labour agreements have not been given any specific hierarchy or priority, they do not occupy any position in the hierarchy of labour law sources negotiated by stakeholders. Therefore, no dependency exists between in-house and in-sector or in national collective labour agreements. Execution of a collective agreement by an employer justifies an application for excluding them from the obligation to abide by the provisions of other (sectoral or national) collective labour agreements. The Member State should build a system of collective labour agreements at all levels, including the national, regional and in-house levels. Collective labour agreements executed at a lower level should correspond to the agreements executed at higher levels. In accordance with the hierarchy of sources of negotiable labour law, observing any collective labour agreements, such as which rank is lower in the same hierarchy, is dependent on conformity with collective agreements ranking higher in the hierarchy. Article 6 §2 of the Charter obliges Member States to promote techniques for voluntary negotiations between stakeholders. However, in accordance with the provisions, Member States are not obliged to create a hierarchic structure of collective labour agreements. When an in-house collective labour agreement executed on a voluntary basis collides with the empowerment of a competent state authority to extend the validity and effectiveness of a sectoral or national collective labour agreement, the priority should be given to the principle of voluntary negotiation of collective labour agreement by the entities interested (representatives of workers and competent employer) in entering into such an agreement.

Another example of the collision of a national regulation with the standards introduced by virtue of Article 6 §2 of the Charter was presented in the justification of the Committee's conclusion on Poland,[1573] where the principle was introduced by Article 241^7 §1 of the Labour Code. The Constitutional Tribunal of the Republic of Poland decided there was non-compliance of the principle with the Polish Constitution, Article 6 §2 of the Charter and the convention No. 98 ILO. In accordance with the principle, after a collective labour agreement expires, its validity will be automatically renewed until the stakeholders enter into a new collective labour agreement.[1574] The automatic extension of the validity of a collective labour agreement that expired with the elapse of the period for which it was entered is in conflict with the obligation to promote the mechanisms for voluntary negotiations between employers and employees' organisations imposed on Member States.

251. On the basis of the clause on promoting 'where necessary and appropriate, the mechanisms for voluntary negotiations', the Committee accepts interventions of Member State authorities in negotiations of work conditions and wages by workers employed directly by state administration and state authorities' organisational units.

1572. Conclusions XVII-1, vol. 2, p. 317.
1573. Conclusions XVII-1, vol. 2, p. 380.
1574. Judgment of the Constitutional Tribunal of 18 Nov. 2002 (The Journal of Laws of 196, item 1660).

A limitation of the rights of workers' representatives to negotiate in collective labour agreements with employers – state administration and state authority organisational units – applies solely to workers who are not employed on work contracts. Theories vary within Member States about work relations, which are entered into directly with the state administration and state authorities' organisational units. The Committee did not analyse the grounds for entering into formal work relations, but it did stress the inequality of the parties entering into them. The subordination of a clerk to his employer – an organisational unit of the state administration and state authorities – justifies independent regulation of employment conditions and wages by the employer. In formal work relations, the rule preventing representatives of civil servants from negotiating collective labour agreements with their employer is continuously accepted.[1575] However, the Committee does emphasise that, in such cases, it is required to guarantee the participation of representatives of civil servants in the process of creating the regulations issued by employers in order to determine their employment conditions.[1576] This obligation of consultation in conditions of employment and wages with workers' representatives is also applicable to police officers.[1577] The Committee is not satisfied with the information presented in the national reports showing police trade unions having the right to express their opinions on acts of law determining conditions of employment and wages, instead demanding the presentation of evidentiary data on the influence of policy trade organisations on the content of regulations issued by a state authorised to regulate the conditions of employment and wages for the police.[1578]

252. With regard to workers employed in the public sector who are not employed directly by state authorities and administrative units, the Committee initially adopted an indirect position. It arrived at the conclusion that the situation of these employees is rather specific since, while their remuneration is financed from the state budget, their traditional level of wages in the sector reflects the level of wages received by workers in the private sector.

In the conclusions issued for the report presented by the authorities of the Netherlands, the Committee presented the trends prevailing in wage policy in the sector

1575. The Committee concludes that the situation in Georgia is not in conformity with Art. 6 §2 of the Charter on the ground that it has not been established that the legal framework allows for the participation of employees in the public sector in the determination of their working conditions. Conclusions 2016, p. 290.

1576. Conclusions III, p. 34 (Germany); Conclusions IV, p. 45 (Austria); Conclusions X-2, p. 73 (Spain); Conclusions XIV-1, p. 299 (Germany); Addendum to Conclusions XV-1, pp. 155–156 (Poland). Conclusions III, p. 34 (Germany); Conclusions IV, p. 45 (Austria); Conclusions X-2, p. 73 (Spain); Conclusions XIV-1, p. 299 (Germany); Addendum to Conclusions XV-1, pp. 155–156 (Poland).

1577. Complaint No. 11/2000, European Council of Police Trade Unions against Portugal. Complaint No. 11/2000, European Council of Police Trade Unions against Portugal. Conclusion of the Committee of 21 May 2002, the Resolution of the Ministers' Council of 17 Jul. 2002, ResChS (2002) 5. European Social Charter. Conclusion of the Committee of 21 May 2002, the Resolution of the Ministers' Council of 17 Jul. 2002, ResChS (2002) 5. European Social Charter, *Collected Texts*, 512–513 (Council of Europe Publishing, 5th ed., 2005).

1578. Conclusions XVII-1, vol. 2, p. 381 (Poland).

by using the phrase 'trend follower sector'.[1579] As the funds which finance the wages of workers in this sector remain at the disposal of the state, Dutch authorities decided to grant the administrative bodies an authorisation to set raise wage limits for stakeholders negotiating collective labour agreements.

The Committee concluded that the problem of negotiating collective labour agreements in this sector should be solved by way of consultation and negotiations conducted by the interested parties: stakeholders and state authority agencies.[1580] It signifies that stakeholders negotiating collective labour agreements should consult agencies of Member State authorities. In such cases, the process of negotiating in collective labour agreement is very complex. The Committee seems to approve a case when a competent labour minister is authorised to raise wage limits negotiable in collective labour agreements executed by stakeholders on the condition that broad consultations with the organisation representing workers' interests are carried out prior to issuing a decision binding the negotiating parties.[1581] Collective labour agreements executed on such grounds may be described as 'trilateral' in opposition to 'bilateral' normative agreements. Use of such terms is justified when the authorities of specific Member States are involved in the process of negotiating collective labour agreements.[1582] Lately, the Committee concludes non-compliance with Article 6 §2 if the civil servants are not entitled to participate in the process that results in the determination of regulations applicable to them.[1583]

The obligation to promote negotiations of collective labour agreements does not apply to the self-employed.

253. In the last - third thematic group - devoted to the rights of employees - it was noticed that the above phenomenon concerned both the public sector and, less surprisingly, the private sector. Thus, it was noted that there were no institutions in the public sector authorised by the state authorities to conduct consultations.[1584] State authorities do not use appropriate criteria for selecting employee representatives to appropriately negotiate on matters relating to the interests of both parties, which should be interested in conducting cooperation negotiations.[1585] In Georgia, for example, the trade union organisation, the Georgian Confederation of Trade Unions, is not just treated as a proper negotiation forum with employers' representatives.[1586] The provisions of the Labour Code which establish the rules for the exchange of information (Articles 70–73) were ignored. In assessing the legal and factual situation, the ECSR clearly noted the 'complete lack of promotion' of joint consultations between social partners.[1587] The country reports did not contain information on bilateral and tripartite consultations on matters of common economic and

1579. Conclusions IX, p. 53.
1580. Conclusions IX-1, p. 54.
1581. Conclusions X-1, p. 73.
1582. Conclusions 2004, vol. 1, pp. 145–146 (Estonia).
1583. Conclusions 2010, vol. 1, p. 36 (Albania), pp. 97–98 (Armenia), vol. 2, p. 424 (Moldova). Conclusions XIX, p. 40 (Croatia), p. 239 (FYROM).
1584. Conclusions 2022 (Albania).
1585. Conclusions 2022 (Portugal).
1586. Conclusions 2022 (Georgia).
1587. Conclusions 2022 (Malta).

social interest.[1588] In one of the three constituent parts of this country's federation – the republic of Srpska – the presented report, which should be treated as a positive exception from the other reports, laconically states that consultations 'are taking place'. Unfortunately, a refusal to grant a trade union organisation or another institution regulated by national labour law that takes care of interests is not *de lege lata* possible, either in national labour law systems or in any European law system established by the Council of Europe. The ECSR noted that the refusal of European Member States to grant any trade union organisation a status that authorises it to represent the interests of workers to trade unions is not subject to judicial review.[1589] This means that at present, joint consultations of employees and employers have no chance of promotion as referred to in Article 6 §1 of the Charter.

In addition to promoting joint consultations where necessary and appropriate, Member States and social partners are required by Article 6 §2 of the Charter to develop, apply and comply with a mechanism set up to enable voluntary negotiations between employers or employers' organisations and workers' organisations. The purpose and effect of supporting an appropriate mechanism are to regulate employment conditions through collective bargaining agreements. The structure of these organisations and the way they are operated by persons managing social partner organizations in the processes operated by representatives of social partners, in particular the degree of transparency of their activities, are of significance. They also make it possible to form an opinion about the chances of continuing the proper promotion of collective bargaining agreements in employment relations. In the 2022 ECSR monitoring cycle of compliance with the standards of Article 6 §2 of the Charter, the majority of the conclusions were that the Member States and organisations representing the competing interests of social partners were ineffective. In 33 cases, the clause on 'promoting collective bargaining is not sufficient' beat the clause where a smaller proportion of other ECSR Member States was able to identify thirteen cases of concordant negotiations by both parties to a collective bargaining agreement. A smaller proportion of other ECSR Member States was able to identify thirteen cases of conformity. In three cases, the ECSR took a neutral position using the technical term 'deferral'. The vast majority of cases of nonconformity are the result of insufficiently promoting the idea of collective labour agreements.[1590] The authorities of these countries avoided specific answers to the ECSR's questions in cases concerning employees whose interests were protected by collective labour agreements at the level at which the rules for the application of labour agreements were negotiated: the whole country, smaller territorial units, specific workplaces, types of groupings run by entrepreneurs or workers in various professions.[1591] The ECSR was interested in how large professional organisations associating employees in specific professional sectors care for the interests of

1588. Conclusions 2022 (Bosnia and Herzegovina).
1589. Conclusions 2022 (Albania).
1590. Conclusions 2022 (Albania), (Armenia), (Azerbaijan). (Bosnia and Herzegovina), (Bulgaria), (Estonia), (Georgia), (Hungary), (Lithuania), (Romania).
1591. Conclusions 2022 (Romania).

employees.[1592] It tried to determine the proportions of workers protected and unprotected by collective labour agreements in a given Member State.[1593] However, the most important issue was the protection of self-employed persons in collective labour agreements.[1594] These countries avoided answering questions about legal instruments that could be used by the authorities to extend the provisions on collective agreements to self-employed workers who do not fall within the definition of 'dependent employees'.[1595] So far, in some Member States, those in power have single-handedly cut off all efforts to bring self-employed workers under the protection of collective bargaining agreements.[1596] They were not considered employees.

It was also not clear why people employed in the public sector were excluded from the right to be covered by the protection guaranteed by collective agreements. It has been argued, not without reason, that the legal extension of the scope of protection provided by collective bargaining agreements also in force in the public sector has a significant impact on employment conditions in the public sector.[1597] Particularly interesting are the situations that took place in two relatively young Member States of the EU: Hungary and Lithuania. The Hungarian report from 2022 states: 'although the report provides detailed figures as to the number of collective agreements concluded during the reference period, it does not provide aggregated figures for collective bargaining coverage rates at the notational level'.[1598] The one for Lithuania stated that in 2021, 329 collective agreements were concluded. One-third of them (104 collective agreements) were concluded in the private sector. The remaining 224 collective labour agreements involved the public sector: national (one agreement), territorial (four), individual sectors of the economy (11) and at the level of individual workplaces (208). This means that the overall collective bargaining coverage in Lithuania might be less than 15% or 20%.[1599] The ECSR asked that the next report provide a comprehensive review of the relevant amendments introduced under the new Labour Code, which came into force on 1 July 2017 and has fundamentally amended the existing regulations concerning collective bargaining. Meanwhile, the Committee reiterated its finding of non-conformity on the grounds that the promotion of collective bargaining is insufficient.

IV. Mediation and Arbitration

254. Member States are obliged to promote the establishment and use of appropriate techniques for the out-of-court settlement of collective labour disputes.[1600] In

1592. Conclusions 2022 (Armenia), (Azerbaijan).
1593. Conclusions 2022 (Bosnia and Herzegovina).
1594. Conclusions 2022 (Bulgaria), (Estonia), (Denmark).
1595. Conclusions 2022 (France), (Italy).
1596. Conclusions 2022 (Georgia).
1597. Conclusions 2022 (Albania), (Malta).
1598. Conclusions 2022 (Hungary), (Lithuania).
1599. Conclusions 2022 (Lithuania).
1600. The Committee concludes that the situation in Georgia is not in conformity with Art. 6 §3 of the Charter on the grounds that there is no effective conciliation, mediation or arbitration service. The Georgian report indicates that in November 2012, the Government adopted a decree establishing

Article 6 §3, such techniques have been labelled as 'conciliatory', naming 'voluntary arbitration' as one such technique. The Committee believes that these techniques can be introduced to the legal systems of Member States and subsequently applied when utilising a law introduced by the state and in normative decisions and collective labour agreements executed by stakeholders or in practice.[1601] Member States are obliged to promote peaceful methods of settling collective labour disputes. Therefore, if the procedure for settling collective labour disputes is regulated independently and spontaneously by stakeholders, there are no reasons or legal grounds for the authorities of the Member States to intervene in such matters.[1602] The Committee requires that the mechanism for the peaceful settlement of collective labour disputes introduced to domestic legislative systems and practice provides the freedom of judgement for stakeholders, in disputable cases, and to the chosen persons or institutions. In connection with the above, conciliatory techniques for settling such labour disputes should be independent of both stakeholders and from the agencies of state administration. In particular, the above applies to social arbitrage, which should be organised in a manner which prevents the authorities of a Member State from influencing the outcomes of the arbitration decisions. For this reason, the Committee believes that domestic regulations governing collective labour law should not provide any instructions, indicate any guidelines or suggest any criteria to be followed by the arbitration commission or an arbitrator when handing down a judgment.[1603] By no means should peaceful techniques of settling collective labour disputes be replaced by labour court proceedings.

The above argument is illustrated by the case of Slovenia. Slovenian law allows courts to appoint an arbitrator or a higher arbitrator when parties to a collective labour dispute or one of the parties refuses to indicate the arbitrator or is delayed in fulfilling the above obligation, which it has voluntarily accepted.[1604] It is equivalent to a violation of Article 6 §3 of the Charter when one of the authorising parties of the collective disputes (chiefly the employer) takes the dispute to court.[1605]

In addition, national collective labour law regulations provide no legal grounds for authorising the party to choose the bodies authorised to try collective labour disputes: arbitration or the court.[1606] Paragraph 2 of Article 6 of the Charter, the authorities of these Member States made no effort to explain why they did not comply with the legal standards set out in the European Social Charter, first and revised.

---

the labour relations and social dialogue commission and this commission deals, *inter alia*, with labour disputes and promotes reconciliation between employers and employees. The Committee asks that the next report provide concrete examples on the role played by the above-mentioned commission with regard to labour disputes. Conclusions 2014 (Georgia).

1601. Conclusions I, p. 37. The Committee concluded that France lacks the regulations governing conflict-free mechanisms for the settlement of collective labour disputes in local government institutions. In practice, employers – local government administration agencies – were appointing mediators to recognise collective labour agreements, the Committee refused to issue a conclusion on non-compliance with the standards set in Art. 6 §3 of the Charter on the part of the French authorities. Conclusions XV-1, vol. 1, pp. 253–254.

1602. *Ibid.*

1603. Conclusions XIV-1, vol. 1, p. 388.

1604. Conclusions 2002, p. 186.

1605. Conclusions 2004, vol. 2, p. 515 (Slovenia).

1606. Conclusions 2004, vol. 2, pp. 346–347 (Lithuania).

With a negative conclusion, the ECSR demanded that the conditions and procedure for voluntary – but not compulsory – arbitration[1607] be discussed in the next report. During the analysis, it also turned out that a Member State may receive a negative conclusion if its authorities impose on the social partners, without their consent, the obligation to conduct arbitration by the national judicial authority.[1608] This leads to the conclusion that the ECSR equally issues negative decisions on countries that either avoid or impose on their authorities the conduct of social dialogue in collective labour relations. In some countries, it turned out that there is a voluntary legal system for settling collective disputes, but disputes still exist.[1609] There are cases where the obligation for voluntary dispute resolution was only practised in either the public or private sector.[1610] Meanwhile, the obligation to submit to the procedures of voluntary termination of collective disputes, initiated much more often by employees and their trade union organisations than by employers, applied equally to both parties to these collective disputes, including entrepreneurs.[1611] No circumstances, except for those listed in Article G of the Charter (listed by the law as necessary to protect rights and freedoms, public interests and safety and public health and morality), justify deviation from the above rules of conduct by the authorities of these countries in collective disputes[1612] cannot replace the model of protecting social peace described in the Social Charter.

255. Article 6 §3 of the Charter has been included in the regulations aimed at inspiring stakeholders by Member States to enter into collective labour agreements. Hence the Committee primarily believes that collective disputes that should have been settled by peaceful methods such as conciliation proceedings and social arbitration arose either during negotiations or during the application of collective labour agreements.[1613] Depending on the subject matter, the disputes arising from the interpretation of the provisions of collective labour agreements should be classified as collective or individual disputes. Collective disputes arising from the interpretation of provisions of collective labour agreements which create obligations are tried in accordance with the legal mechanisms regulated by the collective labour agreement. Therefore, the obligation of supporting peaceful mechanisms of settling disputes, which may arise between stakeholders in the process of negotiating or in the process of entering into collective labour agreements, is broader, and it includes the obligation of peaceful settlement of collective disputes irrespective of whether stakeholders negotiate a collective labour agreement or attempt to amend its provisions. Only a so-called social peace clause, which will be described below, voluntarily introduced to a collective labour agreement can prevent trade unions from requesting that the employer offer different conditions of work and wages more favourable than those regulated by the effective collective labour agreement to the workers represented by a given trade union. In such collective labour relations,

1607. Conclusions 2022 (Albania).
1608. Conclusions 2022 (Malta).
1609. Conclusions 2022 (Bosnia and Herzegovina).
1610. Conclusions 2022 (Bulgaria).
1611. Conclusions 2022 (Moldova).
1612. Conclusions 2022 (Malta), (Portugal), (Italy).
1613. Conclusions V, p. 45.

stakeholders may be bound by the provisions of a collective labour agreement or such an agreement which is not in force or is not accepted by a trade union. Any disputes about interests, i.e., about granting more favourable rights to workers and duties to employers with respect to wages and work conditions, are, in fact, collective labour disputes. The Committee departed from the view that Article 6 §3 of the Charter could only apply to conciliatory proceedings and social arbitration directly related to collective labour agreements in that it solely is applied to collective disputes that may arise in the process of negotiating collective labour agreements by stakeholders[1614] and concluded that, on the basis of Article 6 §3 of the Charter, Member States are obliged to promote legal mechanisms for the peaceful settlement of all collective labour disputes.[1615] The previous, restrictive interpretation of Article 6 §3 of the Charter was based on the statement forming a part of the introduction to Article 6. Initially, the Committee believed that Member State authorities were obliged to promote the development and undertaking of appropriate mechanisms of conciliation and voluntary arbitration for settling collective disputes 'with a view to exercise the right to collective negotiations effectively'. It was as late as during the fourteenth supervisory cycle that the Committee changed its view and concluded that, on the basis of Article 6 §3 of the Charter, peaceful methods of settling collective labour disputes were commonly applied.

256. Common employment of peaceful techniques in the process of solving collective labour disputes should be the subject matter of all deliberations. Conciliation proceedings and social arbitration should be introduced by Member States with a view to settling collective labour disputes of workers in the public sector.[1616] During a number of supervisory cycles, the Committee came to negative conclusions concerning Malta due to an absence of the peaceful techniques required for the settlement of collective labour disputes in the public service sector.[1617] In the case of Malta and Moldova, the Committee ruled that the situation in these countries was incompatible with Article 6 §3 of the 1961 Charter because of the power of public authorities in these countries to order parties to collective labour contracts to submit collective labour disputes to compulsory arbitration in situations not mentioned in Article G of the Charter.[1618] The situation changed during the fifteenth supervisory cycle. In the report on the application of the provisions of Article 6 §3, the authorities of Malta included some information on the introduction of conciliation techniques in the public sector. To examine the above-mentioned amendments of

1614. Conclusions V, p. 46 (Italy).
1615. Conclusions XIV-1, p. 616 (Norway).
1616. Conclusions V, p. 46 (France); Conclusions VIII, pp. 92–93 (Denmark), p. 93 (Iceland). Conclusions 2010, vol. 1, p. 186 (Bulgaria), vol. 2, p. 394 (Malta). Conclusions XIX-3, p. 41 (Croatia).
1617. Conclusions XII-2, pp. 110–111; Conclusions XIII-2, pp. 279–280; Conclusions XIII-3, p. 132; Conclusions XIV-1, p. 530. Due to the absence of procedures for peaceful settlement of collective disputes of public sector workers in Bulgaria, the Committee concluded on non-compliance of collective labour law regulations with Art. 6 §3 of the Charter. Conclusions 2004, vol. 1, p. 42. Conclusions 2014 (Bulgaria). As of 2014, the Committee concludes that the situation in Armenia and Azerbaijan is not in conformity with Art. 6 §3 of the Charter, on the grounds that it has not been established that mediation/conciliation and arbitration procedures exist in the public sector. Conclusions 2014 (Armenia, Azerbaijan).
1618. Activity Report 2018, pp. 36–37.

domestic regulations of the collective labour law, the Committee postponed its conclusion on the observance of Article 6 §3 of the Charter by Malta.[1619] Two examinations of the new peaceful settlement system of collective disputes of the public-sector workers in Malta did not bring about any amendment of the conclusions on non-compliance of national collective labour regulations with the international standards regarding the settlement of collective labour disputes. Conciliation proceedings are conducted by a committee set up on the basis of the principle of parity (four members representing employers – the authorities and their bodies/agencies and four members representing the trade unions representing the largest groups of workers involved in the collective dispute). A collective labour dispute is settled by a unanimous decision of the conciliation commission. In the absence of unanimity, the chairman of the commission is required to refer the case within two months to the industrial tribunal for settlement. Before concluding on compliance or non-compliance of the domestic regulations with the provisions of Article 6 §3 of the Charter, the Committee requested some additional information on the subject of the competences of the conciliation commission to be provided by the authorities of Malta.[1620] According to legislation in force, the Minister has the power to appoint a court of inquiry to establish the causes and circumstances of the dispute. Due to a lack of information, the Committee cannot establish whether the joint consent of the parties is required in this case. Therefore, the Committee maintains its conclusion of non-conformity on the grounds that it has not been established that decisions of the court of inquiry are binding on the parties only with their contents. The Committee recalls that any form of compulsory recourse to arbitration is a violation of this provision if domestic law allows one of the parties to defer the dispute to arbitration without the consent of the other party or allows the government or any other authority to defer the dispute to arbitration without the consent of one party or both.[1621] It did not pay much heed to it, as decisions handed down by the industrial tribunal have implications for all parties involved in a collective labour dispute. The Committee is against the principle of voluntary social arbitration.

257. 244. The Committee's conclusions on mandatory arbitration, with its decisions binding both parties to a collective labour dispute established by Member States, are stabilised. Any introduction of mandatory arbitration procedure without the consent of the interested parties cannot be considered as complying with the provisions of Article 6 §3 of the Charter unless it is limited to the exceptional cases

1619. Conclusions XV-1, p. 407.

1620. Conclusions XVII-1, vol. 2, p. 289.

1621. Conclusions 2014 (Malta). In 2016 the Maltese report states that the Court of Inquiry has the same powers as any other civil court and therefore the power to issue binding decisions irrespective of the consent of the parties. The Committee again concludes that the situation in Malta is not conformity with Charter due to the fact that under Art. 6 §4 of the Charter any form of compulsory recourse to arbitration is a violation of this provision. Conclusions 2016 (Malta), p. 224. Any restriction upon the conciliation and arbitration into the process of collective labour disputes is allowed within the limits prescribed by Art. G of the Charter. Conclusions 2006 (Portugal).

specified in Article 31 §1 ESC or Article G §1 RESC.[1622] The Committee obliges Member State authorities to indicate the extent to which the obligation of observing the arbitration procedure is required for the protection of rights and freedoms of other persons or for the protection of the public order, national security, public health or good practice. A reference to the 'humanitarian interest' as the basis for submitting a petition for trying a collective dispute by social arbitration after 20 days of a strike have elapsed[1623] served as the basis for postponing its conclusion and demanding a presentation of some additional information on possible threats to legal and public order, health or good practice, which could justify the apparent breach of international standards from the authorities of Romania.[1624]

The case of Norway, which, on several occasions, took advantage of the regulation permitting reference of a collective labour dispute to the arbitration for settlement in order to prevent trade unions from conducting a strike of workers employed on the North Sea oil rigs, prompted the Committee of Ministers towards adopting a resolution on non-compliance of the actions taken by the Norwegian government with the international standards for the reasons of exceeding the authorisations formulated in Article 31 §1 ESC and a breach of Article 6 §3 and 4 of the Charter.[1625] The Committee concluded that the situation in Albania and Moldova is not in conformity with Article 6 §3 of the RESC on the grounds that the circumstances in which recourse to compulsory arbitration is authorised to go beyond the limits set out in Article G of the RESC.[1626]

In accordance with the existing conclusions, the Committee examined the practice of appropriating domestic labour law regulations.

In the case of Portugal, the Committee concluded compliance of its domestic labour law regulations with Article 6 §3 of the Charter regardless of the obligation of arbitration imposed by regulations applicable in that country. However, the Committee established that the above-mentioned regulations are non-enforceable. The state authorities failed to prepare a list of arbitrators that should be agreeable stakeholders.[1627]

1622. Conclusions XII-2, p. 110 (Malta); Conclusions XIII-1, p. 152 (Norway); Conclusions XIII-3, p. 133 (Norway); Conclusions XIII-3, p. 278 (Portugal); Conclusions XIV-1, vol. 1, p. 387 (Iceland); Conclusions XIV-1, vol. 2, pp. 616–617 (Norway); Conclusions XV-1, vol. 1, pp. 44–46 (Austria); Conclusions XV-1, vol. 2, p. 430 (Norway); Conclusions 2010, vol. 1, p. 37 (Albania), vol. 2, p. 425 (Moldova); Conclusion 2014 (Portugal, Malta).
1623. The case of Romania. Conclusions 2002, p. 134.
1624. Conclusions 2004, vol. 2, pp. 458–459.
1625. RChS (93)2. 'The right to organise', *supra*, p. 61; Samuel, *supra*, p. 149.
1626. Conclusions 2006, vol. 1, p. 56 (Albania), vol. 2, p. 570 (Moldova).
1627. Conclusions XVII-1, vol. 2, p. 418. As of 2014, the Committee finds that there are three situation where recourse to compulsory arbitration is possible. The Labour Code (CT) defines two situations in which compulsory arbitration is possible: (1) if the Permanent Commission of Social Concentration adopts a recommendation in favour supported by the majority of voting workers and employers; (2) if essential services relating to the protection of life, health and public security are involved. In addition, the Revised Labour Code (2009) allows a new (third) possibility of compulsory arbitration, called 'necessary arbitration', which is only possible if a new collective agreement is adopted twelve months after the expiration of the time limit of the previous collective agreement and there is no collective convention applicable to at least half of the workers covered by the expired collective convention. With regard to the first and third situations, the Committee

The ECSR acknowledged that during the presentation on 23 March 2023 regarding Article 6 §3 of the Charter, there was no reason to discuss and release to the general public the legal problems related to the Member State authorities' failure to support, establish and have social partners use amicable legal techniques for collective and voluntary arbitration in collective labour disputes.[1628] Had this rule been observed, both parties to collective labour relations would probably have been able to avoid strikes and lockouts. The ECSR reviewed 30 reports submitted by thirty Member States. Eight of these countries have been found not to comply with the provisions of paragraph 3 of Article 6 of the Charter. The vast majority of negative conclusions concerned the so-called new Eastern European countries.[1629] The number of Member States only recently beginning to develop democracy on the European continent is of less importance than the types of violations and the reasons why the authorities of some countries showed disfavour to the idea of maintaining social peace in collective labour relations.

V. Right of Workers and Employers to Collective Action

258. Article 6 §4 of the Charter guarantees all stakeholders the right to take part in collective action in the case of a labour dispute. This provision ensures that both parties to the labour dispute (both workers and employers) are granted the right to take part in collective action. It was not mentioned explicitly as to what type of collective action is permitted to all sides of the collective labour relations. However, in the case of the workers, it was specified they had the right to all types of collective action, including the right to strike. The general regulation of stakeholders' rights to take part in collective action when there are cases of conflict of interests meant a legal basis was formed for the Committee to extend its scope of protection of labour rights in cases of collective labour disputes. The Committee's rulings concern the idea of collective action, the definition of a legal strike, the legal restrictions concerned with the utilisation of the right to organise strikes, the procedural requirements of carrying out and pursuing legal collective action and the legal consequences of collective action for workers. The Committee also undertook the steps for the legality of collective action taken up by employers.

A. Collective Action

259. Article 6 §4 of the Charter does not indicate any specific collective actions but for the right to strike that may be undertaken by the workers in order to protect their interests. The Committee did not analyse or discuss the collective actions

concludes that the situation is not in conformity with Art. 6 §3 of the Charter, as compulsory recourse to arbitration is permitted in circumstances which go beyond the limits set out in Art. G of the Charter. Conclusions 2014 (Portugal).

1628. Conclusions 2022, *Press Briefing Elements*, p. 16.

1629. Conclusions 2022 (Albania), (Azerbaijan), (Bosnia and Herzegovina), (Bulgaria), (Italy), (Malta), (Portugal), (Moldova).

which can be organised based on Article 6 §4 of the Charter. Instead, the Committee was only interested to learn about the types of collective action that are considered legal by the domestic collective labour regulations of a given country.[1630] It demanded to know from certain Member States why domestic collective labour laws prohibited certain categories of workers, such as state officials, from partaking in collective action, permitting them only the right to strike.[1631]

Since the first supervisory cycle, the Committee was of the view that Article 6 §4 of the Charter ensured stakeholders the right to carry out collective action. This provision states *expressis verbis* the right to strike, which workers may utilise in the case of a conflict of interest. Although the provision in question did not clearly state that in the case of conflict of interest, employers have the right to carry out collective action, the Committee pointed out that the lockout was the basic, if not the only, means of protecting the employers' interests against the excessive demands made by the trade unions representing the workers.[1632] It is somewhat difficult to determine whether Article 6 §4 of the Charter ensures stakeholders the right to exert pressure on the other party to the collective labour relation in order to regulate the work conditions and the wages for the workers who are represented in such collective labour relations by union organisations, meeting the demands of the trade unions.[1633] The handed-down rulings of the Committee foremost deal with strikes organised by the workers. In its previous conclusions, the Committee stated that the scope for workers to defend their interests through lawful collective action was excessively circumscribed in the UK.[1634] In its last conclusion, the Committee noted that lawful collective action was limited to disputes between workers and their employer, which prevented unions from taking action against a *de facto* employer if this was not the immediate employer.[1635] At present,[1636] the Committee considers that employees nowadays often do not work solely for and under the direction of a single clearly defined employer, as evidenced by outsourcing, work in networked organisations, the formation of inter-organisational partnerships, particularly in public services, but also more use of agency staff, secondments and joint partnership working. The result is a far more diverse and complex matrix of contractual relationships with workers who used to share the same employer being split among different employers, even while they may find themselves simultaneously brought together with workers from other industries under new employment arrangements. As a consequence, trade unions find themselves representing a workforce whose terms and conditions are, to a large extent, not determined by their employer. Therefore, the Committee concludes that the restrictions in terms of the prohibition of secondary action excessively limit the possibilities for workers to defend their interests

1630. Conclusions XV-1, vol. 1, p. 81 (Belgium), p. 121 (Cyprus).
1631. Conclusions XIV-1, vol. 1, p. 21; Conclusions XV-1, vol. 1, p. 202; Conclusions XV-1, vol. 2, p. 477 (Portugal), p. 520 (Spain); Conclusions 2006, vol. 1, p. 104 (Bulgaria), p. 147 (Cyprus), p. 188 (Estonia).
1632. Conclusions I, pp. 38–39.
1633. Conclusions XIX-3, p. 263 (United Kingdom). The scope for workers to defend end their interests through collective action is excessively circumscribed.
1634. Conclusions XVII-1 (2004), XVIII-1 (2006), XIX-3 (2010).
1635. Conclusions XIX-3 (2010).
1636. Conclusions XX-3 (2014).

through lawful collective action.[1637] It should be assumed that the international collective labour law standards of the Council of Europe do not respect the rule of equality when it comes to exerting pressure, which may be executed by stakeholders engaged in collective labour disputes.

260. A necessary requirement in carrying out a collective action in a collective labour relation is the conflict of interest between stakeholders. In accordance with the generally binding labour laws, the Committee is of the opinion that the right to organise collective labour actions cannot exist in cases where there is a difference of opinion among stakeholders with regard to the interpretations and practices of applying the binding labour law regulations or provisions of collective agreements. According to the Committee, this point of view continues to convince even if stakeholders were to unanimously introduce into their collective agreements provisions allowing for discrepancy of opinion to form a necessary requirement justifying the organisation and the carrying out of collective action.[1638] Of the 29 Member States that submitted reports in the last cycle, ending in December 2022, 24 received negative ECSR conclusions. ECSR representatives on 23 March 2023 listed Albania, Armenia, Azerbaijan, Belgium, Bosnia-Herzegovina, Finland, France, Germany, Greece, Hungary, Ireland, Italy, Montenegro, the Netherlands – Caribbean part, Portugal, Romania, Moldova and the United Kingdom. The Charter of Social Rights of the Council of Europe guarantees employees the right to take collective action addressed to specific companies that violate the rights granted to employees, including the right to initiate and conduct strikes. This right is exercised by trade union organisations that represent the interests of employees. Employers, on the other hand, use the right to conduct lockouts. These rights are vested in social partners in situations where they cannot voluntarily obtain consent from the other party to collective employment relations – almost always a company that also acts as an employer – to make a change in favour of their legal, economic and social situation. A strike is a lawful element of pressure exerted by an employees' trade union on the employer in order to meet the demands of employees in matters relating to remuneration, working conditions, social matters and other issues. Employers use lockouts to mitigate the demands made by employee trade union organisations, collective actions regulated by Article 6 §4 of the Charter. Therefore, there are no grounds for employees or their trade union organisations to analyse compliance with the labour law standards regarding the lockout regulated in this Charter. The 24 cases of non-compliance with the law on the right to organise strikes do not concern the conduct of employees and trade union organisations but relate to employers and state authorities. It is the responsibility of these authorities to bring national law in line with the standards set out in the Council of Europe's Charter of Social Rights. The state is also obliged to exercise constant supervision over the observance of national law and its compliance with the standards of the Charter of Social Rights.

1637. Conclusions XX-3 (2014 United Kingdom).
1638. Conclusions I, p. 38.

B. A Legal Strike

261. Article 6 §4 of the Charter does not classify strikes into legal and illegal categories. It only regulates the workers' right to undertake legal collective action, which includes the right to strike.[1639] It therefore provides the ground for such classifications. In accordance with the understanding of the provision, a legal strike is one that falls into the scope of an analysed standard. A strike is a collective action organised by workers in order to exert pressure on the employer who regulates the conditions of work and the wages. The aim of a strike, therefore, is to create more favourable conditions of employment and better wages. Strikes may be organised by workers in order to protect the workers' interests against the actions of the employer. Strikes and other forms of collective action cannot be organised if their aim is to protect the interests of workers who are employed by other employers or to protect the rights of customers or consumers.[1640] A conflict of interest between workers and the employer is,]8 therefore, a requirement in order for a legal strike to be able to be organised.[1641] The provisions of Article 6 §4 and Article 5 are closely interrelated. Collective action and strikes may be organised to meet the same goals, protecting both economic and social interests. In order to achieve such goals, workers join trade union organisations. The Charter does not protect the other interests of workers. Strikes induced by politics do not enjoy legal protection since Article 6 of the Charter is a norm which ensures effective regulations for collective negotiations between stakeholders, while political issues cannot be negotiated through a collective agreement.[1642] Workers organise in trade unions, negotiate with employers and carry out collective action to ensure their economic and professional interests are protected. Therefore the legal protection ensured by Article 6 §4 of the Charter does not protect strikes when they are organised to support the interests of other groups of workers. The Committee has not taken a stand with regard to the legality of solidarity strikes organised by one trade union in support of another union, which demand to be recognised by the authorities of Member States and employer organisations. The Committee stated that the strikes aimed at protecting the interests of the union, which is responsible for organising the strike, enjoy the legal protection guaranteed by Article 6 §4 of the Charter.[1643] Workers are entitled to organise strikes with the view of protecting their economic, social and union-related interests. Such interests do not have to be directly related to the negotiations aimed at entering into a collective agreement.[1644] The boundary of the Committee's

1639. As of 2014, Georgia is the only Member State for which the following conclusion is adopted by the Committee: it has not been established that the right to collective action of workers and employers, including the right to strike, is adequately recognised. On those grounds, the Committee concludes that the situation in Georgia is not in conformity with Art. 6 §4 of the Charter. In Denmark, civil servants employed under the Civil Service Act are denied the right to strike. For that reason, the Committee concludes that the situation in Denmark is not in conformity with Art. 6 §4 of the Charter. Conclusions XX-3 (Denmark).

1640. *Ibid.*

1641. Conclusions XV-1, vol. 2, pp. 637–641 (United Kingdom).

1642. Conclusions II, p. 27.

1643. Conclusions XVII-1, vol. 2, p. 290 (Malta).

1644. Conclusions II, p. 28; Conclusions III, p. 96; Conclusions XII-1, p. 129. Conclusions XIX-3, p. 105 (Germany).

jurisdiction in matters of legality concerning strikes organised and not in direct connection with entering into collective agreements has not changed since the initial supervisory cycles monitoring the compliance of the provisions of the Charter by Member States. The Committee has handed down decisions concerning the failure of some domestic collective labour regulations to meet the requirements of Article 6 §4 of the Charter. It was of the view that some authorities of Member States considered the organisation of a strike which did not exert pressure on employers in connection with the negotiating of collective agreements as illegal.[1645] This was viewed by the Committee as a violation of Article 6 §4 of the Charter.[1646] The Committee claims domestic collective labour regulations, which forbid workers from organising strikes which are unrelated to the negotiations of collective agreements, do not leave any possibility for the fact that stakeholders also negotiate in order to enter into other normative agreements. According to the Committee, any negotiations aimed at regulating any issues that may evoke the interest of stakeholders should be treated as collective negotiations, as understood by the provision of Article 6 §4 of the Charter. This is irrespective of whether such negotiations are supported by domestic collective labour regulations or not.[1647] An example of a legal strike is an action organised by workers in order to exert pressure on the employer to comply with the health and safety regulation requirements and the protection of the health of the worker.[1648]

Legal strikes can be organised by all workers, irrespective of their membership in trade unions. The Committee concludes that the situation is not in conformity with Article 6 §4 of the RESC if only the most representative trade unions have the right to call on strikes[1649] in the public sector.[1650] Granting a monopoly, according to the domestic collective labour law regulations, to a trade union organisation for organising collective actions is a breach of the international labour law standards established by the Committee.[1651] The Committee voiced its opinion that it is in the best interest of both workers and employers to negotiate the work conditions and wages through collective labour agreements and other such normative agreements. Both sides also have the right to exert pressure on the other party in collective agreements. Irrespective of trade union membership, workers have the right to organise and partake in strikes, which are neither supported nor organised by trade unions.

1645. Case of Germany: Conclusions XIII-2, p. 282; Conclusions XIV-1, vol. 1, p. 310, Conclusions XIX, p. 105; Addendum to Conclusions XIV-1, pp. 27–28; Conclusions XVII-1, vol. 1, p. 206; Case of Iceland: Conclusions XIII-3, p. 135; Conclusions XIV-1, p. 390; Conclusions XV-1, p. 335. Case of Finland: Conclusions XV-1, vol. 1, p. 203; Conclusions XVII-1, vol. 1, p. 170; Conclusions XV-1, vol. 1, p. 153 (Denmark); Conclusions XVII-1, vol. 1, p. 103 (Czech Republic).
1646. Conclusions 2006, p. 249 (Finland).
1647. Conclusions IV, p. 50.
1648. Conclusions II, p. 28.
1649. Case of Ireland, Conclusions 2006, vol. 1, p. 267 (France), p. 373. Conclusions 2010, vol. 2, p. 540 (Romania). Conclusions 2014 (Romania).
1650. Conclusions 2006, vol. 1, p. 309 (France). Conclusions 2010, vol. 2, p. 504 (Portugal). Conclusions 2014 (France).
1651. Conclusions XIX-3, p. 105 (Germany).

The Committee views the right to strike as a guarantee of effective collective negotiations by workers.[1652] The Committee's judgments with regard to the opportunity to exercise the right to organise strikes are not uniform. First, the Committee ruled that domestic collective labour law regulations, which would allow the right to organise a legal strike dependent on the decisions of either the trade unions or other organisations representing the workers' interests in the workplace where the majority were not represented by trade unions, was in compliance with Article 6 §4 of the Charter.[1653] However, the Committee soon changed its position and all subsequent cases where such domestic collective labour regulations within Member States legalised strikes only on the premise that they would be organised by trade unions were seen as non-compliance of domestic laws with international standards.[1654] The Committee's position was that a group of workers who had no legal status had a right to organise a legal strike.[1655] The Committee soon adopted a different position with regard to this issue.

The Committee's ruling with regard to the compliance of Member States with Article 6 §4 of the Charter, therefore depends upon the conclusions made from the analysing of Article 5. The subject matters of such analysis are cases solely dealing with the compliance of Member States to the standards established under Article 5 of the Charter. Among the domestic labour law regulations complying with the international standards based on Article 5 of the Charter, the Committee chooses those which have the least requirements to be fulfilled by workers intending to establish a trade union organisation. If domestic labour law regulations do not hinder workers from establishing a trade union with the intention to strike, the Committee is of the opinion that granting a trade union a monopoly in supervising a collective action is in accordance with Article 6 §4 of the Charter. Domestic regulations, which complicate the establishment of a trade union by demanding requirements that are difficult to fulfil, are seen by the Committee as an inconsistency with Article 6 §4 of the Charter. This is exemplified by a scenario in which a trade union is the only institution allowed to organise a strike.[1656] In Conclusions XV-1 (2001), XVI-1 (2003), XVII-1 (2005), XVIII-1 (2006), and XIX-3 (2010), the Committee concluded that the situation in Germany was not compatible with Article 6 §4 of the Charter because the requirements to be met by a group of workers in order to form a union satisfying the conditions for calling a strike constituted an excessive restriction on the right to strike. Germany's case law dealing with the right to collective action deliberately rules out the lawfulness of strikes instigated by a small group of employees outside trade union organisations with collective bargaining powers. This is in line with the principle that effective collective agreements can only be concluded by trade unions with the capacity to bargain collectively within a collective bargaining framework and, if possible, without collective action.[1657] As

1652. Conclusions IV, p. 50; Conclusions XV-1, vol. 1, p. 204.
1653. Case of Portugal: Conclusions XIII-3, pp. 280–281; Conclusions XIII-5, pp. 179–180; Conclusions XIV-1, vol. 2, p. 662, Conclusions 2006, vol. 2, p. 685.
1654. Conclusions XVII-1, vol. 2, p. 420 (Portugal); Conclusions 2002, p. 237 (Sweden); Conclusions 2004, vol. 2, pp. 350–351 (Lithuania). Conclusion 2014 (Portugal).
1655. Conclusions XV-1. Citing: The right to organise, *supra*, p. 65.
1656. Addendum to Conclusions XV-1, pp. 28–29 (Germany).
1657. Conclusions XX-3 (2014 Germany).

of 2015, the Committee consequently concludes that the situation in Germany is not in conformity with Article 6 §4 of the Charter on the grounds that the requirements to be met by a group of workers in order to form a trade union are too complicated.

Prior to handing down a decision with regard to Portuguese collective labour law regulations, which allow for trade unions only to organise strikes, and the compliance of such laws with Article 6 §4 of the Charter, the Committee examined legal requirements concerning workers' rights to establish trade unions as well as how those requirements are put into practice. The Committee focused mainly on how long it took to register a trade union.[1658] It also analysed whether a minority of workers employed by one employer and who do not belong to a trade union nor are represented by a trade union organisation can organise a legal strike in order to protect their rights.[1659]

Public service employees also have the right to organise legal strikes.[1660] Article 6 §4 of the Charter does not limit such a right, but by the first supervisory cycle, the Committee was of the decision that domestic labour law regulations would impose such restrictions, as verified by the reasons stipulated under Article 31 §1 of the European Social Charter, would not be inconsistent with international standards.[1661] In 2018, the Committee rightly pointed out that excessive restrictions on the right to strike created important problems in some Member States.[1662] The Committee considered that the restrictions on the right to strike of employees working in various sectors such as the energy supply services, telecommunication, nuclear facilities, transport are not justified in nine countries: Armenia, Azerbaijan, Bosnia and Herzegovina, Georgia, Republic of Moldova, the Russian Federation, Serbia, Slovak Republic and Ukraine.[1663] The Committee identified the following groups of public servants that may be restricted in organising strikes: policemen,[1664] professional servicemen, the judiciary, high-level public administrators,[1665] firemen and prison wardens.[1666] The Committee regarded the exclusion of all public servants from the right to organise strikes as a breach of Article 6 §4 of the Charter.[1667] The protection of rights stated under Article 31 §1 of the Charter forms the basis for such exclusions of the following rights: protection of rights and liberties, public order, national security, protection of public health and customs. The exemption from the

1658. Conclusions XV-1, vol. 2, pp. 477–478.

1659. The situation is not in conformity with the Charter if the workers who are not members of a trade union, having called a strike, are prevented from participating in the strike unless they join the relevant trade union, and do not enjoy the same protection as trade union members if they participate in a strike. Conclusions XX-3 (Denmark).

1660. Conclusions 2010, vol. 1, p. 40 (Albania), p. 188 (Bulgaria), p. 228 (Estonia), vol. 2, p. 428 (Moldova). Conclusions XIX-3, p. 83 (Denmark).

1661. On the condition there are not excessive. Conclusions 2010, vol. 1, p. 210 (Cyprus), vol. 2, p. 476 (Norway). Conclusions XIX-3, p. 65 (Croatia).

1662. Armenia, the Czech Republic, Malta, the Republic of Moldova (police) the Czech Republic (prison service). Activity Report 2018, p. 37.

1663. *Ibid.*, p. 37.

1664. The Committee concludes that the absolute prohibition of the right to strike of police forces goes beyond the conditions established by Art. G of the Charter. Conclusions 2014 (Ireland).

1665. Conclusions I, pp. 38–39; Conclusions II, p. 187 (Cyprus); Conclusions III, p. 36.

1666. Conclusions V, p. 48 (France); Conclusions XIII-2, p. 282 (Malta).

1667. The situation is not in conformity with the Charter in Azerbaijan, Denmark, Germany and Ukraine on the ground civil servants are denied the right to strike. Activity Report 2018, p. 37.

right to organise strikes concerns the category of public servants whose tasks (falling within the scope of administration and authority of the state) are related to the protection of the principles enumerated under Article 31 §1 of the European Social Charter.[1668]

The Committee found that the Icelandic authorities were consistent with Article 6 §4 in accordance with Article 31 §1 of the Charter when they drew up a list of all public-sector workers deprived of the right to organise strikes.[1669] The Committee demanded, however, that the information concerning the criteria upon which this list was dependent was produced. The Committee became aware that before the list was prepared, the state authorities consulted trade unions and permitted a trade union to appear before a labour court seeking an injunction concerning the addition of a certain category of public servants to the list. The Committee handed down a decision stating the Icelandic labour laws were consistent with international standards.[1670]

262. At first, the Committee maintained that Member States which have ratified Article 6 §4 of the Charter could not effectively make a declaration concerning the exclusion of certain categories of public servants from the scope of the application of the provision in question.[1671] The Committee found that a complete exclusion of certain public servants in Germany[1672] from having the right to organise strikes was a violation of Article 6 §4 of the Charter.[1673] After the Netherlands raised its objection against the inapplicability of this regulation to public service officials, the Committee reached a conclusion (as all Member States accepted the objection) that under Article 20 of the Charter, Member State authorities were entitled to exclude certain categories of public servants from the scope of Article 6 §4 of the Charter.[1674]

On 28 September 1961, German authorities declared they would not apply Article 6 §4 of the Charter to public officials. The Committee, however, regarded that this declaration had no legal basis.[1675] It did, however, change its views after having examined the legal validity of the objections put forth by the Dutch authorities. It came to the conclusion the 1961 declaration could be treated as a reservation for the exclusion of the above-mentioned categories of workers (public servants) from the provision of Article 6 §4 of the Charter.[1676]

263. In summary of the argumentation presented above, proving the Committee's tendency to change its attitude towards the organisation of strikes in the public sector, the exclusions and restrictions of rights may:

1668. Conclusions 2–14 (Azerbaijan, Hungary, Republic of Moldova, Ukraine).
1669. Conclusions XV-1, vol. 1, p. 122.
1670. *Ibid.*
1671. Conclusions I, pp. 184–185 (Germany).
1672. German state officials – *Beamte*. *See* Novitz, *supra*, pp. 307 et seq.
1673. Case of Germany: Conclusions III, p. 336; Conclusions IV, pp. 48–49; Case of Denmark: Conclusions XIV-1, vol. 1, p. 180; Conclusions XV-1, vol. 1, p. 153; Conclusions XVII-1, vol. 1, p. 134; Conclusions 2004, vol. 1, p. 149 (Estonia).
1674. Conclusions VII, p. 39.
1675. Conclusions I, pp. 184–185.
1676. Conclusions VII, p. 39.

– be justified only by the reasons stipulated under Article 31 §1 of the European Social Charter. The Committee maintains the limitations, which extend beyond the scope of the general clause established under Article 31 §1 of the European Social Charter is, inconsistent with international standards;[1677]
– may relate only to some public servants. Granting the right to all public servants to organise symbolic strikes, especially granting the right to public servants who are employed by work agreements in the government sector[1678] and to those employed in privatised public institutions (such as in the postal system or the railways),[1679] is a breach of Article 6 §4 of the Charter.

C. *Illegal Strikes*[1680]

264. Many states were in breach of the right to strike. The ECSR found 24 states to not be in conformity. Five were found to be in conformity pending receipt of requested information.[1681] Some countries (Germany and the United Kingdom) were found to be in non-conformity due to restrictions on the permitted objectives of strikes. The ECSR adopted conclusions of non-conformity with respect to the situation in eight states.[1682] They also found that excessive restrictions on the right to strike were imposed with regard to certain categories of persons in many states. These categories include civil or public servants, police[1683] and employees in essential sectors such as the energy supply services, telecommunications, nuclear facilities, transport and others. Some countries report to the ECSR on criteria defining minimum services and/or authorities competent to reach an agreement on these services. The ECSR concluded that the situation was not in conformity with Article 6 §4 of the Charter because it had not been established that the situation was not in conformity with the Charter.[1684] These findings were based on information repeatedly provided by the states.

As regards the right of the police to strike, the ECSR concluded that eight states were not in conformity due to an absolute ban on strikes.[1685] In the case of North Macedonia, only very restrictive circumstances are permitted in which members of the police may legally organise a strike. In the case of Ireland, the government stated that the unique position of the police (*An Garda Siochána*) is such that any strike action is likely to impact policing, the security of the state or other maintenance of public authority. In this regard, the government stated that following the

1677. Conclusions 2004, vol. 1, p. 97 (Cyprus).
1678. Conclusions 2004, vol. 1, p. 46.
1679. Conclusions XVII-1, vol. 1, p. 207 (Germany).
1680. Conclusions 2022, *Press Briefing Elements*, *supra*, pp. 16–17.
1681. Conclusions 2022 (Belgium), (Finland), (Greece), (Italy), (Netherlands – Caribbean part).
1682. Conclusions 2022 (Armenia), (France), (Germany), (Hungary), (Ireland), (Portugal), (Montenegro).
1683. Conclusions 2022 (Georgia), (Hungary), (Ireland), (Latvia), (Romania).
1684. Conclusions 2022 (Albania), (Armenia), (Azerbaijan), (Bosnia and Herzegovina), (Bulgaria), (Estonia), (Germany), (Hungary), (Ireland), (Malta), (Montenegro), (Moldova), (Serbia), (Slovakia), (Spain), (United Kingdom).
1685. Conclusions 2022 (Armenia), (Georgia), (Hungary), (Ireland), (Latvia), (Malta), (Romania), (Spain).

Committee's previous conclusion of non-conformity, changes were made to the police's internal dispute mechanisms. The Irish Human Rights and Equality Commission (IHRC) noted that the absolute prohibition of strikes remains in place. Since the situation has not changed, the ECSR reiterates its conclusion of non-conformity.

Although the question on the matter of police strikes was reiterated several times, there are still fifteen Member States which have not submitted any information on this matter.[1686]

Legislation and practises related to the consequences of strikes were not in conformity in Ireland and the United Kingdom. The ECSR noted that some states[1687] are in long-standing non-conformity with Article 6 §4 and are not willing to take steps to bring the situation into conformity.[1688]

D. Restricting the Right to Strike

265. The right to strike is not absolute and has some restrictions. In the appendix to Article 6 §4 of the Charter, authorities of Member States were authorised to regulate, to a reasonable extent, the application of the right in question in a way that each further restriction of the law could be justified only by the circumstances stipulated either in Article 31 §1 ESC or Article G §1 of the appendix to ESC. The right to strike may be restricted by: collective agreements, regulations established by Member States and by the judicial decisions of courts. It cannot be restricted through the national statutory framework.[1689] The Foreign Posting of Employees Act in Sweden provides that no form of collective action can be taken by trade unions if the employer shows that workers enjoy conditions of employment (including wage levels and other essential aspects of work) that are at least as favourable as the minimum conditions established in agreements at the central level. The Committee considers that this statutory framework constitutes a disproportionate restriction on the free enjoyment of the right of trade unions to engage in collective action since it prevents trade unions from taking action to improve the employment conditions of posted workers over and beyond the requirements of the abovementioned conditions. Therefore, the Committee concludes that the situation in Sweden is not in conformity with Article 6 §4 of the Charter.

1. Restricting the Right to Strike in Collective Labour Agreements

266. Pursuant to Article 6 §4 of the Charter, the restriction to strike imposed by the stakeholders in a collective agreement is in compliance with international standards. Parties to the negotiation of collective agreements have the right to introduce

1686. Conclusions 2022 (Albania), (Belgium), (Bulgaria), (Estonia), (Finland), (Greece), (Italy), (Netherlands – Caribbean part), (Portugal), (Moldova), (Slovakia), (Spain), (United Kingdom).
1687. Conclusions 2022 (United Kingdom).
1688. *Press Briefing ...* , *supra*, p. 17.
1689. Conclusions 2014 (Sweden).

the so-called social peace clauses, binding the workers' representatives and signatories of collective agreements to voluntarily refrain from any collective actions, including strikes, for as long as the collective agreement is in force. The voluntarily incorporated provision in a collective agreement by all parties, excluding or limiting the right to strike, is in compliance with Article 6 §4 of the Charter.[1690] A social peace clause is binding only upon those workers who are represented by a trade union which has signed a particular collective agreement.[1691] Workers, members of a trade union bound by a social peace clause – have to refrain from collective actions only in matters covered by the collective agreement. The same applies to trade unions, which are signatories to collective agreements. Trade unions may refrain from carrying out collective actions while a collective agreement is in force.[1692] In such cases, the Committee attempts to establish whether the signatories to the agreement have introduced the exclusion of the right to strike during the period when a collective agreement is in force, knowingly and voluntarily.

2. Restricting the Right to Strike, as Introduced by the Domestic Legislation of Member States

267. 253. Member States enact regulations on collective bargaining. The legality of a strike is conditional on the fulfilment of certain procedural requirements by the organisers of a strike action that are introduced by the authorities of Member States. State intervention during the workers' process of carrying out their right to collective action (including a strike) consists of: restrictions on the number of entities entitled to organising strikes; establishing formal requirements, which need to be met before a legal strike may proceed; introducing the obligation to exhaust all possible avenues of arbitration before declaring strike action; introducing the obligation to ensure the continuity of operation within certain workplaces. The right to introduce procedural requirements concerning strikes cannot be considered equivalent to the prohibition of collective actions and strikes.[1693]

268. In the last cycle of ECSR Member State reports, the Committee found that Member State authorities had too often crossed the line set by Article G (Restrictions) of the Charter. The ECSR is of the opinion that the general wording and even some other cases of 'Essential services' mentioned in this part of the study cannot justify all the exceptions listed in Article G of the Charter. For this reason, the Committee concluded that restrictions in some sectors go beyond the limits set by Article G of the Charter.[1694] The Council of Europe cannot accept the exclusion of the right to strike for people employed in such sectors of the national economy as railway transport (Bulgaria), electricity, water supply services, telecommunications, air traffic control, fire protection or prison services (Albania). Likewise, criteria used to

1690. Conclusions I, p. 38; Conclusions VIII, p. 98 (Sweden); Conclusions XV-1, vol. 2, p. 521 (Spain).
1691. Conclusions VII, p. 40 (Sweden); Conclusions XIV-1, vol. 2, p. 619 (Norway).
1692. Conclusions XV-1, vol. 2, p. 432 (Norway); Conclusions XV-1, vol. 2, p. 521 (Spain).
1693. Conclusions XII-1, p. 128 (Iceland).
1694. Conclusions 2022 (Armenia), (Azerbaijan), (Bosnia and Herzegovina)

define civil servant officials who are denied the right to strike exceed the limits set by Article G.[1695] The ECSR considered cases in which strike bans were introduced for a large group of people intending to strike: public officials and/or employees of state offices and national defence, state security and customs, as well as institutions classified as public sector.[1696] Some individuals who are professionally active in France are not entitled to organise strikes. According to the ECSR, the indivisible thirtieth rule applicable to strikes by staff of administrative state bodies goes beyond the limits set by Article G of the Charter. The French authorities also failed to prove why the restrictions on employees working in state kindergartens and primary schools and in the public transport sector fall within the limits established by Article G.

E. Restricting the Number of Entities Entitled to Organise Strikes

269. No Member State guarantees all workers the right to strike. Generally, a precondition for a lawful strike is the establishment of a trade union organisation. Some Member States restrict the right to organise a strike of trade unions that are not considered to be representative of workers.

This requirement, that only representative trade union organisations have the right to organise strikes, is evident in the French labour law.[1697] Only the most representative trade unions can call strikes in the public sector. Whether a trade union is representative or not is determined not only by the level of membership but also by the results achieved in a ballot carried out at a given workplace concerning various trade organisations and voting on the one that is most applicable to be representative of the workers. All workers employed by a given employer participate in such a ballot. The Committee is of the opinion that the above restriction on the right to strike is in breach of Article 6 §4 of the Charter.[1698] The restrictions on the right to strike for certain categories of employees, regardless of the sector (private or public) in which they are employed, have to comply with the conditions imposed by Article G of the Charter.[1699]

1695. Conclusions 2022 (Hungary), (France).
1696. Conclusions 2022 (Slovakia), (Moldova).
1697. Also in Romania. Conclusions 2010, vol. 2, p. 540.
1698. Case of France: Conclusions 2002, pp. 35–36; Conclusions 2004, vol. 1, p. 220.
1699. The Committee concludes as of 2014, that the restrictions in the following Member States do not comply with the conditions provided by Art. G of the Charter given that they are neither prescribed by law nor proportionate to the aims set out in Art. G of the Charter: Slovak Republic – employees of health care or social care facilities, employees operating nuclear power facilities, facilities with fissile material and oil or gas pipeline facilities, judges, prosecutors and air traffic controllers, and employees working in telecommunications operations, members of fire brigade, rescue teams set up under special regulations; Ukraine – employees working in emergency and rescue services, nuclear facilities, underground undertakings, electric power engineering; Republic of Moldova – all employees in electricity and water supply services, telecommunication and air traffic control, employees of the custom authorities; Hungary – civil servant officials; Armenia – employees in the energy supply services; Azerbaijan and Belgium – no list of employees excluded from the right to strike attached.

Workers have the right to carry out collective actions, including strikes, regardless of whether they are unionised or not.[1700]

In the last cycle – at the end of 2022 – requirements for strike organisers, who must be trade union organisations, were considered. The ECSR deemed cases in which trade unions have the right to organise legal strikes to be incompatible with the standards applicable in the Council of Europe. It negatively assessed situations in the Member States in which a trade union can only take collective action if it meets criteria of representativeness and if the strike is approved by at least half of the respective 'members' of the trade union.[1701] In Armenia, the percentage of workers required to call a strike was considered too high. It requires a vote approved by two-thirds of an organisation's (enterprise's) employees or, if the strike is declared by a subdivision of the organisation, a vote approved by two-thirds of the employees of that subdivision, provided that this is no less than half of the total number of the organisation's employees if the strike hampers the activities of other subdivisions.[1702] In France, there is a rule according to which only representative trade unions have the right to call a strike in the public sector.[1703] It is encouraging that in both cases – Romania and France – the ECSR criticised the legal solutions applied by the state authorities. The ECSR also negatively evaluated the situation in Portugal, where trade unions have a complete monopoly on organising strikes. In such a situation, even a few short days are sufficient to organise supporters for a strike, making it possible to bypass the barrier established by the authorities of a Member State. Meanwhile, in Portugal, the period for establishing a trade union organisation is more than thirty days.[1704] The situation of workers in Germany sheds some light on this problem. They must organise a group of people willing to put pressure on the employer and overcome the barriers established by the state authorities, which are obliged to satisfy the inspectors analysing and issuing opinions on the legality of the collective actions taken. It is difficult to implement, although not impossible because 'the conditions for calling a strike constitute an excessive restriction on the right to strike'.[1705] In Estonia, there is no need to consider what conditions must be met by trade unions organising strikes, as workers employed in the public sector are completely prohibited from striking.[1706]

F. Procedural Requirements Needed Prior to the Commencement of a Legal Strike

270. According to the Committee, a requirement which makes the decision to go on strike conditional on the approval (endorsement) of the executive committee

1700. Case of Romania: Conclusions 2002, pp. 135, 137; Conclusions 2004, vol. 2, p. 461.
1701. Conclusions 2022 (Bosnia and Herzegovina), (Montenegro), (Romania).
1702. Conclusions 2022 (Armenia).
1703. Conclusions 2022 (France).
1704. Conclusions 2022 (Portugal).
1705. Conclusions 2022 (Germany).
1706. Conclusions 2022 (Estonia).

of a trade union[1707] or of the majority of workers,[1708] with two-thirds of the votes cast and a quorum requirement of 50% of the employees affected by the agreement,[1709] is considered to be a violation of international standards. It is a breach of Article 6 §4 of the Charter to carry out a ballot making voting obligatory with regard to the undertaking of a strike action among workers who are employed by the one and only employer against whom the strike is being organised.[1710] The requirement to give notice to an employer of a ballot on industrial action is also excessive since, in any case, unions must issue an additional strike notice before taking action.[1711] In 2018, the Committee found that the obligation to notify the employer of preparations for a strike imposed by national law on a trade union organisation intending to organise a strike was excessive.[1712] In particular, the Committee found the obligation to inform the employer about the results of the pre-strike referendum as inconsistent with trade union freedom to organise strikes. A specific restriction on the right to strike, as well as procedural requirements, has been instigated in Serbia. The Serbian report states that the Law on Strike Action limits strikes in a number of sectors, namely those of 'public interest' or those in which a strike 'could jeopardise the lives or health of the population or cause extensive damage'. In these sectors, strikes are allowed only under certain conditions stipulated by the law. According to the law, these sectors are: the electricity-generating industry, water management, transport, media (radio and television), postal services, public and municipal services, production of staple foodstuff, healthcare and veterinary services, education, childcare, social security and social protection, essential activities for national defence and security, the performance of Serbia's international obligations and activities, or activities interruption of which may – bearing in mind the very nature of the activity – jeopardise people's lives or health, or cause extensive damage (for example, in the chemical, steel, ferrous on non-ferrous metallurgy industries). In the case of strikes involving the above-mentioned 'general interest', employers have the power to unilaterally determine the minimum service required after having consulted the trade union. If such services are not determined within a five-day period before a strike, the competent public or local authority takes the necessary decision. The International Trade Union Confederation (ITUC) states that the notion of 'essential services' is very broad and that the procedures for determining the minimum service are set out in the government regulations and can even lead to a total ban on strike action. The Committee concludes that the situation in Serbia is not in conformity with Article 6 §4 of the Charter on the grounds that workers are

1707. Case of Cyprus: Conclusions 2002, vol. 1, p. 97, Conclusions 2006, vol. 1, p. 147. Conclusions 2010, vol. 1, p. 210 (Cyprus). Conclusions 2014 (Cyprus).
1708. In the case of Romania, 50% of workers. Conclusions 2002, p. 137; Conclusions 2004, vol. 2, p. 461, Conclusions 2006, vol. 2, p. 753. In the case of Lithuania, however, it is 75% of workers. Conclusions 2004, vol. 2, p. 461, Conclusions 2006, vol. 2, p. 505. Conclusions 2014 (Hungary, Armenia) – a vote by two-thirds of the organisation's (enterprise's) employees is required, by secret ballot.
1709. Conclusions 2014 (Czech Republic).
1710. Conclusions XV-1, vol. 2, p. 641 (United Kingdom). Conclusions XIX, p. 263 (United Kingdom).
1711. Conclusions XVII-1, 2010, XX-3, 2014, United Kingdom).
1712. Armenia, Czech Republic, Germany, Romania, the Russian Federation, and the United Kingdom. Activity Report 2018, p. 37.

not involved on the same footing as employers during the procedures that are conducted to determine the 'minimum services' required in connection with the restrictions on the right to strike pertaining to some 'general interest' services.[1713]

The case of the United Kingdom is unique in this respect since, in the earlier supervisory cycles, the Committee was of the view that Member States had the right to impose on the strike organisers an obligation to carry out a secret ballot among the workers over a planned strike action.[1714] The Committee found the requirements imposed by the British authorities to be too strict. Trade unions intending to organise strikes are obliged to notify the employer, at least seven days in advance, of the planned strike ballot[1715] and to provide a list of workers participating in the ballot.[1716] The Committee found the above requirements to be too complicated.

The Committee based its conclusion that such requirements were in breach of Article 6 §4 of the Charter on the assumption the said requirements were introduced with the view to enable the employer to exert pressure on the workers entitled to call on the strike.

The Committee did not, however, question the compliance of the domestic regulations with the international standards regarding the notice period required when there is a planned strike action. The Committee was of the opinion that in the case of a planned collective action, particularly a strike action, notice periods help calm down the emotions and help to consider what is involved in organising a strike (cooling off period). The Committee claims the obligation to notify the employer of the planned collective action and its period in advance cannot be considered as a restriction on the right to strike.[1717] However, the length of the notice period may be restrictive. The Committee, by definition, does not establish a model of legal solutions and therefore does not specify what notice periods are in line with international standards. It only assesses the labour legislation enacted within the Member States. The Committee handed down the following decision concerning Member States imposing extended notice periods. When domestic labour law requires prolonged notice periods (lasting for several weeks) prior to the commencement of planned strike actions, especially on the request of the employer or a public administrative body, and also requires the plan to be presented to a court or an arbitration tribunal, the Committee sees this as a violation of Article 6 §4 of the Charter.[1718]

In some Member States of the Council of Europe, trade union organizations are obliged not only to warn the company entrepreneur against whom a protest action will be organized and then, possibly, a strike, of this fact but also to notify him of the decision taken by the trade union organization to stop working in connection with the planned strike – by employees, but also have an obligation to inform the employer about the results of employee votes among employees (voting age) on the

1713. Conclusions 2014 (Serbia).
1714. Conclusions II, p. 187, Conclusions XIV-1, vol. 1, p. 389 (Iceland).
1715. Conclusions XII-1, p. 131; Conclusions XIV-1, p. 805; Conclusions XV-1, vol. 2, p 639.
1716. Conclusions XV-1, vol. 2, 639.
1717. Conclusions I, p. 38. However, an obligation to limit the strike to 30 days is contrary to the Art. 6 §4 of the ESC. Conclusions XIX-3, p. 65 (Czech Republic). Conclusions 2010, vol. 1, p. 326 (Italy). Conclusions 2014 (Italy).
1718. Conclusions XIV, vol. 1, p. 157; Conclusions XV-1, p. 123.

idea of a strike.[1719] In Bulgaria, national labour law requires an employer to be informed of how long the strike will last.[1720] In all the cases mentioned above, the ECSR found that these obligations imposed on strikers go beyond the limits set by Article G of the Charter.

G. Compulsory Referral of Collective Disputes to an Arbitration Tribunal

271. Some Member States make it compulsory for collective dispute cases to undergo arbitration. The purpose of such a procedure is to defer a collective action or a strike.[1721] Compulsory arbitration stipulated under the legislation of Member States is permissible if it serves to protect the rights and liberties referred to in Article 31 §1 ESC or in Article G §1 RESC. Such restrictions placed upon the right to strike, based on the provisions of the Charter, should not be excessive.[1722] The timeframe within which they are utilised should be limited. The Committee stated that the restrictions on the right to strike for public officials and employees in public sectors may not go beyond those permitted by Article G of the RESC.[1723] Under no circumstances should such restrictions exceed that which is needed to return the situation to normal.[1724] If there is an absence of the circumstances that are stipulated under Article 31 §1 ESC and Article G §1 RESC, the Committee may conclude domestic labour legislation of Member States is non-compliant with international standards in the following situations: if state authorities prolong the existence of a collective agreement that is in place (generalisation),[1725] issue injunctions or orders restricting strikes in essential public services,[1726] and when there is an imposition of compulsory arbitration before a trade union is entitled to pass a resolution to call a strike.[1727] A similar stand was adopted in cases where collective disputes had to be referred by trade unions to mediation,[1728] in cases when the mediation period was extended by Member States to 30 days[1729] or when the mediator was authorised by way of a ballot to suggest a resolution of the collective dispute in the manner which the mediator saw as most appropriate, and not in a way

1719. Conclusions 2022 (United Kingdom).
1720. Conclusions 2022 (Bulgaria).
1721. It was declared illegal by the Committee. Conclusions XIX-3, p. 221 (Spain). Conclusions 2014 (Norway, Portugal, Spain). The Committee observes that even though the strike may have had important consequences for the economy, this being the primary consideration on which state intervention to terminate the strikes was based, the intervention (which brought the collective action to an end) was not necessary for the protection of the rights and freedoms of others or for the protection of the public interest, national security, public health or morals. Conclusions 2014 (Norway).
1722. Spain and Island, Activity Report 2018, p. 37.
1723. Conclusions 2006, vol. 2, p. 577 (Moldova), p. 629 (Norway).
1724. Conclusions X-1, pp. 74–75.
1725. Case of Denmark: Conclusions XI-1, p. 87; Conclusions XII-1, p. 127.
1726. Conclusions 2014 (Italy).
1727. Case of Norway: Conclusions XI-1, pp. 89–90; Conclusions XII-1, p. 130; Conclusions XIII-1, pp. 158–159; Conclusions XIV-1, pp. 622–623; Conclusions XV-1, p. 432.
1728. Conclusions 2002, p. 136 (Romania).
1729. Conclusions XVII-1, vol. 1, p. 103 (Czech Republic). Conclusions 2014 (Czech Republic).

presented by a trade union representing workers. The mediator is bound by the position taken up by the trade union. However, when more than one trade union participates in the dispute on behalf of the workers, each having the right to propose different methods of solving the dispute, Danish labour law authorises the mediator to decide the several solution proposals are to be considered as a whole for voting purposes (linkage rule). This procedure was considered by the Committee to be a violation of Article 6 §4 of the Charter.[1730]

H. The Obligation to Ensure Continuous Operation of Certain Workplaces

272. Member States may restrict the right to strike with regard to workers employed in private employment in order for the rights and liberties as are stipulated under Article 31 §1 ESC and Article G §1 RESC to be protected. The Committee is adopting the same approach as it did in relation to workers engaged in public services and the interpretation of Article 6 §4 of the Charter. The scope of restrictions to the right to strike for workers employed in the private sector depends upon the level of services provided to local communities by such workers. The Committee takes the view that the restriction to the right to strike is permissible only in situations when the cessation of work within such a workplace constitutes a serious danger to the existence of a given community.[1731] When reviewing the restrictions on the right to strike imposed by Member States, the Committee examines whether such restrictions apply to workers in employment that is crucial to local communities[1732] and whether, instead of restricting the right to strike, it would be possible to oblige the striking participants to provide necessary services.[1733] The

1730. Conclusions XVII-1, vol. 1, pp. 132, 134 (Denmark). Conclusions XIX, p. 83 (Denmark).
1731. Conclusions I, p. 38.
1732. The Committee sought information on a number of issues pertaining to the right to strike in Georgia namely: (1) who has the right to call a strike and whether this right is reserved for trade unions; (2) which are the categories of workers that are denied the right to strike, in order to asses that restrictions are in accordance with Art. G of the Charter; (3) what sectors the relevant information is intended to cover when banning the right to strike of employees whose work is related to human life and health or which, due to its technology, cannot be suspended; (4) whether strikes of the above-mentioned workers are totally banned or whether is made for minimum service; (5) the practical circumstances in which courts actually postpone or suspend a strike; (6) the meaning of the provision providing that the maximum duration of a strike cannot be longer than a number of days (ninety in case of Georgia); (7) further procedural requirements, for example on those subjecting the exercise of the right to strike to prior approval by a certain percentage of workers. In response, the Georgian report stated that the Constitution recognises the right to strike. Art. 51 of the amended Labour Code provides that the right to strike cannot be exercised by employees whose work/activity involves the safety of human live or health or if the activity cannot be suspended due to the nature of the work process. The Committee notes that the report fails to provide much of the information requested. At the end the Committee concludes that the situation in Georgia is not in conformity with Art. 6 §2 of the Charter, on the grounds that it has not been established that the right to the collective action of workers and employers including the right to strike, is adequately protected. Conclusions 2016 (Georgia), pp. 225–226.
1733. The Committee concludes that the restrictions on the right to strike in the energy supply services (electricity, gas etc.) do not comply with the conditions laid down by the Art. G of the Charter. Conclusions 2016 (Armenia), p. 227. Similar decision is handed down by the Committee in case on the restrictions the right to strike of the employees of customs authorities. Conclusions 2016

Committee opposes the idea that authorities of Member States reserve the right to define the minimum range of services which would be provided during a strike action.[1734] It also emphasises the manner in which such restrictions are being introduced. The Committee notes that during the reference period, the Icelandic Parliament adopted legislation to terminate a strike. The Act put an end to the strike, prolonging collective agreement that was then in force between the parties if no new agreement was concluded between them. The Committee concludes that the situation in Iceland is not in conformity with Article 6 §4 of the Charter on the grounds that during the reference period, the legislature intervened in order to terminate collective action in circumstances which went beyond those permitted by Article 31 of the Charter.[1735] Special attention is drawn to ensuring strike organisers are entitled to appeal against the decisions handed down obliging workers to provide continuous operation of a workplace during the period of a strike.[1736] Analysing the Committee's conclusions with regard to the argument in question leads to the point the following factors justify the introduction of such restrictions to the right to strike: the scope, the length of the strike and the importance of the workplace and the services it provides to the local community, which is carrying out a strike.[1737] In cases where a strike could have irremediable effects on the life of a local community, the Committee formed an opinion that the restrictions imposed on the right to strike were in line with international standards. When such restrictions, however, encompassed various workplaces within various sectors of the market or when they were too broadly defined, the Committee's ruling in this respect was negative.[1738] The Committee claimed the default on the obligation stipulated under Article 6 §4 of the

---

(Moldova), p. 267. The Committee previously noted that employees of a particular grade in the customs authorities are denied the right to strike. Conclusions 2006, 2010 (Moldova). It asked whether the duties and functions of the employees concerned, given their nature or level of responsibility, are directly related to national security or the protection of public order (Conclusions 2014). The most current report presented by the Moldovan government simply states that the Committee's conclusions regarding restrictions on the right to strike will be examined by a tripartite group, and then Committee will be informed of any developments. The Committee in 2016 decides: 'As there have been no changes in the situation the Committee is obliged to reiterate its previous conclusions.'

1734. Conclusions XVII-1, vol. 2, p. 420 (Portugal). The Committee concluded that the situation in Albania and in Lithuania is not in conformity because strikes are forbidden in electricity and water supply services (Albania), public electricity, district heating and gas supply enterprises (Lithuania). Conclusions 2006, vol. 1, p. 51 (Albania), vol. 2, p. 505 (Lithuania). Conclusions 2010, vol. 1, p. 40 (Albania), p. 188 (Bulgaria), p. 326 (Italy). Conclusions XIX, p. 65 (Czech Republic), p. 199 (Slovakia).

1735. Conclusions XX-3 (2014, Iceland).

1736. Conclusions XII-2, p. 114; Conclusions XIII-1, pp. 156–157; Conclusions XIII-3, p. 137; Conclusions XV-1, vol. 2, p. 480.

1737. Case of Portugal: Conclusions XIII-3, p. 281; Conclusions XIII-5, p. 181; Conclusions XIV-1, vol. 2, p. 663; Conclusions XV-1, vol. 2, p. 479; Conclusions XV-1, vol. 2, pp. 367–368 (Italy); Conclusions XV-1, vol. 2, p. 523 (Spain); Addendum to Conclusions XV-1, p. 30 (Germany).

1738. Case of Portugal: *see* 'The right to organise', *supra*, p. 71; Conclusions 2004, vol. 1, p. 46 (Bulgaria), which declared the unlawfulness of strike in the public health care, in the power industry and in the telecommunications sector. Conclusions 2004, vol. 2, p. 351 (Lithuania) – due to the ban of strikes in power plants and in the gasworks.

Charter is related to the provision Article 1 §2 of the Charter, which would violate the prohibition against forced labour that is stipulated under that provision.[1739]

To ensure the continuity of operation within a workplace, authorities of some Member States replace the striking workers with strikebreakers. The Committee has dealt with three such cases.

The case of Germany has served twice as a basis for disparate conclusions of the Committee. Initially, the Committee took the view the replacement of workers striking in public workplaces, employed on work agreements and civil servants being appointed was in compliance with international standards, provided there was no breach of Article 31 §1 ESC.[1740] In the following supervisory cycle, the Committee handed down a ruling, stating the German Constitutional Tribunal, which found on 2 March 1993 that the provision allowing for the replacement of striking workers with new employees was unlawful, was in breach as were the domestic labour law regulations with Article 6 §4 of the Charter since such a claim could not be grounded by Article 31 of the Charter.[1741]

The Committee has not changed its position in this respect, as can be seen in the rulings handed down with regard to Slovenia.[1742]

In order to ensure the uninterrupted continuation of a significant number of jobs, the authorities of some Member States have imposed a total ban on strikes. In Germany, for example, it is absolutely forbidden to organise strikes and other collective actions while the parties to collective labour disputes are negotiating the possibility of concluding collective bargaining agreements. This prohibition is intended to prevent trade union organisations from violating social peace in collective labour relations. However, the German authorities do not take into account the policy used by enterprises of fictitiously starting and formally continuing negotiations to ostensibly conclude a collective bargaining agreement. Such a situation may go on for a long time because the regulations do not specify or regulate the cases in which the above prohibition loses its meaning. For this reason, the ECSR concluded that sham negotiations on a collective bargaining agreement do not precede real efforts to restore social peace in labour relations. Thus, in 2022, the ECSR correctly defined this case as 'an excessive restriction on the right to strike'.[1743] A similar situation also occurred in Spain. The national labour legislation authorised the Spanish government to take an administrative decision to immediately stop a strike and to initiate arbitration in order to immediately restore social peace in collective labour relations. A slightly better, although less controversial, solution is for one of the parties to a dispute (trade union or enterprise) to refer the dispute to the court adjudicating in collective labour disputes. The problem, however, is that in the Council of Europe, such disputes are generally not resolved by judicial authorities. In the cases

1739. Conclusions XIV-1, vol. 1, p. 110 (Belgium); p. 158 (Cyprus).
1740. Conclusions XII-2, pp. 113–114.
1741. Conclusions XIII-2, p. 282.
1742. Conclusions 2004, vol. 2, p. 282. The decision was deferred until information was provided, concerning the legal consequences of the unlawful dismissal of employees by employers during a lawful strike.
1743. Conclusions 2022 (Germany).

analysed by the ECSR in the cycle that ended on 31 December 2022, the only country where the model of dealing with strikers was assessed negatively was the overseas part of the Netherlands, Curaçao. According to the report, 'the right to strike is not absolute, and the legitimacy of a strike may be assessed by the courts'.[1744] The ECSR therefore issued a negative ruling addressed to the Dutch state authorities.

I. The Legal Consequences of Collective Action with Regard to Individual Work Agreements

273. Participation in a lawful strike should not bring about any negative legal consequences for workers. While analysing the reports of Member States, the Committee generally concluded Member States had accepted or regulated legal solutions provided for the legal consequences of the participation in a strike in cases related to the termination of employment contracts, loss of remuneration and civil liability or even criminal responsibility.

1. Strike and the Termination of a Work Agreement

274. During the first supervisory cycle, the Committee concluded that participation in a lawful strike action cannot result in the termination of a work agreement, nor can it justify the dissolution of such a contract.[1745] The legal regulations in Member States, which do not agree with the above principle, are also in breach of Article 6 §4 of the Charter. Due to the differences in labour law provisions of various Member States with regard to the termination and restoration of work agreements, the Committee concluded in cases where labour regulations provide for automatic termination of a work agreement in the event of a strike but also oblige the employer to reinstate all the participating workers *post* strike, as being in compliance with international standards. The Committee is of the opinion if those who are participating in a strike and who have their employment terminated are then reinstated to their former positions after the strike has ended and have none of their acquired rights impaired, such a formal termination is not regarded as a breach of the Charter.[1746] When considering their decision concerning the consequences of a strike on individual work agreements, the Committee requested the Member State authorities to provide information confirming their domestic labour legislation ensures the existence of a legal relationship between the parties in the individual work contract when there is a strike. The Committee also requested information showing legislation ensuring workers are reinstated and that their acquired rights are

1744. Conclusions *2022* (Netherlands – Curaçao).
1745. Conclusions I, p. 39.
1746. As above; Conclusions II, p. 29 (Norway); Conclusions XII-2, p. 116.

not impaired. The Committee takes the view that strike action should not bring any negative legal consequences with regard to individual work agreements.[1747]

The Committee therefore ruled against Great Britain and Ireland, whose domestic labour law, based on the common law, regards a strike as a breach of workers' obligations under a work agreement and therefore in turn gives an employer the right to dismiss a worker immediately and every employee participating in such a collective action.

The ruling was handed down by the Commission against the British[1748] and Irish[1749] authorities whose labour law legislation was not in compliance with Article 6 §4 of the Charter as the regulations provided the employer with the freedom to choose whether he/she would reemploy their striking workers.

The British labour law regulations allowed an employer to dismiss all workers taking part in a strike and reemploy workers selectively three months after the dismissal.

The Committee came to the conclusion the certainty entailed with the termination of a work agreement for workers partaking in a strike, accompanied by the uncertainty as to who is going to be reemployed, constituted a serious threat to the right to organise and participate in strike action, protected under Article 6 §4 of the Charter.[1750] In 2018, the Committee found that the situation in the United Kingdom is not in conformity with the Charter, as workers are not adequately protected against dismissal in the event of participating in a strike.[1751]

Identical was the conclusion of the Committee concerning the provisions of the Danish labour law, which did not ensure reinstatement of the workers dismissed on the grounds of participation in a strike action.[1752]

1747. The Committee concludes that the situation is not in conformity with Art. 6 §4 of the Charter, on the grounds that: under the Unfair Dismissal Act, an employer may dismiss all employees for taking part in a strike (Conclusions 2014, Ireland); it has been established that striking workers are protected from dismissal after the strike (Conclusions 2014, Armenia); the protection of workers against dismissal when taking industrial action is insufficient. Workers participating in lawful industrial action are protected against dismissal for twelve weeks (Conclusions XX-3, 2014, United Kingdom). In its previous conclusion (Conclusions XVIII-1, 2010, United Kingdom) the Committee held that the period of twelve weeks after which those concerned lost their employment protection was arbitrary, and reiterated its conclusion of non-conformity. As of 2014, the Committee does not accept the government view that the statutory protection against dismissal for workers taking industrial action is substantial, and concludes that the situation in the United Kingdom is not in conformity with Art. 6 §4 of the Charter.

1748. Conclusions XIII-1, p. 160; Conclusions XIV-1, vol. 2, p. 804; Conclusions XV-1, p. 638. On the basis of the opinion issued by the Committee, the Committee of Ministers of the Council of Europe adopted two recommendations addressed to the authorities of the United Kingdom: No. RSChS (93) 3, No. RSChS (97) 3. Conclusion XIX-3, p. 263 (United Kingdom).

1749. Conclusions XIV-1, vol. 1, p. 422; Addendum to Conclusions XV-1, p. 18, Conclusions 2006, vol. 1, p. 373.

1750. Conclusions XI-1, p. 90; Conclusions XIII-3, pp. 144–145; Conclusions XIV-1, p. 804; Conclusions XV-1, pp. 638–639.

1751. The United Kingdom, Activity Report 2018, p. 36.

1752. Conclusions XIV-1, vol. 1, p. 181; Conclusions XV-1, vol. 1, p. 156.

As a result of the Committee's conclusions, the provisions discriminating against the participants of lawful strikes have been changed. The Committee was interested in information on whether there are any practical examples of unequal treatment by employees involved in strike actions.[1753]

The situation in Ireland has not changed to date. In the latest report, presented to the ECSR in 2022, the situation had not been brought into conformity with Article 6 §4 of the Charter since, under Irish law (the Unfair Dismissal Act), an employer can dismiss all employees for taking part in a strike. The Committee points out that its 'Statement on COVID-19 and social rights', adopted on 24 March 2021, specifies that Article 6 §4 of the Charter entails the right of workers to take collective action (e.g., work stoppage) for occupational health and safety reasons. This means that strikes in response to a lack of adequate personal protective equipment or inadequate distancing, disinfection and cleaning protocols in the workplace would fall under the protection afforded by the Charter. The Irish government states that no specific measures were taken in connection with the COVID-19 crisis to ensure the right to strike or to restrict the right to take industrial action. The ECSR found that the situation had not been brought into conformity with Article 6 §4 of the Charter.

2. Strike Action and the Right to Fair Remuneration

275. Wages are paid for work performed. During a strike, workers do not work, and therefore, they are not entitled to a salary. Therefore Member States, without violating international standards, may grant employers the right to deduct from employees' salaries amounts due for the periods when workers were not at work due to the strike action.

The Committee has adopted the view that such deductions should be proportional to the length of the strike, but in principle, such deductions also function as penalties.[1754] The Committee declared the French labour provision allowing employers to deduct from workers' salaries (engaged the public sector receiving monthly wages) 1/30th of their wage per day of the strike action, regardless of whether the strike lasted the whole day or only one hour, constitutes a breach of Article 6 §4 of the Charter.[1755]

3. Strikes: Civil Liability and Criminal Responsibility

276. During the first supervisory cycle, the Committee decided the domestic labour legislation providing for civil liability (for damages) and criminal responsibility for unlawful acts committed during a strike cannot be considered as a violation of Article 6 §4 of the Charter.[1756] In the case of Member States where the legal

1753. Conclusions XV-1, vol. 2, p. 619 (Norway).
1754. Conclusions XIII-1, p. 153.
1755. Conclusions XIII-1, p. 154; Conclusions XIII-3, p. 135; Conclusions XIV-1, vol. 1, p. 258; Conclusions 2002, p. 36, Conclusions 2006, vol. 1, p. 309. Conclusions 2010, p. 267 (France).
1756. Conclusions I, p. 39.

system is based on the common law, the organisers and participants of lawful industrial actions are granted immunity from civil liability and criminal responsibility for the consequences of any events during strikes. The restriction imposed on the above rule led the Committee to the conclusion these domestic provisions constitute a breach of international standards.

Although employers participating in lawful strikes were absolved from civil liability and criminal responsibility,[1757] in Irish legislation, the participation of civil servants in a lawful strike action was classified as an offence against the state.

Similarly, this was appropriated in the circumstances of merchant seamen.

Under Irish criminal law, a strike action of merchant seamen constitutes a breach or neglect of duty or even an act of criminal conspiracy.[1758]

The Committee has taken the view the above-cited provisions constitute an impediment to the effective execution of the right to strike by merchant seamen. The Committee recalled public authorities were only entitled to establish procedural requirements regulating the exercise of the right to collective action, and any restriction on this right could only be justified according to the relevant conditions laid down in Article 31 §1 ESC.[1759] Although the provisions subject to which participation in a lawful strike action by civil servants and seamen were acts prohibited by criminal law had no practical application, the Committee pointed out the maintaining of such provisions constitutes a serious threat to the right to strike.[1760] During the following supervisory cycles, the Committee was informed that the provisions constituting the basis for the Committee's negative opinion with regard to Irish compliance with international standards of the protection of the right to strike had been repealed.[1761]

Irish law does not provide immunity from civil liability and criminal responsibility for participating in a strike action organised by a trade union, which does not have the status of a representative organisation.[1762] Domestic labour legislation, which gives employers the right to dismiss the striking employees, is in breach of Article 6 §4 of the Charter.[1763]

277. The Committee concluded keeping such provisions in force under which only trade unions holding a negotiating licence are entitled to carry out collective action, including strikes, was a violation of the provisions under Article 6 §4 of the Charter.[1764] As pointed out earlier, the Committee was of the opinion that a group of employees who are not members of a trade union have the right to organise a

1757. Addendum to Conclusions XI-2, p. 26.
1758. The Conspiracy and Protection Act of 1875. This Act was amended to The Merchant Shipping (Miscellaneous Provisions Act) 1998.
1759. Conclusions II, p. 27; Conclusions X-1, pp. 74–75; Conclusions X-2, p. 75; Conclusions XI-1, p. 76; Addendum to Conclusions XI-2, p. 26; Conclusions XIII-1, p. 156; Conclusions XIII-3, p. 136.
1760. Addendum to Conclusions XI-2, pp. 24–26; Conclusions XIII-1, p. 156; Conclusions XIII-3, p. 136.
1761. Addendum to Conclusions XV-1, p. 27.
1762. Conclusions 2014 (Ireland).
1763. Conclusions 2004, vol. 1, p. 265.
1764. Conclusions XIII-1, p. 156; Conclusions XIII-3, p. 136.

lawful strike. Therefore, depriving such workers of immunity from civil liability and criminal responsibility for participating in a lawful action is not in compliance with international protection standards.[1765]

Although the Committee did not actually deal with the cases of compliance with international standards of industrial action taken up by workers wanting to protect the economic and social interests of employees employed by other employers, it nonetheless stated that excluding those workers from liability striking in a legal collective action against an employer for whom they work, although they have been formally employed by an intermediary company, is a violation of the right to strike protected under Article 6 §4 of the Charter. A similar stand was adopted in the case of industrial action carried out in order to protect employees hired by a different intermediary company than the striking employees, although working for the same employer.[1766]

278. The immunity from civil liability and criminal responsibility for participating in a lawful strike should be granted to all workers, regardless of trade union membership. The Committee is of the opinion the authorities of Members States should ensure legal protection of all workers involved, either as organisers or as participants, in a lawful industrial collective action.[1767] The exclusion from this protection of striking workers who are not members of a trade union is incompatible with the international standards protecting the rights of the workers.[1768]

The Committee also dealt with the liability of the strike organisers and concluded the power of the state authorities to impose excessive financial sanctions for the violation of the procedural requirements with regard to collective action constitutes a breach of Article 6 §4 of the Charter. Only authorised trade unions and their officials and members are granted immunity from civil liability in the event of a strike.[1769]

Under Swedish labour law legislation, failure to give requisite notice of a collective action may lead to a fine between SEK 30,000 and SEK 100,000 (SEK 3,301–EUR 10,831) and litigation for the violation of a postponement order (discussed in detail in the subsequent paragraph) may entail liability ranging from a minimum of 300,000 SEK (EUR 33,008) up to a maximum of SEK 1 million SEK (EUR 108,310).[1770]

4. Restrictions on the Right to Strike as Imposed by the Courts

279. In some Member States, the courts have the power to restrict the right of workers to strike. In such cases, the Committee found itself competent to review the

1765. Conclusions XIV-1, p. 422; Addendum to Conclusions XV-1, p. 27.
1766. Case of the United Kingdom: Conclusions XII-1, pp. 131–132; Conclusions XIII-1, pp. 159–160; Conclusions XIV-1, vol. 2, p. 805; Conclusions XV-1, vol. 2, p. 637.
1767. Conclusions 2004, vol. 2, p. 405 (Norway).
1768. Conclusions XVII-1, vol. 1, p. 135 (Denmark).
1769. Conclusions 2022 (Ireland).
1770. Conclusions 2002, p. 237; Conclusions 2004, vol. 2, p. 566.

rulings of domestic labour courts with regard to their compliance with the international standards set by the Charter.[1771] During the following nine supervisory cycles, the Committee did not make use of this power.

By the eleventh supervisory cycle, the Committee assessed the judicature of the Danish courts with regard to their compliance with Article 6 §4 of the Charter and with Article 31 §1 ESC. This move was consequent to the judgment handed down by the Netherlands Supreme Court on 30 March 1986, which ruled the abovementioned provisions were directly applicable to the Dutch labour law.

The Committee was of the opinion allowing direct applicability in domestic regulations. Article 31 §1 ESC led to the situation where the provisions of an international treaty create a legal possibility to restrict the right to strike. Therefore, the Committee's interest in the rulings handed down by national courts dealing with collective labour relations is justified.[1772] While examining the judgments of the Dutch courts the Committee came to the conclusion that in order to protect financial interests of third parties (consumers, clients) and employers, the courts had been imposing restrictions on both the duration and the measures taken in collective actions initiated by the workers. The Committee claimed on the basis of Article 31 of the Charter that the protection of economic interests of third parties could only be taken into consideration in exceptional cases. The Committee also required to know who made requests before the courts to have the measures and the duration of a collective action limited and whether it was possible to appeal against the judgments of first-instance courts in this field.[1773] In the absence of sufficient information with regard to the appeal avenues against interim judgments concerning restrictions of duration of lawful collective actions, the Committee postponed its conclusions concerning the compliance by the Dutch court with Article 6 §4 of the Charter during the following two supervisory cycles.[1774]

The failure of Member States to submit information requested by the Committee, therefore forcing the Committee to postpone its conclusions in three subsequent supervisory cycles, constitutes sufficient grounds for the Committee to declare a violation of domestic legislation of those Member States with international standards. Having received the required information, the Committee stated the Dutch courts' power to determine whether a strike was premature, confirmed in the judicial practices and rulings of the Netherlands Supreme Court,[1775] restrict the right to strike, which confirms the Netherlands do not comply with Article 6 §4 of the Charter.[1776]

The Committee has found similar examples of court-imposed controls over industrial actions in Belgian reports.

Although the power to monitor the lawfulness of industrial actions is not formally granted to the Belgian courts, the judges have the right to assess the behaviour of workers participating in such actions. Even if a strike or a picket line is

1771. Conclusions I, p. 38.
1772. Conclusions XI-1, p. 88.
1773. Conclusions XIII-1, p. 158; Conclusions XIII-3, pp. 139–140.
1774. Conclusions XIV-1, pp. 555–556; Addendum to Conclusions XV-1, pp. 93–94
1775. Judgment of 28 Jan. 2000 cited in Conclusions XVI-1, p. 471.
1776. Conclusions XVII-1, vol. 2, p. 320.

lawful from a formal point of view, courts may decide workers participating in a lawful collective action are guilty of criminal behaviour.

The Committee observed the above right allows courts to assess collective action and therefore causes judges to be the determiners on whether a strike is appropriate or not, consequently deciding its legality. The outcome is such rulings handed down by the judiciary results in the restriction of the right to strike.[1777]

5. Lockouts

280. Article 6 §4 of the Charter also provides employers the right to take industrial action. It ensures them the right to a lockout which, in the Committee's opinion, exists as the major, if not the only, form of employers' collective action concerning collective labour relations.[1778] Since the employers' right to lockout has not been explicitly formulated in Article 6 §4 of the Charter, the Committee has come to the conclusion the right in question is not on an equal footing of protection when compared to the right to strike under the Charter.[1779] The fact Article 6 §4 of the Charter does not in any way authorise Member States to enact regulations concerning the right of the employer to lockouts should not be used as evidence supporting the claim the Charter does not protect the right to lockout as it does the right to strike. The absence of any legal basis in the domestic labour legislation for regulations concerning the procedure for executing the right to lockouts does not justify, in the Committee's opinion, the statement a Member State does not comply with international standards if the right to lockout is not explicitly recognised in its domestic legislation.[1780] The Committee is of the view that judicial bodies of Member States may be granted authorisation to impose certain restrictions on the employers' right to lockout.[1781] In its decisions, the Committee does not apply the principle of equal means to be used by the parties in collective work agreements (who, in a period of social peace, are defined as stakeholders), i.e., by employers and employees, to exert pressure on each other. The Committee does not regard Article 6 §4 of the Charter as an international labour law standard established with a view to ensure and maintain balance with regard to collective work agreements. The Committee does not impose any obligation on Member States to explicitly recognise the employers' right to lockout. It is of the opinion that domestic labour legislation under which a lockout is a tortuous act punishable by a fine imposed on an employer, who makes use of an illegal form of exerting pressure, violates international standards in this respect.[1782] Also, domestic legislation where lockouts are considered to be a breach of a work agreement by employers is a non-compliance with international standards. An exception may be the Committee's decision on the non-compliance of domestic labour law with Article 6 §4 of the Charter, resulting

1777. Conclusions XVI-1, pp. 71 et seq.; Conclusions XVII-1, vol. 1, pp. 68–69.
1778. Conclusions I, p. 38.
1779. Conclusions VIII, p. 95.
1780. Conclusions II, p. 187 (Cyprus).
1781. Conclusions VIII, p. 95.
1782. Case of Italy: Conclusions III, p. 38; Conclusions VI, p. 40; Conclusions IX-2, pp. 48–49; Conclusions XV-1, vol. 2, p. 367.

from the absence of regulations legitimising the right to lockout in such legislation.[1783] The Committee regards lockouts as deliberate actions taken by employers in cases of *force majeure*. In the Committee's conclusion, lockouts are regarded as a lawful method of protecting employers' interests threatened by collective industrial action initiated by workers.[1784] Therefore the Committee approves of defensive lockouts.[1785] However, it has not expressed an opinion on the compatibility of defensive lockouts with international standards.[1786]

§3. The Right to Information and Consultation

281. Article 21 obliges Member States to undertake or to encourage measures enabling workers or their representatives to attain information concerning the financial and economic situation of the undertaking employing them and being consulted on proposed decisions which could substantially affect their interests. First and foremost, employers should consult with their workers or with their representatives about the decisions which may seriously influence the level of employment within their industry. The right to information and consultation introduced by the Additional Protocol into the European Social Charter in 1988 (Article 2) was a prototype for Directive No. 14 of the European Parliament and the Council on 11 March 2002 (2002/14.EC), which formulated the basic grounds for information and consultation among the workers of the European Community.[1787] Under Article 21 of the Charter, employees and/or their representatives (trade unions, staff communities, work councils or health and safety committees) have the right to be informed about any issue which might affect their working environment unless the disclosure of such information could be prejudicial to the undertaking. They must also be consulted in good time on proposed decisions which could substantially affect the interests of workers, particularly on those decisions which could have an important impact on the employment situation in the undertaking.[1788]

The prototype for Article 21 RESC (Article 2 Additional Protocol of 1988) is a directive project of the Vredeling community dedicated to the processes of information and consultation in industries.[1789] Differentiated from the EU directive, neither Article 2 of the Additional Protocol nor Article 21 RESC considers workers' rights

1783. Case of France: Conclusions V, p. 48; Conclusions VI, p. 39.

1784. Conclusions IX-2, pp. 47–48 (France); pp. 48–49 (Italy).

1785. Addendum to Conclusions XV-1, p. 27 (Germany).

1786. As of 2014, the Committee notes that employers in Azerbaijan have the right to a lockout under the certain conditions, such as in response to an illegal strike, or where the demands of the employees are beyond their production, financial, or other capabilities. An employer must give ten days' written notice to the employees/trade unions and other relevant authorities, and must try to reach a settlement before resorting to a lockout. Pursuant to Art. 285 of the Labour Code, upon the request of employees, the Court shall decide if a lockout is legal. If the Court declares that a lockout is illegal, employees must be compensated for damages suffered, and the employer shall be held liable for the violation of the law on lockout. Conclusions 2014 (Azerbaijan).

1787. OJ L.80, 23 Mar. 2002.

1788. Conclusions 2014 (Italy).

1789. Directive on Information and Consultation Procedures for Employees, 1980 OJ (C 197), p. 3.

or their representatives to information concerning their employers as a personal right available to each employed individual.

The analysed provisions of the Charter are treated as a standard, which may be utilised by labour collectives or by their representatives. The analysis of the Committee's judgment allowed for the formation of the hypothesis that Article 21 RESC is also considered a legal standard which certain employees may utilise.[1790] The Committee, which not only supervises the compliance of domestic labour legislation with the international standards established by the Charter, decided the right to information and consultation should be ensured by domestic legislation, which would allow its beneficiaries effective use. To guarantee this, the regulation present in domestic labour legislation must allow for an independent body to deal with claims and complaints that may arise from the inability to make use of such a right to information and consultation by workers who have attained such a right.[1791] The Committee noted in 2010 that in the event of infringements of the right to information and consultation, labour courts could order employers to carry out their obligations and declare any decision taken in violation of these obligations void. Employers who do not execute labour court orders are liable to face criminal prosecution.[1792] This above entitlement should be ensured to workers and their representatives.[1793] The right should not be limited to bodies, which in turn pursue those employers who are violating provisions concerning information and consultation. In certain situations, the beneficiaries whose right to information and consultation has been breached should be able to file a claim seeking damages.[1794] In the view of the Committee, penalties imposed should support civil liability claims and pay for damages and annul decisions[1795] carried out by employers without consulting and informing the workers or their representatives. Having in mind the protection of employers' rights who have acted criminally or in a white-collar crime capacity, which resulted in penalties imposed on the employer for breaching the obligation to inform and consult the workers or their representatives, the Committee was interested in receiving information concerning the decisions handed down by courts or work inspectors.[1796] It demanded information from Member State authorities, which entities (particular workers or organisations) have the right to litigate and file claims against employers who have breached domestic legislation stipulating the obligation of informing and consulting with workers or their representatives under Article 21 RESC.[1797] As of 2015, the Committee concludes that the situation in France, Italy and Norway is not in conformity with Article 21 of the Charter on the grounds that: (1) some employees are excluded from the calculation of staff numbers carried

1790. The Committee concludes that the situation in Moldova is not in conformity with Art. 21 of the RESC because it has not been established that sanctions are applicable in case of employers fail to fulfil their obligation to inform and consult workers within the undertaking. Conclusions 2010, vol. 2, p. 429.
1791. Conclusions XIII-3, p. 440.
1792. Conclusions 2010 (Italy).
1793. Conclusions XIII-5, p. 288 (Sweden).
1794. Conclusions XIII-5, p. 278 (Finland).
1795. Conclusions 2003, vol. 1, p. 311 (Italy).
1796. Conclusions XVI-2, vol. 1, p. 365 (Greece); Conclusions XVI-2, vol. 2, pp. 594–595 (Norway).
1797. Conclusions 2003, vol. 1, p. 72 (Bulgaria); Conclusions 2003, vol. 2, p. 420 (Romania).

out to determine the minimum thresholds beyond which staff representative bodies must be set to ensure the information and consultation of workers;[1798] (2) it has not been established that the rules on information and consultation cover all categories of employee.[1799]

The position of the Committee, which demanded from Bulgarian and Romanian authorities detailed information concerning the entities entitled to file claims regulated by labour law in the case when an employer breaches the obligation outlined under Article 21 RESC, sought its information by way of a questionnaire whether the above provision is guaranteed to all workers or solely to their representatives. Exactly the same situation took place in 2018. Due to the lack of information, the government of Serbia and Herzegovina was obliged to inform the Committee whether all employees have the right to information and consultation on the economic and financial situation of the employer and on other matters listed in Article 21 lit. (a) and (b) the Committee concluded that the situation in this country was not in line with the RESC provisions.[1800] The Committee proves the statement on the interpretation of the analysed provisions of the Charter as standards, which regard the right to information as a right particular workers are entitled to and not only groups of workers employed by particular employers or their representatives.

282. In executing the plan for information and consultation, authorities of Member States should either independently formulate provisions dealing with the principles of information and consultation by industries with workers or their representatives or encourage stakeholders to define the above principles in collective labour agreements or in other normative agreements. Informing and consulting about matters stipulated under Article 21 RESC does not require legislative regulation. It may, depending on the individual customs of particular Member States concerning collective labour relations, be ensured by the judiciary or be customary in its nature. The undertaken methods of regulating information and consultation by each Member State through employers, workers or their representatives should be effective and adequate.[1801] To determine whether such mechanisms dealing with information and consultation for workers and/or their representatives are effective, the Committee demands detailed information concerning the established procedures

1798. Conclusions 2014 (France). The employees not dealt with in the French labour law are mostly employed by companies with fewer than eleven employees, and this is the case for about a fifth of all employees, including public-sector employees. The French report stated that this exclusion makes it possible to ensure that the recruitment of workers on state-subsidised contracts (*contrats initiative-emploi* and *contrats d'accompagnement dans l'emploi*) does not subject employers to additional administrative and financial constraints by making them overstep thresholds beyond which they must set up staff representative bodies.

1799. Conclusions 2014 (Italy, Norway). In Norway, in companies with more than thirty employees, employees may demand that one member and one observer be elected to the board of the company by and among employees. In companies more than 200 employees, there shall be a corporate assemble where one-third of the members shall be elected by and among the employees. The corporate assembly shall then elect the board. In cases where an agreement not to establish a corporate assembly is concluded between the company and local trade unions, the employees shall elect an additional board member or two observers.

1800. Activity Report 2018, p. 38.

1801. Explanatory report to the 1988 Additional Protocol, European Social Charter, *supra*, p. 132.

of the issue at hand.[1802] Article 21 RESC obliges Member States to undertake or encourage measures which will ensure workers or their representatives the right to information and consultation. This obligation is considered fulfilled when the existing regulations within a country are established by the state, negotiated by stakeholders, the judiciary or the binding customs, and warrant employers to inform workers or their representatives, or both.[1803] The word 'or' included in the analysed provision does not demand Member States utilise only one or the other option – to inform and consult workers or their representatives. This does not indicate, however, the right to information and the consultation of workers as to changes in its nature. It becomes dependent upon whom the employer is informing and consulting the matters stipulated under Article 21 RESC, a right which can be utilised by either individuals, particular workers or their representatives. The beneficiaries of this provision are the workers. This provision allows them to utilise the right either individually or collectively. In the latter case, the workers' representatives usually carry out this right. In the case where a workplace fails to organise representation, the state or the stakeholders may establish that an employer will be obligated to inform the workplace of the matters raised in Article 21 RESC. Consulting with a group of workers may function according to various legal-admin formats, such as a referendum. Neither the obligation to inform nor to consult with workers and/or their representatives within the workplace deprives the employer of carrying out decisions in matters stipulated in Article 21 RESC. The employer has the right to inform workers and/or their representatives. He also has the right to consult the workers, their representatives and the workplace about intended decisions. The state and stakeholders decide which of the above options will be carried out. There are no law-based barriers which might impinge all the options from being executed. In such cases whereby the report has indicated that the trade union, an authorised body, is responsible for receiving the information from the employers and stating its opinion in the name of the workers, the Committee demands from information Member State authorities concerning the laws protecting information and consultation of workers who are not represented by a trade union.[1804] In particular, the Committee is interested in attaining information dealing with the guarantees of the right in question for workers who are citizens of other Member States which are parties to the Charter.[1805]

283. If a state or the stakeholders decide that an employer has an obligation to inform and consult workers' representatives, in the appendix to Article 21 RESC, it was stipulated that what is understood by a representative in the Charter is a body entitled to representative status thanks to domestic regulations. If the other authorised bodies from the side of the workers partaking in the consultative process happen to be entities other than trade union entities, the Committee is interested in gaining information about their legal status, in particular, interested in its ability to

1802. Conclusions 2003, vol. 1, pp. 71–72 (Bulgaria); Conclusions 2003, vol. 2, p. 419 (Romania).
1803. *Ibid.*, p. 131.
1804. Conclusions 2003, vol. 1, pp. 71–72 (Bulgaria); Conclusions 2003, vol. 2, p. 625 (Sweden).
1805. Conclusions 2003, vol. 1, p. 72.

attain information, whether it falls under the protection of the law ensuring independence in work relations with the employers.[1806] Workers' representatives are bodies which are recognised as such by domestic labour laws. The technique of electing workers' representatives and the level of conducting consultations (the level of the workplace, local, regional or national) were left for Member States to deal with, who in turn were authorised to pass on the decisions in serious matters to the interested parties, i.e., the stakeholders.[1807] It is not sought for the consultations to be carried out at the same level as those of the decision-making level within the workplace.[1808] Workers' representative bodies, in the understanding of the given provision, may be trade unions and/or advisory councils.[1809] In most of the Member States, the representative function is fulfilled by trade unions. With regard to such unions, the Committee attempts to ensure Member States abide by the principle that all trade organisations, without exception and regardless of their status (representative or non-representative), are treated equally.[1810]

284. Article 21 RESC obligates Member States to inform and consult workers employed in industries. In the appendix to the Additional Protocol of 1988, an industry was redefined as a 'set of tangible and intangible components, with or without legal personality, formed to produce or provide services for financial gain and with power to determine its own market policy'. The right to information and consultation is enjoyed solely by those workers who are employed in an industry as defined by the Additional Protocol of 1988. In the situation when an industry has an established organisational structure, an industry, by definition of the provision in question, is an organisational unit with the purpose of producing goods or rendering services.[1811] The scope of the effect of the provision of Article 21 RESC encompasses solely the employers, not the public sector. The terms 'produce goods' and 'provide services' used to identify the entities who are encompassed by the provision in question stand in the way of the public-sector workers to be encompassed by the provision also.[1812] The scope of the effect of these public undertakings' are carried out by public administrative bodies.[1813]

285. Article 21 RESC allows the authorities of Member States to exclude from the scope of application of this provision those undertakings which employ a small number of workers. The Committee regards the exclusion of undertakings employing twenty,[1814] fifty[1815] or even one hundred[1816] workers as being in accordance with international standards. Undertakings which may be excluded from the scope of the

1806. Conclusions 2003, vol. 1, p. 71 (Bulgaria).
1807. As above, Conclusions XIII-3, p. 447 (Sweden).
1808. *Ibid.*
1809. Conclusions XIII-3, p. 443 (the Netherlands).
1810. Conclusions XIII-3, p. 447 (Sweden).
1811. Explanatory report, *supra*, p. 133.
1812. Conclusions XIII-5, p. 284 (Norway).
1813. Conclusions XV-1, pp. 176–177 (Denmark).
1814. Conclusions XIII-5, p. 270 (Finland).
1815. Conclusions XVI-2, vol. 1, p. 363 (Greece).
1816. Conclusions XVI-2, vol. 2, p. 594 (Norway).

application of the above provision, regardless of the number of workers employed, are those which are established and organised by associations and religious organisations. Further, undertakings which are carried out by organisations inspired by ideals or moral viewpoints or approaches subject to legal protection by the legislation of Member States may be excluded from the scope of Article 21 RESC to such a point that it is necessary to protect the reason as to why the undertaking was established in the first place. The exclusion from the encompassing obligation of Article 21 RESC are undertakings functioning solely for educational, artistic or charitable purposes.[1817] Article 21 RESC is a standard on which the principle of the 'majority of interested workers' (Article 7 §2 Additional Protocol of 1988) is based. It is an indication that a Member State fulfils its obligations specified by the provisions of the Charter to which the above principle is applicable (if such a matter includes information and consultation) if 80% of the workers use their right to information and consultation.[1818] In the understanding of the provision in question, the 'interested workers' are all those employed in undertakings which utilise the right to information and consultation. To the category of those employed in undertakings, which form the basis for calculating the number of workers Member States should guarantee the right to information and consultation workers who are not included or employed in the public sector or in small undertakings to which Article 21 RESC cannot be applied on the grounds of domestic legislation or established collective labour agreements.

286. Employers should be obliged to inform workers and/or their representatives regularly or in a reasonable timeframe. Member States and stakeholders have the choice of how frequently employers should inform and consult their workers concerning matters stipulated under Article 21 RESC. Depending on how the obligation to inform and consult is regulated, employers may be obliged to provide information and seek opinions from workers and/or their representatives at regular, previously established intervals (monthly, quarterly, half-yearly or even annually[1819] or if required from time to time) Domestic labour legislation, or the standards, which are negotiated by stakeholders, should specify the frequency of the consultations.[1820] This analysed provision is a legal basis for certain obligations and how these legal obligations are to be carried out in a legal framework. The frequency of fulfilling these obligations, as stated in the provision, is dependent upon the necessity of the employer offering information to the workers and/or their representatives. The information should be passed on to the workers and/or their representatives in an accessible fashion. Because Article 21 (1)(a) RESC demands employers inform their workers and/or their representatives about the economic and financial situation of the workplace in which the workers are employed as well as

1817. Harris & Darcy, *supra*, p. 246.

1818. Conclusions XIII-3, p. 442 (Finland). The Committee concluded that in the case of Italy and Norway it has not been established that the rules on the information and consultation of workers applicable during the reference period cover the great majority of workers concerned. Conclusions 2007, vol. 2, p. 732 (Italy), p. 937 (Norway). Conclusions 2010, vol. 1, p. 329 (Italy). Conclusions XIX-3, p. 45.

1819. Case of Finland: as above, p. 441; Conclusions XIII-5, p. 277.

1820. Conclusions 2003, vol. 1, p. 71 (Bulgaria).

inform them about the planned decisions, which may have an impact on the workers' interests, employers should provide such in an accessible fashion so that it may be understood by individuals who have not completed any specialist education.[1821] Consultations regarding planned decisions by the employer should be conducted in 'good time' (Article 21(1)(b) RESC). Aside from the provisions which regulate the obligation to inform and consult workers and/or their representatives, there is also the strict labour relationship. Therefore, employers have an obligation to consult with the workers and/or their representatives in matters that they must inform. This includes the financial and economic situation of the workplace in which the workers are employed. The interdependency between the obligation to inform and the obligation to consult is very particular. The employers should inform the workers and/or their representatives of all matters concerning the financial and economic situation of the place of employment. However, employers are only obliged to consult on those financial and economic matters which form a part of the planned decisions, which may, in turn, affect the interests of the workers. Consultations should be carried out before the employer makes any decisions where the consequences of such decisions may have a serious effect on employment in the industry.

The Charter analysts present the following examples of such decisions: liquidation of the workplace, transferring the production sector or its services to another region[1822] and changing the production profile. The obligation to consult should be fulfilled by the employer in such a way that all parties taking advantage of this entitlement may accomplish positive benefits. Such consultations will not be effective if they are conducted at a late period, so much so that the decision-makers are unable to take into account the views and proposals of the workers and/or their representatives. Informing the workers and/or their representatives about the proposed decisions and also inviting them to express their opinions in such matters, the employer should enable consultative contemplation and expression of opinion. Only certain information may not be released to the workers and/or their representatives if such information, when disclosed, would cause the workplace grave damages. The employer decides which information will be disclosed. An employer should be conscious of the fact the failure to disclose certain information to workers and/or their representatives may lead to a violation of the obligation specified under Article 21 §1 RESC. Judicial bodies or those administrative institutions equipped to deal with labour matters (work inspectors) that have been mentioned in the introduction of this section are delegated to analyse the reasons for the refusal to provide information or disallow workers and/or their representatives' opinion to be taken into account concerning matters specified in the provision. The necessary requirement for the effectiveness of the consultation is the availability of crucial and important information concerning the economy and financial situation of the workplace before the employer can reach any decision.[1823] Employers who fear the disclosure of certain details may be detrimental to the workplace may oblige workers and/or their representatives to confidentiality.

1821. Harris & Darcy, *supra*, p. 247.
1822. *Ibid.*
1823. Explanatory report to the 1988 Additional Protocol, *supra*, p. 133.

274. The ECSR analysed the compliance of companies in the Member States with the obligation to take or support measures that enable employees or their representatives to receive information about the economic and financial situation of the workplace in which they are employed on a regular basis, in an appropriate manner and in an accessible form. It is the duty of employers to inform employees and their representatives about planning and decision-making in the near future on economic and financial matters of the workplace, which may significantly affect the interests of employees in matters related to employment in the company. The Committee examined and discussed the situation of twenty-one Member States. Slightly more than half of the 12 countries visited met the requirements set by the ECSR. Some countries – Albania, Bosnia and Herzegovina, Serbia and Türkiye[1824] – received negative feedback. Their situation was found to be incompatible with Article 21(a) and (b) of the Charter. A 'suspension' of the decision was applied for the remaining four countries until the next case can be reviewed. The situation presented to the public in Strasbourg on 23 March 2023 is unusual because almost all of the negatively assessed Member States had evaded the obligation to present the actual state of affairs in cases involving the right to information and consultation. As a result, the ECSR was forced to repeat several consecutive times that the cases relating to the above-mentioned Member States were the result of the failure of the authorities of these Member States to comply with the provisions of Article 21 of the Charter and the recommendations issued by the Committee to respect these provisions. The standard case for a negative decision, in conclusion, was as follows:

The Committee concludes that the situation is incompatible with Article 21 of the Charter on the grounds that it has not been established that:

- effective remedies are available to employees or their representatives who believe that their right to information and consultation within the company has not been respected[1825]
- some employees are excluded from the calculation of staff numbers which is carried out to determine the minimum thresholds beyond which staff representative bodies must be set up to ensure that information and consultation are provided to workers[1826]
- the material scope of the right to information and consultation under the law does not cover information on the economic and financial situation of the company.[1827]

The case of Albania, which was alleged to have failed to comply with the three obligations, is unusual in that the ECSR was unable to determine whether 1) the law effectively secures the right of workers to information and consultation within a company, 2) the personal and material scope of the right to information and consultation within a company complies with the requirements of the Charter and 3) there are effective sanctions and remedies available when employers have failed to

1824. Conclusions 2022 (Albania), (Bosnia and Herzegovina), (Serbia), (Türkiye).
1825. Conclusions 2022 (Bosnia and Herzegovina), (Serbia).
1826. Conclusions 2022 (France).
1827. Conclusions 2022 (Türkiye).

respect their employees' right to be informed and consulted.[1828] In the section on the negative conclusions of the reports analysed in 2022, the Federation of Bosnia and Herzegovina was discussed extensively. In the Conclusions for 2018,[1829] the Committee stated that not all employees have the right to information and consultation with their employer. The state authorities did not make any efforts to improve the situation. In particular, in the federation's Republic of Srpska, police officers, judges, prosecutors and others working in the judiciary and public administration are not notified of the possibility of exercising their right to information and consultation.[1830] Moreover, the federal state does not have an institution authorised to provide information and discuss matters of interest to employees. The federal authorities defended themselves by claiming that the above-mentioned categories of employees did not have the legal status of public servants, but were considered holders of judicial functions, the police and army officers. The authorities indicated that the Law on Employees' Councils provides all employees with the right to express their opinions and suggests the need for the employer to take action in order to improve working conditions and safety, guarantees them food, organises transport from work to the plant and back and helps poorer employees financially. Employers are obliged to inform the council about all important issues related to work and the employees. In the event of a failure to fulfil these obligations, employers may be fined for misconduct by the relevant administrative or judicial institutions. The central state authorities, the Ministry of Justice and its administrative inspectorate supervise compliance with the standards in Article 21 of the Charter. The arguments of the federation authorities were rejected by the ECSR. Once again, these explanations were not given credence. They were not confirmed by the facts contained in the report on compliance with employee rights to information and consultation.

The case of Türkiye was slightly different.[1831] The state report was submitted to the Committee in a report on special measures during the COVID-19 pandemic. The ECSR obtained information and commentary from the Human Rights Association (HRA), an objective organisation, on cases of state assistance to people in need during the pandemic. It reads as follows: 'According to the HRA, the government had discriminatory conduct in the committees formed to take pandemic measures and prevented all social partners from being represented. The Committee refers to its statement on COVID-19 and social rights of 24 March 2021 in that it recalled that social dialogue has taken on new dimensions and new importance during the COVID-19 crisis. Trade unions and employers' organisations should be consulted at all levels on both employment-related measures focused on fighting and containing COVID-19 in the short term and efforts directed towards recovery.' This information did not convince the Committee because it was not sufficiently specific and precise. As written in the Conclusion, 'the material scope of the right of information and consultation under the legal framework does not cover information with regard to the economic and financial situation of the undertaking'.

1828. Conclusions 2022 (Albania).
1829. Conclusion 2018 (Bosnia and Herzegovina).
1830. Conclusions 2022 (Bosnia and Herzegovina).
1831. Conclusions 2022 (Türkiye).

§4. The Right to Take Part in the Determination and Improvement of Working Conditions and Working Environment

287. This provision was enacted to ensure workers effectively utilised the right to participate in the determination and improvement of the working conditions and the working environment within the workplace. In order to achieve this effectiveness, Member States are obliged to undertake or support measures which will enable workers and/or their representatives to partake in the following improvements to the workplace: working conditions, work organisation or working environment, protection of health and safety, organising social and socio-cultural services as well as supervising practices that are used to comply with the provisions in such matters. This regulation places similar obligations on the authorities of Member States as those established in Article 2 Additional Protocol of 1988 as well as Article 21 RESC. The obligatory conditions are identical in this provision. In Article 22 RESC, the same terms were utilised as in Article 21 RESC. In both provisions, Member States were obligated to undertake or specify measures which would lead to the attainment of the desired goals. In the case of Article 22 RESC, the effect of these measures should enable workers and/or their representatives to partake in the determination and improvement of the working conditions and the working environment in the workplace. With regard to the other terms used in the provision, such as 'the undertaking' and 'workers' representatives', they carry the same connotations as in Article 21 RESC. Article 22 RESC, therefore, solely encompasses the employees of an undertaking. It is not applicable to civil services, but it is applicable to undertakings which are run by administrative bodies. Despite the fact that it is more difficult to derive from Article 22 RESC, the assurance concerning the guarantee of rights to particular workers to partake in the determination and improvement of the working conditions and working environment, the Committee examines whether complying with this provision has been secured by claims filed either by the interested workers or by their representatives.[1832] There is a possibility that Member States are obliged to ensure the employer has the ability to appeal the decision.[1833] Member States are obliged to enable workers and/or their representatives to partake in the decision-making process carried out by the employer in matters concerning the improvement of the working conditions and the working environment, as well as in organising work, in issues concerning health and security protection at the workplace, organising social matters and meeting the socio-cultural needs of the workers. Member States are also obliged to enable workers and/or their representatives to oversee the employers' compliance with the provisions in question. The right of workers to partake in the determination and improvement of the working conditions and the working environment in the undertaking does not entitle them to make decisions with regard to these matters. Article 22 RESC demands authorities of Member States enable workers to take part in such decisions. It does not mean, however, that workers and/or their representatives have, according to the provision, the right to make decisions together with the employer in the matters stipulated in points (a) to (c) of the provision in question, nor are they authorised to voice their

1832. Conclusions XIII-3, p. 440.
1833. Conclusions XIII-5, p. 293 (Finland).

objections with regard to the decisions made by the employers.[1834] The result of the workers and/or their representatives determining and improving the working conditions, the organisation of work and the working environment, protecting health and safety in the workplace, organising social services as well as fulfilling the socio-cultural needs of the workers, cannot be identified with negotiating and reaching collective work agreements. The element raised in Article 22 RESC is often the subject of negotiations conducted by stakeholders and is regulated by collective labour relations or by other agreements of stakeholders.[1835] By signing collective labour agreements, the workers' representatives do not automatically partake in the determination and improvements of the work conditions and work environment conditions. However, Member States that ratified Article 22 are obligated to ensure workers and/or their representatives, legal avenues (other than collective labour agreements) resulting in the determination and improvements of the work conditions and work environment conditions, as well as supervising compliance of the provisions concerning these issues. In the Additional Protocol of 1988, in which Article 3 was included, repealed by Article 22 RESC, it was decided that the provisions of this Protocol were not in breach of the provisions of the Charter (Article §1 Additional Protocol 1988).[1836] In view of this, it is possible to conclude the provisions of Article 22 RESC do not breach either provision §1 or §2 of Article 6 RESC.

In relation to Article 3 Additional Protocol 1988, there were differences introduced to Article 22 RESC. Article 3 §2 Additional Protocol allowed for the authorities of Member States to solely exclude from the scope of application of this provision undertaking in which the number of employers does not reach the limit specified in the domestic legislation or in its practices. Article 22 RESC does not include such an approach. In light of this provision, workers and/or their representatives have a right to contribute to the improvement of the working conditions in all sectors of the industry regardless of the number of workers employed.

Contributing to the improvement of working conditions, the health and safety of the workplace and the improvement of social matters within the workplace takes on the form of an institutional structure with a commission overlooking the above matters. Generally, workers' representatives delegate managerial trade union organisations to work with such commissions. The Committee is interested in gaining information with regard to how workers' interests are protected and who the members of the trade union may be.[1837] Member States do not provide information in relation to the contributions made by workers' representatives concerning the improvement of the work conditions and the organisation of work, and the working environment.[1838] The same attention may be paid to the definition of socio-cultural issues within the undertaking and fulfilling such socio-cultural needs of the workers,[1839] despite the fact that in Article 3 of the Additional Protocol of 1988, it was

1834. Explanatory report to the 1988 Additional Protocol, *supra*, p. 134.
1835. *Ibid.*
1836. *Ibid.*
1837. Conclusions XVI-2, vol. 1, p. 184 (Czech Republic); Conclusions XVI-2, vol. 2, p. 819 (Slovakia); Conclusions 2003, vol. 1, p. 73 (Bulgaria); p. 313 (Italy).
1838. Conclusions XVI-2, vol. 1, p. 184 (Czech Republic).
1839. As above, p. 185; Conclusions 2003, vol. 1, p. 75 (Bulgaria); p. 313 (Italy).

suggested that fitting under the definition were all socio-cultural matters, which aid in the convenience of the following: social assistance, sporting grounds, available areas for mothers feeding their young, libraries, holiday camps for children. There are no set indications of how to carry out the procedure of decision-making with regard to these issues. Postponing its ruling in matters of domestic labour law compliance with international standards, the Committee obligated the given Member States to present detailed information with regard to the issues in question. The most developed techniques of contributions by workers' representatives are seen in the area of improving the protection of health and safety within the workplace. Usually, Member States obligate employers to create security and health commissions, and workers' representatives selected by the trade organisations are part of them. This is the most widely encountered technique incorporated by authorities of Member States obligated by Article 22 (b) RESC.[1840] It is important to stress that Article 22 (b) RESC does not influence the rights and obligations of a Member State in the area of health and safety responsibilities within the workplace. Workers' and/or their representatives' input in the monitoring of the compliance of their employers of the obligations stipulated under Article 22 (a)(b)(c) RESC does not absolve the employers (nor their representatives) from their obligations to improve working conditions, the organisation of work, the protection of the working environment, the protection of health and safety within the workplace as well as fulfilling the social and cultural needs of the workers.[1841] The commissions created by the employers (including workers' representatives), which monitor employer compliance with obligations under the Charter, cannot free the employers of such obligations; instead, they assist in improving the supervisory institutions within the workplace.[1842] As of 2015, the Committee concludes that the situation in Armenia is not in conformity with Article 22 of the Charter on the four following grounds that it has not been established (1) that the right of workers to take part in the determination and improvement of working condition and the working environment is effective; (2) that the right of workers to take part in the determination and improvement of the protection of health and safety is effective; (3) that workers' representatives have legal remedies when their right to take part in the determination and improvement of working conditions and the working environment is not respected; and (4) that sanctions exist for employers who fail to fulfil their obligations under this article.[1843] In the case of two other Member States, Azerbaijan and Italy, the Committee concludes that it has not been established that (1) workers and/or their representatives have an effective right to take part in the decision-making process in undertakings with regard to working conditions, work organisation and the working environment; (2) legal remedies are

1840. Conclusions XIII-3, p. 453 (Sweden).
1841. The Committee concluded that Albania, Italy and Norway have not established the great majority of workers are granted an effective right to participate in the decision-making process within the undertaking concerning the matters referred to in Art. 22 of the RESC. Conclusions 2007, vol. 1, pp. 67–68 (Albania), vol. 2, pp. 754–755 (Italy), p. 938 (Norway). The very same conclusion is reached in 2010 in case of Albania, Bulgaria, Estonia and Italy. Conclusions 2010, vol. 1, p. 44 (Albania), p. 192 (Bulgaria), pp. 233–234 (Estonia), p. 331 (Italy).
1842. Conclusions XIII-3, p. 453 (Sweden).
1843. Conclusions 2014 (Armenia).

available in the event of infringements of their right to take part in the determination and improvement of working conditions and the working environment.[1844] In the case of another three countries, Bulgaria, Norway and Turkey, the Committee concludes that it has not been established that (1) the right of workers to participate in the determination and improvement of the working conditions, work organisation and working environment is ensured,[1845] (2) legal remedies are available to workers and/or their representatives when their rights protected by Article 22 of the Charter are not granted or respected.[1846] In 2018, in three countries, the Committee concluded that the situation was inconsistent with Article 22 of the RSC because workers had not been granted an effective right to participate in the process of deciding on working conditions, work organisation rules, the working environment and legal remedies that they could use to obtain the above information.[1847]

288. Article 22 of the Charter requires the ratifying Member States to enable employees to actively participate in defining and improving working conditions and the working environment in the enterprise. The authorities of those countries should take or encourage measures to enable workers or their representatives, acting in accordance with national laws and practices, to contribute to (a) defining and improving working conditions, organisation of work and the working environment, (b) protecting health and safety in the company, c) organising social and socio-cultural services and facilities in the company and d) exercising control over employers' compliance with these provisions. The ECSR assessed compliance with this provision in 2022. Eleven Member States received positive feedback confirming the compliance of national social policies with the standards set out in Article 22 (a)–(d). Six countries, i.e., slightly more than half of the countries that act in accordance with Article 22 of this Charter, were assessed negatively by the ECSR. Of these six countries, Azerbaijan, Bosnia and Herzegovina and Serbia[1848] were warned and had previously been warned, mainly in 2018, that further ignorance or disregard for the duties that these authorities assumed would result in the ECSR issuing a negative Conclusion. In 2022, such changes to law compliance policies in work environments were also negatively assessed because they were not undertaken or were implemented incorrectly. Since the violation of Article 22 of the Charter was serious, the Committee did not repeat the previous practice for the two remaining negatively assessed countries, Hungary and Tūrkiye. Without prior notice, the Committee issued two negative decisions in the cases of Hungary and Türkiye. This time, the previous deferral method was used against three other countries: Ireland, Spain and France.

The cases of non-compliance with Article 22 of the Charter against six Member States are presented in alphabetical order. In previous negative rulings inform 2010 and 2018, the Committee accused Albania, Azerbaijan and Bosnia and Herzegovina that the situation was not in conformity with Article 22 of the Charter on the

1844. Conclusions 2014 (Azerbaijan, Italy). Conclusions 2016 (Azerbaijan, Bulgaria).
1845. Conclusions 2014 (Bulgaria).
1846. Conclusions 2014 (Norway, Turkey). Conclusions 1016 (Turkey).
1847. Azerbaijan, Bosnia and Herzegovina and Serbia. Activity Report 2018, p. 38.
1848. Conclusions 2022 (Azerbaijan), (Bosnia and Herzegovina), (Serbia).

grounds that employees are not granted an effective right to participate in the decision-making process concerning their working environment. It turned out that the negative evaluation was also repeated in the next cycle.

A good example of this is the attitude of Member State authorities towards informing the ECSR about measures taken in connection with the COVID-19 pandemic. The Committee referred to its 24 March 2021 statement on COVID-19 and social rights in which it recalled that social dialogue took on new dimensions and new importance during the COVID-19 crisis. In particular, the Committee requested specific reference to the situation and arrangements in the sectors most affected by the crisis, whether as a result of the inability to continue operations, the need for a broad shift to remote work or telework or their nature as frontline operations, such as health care, law enforcement, transport, the food sector, essential retail and other essential services. The ECSR noted that that report does not provide any information in this respect.[1849] In Azerbaijan,[1850] employees 1) are not granted an effective right to participate in the decision-making process regarding working conditions, organisation of work or the working environment; and 2) do not have access to legal remedies in the event of an infringement of their right to take part in the determination and improvement of working conditions and the working environment. However, the report incorrectly stated that this right is regulated by labour law. In the previous (2018) and current (2022) cycles, Bosnia and Herzegovina, Serbia, Hungary, and Türkiye informed about practices for protecting the health and safety of employees. The Committee assessed that the above efforts are unproductive because the state authorities of Bosnia and Herzegovina had not established institutions that would supervise national institutions that do not comply with environmental protection or health and safety standards for workers. The situation is similar in Serbia, Hungary and Türkiye. The employee rights listed in Article 22 of the Charter have not been effectively implemented or guaranteed[1851] by the law and the practice of its application[1852] or by legal remedies.[1853]

§5. The Right of Workers to Information and Consultation in Collective Redundancy Procedures

289. Article 29 RESC obliges the authorities of Member States to introduce regulations which oblige employers to inform and consult workers' representatives about t collective redundancy procedures. Article 29 RESC is somewhat different to Article 21 RESC, which obliges the authorities of Member States to ensure that employers regularly inform workers' representatives about the economic and financial situation of the workplace, as well as consulting them about the planned decisions which may impinge on workers' interests.

1849. Conclusions 2022 (Albania).
1850. Conclusions 2022 (Azerbaijan).
1851. Conclusions 2022 (Serbia).
1852. Conclusions 2022 (Türkiye).
1853. Conclusions 2022 (Hungary).

Consultations in matters in collective redundancy procedures should be carried out in 'good time'. In most cases, Member States comply with the standards set out in Article 29 of the RESC. In 2018, the Committee issued two negative conclusions. One for Georgia, which does not guarantee workers' representatives a timely consultation on collective redundancies before starting the redundancy procedure. The other is for Azerbaijan, where the authorities have failed to demonstrate that the widely available and required protective provisions against collective redundancies can only be applied after the social partners (employers 'representatives and workers' representatives) have completed the social dialogue on collective redundancies.[1854] The goal of such consultations is to understand the position of the workers' representatives in the planned collective redundancy. A necessary requirement for the consultations to be effective is to provide the workers' representatives with all appropriate information dealing with the causes upon which the collective redundancy is based, how the redundancy is planned, the selection criteria in choosing which employees will be made redundant during the collective proceedings (and the sequence with which following employees will be let off). The Committee considers that in order for there to be an adequate dialogue between employer and workers' representatives on ways of avoiding redundancies or limiting their number and mitigating their effects, all relevant documents must be supplied before consultation starts. To that end, prior information must cover not only the reasons, time period and category of workers concerned but also proposed social measures, criteria for dismissals and the order of dismissals. In the event information provided to workers' representatives is restricted, the Committee considers that the situation is not in conformity with Article 29 RESC.[1855] An employer planning collective redundancy proceedings should inform workers' representatives by way of writing stating the above information.

290. Article 29 RESC does not define the term 'collective redundancy'. This term was also not defined by the appendix to the RESC. The Committee is of the position that the case of collective redundancy is evident when, during a given period regulated by domestic labour legislation, a group of employees have their work agreements terminated for reasons not associated with the given employees.[1856] When defining collective redundancy, the Committee took into consideration the concept of *acquis communautaire*. During one of the completed control cycles, finalised with an annual report and accepted by the Committee of Ministers in 2003, the Committee analysed six such state reports, which dealt with the compliance of standards established by Article 29 RESC.[1857] In several of the cases, the Committee handed down a decision concerning the non-compliance of domestic labour legislation with the demands stipulated under Article 29 RESC.[1858] One of

1854. Activity Report 2018, p. 39.
1855. Case of Lithuania: Conclusions 2005, vol. 1, pp. 404–405.
1856. Conclusions 2003, vol. 1, *supra*, pp. 92, 210, 332; Conclusions 2003, vol. 2, *supra,* pp. 429, 546, 640.
1857. Reports filed by Romania, Slovenia, Sweden, Bulgaria, France and Italy.
1858. Romania. Conclusions 2003, vol. 2, *supra*, pp. 429–431, Conclusions 2007, vol. 2, p. 1098 (Sweden). In the latter case the Committee concludes that the situation in Sweden is not in conformity with Art. 29 of the RESC on the grounds that no provision is made for some possibility of recourse

the reports exemplified compliance.[1859] The remaining four decisions concerning the presented reports were adjourned, and the Committee sought further information from those countries.

Complying with the international standards stipulated under Article 29 RESC is France, where the domestic labour law legislation regards collective redundancies as redundancies executed by the employer due to economic reasons, affecting at least two employees within a period of 30 days. Before making a decision involving such redundancy, the employer is obligated to consult with workers' representatives, and such consultations must be carried out within a workplace employing at least fifty workers. In small plants where there are more than eleven workers employed, there is an obligation for the appointment of workers' representatives. In workplaces where the workers do not have the obligation to appoint their representatives, the employer has an obligation to carry out consultations with the workers he intends to lay off as part of the collective redundancy. The French labour code specifies the scope of information that has to be presented to workers' representatives by the employer. The workers' representatives have to be informed about the reasons for the redundancies. The information has to specify the type of reasons (economic, financial or technical) responsible for the collective redundancy. The workers' representatives have to be informed about the number of workers and the categories of employment from which the collective redundancies will take place. They also have to be made aware of the selection criteria for workers being laid off during the collective redundancy process. The workers' representatives also have to be familiar with the order of the redundancies. The employer also has to inform about the period in which all this will take place. In order for workers' representatives to be familiarised with the structure and scale of the collective redundancy, the employer should inform them about the amount of typical and atypical work agreements the workers have signed within the workplace.

291. Workers‘ representatives are obliged to inform the employer about their opinion in relation to the collective redundancy. The responsibility of the employer is to carry out an analysis of the workers‘ representatives' position and to familiarise workers' representatives with any of the decisions made. The Committee underlined that Article 29 RESC obliges employers to 'inform and consult' with workers' representatives in cases where there is a planned collective redundancy. The goal of this process is to avoid collective redundancies or to limit its extent. Furthermore, the consultation process cannot simply limit the employer to providing workers‘ representatives with information or allow them to take a standpoint or (as it is in France) obligate the employer to inform the workers' representatives with details concerning the decision of the collective redundancy. The Committee is of the opinion that consultations with stakeholders should employ a legal format of 'balanced

---

to administrative or judicial proceedings before redundancies are made to ensure that they are not put into effect before the consultation requirement is met.

1859. France. Conclusions 2003, vol. 1, *supra*, pp. 210–213. Conclusions 2010, vol. 2, p. 431 (Moldova).

social dialogue'. It cannot therefore be a case of presenting and receiving information.[1860] The Committee obligated French authorities to provide more detailed information in the following supervisory cycle concerning the dialogue carried out before an employer in matters of collective redundancies makes a decision.

The French labour law code regulations order those employers who intend to lay off at least ten workers within thirty days to provide the appropriate institutions, which monitor labour law compliance, a copy of the same information provided to workers' representatives. Such competent authorities, like national workplace inspectors, do not examine the reasons for collective redundancy decisions. They only control the procedure, which takes place before the decision is made. Independent from the functions carried out by such administrative, supervisory institutions prior to when a final decision is handed down, workers' representative bodies have the right to appear in court seeking an injunction for the information to be provided by the employer concerning the collective redundancy. Unless the obligations set by domestic labour regulations are met, meeting the various standards stipulated under Article 29 RESC, the court is able to grant an injunction and suspend the collective redundancy process.

292. The employers' obligation to carry out consultations with workers' representatives with regard to collective redundancy is also protected by penal provisions. Appropriate workers' representatives who are not fully informed by the employer about the planned redundancies are regarded as aggrieved. Violating the obligation to inform and consult about planned group redundancies by an employer means that workers' representatives are unable to carry out their own statutory obligations. Such a violation by the employer carries a maximum sentence of one-year imprisonment and/or a fine of EUR 3,811.

293. The legal right protected by Article 29 RESC is the social dialogue between the employer and the workers' representatives before any final decision is made about collective redundancies. Information and consultation as a legal basis for the above dialogue are necessary to limit or even avoid collective redundancies. In such cases where collective redundancy cannot be avoided, the social dialogue carried out by the social partners within the workplace is utilised to smooth the inevitable consequences of such an action. This may occur via certain social benefits provided for by the employer, who will be obligated by the workers' representative to provide assistance for those workers who will suffer the collective redundancy. The scope of such assistance is usually established by the social pact, an effect of the social dialogue carried out by the social partners. Article 29 RESC refers to such assistance in the form of redeployment or the reintegration of the workers who are being made redundant.

The remainder of the reports differs from the obligations stipulated under Article 29 RESC.

The Romanian report indicates the information an employer provides workers' representatives is limited. It is limited to the reasons provided for the collective redundancies as well as to the number of workers who will make redundant. It does

1860. Conclusions 2003, vol. 1, *supra*, p. 212.

not provide any information about the legal consequences involved when collective redundancy procedures are not followed.[1861] The Slovenian[1862] and Bulgarian[1863] reports inform about the change in collective law regulations and how those changes are adapted to the standards stipulated under Article 29 RESC. In accordance with the informal rigueur accepted by the Committee during supervision and assessment of the annual domestic reports, the information justified the adjournment of a decision being made against Bulgaria's and Slovenia's existing labour regulations concerning the procedures involved in collective redundancy situations and left until the next supervisory cycle.

294. The Committee does not only examine the existing regulations within Member States of the Council of Europe but their practices and how they are applied as well. For this reason, the Committee is able to adjourn its decision until all the information concerning the actions committed prior to a collective redundancy is provided. Examining the case of Sweden, the Committee was interested in whether the trade unions involved were entitled to file claims for compensation in court from the employers who did not fulfil their obligations to consult about their intention to carry out collective redundancies and if they were, whether they took advantage of this right.[1864]

A more interesting case is that of Italy. The report presented by the Italian authorities informed that besides the penal consequences involved for employers who do not fulfil their obligation to consult with workers' representatives about the intended collective redundancies, such collective redundancy action by force of law is transformed into individual work agreement terminations.[1865] The Committee demanded information from the Italian authorities to clarify the above situation in their next report. Collective redundancy is a summing up of individual terminations. The scope of workers' protection against the termination of their work agreements is Article 24 RESC. This provision does not demand consultations to be carried out between employers and workers' representatives due to the fact that in individual terminations, there is no need for social dialogue to take place, as is the case in collective redundancies.

295. In 2022, the Committee audited 22 Member States. It found 13 of them to be in compliance. Of the remaining nine, the decision was postponed in five cases[1866] and in four, a negative assessment was handed down.[1867] The states which have ratified Article 29 of the Charter are obliged to protect the interests of employees when employers intend to carry out collective redundancies in their workplaces. Article 29 of the Charter imposes the following obligations on such employers. They are to share with the workers and their representatives, the trade unions, news about the planned reduction of staff. Employees and trade union organisations

1861. Conclusions 2003, vol. 2, *supra*, pp. 430–431.
1862. As above, pp. 546–547.
1863. Conclusions 2003, vol. 1, *supra*, pp. 92–93.
1864. Conclusions 2003, vol. 2, *supra*, pp. 642–643.
1865. Conclusions 2003, vol. 1, *supra*, p. 334.
1866. Conclusions 2022 (Albania), (Bulgaria), (Greece), (Portugal), (Slovakia).
1867. Conclusions 2022 (Azerbaijan), (Georgia), (North Macedonia), (Serbia).

should be informed in due time, i.e., before the decision is taken and the layoffs begin. Organisations representing the professional interests of employees in the company should have the opportunity to take a position on the planned redundancies. Such an opportunity is the right of trade unions, set out in Article 29 of the Charter, to be consulted about an employer's plans. The goal is to work out a common position between employers and employees as well as their representatives, which may allow the employer to withdraw from the plans to dismiss an unnecessary – in their opinion – group of employees from work. Compliance with this requirement may make it possible to limit the scope of these redundancies and sometimes may even persuade the employer to avoid the intended collective redundancies. It may also prove possible for employees' and employers' representatives to take action to mitigate the effects of the redundancies. This is possible due to the wide variety of options provided by the social law applicable in a given Member State. Redundant workers can be encouraged and assisted in exercising their rights under Articles 9 and 10 of the Charter: the right to vocational guidance and training. It is clear from previous ECSR jurisprudence that, in addition to respecting the right to be informed and consulted on actions taken by employers in the interest of dismissed employees, employers are obliged to ensure that all measures that should be taken to protect redundant employees are effective. The principle of effective action was recognised by the Committee as the most important duty of employers who are forced to make some of their employees redundant for economic or organisational reasons.

The second such principle is the obligation to take preventive action against employers who are obliged by Article 29 of the Charter to protect the interests of those employees who are to be made redundant. In 2022, out of the 22 Member States that were audited, Azerbaijan, Georgia, North Macedonia and Serbia were assessed negatively according to one of the two standard statements used by the ECSR: 'the situation is not in conformity with Article 29 of the Charter on the ground that it has not been established that there are preventive measures to ensure that redundancies do not take effect until the employers have met their obligation to inform and consult employee representatives'. Such a decision was made for North Macedonia and Serbia.[1868] In the case of North Macedonia, the national report was prepared not in accordance with the requirements listed in Article 29 of the Charter but in accordance with Article 21 of the Charter: the right to information and consultation. Therefore, it did not refer to the ECSR requirements from the 2018 decision when the Committee postponed its decision until the next inspection in 2022 instead of issuing a negative or positive decision for North Macedonia. The same was true for Serbia.[1869] In its 2018 Conclusions, the Committee asked the authorities of that country for information on protective measures taken by employers during collective redundancies. Due to the lack of response from the authorities, the Committee deferred issuing an opinion and repeated the questions it had asked. As it did not receive an answer once again, it issued a negative decision. The second standard statement applied to negatively assessed Member States has the following legal wording: 'the Community concludes that the situation is not in conformity

1868. Conclusions 2022 (North Macedonia), (Serbia).
1869. Conclusions 2022 (Serbia).

with Article 29 of the Charter on the ground that domestic law makes no provisions for sanctions in case of non-compliance by the employer with their obligations in procedures of collective redundancies.' Such a case occurred in 2022 against Georgia and Azerbaijan.[1870] The Georgian authorities did not deal with the sanctions applied to enterprises that failed to comply with the standards set out in Article 29 of the Charter. The report indicates that in case of an employer's failure to comply with an obligation imposed by law, employees can appeal to the courts. However, the report also indicates that the law does not provide for any sanctions for an employer's non-compliance.[1871] On the other hand, Azerbaijan's report indicates that according to the Labour Code, in the event of a reduction in the number of employees, the employee must be officially notified in advance by the employer, depending on the length of service specified in the employment contract. If the length of service is up to one year, the employee must be notified at least two calendar weeks before the termination of the contract. If the length of service is more than ten years, the employee must be notified at least nine calendar weeks before the termination. The Committee concluded that it was not established that there were measures in place that would prevent redundancies from taking effect before the obligation to inform and consult was fulfilled. In reply, the report merely indicates that under the Labour Code, the parties may include in a collective agreement an obligation to take measures to prevent mass layoffs and dismissals. However, the Committee considers this information insufficient for it to assess the situation. Given the ongoing failure to provide the requested information, the Committee concluded that there are no measures and sanctions to ensure that redundancies do not take effect before employers fulfil their obligation to inform workers' representatives. The result that one-third of the 22 compliance decisions were negative is relatively good. In the majority of the countries under examination, the situations were in conformity with Article 29. In countries where non-compliance was found, there were no preventive measures to ensure that redundancies do not take effect before employers fulfil their obligations to inform and consult (such as recourse to administrative and judicial proceedings), and there were no effective measures applicable in cases where employers fail to fulfil their obligations under Article 29.

§6. The Right of Workers' Representatives to Protection

296. Article 28 RESC has a functional nature. It was introduced in order to enable workers' representatives to carry out their functions and statutory goals within the workplace. Member States that ratified Article 28 RESC are obligated to ensure workers' representatives' effective protection against acts prejudicial to them by employers, especially actions which may cause their dismissal based on their status or activities as workers' representatives within the workplace. They are also obligated to facilitate workers' representatives in carrying out their statutory functions.

1870. Conclusions 2022 (Azerbaijan), (Georgia).
1871. Conclusions 2022 (Georgia).

The Committee recalls that the rights recognised by the Charter must take a practical and effective rather than purely theoretical form.[1872] The protection afforded to workers' representatives shall be extended for a reasonable period after the effective end of the period of their office.[1873] The Committee has found the situation to be in conformity with the requirements of Article 28 of the Charter in countries such as Estonia[1874] and Slovenia,[1875] where the protection is extended for one year after the end of the mandate of workers' representatives, but not in Bulgaria,[1876] where the protection granted to workers' representatives is extended for six months after the end of their mandate. The Committee considers that the protection granted to workers' representatives is not extended for a reasonable period after the end of the period of their mandate. As of 2010, the Committee declares that the protection granted to workers' representatives is not extended for a reasonable period after the end of the period of their mandate in the following Member States: Armenia,[1877] Azerbaijan,[1878] Austria,[1879] Norway[1880] and Romania.[1881] In 2016 the Committee found that there have been no changes to this situation in Armenia,[1882] Azerbaijan,[1883] Moldova,[1884] Norway[1885] and Ukraine.[1886] According to the Finnish

1872. *International Movement ATD Fourth World v. France*, Complaint No. 33/2006, decision on merits of 5 Dec. 2007, §59.
1873. Conclusions 2010, Statement of Interpretation of Art. 28.
1874. Conclusions 2010.
1875. Conclusions 2010.
1876. Conclusions 2010.
1877. Conclusions 2014 (the protection is afforded to workers' representatives only during the period of their mandate).
1878. Conclusions 2014 (no information in the report).
1879. Conclusions 2014 (the special protection applied from the time of acceptance of being elected a works council member to three months after expiry of works council membership).
1880. Conclusions 2014 (the government only provides information on the period of notice required before dismissing a shop steward (twelve weeks) and does not provide an answer as to how long the protection for workers' representatives lasts after cessation of their function).
1881. Conclusions 2014 (the protection is afforded to workers' representatives only during their mandate, but not after the end of the period of their office as workers' representatives).
1882. Conclusions 2016, p. 237. The report recalls that representatives are protected against dismissal and that Art. 3 of the Labour Code, prohibits, *inter alia*, discrimination on ground of trade union membership. However, the Committee need more precise information on the protection of representatives against detriment in employment other than dismissal.
1883. Conclusions 2016, p. 238. The report fails to provide any information specifically addressing the issue of protection granted to workers' representatives.
1884. *Ibid.*, p. 239. The report states that there has been no change to this situation; however, consideration is being given to modifying the situation.
1885. *Ibid.*, p. 241. The report does not provide any information on any specific protection against dismissal afforded to workers representatives after the end of their mandate. It recalls employees may not be dismissed unless is objectively justified on the basis of circumstances relating to the undertaking, the employer or the employee. The above-mentioned rules apply generally to all dismissals, also in cases of dismissal of shop stewards. According to Basic Agreements, shop stewards may not be given notice to leave or be summarily dismissed without just cause. Due regard shall be taken to the special position the shop stewards have in the enterprise. Most shop stewards' rights are afforded in respect of acting shop stewards during their mandate.
1886. Conclusions 2016, p. 240. The report states that new legislation is currently being adopted. No further details on the right of workers' representatives to protection in the undertaking are provided.

report, the rights and the protection granted to workers' representatives and shop stewards are covered by the Employment Contracts Act of 2001 as well as collective agreements concerning shop stewards. An employer must be ordered to pay compensation for any unjust termination of the employment contract. The maximum amount due to be paid to a shop steward or elected representative is equivalent to the pay due for 30 months. The Employment Contracts Act makes no provisions for reinstatement. Safety delegates enjoy the same protection as other worker representatives. The Committee concludes as there is no possibility for the reinstatement of representatives who have been unlawfully dismissed in Finland that the situation is not in conformity with the Charter.[1887]

297. Article 28 RESC is composed of two standards. The addressees of these two standards are the authorities of Member States of the Council of Europe. They should ensure particular protection of the functions carried out by workers' representatives. Article 28(a) RESC deals with this element. Member States are also obliged to afford facilities for workers' representatives to carry out their functions promptly and efficiently (Article 28(b) RESC). Article 5 of both Social Charters (ESC and RESC), ensuring workers the right to organise in trade unions, is interpreted by the Committee as a standard ensuring the increased protection of the right of the workers' representatives protection and obligates Member States to afford such facilities for them so the workers' representatives are able to carry out their functions.[1888]

298. In 2022, the ECSR examined the situation in twenty-four European countries regarding Article 28, the provision that guarantees the effective exercise of the right of workers' representatives to carry out their functions. It states that workers' representatives must enjoy effective protection against acts prejudicial to them, including dismissal based on their position.[1889] They must also be provided with the necessary facilities to carry out their functions promptly and efficiently. The ECSR examined the protection against prejudicial acts other than dismissal, such as denial of certain benefits, training opportunities, promotions or transfers, discrimination in lay-offs, reassignment of retirement options, reduction of shifts or any other ill-treatment or abuse. In order to ensure that such protection is effective, the Charter requires that it be extended for a reasonable period of at least six months after the expiry of the representatives' mandate. The ECSR also examined whether the countries in question grant employee and trade union representatives facilities to allow them to carry out their functions effectively. Those facilities include paid time off to represent employees, financial contributions to work councils and the use of premises and materials for work councils.

1887. Conclusions 2016, pp. 242–243.
1888. Samuel, *supra*, pp. 118–119.
1889. Conclusions 2022, *Press Briefing* … , *supra*, pp. 20–22.

299. In 2022, out of the 24 countries examined by the ECSR, there were 13 with non-conformity decisions.[1890] The non-conformity decisions were issued due to the following:

(1) failure to extend the protection granted to employee and trade union representatives for a reasonable period after the end of their mandate
(2) lack of sufficient protection against prejudicial acts short of dismissal
(3) lack of legal remedies to allow employee and trade union representatives to contest their dismissal and other prejudicial acts short of dismissal
(4) lack of legal provisions for the reinstatement of unlawfully dismissed representatives of workers and trade unions
(5) failure to establish that the facilities granted to employee and trade union representatives were adequate
(6) failure to establish that facilities identical to those afforded to trade union representatives are not made available to other workers' representatives
(7) lack of provisions for the reinstatement of unlawfully dismissed workers' representatives.[1891]

300. An overview of the negative Conclusions regarding the rights of employee representatives to protection in the workplace and facilitating their functions as employee representatives can be presented in four separate groups of employees performing functions and tasks that protect all interests, not only professional but also other work-related interests. The first and smallest group includes employees from Austria and Slovakia. The ECSR issued a negative decision based on one legal reason: the lack of applicable legal protection against the illegal dismissal of employee representatives in the workplace.[1892] The second group includes representatives of Albania, Azerbaijan, Bulgaria, Montenegro, Moldova, Romania and Türkiye. Two charges were brought against them, namely 1) the protection against dismissal granted to workers' representatives is not extended for a reasonable period after the end of their mandate, and 2) the protection to workers' representatives against prejudicial acts short of dismissal is not afforded outside the period of collective bargaining.[1893] The third group represents the following grounds for dismissal: 1) the protection granted to workers' representatives against dismissal is not effective and is not extended for a reasonable period after the end of their mandate, 2) workers' representatives are not effectively protected against prejudicial acts short of dismissal and 3) the facilities granted to workers' representatives are not adequate.[1894] In the last and largest group, comprising two European countries, Bosnia and Herzegovina and North Macedonia, all the grounds listed in groups one through three that were found to be inconsistent with the Charter were present: 1) it has not been established that adequate forms of representation are available to all

1890. Albania, Armenia, Austria, Azerbaijan, Bosnia and Herzegovina, Bulgaria, Finland, Montenegro, North Macedonia, Moldova, Romania, Slovakia and Türkiye.
1891. Conclusions 2022 (Finland).
1892. Conclusions 2022 (Austria), (Slovakia).
1893. Conclusions 2022 (Albania), (Azerbaijan), (Bulgaria), (Montenegro), (Moldova), (Romania).
1894. Conclusions 2022 (Armenia).

employees, both within and outside the scope of collective bargaining, 2) the protection of trade union representatives against dismissal does not extend for a reasonable period after the expiry of their mandate, 3) trade union and employee representatives do not enjoy adequate protection from prejudicial acts short of dismissal and 4) the facilities afforded to workers' representatives are not adequate.

301. The most common reason for non-conformity was that the protection granted to employee and trade union representatives was not extended for a reasonable period after the end of their mandate.[1895] In many European countries, this protection is limited to the duration of the representative's mandate and is not extended at all afterwards. In Austria, termination or dismissal without court approval is invalid. The court only gives consent to the dismissal of a workers' representative in cases specified by the law. In some serious and exceptional cases, the workers' representative may be dismissed without a court decision, but the approval of the court is required after the dismissal. After the expiry of the three-month period, the employer should notify the former employee representative of the dismissal. Even after the expiry of the three-month period, domestic law may provide some guarantees in order to prevent an employer from dismissing a former workers' representative based on actions taken during their mandate. The three-month period of protection is not reasonable and hence is not in conformity with the Charter.

302. Concerning the protection of workers against detrimental actions other than dismissal, in some Member States, this protection is not afforded outside the period of collective bargaining.[1896] Workers' representatives other than trade union representatives are not granted such protection.[1897] Legal remedies available to workers' representatives to contest their dismissals and to challenge other prejudicial acts were deemed to be ineffective. Sometimes this was due to a total lack of legal remedies to contest dismissals,[1898] while sometimes, it was due to the inadequacy of the compensation awarded in cases of wrongful dismissal.[1899]

303. For Finland, the non-conformity was due to the impossibility of reinstatement in cases of unlawful dismissal. The Committee reiterated its case law that ordering reinstatement is an important element of the protection afforded to workers' representatives against illegal dismissal.[1900] The inadequacy of the facilities granted to employee and trade union representatives was the basis for non-conformity in eight countries. In some countries, this was due to a lack of information on the subject.[1901] In others, it was due to insufficient information being

1895. Conclusions 2022 (Albania), (Armenia), (Azerbaijan), (Bosnia and Herzegovina – Brcko District), (Bulgaria), (North Macedonia), (Romania), (Türkiye).
1896. Conclusions 2022 (Azerbaijan).
1897. Conclusions 2022 (Montenegro), (Moldova).
1898. Conclusions 2022 (Bosnia and Herzegovina – Brcko District).
1899. Conclusions 2022 (Bulgaria), (Slovakia).
1900. Conclusions 2022 (Finland).
1901. Conclusions 2022 (Albania), (Bosnia and Herzegovina – Brcko District), (Montenegro), (North Macedonia), (Moldova).

provided,[1902] as it did cover such areas as access to premises, use of materials, distribution of information, support in terms of benefits and training costs. According to the ECSR, the most common problem with Article 28 of the Charter is the failure to extend the protection afforded for a reasonable period after the end of the mandate.

I. An Obligation to Ensure Workers' Representatives the Protection of Endurance in the Undertaking

304. The Committee underlines the necessity of ensuring workers' representatives the protection of endurance in the undertaking. It is possible to increase the scope of protection of such endurance in the undertaking of workers' representatives through the mechanism of the Committee decisions based on Article 5 RESC. This provision protects the rights of workers who are active within trade unions and forbids any discrimination based on such trade union activity by the employers in any of the decisions made concerning labour relations (signing, changing or terminating work agreements).[1903] Increased protection of endurance in the undertaking should be ensured to all workers carrying out functions within trade unions and not only to workers of employers employing more than the number of workers stipulated by domestic legislation. The Committee, on many occasions, underlined that the domestic labour regulations, which exclude any of the workers from the protection of endurance in the undertaking due to being employed in a workplace of fewer than five workers, are not in compliance with Article 5 1961 ESC and 1996 RESC.[1904] Workers and trade unionists should take advantage of the protection of their rights regardless of the trade union they represent (representative and authorised to reach collective labour agreements or others without such legal status).[1905] The Committee continues to examine whether workers' representatives take advantage of this protection of rights in light of domestic labour legislation.[1906] The Committee demands from authorities of Member States additional information when it is evident that such protection is used.[1907] It is important to mention the Committee

1902. Conclusions 2022 (Armenia), (Romania), (Türkiye).

1903. *The Right to Organise and Bargain Collectively.* Study drawn up on the basis of case law of the European Social Charter, 35, Council of Europe Publishing, 2d ed., 2001).

1904. Case of Austria: Conclusions XI-2, p. 73; Conclusions XIII-3, p. 96; Conclusions XIV-1, pp. 73–74; Conclusions XV-1, p. 39.

1905. Addendum to Conclusions XV-1, pp. 14–15.

1906. The Committee concludes that it has not been established that national labour legislation in Albania, Armenia, and Bulgaria does not provide for adequate protection in the event of unlawful dismissal based on the employee's status as a trade union representative or activities linked to this status. Conclusions 2010, vol. 1, p. 49 (Albania), p. 106 (Armenia), p. 197 (Bulgaria). In addition, in Albania and Armenia, the protection is guaranteed only until the mandate expires. In case of Moldova it has not been established that employees' representatives, other than trade union representatives are guaranteed protection against dismissal or prejudicial acts short of dismissal where they exercising their functions outside the scope of collective bargaining. Conclusions 2010, vol. 2, p. 431 (Moldova).

1907. Case of France: Conclusions XIV-1, vol. 1, pp. 254–255; Conclusions XV-1, vol. 1, p. 243.

is not content with information which shows that such protection is solely applicable to workers who are trade unionists. Article 28 RESC obligates the authorities of Member States to protect workers' representatives. Aside from trade unionists, workers who are active in non-trade union organisations representing workers should also receive increased protection. Given the lack of information, the Committee concludes that the situation is not in conformity, as it has not been established that workers' representatives, other than trade union representatives, are granted adequate protection.[1908] In such cases (as seen in the report filed by the Romanian authorities), when a Member State issues information dealing only with particular rights protection of workers who are members of trade union organisations, the Committee adjourns its decision and demands further information concerning the legal situation of workers who are active in organisations other than representative trade union within the workplace.[1909]

The Committee is interested in situations in which workers are members of health and safety committees and in workers who are members of general assemblies of workers within a workplace owned by the state treasury.[1910] It is of the position, in the light of the legal regulation established by Article 28 of RESC, that the definition 'workers' representatives' has no international meaning encompassing solely those organisations that are authorised by domestic labour legislation to represent the interests of the workers and protect their rights. On the other hand, the position of the authorities of Member States is that a given labour legislation only authorises a trade union to represent workers' interests and protect their rights and is binding in its nature. In such a case, the Committee has no basis for further examination of reasons why solely a trade union or other representative organisation is authorised to represent workers' interests or protect their rights.

The Committee does not express itself about the particular scope of protection of rights of a representative team within a workplace carrying outs its functions. It is of the conviction any form of rights protection especially concerned with the protection of lasting labour relations that may be moving away from the protection regulations established by a given Member State yet benefiting the worker, are in accordance with the standards stipulated under Article 28 RESC. The Committee accepts adequate compensation – proportionate to the damage suffered by the victim of unfair dismissal based on the grounds of his/her activities as a representative

1908. Conclusions 2014 (Armenia, Bulgaria, Finland, Ukraine, Republic of Moldova). In the case of Armenia, it has not been established that workers representatives are granted adequate protection against prejudicial acts other than dismissal. The Committee finds out that in the Republic of Moldova workers' representatives, other than trade union representatives, are guaranteed protection against dismissal or prejudicial acts other than dismissal where they are exercising their functions outside of the scope of collective bargaining. In Finland and Ukraine the Committee concludes that legislation does not provide for adequate protection. In Bulgaria the Committee concludes that the situation is not in conformity with Art. 28 of RESC, on the grounds that legislation does not provide for adequate protection in the event of an unlawful dismissal based on trade union membership or activities.

1909. Conclusions 2003, vol. 2, p. 428.

1910. Case of Bulgaria: Conclusions 2003 vol. 1, p. 91.

of personnel.[1911] The protection of lasting labour relations should be taken advantage of by those workers who are representing the interests of workers and are protecting their rights. The increased protection therefore is not applicable to workers who are not carrying out their responsibilities stipulated in their work agreement. In 2018, the Committee recalled that Article 28 RESC 'protects workers' representatives in undertakings from dismissal or other prejudicial acts and requires that they are afforded appropriate facilities to carry out their functions. All forms of employee representation, not exclusively trade unions, should benefit from the rights guaranteed by this article. In order to ensure that such protection is effective, the Charter requires that it is extended for a reasonable period, at least six months after the expiry of the representative's mandate.

The most frequent ground of non-conformity with the Charter under this provision was the absence of such extended protection.[1912]

In several cases, the Committee found that workers' representatives were not adequately protected from prejudicial acts, which may entail, for instance, denial of certain benefits, training opportunities, promotions or transfers, discrimination when issuing lay-offs or assigning retirement options, being subjected to shifts cut-down or any other taunts or abuse[1913] In addition, in one country, workers' representatives other than trade union members were also insufficiently protected against dismissal.[1914]

In its case law, the Committee set examples of facilities which workers' representatives should be afforded and which entail, i.e., access to premises and office equipment, authorisation to distribute information or financial contributions. The Committee found that the situation was not in conformity in this respect in certain number of Eastern European countries.[1915]

II. The Obligation to Afford Workers' Representatives Facilities to Carry Out Their Statutory Functions

305. A necessary condition for workers' representatives to appropriately carry out their functions and statutory goals is for employers to allow workers' representatives entry onto the work plant and allow them to organise meetings within the workplace. The Committee claimed the obligation of an employer to allow representatives of union organisations access to the workplace is not strict in its nature. Examining the methods of allowing workers' representatives access to the workplace, the Committee is obliged to take into consideration some of the employer demands, such as the necessity of assured management of the workplace, protection of confidential information as well as the obligation of protecting health and safety

1911. Case of Bulgaria, Conclusions 2007, vol. 1, pp. 303, 305.
1912. Austria, Azerbaijan, Bosnia and Herzegovina, Lithuania, North Macedonia, Norway, Romania, Russian Federation, Turkey. Activity Report 2018, p. 39.
1913. Armenia, Azerbaijan, Republic of Moldova, North Macedonia, Turkey, Ukraine. *Ibid.*
1914. Ukraine. *Ibid.*
1915. Armenia, Bosnia and Herzegovina, Moldova, Romania, North Macedonia and Russian Federation.

of every person within the workplace.[1916] During the twelfth and thirteenth supervisory cycles, the Committee concluded that the German authorities ensured trade unionists limited access to the workplace in such cases when the workplace employs only one or a few members of the particular union organisation.[1917] During the fifteenth supervisory cycle, the Committee changed its position. It came to the conclusion that the right to access the grounds of a workplace should be applicable to workers' representatives of trade unions. Regardless of the type of workplace (whether it is public or private) and the number of workers employed (over or under five workers), workers' representatives of union organisations gained the right of access to the grounds of a workplace in order to be able to carry out trade union activities.[1918] As of 2015, the Committee concludes that the situation is not in conformity with Article 28 of RESC, as it has not been established that appropriate facilities are granted to workers' representatives[1919] or that facilities identical to those afforded to trade union representatives are provided to other workers' representatives.[1920] In 2016, the Committee concluded that the situation in Armenia, Moldova and Ukraine was not in conformity with the Charter as it had not been established that appropriate facilities were granted to worker representatives.[1921]

A direct connection of the rights of the workers' representatives being able to enter the grounds of a workplace is to be able to organise meetings. The questionnaire prepared by the Committee, which is to be used as a basis for authorities of Member States in preparing reports and then used by the Committee to examine domestic standards to the international model established by Article 28 RESC, contains the questions concerning the ease with which workers can organise as well as the limitations of being able to take advantage of this right. Despite this question, The Committee did not concern itself[1922] with the matter of trade union meetings being organised within on the grounds of a workplace. For this reason, in the official publication regarding Committee decisions was the inclusion of an official lack of position in this matter.[1923] In reality, the Committee indeed was concerned with this matter.

1916. Conclusions XII-2, p. 98.
1917. *Ibid.*; Conclusions XIII-2, p. 269.
1918. Addendum to Conclusions XV-1, p. 22.
1919. Conclusions (Ukraine).
1920. Conclusions (Republic of Moldova).
1921. Conclusions 2016 (Armenia), p. 237. The report states that pursuant to the Labour Code, employee representatives shall be exempted from employment duties for up to six working days per year, to attend various events organised by the employees' representative bodies or to improve their qualifications as members of the representative bodies of employees. The Committee takes note of this information, but in order to assess the situation still needs further information on other facilities to be afforded to worker representatives. The Moldovan report declares that there has been no change to the previous situation; however, consideration is being given to modifying the situation. Therefore, the Committee reiterates its previous negative conclusion. The Ukrainian report states that the new legislation has been adopted. No further details on the obligation to afford workers' representatives facilities to carry out their statutory functions has been supplied.
1922. During the third supervisory cycle the Committee concerned itself with the accusations of destabilisation of trade union meeting in Austria. Conclusions III, p. 30.
1923. The right to organise, *supra*, p. 34.

Examining the case of Finland, the Committee came to the conclusion that an employer employing more than ten workers has an obligation to make available (and have under control) a room and facilities within the workplace for after-hours trade union meetings.[1924]

Despite the minimum experience of the Committee in this field concerning the accessibility of rooms and facilities within the workplace for after-hours trade union meetings, this right has to be made available to other workers' representatives' organisations to be able to carry out meetings.[1925]

1924. Conclusions XIV-1, vol. 1, p. 215.

1925. The Committee concludes that in Moldova it has not been established that facilities identical to those afforded to trade union representatives are provided to the other employees' representatives. Conclusions 2010, vol. 2, p. 431.

Chapter 3. Necessary Derogations

306. Exclusions and limitations are accepted in the case of war or other public emergencies threatening the life of the nation (Article 30 ESC, Article F RESC). Exclusions and limitations of some of the Charter provisions are possible in cases of the necessity of protection of the rights and freedoms of others or for the protection of public interest, national security, public health, or morals (Article 31 §1 ESC; Article G §1 RESC). Stakeholders or the authorities of the Member States have a right to introduce exclusions and limitations with regard to some of the provisions of the Charter (Article 2 §1, 2, 3, 4, 5; Article 7 §4, 6, 7; Article 10 §1, 2, 3, 4) as far as the majority of interested workers is concerned (Article 33 §1 ESC; Article I §2 RESC). The authorities of the Member States decide upon the territorial range of the Charter's application (Article 34 ESC; Article E RESC).

§1. Temporary Derogations of the Charter in Case of War or National Security Threats

307. In cases of war or other public emergency threatening the life of the nation, the authorities of every Member State, which are parties to the Charter, can undertake measures required by the exigencies of the situation, exempting it from its commitments under the ratification of the Charter. The necessary condition of temporary derogation from abiding by the Charter provisions is the occurrence of the conditions determined in Article 30 §1 ESC or Article F RESC, defined in terms of international public law. The appendix to the Charter allows the authorities of a Member State not in a state of war but prior to it (threatened by war) for temporary derogations of the Charter. Public security threats are defined as an exceptional state of crisis embracing whole of society, dangerous to public order.[1926] The authorities of a Member State have a right to make decisions about the derogations of the Charter in the cases listed above. Once the decision is made, it is subject to the control of the Council of Europe and its bodies. The authorities of the Member States enjoy the right of the evaluation of the situation as well as a relatively wide margin of appreciation.[1927] Any party which has availed itself of this right of exemption shall, within a reasonable lapse of time, inform the Secretary General of the Council of Europe in detail about the measures taken. The notice should compile the time when the provisions of the Charter have ceased to operate and the period when these provisions would be derogated on the territory of a particular Member State. Violating of this obligation formulated in Article 30 §2 ESC and in Article F RESC does not imply the invalidity of the decision upon the temporary derogation of the provisions of the Charter. The Secretary General will inform the authorities of the Member States who are parties to the Charter as well as the Director General of the

1926. *See* the verdicts of the European Tribunal of Human Rights in the cases: *Lawless v. Ireland*, 3 ECtHR (ser. A) 1961; *Ireland v. United Kingdom*, 25 ECtHR (ser. A) 1978.

1927. *See* the verdict of the European Tribunal of Human Rights in the case: *Branningan and Mc Bride v. United Kingdom*, 258 ECtHR (Ser. A), 1993.

International Labour Office about the decisions made. The Secretary General will forward the information delivered by a Member State that made the above-mentioned decision.[1928]

§2. Derogations Necessary for the Protection of the Rights and Freedoms of Others or for the Protection of Public Interest, National Security, Public Health, or Morals

308. Article 31 §1 ESC and Article G §1 RESC confirm the rule the efficient enforcement of the rights established by Parts I and II of the Charter cannot be subject to any limitations that are not listed in the above-mentioned parts of the Charter, with the exception of these determined by law legislated in Member States and inevitable for the democratic society for the protection of public interest, national security, public health, or morals. The Committee declared derogations of the Charter should be well-founded and lead to the achievement of one of the above-mentioned aims.[1929] Within the analysed jurisdiction of the Committee, it is not a single case for the authorities of Member States to refer to the above-mentioned grounds as a reason for not abiding by or partially following the provisions of the Charter. It was with regard to the right to strike colliding with the rights of other persons: patients in hospitals,[1930] financial situation of employers,[1931] limitations of the right to negotiate collective work agreements, introduction of the compulsory arbitration in cases of collective work disputes on the basis of protection of public interest.[1932]

National security gave grounds to derogate the rights to associate with the governmental telecommunications centre in the United Kingdom.[1933] Security reasons were used as the explanation for destroying housing resources by the Turkish authorities.[1934]

309. The Committee, in the early stage of the supervisory cycle, made a ruling which became a firm precedence for the following supervisory cycles, stating the reasons for derogations of the provisions of the Charter by the Member States listed in this document cannot be applied to any purpose other than that for which they have been prescribed. The limitations are necessary. They also should be well proportioned to the aims they are introduced for. These aims cannot be flagrantly disproportional to the labour rights guaranteed by the Charter. In the literature devoted

1928. The history of the Council of Europe does not know a case of temporary derogation of the provisions of the Charter caused by the above-mentioned reasons. Neither the Turkish invasion of Cyprus of 1974 nor the threatening of public security in Northern Ireland initiated the analysed legal mechanism.
1929. Conclusions XIV-1, p. 622 (Norway).
1930. As above, in case of limitations of the right to strike for the hospital personnel.
1931. Conclusions XIV-1, p. 555 (the Netherlands).
1932. Conclusions XII, pp. 122–123 (the Netherlands); Conclusions XIV-1, p. 387 (Iceland); p. 623 (Norway).
1933. Conclusions XI, p. 80.
1934. Conclusions XIII-3, p. 466.

to the labour rights regulated by the Charter, the terms deriving from the terminology of labour law are used *expressis verbis,* for example forbidding the authorities of the Member States to abuse power (*détournement de pouvoir*).[1935] The rulings presented in the previous chapters of this monograph give evidence the authorities of the Member States have groundlessly referred to the analysed provisions of the Charter (Article 31 §1 ESC and Article G §1 RESC) several times in order to limit the application of some provisions in particular situations. Derogations of the Charter are exceptionally permissible in a 'democratic society'. The Committee did not interpret this term. It was agreed by all Member States of the Council of Europe to meet the requirements in order to be considered democratic.[1936] Membership of the Council of Europe gives each of the states the right to introduce derogations of the Charter in order to protect values listed in Article 31 §1 ESC and Article G §1 RESC.

§3. Derogations of the Provisions Specified by the Charter to the Significant Majority of Workers

310. The Charter, which is listed among international sources of labour law and social security law, can be implemented into an internal legal system of Member States either by legal provisions legislated by the relevant state institutions (acts, decrees) or by collective work agreements or other normative acts negotiated by stakeholders. The Charter does not exclude other methods of the implementation of its provisions into the national legal system where the enforcement of these provisions is guaranteed. Implementation of the provisions of the Charter is possible and accepted when a Member State uses a combined technique (partly legislated law, partly negotiated collective work agreements) or employs other adequate measures (custom). Regardless of the legislative technique, the authorities of the Member States are responsible for adjusting the national regulations to the ratified provisions of the Charter. Article 33 ESC and Article I RESC introduce some exceptions to this rule. They allow for the implementation of some provisions (Article 2 §1, 2, 3, 4; Article 7 §4, 6, 7; Article 10 §1, 2, 3, 4 of the Charter) while the appendixes to the Charter broaden the range of this exemption onto Article 5 §5 and Article 7 §8 of the Charter as far as the 'great majority of the workers' is concerned. The Committee declares that Member States which utilise the above-mentioned exceptions do not abuse their entitlements when provisions listed in Article 33 ESC and Article I RESC are complied with for the 80% of workers concerned.[1937]

The provisions of the Charter allow the authorities of the Member States to introduce the exceptions from the obligation of the enforcement of the provisions of the Charter, including the analysed provisions of Article 33 ESC and Article I RESC, as well as the appendixes to these Charters, cannot be abused. Abuse of the latter takes place when 20% of the workers protected are located within one national or ethnic

1935. Darcy & Harris, *supra*, p. 382.
1936. As above, p. 381.
1937. Conclusions XIII-5, p. 47 (Finland); p. 158 (Portugal).

group.[1938] To avoid the abuse of the above-mentioned provision, the requirement of enforcement of the provisions guaranteeing particular labour rights to the great majority (at least 80%) of workers concerned has been introduced. This term stands for all categories of workers whose rights should be protected under the provisions listed in Article 33 ESC and Article I RESC. It is of no significance for the Committee that the majority of workers on the national, occupational or regional scale are encompassed by legal protection if they are not, for example, young workers who should be legally protected under Article 7 §4, 6, and 7 of the Charter.

§4. Territorial Application of the Charter

311. The Charter is applied to the metropolitan territory of the Member States (Article 34 §1 ESC and Article L §1 RESC). The territory, which shall be considered to be a particular state metropolitan territory, is determined by the authorities of the Member State by sending a declaration addressed to the Secretary General of the Council of Europe. The application of the Charter can be extended in whole or in part to a non-metropolitan territory or territories for whose international relations a particular Member State, party to the Charter, is responsible or for which it assumes international responsibility (Article 34 §2 ESC and Article L §2 RESC).[1939] Member States with no metropolitan territories are not obliged to deliver reports on the lack of application of some parts or the whole Charter on such territories. Article 34 §2 ESC and Article L §2 RESC as the necessary condition of application of the Charter outside the metropolitan territory of a given Member State request for a special notice with regard to this matter. Some of the Member States deliver the declaration on not applying the Charter on the territory of non-metropolitan areas.[1940]

Changes to the metropolitan territories of the Member States imply automatic changes in the Charters application. Incorporating a state by a Member State, as it occurred in the case of the unification of Germany, causes the obligations of the Charter to be applied to the new metropolitan territory.[1941] The loss of a part of a territory by a Member State would eventuate in cessation of de facto responsibility on behalf of the authorities of the said state for the Charter enforcement if a territory that has divided itself off did not obtain international status.[1942] In cases of obtaining a legal entity in terms of international law, new states themselves decide upon the ratification of the Charter and accept duties of abiding by its provisions on

1938. Conclusions VIII, p. 139 (Austria).

1939. Making use of this provision the United Kingdom extended the application of the Charter for the Isle of Man. The Netherlands introduced Arts 1, 5 and 6 (with the exception of civil servants) and Art. 16 of the Charter as well as Art. 1 of the Additional Protocol and Art. 1 of the Additional Protocol of 1988 on the Dutch Antilles and Aruba. France extended all provisions of the Additional Protocol of 1988 for all overseas districts.

1940. Norway sent a declaration informing the Charter is not applied on the 'subsidiary territories'.

1941. Conclusions XII-2, p. 11; Conclusions XIII-2, p. 23.

1942. Case of the northern part of Cyprus which, as a consequence of the Turkish invasion of 1974, tore off from Cyprus but is not a legal entity of international law.

their metropolitan territories.[1943] Changes in the territories have a significant impact on the application or derogation of the Charter or its irrelevance.

312. The Charter does not allow for the possibility of sending a declaration informing about the derogation of the ratified provisions as far as the specified categories of workers are concerned. Some of the Member States (France, the Netherlands, Germany and Norway) delivered a declaration regarding the exemption of some of the provisions of the Charter in cases of the specified categories of workers.[1944] The remaining Member States that were informed about the above-mentioned reservations did not respond. The Committee accepted the notified reservations and declarations as fact and made a ruling on the basis of a formal distinction between the said types of notices delivered by the Member States authorities, stating the case of violation of Article 6 §4 by Germany as the deprivation of civil servants of the right to participate in collective actions expressed in the declaration of not abiding by Article 6 §4 of the Charter was not regarded as a reservation.[1945] From the above-mentioned cases, it can be derived that, although there is a lack of a reservation clause in the Charter, the authorities of the Member States are capable, by the formal notification, of limiting the Charter application (or at least some of its provisions) in cases of particular categories of workers.

1943. Cases of the European states which came into being from the former republics of the Soviet Union and Yugoslavia.

1944. The Netherlands and Germany ratified Art. 6 §4 of Charter with reservation that the right to strike cannot be utilised by civil servants.

1945. Conclusions IV, p. 49.

Part III. The Supervision of Complying with the Laws of the European Social Charter

Chapter 1. Supervisory Bodies

§1. The Committee

313. The Committee performs three basic functions: establishes the European standards in terms of labour law, social security and social policy; examines the reports delivered by the authorities of the Member States and declares compliance or non-compliance of the national regulations with the standards established under the Charter; recognises collective complaints registered by international workers and employers organisations as well as other non-governmental organisations against the Member States.

314. The Committee consists of professors of labour law and social security law as well as the former judges of the highest courts in the Member States.[1946] Candidates for Committee members are proposed by the authorities of the Member States. Given the increased number of the Member States of the Council of Europe and the new competences of the Committee, which since passing the Additional Protocol to the European Social Charter in 1995 introducing the system of collective complaints, started acting as an international quasi-judicial body, the number of the Committee members was increased to 9[1947] and then to 15.[1948] In comparison, the number of Member States (forty-seven) with the number of the Committee

1946. Members of the Committee are: the former President of the national Norwegian labour court, the former judge of the Belgian Constitutional Tribunal (*Cour d'arbitrage*), the judge of the French State Council (*Conseil d'Etat*). F. Sur writes about the qualifications of the first members of the Committee in 'La Charte sociale européenne: Dix années d'application 1965–1975', *Annuaire européen*, vol. 12, M. Nijhoff, La Haye 1974, p. 91. In the past the members of the Committee had experience in the International Labour Organisation. The members of the Committee were: the Belgian, L. Troclet (1972–1978), the former President of ILO, the British: W. James (1980–1982), the former President of the International Labour Conference, M. Morgan (1976–1980), the former representative of the government to the Administrative Council of ILO. Among the members of the Committee there were also outstanding scholars specialising in labour law: Sir Otto Kahn Freund, United Kingdom (1966–1972); Rudolf Strasser, Austria (1970–1973).
1947. Decision of the Committee of Ministers made during the 509th sitting in March 1994, European Social Charter, *supra*, p. 189.
1948. Decision of the Committee of Ministers made during the 751st sitting on 2–7 May 2001 as above.

members (fifteen) leads to the conclusion that only citizens of some Members States of the European Council sit on the Committee. Unlike the judges of the European Tribunal of Human Rights, who are equal in number to the number of Member States of the European Council, the members of the Committee do not act as the representatives of the Member States according to their citizenship. They hold the seat 'on their own behalf'. While serving their mandate, they are not allowed to perform any functions which are impossible to reconcile with the requirements of independence, objectivity and availability connected with the above role (Article 3 of Amending Protocol ESC of 21 October 1991).[1949] Taking into consideration the rule the members of the Committee do not represent the Member States, the Committee of Ministers attempt to gather the representation of different geographical regions of Europe within the Committee. This tendency can be seen in the elective proceedings. The Committee members are elected for a six-year-long tenure. They can be re-elected. The members chosen to fill in for those who have left will stay for the remaining time of the tenure of the predecessor (Article 25 ESC). The Committee of Ministers regulates the electing procedure dividing the Member States of the Council of Europe into five groups and determines the number of future Committee members belonging to each group. The last Committee election took place in 2012, and the said groups were divided as follows:[1950]

- Group 1 (three seats in the Committee): Armenia, Austria, Czech Republic, Liechtenstein, Germany, Slovakia, Switzerland, and Hungary;
- Group 2 (two seats in the Committee): Azerbaijan, Belgium, Bulgaria, France, the Netherlands, Luxembourg, Moldova, Romania, and Turkey;
- Group 3 (three seats in the Committee): Denmark, Finland, Ireland, Iceland, Norway, Sweden, and Great Britain;
- Group 4 (three seats in the Committee): Albania, Andorra, Cyprus, Georgia, Greece, Spain, Malta, Portugal, Italy and San Marino;
- Group 5 (three seats in the Committee): Bosnia and Herzegovina, Croatia, Estonia, Lithuania, Latvia, the former republic of Yugoslavia, now North Macedonia, Poland, the Russian Federation, Slovenia and Ukraine.

315. The Committee sits on plenary sessions as well as in two working groups, which take place on average seven to eight times during the calendar year. The sittings of the Committee are closed sittings, and the Committee members are obligated to keep the debates confidential. The Committee is in charge of deciding upon the public session when it deals with collective complaints. The work of the Committee is managed and administrated by the board consisting of the chairman, the two vice-chairmen, the general reporter and the secretary executive. The rules of conduct for the Committee and its members are listed in the statute of conduct

1949. Because of acceding the role of vice Commissary of Employment and Social Matters of the EU L. Samuel resigned from being the member of the Committee in May 2005. Previously, to become a member of the Committee L. Samuel gave up the role of the Secretary of State in the Labour Ministry of Cyprus. Her place was taken by Ms. E. Spatafora from Italy. In March 2006, Mr. G. Quinn stood down from The Committee.

1950. 4.3 decision of the Committee of Ministers made during the 881st sitting on 14 Apr. 2004, European Social Charter, *supra*, pp. 190–191.

passed on 29 March 2004.[1951] It specifies the procedure employed in the process of analysing the reports delivered by the authorities of the Member States. The Member States are obligated to deliver reports of two kinds, one under Article 21 about the ratified provisions of the Charter and the other under Article 22 about the provisions of the Charter that have not been ratified. The above-mentioned provisions of the European Social Charter create legal grounds for delivering the reports by the Member States. According to the regulation of Article C of the Revised European Social Charter, the controlling mechanism determined in Articles 21 and 22 ESC has the application in the process of supervision over the enforcement of the ratified provisions of the Revised European Social Charter. In the process of the supervision of the enforcement of the Charter by the Member States, the Committee operating on the basis of Article 21 of the Charter, analyses the reports of the authorities of the Member States and makes a ruling declaring compliance or non-compliance with the national regulations and the practice of their application with the Charter. According to Article 22, the Committee familiarises itself with the reasons why the authorities of the Member States did not ratify the provisions of the Charter.

I. Reports Concerning the Ratified Provisions of the Charter

316. The authorities of the Member States are obligated to present to the Secretary General of the Council of Europe reports from the enforcement of the provisions of the Charter once every two years. The Secretary General forwards these reports to the Committee, which performs a content-related examination. In the period of the first eight supervisory cycles, the Member States delivered reports concerning the enforcement of all ratified provisions of the Charter. In order to improve the supervisory process, the Committee of Ministers divided the Member States into two groups, deciding upon this during the 336th session on the 27th day of 1984. From the ninth supervisory cycle in 1985, the Member States of Group 1 were obligated to deliver reports in uneven years.[1952] The Member States of the second group were obligated to deliver reports in even years. The division of the Charter's provisions into two categories was made: the first category encompasses the provisions listed in Article 20 §1(b) ESC[1953] and in Article A §1(b) RESC[1954] (hardcore provisions); the remaining provisions of the Charter were classified to the second category. The authorities of Member States were obligated to present the reports on the enforcement of the provisions of the Charter classified to the first category in four-year cycles. The frequency of these reports was set at the level of two years. The further division into the two groups was made. The first group consisted of Articles 2, 3, 4, 9 and 10 ESC and the Additional Protocol of 1988, while the second group compiled Articles 7, 8, 11, 14, 17 and 18 ESC, as well as Article 1 §4 of the Additional Protocol of 1988.

1951. Rules of procedure (in:) European Social Charter, *supra*, pp. 193 et seq.
1952. Supervision of the application of the European Social Charter (in:) European Social Charter, *supra*, pp. 408 et seq.
1953. Articles 1, 5, 6, 12, 13, 16 and 19.
1954. Articles 1, 5–7, 12, 13, 16, 19 and 20.

317. The complicated system of supervision has been criticised by the authorities of the Member States.[1955] Following a decision taken by the Committee in 2006, under the current reporting system, the provisions of both Charters have been divided into four thematic groups. Two of them deal with labour rights: Group 1, 'Employment, training and equal opportunities' (Articles 1, 9, 10, 15, 18, 20, 24, 25) and Group 3 ', Labour rights' (Articles 2, 4, 5, 6, 21, 22, 26, 28,29). Some provisions related to labour rights are included in Group 2, 'Health, social security and social protection' (Article 3 – safe and healthy working conditions) and Group 4 (Article. 8 – protection of maternity, Article 27 – equal opportunities and equal treatment of workers with family responsibilities). States present a report on the provisions relating to one of the above-mentioned thematic groups on an annual basis. Consequently, each provision of the Charter is reported once every four years.

In April 2014, the Committee of Ministers adopted new changes to the Charter's monitoring system. The most important goal of the changes was to simplify the reporting system for States Parties that accepted the Collective Complaints procedure (see the relevant list). Following these modifications, **states that accepted the Collective Complaints procedure must submit a simplified report every two years.** In order to prevent excessive fluctuations in the workload of the European Committee of Social Rights from year to year, the **states that have so far adopted the collective complaints procedure were divided into two groups.** The groups were formed according to the number of complaints registered against the states (from the highest to the lowest), as follows:

- **Group A** is made up of eight states: France, Greece, Portugal, Italy, Belgium, Bulgaria, Ireland and Finland.
- **Group B** is made up of eight states: the Netherlands, Sweden, Croatia, Norway, Slovenia, Cyprus, the Czech Republic and Spain.

318. The delivery dates for the reports are: 31 October 2012 (Group 2), 2013 (Group 3), 2013 (Group 3), and 2014 (Group 1). Conclusions of the Committee are due as follows: December 2013 (Group 2), December 2014 (Group 3), December 2015 (Group 1), and December 2016 (Group 1). A new system for the presentation of reports concerning the application of the European Social Charter was adopted by the Committee of Ministers during their 1196th meeting (2–3 April 2014).[1956] The new reporting system of the ESC for Member States that have accepted the collective complaints procedure is based on the following principles: (1) a significant simplification for Member States which have accepted the collective complaints procedure and hence are subject to more comprehension examination of their national situation by the European Committee of Social Rights (ECSR) and therefore have a greater workload than other state parties; (2) a relatively simple and predictable system, so that there is no discussion or ambiguity about the exact nature of the state parties' reporting obligations; (3) a system that is manageable over time, particularly for state parties that accept the collective complaints procedure in the

1955. Governmental Committee XIII-3, p. 10.
1956. CM(2014)26. European Social Charter. Collected Text[s] (seventh edition), updated 1 Jan. 2015, Council of Europe, Strasbourg 2015, pp. 214–215.

future. For this purpose, the states which have accepted the collective complaints procedure will submit a simplified report every two years. To prevent this simplification from causing excessive fluctuations in the workload of the ECSR and the Governmental Committee (GC), from this year, the sixteen states which have accepted the collective complaints procedure are divided into two groups, A and B. The groups will be composed by distributing the States according to the number of complaints registered against them (from the highest to the lowest), as follows:

- Group A is made up of eight States: France, Greece, Portugal, Italy, Belgium, Bulgaria, Ireland, and Finland;
- Group B is made up of seven States: the Netherlands, Sweden, Croatia, Norway, Slovenia, Cyprus, and the Czech Republic.

The system would function as follows:

Reference Period	*Thematic Groups/ Articles*	*Deadline to Submit Reports*	*Regular Report*	*Simplified Report*	*Adoption of Conclusions*
1 January 2015–31 December 2018	Group 1 Employment, training and equal opportunities Articles 1, 9, 10, 15, 18, 20*, 24 and 25	31 December 2019	All states except Group A	States from Group A	January 2021
1 January 2016–31 December 2019	Group 2 Health, social security and social protection Articles 3, 11, 12, 13, 14, 23* and 30	31 December 2020	All states except Group A	States from Group A	January 2022
1 January 2017–31 December 2020	Group 3 Labour rights Articles 2, 4, 5, 6, 21*, 22*, 26, 28 and 29	31 December 2021	All states except Group B	States from Group B	January 2023
1 January 2018–31 December 2021	Group 4 Children, family and migrants Articles 7, 8, 16, 17, 19, 27 and 31	31 December 2022	All states except Group A	States from Group A	January 2024

Reference Period	*Thematic Groups/ Articles*	*Deadline to Submit Reports*	*Regular Report*	*Simplified Report*	*Adoption of Conclusions*
1 January 2019–31 December 2022	Group 1 Employment, training and equal opportunities Articles 1, 9, 10, 15, 18, 20*, 24 and 25	31 December 2023	All states except Group B	States from Group B	January 2025
1 January 2020–31 December 2023	Group 2 Health, social security and social protection Articles 3, 11, 12, 13, 14, 23* and 30	31 December 2024	All states except group B	States from Group B	January 2026

* NB: Articles 20–23 of the Revised Charter correspond to Articles 1–4 of the 1998 Additional Protocol.

States which draw up a simplified report would be required to state what follow-up action has been taken in response to the decisions of the ECSR on the collective complaints and reply to any questions put in the event of deferrals of the relevant provision. As new states accept the collective complaints procedure, they will be assigned on an alternating basis to Group B, then Group A again, and so on. The new system enters into force for all states which have already accepted the procedure from October 2014 onwards and for other states one year after acceptance.

319. The Committee of Ministers regulates the form of the reports. The reports are presented in one of the two official languages of the Council of Europe, English or in French. The reports are usually exhaustive studies with the attached provisions written in the language of the state delivering the report. The authorities of the Member States can present copies or summaries of the reports to the International Labour Organisation. As the Committee also supervises the practice of abiding by the provisions of the Charter, it demands from the authorities of the Member States the quotation of the original statistical data. The above obligation is especially required while checking on the enforcement of Article 2 §1, 2, 3, 4, 5, Article 7 §1, 2, 3, 4, Article 10 of the Charter and the standards ordering the fulfilment of the obligation to the great majority of the workers concerned. During the first three supervisory cycles, the Committee rigorously demanded this obligation be met. In the fourth supervisory cycle, the Committee reduced the requirements and declared the authorities of the Member States, in order to reduce the costs, could deliver their own statistical data from a different source.[1957] The lack of delivery of the above data justifies the delay in making a ruling on the compliance or non-compliance of the national regulations and practices with international standards. The Committee has elaborated the practice of warning a Member State when it does not deliver the required information for the second time. When this occurs, the Committee informs about the postponed ruling stating compliance or non-compliance of the national regulations and practices with the international standards gives a notification that not fulfilling this obligation for the third time will eventuate in the negative ruling declaring non-compliance of the particular provisions of the Charter by a given Member State.[1958] The Amending Protocol to the European Social Charter passed on 21 October 1991 revises Article 24 ESC and authorises the Committee to communicate directly with the Member States and make requests for the delivery of additional information and clarifications. It also allows for the organisation of direct meetings with the representatives of the authorities of the Member States when it is necessary. Organisers of such meetings can be both the Committee and the authorities of the interested states (Article 24 §3 ESC in relation to Article C RESC)

320. The rulings of the Committee are not of a binding character. They are opinions which have been well-prepared by a group of international experts on labour and social security law as well as social policies, which allows the Committee of Ministers to take a position about a Member State not abiding by the human rights protected under the Charter.

1957. Conclusions IV, p. xvi.
1958. Conclusions V, p. xvi.

II. Reports Concerning Provisions of the Charter That Have Not Been Ratified

321. The Committee of Ministers have a right to request the authorities of the Member States to deliver the reports concerning the relationship between the national regulations and the practice of their application and the provisions of the Charter that have not been ratified. Until 1978, the Committee of Ministers never utilised this right. In 1978 it obligated the authorities of the Member States to deliver the reports concerning Article 4 §3, Article 7 §1, Article 8 §1 and 2 of the Charter. In 1981 it demanded from the Member States the delivery of the reports concerning Article 2 §4, Article 7 §4, Article 8 §4 and Article 19 of the Charter. In 1993 the report concerned Article 7 §9 and Article 19 §4 of the Charter. In 1995, Article 4 §4 and, in 1997, Article 5 of the Charter. The decision passed by the Committee of Ministers during the 821st session on 11 December 2002 obliged the authorities of the Member States to deliver the reports concerning the national legal regulations and the practice of the application of these provisions in relation to the not ratified provisions of the Revised European Social Charter every five years.[1959] The Committee of Ministers authorised the Committee to analyse the reports delivered on the basis of Article 22 of the Charter.

On the basis of Article 22 of the Charter, the Committee analysed the reports and attended meetings with the authorities of the following Member States: Sweden[1960] (2003), Romania,[1961] Slovenia[1962] and Italy[1963] (2004) and Estonia[1964] (2005). In 2005 within the confines of the procedure regulated under Article 22 of the Charter, the Committee was carried on in: Bulgaria,[1965] Ireland[1966] and Cyprus.[1967] The procedure on non-accepted provisions was carried out with respect to: Albania[1968] and Lithuania[1969] (2006), Finland[1970] and Sweden[1971] (2008), Azerbaijan,[1972] Belgium,[1973] Romania[1974] (2009), Estonia,[1975] Malta[1976] (2010), Moldova,[1977]

1959. Implementation of Art. 22 for states having ratified the Revised European Social Charter as from 2003 (in:) European Social Charter, *supra,* pp. 501–502.
1960. Sweden did not ratify 15 provisions of RESC.
1961. Romania did not ratify 33 provisions of RESC.
1962. Slovenia did not ratify provisions of RESC.
1963. Italy did not ratify provisions of RESC.
1964. Estonia did not ratify 19 provisions of RESC.
1965. Bulgaria did not ratify 37 provisions of RESC.
1966. Ireland did not ratify 6 provisions of RESC.
1967. Cyprus did not ratify 34 provisions of RESC.
1968. Albania did not ratify 34 provisions of RESC.
1969. Lithuania did not ratify 12 provisions of RESC.
1970. Finland did not ratify 10 provisions of RESC.
1971. Sweden did not ratify 15 provisions of RESC.
1972. Azerbaijan did not ratify 51 provisions of RESC.
1973. Belgium did not ratify 11 provisions of RESC.
1974. Romania did not ratify 33 provisions of RESC.
1975. Estonia did not ratify 19 provisions of RESC.
1976. Malta did not ratify 26 provisions of RESC.
1977. Moldova did not ratify 35 provisions of RESC.

Netherlands[1978] (2011), Albania, Andorra,[1979] Bulgaria, Cyprus, Finland, Georgia,[1980] Ireland (2012), Bosnia and Herzegovina,[1981] Norway and Turkey[1982] (2013). In addition, the following countries were concerned in 2015: Andorra, Armenia, Azerbaijan, Belgium, France, Italy, Romania, the Russian Federation,[1983] Serbia,[1984] the Slovak Republic,[1985] Slovenia and Sweden.[1986]

322. The procedure determined in Article 22 of the Charter allows the authorities of this state to acknowledge the judicial decisions of the Committee concerning issues of the provisions of the Revised European Social Charter, which have not been ratified. The members of the Committee act as technical advisors. They examine the national regulations of labour and social security law, as well as the practices of their application, and are able to evaluate what the chances are for the Committee to make a ruling stating the conformity of the analysed provisions with the international standards. The opinions expressed by them are not binding to the Committee.

The copies of the report presented to the Committee by the Member States on the basis of Article 21 and Article 22 of the Charter should be forwarded to the national organisations of workers and employers – the participants of the international organisations of stakeholders – who are invited, according to Article 27 §2 ESC, to partake in the sittings of the Subcommittee of the Governmental Social Committee. The copies of the national reports are also sent to the international non-governmental organisation, relevant in terms of issues regulated by the Charter, being the advisory bodies to the Council of Europe (Article 23 §1 of the Charter). The above bodies have the right to present their remarks with regard to the reports to the Secretary General of the Council of Europe. The authorities of the Member States can inform the Secretary General about their comments on the said remarks. Supervisory rights granted to the stakeholders under Article 23 of the Charter create the fundamental element of the supervisory mechanism employed by the Committee to control the enforcement of the provisions of the Charter by the Member States. The reports, remarks and comments are available once they are published.

§2. THE GOVERNMENTAL COMMITTEE

323. The Governmental Committee consists of the representatives of the authorities of the Member States. Each state has one representative on the Committee. They are civil servants of the relevant ministries dealing with issues of labour

1978. Netherlands did not ratify 1 provision of RESC.
1979. Andorra did not ratify 23 provisions of RESC.
1980. Georgia did not ratify 35 provisions of RESC.
1981. Bosnia and Herzegovina did not ratify 47 provisions of RESC.
1982. Turkey did not ratify 7 provisions of RESC.
1983. Russian Federation did not ratify 31 provisions of RESC.
1984. Serbia did not ratify 10 provisions of RESC.
1985. Slovak Republic did not ratify 12 provisions of RESC.
1986. Information furnished on 25 Sep. 2012 by the Deputy Executive Secretary of the Committee Mr Henrik Kristensen.

and social policies. The authorities of the Member States that did not ratify the Charter, having only signed this document, have a right to delegate an observer to the sittings of the Governmental Committee. The status of the observer is also enjoyed by no more than two international organisations of employers and two international organisations of workers (trade unions) invited to participate in the sittings of the Governmental Committee. The international non-governmental organisations, being the consultative bodies to the Council of Europe which are relevant in terms of issues regulated by the Charter, can present their opinions concerning the matters being on the agenda of a particular session of the Committee upon request.

324. The Governmental Committee is the political consultative body of the Committee of Ministers. Article 27 §3 of the Charter, revised by the Amending Protocol to the European Social Charter passed on 21 October 1991, states that the Governmental Committee is obligated to prepare the decisions of the Committee of Ministers. Within the confines of the above competence, the Governmental Committee is obligated to perform the selection of cases which should be referred to in the recommendations issued by the Committee of Ministers addressed to the Member States who are not abiding by the provisions of the Charter. Presenting the cases of non-compliance with the provisions of the Charter by the Member States, the Governmental Committee chooses 'in a well-grounded way the basis of the examination concerning social and economic policies' situations which, in its opinion, should be commented upon within the recommendations addressed to the interested party according to Article 28 of the Charter (Article 27 §3 of the Charter) In choosing the above cases, the Governmental Committee should be guided by the evaluation and rulings made by the Committee. For a long period of time, there were contrasting differences between the Governmental Committee and the Committee of Social Rights (previously the Committee of Independent Experts). As early as during the first supervisory cycle, it declared a lack of enforcement of a significant number of provisions in the case of the majority of the Member States that had either delivered reports or where it had postponed decisions due to missing information.

It caused the Governmental Committee to react. From the first supervisory cycle, the Governmental Committee accused the Committee of Independent Experts of too rigorous interpretations of the provisions of the Charter and produced its independent interpretation. The rivalry between the said Committees was caused by the unclear division of their competences. From the first to the eleventh supervisory cycle, the report of the Member States were evaluated differently by the said Committees, as the Governmental Committee claimed it had a right to make content-related evaluations of the reports previously evaluated by the Committee of Independent Experts. Like the Committee of Independent Experts, the Governmental Committee took into consideration political issues. According to the original version of Article 27 §1 ESC, conclusions of the Committee of Independent Experts were forwarded for examination to the Subcommittee of the Governmental Social Committee of the Council of Europe. The Subcommittee delivered the report, including its remarks, to the Committee of Ministers. To its own report, the report of the Committee of Independent Experts was attached (Article 27 §3 ESC). Until the day when the Amending Protocol to the European Social Charter of 21 October 1991 came into force, the Consultative Assembly of the Council of Europe, renamed in 1973 to the Parliamentary Assembly, also partook in the supervisory process over the enforcement of the provisions of the Charter. It was entitled to pass the remarks regarding the report of the Committee of Independent Experts onto the Committee of Ministers. The supervisory process over the enforcement of international standards in terms of the protection of labour rights by the Member States was complicated. The content-related evaluation made by the Committee of Independent Experts was given lesser importance because of the remarks made by the political bodies.

325. The Amending Protocol to the European Social Charter of 21 October 1991 revised the content of Articles 27 and 28 of the Charter. It excluded the Parliamentary Assembly from participation in the supervisory process over the enforcement of provisions of the Charter by the Member States. It specified the competence of the Governmental Committee. It changed the Committee into a body solely entitled to make decisions regarding cases violating the provisions of the Charter by the Member States, declared by the Committee of Independent Experts, later renamed for the Committee and presented to the Committee of Ministers. By the Amending Protocol to the European Social Charter of 21 October 1991, the mechanism of supervision over the enforcement of the provisions of the Charter by Member States was regulated. The Governmental Committee examines the negative rulings made by the Committee and, on the basis of economic and social reasons, decides which of these cases should be presented to the Committee of Ministers. In making a decision on these matters, the Governmental Committee only takes into account political reasons. The high level of unemployment, which according to the Committee, is evidence of violating Article 1 §1 of the Charter, can be justified by the Governmental Committee through measures aimed at economic reform. The Governmental Committee pays attention to whether the provisions belonging to the first or the second group of the provisions of the Charter have been breached, what the position of the stakeholders was, from what supervisory cycle the Committee of Social Rights makes such rulings on the non-compliance of a particular provision of the Charter. First, it is interested in the reaction of the authorities of a Member State following a negative ruling by the Committee. The Governmental Committee has elaborated the practice of warning the Member State authorities that in cases of not adjusting the national regulations and the practices of their application to the international standards determined by the Charter, the next supervisory cycle will bring the matter before the Committee of Ministers with the request to pass the motion. The decision about the issuing of a warning is passed by a two-thirds qualified majority of votes of the Governmental Committee.[1987] The practice of warning the authorities of the Member States was taken as a fact and accepted by the European Tribunal of Human Rights.[1988]

1987. Governmental Conclusions XII-1, p. 14.
1988. *Sigurjonsson v. Iceland*, 264 ECtHR (ser. A) (1993).

326. The reports of the authorities of the Member States on the relation between the national regulation, the practice of their application and the provisions of the Charter not ratified by a particular Member State are also presented to the Governmental Committee (Article 27 §1 of the Charter). The Governmental Committee presents its report to the Committee of Ministers. On the basis of this report, the Committee of Ministers is entitled to pass a resolution. The reports of the Governmental Committee are available to the public (Article 27 §3 in a version revised by the Amending Protocol to the European Social Charter). The reports of the Governmental Committee concerning the introductions of the provisions of the Charter in the Member States can provide the grounds to elaborate proposals suggesting undertaking research on social issues and the provisions of the Charter. The addressee of these proposals is the Committee of Ministers. The Governmental Committee operates as the consultative body to the Committee of Ministers in matters concerning the range and protection of labour rights.

327. In 2018, the Governmental Committee examined follow-up measures taken by the Governments with respect to conclusions of non-conformity issued by the European Committee of Social Rights on articles of the European Social Charter relating to 'Health, social security and social protection' (Conclusions 2017). In its examination, the Governmental Committee applied the procedures adopted by the Committee of Ministers at its 1196th meeting on 2 April 2014 and focused on certain conclusions of non-conformity as selected by the European Committee of Social Rights.

The Governmental Committee voted, among others, several warnings as follows: Article 3 §2 (to issue safety and health regulations) in respect of Hungary; Article 3 §3 (to provide for the enforcement of safety and health regulation by measures of supervision) in respect of Republic of Moldova.[1989]

In 2019, the Governmental Committee examined follow-up measures taken by the Governments with respect to conclusions of non-conformity issued by the European Committee of Social Rights on articles of the European Social Charter relating to 'Labour rights' (Articles 2, 4, 5, 6, 21, 22, 26, 28 and 29) covering the reference period 1 January 2013–31 December 2016, related to ECSR Conclusions XXI-3(2018) of the 1961 Charter and Conclusions 2018 of the Revised European Social Charter.

The Governmental Committee examined 119 situations not in conformity with the Charter as selected by the ECSR: 34 concerned countries bound by the 1961 Social Charter and 85 countries bound by the Revised European Social Charter. The detailed reports of the Governmental Committee meetings contain more extensive information regarding the cases of non-conformity examined and may be consulted at www.coe.int/socialcharter.

The Governmental Committee adopted thirty-seven warnings: twenty-eight warnings in respect of the nine countries bound by the Revised European Social Charter: Azerbaijan (12), Armenia (4), Ukraine (4), Georgia (2), Republic of Moldova (2),

1989. Activity Report 2018, p. 48.

Estonia (1), Lithuania (1), Netherlands (1) and Romania (1) and nine warnings in respect of the three countries bound by the 1961 Charter: United Kingdom (7), Germany (1) and Poland (1).[1990]

The findings published by the European Committee of Social Rights on 24 March 2020 concern eight Member States: Belgium, Bulgaria, Finland, France, Greece, Ireland, Italy and Portugal. A total of 51 decisions of the ECSR were examined. In matters of employment law, social security and industrial relations, the Committee scrutinised decisions taken by five Member States: Finland, France, Greece, Ireland and Italy.

In respect of Finland, one decision was examined on the issue of upper limits on compensation in cases of illegal dismissal as well as lack of provisions for the possibility of reinstatement (Article 24 RESC).[1991] The Committee found that the situation has still not been brought fully into conformity.

In respect of France, three decisions out of sixteen: overtime compensation for members of the national police force (Article 4 §2 of the Charter),[1992] the right to organise and collective bargaining in the National Gendarmerie and the military[1993] (Articles 5 and 6 §2 of the Charter) and so-called designating clauses concerning supplementary pension schemes in collective agreements (Article 6 §2 of the Charter)[1994] were examined. In all these cases, the situation has not been brought into conformity with the Charter provisions invoked.

In respect of Greece, three decisions out of twelve were examined on issues such as the right to a healthy environment and health and safety at work[1995] I, austerity measures relating to the labour market (working time – Article 2 §1, remuneration – Article 4 §§1–3, vocational training – Article 10) and social security benefits (Article 13)[1996] have been examined. Only in Collective Complaints 66, the ECSR noted that the age discrimination identified in respect of remuneration had been removed.

In respect of Ireland, three decisions examined issues of the right to organise and collective bargaining, including the strike of members of the police force (Article 5 and Article 6 §§1–4)[1997] and the right to organise and collective bargaining in the military (Articles 5 and 6 §§1–4)[1998] were examined. In all these cases, the ECSR found that the situation has still not been brought fully into conformity with the Charter provisions invoked, although progress was noted in certain cases. In Collective Complaint 112, the situation as regards collective bargaining in military has been solved, while other weaknesses have not been resolved.

1990. Activity Report 2019, pp. 41–42.
1991. Collective Complaint 106.
1992. Collective Complaints 38, 57, 68.
1993. Collective Complaint 101.
1994. Collective Complaints 118.
1995. Collective Complaints 30 and 72.
1996. Collective Complaints 66, 111.
1997. Collective Complaint 83.
1998. Collective Complaint 112.

In respect of Italy, only one decision on work and social security issues, such as the right to coverage for persons performing the duties of Justice of the Peace,[1999] was now made compatible with the Charter.

§3. The Committee of Ministers

328. The Committee of Ministers adopts a resolution concerning the whole supervisory cycle by a two-thirds qualified majority of votes of the representatives of states which are parties to the Charter[2000] as well as the individual recommendations addressed to particular Member States. The basis for the resolution passed by the Committee of Ministers is the report of the Governmental Committee (Article 28 §1 a version revised by the Amending Protocol to the European Social Charter of 21 October 1991). The Charter does not specify any guidelines for the Governmental Committee in terms of adapting resolutions and recommendations. Article 28 §2 of the Charter states the Committee of Ministers 'shall take such decisions as it deems appropriate'. The alteration of the procedure eventuated in a situation when the Committee of Ministers from the twelfth supervisory cycle in 1993 started passing resolutions and individual recommendations on the basis of the rulings of the Committee of Independent Experts (the Committee) concerning nonconformity between the national legal regulations, the practice of their application and the international standards. The two first individual recommendations were general. They obligated the authorities of the Member States to inform about measures undertaken in relation to the negative ruling of the Committee of Independent Experts.[2001] The Committee of Ministers, in its third recommendation, obligated the Norwegian authorities to change the regulation regarded by the Committee of Independent Experts as contradicting Article 6 §4 and Article 7 §3 of the Charter.[2002] During the thirteenth supervisory cycle, the Committee of Ministers adopted twenty-two individual recommendations sent to the authorities of twelve Member States.[2003] During the fourteenth supervisory cycle, the Committee of Ministers adopted three individual recommendations.[2004] During the last two supervisory

1999. Collective Complaint 102.

2000. Decision on voting in the Committee of Ministers Adopted by the Committee of Ministers in April 1993 at the 492nd meeting of the Ministers' Deputies (in:) European Social Charter, *supra,* p. 225; Decision on the adoption of recommendations under the European Social Charter Adopted by the Committee of Ministers on 22 Jun. 1995 at the 541st meeting of the Ministers' Deputies, as above, p. 227; Rules of Procedure for the adoption of recommendations under the European Social Charter. Adopted by the Committee of Ministers on 17 Dec. 1998 at the 653rd meeting of the Ministers' Deputies, as above, p. 229.

2001. Recommendations: No. R ChS (93)1 adopted on 7 Sep. 1993 addressed to Greece (Art. 1 §2, Art. 13 §§1 and 4) Supervision of the Application of the European Social Charter (in:) European Social Charter, *supra*, pp. 427–428; No. R ChS (93) 3 (United Kingdom, Art. 6 §4, Art 8 §1).

2002. Recommendation No. R ChS (93) 3, as above, pp. 430–431.

2003. Austria (Art. 5), Denmark (Arts 5, 6 §§2 and 4); France (Art. 1 §2, Art. 17); Greece Art. 7 §§1, 3, Art. 18 §2, Art. 19 §§1 and 8; Ireland (Art. 1 §2, Art. 4 §4, Art. 6 §4, Art. 7 §3, Art. 19 §8); Italy (Art. 1 §2, Art. 3 §2, Art. 4 §§4 and 5, Art. 7 §§2, 4); Spain (Art. 1 §2); Malta (Arts 5, 6 §4); Germany (Art. 6 §4); Norway (Art. 7 §3); Portugal (Art. 7 §1); Sweden (Art. 19 §8); Turkey (Art. 11 §1, Art. 16), as above, pp. 439 et seq.

2004. Austria (Art. 5); Ireland (Arts 5, 6 §2); Turkey (Art. 4 §3), as above, pp. 469 et seq.

cycles (fifteenth and sixteenth), the Committee of Ministers adopted the individual recommendations sent to the authorities of Ireland,[2005] Malta,[2006] Germany,[2007] and Turkey.[2008]

329. In 2005 during the supervision over the enforcement of the provisions of the Revised European Social Charter, the Committee of Ministers passed a resolution addressed to the authorities of all Member States who ratified the above international treaty and prescribed taking into consideration observations made by The Committee published after the supervisory cycle had finished.[2009] In 2003 the Committee addressed one individual recommendation to the Italian authorities.[2010] The individual recommendations are not of a binding character. The Member States that have representatives within the Committee of Ministers act as judges in their own matters. Taking part in the resolution process is based on political and substantial reasons. The level of the influence of the resolution of the Committee of Ministers on the said authorities of the Member States is decided by the international pressure of the opinions of these Member States that are adapting to the international standards of human rights protection regulated by the Charter.

2005. ResChS (2001) 2, Art. 6 §4, as above, pp. 477–478; ResChS (2002)1, Art. 7 §3, as above, pp. 480–481; ResChS (2004) 4, Arts 5, 6 §2, Art. 19 §8, as above, pp. 482–483.
2006. RecChS (2001)3, Art. 6 §2, as above, pp. 478–479.
2007. Addendum to Resolution ResChS (2001)5, Art. 19 §6, as above, pp. 479–490.
2008. ResChS (2002) 1, Art. 11 §1, as above, pp. 481–482.
2009. ResChS (2002) 7, as above, p. 485.
2010. ResChS (2004) 3, as above, pp. 486–487.

Chapter 2. Adjudicating Collective Complaints

§1. Introduction

330. The Additional Protocol of 1995 to the European Social Charter introducing the collective complaint procedure gave the Committee the status of a *quasi*-judicial body.[2011] The Committee was vested with the power to examine collective complaints lodged by selected international and national organisations against the authorities of the Member States violating the provisions of the European Social Charter or the Revised European Social Charter, which do not adapt their domestic labour and social insurance legislation to the European standards. The Additional Protocol of 1995 was made available for signing on 9 November 1995.

It came into force on 1 July 1998 upon ratification by eight European states.[2012] The signatories of the Protocol could only be the states which ratified the European Social Charter of 1961. Five states, the signatories of the European Social Charter of 1961, signed the Additional Protocol of 1995, undertaking to comply with its provisions.[2013] Two other states, the signatories of the Revised European Social Charter of 1996, declared that they would abide by the provisions of the Protocol.[2014] Therefore, the examination procedure for collective complaints followed by the Committee applies to fifteen out of forty-seven Member States of the Council of Europe. The Department of Social Rights of the Council of Europe was pleased to celebrate and mark the 25th anniversary of the entry into force of the Additional Protocol to the European Social Charter Providing for a System of Collective Complaints (ETS No. 158) in 1998. The event 'The Collective Complaints Procedure: 25 Years in Pursuit of Human Rights and Social Justice' took place on 6 July 2023 at the Council of Europe in Strasbourg.

The Committee examines collective complaints lodged against the authorities of Member States of the Council of Europe concerning the violation of economic and labour rights, including the freedom to organise in trade unions and in employers' organisations (Article 5) guaranteed under the Social Charters. In total, in 1998-2018, 173 collective complaints were lodged with the European Committee of Social Rights. A total of fifteen new complaints were lodged in 2019. The European Committee of Social Rights did not distinguish collective complaints on employment rights from other complaints relating to rights in the field of social security and social policy. Information presented in Activity Reports when collective complaints procedures and decisions on the merits were discussed in the last edition of this monograph is included in cases falling within thematic groups in the field of individual and collective labour law.

2011. A. Świątkowski, 'Funciones causi jurisdiccionales', *supra*, pp. 533 et seq.; R. Brillat, *The Supervisory Machinery of the European Social Charter: Recent Developments and Their Impact*, in *Labour Rights in Europe*, 31 ff. (G. de Búrca, B. de Witte & L. Ogertschnig eds, 2005).
2012. Cyprus, Finland, France, Greece, Norway, Portugal, Sweden and Italy.
2013. Austria, Belgium, Croatia, Denmark, Slovakia.
2014. Bulgaria and Slovenia.

§2. Entities Entitled to Initiate Collective Complaint Proceedings

331. Under the Additional Protocol of 1995, the following types of organisations are entitled to lodge collective complaints:

- International employers' organisations and trade unions invited by the Subcommittee of the Governmental Committee[2015] (Article 27 §2 the RESC). The cited provision provides for the invitation of no more than two international organisations of employers and no more than two international trade union organisations to be represented as observers in a consultative capacity at meetings of the Governmental Committee. Although the European Social Charter protects mainly the rights of employees,[2016] one international trade union organisation (The European Trade Union Confederation – ETUC) and two international employers' associations (the Union of the Confederation of Industry and Employers of Europe – UNICE and the International Organisation of Employers – IOE) have been invited to participate in the procedures of the Governmental Committee. These organisations are entitled to initiate proceedings in collective complaints (Article 1 (a) Additional Protocol of 1995).
- Other international non-governmental organisations (INGOs) having a consultative status with the Council of Europe and are placed on a list established for this purpose by the Governmental Committee (Article 1 (b) of the Protocol).[2017] To be included in the list, an organisation has to fulfil certain conditions stipulated in the decisions of the Committee of Ministers of the Council of Europe of 22 June 1995.[2018] All the INGOs having consultative status with the Council of Europe, competent in matters governed by the European Social Charter, which have access to sources of information and are able to draw up and professionally (from a legal point of view) present their position in matters examined by The Committee of the Council of Europe, are entitled to apply for the right to lodge collective complaints.[2019] The Secretary General of the Council of Europe examines the applications for inclusion in the list of INGOs entitled to lodge collective

2015. The former name of the Committee was the Governmental Social Committee.

2016. Article 6 §4 of the European Social Charter guarantees the employers the right to undertake collective action hence, it gives them the right to organise defensive lockouts. *See*: European Social Charter, Committee of Independent Experts, Conclusions I, 1969–70, Council of Europe Press, Strasbourg 1995, pp. 38,40; Conclusions III, p. 38; Conclusions V, p. 48; Conclusions VI, pp. 39–40; Conclusions VIII, p. 95; Conclusions IX-2, pp. 47–49; Conclusions XV-1, vol. 1 (Belgium), p. 81 (Cyprus), p. 123; Addendum to Conclusions XV-1 (Germany), p. 27. *See* the right to organise and to bargain collectively. Study drawn up based on case law of the European Social Charter, Council of Europe Publishing, 2nd ed., 2001, pp. 79–81; L. Samuel, *Fundamental Labour Rights: Case Law of the European Social Charter*, pp. 167 et seq. (Council of Europe Publishing, 2d ed., 2002).

2017. Register of forty-six organisations placed on the list in Przewodnik po Europejskiej Karcie Społecznej, Wydawnictwo Prawnicze (Guide to the European Social Charter) LexisNexis, Warsaw 2001, pp. 59 et seq.

2018. Explanatory report to the 1995 Protocol (in:) European Social Charter. *Collected Texts*, 149 et seq. (Council of Europe Publishing, 4th ed., 2003); *Podstawowe dokumenty Rady Europy* … (*Primary documents of the Council of Europe* …), *supra*, p. 49.

2019. Several hundreds of international non-governmental organisations have the right to express their opinions in the Council of Europe.

complaints in The Committee. An application is considered accepted by the Governmental Committee unless it is rejected in a ballot by a simple majority of cast votes.[2020] An INGO can be placed on the list for a period of four years. After the elapse of this period, an organisation has the right to apply for renewal. The above-described procedure is applicable in cases of renewing applications.

- National employers' representative organisations and trade unions have the right to act within the jurisdiction of a Member State of the Council of Europe, against a state, which they will be entitled to lodge a collective complaint (Article 1 (c) of the Protocol). Only employers' and employees' organisations are entitled to apply to be placed on the list. Therefore, those employers who are not members of any employers' organisation or association do not have the right to lodge any collective complaints. Trade unions enjoy the status of organisations, and hence, trade unions and associations of trade unions are entitled to apply for entry. Article 1 (c) of the Additional Protocol of 1995 also entitles for application for entry to the list of national organisations. The decision to admit an organisation to apply for entry is not conditional upon membership of a national employers' organisation or a trade union in an international organisation of similar character. Only 'represented' employers' organisations, and trade unions are eligible for inclusion on the list. None of the cited international documents specify any criteria for establishing whether an organisation is or is not represented. Neither do they specify a body which would be entitled to make such decisions. The Committee of Ministers of the Council of Europe would rather leave this issue to the authorities of its Member States. Thus, an employers' organisation or a trade union, which, under domestic legislation, enjoys the status of a representative organisation, retains this status for the purpose of the Social Charter of the Council of Europe. Yet, in the absence of any criteria for assessing whether an organisation is or is not a representative on a national level, the power to make decisions concerning the status of a national organisation applying for entry to the list of organisations entitled to lodge collective complaints is vested in the Committee. Factors such as the number of members and the organisation's actual role in national negotiations with stakeholders should be taken into account.[2021]
- Representative national non-governmental organisations (NGOs) are entitled to carry out their statutory activities within the jurisdiction of the Member State of the Council of Europe, against which their complaint is made (Article 2 §1 of the Protocol) if the state in question has previously issued a declaration in this respect. The Committee has been authorised to verify whether the NGOs other

2020. Three organisations, which applied for the right to lodge collective complaints, have not been included in the list by the Governmental Committee.

2021. Explanatory report, *supra*, p. 153. R. Birk, *The Collective Complaint: A New Procedure in the European Social Charter*, in *Labour Law and Industrial Relations at the Turn of the Century. Liber Amicorum in Honour of Roger Blanpain*, 265–266 (C. Engels & M. Weiss eds, Kluwer Law International, 1998) points out that the Additional Protocol has the status of an international treaty which should apply identical criteria while assessing employers' organisations and trade unions. The report also postulates that the Committee should be vested with the power to assess all employers' organisations and trade unions – also those, which, pursuant to their domestic legislation, already enjoy the status of representative organisations. *See also*: D. Harris & J. Darcy, *The European Social Charter*, 358 (Transnational Publishers, Inc., 2nd ed., 2001).

than the organisations of employers and trade unions, referred to in Article 1 (c) of the Additional Protocol of 1995, entitled by the authorities of the Member States to lodge collective complaints, have the status of a representative organisation, as construed under Article 2 §1 of the Protocol. The authorities of the Member States have the right to authorise representative NGOs to initiate proceedings in accordance with the procedures laid down in the Additional Protocol of 1995. The authorisation is valid for the period stated in the relevant authorising document or for an unlimited period. An authorisation to lodge collective complaints can be revoked by way of denouncement of the Protocol.[2022] Finland is the only country among the states, which ratified or signed the Additional Protocol, to authorise its representative NGOs to lodge collective complaints. None of the Finnish NGOs has ever exercised this power.

332. The Additional Protocol of 1995 makes a clear distinction between the organisations entitled to lodge collective complaints against their own state. Organisations of employers and trade unions falling within one of the four categories of organisations entitled to lodge collective complaints have the right to make use of the powers vested in them with respect to every matter governed by the provisions of the European Social Charter. Other organisations falling within any of the categories mentioned in the Additional Protocol are entitled to lodge collective complaints solely on those matters which have been recognised by The Committee as those having particular competence (Article 3 of the Additional Protocol).

§3. Examining the Admissibility of the Collective Complaint

333. The Committee plays a quasi-judicial role during the examination of the status of an organisation lodging a collective complaint (a representative or non-representative), active or not, in the areas regulated by the European Social Charter. Another important element of the quasi-judicial proceedings carried out with respect to collective complaints is the initial examination of a complaint and deciding upon its admissibility. Out of a total of 197 collective complaints received by the Commission between 1998 and 2020, 7 were examined (processed).

Processed complaints

No. 194/2020 *Sindacato Autonomo Europeo Scuola ed Ecologia (SAESE) v. Italy.*
No. 186/2019 *Sindacato Autonomo Europeo Scuola ed Ecologia (SAESE) v. Italy.*
No. 184/2019 *Syndicato CGT FORD Blanquefort v. France.*
No. 183/2019 *Syndicato CGT YTO France v. France.*
No. 177/2019 *Associazione Medici Liberi v. Italy.*
No. 174/2019 *Syndicat oCGT YTO France v. France.*
No. 166/2018 *Sindacato Autonomo Europeo Scuola ed Ecologia (SAESE) v. Italy.*

2022. The notice period for denouncement is twelve months.

No. 164/2018 *European Organisation of Military Associations (EUROMIL) v. Ireland.*
No. 163/2018 *ATTAC ry, Globaali sosiaalityö ry and Maan ystävät ry v. Finland.*
No. 162/2018 *International Federation of Associations of the Elderly (FIAPA) v. France.*
No. 158/2017 *Confederazione Generale Italiana del Lavoro (CGIL) v. Italy.*
No. 157/2017 *European Roma Rights Centre (ERRC) and Mental Disability Advocacy Centre (MDAC) v. Czech Republic.*
No. 156/2017 *Panhellenic Association of Pensioners of the OTE Group Telecommunications v. Greece.*
No. 154/2017 *Confédération générale du travail (CGT) v. France.*
No. 151/2017 *European Roma Rights Centre (ERRC) v. Bulgaria.*
No. 148/2017 *International Commission of Jurists (ICJ) v. Czech Republic.*
No. 146/2017 *Associazione Professionale e Sindacale (ANIEF) v. Italy.*
No. 145/2017 *International Federation of Associations of the Elderly (FIAPA) v. France.*
No. 144/2017 *Confederazione Generale Sindacale (CGS) v. Italy.*
No. 143/2017 *UGL-CFS and SAPAF v. Italy.*
No. 142/2017 *Fédération FIECI and Syndicat SNEPI CFE-CGC v. France.*
No. 141/2017 *International Federation for Human Rights (FIDH) and Inclusion Europe v. Belgium.*
No. 140/2016 *Confederazione Generale Italiana del Lavoro (CGIL) v. Italy.*
No. 139/2016 *Central Union for Child Welfare (CUCW) v. Finland.*
No. 138/2016 *University Women of Europe (UWE) v. Sweden.*
No. 137/2016 *University Women of Europe (UWE) v. Slovenia.*
No. 136/2016 *University Women of Europe (UWE) v. Portugal.*
No. 135/2016 *University Women of Europe (UWE) v. Norway.*
No. 134/2016 *University Women of Europe (UWE) v. the Netherlands.*
No. 133/2016 *University Women of Europe (UWE) v. Italy.*
No. 132/2016 *University Women of Europe (UWE) v. Ireland.*
No. 131/2016 *University Women of Europe (UWE) v. Greece.*
No. 130/2016 *University Women of Europe (UWE) v. France.*
No. 129/2016 *University Women of Europe (UWE) v. Finland.*
No. 128/2016 *University Women of Europe (UWE) v. Czech Republic.*
No. 127/2016 *University Women of Europe (UWE) v. Cyprus.*
No. 126/2016 *University Women of Europe (UWE) v. Croatia.*
No. 125/2016 *University Women of Europe (UWE) v. Bulgaria.*
No. 124/2016 *University Women of Europe (UWE) v. Belgium.*
No. 123/2016 *Irish Congress of Trade Unions v. Ireland.*
No. 122/2016 *Movimento per la libertà della psicanalisi – Associazione culturale v. Italy.*
No. 121/2016 *Equal Rights Trust (ERT) v. Bulgaria.*
No. 120/2016 *Fellesforbundet for Sjøfolk (FFFS) v. Norway.*
No. 119/2015 *European Roma and Travellers Forum (ERTF) v. France.*
No. 118/2015 *Confédération Générale du Travail Force Ouvrière (CGT-FO) v. France.*

No. 117/2015 *Transgender-Europe and ILGA-Europe v. Czech Republic.*
No. 116/2015 *Matica hrvatskih sindikata v. Croatia.*
No. 115/2015 *European Federation of Employees in Public Services (EUROFEDOP) v. Greece.*
No. 114/2015 *European Committee for Home-Based Priority Action for the Child and the Family (EUROCEF) v. France.*
No. 113/2014 *Unione Italiana del Lavoro U.I.L. Scuola – Sicilia v. Italy.*
No. 112/2014 *European Organisation of Military Associations (EUROMIL) v. Ireland.*
No. 111/2014 *Greek General Confederation of Labour (GSEE) v. Greece.*
No. 110/2014 *International Federation for Human Rights (FIDH) v. Ireland.*
No. 109/2014 *Mental Disability Advocacy Center (MDAC) v. Belgium.*
No. 108/2014 *Finnish Society of Social Rights v. Finland.*
No. 107/2014 *Finnish Society of Social Rights v. Finland.*
No. 106/2014 *Finnish Society of Social Rights v. Finland.*
No. 105/2014 *Associazione sindacale 'La Voce dei Giusti' v. Italy.*
No. 104/2014 *European Roma and Travellers Forum (ERTF) v. Czech Republic.*
No. 103/2013 *Bedriftsforbundet v. Norway.*
No. 102/2013 *Associazione Nazionale Giudici di Pace v. Italy.*
No. 101/2013 *European Council of Police Trade Unions (CESP) v. France.*
No. 100/2013 *European Roma Rights Centre (ERRC) v. Ireland.*
No. 99/2013 *Federation of Catholic Family Associations in Europe (FAFCE) v. Sweden.*
No. 98/2013 *Association for the Protection of All Children (APPROACH) Ltd v. Belgium.*
No. 97/2013 *Association for the Protection of All Children (APPROACH) Ltd v. Cyprus.*
No. 96/2013 *Association for the Protection of All Children (APPROACH) Ltd v. Czech Republic.*
No. 95/2013 *Association for the Protection of All Children (APPROACH) Ltd v. Slovenia.*
No. 94/2013 *Association for the Protection of All Children (APPROACH) Ltd v. Italy.*
No. 93/2013 *Association for the Protection of All Children (APPROACH) Ltd v. Ireland.*
No. 92/2013 *Association for the Protection of All Children (APPROACH) Ltd v. France.*
No. 91/2013 *Confederazione Generale Italiana del Lavoro (CGIL) v. Italy.*
No. 90/2013 *Conference of European Churches (CEC) v. The Netherlands.*
No. 89/2013 *Federation of Catholic Family Associations in Europe (FAFCE) v. Ireland.*
No. 88/2012 *Finnish Society of Social Rights v. Finland.*
No. 87/2012 *International Planned Parenthood Federation European Network (IPPF EN) v. Italy.*

No. 86/2012 *European Federation of National Organisations working with the Homeless (FEANTSA) v. The Netherlands.*
No. 85/2012 *Swedish Trade Union Confederation (LO) and Swedish Confederation of Professional Employees (TCO) v. Sweden.*
No. 84/2012 *Union syndicale des magistrats administratifs (USMA) v. France.*
No. 83/2012 *European Confederation of Police (EUROCOP) v. Ireland.*
No. 82/2012 *Comité européen d'action spécialisée pour l'Enfant et la Famille dans leur milieu de vie (EUROCEF) v. France.*
No. 81/2012 *Action européenne des handicapés (AEH) v. France.*
No. 80/2012 *Pensioner's Union of the Agricultural Bank of Greece (ATE) v. Greece.*
No. 79/2012 *Panhellenic Federation of pensioners of the public electricity corporation (POS-DEI) v. Greece.*
No. 78/2012 *Pensioners' Union of the Athens-Piraeus Electric Railways (I.S.A.P.) v. Greece.*
No. 77/2012 *Panhellenic Federation of Public Service Pensioners v. Greece.*
No. 76/2012 *Federation of employed pensioners of Greece (IKA –ETAM) v. Greece.*
No. 75/2011 *International Federation of Human Rights (FIDH) v. Belgium.*
No. 74/2011 *Fellesforbundet for Sjøfolk (FFFS) v. Norway.*
No. 73/2011 *Syndicat de Défense des Fonctionnaires v. France.*
No. 72/2011 *International Federation for Human Rights (FIDH) v. Greece.*
No. 71/2011 *The Central Association of Carers in Finland v. Finland.*
No. 70/2011 *The Central Association of Carers in Finland v. Finland.*
No. 69/2011 *Defence for Children International (DCI) v. Belgium.*
No. 68/2011 *European Council of Police Trade Unions (CESP) v. France.*
No. 67/2011 *Médecins du Monde – International v. France.*
No. 66/2011 *General Federation of employees of the national electric power corporation (GENOP-DEI) / Confederation of Greek Civil Servants' Trade Unions (ADEDY) v. Greece.*
No. 65/2011 *General Federation of employees of the national electric power corporation (GENOP-DEI) / Confederation of Greek Civil Servants' Trade Unions (ADEDY) v. Greece.*
No. 64/2011 *European Roma and Travellers Forum (ERTF) v. France.*
No. 63/2010 *Centre on Housing Rights and Evictions (COHRE) v. France.*
No. 62/2010 *International Federation of Human Rights (FIDH) v. Belgium.*
No. 61/2010 *European Roma Rights Centre (ERRC) v. Portugal.*
No. 60/2010 *European Council of Police Trade Unions (CESP) v. Portugal.*
No. 59/2009 *European Trade Union Confederation (ETUC)/ Centrale Générale des Syndicats Libéraux de Belgique (CGSLB)/ Confédération des Syndicats chrétiens de Belgique (CSC)/ Fédération Générale du Travail de Belgique (FGTB) v. Belgium.*
No. 58/2009 *Centre on Housing Rights and Evictions (COHRE) v. Italy.*
No. 57/2009 *European Council of Police Trade Unions (CESP) v. France.*

No. 56/2009 *Confédération Française de l'Encadrement (CFE-CGC) v. France.*
No. 55/2009 *Confédération Générale du Travail (CGT) v. France.*
No. 54/2008 *European Council of Police Trade Unions (CESP) v. France.*
No. 53/2008 *European Federation of National Organisations working with the Homeless (FEANTSA) v. Slovenia.*
No. 52/2008 *Centre on Housing Rights and Evictions (COHRE) v. Croatia.*
No. 51/2008 *European Roma Rights Centre (ERRC) v. France.*
No. 50/2008 *Confédération française démocratique du travail (CFDT) v. France.*
No. 49/2008 *International Centre for the Legal Protection of Human Rights (INTERIGHTS) v. Greece.*
No. 48/2008 *European Roma Rights Centre (ERRC) v. Bulgaria.*
No. 47/2008 *Defence for Children International v. The Netherlands.*
No. 46/2007 *European Roma Rights Centre (ERRC) v. Bulgaria.*
No. 45/2007 *International Centre for the Legal Protection of Human Rights (INTERIGHTS) v. Croatia.*
No. 44/2007 *International Helsinki Federation for Human Rights (IHF) v. Bulgaria.*
No. 43/2007 *Sindicato dos Magistrados do Ministério Público (SMMP) v. Portugal.*
No. 42/2007 *International Federation of Human Rights (FIDH) v. Ireland.*
No. 41/2007 *Mental Disability Advocacy Center (MDAC) v. Bulgaria.*
No. 40/2007 *European Council of Police Trade Unions (CESP) v. Portugal.*
No. 39/2006 *European Federation of National Organisations Working with the Homeless (FEANTSA) v. France.*
No. 38/2006 *European Council of Police Trade Unions (CESP) v. France.*
No. 37/2006 *European Council of Police Trade Unions (CESP) v. Portugal.*
No. 36/2006 *Frente Comum de Sindicatos da Administração Pública v. Portugal.*
No. 35/2006 *Federation of Finnish Enterprises v. Finland.*
No. 34/2006 *World Organisation Against Torture v. Portugal.*
No. 33/2006 *International Movement ATD Fourth World v. France.*
No. 32/2005 *European Trade Union Confederation (ETUC), Confederation of Independent Trade Unions in Bulgaria (CITUB), Confederation of Labour 'Podkrepa' (CL 'Podkrepa') v. Bulgaria.*
No. 31/2005 *European Roma Rights Center (ERRC) v. Bulgaria.*
No. 30/2005 *Marangopoulos Foundation for Human Rights (MFHR) v. Greece.*
No. 29/2005 *Syndicat des hauts fonctionnaires (SAIGI) v. France.*
No. 28/2004 *Syndicat national des dermato-vénérologues (SNDV) v. France.*
No. 27/2004 *European Roma Rights Center (ERRC) v. Italy.*
No. 26/2004 *Syndicat des Agrégés de l'Enseignement Supérieur (SAGES) v. France.*
No. 25/2004 *Centrale générale des services publics v. Belgium.*
No. 24/2004 *Syndicat SUD Travail Affaires Sociales v. France.*

No. 23/2003 *Syndicat occitan de l'éducation v. France.*
No. 22/2003 *Confédération générale du travail (CGT) v. France.*
No. 21/2003 *World Organisation against Torture (OMCT) v. Belgium.*
No. 20/2003 *World Organisation against Torture (OMCT) v. Portugal.*
No. 19/2003 *World Organisation against Torture (OMCT) v. Italy.*
No. 18/2003 *World Organisation against Torture (OMCT) v. Ireland.*
No. 17/2003 *World Organisation against Torture (OMCT) v. Greece.*
No. 16/2003 *Confédération Française de l'Encadrement (CFE-CGC) v. France*
No. 15/2003 *European Roma Rights Centre (ERRC) v. Greece.*
No. 14/2003 *International Federation of Human Rights Leagues (FIDH) v. France.*
No. 13/2002 *International Association Autism-Europe (IAAE) v. France.*
No. 12/2002 *Confederation of Swedish Enterprise v. Sweden.*
No. 11/2001 *European Council of Police Trade Unions v. Portugal.*
No. 10/2000 *Tehy ry and STTK ry v. Finland.*
No. 09/2000 *Confédération Française de l'Encadrement (CFE-CGC) v. France.*
No. 08/2000 *Quaker Council for European Affairs (QCEA) v. Greece.*
No. 07/2000 *International Federation of Human Rights Leagues (FIDH) v. Greece.*
No. 06/1999 *Syndicat national des professions du tourisme v. France.*
No. 05/1999 *European Federation of Employees in Public Services (EURO-FEDOP) v. Portugal.*
No. 04/1999 *European Federation of Employees in Public Services (EURO-FEDOP) v. Italy.*
No. 03/1999 *European Federation of Employees in Public Services (EURO-FEDOP) v. Greece.*
No. 02/1999 *European Federation of Employees in Public Services (EURO-FEDOP) v. France.*
No. 01/1998 *International Commission of Jurists (ICJ) v. Portugal.*
No. 197/2020 *Validity v. Finland No. 196/2020 Greek Bar Associations v. Greece.*
No. 195/2020 European Roma Rights Centre (ERRC) v. Belgium.
No. 193/2020 *Union Syndicale Solidaires SDIS v. France.*
No. 192/2020 Confederazione Generale Sindacale CGS, Federazione GILDA-UNAMS and Sindacato Nazionale Insegnanti Di Religione Cattolica v. Italy.
No. 191/2020 European Federation of National Organisations working with the Homeless (FEANTSA) v. Czech Republic.
No. 190/2020 European Roma Rights Centre (ERRC) v. Czech Republic.
No. 189/2020 Confédération française démocratique du travail (CFDT) v. France.
No. 188/2019 Validity Foundation – Mental Disability Advocacy Centre v. Czech Republic.
No. 187/2019 Sindacato autonomo Pensionati Or.S.A. v. Italy.
No. 185/2019 European Roma Rights Centre (ERRC) v. Belgium.

No. 182/2019 Syndicat CFDT de la métallurgie de la Meuse v. France.
No. 181/2019 Syndicat CFDT général des transports et de l'environnement de l'Aube v. France.
No. 180/2019 Association of Secondary Teachers Ireland (ASTI) v. Ireland.
No. 179/2019 Associação Sindical dos Profissionais da Polícia (ASPP/PSP) v. Portugal.
No. 178/2019 Amnesty International v. Italy.
No. 176/2019 Union Syndicale Solidaires SDIS v. France.
No. 175/2019 Syndicat CFDT de la métallurgie de la Meuse v. France.
No. 173/2018 International Commission of Jurists (ICJ) and European Council for Refugees and Exiles (ECRE) v. Greece.
No. 172/2018 Finnish Society of Social Rights v. Finland.
No. 171/2018 Confédération générale du travail (CGT) v. France.
No. 170/2018 Unione sindacale di base (USB) v. Italy.
No. 169/2018 Nursing Up v. Italy.
No. 168/2018 European Disability Forum and Inclusion Europe v. France.
No. 167/2018 Sindacato autonomo Pensionati Or.S.A. v. Italy.
No. 165/2018 Panhellenic Association of Pensioners of the OTE Group Telecommunications v. Greece.
No. 161/2018 Confederazione Generale Sindacale (CGS) and Federazione dei Lavoratori Pubblici e Funzioni pubbliche (FLP) v. Italy.
No. 160/2018 Confédération Générale du Travail Force Ouvrière (CGT-FO) v. France.
No. 159/2018 Associazione Professionale e Sindacale (ANIEF) v. Italy.
No. 155/2017 Confédération générale du travail (CGT) v. France.
No. 153/2017 Unione sindacale di base –settore pubblico impiego (USB) v. Italy.
No. 152/2017 Unione sindacale di base –settore pubblico impiego (USB) v. Italy.
No. 150/2017 European Youth Forum (YFJ) v. Belgium.
No. 149/2017 Confédération générale du travail (CGT) et Confédération française de l'encadrement-CGC (CFE-CGC) v. France.
No. 147/2017 Unione Nazionale Dirigenti dello Stato (UNADIS) v. Italy.
From 2021 to 2022, another 38 cases were submitted to the Committee.
No. 224/2023 European Federation of National Organisations working with the Homeless (FEANTSA) and International Federation for Human Rights (FIDH) v. France.
No. 223/2023 Associazione professionale sindacale dirigenti area istruzione e ricerca (Dirigentiscuola) v. Italy.
No. 222/2023 Fédération nationale des syndicats de salariés des mines et de l'énergie - Confédération générale du travail (FNME-CGT) v. France.
No. 221/2023 Eurochild v. Bulgaria.
No. 220/2023 European Roma Rights Centre (ERRC) v. Czech Republic.
No. 219/2022 European Organisation of Military Associations and Trade Unions (EUROMIL) v. Spain.
No. 218/2022 Confederación Sindical de Commissions Obreras (CCOO) v. Spain.

No. 217/2022 Amnesty International v. Greece.
No. 216-2022 Federação Nacional dos Professores (FENPROF) v. Portugal.
No. 215/2022 Sindacato Autonomo Comitato Nazionale Pompieri (CO.NA.PO.) v. Italy.
No. 214/2022 Sindacato Autonomo Comitato Nazionale Pompieri (CO.NA.PO.) v. Italy.
No. 213/2022 Associazione Sindacale Militari (ASSO.MIL.) v. Italy.
No. 212/2022 European Organisation of Military Associations and Trade Unions (EUROMIL) v. Ireland.
No. 211/2022 Syndicat des Agrégés de l'Enseignement Supérieur (SAGES) v. France.
No. 210/2022 International Federation of Associations of the Elderly (FIAPA) v. France.
No. 209/2022 Fellesforbundet for Sjøfolk (FFFS) v. Norway.
No. 208/2022 Unione sindacale di base (USB) v. Italy.
No. 207/2022 Unión General de Trabajadores (UGT) v. Spain.
No. 206/2022 Defence for Children International (DCI), European Federation of National Organisations working with the Homeless (FEANTSA), Magistrats Européens pour la Démocratie et les Libertés (MEDEL), Confederación Sindical de Comisiones Obreras (CCOO), and International Movement ATD Fourth World v. Spain.
No. 205/2022 International Federation of Associations of the Elderly (FIAPA) v. France.
No. 204/2022 Open Society European Policy Institute (OSEPI) v. Bulgaria.
No. 203/2021 European Federation of National Organizations Working with the Homeless (FEANTSA) v. Belgium.
No. 201/2021 European Trade Union Confederation (ETUC), Netherlands Trade Union Confederation (FNV) and National Federation of Christian Trade Unions (CNV) v. the Netherlands.
No. 200/2021 Associazione Professionale e Sindacale (ANIEF) v. Italy.
No. 199/2021 European Organisation of Military Associations and Trade Unions (EUROMIL) v. Portugal.
No. 198/2021 Norwegian Association of Small & Medium Enterprises (SMB Norge) v. Norway.
No. 195/2020 European Roma Rights Centre (ERRC) v. Belgium.
No. 193/2020 Union Syndicale Solidaires SDIS v. France.
No. 192/2020 Confederazione Generale Sindacale CGS, Federazione GILDA-UNAMS and Sindacato Nazionale Insegnanti Di Religione Cattolica v. Italy.
No. 191/2020 European Federation of National Organisations working with the Homeless (FEANTSA) v. Czech Republic.
No. 190/2020 European Roma Rights Centre (ERRC) v. Czech Republic.
No. 189/2020, Confédération française démocratique du travail (CFDT) v. France.
No. 188/2019 Validity Foundation – Mental Disability Advocacy Centre v. Czech Republic.

No. 187/2019 Sindacato autonomo Pensionati Or.S.A. v. Italy.
No. 180/2019 Association of Secondary Teachers Ireland (ASTI) v. Ireland.
No. 179/2019 Associação Sindical dos Profissionais da Polícia (ASPP/PSP) v. Portugal.
No. 178/2019 Amnesty International v. Italy.
No. 176/2019 Union Syndicale Solidaires SDIS v. France.

In total, from the establishment of collective complaints until the last day of 2022, the Committee adjudicated 269 cases.

In this monograph, I only discuss collective labour law complaints. Very few were lodged by an organisation of employers[2023] Most of the collective complaints were brought by non-profit organisations (NGOs)[2024], trade unions and other organisations representing workers' interests.[2025] During the 'pre-court' proceedings, the Committee examined the right of an international lawyers' association to lodge a collective complaint against the authorities of Portugal, who allow employers to employ children younger than 15 years of age, which constitutes a violation of Article 7 §1 of the European Social Charter.[2026] The Committee also had to decide whether a Quaker organisation had the right to lodge a collective complaint against Greece which violated the provision prohibiting forced labour (Article 1 §2 of the European Social Charter) by introducing some alternative forms of compulsory military service. With regard to the complaints examined so far, the Committee has pronounced that INGOs making collective complaints meet the requirements laid down in the Additional Protocol of 1995. They have been established either to represent and defend economic and labour rights expressed in the European Social

2023. *Confederation of Swedish Enterprise v. Sweden*, Complaint No. 12/2002. *See*: European Social Charter. Collected texts, *supra*, p. 500.

2024. *International Commission of Jurists v. Portugal*, Complaint No. 1998; *International Federation of Human Rights Leagues v. Greece*, Complaint No. 2000; *Quaker Council for European Affairs v. Greece*, Complaint No. 2000; *Autisme-Europe v. France*, Complaint No. 13/2002; *International Federation for Human Rights (IFHR) v. France*, Complaint No. 14/2003; *European Roma Rights Centre v. Greece*, Complaint No. 15/2003; *World Organisation Against Torture (OMCT) v. Greece*, Complaint No. 17/2003; *OMCT v. Ireland*, Complaint No. 18/2003; *OMCT v. Italy*, Complaint No. 19/2003; *OMCT v. Portugal*, Complaint No. 20/2003; *OMCT v. Belgium*, Complaint No. 21/2003, European Social, *supra*, pp. 500 et seq., http://.coe.int/en/web/turin-european-social-charter/collective-complaints-procedure.

2025. *European Federation of Employees in Public Services (EFEPS) v. France*, Complaint No.2/1999; *EFEPS v. Greece*, Complaint No. 3/1999; *EFEPS v. Italy*, Complaint No. 4/1999; *EFEPS v. Portugal*, Complaint No. 5/1999; *Syndicat national des professions du tourisme v. France*, Complaint No. 6/1999; *Confédération Française de l'Encadrement – (CFE) CGC v. France*, Complaint No. 9/2000; *They ry and STTK ry v. Finland*, Complaint No. 10/2000; *European Council of Police Trade Unions v. Portugal*, Complaint No. 11/2001; *CFE CGS v. France*, Complaint No. 16/2003; *Confédération Générale du Travail v. France*, Complaint No. 22/2003; *Syndicat Occitan de l'education v. France*, Complaint No. 23/2003; *Synidicat Sud Travail Affaires Sociales v. France*, Complaint No. 24/2004; *Centrale générale des services publics (CGSP) v. Belgium*, Complaint No. 25/2004, *European Social …*, *supra*, pp. 500 et seq.; http://.coe.int/en/web/turin-european-social-charter/collective-complaints-procedure.

2026. *See*: Complaint No. 1/1998: *International Commission of Jurists v. Portugal*. Documents, Council of Europe Publishing, Strasbourg 2000, pp. 13 et seq.

Charter or to protect the rights of a particular social group, e.g., children or immigrants. The Committee makes decisions concerning the admission for further examination or the rejection of a collective complaint during a plenary discussion. A report prepared by a member of the Committee selected by the President to be a spokesperson in a particular case serves as a basis for the discussion. The fifteen complaints registered in 2018 were lodged against five States Parties: Italy (6), France (4), Finland (2), Greece (2) and Ireland (1). They were submitted by national trade unions and by international and national NGOs.[2027] Further, fifteen new complaints were lodged in 2019 against six States Parties: France (7), Italy (4), Belgium (1), Czech Republic (1), Ireland (1), and Portugal (1); twelve complaints were submitted by national trade unions and three by international NGOs.[2028] In 2020, seven new actions were brought against Finland, Greece, Belgium, France (one each) and two against the Czech Republic and Italy. The last one, against Italy (No. 194/2020), was closed.

§4. Grounds for Collective Complaint

334. A collective complaint can only be made in the event of an alleged unsatisfactory application of the European Social Charter by the authorities of a Member

2027. Activity Report 2018, p. 15. Appendices, p. 65. In 2018, the Committee registered the following fifteen complaints: *Associazione Professionale e Sindacale (ANIEF) v. Italy*, Complaint No. 159/2018; *Confédération générale du Travail Force Ouvrière v. France*, Complaint No. 160/2018; *Confederazione Generale Sindacale (CGS) and Federazione dei Lavoratori Pubblici e Funzioni pubbliche (FLP) v. Italy*, Complaint No. 161/2018; *International Federation of Associations of the Elderly (FIAPA) v. France*, Complaint No. 162/2018; *ATTAC ry, Globaali sosiaalityö ry et Maan ystävät ry v. Finland*, Complaint No. 163/2018; *European Organisation of Military Associations (EUROMIL) v. Ireland*, Complaint No. 164/2018; *Panhellenic Association of Pensioners of the OTE Group Telecommunications v. Greece*, Complaint No. 165/2018; *Sindacato Autonomo Europeo Scuola ed Ecologia (SAESE) v. Italy*, Complaint No. 166/2018; *Sindacato autonomo Pensionati Or.S.A. v. Italy*, Complaint No. 167/2018; *European Disability Forum and Inclusion Europe v. France*, Complaint No. 168/2018; *Nursing Up v. Italy*, Complaint No. 169/2018; *Unione sindacale di base (USB) v. Italy*, Complaint No. 170/2018; *Confédération générale du travail (CGT) v. France*, Complaint No. 171/2018; *Finnish Society of Social Rights v. Finland*, Complaint No. 172/2018; *International Commission of Jurists (ICJ) and European Council for Refugees and Exiles (ECRE) v. Grèce*, Complaint No. 173/2018.

2028. Activity Report 2019, p. 15. In 2019, the Committee registered the following fifteen complaints:

Syndicat CGT YTO France v. France, Complaint No. 174/2019; *Syndicat CFDT de la métallurgie de la Meuse v. France*, Complaint No. 175/2019; *Union Syndicale Solidaires SDIS v. France*, Complaint No. 176/2019; *Associazione Medici Liberi v. Italy*, Complaint No. 177/2019; *Amnesty International v. Italy*, Complaint No. 178/2019; *Associação Sindical dos Profissionais da Polícia (ASPP/PSP) v. Portugal*, Complaint No. 179/2019; *Association of Secondary Teachers lreland (ASTI) v. Ireland*, Complaint No. 180/2019; *Syndicat CFDT général des transports et de l'environnement de l'Aube v. France*, Complaint No. 181/2019; *Syndicat CFDT de la métallurgie de la Meuse v. France*, Complaint No. 182/2019; *Syndicat CGT YTO France v. France*, Complaint No. 183/2019; *Syndicat CGT Ford Aquitaine Industrie v France*, Complaint No. 184/2019; *European Roma Rights Centre (ERRC) v. Belgium*, Complaint No. 185/2019; *Sindacato Autonomo Europeo Scuola ed Ecologia (SAESE) v. Italy*, Complaint No. 186/2019; *Sindacato autonomo Pensionati Or.S.A. v. Italy*, Complaint No. 187/2019; *Validity Foundation – Mental Disability Advocacy Centre v. Czech Republic*, Complaint No. 188/2019.

State (Article 1 of the Additional Protocol). Since Member States do not 'apply' the Charter and are only obliged to abide by the Charter's provisions, on the basis of which the Committee formulates European standards for social and economic rights, the phrase used in Article 1 of the Additional Protocol should be construed as stating that a collective complaint may be lodged whenever the authorities of Member States fail to fulfil their obligations arising from the European Social Charter, which they have voluntarily accepted for implementation. When lodging a collective complaint, a complaining party should identify particular provisions of the Charter and indicate in what respect the state has not ensured their satisfactory application (Article 4 of the Additional Protocol). Presenting its conclusions, the Committee has to assess whether or not the Member State concerned has ensured the satisfactory application of the provision of the Charter referred to in the complaint – Article 8 (1) of the Additional Protocol. With regard to the supervision over the reports presented by the Member States, the Committee assesses whether the provisions of labour law and social security law and the common practice in this respect by Member States comply with the European standards set out in the Social Charters of the Council of Europe. Hence, a collective complaint can be made in the event of an alleged unsatisfactory application of the provisions of the European Social Charter and of the standards laid down by The Committee by a Member State.

335. The allegations made in a collective complaint should be general in their nature. They ought to refer to a specific case of an unsatisfactory application by a Member State of a particular provision of the European Social Charter or non-compliance with a particular European standard laid down by the Committee on the basis of the Charter. The Committee of Ministers of the Council of Europe, in the above-cited decision, ruled out the possibility of admitting complaints concerning individual cases where the state authorities or state administration violate any social or economic right included in the European Social Charter.[2029] The analysis of 120 collective complaints examined by the Committee during 1999-2013 shows that 50 collective complaints (42%) were concerned with unsatisfactory applications of the following provisions of the European Social Charter by Member States: Article 7 §1 (ban on child labour),[2030] Article 5 (the right to organise),[2031] Article 6 (the right

2029. Explanatory, *supra*, p. 155.

2030. Complaint No. 1/1998; No. 114/; No. 111/2014.

2031. Complaint No. 2/1999 *European Federation of Employees in Public Services (EUROFEDOP) v. France*; No. 3/1999, *European Federation of Employees in Public Services (EUROFEDOP) v. Greece*; No. 4/1999 *European Federation of Employees in Public Services (EUROFEDOP) v. Italy*; No. 5/1999 *European Federation of Employees in Public Services (EUROFEDOP) v. Portugal*; No. 11/2001 *European Council of Police Trade Unions (CESP) v. Portugal*; No. 12/2002 *Confederation of Swedish Entreprise v. Sweden*; No. 23/2003 *Syndicat occitan de l'éducation v. France*; No. 26/2004 *Syndicat des Agréés de l'Enseignement Supérieur (SAGES) v. France*; No. 35/2006 *Federation of Finnish Entreprises v. Finland*; No.83/2012 *European Confederation of Police (EUROCOP) v. Ireland*; No. 85/2012 *Swedish Trade Union Confederation (LO) and Swedish Confederation of Professional Employees (TCO) v. Sweden*; No. 101/2013 *European Council of Police Trade Unions (CESP) v. France*; No. 116 *Matica hrvatskih sindicata v. Croatia*; No. 112/2014 *European Organisation of Military Associations (EUROMIL) v. Ireland*; No. 103 *Bedriftsforbundet v. Norway*.

to bargain collectively),[2032] Article 6 §4 (the right to strike),[2033] Article 1 §2 (non-discrimination with regard to the right to work and prohibition of forced labour),[2034] Article 10 (the right to vocational training),[2035] Article 2 (the right to just conditions of work),[2036] Article 2 §4 (the right to work in safe conditions),[2037] Article 3 (the right to safe and healthy working conditions),[2038] Article 4 (the right to a fair remuneration),[2039] Article 20 (the right to equal opportunities and equal treatment in matters of employment and occupation without discrimination on the grounds of sex),[2040] Article 21 (the right to information and consultation),[2041] Article 22 (the right to take part in the determination and improvement of the working conditions and working environment),[2042] Article 24 (the right to protection in cases of

---

2032. Complaint No. 2/1999; No. 3/1999; No. 4/1999; No. 5/1999; No. 9/2000 *Confédération Française de l'Encadrement (CFE-CGC) v. France*; No. 11/2001; No. 16/2003 *Confédération Française de l'Encadrement (CFE-CGC) v. France*; No. 25/2004 *Centrale générale de services public v. Belgium*; No. 36/2006 *Frente Comum de Sindicatos da Administração Pública v. Portugal*; No. 40/2007 *European Council of Police Trade Unions (CESP) v. Portugal*; No. 83/2012; No. 118 *Confédération Générale du Travail Force Ouvrière (CGT-FO) v. France*; No. 116 *Matica hrvatskih sindicata v. Croatia*; No. 112/2014 *European Organisation of Military Associations (EUROMIL) v. Ireland.*
2033. Complaint No. 9/2000; No. 16/2003; No. 32/2005 *European Trade Union Confederation (ETUC), Confederation of Independent Trade Unions in Bulgaria, Confederation of Labour 'Podkrepa' (CL 'Podkrepa') v. Bulgaria*; No. 59/2009 *European Trade Union Confederation (ETUC)/ Centrale Générale des Syndicats Libéraux de Belgique (CGSLB)/ Confédération des Syndicats chrétiens de Belgique (CSC)/Fédération Générale du Travail de Belgique (FGTB) v. Belgium*; No. 65/2011
2034. Complaint No. 6/1999 *Syndicat national des professions du tourisme v. France*; No. 7/2000 *International Federation of Human Rights Leagues (FIDH) v. Greece*; No. 8/2000 *Quaker Council of European Affairs (QCEA) v. Greece*; No. 24/2004 *Syndicat SUD Travail Affaires Sociales v. France*; No. 56/2009 *Confédération Française de l'Encadrement (CFE-CGC) v. France*; 74/2011 *Fellesforbundet for Sjofolk (FFFS) v. Norway*; No. 91/2013 *Confederatione Generale Italiana del Lavoro (CGIL) v. Italy*; No. 115 *European Federation of Employees in Public Services (EUROFEDOP) v. Greece*; No. 111/2014 *Greek General Confederation of Labour (GSEE) v. Greece.*
2035. Complaint No. 6/1999; No. 119 *European Roma and Travellers Forum (ERTF) v. France*; No. 105/2014 *Associazione sindicale 'La Voce dei Giusti' v. Italy.*
2036. Complaint No. 9/2000; No. 16/2003 *Tehy ry and STTK ry v. Finland*; No. 22/2003 *Confédération général du travail (CGT) v. France*; No. 54/2008; No. 56/2009; No. 73/2011 *Syndicat de Défense des fonctionnaires v. France*; No. 91/2013; No. 111/2014 *Greek General Confederation of Labour (GSEE) v. Greece.*
2037. Complaint No. 10/2000 *Tehy ry and STTK ry v. Finland*; No. 30/2005 *Marangopoulos Foundation for Human Rights (MFHR) v. Greece.*
2038. No. 22/2003; No. 30/2005; No. 56/2009; No. 91/2013.
2039. Complaint No. 9/2000; No. 37/2006 *European Council of Police Trade Unions (CESP) v. Portugal*; No. 38/2006 *European Council of Police Trade Unions (CESP) v. France*; No. 50/2008 *Confédération française démocratique du travail (CFDT) v. France*; No. 57/2009 *European Council of Police Trade Unions (CESP) v. France*; No. 60/2010 *European Council of Police Trade Unions (CESP) v. Portugal*; No. 65/2011 *General Federation of employees of the national electric power corporation (GENOP-DEI)/Confederation of Greek Civil Servants Trade Unions (ADEDY) v. Greece*; No. 68/2011 *European Council of Police Trade Unions (CESP) v. France*; No. 84/2012 *Union syndicale des magistrats administratifs (USMA) v. France*; No. 85/2012; No. 111/2014 *Greek General Confederation of Labour (GSEE) v. Greece.*
2040. Complaint No. 73/2011.
2041. Complaint No. 83/2012.
2042. Complaint No. 40/2007.

termination of employment),[2043] Article 25 (the right of workers to the protection of their claims in the event of the insolvency of their employer),[2044] Article 27 (the right of workers with family responsibilities to equal opportunities and equal treatment).[2045] Collective complaints include some allegations of the violation of certain labour rights guaranteed in the above-mentioned provisions of the European Social Charter against authorities of some Member States of the Council of Europe. As construed in the Additional Protocol, the admission of a complaint as a collective complaint does not exclude the possibility of identifying persons against whom the complaint has been made. In the next two years (2016–2017), 37 collective complaints were submitted either by NGOs or by trade union organisations. The growing number of collective complaints stems from the new rules for the functioning of the reporting system. Fifteen Member States which accepted the collective complaints procedure shall henceforth submit simplified reports every two years. Those fifteen states were divided into two groups as follows: Group A, made up of the eight states: France, Greece, Portugal, Italy, Belgium, Bulgaria, Ireland, and Finland; Group B, made up of seven states: the Netherlands, Sweden, Croatia, Norway, Slovenia, Cyprus, and the Czech Republic.

336. Under the current rules of the reporting system, the collective complaint procedure is considered the principal instrument in terms of legal control as to whether or not Member States' governments follow labour law standards established by the Council of Europe. At the end of 2017, forty-six collective complaints were pending,[2046] and 112 had been registered as processed complaints.[2047] During the last, most current period (2018–2020), ten collective complaints were processed. Six against three Member States: Italy, France and Czech Republic (two each country), three against Finland, Greece and Belgium (one each country).

In the previous edition of the monograph, there are five decisions on the admissibility and merits of the collective complaints published during the last two years, 2016–2017: No. 91/2013 *Confederazione Generale Italiana del Lavoro (CGIL) v. Italy*; No. 101/2013 *European Council of Police Trade Unions (CESP) v. France*; No. 103/2013, *Bedriftsforbundet v. Norway*; No. 106/2014 *Finnish Society of Social Right v. Finland.* Complaint No.91/2013 alleges that section 9 of Act No. 194, which governs the conscientious objection of medical practitioners and other medical personnel in relation to abortion services, violates Article 11 (the right to health) RESC, Article 1 (the right to work), as well as Article 2 (the right to just conditions of work), 3 (the right to safe and healthy working conditions) and 26 (the right to dignity at work) of the Charter, the latter Articles read either alone or in conjunction with Article E (non-discrimination). The allegations of CGIL are based on a demonstration of the inadequacy of section 9 of Act No. 194 due to the fact that the vast majority of medical practitioners and other health personnel exercise their right to conscientious objection. CGIL underlines that this situation prevents effective

2043. Complaint No. 74/2011; No. 106/2014 *Finnish Society of Social Rights v. Finland*; No. 107/2014 *Finnish Society of Social Rights v. Finland.*

2044. No. 113/ 2014 *Unione Italiana del Lavoro U.I.L. Scuola-Sicilia v. Italy.*

2045. Complaint No. 9/2000.

2046. Nos 109/2014–158/2017.

2047. Nos 01/1998–122/2016.

access to abortion procedures in Italy and undermines the right of women to the protection of their health. Given the urgent character of the procedures, women wishing to seek an abortion may be forced to move to other health facilities in Italy or abroad, terminate their pregnancy without the support or control of competent health authorities, or may be deterred from accessing abortion services which they have a legal entitlement to receive. The Committee emphasises that this situation may involve considerable risks to the health and well-being of the women concerned, which is contrary to the protection of health as guaranteed by Article 11 of the Charter. For all these reasons, the Committee holds that there is a violation of Article 11 §1 of the Charter. It also found that discrimination exists on the grounds of health status between women seeking access to lawful abortion services and women seeking access to other lawful forms of medical procedures, which are not provided on a restricted basis. The Committee considers that due to the specific conditions to access abortion services, the situation amounts to denial of access to these services. As a consequence, the difference in treatment constitutes discrimination and, therefore, a violation of Article E in conjunction with Article 11 of the Charter. The Committee also holds that the difference in treatment between the objecting and non-objecting medical practitioners amounts to discrimination in violation of Article 1 §2 of the Charter. The complaint does not raise issues relating to forced labour or any other aspect of the right to earn one's living in an occupation freely entered up. The Committee observes that it has not been provided with any information on the average working time of non-objecting medical practitioners. Therefore holds that there is a violation of Article 2 §1 of the Charter. The same conclusion goes for the provisions of Articles 3 §3 and 26 of the Charter.

In case No. 101/2013, the European Council of Police Trade Unions (CESP) alleges that in France, officers, non-commissioned officers and volunteers of the National Gendarmerie are conferred military status and do not enjoy trade union rights, in violation of Article 5 (right to organise) and 6 (right to bargain collectively) of the Revised European Social Charter. The Committee considers that the National Gendarmerie may be functionally equivalent either to the police or to an armed force, depending on the duties assigned and authority tasks performed. It depends on an individual's concrete situation with regard to the combination of thesis connecting factors that each member of the Gendarmerie does or does not qualify as a member of the armed forces under Article 5 of the Charter. Consequently, there is no violation of Article 5 of the Charter where the National Gendarmerie is functionally equivalent to an armed force. The Committee recalls that under Article 6 §1 of the Charter, Member States must take positive steps to encourage joint consultation within bodies, in which both sides are represented on an equal footing and engage in consultation regardless of the presence of Government representatives. Therefore, the Committee concludes that there is no violation of Article 6 §1 and 2 of the Charter. In complaint No. 103/2013, Bediffsforbundet alleges a violation of Article 5 of the Revised European Charter on the grounds that closed-shop practices exist in the dock sector. In order to be recruited and continue to be employed, dock workers must be a member of the Norwegian Transport Workers (NTF). There is a violation of Article 5 on the ground that NTF have a monopoly, in that they are given preference by the collective agreements in force. The Committee notes that Norwegian law protects negative freedom of association, the right not to join. Also notes that the relevant collective agreement covering dock workers, providing for the registration of dock workers with priority rights, contains no provision requiring registered dock workers to be members of NTF or any other trade union. The Committee finds that evidence at its disposal is not sufficient to prove the existence of a closed shop in practice. There is no conclusive evidence that dock workers are compelled to be members of NTF.

Complaint No. 106/2014 demands the Committee to find that Finland is in breach of Article 24 of the Charter on the grounds that Finnish legislation makes no provision for reinstatement in the event of unlawful dismissal and the Employment Contracts Act provides for a ceiling on the amount of compensation that may be awarded in the event of unlawful dismissal. The Committee states that the possibility of awarding the remedy recognises the importance of placing the employee back into an employment situation no less favourable than he/she previously enjoyed. Whether reinstatement is appropriate in a particular case is a matter for the domestic courts to decide. The Committee considers that the upper limit to compensation provided for by the Employment Contracts Act the Committee may result in situations where compensation awarded is not commensurate with the loss suffered. Therefore, the Committee holds that there is a violation of Article 24 of the Charter.

The same plaintiff, the Finnish Society of Social Rights, invites the Committee to find that Finland is in breach of Article 24 on the grounds that employees may be dismissed in circumstances which go beyond those permitted by Article 24 of the Charter.[2048] It maintains that it is very easy to legally dismiss employees in Finland. The employer must respect the notice period laid down by law or collective agreement but then may dismiss employees on production or economic grounds without further constraints. The plaintiff argues that enterprises considering that they wish to increase profits may justify dismissal on economic and production grounds, even where the enterprise is already profitable. Finnish enterprises have no duty to take into account the interests of their employees. The Committee recalls that economic reasons for dismissal must be based on the operational requirements of the undertaking and establishment of services. The assessment relies on the domestic courts' interpretation of law.[2049] The Committee notes that the term 'operational requirements' found in Article 24 of the Charter may cover different situations, in particular, may cover industrial or strategic measures necessary by the enterprise to maintain or improve competitiveness in a globalised market even when the enterprise is not in economic difficulty. Article 24 requires a balance to be struck between employer's right to manage their enterprise as they see fit and the need to protect the rights of the employees. The Committee finds out that Finnish legislation strikes such a balance. It notes that under the Employment Contracts Act, employers may dismiss employees for economic or production-related grounds, but in addition, there must be a proper and weighty reason, and the work must have diminished substantially and permanently. Furthermore, it notes the factors which must be taken into account when assessing whether a dismissal fulfils the conditions: decline in

2048. Conclusions 107/2014.
2049. Conclusions 2012 (Turkey).

demand, obsolete products, increased competition or restructuring of the business. Taking that argument into account, the Committee concludes that there is no violation of Article 24 of the Charter.

The Committee admits the possibility of making a complaint on behalf of employees of a particular establishment, as in the case of employees of the British Governmental Communications Headquarters (GCHQ) – an organisation responsible for intelligence, security and military communication systems – deprived of the right to organise in trade unions, guaranteed by Article 5 of the European Social Charter.[2050] Another specific social group, for the benefit of which the Committee could admit a collective complaint, was a group of Norwegian workers employed in the oil drilling industry and nurses working on the drilling platforms, who were made to submit to a collective dispute to be settlement by an arbitration tribunal before they could decide to go on strike, which constituted a violation of Article 6 §4 of the European Social Charter.[2051]

In 2018, the following decisions taken by the Committee were made public: (1) The decision on admissibility and the merits in the *European Organisation of Military Associations (EUROMIL) v. Ireland*, Complaint No. 112/2014, became public on 12 February 2018. The complainant organisation alleged that Ireland is in violation of Articles 5 and 6 of the Charter on the grounds that the defence force representative association does not possess proper trade union rights. In its decision on merits, the Committee concluded by 11 votes to 2 that there is a violation of Article 5 of the Charter; unanimously that there is a violation of Article 6 §2 of the Charter; by nine votes to 4 that there is no violation of Article 6 §4 of the Charter. (2) The decision on the merits in *Matica Hrvatskih Sindikata v. Croatia*, Complaint No. 116/2015. Matica Hrvatskih Sindikata alleged that Croatia is in violation of Articles 5 and 6 of the European Social Charter of 1961 on the grounds that the Act on Withdrawal of Certain Material Rights of the Employed in Public Services, Official Gazette No. 143/2012, and other legislation enacted and implemented by the Government of Croatia on 20 December 2012 infringe the right to organise and the right to bargain collectively. In its decision on the merits adopted on 21 March 2018, the Committee concluded: unanimously that there is no violation of Article 5 of the 1961 Charter; by 13 votes to 1 that there is a violation of Article 6 §2 of the 1961 Charter; by 13 votes to 1 that there is no violation of Article 6 §1 of the 1961 Charter; by 13 votes to 1 that there is no violation of Article 6 §3 of the 1961 Charter; by 12 votes to 2 that there is no violation of Article 6 §4 of the 1961 Charter. (3) the merits in *Confédération Générale du Travail Force Ouvrière (CGT-FO) v. France*, Complaint No. 118/2015, became public on 26 November 2018. CGT-FO alleged a violation of Article 6 §2 of the revised European Social Charter with respect to the conditions under the French legislation concerning complementary social protection of employees with regard to the choice of an insurer. In its decision on the merits, adopted on 3 July 2018, the Committee concluded: unanimously that there is a violation of Article 6 §2 of the Charter. (4) The decision on the merits in *Irish Congress of Trade Unions (ICTU) v. Ireland*, Complaint No. 123/2015, became public on 12 December 2018. The complainant organisation alleged that the decision of the

2050. Conclusions XI-1, p. 80. The right to organise, *supra*, p. 38.
2051. Conclusions XII-1, p. 130; Conclusions XIII-1, p. 38.

Irish Competition Authority prohibiting certain workers – deemed self-employed – such as voiceover actors, freelance journalists, and some musicians, from concluding collective agreements setting out minimum rates of pay and other working conditions, as this would amount to a breach of competition law, is in violation of Article 6 of the Charter. In its decision on the merits, adopted on 12 September 2018, the Committee concluded by 11 votes to 2 that there is no violation of Article 6 §2 of the Charter.

In 2019, two collective complaints decisions in the field of labour law were made public: (1) The decision on the merits in *Confédération générale du travail (CGT)*, Complaint No. 154/20174, became public on 15 March 2019. CGT alleged that France failed to fulfil its obligations under Article 4 §2 of the Charter with regard to increased remuneration for overtime work due to legislation which authorises the adjustment of working time for a period longer than a week and up to three years. In its decision on the merits, adopted on 18 October 2018, the Committee concluded unanimously that there is a violation of Article 4 §2 of the Charter in respect of the reasonableness of the reference period but that there is no violation of Article 4 §2 of the Charter in respect of the right of workers to be informed of any changes to their working time. (2) The decision on the merits in *Confederazione Generale Italiana del Lavoro (CGIL) v. Italy*, Complaint No. 140/2016, became public on 7 June 2019. CGIL alleged that Italy was in violation of Article 5 of the Charter because it prohibits the members of the *Guardia di Finanza* from establishing professional trade unions or joining other trade unions; Article 6 §1 of the Charter because it does not promote joint consultations between the members of the *Guardia di Finanza* and the Ministry of Economy and Finances/employer; Article 6 §2 of the Charter because it does not promote voluntary negotiations between the members of the *Guardia di Finanza* and the Ministry of Economy and Finances/employer in order to regulate employment conditions by collective agreements; Article 6 §4 of the Charter because it prohibits members of the *Guardia di Finanza* from exercising the right to strike. In its decision on the merits, adopted on 22 January 2019, the Committee concluded – by nine votes to two that there is a violation of Article 5 of the Charter – unanimously that there is no violation of Article 6 §1 of the Charter – unanimously, that there is a violation of Article 6 §2 of the Charter; by nine votes to 2, that there is a violation of Article 6 §4 of the Charter.

In 2020, in the collective complaint *Confederazione Generale Sindacale (CGS) v. Italy*, by maintaining hundreds of thousands of public-sector workers – in particular, public education staff (teachers and ATA staff) – on fixed-term contracts, Italy violates Article 1 §2 of the Charter, insofar as it does not protect the right of these workers to earn their living in an occupation freely entered upon.[2052] By thirteen votes to two that there is no violation of Article 1 §2 of the Charter in respect of public-sector staff, including public education staff registered in the ERE lists, recruited under successive contracts for an overall length of more than thirty-six months. In view of these elements, the Committee considers that the situation of public-sector staff and of public education staff registered in the ERE lists and

2052. Complaint No. 144/2017, Adoption: 9 Sep. 2020, Notification: 8 Oct. 2020, Publicity: 9 Feb. 2021.

recruited on annual contracts does not constitute a discriminatory treatment, in comparison to private-sector workers, which would be incompatible with Article 1 §2 of the Charter. It accordingly considers that the situation of public-sector staff and public education staff registered in the ERE lists is in conformity with Article 1 §2 of the Charter. Unanimously, the Committee decides that there is a violation of Article 1 §2 of the Charter in respect of public education staff not registered in the ERE lists and recruited under successive contracts with interruptions for an overall length of more than 36 months.

Having regard to the situation of public education staff not registered in the ERE lists and recruited under successive contracts with interruptions for an overall length of more than 36 months, the Committee considers that there has been a disproportionate interference with their rights to earn their living in an occupation freely entered upon, on account of:

- the absence of effective preventive and remedial safeguards against abuse arising from the undue recourse to fixed-term contracts, combined with
- the legal uncertainty resulting from the repeated changes to legislation and case law; and
- the restricted chances of obtaining indefinite duration contracts regardless of actual competences and working experience.

Fédération de syndicats des métiers de l'ingénierie, de l'informatique, du conseil, de la formation, des bureaux et d'études (FIECI) and *Syndicat National de l'Encadrement du Personnel de l'Ingénierie (SNEPI CFE-CGC) v. France.*[2053] The complainant organisations allege that Article L. 2143-3 of the Labour Code as modified by Law of 20 August 2008, which added extra requirements for the appointment of trade union representatives, is contrary to Article 5 of the Charter as it may, following interpretation by the courts, create a situation in which a trade union purely and simply loses its right to appoint its representative. The Committee notes that Article L. 2143-3 of the Labour Code was amended on 29 March 2018, i.e., after the lodging of the present complaint. According to this amendment, a new exemption from the 10% rule was added, and a representative trade union can now choose its representatives from among its members if all of the elected representatives who fulfil the 10% requirement waive in writing their right to be appointed as a trade union representative. The Committee considers that this amendment removes the excessive restrictions imposed on trade unions with respect to the appointment of their representatives that are the subject of this complaint and thus removes the invoked circumstances in which trade unions may lose their right to appoint their representatives. In this respect, the Committee also takes note of the report of the ILO Committee on Freedom of Association No. 389 of June 2019 which considered that the amendment in question contributes, in conformity with the principles of freedom of association, to the preservation of the right of trade

2053. In the opinion of the Committee, only a privileged system supplemented by an alternative mechanism effectively guarantees the satisfaction of pecuniary claims of those employed by entrepreneurs who do not own any assets.

union organisations to freely choose their trade union representatives. Therefore, the Committee holds that there is no violation of Article 5 of the Charter.

Associazione Professionale e Sindacale (ANIEF) v. Italy[2054] ANIEF alleges that Italian legislation and case law do not adequately protect public education staff (teaching and non-teaching staff) from abuses arising from the successive renewal of their fixed-term employment contracts, insofar as such contracts cannot be converted into indefinite duration contracts upon completion of a certain length of service, contrary to what applies in the private sector. ANIEF alleges that through a series of legislative changes and decisions of the Court of Cassation which affected the employment situation of public education staff working under fixed-term contracts Italy has violated the following provisions of the Charter: (a) Article 1 §1, as the precarious employment situation of public education staff does not correspond to the engagement of achieving and maintaining a level of employment as high and stable as possible; (b) Article 1 §2, as the above-mentioned precarious situation also infringes upon the right of public education staff to earn their living in an occupation freely entered upon; (c) Article 4 §1, as the recourse to fixed-term contracts not covering the whole year and not taking into account the service already carried out under previous contracts does not ensure a fair and decent remuneration to public education staff; (d) Article 4 §4, as the recourse to fixed-term contracts also infringes upon the right of public education staff to a reasonable period of notice for termination of employment; (e) Article 5, as the legislation and the Court of Cassation's decisions allegedly impair the freedom of public education staff to form national trade union organisations such as ANIEF and to join them; (f) Article 6 §4, as the legislation and the judiciary, by depriving of effect the case brought by ANIEF before the CJEU, undermine the right of public education staff to collective action through ANIEF; (g) Article 24, as the abusive recourse to fixed-term contracts in the public education sector infringes upon the right of the staff concerned not to have their employment terminated for reasons not connected with their capacity or conduct or based on the operational requirements of the public offices or service, as well as their right to get in such cases an adequate compensation or other appropriate relief by appeal to an impartial body; (h) Article E taken together with each of these provisions on account of discrimination of public education staff with more than 36 months length of service under fixed-term contracts as regards access to indefinite duration contracts and remedies in case of abuse arising from the recourse to fixed-term contracts in comparison to private-sector workers and to teaching staff registered on the ERE lists.

The Committee considers that the non-renewal of fixed-term contracts or the fact that such contracts are not converted into indefinite duration contracts under the conditions referred to in the present complaint cannot be regarded as dismissals contrary to Article 24 of the Charter. Moreover, the arguments of the parties do not disclose any violation of Article E in conjunction with Article 24 of the Charter. The Committee accordingly holds that there is no violation of Article E in conjunction with Article 24 of the Charter.

For these reasons, the Committee concludes:

2054. Complaint No. 146/2017, Adoption: 7 Jul. 2020, Notification: 18 Sep. 2020, Publicity: 19 Jan. 2021.

- by nine votes to five, that there is no violation of Article 1 §2 of the Charter in respect of public education staff registered in the ERE lists and recruited under successive contracts for an overall length of more than 36 months;
- unanimously, that there is a violation of Article 1 §2 of the Charter in respect of public education staff not registered in the ERE lists and recruited under successive contracts with interruptions for an overall length of more than 36 months;
- by ten votes to four, that there is no violation of Article E in conjunction with Article 24 of the Charter.

University Women of Europe (UWE) v. Belgium[2055]

337. UWE alleges that the situation in Belgium is in violation of Articles 1, 4§3, 20 and E of the Revised European Social Charter ('the Charter') having regard to the pay gap between men and women and the under-representation of women in decision-making positions within private companies in Belgium and other private institutions in other European States which ratified Collective Complaints Procedure.[2056]

The Committee considers that Article 20 (d) of the Charter imposes positive obligations on States to tackle vertical segregation in the labour market by means of, *inter alia*, promoting the advancement of women in decision-making positions in private companies. This obligation may entail the introduction of binding legislative measures to ensure equal access to management boards of companies. Measures designed to promote equal opportunities for women and men in the labour market must include promoting effective parity in the representation of women and men in decision-making positions in both the public and private sectors.[2057] The Committee observes that according to the European Commission's 2019 Report on equality between women and men, the proportion of women on management boards of the largest publicly listed companies in countries with binding legislative measures has risen from an average of 9.8% in 2010 to 37.5% in 2018. In countries with non-binding measures, including positive action to promote gender balance, the corresponding percentages were 12.8% in 2010 and 25.6% in 2018, whereas, in countries where no particular Action (apart from self-regulation by companies) has been taken, the situation remained almost stagnant with 12.8% on average in 2010 and 14.3% in 2018. The overall EU-28 average was 26.7% in 2018. The Committee further observes that PACE Resolution 1715(2010) recommends that the proportion of women on management boards of companies should be at least 40%. The Committee recalls that in respect of Article 20.d, as for Article 20.c, States must take measures that enable the achievement of the objectives of the Charter within a reasonable time, with measurable progress and to an extent consistent with the

2055. Complaint No. 124/2016 Adoption: 6 Dec. 2019, Notification: 28 Feb. 2020, Publicity: 29 Jun. 2020.
2056. Bulgaria (No. 125/2016), Croatia (No. 126/2016), Cyprus (No. 127/2017), Czech Republic (No. 128/2016), Finland (No. 129/2016), France (No. 130/2016), Greece (No. 131/2016), Ireland (No. 132/2016), Italy (No. 133/2016), the Netherlands (No. 134/2016), Norway (No. 135/2016), Portugal (No. 136/2016), Slovenia (No. 137/2016).
2057. Conclusions 2016, Art. 20, Portugal.

maximum use of available resources. The Committee observes that according to data provided by the European Institute for Gender Equality (EIGE) up to April 2019, the proportion of women on the management boards of Belgium's largest listed companies is 34.4%. It was 29.4% in 2017. In 2010, women represented 10.5% of board members in the largest listed companies. The Committee notes that the introduction of the so-called Quota Law (law of 28 July 2011) has had a clear positive impact on the number of women on the management boards of the largest listed companies and that the figures have evolved positively. The Committee considers, therefore, that the Government has taken measures to meet its positive obligations to tackle vertical segregation in the labour market and has advanced in promoting the presence of women in decision-making positions of private companies. Although there is still progress to be made, as the PACE in its Resolution 1715 (2010) has recommended a goal of at least 40% of women representation which is not yet achieved, the legislation and the policies adopted have clearly improved the situation and contributed to tackling the existing obstacles.

Therefore, the Committee holds that there is no violation of Article 20(d) of the Charter concerning the measures taken to ensure a balanced representation of women in decision-making positions within private companies.

For these reasons, the Committee concludes – with regard to recognition and enforcement of the right to equal pay for work of equal value:

- unanimously, that there is no violation of Articles 4§3 and 20(c) of the Charter as regards recognition of the right to equal pay in the legislation;
- by nine votes to six, that there is no violation of Articles 4§3 and 20(c) of the Charter as regards access to effective remedies;
- unanimously, that there is a violation of Articles 4§3 and 20 (c) of the Charter on the ground that pay transparency is not ensured;
- unanimously, that there is no violation of Articles 4§3 and 20 (c) of the Charter as regards equality bodies;
- unanimously, that there is no violation of Article 20(c) of the Charter with regard to promotion of equal opportunities between women and men in respect of equal pay;
- unanimously, that there is no violation of Article 20(d) of the Charter as regards measures to ensure a balanced representation of women in decision-making positions within private companies.

In the remaining fourteen cases of University Women of Europe[2058] versus various European countries, the distribution of votes was as follows:

- there is (no) violation: 6 times, Complaint No. 138/2016; 3 times, No. 137/2016; 5 times, No. 136/2016; 3 times No. 136/20216; 3 times, No. 135/2016; 4 times, No. 134/2016; 4 times, No.133/2016; 3 times, No. 132/2016; 2 times, No. 131/2016; 5 times, No. 130/2016 and partly one dissenting opinion; 4 times, No. 129/2016; 3 times, No. 128/20216; 4 times, No. 127/2016; 2 times, No. 126/2016; 1 time, No. 125/2016; 5 times, No. 124/2016.

2058. *Decisions on the merits*. Adopted: 6 Dec. 2019; Notified: 28 Feb. 2020; Published: 29 Jun. 2020.

– there is a (yes) violation: 3 times, Complaint No. 137/2016; 1 time, No. 136/ 2016; 2 times, No. 135; 2 times, No. 134/2016; 2 times No.133/2016; 3 times, No. 132/2016; 4 times, No. 131/2016; 1 time, No. 130/2016 and partly one dissenting opinion; 2 times, No. 129/2016; 3 times, No. 128/2016; 2 times, No. 127/ 2016; 4 times, No. 126/2016; 5 times, No. 125/2016; 1 time, No. 124/2016.

Central Union for Child Welfare (CUCW) v. Finland.[2059] The Central Union for Child Welfare invites the Committee to find a violation of Articles 16, 17 and 27§1(c) taken alone and Article E in conjunction with each of these provisions of the Charter, on the ground that because of the amendments to its Act on Early Childhood Education and Care, which came into force on 1 August 2016, Finland has:

– infringed the rights of children of unemployed parents or parents on maternity, paternity or parental leave, in breach of Articles 16, 17, 27§1(c) and E of the Charter;
– infringed the rights of the parents referred to above, in breach of Articles 16, 17, 27§1(c) and E of the Charter;
– created geographical inequalities between children and between parents depending on the municipality where they live, discriminating, in particular, against children and their parents in the economically least advantaged municipalities in breach of Articles 16, 27§1(c) and E of the Charter.

The Committee takes note of the Government's intention to amend the Act on Early Childhood Education and Care and restore the earlier subjective right of children to full-time early childhood education and care. The Committee considers that should the new law come into force and be properly implemented, the situation would no longer be in violation of Article E, read in conjunction with Article 17 §1(a), Article 27 §1(c) and Article E read in conjunction with Article 16 of the Charter. The Committee decided that there is a violation of Article E taken in conjunction with Article 17 §1(a) of the Charter, Article 27 §1(c) of the Charter, and Article E taken in conjunction with Article 16 of the Charter.

338. In the period 2016–2020, twenty decisions were issued in matters relating to labour and employee protection. These are substantive decisions caused by the following quasi-judgments issued by the European Committee of Social Rights:

– Complaint No. 143/2017 Union Generale Lavoratori – Federazione Nazionale Corpo forestale Dello Stato (UGL CFS) and Sidicato autonomo polizia ambientale forestale (SAPAF) v. Italy, Articles 1 §2, 5 and 6 §2 (adopted 3 July 2019; notified 25 July 2019; published 26 November 2019)
– Complaint No. 158/2017 Confederatione Generale Italiana del Lavoro (CGIL) v. Italy, Article 24 (adopted 22 January 2019; notified 6 February; published 7 June 2019)

2059. Complaint No. 139/2016, Adoption: 11 Sep. 2019, Notification: 3 Oct. 2019, Publicity: 4 Feb. 2020.

- Complaint No. 118/2015 Confédération Générale du Travail Force Ouvrière (FO) v. France, Article 6 §2 (adopted 3 July 2018; notified 25 July 2018; published 26 November 2018)
- Complaint No. 123/2016, Article 6 (adopted 12 September 2018; notified 4 October 2018; published 12 December 2018)
- Complaint No. 162/2018 International Federation of Associations of the Elderly (FIAPA) v. France, Articles 5, 23 and E (adopted 10 December 2020; notified 11 January 2021; published 12 May 2021)
- Complaint No. 169/2018 Associazione nazionale sindicato professionanisti sanitari della funzione infermieristica-Nursing UP v. Italy, Articles 5, 6 §2, 21 (a)–(c), as well as Articles G and E (adopted 19 October 2022; notified 19 December 2022; published 22 February 2023)
- Complaint No. 164/2018 European Organisation of Military Associations and Trade Unions (EUROMIL) v. Ireland, Articles 1 §2 and 26 §2 (adopted 21 October 2020; notified 17 November 2020; published 18 March 2021)
- Complaint No. 144/2017 Confederatione Generale Italiana del Lavoro (CGIL) v. Italy, Articles 1 §1, 1 §2, 4 §1, 4 §4, 5, 6 §4, 24 and E (adopted 9 September 2020; notified 8 October 2020; published 9 February 2021)
- Complaint No. 147/2017 Unione Nazionale Dirigenti dell Stato (UNADIS) v. Italy, Articles 1, 4, 5, 6 and 24 as well as Article E (adopted 30 June 2021; notified 3 September 2021; published 10 November 2021)
- Complaint No. 153/2017 Unione sindacale di base – settore pubblico impiego (USB) v. Italy, Articles 1 §1, 1 §2, 4 §1, 4 §4, 5, 6 §4, 24 and Article E (adopted 8 December 2021; notified 24 January 2022; published 20 April 2022)
- Complaint No. 150/217 European Youth Forum (YFJ) v. Belgium, Articles 4 §1, 7 §5 and Article E (adopted 8 September 2021; notified 15 October 2021; published 16 February 2022)
- Complaint No. 149/2017 Confédération générale du travail (CGT) and Confédération française de l'encadrement-CGC (CFE-CGC) v. France, Articles 2 §1, 5, 4 §2 (adopted 19 May 2021; notified 9 July 2021; published 10 November 2021)
- Complaint No. 161/2018 Conferezione Generale Sindicale (CGS) and Federazione dei Lavoratori Pubblicie e Fuzioni pubbliche (FLP) v. Italy, Articles 5, 6 §2, 21 (a)–(c) (adopted 19 October; notified 2 December 2022; published 22 February 2023)
- Complaint No. 155/2017 Confédération générale du travail (GT) v. France, Article 6 §4 (adopted 14 September 2022; notified 13 October 2022; published 14 February 2023
- Complaint No. 175/2019 Syndicat CFDT da la métallurgie de la Meuse v. France, Article 24 (adopted 5 July 2022; notified 29 July 2022; published 30 November 2022)
- Complaint No. 170/2018 Unione sindicale di base (USB) v. Italy, Articles 1 §1, 1 §2, 4 §1, 4 §4, 5, 6 §4, 12 §1 and 24 as well as Article E (adopted 26 January 2022; notified 4 March 2022; published 5 July 2022)
- Complaint No. 146/2017 Associazione Professionale e Sindacale (ANIEF) v. Italy, Articles 1 §1, 1 §2, 4 §1, 4 §4, 5, 6 §4, 12 §1 and 24 as well as Article E (adopted 7 July 2020; notified 18 September 2020; published 19 January 2021)

- Complaint No. 159/2018 Associazione Professionale e Sindacale (ANIEF) v. Italy, Articles 1 §1, 1 §2, 4 §1, 4 §4, 5, 6 §4, 12 § and 24 as well as Article E (adopted 2 March 2022; notified 22 April 2022; published 23 August 2022)
- Complaint No. 152/2017 Unione Sindicale di Base – Settore public impiego (USB) v. Italy, Articles 1 §2, 4 §4, 10 §1 and 3 as well as Article E (adopted 18 May 2022; notified 27 June 2022; published 14 September 2022)
- Complaint No. 171/2018 Confédération générale du travail (CGT) v. France, Article 24 (adopted 23 March 2022; notified 25 May 2022; published 26 September 2022)

The position of the Committee on contentious matters in the field of labour law will be presented in the fifth edition of the monograph on the Council of Europe and the European labour laws of individual Member States in the order that was applied by the European Committee of Social Rights towards persons and entities submitting applications to initiate proceedings and resolve disputed cases in the period from 2018–2022. The cases are discussed in the order in which they were presented to the Committee – by number and date – by the institutions authorised to submit requests for rulings in the years 2016 through 2020.

Complaint No. 118/2015. Force Ouvrière (FO) alleges a violation of Article 6 §2 of the Charter with respect to the French law concerning complementary social protection of employees with regard to the choice of an insurer, in particular Article L.912-1 of the Social Security Code, as amended by Law No. 2013-1203 of 23 December 2013 on social security financing for 2014 and the implementing decrees. FO asks the Committee to find violations of Article 6 §2 due to 1) the prohibition of designation clauses, 2) the reduction in the number of collective social insurance agreements, 3) the belated adoption of the implementing decrees, 4) the prior competitive bidding procedure and 5) the rules on conflicts of interest. Under the current legislation, sectorial social partners can only recommend insurers with which companies may sign a complementary insurance contract within the operator of their choice. However, companies representing a 'bad risk' will have an interest in using a recommended organisation, which cannot refuse the affiliation of a company falling within the scope of the agreement. Conversely, companies in the opposite situation, with fewer potential claims, can negotiate an insurance contract with a non-recommended organisation at more advantageous rates, or an insurance contract with a non-recommended insurer at more advantageous rates, or even improved coverage. This would jeopardise the financial equilibrium of the supplementary insurance scheme that the mechanism of the recommendation leads to a complementary 'two-track' social protection scheme. For the Committee, the impossibility of using designation clauses limits the bargaining powers of the social partner at the industry level. In this respect, the government does not demonstrate how the recommendation of one or more insurers can guarantee the actual effectiveness of collective bargaining of the social partners, contrary to the designation, which leads to a binding agreement on supplementary social protection. The Committee notes that the prohibition of designation clauses is very general and does not take into account certain industries with specific needs, presenting a 'bad risk' or involving activities where employees frequently change employers – such as with hotels, restaurants and intermittent shows. For this reason, the Committee considers that the general prohibition of designation clauses is not proportionate to the legitimate aim being pursued. Such a restriction cannot be regarded as necessary in a democratic society within the meaning of Article G. Therefore, the Committee holds that there is a violation of Article 6 §2 of the Charter on the issue of prohibiting designation clauses. There is no violation of Article 6 §2 of the Charter on the issues of the number of collective social insurance agreements, implementing decrees or rules of competition.

Complaint No. 123/2016. The complainant, the Irish Congress of Trade Unions (ICTU) v. Ireland, alleges that the decision of the Irish Competition Authority to prohibit certain workers – deemed self-employed, such as voiceover actors, freelance journalists and some musicians – from concluding collective agreements setting out minimum rates of pay and other working conditions amounts to a breach of competition law and is in violation of Article 6 §2 of the Charter. The ICTU asks the Committee to find the situation in Ireland to be in breach of Article 6 of the Charter on the grounds that certain categories of workers are denied the right to bargain collectively. A trade union which represents a class of falls- or fully self-employed workers, for the purposes of collective bargaining and agreements on behalf of the class of worker so represented may apply to the Minister to proscribe such a class of self-employed workers for the purposes of collecting bargaining. For that reason, the Committee concluded that there is no violation of Article 6 §2 of the Charter.

Complaint No. 140/2016. The Complainant alleges that members of the Guardia di Finanza do not enjoy trade union rights. The corps of Guardia di Finanza is defined by domestic legislation as a military police force with general competence over economic and financial matters. The members of the Guardia di Finanza are subject to military discipline as applies to the army, and therefore the Military Code is applicable to them. Under that Code, military personnel are prohibited from striking. The Committee recalls that restrictions on fundamental rights and rights guaranteed by the Charter must be interpreted narrowly and must comply with the requirements of Article G of the Charter. The Committee decided that there is a violation of Article 6 §4 but no violation of Article 6 §1 of the Charter.

Complaint No. 143/17. UGL-CFS and SAPAF allege that the incorporation of the (formerly civilian) State Forestry Corps into the Carabinieri Force (military police) violates the rights of the personnel concerned, in particular as regards:

- their rights to earn their living in an occupation freely entered into, in violation of Article 1 §2 of the Charter, as the contested measure substantially affects their conditions of work and whether they accept military status or opt for reassignment to a civilian post;
- the right to organise, in violation of Article 5 of the Charter, taken separately or together with Article G of the Charter because the trade union rights of the individuals transferred to the Carabinieri Force of the Guardia di Finanza are restricted as a result of their acquiring military status; and
- their right to bargain collectively, in violation of Article 6 §2 of the Charter, on account of the excessive restrictions imposed on the individuals transferred to the Carabinieri Force of the Guardia di Finanza as a result of their acquiring military status.

The Committee found that the restrictions provided by the legislation at issue were excessive because the establishment of trade unions or professional organisations by members of the Guardia di Finanza is subject to the prior consent of the Minister of Defence and because of the complete prohibition on members of Guardia di Finanza to join trade unions. As the provisions at issue have not changed, the Committee maintains its finding and holds that there is a violation of Article 5 of the Charter. The Committee recalls that the wording of Article 6 of the Charter entitles States Parties to enact restrictions on the right of the police or armed forces to bargain collectively. Under Article 6 §2 of the Charter, States Parties are obliged to promote, where necessary and appropriate, mechanisms for voluntary negotiations on the regulation of terms and conditions of employment, among other things. For these reasons, the Committee concludes that Article 1 §2 of the Charter is not applicable.

Complaint No. 144/2017. CGS alleges that while Italian law provides that private-sector workers can obtain contracts of indefinite duration when their fixed-term contracts are renewed beyond a certain point, this does not apply to public-sector workers, in particular teaching and non-teaching staff (administrative, technical and auxiliary staff) in public education (nursery, primary and secondary schools), thus discriminating against them and jeopardising their situation in violation of Articles 1 §1, 1 §2, 4 §1, 4 §4, 5, 6 §4, 24 and E in conjunctions with each the provisions concerned of the Charter. The Committee concludes that there is no violation of Article 1 §2 of the Charter in respect of public education staff registered in the ERE list and recruited under successive contracts of an overall length of more than thirty-six months. However, there is a violation of Article 1 §2 of the Charter in respect of public education staff not registered in the ERE list and recruited under successive contracts with interruptions for an overall length of more than thirty-six months.

Complaint No. 146/2017. ANIEF alleges that, while Italian law provides that private-sector workers obtain contracts of indefinite duration when their fixed-term contracts are renewed beyond a certain point, this does not apply to teaching and non-teaching staff (administrative, technical and auxiliary staff) in public education (nursery, primary and secondary schools), thus discriminating against them and their situation in violation of Articles 1 §1, 1 §2, 4 §1, 4 §4, 5, 6 §4, 24 and E in conjunctions with each the provisions concerned of the Charter. The Committee considers that the non-renewal of fixed-term contracts or the fact that such contracts are not converted into contracts of indefinite duration under the conditions referred to in the complaint cannot be regarded as dismissal contrary to Article 24 of the Charter. Moreover, the arguments of the parties do not disclose any violation of Article E in conjunction with Article 24 of the Charter. The Committee accordingly holds that there is no violation of Article E in conjunction with Article 24 of the Charter, while the rest of the situation is identical to that presented in the previous case (Complaint No. 144/2017).

Complaint No. 147/2017. UNADIS alleges that Italy has violated Articles 1, 4, 5, 6 and 24 of the Charter as well as Article U in conjunction with each of the aforementioned provisions as regards the situation of some 800 public employees of tax agencies who, after exercising fixed-term contracts higher functions than those for which they had been initially recruited, have lost such sanctions due to changes in the legislation and case law, without being entitled to normalise their position in the managerial posts they occupied. The Commission notes that the substantive complaint about the staffing situation of tax officials appointed to managerial positions is based on fixed-term employment contracts.

The Commission notes that the substantive complaint about the staffing situation of tax officials appointed to managerial positions concerns employees employed on the basis of fixed-term employment contracts. The Committee observes that fixed-term contracts may result in a certain disadvantage for the employee compared to an indefinite contract. Moreover, the Committee finds that the situation is not comparable to that of workers in the private sector. The Committee notes the measures taken by Italy, even after the introduction of the complaint, aimed at both facilitating the permanent appointment to managerial positions of the tax officials in question and at enabling their previous experience as temporary managers to be taken into account. For these reasons, the Committee concludes that there is no violation of Article 1 §2 of the Charter.

Complaint No. 149/2017. CGT and CFE_CGC allege that the provisions of Act No. 2016-1088 of 8 August 2016 on labour, modernisation of the social dialogue and professional career security fail to comply with Articles 2 §1, 5, and 4 §2 of the revised European Social Charter. The Committee found that an absence of effective work determined a posteriori for a period of time that the employees a priori did not have at their disposal, cannot constitute an adequate criterion for regarding such a period as a rest period. The Committee held that the *equi* validation of an inactive part of an on-call period, in its entirety, constituted a violation of the rights to reasonable working hours, both in respect of stand-by duty at the employer's premises as well as on-call time spent at home. The Committee notes that a change has been made to the French legislation, which was previously considered to be in breach of the Charter. The Committee considers that the situation remains essentially unchanged and therefore holds that there is a violation of Article 2 §5 of the Charter on the ground that on-call periods they are assimilated to rest periods can occur on Sundays. The Committee emphasises that Article 4 §2 is inextricably linked to Article 2 §1 of the Charter, which guarantees the right to reasonable daily and weekly working hours. The Committee considers that the number of working hours performed by managers who work under an annual working days system and who do not benefit from a higher rate for overtime under a flexible working time system is abnormally high. The situation was, therefore, contrary to Article 4 §2 of the Charter. The Committee considers that the new legal framework introduced by Act No. 2016-1088 does not fundamentally change the situation, which the Committee had already considered to be in violation of Article 4 §2 of the Charter. For this reason, the Committee concludes that there is a violation of Article 2 §1 of the Charter on the following grounds:

(a) the assimilation of an on-call period to a rest period in its seniority; and
(b) as regards the annual working days system:
   - the absence of statutory limitations to the maximum permissible weekly working hours;

- the absence of adequate safeguards to guarantee reasonable working time; and
- the reference period of twelve months.

There is a violation of Article 2 §5 and 4 §2 of the Charter.

Complaint No. 150/2017. YFJ alleges that the Volunteer Rights Act of 3 July 2005, permitting the practice of unpaid internships and the lack of enforcement of a number of provisions in the national legislation regulating internships, violates the right of workers to remuneration such as will give them and their families a decent standard of living under Article 4 §1 and the right of young workers and apprentices to a fair wage or other appropriate allowances under Article 7 §5 in conjunction with Article E (non-discrimination) of the Charter. The Committee notes that the complaint includes an allegation of Article E in conjunction with Article 4 §1 of the Charter. Therefore, the Committee will examine the complaint only on the basis of those provisions, without expanding its analysis to other Charter provisions that may arise in the context of the complaint. The Committee acknowledges that unpaid internship schemes might place young people without financial resources at a disadvantage (compared to those who can afford such internships) and that states should strive to prevent or reduce such inequality. The Committee also recalls that where it is known that a certain category of persons is or might be discriminated against, it is the duty of the national authorities to collect data to assess the extent of the problem. The Committee considers that the insufficient efficiency of the Labour Inspectorate in this respect will inevitably have discriminatory consequences in respect of 'bogus interns', as this category of workers is, in practice, deprived of the effective right to fair remuneration guaranteed to other workers who perform similar work under a regular employment contract.

For these reasons, the Committee concludes that there is a violation of Article 4 §1 and a violation of Article E in conjunction with Article 4 §1 of the Charter.

Complaint No. 152/2017. USB also alleges that the existing legislation does not allow public servants who are support staff to undertake vocational training made necessary by the technological innovations of recent years. It further alleges that the Italian government does not guarantee the right of these public servants to collective action. The Committee notes that USB has not put forward any arguments to the effect that support staff are discriminated against by comparison with other categories of public servants, as the latter have received training that enables them to gain the professional experience necessary to develop their careers while support staff have not received any training. Consequently, the Committee considers that no issue arises under Article E taken in conjunction with Article 10 §3. In light of the above, the Committee considers that the allegation that the Italian government has failed to provide training to support staff at the Ministry of Justice is unsubstantiated. It, therefore, concludes that there is no violation of Article 1 §2 or 10 §3 of the Charter.

Complaint No. 153/2017. USB alleges that the right of workers employed on fixed-term contracts by the municipalities of Sicily are violated because, in cases of abuse arising from the recourse to fixed-term contracts, the regional and national law and case law do not allow contracts of indefinite duration, as is the case when such abuses occur in the private sector. ESB alleges that this situation is in violation of Articles 1 §1, 1 §2, 4 §1, 4 §4, 5, 6 §4, 24 and E in conjunctions with each of the provisions concerned of the Charter. The Committee considers that this situation falls within the scope of Article 1 §2 of the Charter. In this regard, the Committee recalls that Article 1 §2 of the Charter requires States Parties to effectively protect the right of workers to earn their living in an occupation freely entered into. The Committee points out that Article 1 §2 of the Charter does not imply, as such, that the private and public sectors should apply the same rules as regards access to indefinite employment. The worker concerned is entitled to compensation for damages incurred as a result of working in breach of binding provisions. The authorities must recover from the managers responsible any sums paid, whether the infringement was intentional or the result of gross negligence. The Committee did not find sufficient evidence supporting the allegation on this point. The situation does not constitute discriminatory treatment. The situation of such workers does not amount to a violation of Article 1 §2 of the Charter.

Complaint No. 154/2017. CGT alleges that Law No. 2016-1088 of 8 August 2016 on labour, modernisation of social dialogue and professional career security, called ‘the Labour Law’, which permits flexible working time arrangements for a period superior to a week for up to three years is contrary to Article 4 §2 of the Charter because it deprives workers of their right to fair remuneration and, in particular, to a higher rate of remuneration for overtime work. The Committee considers that the guarantees provided by the Labour Code for informing the workers of changes to their working time are appropriate and in conformity with the Charter. The is no violation of Article 4 §2 of the Charter. Instead, it is the basis for finding a violation of Article 4 §2 of the Charter in respect of the right of workers to be informed of any changes to their working time.

Complaint No. 155/2017. CGT alleges that the ‘indivisible thirtieth’ rule, which is laid down by Law No. 87-588 of July 1987 (whereby any non-preferment of service during a part of one day gives rise to a deduction of earnings equal to the indivisible fraction of one-thirtieth of the monthly salary, each month being deemed to have thirty days) and which applies to strikes lasting less than one day in the state civil service has the aim and effect of unjustifiably infringing the right of public servants to strike under Article 6 §4 of the Charter. CGT asks the Committee to find that France is in breach of its obligation under Article 6 §4 of the Charter concerning the right to strike because the ‘indivisible thirtieth’ rule is applicable to strikes lasting less than one day in the state civil service and the national public service. The Committee considers that the difference in treatment between different categories of staff with respect to the application of this rule in the case of strikes has not been shown to have an objective and reasonable justification; it, therefore, holds that there is a violation of Article E in conjunction with Article 6 §4 of the Charter.

Complaint No. 158/2017. The CGIL alleges that the situation in Italy constitutes a violation of Article 24 of the Charter (right to protection in cases of termination of employment) on the grounds that the predefined compensation mechanism set up by Legislative Decree No. 23/205 (Articles 3, 4, 9 and 10) does not allow victims of unlawful dismissal to obtain compensation through the domestic judicial procedure that would adequately cover the damage suffered and be dissuasive for employers, as there is a ceiling on the compensation and the amount awarded is automatically calculated according to the length of service. The Committee points out that any ceiling for compensation that may preclude damages from being commensurate with the loss suffered and be sufficiently dissuasive is, in principle, contrary to the Charter. The government mentions the possibility of workers claiming additional compensation on the basis of the general rules of civil liability. The Committee notes that the government has not provided any examples of cases in which compensation has been granted for unlawful dismissal on the rule of civil liability. Yet, it notes that in the event of illegal dismissal, victims may choose between two options of compensation for their pecuniary damages – a judicial remedy and a non-judicial one – which are subject to a ceiling and do not cover the financial losses actually incurred since the dismissal date. In the event of a dismissal, the conciliatory measures provided for in Italy enable employers to avoid judicial proceedings and curb the cost of dismissals, whereas victims waive their right to initiate any subsequent proceedings, their sole benefit being that they are certain to receive compensation within a short time span. Thus, over time the compensation becomes inadequate to the damage suffered. In light of the above, the Committee considers that neither the alternative legal remedies offering victims of unlawful dismissal the possibility of compensation exceeding the upper limit set by the law in force and not the conciliation mechanism as laid down in the provision in question make it possible in all cases of dismissal without valid reason to obtain appropriate redress proportionate to the damage suffered and apt to discourage employers from resorting to illegal dismissal. Consequently, the Committee holds that there is a violation of Article 24 of the Charter.

Complaint No. 159/2018. ANIEF alleges that Italy violated Articles 1 §1, 1 §2, 4 §1, 4 §4, 5, 6 §4 and 24 as well as Article E in conjunction with each of the provisions concerned of the Charter as regards the situation of some 50,000 teachers who obtained primary school teaching certificates during or before 2001–2002, i.e., before stricter qualifications for teaching were required by law. ANIEF points out that even if such teachers have been regularly working as supply teachers in public nurseries and primary schools under fixed-term contracts, as of 1 September 2016, they cannot have their fixed-term contracts extended beyond thirty-six months (as established by Law No. 107/2015 at the time the collective complaint was lodged). ANIEF also points out that these teachers are not entitled to be registered in the eligibility ranking lists to be drawn upon exhaustion (henceforth 'ERE list'), from which teachers can be recruited under contracts of indefinite duration because their qualification was not recognised as sufficient by the Council of State.[2060] The Committee considers that the situation of the holders of primary school teaching certificates received during or before the 2001–2002 academic year who are entitled to be automatically included in the ERE lists following Judgment No. 11/2017 does not amount to discriminatory treatment, compared to that of holders of primary school teaching certificates received during or before the 2001–2002 academic year who are on the ERE list. For these reasons, the Committee concludes that there is no violation of Article 1 §2.

Complaint No. 161/2018. CGS and FLP allege that Italy has violated Articles 5, 6 §2, 21 (a) and (b), 22 (a) and (b) as well as Articles E and G in conjunction with each of the aforementioned provisions of the Charter, on the grounds that the

2060. Judgment No. 11/2017 of the Council of State in Plenary Session, 20 Dec. 2017.

National Collective Agreement of 12 February 2018 for public-sector workers and public functions of the Central Functions Branch for the three-year period 2016 to 2018 deprived them of their trade union rights by excluding them from subsequent participation in collective bargaining as a result of their decision not to sign the agreement. The Committee recalls that collective agreement is a negotiation process where not all conditions demanded by one party are likely to be accepted by the other. Under Italian law, only the intervention of the unitary staff representation body is necessary for supplementary collective bargaining. The Committee also notes that only the trade unions which signed National Collective Agreements were recognised as having the right to conduct supplementary collective bargaining. The Committee accordingly holds that there is no violation of Article 6 §2 of the Charter as regards the right to supplementary collective bargaining of trade union representatives that did not sign the National Collective Agreement.

Complaint No. 162/208. FIAPA alleges that Ordinance No. 2017-192 of 16 February, which sets an age limit of 71 years for candidates for an election to the board of the Order of Healthcare Professionals, is contrary to Articles 5, 23 and Article E, read in conjunction with each of these provisions of the Charter. Article 5 covers not only workers in activated but also personas who exercise rights resulting from work (pensioners and unemployed persons). The Committee considers that the age limit of 71 imposed on candidates for election to the councils of the Order of Healthcare Professionals represented different treatment of persons in this age group as compared to others with respect to their right to organise. The Committee observes that the aim pursued by the government was to reduce the over-representation of inactive members and to support the renewal of leaders at the top of so-called frozen structures. It nevertheless considers that the means chosen were neither reasonable nor proportionate to the aims pursued. The government itself states that a person affected by the prohibition to stand as a candidate to the council of the professional order may nevertheless continue to be involved in their profession and the bodies with which they are affiliated. This statement demonstrates that the age limit introduced by the impugned Ordinance is not based on sufficient justification. Accordingly, the Committee considers that these measures represented direct discrimination on the basis of age that denied the individuals concerned the benefit of the right guaranteed by Article 5 of the Charter. Therefore, there was a violation of Article E in conjunction with Article 5 of the Charter.

Complaint No. 164/2018. EUROMIL alleges that the situation in Ireland is in violation of Articles 1 §2 and 26 §2 of the Charter due to the fact that there is no provision in Irish law that would enable members of the Irish Defence Forces to be discharged from the armed forces on the grounds of conscientious objection. Article 1 §2 of the Charter implies that all forms of forced or compulsory labour must be prohibited. The Committee has previously considered that Article 1 §2 may be infringed in cases related to the ability of military personnel to be discharged from service even if they initially entered into the occupation freely. The lack of an explicit provision in domestic law providing for discharge from the military on the grounds of conscientious objection amounts *per se* to a violation of Article 1 §2 of the Charter. In light of these considerations and with regard to the fact that the restriction imposed on discharge from the Defence Forces during a period of emergency is prescribed by law with sufficient clarity, pursues a legitimate aim and can be deemed to be necessary in a democratic society for reasons of national security, the Committee considers that the situation is compatible with the Charter. The Committee concludes that there is no violation of Article 1 §2 of the Charter.

Complaint 169/2018. Nursing Up alleges that pursuant to Legislative Decree No. 165/2001 and the Collective Agreement for Public-Sector Workers (NCLA) of 21 May 2018, representative trade unions, Nursing Up being among them, have been excluded from any subsequent participation in collective bargaining because of their refusal to sign the NCLA. The complainant alleges that this situation violates Articles 5, 6 §2, 21 (a)–(c), as well as Articles G and E in conjunction with each of the provisions concerned of the Charter. The Committee considers the fact that the effective exercise of the right of trade unions to supplementary collective bargaining is linked to the signing of a previous national agreement, a restriction of the right to collective bargaining set out in Article 6 §2 of the Charter. However, such restriction could be regarded as compatible with the Charter if it is reasonably justified and proportionate. There is no violation of Article 6 §2 of the Charter.

Complaint No. 170/2018. USB alleges that the situation in Italy, where municipalities and public bodies in Sicily and Campania make abusive use of contracts for 'socially useful workers', whereas these workers carry out regular work which should be assigned to employees under permanent or fixed-term contracts, amounts to a violation of Articles 1 §1, 1 §2, 4 §1, 4 §4, 5, 6 §4, 12 §1, 24 as well as Article E of the Charter. The Committee finds that where persons perform their duties within public administrations as 'socially useful workers' for twenty hours per week and where they receive benefits for their work, the differential treatment does affect their entitlement to social security, namely the amount of old-age pension, the right to receive early retirement and other pensions under Article 12 §1. Consequently, the Committee holds that there is a violation of Article 1 §2 and Article E in conjunction with Article 12 §1 of the Charter.

Complaint No. 171/2018. CGT-FO alleges that Order No. 2017-1387 of 22 September 2017, which introduced a ceiling on the amount of compensation that may be awarded to an unlawfully dismissed employee, is contrary to Article 24 of the Charter. The Committee considers that the ceilings set by Article L.1235-3 of the Labour Code are not sufficiently high to compensate for the damage suffered by the victim and to be dissuasive for the employer. Moreover, the courts have a narrow margin of manoeuvre in deciding the case on its merits by considering individual circumstances of unjustified dismissal. For this reason, the real damage suffered by the workers in question may be neglected and, therefore, not be made good. In addition, other legal avenues are limited to certain cases. The Committee considers in light of all of the above elements that the right to adequate compensation or other appropriate relief within the meaning of Article 24 (b) of the Charter is not guaranteed. Therefore, there is a violation of Article 24 (b) of the Charter.

Complaint No. 175/2019. CFDT Meuse Metallurgy alleges that the provision of the Law of 13 July 1973 and Order No. 2017-1387 of 22 September 2027 on the predictability and increased security of employment relationships, as inserted in paragraphs 1 and 2 of Article L.1235-3 of the Labour Code – which amended the provisions relating to financial compensation for dismissal without a valid reason by setting mandatory compensation ranges according to the worker's length of service and the size of the undertaking – constitute a violation of Article 24 of the

Charter, both on the issue of adequate compensation in case of unfair dismissal and on the issue of the right to reinstatement. The Committee considers in light of all of the above elements that because in the French domestic legal order, Article 24 cannot be directly applied by national courts to guarantee adequate compensation to workers dismissed without valid reasons. The right to adequate compensation within the meaning of Article 24 (b) of the Charter is not guaranteed as a result of the callings set by Article L.12353 of the Labour Code. For these reasons, the Committee concludes unanimously that there is a violation of Article 24 (b) of the Charter with respect to adequate compensation.

§5. Formal Requirements for Collective Complaint Proceedings

339. A collective complaint is addressed to the Secretary General of the Council of Europe. The Additional Protocol requires the Secretary General to acknowledge the receipt of the complaint, to notify the Member State concerned of this fact and to immediately forward the complaint to The Committee (Article 5). Formal requirements for making collective complaints have been laid down in the Rules of Procedure of the Committee.[2061] A collective complaint should be made in writing, in one of the two official languages of the Council of Europe (English or French) and signed by a person authorised to represent the entities entitled to lodge collective complaints.

340. The fact that the case is pending before other authorities or that a judgment has already been passed (*res indicate*) does not constitute any formal impediment to the examination of a complaint. There is no time limit, in the case of individual complaints, that would result in the loss of the right to demand certain benefits. A collective complaint can be lodged even if not all available forms of legal action before domestic state authorities, against which the complaint is lodged have been exhausted. The *ne bis in idem* principle (the prohibition on double jeopardy) does not apply either in the case of collective complaints. The Committee of Ministers of the Council of Europe has clearly stated that a collective complaint may be declared admissible by the Committee, even if a similar case has already been submitted to another national or international body. The cases on the violation of the right to organise are dealt with by the ILO Committee on Freedom of Association and by the Committee of the Council of Europe. Making a complaint in one of these institutions does not exclude the possibility of referring to legal opinion on domestic legislation concerning collective labour law and common practice in this respect to another institution authorised to assess the compliance of national collective labour law with the international standards laid down in the ILO Conventions and one of the Social Charters of the CoE (ESC or RESC). The examination of a collective complaint, subject to the provisions of the Additional Protocol of 1995, is also possible when the Committee had already presented its opinion on the subject in the

2061. Rules of Procedure of the Committee. A legal basis for the Rules of Procedure is the provisions of Arts 24 and 25 of the European Social Charter amended by the Amending Protocol of 1991. *See*: European Social, *supra*, pp. 189 et seq.

course of its regular supervision over the reports submitted by the authorities of the Member States, concerning their compliance with the provisions of the Social Charters. The Committee has two roles: it acts as a body setting the standards and supervising the compliance with these standards; and as a body authorised to examine collective complaints lodged against authorities of the Member States which do not comply with the standards concerning the protection of social and economic rights. As a supervisory body, the Committee evaluates situations in Member States in legal terms, and the evaluation is mainly based on reports submitted by the authorities of the states concerned. On occasion, stakeholders, especially trade unions, attach their own opinions to the reports. In the case of collective complaint proceedings, a different approach is followed. Proceedings initiated by an entity entitled to lodge collective complaints are contradictory in its nature. Every party has to present statements and evidence justifying the allegations raised in a collective complaint (the complainant) and in response to the allegations (the authorities of the state against which the complaint is made). If a collective complaint is made by a national employers' organisations, national trade unions or national or international NGOs, The Committee has to notify – through the Secretary General of the Council of Europe – the international employers' organisations and trade unions referred to in Article 27 §2 of the European Social Charter of the proceedings and invited them to submit their observations on the subject and to consider the position expressed by the organisation acting in the collective complaint proceedings as *amici curiae*.

341. The specific quasi-judicial role of the Committee results from a lack of any formal impediments to the examination of the case already examined or currently being examined by another organisation or by the Committee itself. This opinion on the nature of the legal character of the role played by the Committee, as a body authorised to examine collective complaints, is further justified by little formalisation of the proceedings and the non-binding (for the parties) character of the Committee's conclusions.

§6. Collective Complaint Proceedings

342. The Committee may examine a collective complaint during a trial with the participation of the parties. The Committee makes the decision in the form of an examination during a plenary session. The Committee decides to proceed with the participation of the parties before expressing the conclusions whenever it believes that such procedure is 'necessary'. The trial enables the Committee to establish the facts which cannot be established on the basis of the procedural writs and documents.[2062] Trials are open to the public and are held in the courtroom of the European Tribunal of Human Rights. The Parties and their representatives put forward their arguments and offer additional explanations. The right to present arguments during the trial is also given to the organisations acting as *amici curiae*.

2062. Explanatory report, *supra*, p. 156.

343. The proceedings of the Committee are concluded with a report stating the findings of the Committee and the rulings concerning the collective complaint. The report of the Committee is presented to the Committee of Ministers of the Council of Europe and to the parties. On the basis of the findings and report of the Committee, the Committee of Ministers passes a resolution or a recommendation. A resolution stating the compliance of domestic labour legislation with the ESC or the RESC is passed by a simple majority vote of the Committee of Ministers. A recommendation stating the unsatisfactory application of one of the two Charters requires a qualified majority of two-thirds of those voting. A report of the Committee, accompanied by the resolution or recommendation of the Committee of Ministers, is forwarded to the Parliamentary Assembly of the Council of Europe and to the parties engaged in the collective complaint.

344. The authorities of the Member State against which a collective complaint is lodged have the right to apply to the Committee of Ministers to consult the Governmental Committee of the Council of Europe before adopting a recommendation. An opinion of the Governmental Committee is required when the report of The Committee raises some 'new issues', or when the qualified majority of the Committee of Ministers wishes it so (Article 9 §2 of the Additional Protocol). The 'new issues', which require the Committee of Ministers to consult the Governmental Committee, are legal issues which have not been dealt with thus far by The Committee while performing its supervisory role over the compliance by Member States with the provisions of the ESC or RESC. The Governmental Committee made up of the representatives of the Member States' authorities, is a political body. The Committee of Ministers is of identical nature. Additional political body in the proceedings counterbalances the assessment of findings made by the Committee of Social Rights, which is independent of national authorities of the Member States. Although the recommendations of the Committee of Ministers are not binding upon the Member States of the Council of Europe, the authorities of the states against which proceedings have been initiated as a result of a collective complaint postulate that the Governmental Committee should participate in the proceedings to counterbalance the legal evaluation of the Committee with a political opinion.

§7. Conclusion

345. The Committee is not a judicial body, and it does not deal with any individual complaints concerning instances of violation of the provisions of the European Social Charters by Member States of the Council of Europe. With regard to collective complaints, the Committee does not adjudicate but gathers information and adopts a stand whenever an entitled entity lodges a complaint against a Member State which has ratified the Additional Protocol of 1995 and, thus, submitted its national labour and social insurance legislation and practice to the supervision and assessment by an independent international body. The procedure followed for the examination of collective complaints, as presented above, shows that the Committee follows the path of international bodies of justice competent to examine complaints in matters governed by labour and social security legislation. Hence, the opinion is that the Committee plays a quasi-judicial role which is therefore justified. This role is supplementary to the main function of the Committee, which mainly serves as an international body established to set European standards with regard to labour and social insurance legislation and to supervise the compliance of the Member States of the Council of Europe with the provisions of the European Social Charter of 1961, the Revised European Social Charter 1996 and by the standards set on the basis of the said Charters.

346. The Committee and its predecessor, the Committee of Independent Experts, is sometimes regarded as a body which is less influential than the European Court of Human Rights – the body supervising the compliance of the Member States of the Council of Europe with the provisions of the European Human Rights Convention.[2063] The Committee voices criticism in connection with the effective supervision over the compliance of the Member States of the Council of Europe with the standards concerning labour law established on the basis of the European Social Charter and the Revised European Social Charter.[2064] The Committee, as an independent, professional body, does not issue any binding adjudications. It presents its position on the technical aspects and is subject to the political control of the Governmental Committee and to the Committee of Ministers of the Council of Europe. The above opinion concerning the *quasi*-judicial role of the Committee does not influence the number of collective complaints examined by this body of the Council of Europe. As of 9 September 2013, the Committee admitted 120 collective complaints for examination.[2065] With an increase in the number of Member States deciding to ratify the Additional Protocol of 9 November 1995 to the European Social Charter providing for a system of collective complaints, the methods applied by the Committee for supervision over the compliance of the Member States with the Charters will also change. The reports of Member States on compliance with international standards will be replaced with collective complaints lodged by stakeholders active in the national or international arena and by the international NGOs included in the list drawn up by the Council of Europe. The roles and the nature of the Committee will change as well. The Committee will be transformed from a supervisory body monitoring compliance with the provisions of the Charters to a judicial body.

2063. Ph. Alston & J. Crawford, *The Future of UN Human Rights Treaty Monitoring* (Cambridge University Press, 2000); M.C.R. Craven, *The International Covenant on Economic, Social and Cultural Rights: A Perspective on Its Development* (Clarendon Press, 2002); R.R. Churchill & U. Khaliq, *The Collective Complaints System of the European Social Charter: An Effective Mechanism for Ensuring Compliance with Economic and Labour Rights?*, 15(3) European Journal of International Law 417 (2004).

2064. L. Betten, International Labour Law: Selected Issues, ss 416–417 (Kluwer, 1993); T. Novitz, International and European Protection of the Right to Strike: A Comparative Study of Standards Set by the International Labour Organisation, the Council of Europe and the European Union, Oxford Monographs on Labour Law, 212 et seq. (Oxford University Press, 2003).

2065. List of registered collective complaints and state of procedure. http://www.coe.int/en/web/turin-european-social charter/collective-complaints-procedure.

Selected Bibliography

Aliprantis N. & I. Papageorgiou (eds). *Social Rights at European Regional and International Level*. Bruxelles: Bruylant, 2010.

Belorgey J.M. La Charte sociale en pratique: la jurisprudence du Comité européen des Droits sociaux, 'Revista Europea de Derechos Fundamentales', No. 13 (2009).

Birk, R. *The Collective Complaint: A New Procedure in the European Social Charter. Labour Law and Industrial Relations at the Turn of the Century, Liber Amicorum in Honour of Prof. Dr. Roger Blanpain*, Alphen aan den Rijn: Kluwer, 1998.

Birk, R. *European Social Charter*. Alphen aan den Rijn: Kluwer Law International, 2007.

Brillat, R. 'A New Protocol to the European Social Charter Providing for the Collective Complaints'. *European Human Rights Law Review*, No. 1 (1996).

Blanpain, R. (ed.). *The Council of Europe and the Social Challenges of the XXIst Century*. Bulletin of Comparative Labour Relations, vol. 39. Alphen aan den Rijn: Kluwer Law International, 2001.

Charte sociale européenne Vademecum, Strasbourg: Editions du Conseil de l'Europe, 2000.

Charte sociale européenne, Recueil de textes, 7th edn. Strasbourg: Editions du Conseil de l'Europe, 2015.

Courts and the Legal Enforcement of Economic, Social and Cultural Rights. *Comparative Experiences of Justiciability*, Geneva: International Commission of Jurists, 2008.

Darcy J., & D. Harris. *The European Social Charter*, 2nd edn. Ardsley, N.Y.: Transnational Publishers, 2001.

Deliyanni-Dimitrakou, Ch. & Petros Stangos, 'Hommage à Jean-Michel Belorgey: Tribute to Jean-Michel Belorgey: 'Parcours en Europe sociale, à bord du Comité européen des droits sociaux'. *Journeys in Social Europe, on Board of the European Committee of Social Rights*. Sakkoulas 2018.

Deliyanni-Dimitrakou, Ch. & Petros Stangos (eds). Hommage à Jean-Michel Belorgey/ Tribute to Jean-Michel Belorgey, Parcur en Europe sociale, à bord européen des droits sociaux/Journes in Social Europe, on board of the European Committee of Social Rights, Sakkoulas Publications, 2018.

de Búrca & de Witte, eds. with the assistance L. Ogertschnig. *Social Rights in Europe*. Oxford: Oxford University Press, 2005.

Selected Bibliography

De Schutter, O. (Coord.), The European Social Charter: A Social Constitution for Europe/La Charte sociale européenne: Une constitution sociale pour L'Europe. Bruxelles: Bruylant, 2010.

European Social Charter: Collected Texts. 7th edn. Strasbourg: Council of Europe Publishing, 2015.

European Social Charter: Short Guide. Strasbourg: Council of Europe Publishing, 2000.

Gomien, D., D. Harris & L. Zwaak. *Law and Practice of the European Convention on Human Rights and the European Social Charter*. Strasbourg: Council of Europe Publishing/Editions du Conseil de l'Europe 1999.

Harris, D. *The Procedural Aspects of International Law Book Series* vol. 25, Arsdley, New York: Transnational Publishers Inc., 2001.

Kahn Freund, O., 'The European Social Charter'. In *European Law and the Individual*, edited by F.G. Jacobs. Amsterdam, New York, Oxford: Elsevier, 1976.

Lukas, K. *The Revised European Social Charter: An Article by Article Commentary*. Cheltenham UK, Northampton US: EE Elgar Publishing, 2021.

Mikkola, M. *Social Human Rights of Europe*. Porvoo: Bookwell Ltd, 2010.

Samuel, L. *Fundamental Labour Rights: Case Law of the European Social Charter*. Strasbourg: Council of Europe Publishing, 1997.

Samuel, L. *Droits sociaux fondamentaux – jurisprudence de la Charte socialeeuropéenne*. Editions du Conseil de l'Europe, 1997.

Strasser, R. *European Social Charter*, Encyclopedia of International Public Law, Instalment 8, Amsterdam: Ed. Bernhardt, 1985.

Świątkowski, A.-M. *Charter of Social Rights of the Council of Europe*. Alphen aan den Rijn: Kluwer Law International, 2007.

Świątkowski, A.-M. *Carta de Los Derechos Sociales Europeos*. Buenos Aires: EDUNTREF, 2007.

The Social Charter of the 21st Century. Colloquy organised by the Secretariat of the Council of Europe, Council of Europe Publishing, 1997.

Valticos, N. 'La Charte sociale européenne. Sa structure, son contenu, le contrôle de son application'. *Droit social*, No. 9, 26e Année, 10 September-October 1963, pp. 466–482.

Vandamme, F. 'The Revision of the European Social Charter'. *International Labour Review* 133, nos 5–6 (1994): 635–655.

Vogel-Polsky, E. 'L'Article 6 de la Charte sociale européenne'. *La Charte sociale européenne,* Numéro spécial de la Revue de l'Institut de Sociologie No. 1, Bruxelles, 1966, pp. 83–107.

Wiebringhaus, H. *Council of Europe*, EEL-Suppl. 42 (March 1984).

Zacher, H.F. *Europäische Sozialcharta Staatslexikon (Görres-Gesellschaft)*, 7th edn, vol. 2 (Freiburg, Basel, Vienna: Editions Herder, 1986).

Index

The numbers given refer to paragraphs

Carrying out trade union activities, 230–231
- access for trade unionists to workplace grounds, 230
- fees for administrative costs and services, 228
- licence for negotiating purposes, 228
- Member States' right to regulate the negotiating rights, 229
- negotiating collective labour agreements, 227–229, 248–253
- representative status of a trade union, 229

Collective bargaining
- collective labour agreements, 248–253
- execution of collective labour agreement, 250
- generalisation of collective agreements, 250
- Member States' interventions in negotiations of work conditions, 251, 259, 287
- Member States' obligation to promote negotiations on collective labour agreements, 252
- Member States' obligation to provide information about collective labour agreements, 256
- public-sector and collective labour agreements, 261, 284, 336
- restrictions of the freedom to negotiate in collective labour agreements
- joint consultations, 242–247
- conducting joint consultations, 242–247
- joint consultations' conducting levels, 242–247
- scope of the matters subject to joint consultations, 245

mediation and arbitration, 254–257
collective disputes, 254–257, 271
conciliatory proceedings, 254–255
mandatory arbitration, 257
Member States' obligation to promote voluntary arbitration, 254
public sector, 248
social arbitration, 255–257
social peace clause, 255, 266
right of workers and employers to collective action, 258–280
arbitrational tribunal, 271
civil liability and criminal responsibility, 276–278
collective action, 259–260
commencement of a legal strike, 270
conflict of interests, 258–261
cooling off period, 270
ensuring continuous operation of certain workplaces, 272
legal consequences of collective action with regard to individual work agreement, 273–280
legal strike, 261–263
lockout, 280
monopoly for organising collective actions, 261
public sector, 246–248, 252. 253, 256, 261
restricting the right to strike, 265–268
restrictions in organising strikes, 261
restrictions to the right of strike as imposed by the courts, 279
right to strike, 265–268
strike action and the right to fair remuneration, 275
strike and the termination of a work agreement, 274

Index

Collective complaints, 330
  examining the admissibility, 333
  grounds, 334–338
  formal requirements, 339–341
  proceedings, 331–332
Collective redundancy procedures, 289–295
  employers' obligations, 291, 292
  Member States' obligations, 287
  obligations of workers' representatives, 290–292
  scope of information and consultation, 290
  social dialogue, 289, 291, 293, 294
Conditions of work, 76–97
  annual holiday with pay, 85–90, 149–150
  dangerous or unhealthy occupations, 91–93
  information in written form of the work agreement, 96
  night work, 97, 151, 155, 167, 213
  public holidays with pay, 82–84
  weekly rest period, 94–95
  working hours, 77–81
Council of Europe, 1
  aims and functions, 9–11
  Commissioner for Human Rights, 8
  Committee of Ministers, 8, 13, 20, 21, 25, 27–28, 33, 35, 37, 42, 46, 112, 225, 257, 290, 314, 317–321, 324-329, 331, 335, 340, 343, 344, 346
  Conference of International Non-Governmental Organisations (INGOs), 8, 331, 333
  Congress of Local and Regional Authorities, 8, 12
  European Anthem, 13, 14
  European Court of Human Rights in Strasbourg, 6, 8
  European flag, 13
  headquarters, 12
  Member States, 4
  non-Member States, 5
  Parliamentary Assembly (PACE), 8
  permanent committees, 11
  European Commission Against Racism and Intolerance (ECRI), 11
  European Committee for the Prevention of Torture and Inhuman Degrading Treatment or Punishment (CPT), 11
  European Committee of Social Rights (ECSR), 11
  Group of Experts on Action Against Trafficking in Human Beings (GRETA), 11
  Secretariat, 8
  Secretary General, 8
  Treaty of London, 4
Council of Europe's major conventions, 10
  Convention on Preventing and Combating Violence against Women and Domestic Violence, 10
  Convention on the Protection of Children against Sexual Exploitation and Sexual Abuse, 10
  European Convention for the Prevention of Torture and Inhuman or Degrading Treatment or Punishment, 10
  European Convention of Human Rights (ECHR), 6, 8, 10, 25, 32, 55, 99
  European Convention on Action against Trafficking in Human Beings, 10
  European Convention on Human Rights and Biomedicine, 10
  European Cultural Convention, 10
  Equal opportunities in matters of employment, 192–197
  European Social Charter, 10, 15–23, 91–94, 345–346
  Additional Protocol to the European Social Charter from 5 May 1988, 15, 20
  Additional Protocol to the European Social Charter providing for a system of collective complaints, from 9 November 1995, 15, 27–28
  collective complaints against Member States, 27, 32
  Amending Protocol to the European Social Charter from 21 October 1991, 25–26
  European Social Charter from 18 October 1961, 15, 17–23
  amendments, 21
  Appendix, 23
  categories of rights protected by the Charter, 20
  denunciation, 22
  obligations to Member States, 18
  ratifying, 19
  reports of Member States, 20
  restrictions and exclusions, 279
  standards of social policy, 18

supervising Member States, 20, 39, 43, 248
Advisory Assembly, 20
Committee of Experts, 20
Governmental Social Committee, 20, 322, 324
temporary derogations, 307
territorial scope of the Charter application, 21, 311–312
Framework Convention for the Protection on National Minorities, 10
Court of Justice in Luxembourg, 6
Dignity at work, 209-213
mobbing, 209
sexual harassment, 209–212
Revised European Social Charter from 3 May 1996, 29–34
amendments, 33
Appendix, 33
denunciation, 33
discrimination, 32
introducing restrictions in utilising labour rights, 32
introducing the provisions and its coming into force, 33
ratifying, 33
right of workers to dignity at work, 31, 209–213
right of workers to protect their pecuniary claims in cases of insolvency of their employer, 31
right of workers to protection of their employment durability, 31
right of workers with family responsibilities to equal opportunities and equal treatment, 31, 214–215
right of workers' representatives to protection in the undertaking and facilities to be accorded to them, 31
temporary exemption from obligations, 32
territorial scope of the Charter application, 33, 311–312
right of workers and/ or their representatives to information and consultation in collective redundancy procedures, 31
rights through collective labour laws, 16
rights through individual labour laws, 16

Freedom of association in trade union, 235
civil servants' trade union freedom, 236
establishing the protection of workers by Member States, 223
migrant workers' and citizens' of a Member State right to organise, 239
negative trade union freedom, 225
police officers' right to organise, 237
professional militia's trade union freedom, 238
regulation the intake of members, 224
restricting trade union freedoms, 236, 237
right not to join a trade union, 225
right to join trade unions, 224

Guarantees of free association in trade unions
Member States' obligations, 287
prohibiting discrimination, 232–233
scope of protection, 253
workers' duties and participation in a legal strike action, 234

Health and morals, 134, 254, 308–309

Information and consultation duties, 281–286
employers with a small number of workers, 285
employers' obligations, 292
employment in industries, 284
exclusions, 285
Member States' obligations, 282, 286
normative agreements, 282
workers' representatives, 282
Insolvency of employer
right of workers to the protection of their claims, 205–208
International employers' organisations, 331, 340

Labour human rights, 38–312
regulation of labour human rights, 38–312

Majority of the workers, 310, 319

Index

National employers' representative organisations, 331
National security threats, 307

Occupation on the territories of other countries, 65–75
  administrative fees, 73
  existing formalities, 71–73

Participation in the determination and improvement of the working conditions and working environment, 287
  exclusions, 287
  Member States' obligations, 287
  workers' commissions, 287
  workers' participation, 287
Protection in cases of termination of employment, 198–204
Protection of children and young persons, 133
  ban of employing persons under the age of 18 years, 137–138
  ban on employing children, 134–136
  medical control of young workers, 152–153
  physical and moral dangers, 154
  vocational training, 148
  young workers, 142–144
Protection of employed women, 155–156
  maternity leave, 157–161
  mothers nursing, 165–166
  pregnant women, 167–168
  prohibiting the employment of women, 170171
  prohibiting the termination of a work agreements, 162–164
  underground mining, 172
Protection of workers' representatives
  affording workers' representatives facilities to carry out their statutory functions, 305
  ensuring workers' representatives the protection of endurance in the undertaking, 304
  Member States' obligations, 297
  scope of protection, 300
Public interest, 308–309

Remuneration, 108
  decent remuneration, 109–113
  deduction from wages, 130–132
  equal remuneration for work of equal value, 119–122
  overtime work, 114–118
  period of notice, 123–129
Reports
  ratified provisions of the Charter, 316–320
  provisions of the Charter that have not been ratified, 321–322
Right to work, 41
  freedom of work, 45
  eliminating forms of discrimination in employment, 48–57
  prohibition of forced labour, 46–47
  full employment, 42–44
  function of general access to free employment services, 58–60
  vocational guidance, training and rehabilitation, 61–64

Safe and healthy working conditions, 98
  consultation of industrial health and safety, 103
  measures of supervision with health and safety work, 100–102
  occupational health services, 107
  regulations with health and safety at work, 99

Trade unions, 218–240
Trade union's organisation
  electing trade unions' representatives, 221
  establishing formal demands, 219
  forming trade unions, 218–219
  freedom of trade unions, 220–222
  freedom to start federations or confederations and international unions, 222
  internal organisational affairs, 220–222
  minimum number of members, 219
  obligation of registering an organisation, 219
  property of the union organisation, 222

United Nations, 7

Vocational guidance, 61–64, 173–175
Vocational training, 148, 176–177
  apprenticeship for young persons, 181

higher technical and university education, 178–180
retraining and reintegration, 185–186
unemployed, 185–186

War, 307
Workers with family responsibilities, 214
discrimination based on sex, 119, 122, 192, 195, 202, 214
equal treatment of both men and women, 214
right to equal opportunities and equal treatment, 192–197

Index

www.ingramcontent.com/pod-product-compliance
Lightning Source LLC
Chambersburg PA
CBHW071410230926
51846CB00001B/45
* 9 7 8 9 4 0 3 5 4 8 0 7 4 *